THE WORLD ALMANAC OF THE U.S.A.®

Allan Carpenter and Carl Provorse

WORLD ALMANAC BOOKS
A PRIMEDIA Company

World Almanac Books

Vice President and Publisher: Richard W. Eiger

Vice President–Sales
and Marketing:
James R. Keenley

Deputy Editor:
William McGeveran

Marketing & Licensing
Administrator:
Jacqueline J. Sloan

Editorial Staff: Lori P. Wiesenfeld, Senior Editor; Beth R. Ellis, Mark S. O'Malley,
Associate Editors; Melissa Janssens, Desktop Publishing Associate

PRIMEDIA Reference Inc.

Vice President and Editorial Director: Robert Famighetti
Director of Editorial Production: Andrea J. Pitluk
Director–Purchasing and Production: Edward Thomas
Director of Indexing Services: Marjorie B. Bank
Indexer: Walter Kronenberg
Desktop Publishing Assistant: Hana Shaki

Contributors

Editorial Project Manager: Jacqueline Laks Gorman
Cover Design: Ron Leighton, Bill Smith Studio
Proofreading: Aidan C. O'Reilly

CONTENTS

AUTHORS' NOTE

The newly revised 1998 edition of *The World Almanac of the U.S.A.* continues the success of its predecessors as the most up-to-date and most varied single-volume reference work on the United States as a whole, the fifty states, the District of Columbia, Puerto Rico, and other U.S.-associated regions.

Part I, Portrait of the U.S.A., again presents a concise overview of the nation as a whole. In addition to the expanded text and statistical data, this edition looks forward to the forthcoming millennium with new statistics that anticipate the state of the "U.S.A. in the Next Millennium." Also included are comparison rankings that offer unique insight into the standing of the U.S.A. vis à vis other major nations.

Part II, Portraits of the States, broadens the scope of the work with succinct and in-depth profiles of each state. The work is enlivened by significant quotations and intriguing facts presented in boxed format. General information on each state, the District of Columbia, and the associated outlying regions includes, among other data, individual state capital, nicknames, mottos, slogans, songs, and symbols. The factual/statistical information provides hundreds of items of information about each state in such categories as land, climate and environment, major cities, people, vital statistics, health, housing, crime, teaching and learning, law enforcement, religion, personal income, economy and business, travel and transportation, government, law, attractions, and sports.

Also included, at the end of each state chapter, are one or more addresses for appropriate sites on the World Wide Web, where a variety of further information can be found. The sites listed may be official state government sites or unofficial sites created by a college or university, commercial enterprise, or some other source. Readers are reminded that the address must be typed exactly as it appears in order to gain access; if you are still unable to connect to a particular site, the site may be busy or it may have moved or gone out of existence.

Part III, The States Compared, enables the reader to compare the status of the states in a unique ranking system provided for a careful selection of important topics.

The authors intend the work not only as an invaluable reference tool but also as an enjoyable resource for browsing, providing both interest and enlightenment time and time again.

The statistical information is the latest known to be available at press time. When no date is provided, the information is based on 1990 figures, drawn from the latest census. Quick access to the entire work is ensured by the separate indexes to people, places, and topics.

Allan Carpenter
Carl Provorse

Allan Carpenter's authorship now extends to 228 volumes bearing his name, including 122 on the U.S.A. His latest work is the third edition of his first book, a history of Iowa. Among his current projects is the development of a new history of Cook County, Illinois.

Carl Provorse has joined with Allan Carpenter as coauthor in six of his recent works. He is recognized for his expertise in the collection and organization of statistical and other data.

ACKNOWLEDGMENTS

Recording the extraordinary volume of detail in *The World Almanac of the U.S.A.* would not have been possible without the generous assistance of the numerous government and other sources. Particular thanks are extended to the U.S. Census Bureau, especially to Glenn King and his associates, who provided a wide variety of data selected by the authors.

PART I: PORTRAIT OF THE U.S.A.

O beautiful for spacious skies,
For amber waves of grain,
For purple mountain majesties
Above the fruited plain.
America! America!
God shed His grace on thee,
And crown thy good with brotherhood
From sea to shining sea.

Katharine Lee Bates

"As yet we only crawl along the outer shell of our country, the interior excels the part we inhabit in soil, in climate, in everything. The proudest empire in Europe is but a bauble compared to what America will be, must be, in the course of two centuries, perhaps one!"

Gouverneur Morris, American statesman (1801)

Two views of our great country are presented above, both almost prescient in their forecast of what was to come. Yet Katharine Lee Bates, the professor-poet, was able to express her thoughts in a way that perhaps has never been equaled.

On a visit to Colorado in 1893, Bates—a Wellesley College professor—stood on the summit of Pikes Peak and gazed at an expanse of purple mountains and waves of grain. The dramatic view inspired perhaps the most descriptive brief word "portrait" of the United States ever made—"America the Beautiful."

FROM SEA TO SHINING SEA—A NATION OF VAST EXTENT

The United States is indeed, as Katharine Lee Bates proclaimed, a land of spacious skies, majestic mountains, and rich plains. The country's 50 states encompass a total area of 3,717,522 square miles (including inland, coastal, and Great Lakes waters). The conterminous (48 contiguous) states are made up of a vast central plain, mountains in the west, and hills and low mountains in the east, along with numerous rivers and lakes, deep gorges, and even active volcanoes. Of the two noncontiguous states, Alaska is characterized by tall mountains and broad river valleys, Hawaii by rugged volcanic peaks. Structural additions made to the landscape of the United States include some of the world's tallest buildings, longest bridges, and grandest dams. Alaska is the largest of the 50 states, with Rhode Island being the smallest.

The conterminous United States is bounded by Canada to the north, Mexico and the Gulf of Mexico to the south, the Atlantic Ocean to the east, and the Pacific Ocean to the west.

If all 50 states could be fitted into a gigantic rectangle, the tip of Point Barrow, Alaska, would stand at the northernmost edge of that figure, with the southern beaches of Hawaii at the southern perimeter. Quoddy Head, Maine, on the eastern limit and Cape Prince of Wales in Alaska on the west would complete the great quadrangle.

However, the nation's reach extends much farther—all the way to Guam in the west, to American Samoa in the far south, and to the Virgin Islands in the east. Largest and most populous of U.S. "territories" is Puerto Rico, now under much discussion as to its future relationship with the United States. Less well-known to most Americans are other dots of U.S. land scattered about the Pacific, such as Wake Island and its sister islands of Wilkes and Peale, or the tiny Johnston Atoll, administered by the U.S. federal government.

SUPERLATIVES

- The world's only remaining superpower.
- Third most populous nation, after China and India.
- Initiated the atomic age.
- Landed the first and only men on the moon.
- *Mariner 9*—first spacecraft to orbit Mars, 1971.
- Largest portrait art—Mount Rushmore.
- World's first air mail.
- One of the world's greatest engineering feats—the reversal of the Chicago River, creating a water route from the Great Lakes to the Gulf of Mexico.
- World's first oil well.
- World's first powered air flight.
- World's largest cavern—Carlsbad, in New Mexico.
- The Declaration of Independence, whose statement of the right of self-determination was a landmark in the history of freedom.
- World's largest economy, or biggest gross domestic product.

THE EARLIEST TIMES

From Time Immemorial. When did humans first reach what is present-day America? The estimates cover an almost ridiculous range, from 12,000 to 40,000 years ago. These ancient peoples may first have trudged over a "land bridge" that is now covered by the Bering Strait. Such a land route was formed when the seas were lower at the point of Alaska where the United States "touches fingers with Siberia." (Today this icy strait separates the mainland of Asia and the Americas by only about 50 miles.)

Actually, Russia and the United States lie even closer together, with only three miles of ocean separating Russia's Big Diomede Island from America's Little Diomede Island. Experts point out that human wanderers could have crossed the narrow waters without a land bridge. Following the crossing—whenever it took place—men and women made their way across and down the Western Hemisphere, until they finally reached the easternmost and southernmost extent of the current United States.

Known Only to Archaeology. The prehistoric Americans produced many well-developed civilizations about which modern archaeologists continue to make exciting discoveries. Remains that permit continuing study were left by the native peoples of the far north, who were skilled hunters and craftsmen, and by the ancestral Hawaiians, the Pueblo peoples of the Southwest, the Mound Builders of the Midwest, and others.

The Fringes of History. History is vague about the earliest Europeans who touched what is now U.S. soil. Phoenician sailors may possibly have reached U.S. soil in ancient times, and finds continue to be made that shed light on pre-Columbian discoveries. The famed Kensington Runestone, dug up on a Minnesota farm in 1898, may have been one of these discoveries, or it may be a fraud. In any case, it appears that Norse adventurers visited North America around the 11th century. The voyages of Christopher Columbus to the Caribbean region in the late 15th century finally brought Europe and the Americas together.

So They Say

"Eight Goths [Swedes] and twenty-two Norwegians, on a journey of discovery from Vinland westward. We had a camp by two skarries [islands] one day's journey north of this stone. We were out fishing one day. When we returned home, we found ten men red of blood and dead. Ave Virgo Maria. Save us from evil...[We] have ten men by the sea to look after our ships fourteen days' journeys from this island [in the year of our Lord] 1362."

Transcription of a portion of the Kensington Runestone

The Indian Nations. Early explorers and settlers were introduced to the diverse Indian tribes, many of whom had created highly civilized nations which even today have not been adequately recognized. Among the most important of these were the powerful confederacies of the Six Nations and of Chief Powhatan. Other indigenous groups include the Pueblo, Caddo, Algonquin, and Iroquois nations and the many remarkable aboriginal peoples of the Pacific areas associated with the United States.

MOMENTS IN RECORDED HISTORY

Early Recorded History (1497-1619)

1497—John Cabot reaches present-day Massachusetts

1519—Alvarez de Pineda may have discovered the Mississippi River

1524—Giovanni de Verrazano enters New York harbor

1539—Father Marcos de Niza explores Southwest, brags of cities of gold

1540—Francisco Vásquez de Coronado's great party begins exploration of Southwest

1541—Hernando de Soto reaches the Mississippi River

1542—Juan Rodriguez Cabrillo discovers San Diego Bay

1565—St. Augustine, Florida, founded

1570—(approx.) Iroquois Federation founded

1579—Sir Francis Drake explores Pacific coast

1586—Drake plunders St. Augustine

1587—First English colony in North America is established in North Carolina, at Roanoke

1598—Don Juan de Onate explores Southwest

1607—Jamestown, Virginia, founded; first permanent English settlement in North America

1609—Santa Fe, New Mexico, founded
—Henry Hudson explores the Hudson River
—Samuel de Champlain explores the Northeast

1614—Captain John Smith explores New Hampshire region

1619—House of Burgesses formed in Jamestown

Growth Continues (1620-1735)

1620—Plymouth, Massachusetts, founded by Pilgrims

1624—New Amsterdam (New York City) founded

1630—Puritans settle Boston area

1632—King grants Lord Baltimore a charter for Maryland

1634—Benjamin Syms endows first U.S. free school, in Hampton, Virginia
—Jean Nicolet passes through straits of Mackinac

1636—Harvard University founded, first university in United States
—Rhode Island is acquired by Roger Williams, who founds Providence

1638—Swedes begin settlement at what is now Wilmington, Delaware

1643—Tinicum Island is site of first European settlement in Pennsylvania

1664—British conquer New Netherland (becomes New York)

1670—Charleston, South Carolina, founded, soon becomes early cultural center

1673—Jacques Marquette and Louis Jolliet discover upper Mississippi, explore vast area

1675—King Philip's War with the Wampanoag Indians begins

1676—Nathaniel Bacon leads Virginia planters in the first conflict over British rule

1682—Robert Cavelier, Sieur de La Salle, claims vast Louisiana region for France
—Ysleta founded, first permanent European settlement in Texas

1692—Witchcraft trials and executions take place in Salem, Massachusetts

1701—Detroit founded by Antoine de la Mothe, Sieur de Cadillac

1704—First regular newspaper in colonies published, in Boston

1718—Sieur de Bienville founds New Orleans, Louisiana

1729—Baltimore, Maryland, founded

1733—James Oglethorpe begins establishment of Georgia

1735—Trial of John Peter Zenger recognizes freedom of the press

The Early Frontier (1736-1764)

1741—Vitus Bering becomes first explorer known to reach Alaska

1748—Ohio Company of Virginia organized to begin Ohio settlement

1754—French and Indian War begins

1760—French rule in Detroit ends

1761—First regular U.S. stagecoach run is begun, from Boston to Portsmouth, New Hampshire

1763—French control in North America ends with British victory in French and Indian War

    —Chief Pontiac's siege of Detroit begins

1764—St. Louis, Missouri, established

Seeds of Rebellion (1765-1774)

1765—Stamp Act incites the colonists against taxation without representation

    —Patrick Henry fans the flames of the colonists' discontent

1769—First visit made by Daniel Boone to Kentucky

1770—Boston Massacre occurs

1772—Rhode Island residents burn British ship *Gaspee* to protest tax laws

1773—Boston Tea Party takes place

1774—Rhode Island abolishes slavery

    —First Continental Congress meets in Philadelphia

So They Say

John Adams estimated that one-third of the population was against the American Revolution, one-third for it, and one-third indifferent.

The Revolution (1775-1783)

1775—Coxsackie declaration of independence signed

    —Bruno Heceta discovers the Columbia River

    —Midnight ride of Paul Revere alerts patriots to approach of British troops; battles of Lexington and Concord fought

    —Battle of Bunker Hill, first major battle of Revolution, takes place

    —Second Continental Congress names George Washington commander in chief of Continental Army

1776—Enemy troops enter, then are forced to withdraw from Boston

    —Declaration of Independence is approved by the Continental Congress on July 4

    —Colonists driven back and defeated in Battle of Long Island

    —General Washington crosses Delaware River, wins Battle of Trenton

1777—Washington loses Battle of Brandywine

    —British troops led by Lord William Howe enter Philadelphia

    —Continental Congress flees to York

    —Desperate winter spent by Continental Army at Valley Forge

    —Decisive Battle of Saratoga won by Americans

    —Articles of Confederation adopted by Continental Congress

1778—Battle of Rhode Island fought

    —Captain James Cook arrives in Hawaii

    —Savannah, Georgia, is captured by the British

    —Benjamin Franklin brings about alliance with France

1779—George Rogers Clark's capture of Vincennes, Indiana, confirms U.S. control in Midwest

1780—French army of over 5,000 lands at Newport, Rhode Island

    —British fleet arrives at Newport and blocks Washington's attempt to retake New York

1781—Lord Cornwallis arrives in Virginia, is overtaken by Washington and allies; surrenders at Yorktown

    —Los Angeles founded

1782—Americans recapture Georgia

1783—Treaty of Paris officially ends Revolutionary War

Becoming a Nation (1784-1815)

1784—"State of Franklin" proclaimed in Tennessee

    —Russia establishes settlement in Kodiak, Alaska

1786—Last of the eastern states cede western land claims

1787—Constitutional convention adopts Constitution of the United States

    —Delaware is first state to ratify new Constitution

    —Northwest Ordinance establishes Northwest Territory

1788—Cincinnati founded, becomes "Queen City of the West"

1789—Washington is inaugurated as first U.S. president

1790—Rhode Island is last of the 13 original colonies to ratify Constitution

1791—Vermont becomes a state

1792—Kentucky becomes a state

—American explorer Captain Robert Gray passes the treacherous Columbia River mouth

1793—Eli Whitney invents the cotton gin

1795—King Kamehameha I conquers most of Hawaii

1796—Tennessee becomes a state

1800—U.S. government moves to District of Columbia

1803—Ohio becomes a state

—Vast Louisiana Territory purchased from France

1804—Great expedition of Meriwether Lewis and William Clark leaves St. Louis

—Duel between Alexander Hamilton and Aaron Burr; Hamilton is killed, Burr becomes a fugitive

1805—Lewis and Clark expedition reaches the Pacific

—Zebulon Pike begins two years of exploration of the Southwest

1806—Lewis and Clark bring back much knowledge of the Northwest

1807—Robert Fulton's steamboat *Clermont* sails up the Hudson River

1811—First steamship sails on Ohio River

—Indians under the Prophet defeated by William Henry Harrison at Battle of Tippecanoe

—Strong U.S. earthquake devastates central Mississippi River region, forms Reelfoot Lake in what is now Tennessee

1812—Fort Ross is built by the Russians in what is now California

—War of 1812 begins

—Louisiana becomes a state

—Fort Dearborn (Chicago) massacre by Potawatomi Indians

1813—Detroit recaptured by United States

—Oliver Hazard Perry's victory over the British at Put-in-Bay ensures U.S. control of Great Lakes

1814—British attack, are defeated at Fort McHenry; "Star-Spangled Banner" is composed

—British burn Washington, DC

—Battle of Plattsburgh brings U.S. control of Lake Champlain

1815—Treaty of Ghent ends War of 1812

—Andrew Jackson wins Battle of New Orleans after War of 1812 ends

Expansion and Controversy (1816-1860)

1816—Indiana enters the Union

1817—Mississippi enters the Union

—Indian resettlement begins in Oklahoma

1818—Illinois enters the Union

—First steamboat sails on the Great Lakes

1819—Alabama enters the Union

1820—Maine becomes a state

1821—Andrew Jackson's successes in Indian wars bring Florida to the United States

—Missouri becomes a state (after Missouri Compromise on slavery is reached)

1822—Santa Fe Trail blazed

1824—First great annual fur "rendezvous" held in West

—Dr. John McLoughlin establishes Fort Vancouver, Washington

1825—Mexico takes control in California

—Erie Canal opens

1827—Mechanics Union of Trade Associations formed, in Philadelphia

1828—America's first passenger railroad, which is horse-drawn, begins operation

—Gold discovered in northern Georgia

1830—Country's first railroad built for a steam engine begins operation in South Carolina

1832—Black Hawk War pushes Indians west

—Henry R. Schoolcraft discovers source of Mississippi River: Lake Itasca, in Minnesota

1834—Indian Territory established in present-day Oklahoma

—Cyrus McCormick invents reaper, revolutionizing agriculture

1835—Fire destroys 600 New York City buildings

1836—Texans besieged by Mexican troops at the Alamo

—Seminole War begins in Florida, as Indians protest forced removal

—Sam Houston's Texans defeat Mexican leader Santa Anna in Battle of San Jacinto

—Texas becomes an independent republic

—Arkansas becomes a state

1837—Electric motor invented by Thomas Davenport, in Vermont

—John Deere invents steel plow

—Michigan becomes a state

1838—Last of Cherokee forced over infamous "Trail of Tears" to Oklahoma, where Indian nations begin their great advances

1841—William Henry Harrison becomes the first president to die in office

1842—Webster-Ashburton Treaty establishes northeast border with Canada

1843—First major westward immigration begins, from Missouri
—Hawaii recognized as an independent nation

1844—Mormon leader Joseph Smith murdered; Mormons leave Iowa

1845—Texas and Florida become states
—Naval Academy founded at Annapolis
—California Republic is formed

1846—Oregon and Washington come under U.S. control after agreement with Britain; expansionists had called for "54° 40′ or fight" boundary
—War with Mexico over disputed southwest lands
—Iowa becomes a state
—Elias Howe invents sewing machine

1847—Mormon pioneer refugees found Salt Lake City

1848—Treaty of Guadalupe Hidalgo with Mexico adds Southwest region to United States
—Wisconsin becomes a state

1849—Unparalleled gold rush begins, with arrival of California 49ers

1850—California becomes a state

So They Say

"....four wagons, with nine men.... traveled together for a thousand miles, and separated only when our roads parted, the one to California and the other to Oregon. And yet we were all the while in one great train, never out of the sight or hearing of others. In fact, at times the road would be so full of wagons that all could not travel in one track, and this accounts for the double road-beds seen in so many places on the trail."   Ezra Meeker, a traveler on the Mormon Trail (1852)

1853—Gadsden Purchase completes U.S. lands in the Southwest
—New York holds nation's first world's fair

1854—Republican Party formed

1855—Sault Ste. Marie canal opens, eventually becomes world's busiest

1856—Slave disagreement grows, flares into Kansas/Missouri guerrilla war

1858—Minnesota becomes a state
—Debates between Stephen Douglas and Abraham Lincoln focus national attention on Lincoln

1859—Comstock silver boom begins in Nevada
—Five Civilized Tribes hold council, consolidate their gains, in present-day Oklahoma
—John Brown seizes federal arsenal at Harpers Ferry, West Virginia; is tried and executed
—Oregon becomes a state
—World's first petroleum well pumps in Titusville, Pennsylvania

1860—Pony Express begins its brief life
—Regular steamboat runs begin in upper Missouri River
—Lincoln elected president

Times of Great Travail (1861-1865)

1861—Kansas enters the Union as a free state
—Southern states, eventually numbering 11, form Confederacy
—Civil War begins with Confederate attack at Fort Sumter, South Carolina
—North American continent is spanned by telegraph
—Northern forces routed at first Battle of Bull Run
—Confederates seize Fort Pulaski, Georgia, many other strongholds

1862—Northern drive on Richmond, Virginia, fails
—Battle of the *Monitor* and *Merrimac*
—Battle of Antietam, Maryland, halts Confederates' northern advance
—Union drive defeated by Robert E. Lee at Fredericksburg, Virginia
—Battles of Pea Ridge and Prairie Grove, Arkansas
—Battles of Shiloh, Iuka, Booneville, Mississippi
—Union forces capture New Orleans

1863—Lincoln issues Emancipation Proclamation, freeing slaves
—Ulysses S. Grant lays siege to Southern stronghold of Vicksburg, Mississippi
—Battle of Gettysburg halts Lee's drive north, is turning point of Civil War
—Federal forces defeated at Chickamauga

—William Clarke Quantrill burns Lawrence, Kansas

—Vicksburg, Jackson, and Natchez fall to North; Union forces completely control Mississippi River

—West Virginia becomes a state, maintains Union sympathies

—Battle of Missionary Ridge provides an important Union victory

1864—Grant placed at head of all Union armies

—Captain David Farragut captures Mobile Bay (Alabama)

—Sand Creek massacre of Indians in Colorado

—General William Tecumseh Sherman captures and burns Atlanta, captures Savannah

—Nevada becomes a state

1865—Petersburg and Richmond fall to Union forces

—Lee surrenders at Appomattox Court House, Virginia

—Lincoln is assassinated

—Jefferson Davis captured in Irwinville, Georgia

—Jesse Chisholm blazes Chisholm Trail

Reconstruction, Recovery, Road to Greatness (1866-1899)

1866—First bridge built across Ohio River

1867—Alaska purchased from Russia by the United States

—Nebraska enters the Union

1868—President Andrew Johnson is impeached, cleared by Senate

1869—First transcontinental railroad connects east and west coasts

1871—Great Chicago fire

1872—Yellowstone becomes first national park

1874—George Armstrong Custer expedition finds Black Hills gold in South Dakota

1875—First Kentucky Derby in Louisville

1876—Custer defeated, his troops wiped out, at Battle of Little Bighorn, Montana

—Centennial Exposition held in Philadelphia

—Colorado becomes a state

1877—Thomas Edison invents the phonograph

—Chief Joseph defeated in Nez Percé War

So They Say

"Our chiefs are dead; the little children are freezing. My people have no blankets, no food. From where the sun now stands, I will fight no more, forever." He later explained, "My people needed rest—we wanted peace."

Chief Joseph of the Nez Percé

1878—Devastating yellow fever epidemic strikes the South

1880—Gold rush in Juneau, Alaska

1881—President James Garfield is assassinated in Washington, DC

1884—Cigarette-making machinery fuels growth of smoking

—First U.S. golf course opens in White Sulphur Springs, West Virginia

—Minnesota iron ore dominance begins

1885—Washington Monument dedicated

—World's first steel frame skyscraper rises in Chicago

1886—Coca-Cola is formulated and introduced in Atlanta

—Statue of Liberty dedicated

—American Federation of Labor formed, in Pittsburgh

1887—Bauxite (aluminum) discovered in Arkansas

1888—Great Blizzard causes 400 deaths in eastern United States

1889—First "run" for land titles begins Oklahoma land boom

—Johnstown, Pennsylvania, flood kills 2,200 people

—North and South Dakota, Montana, and Washington enter the Union

1890—Sioux leader Sitting Bull is killed by U.S. forces

—South Dakota is site of last Indian battle in United States, at Wounded Knee

—Wyoming and Idaho enter the Union

So They Say

President and Mrs. Benjamin Harrison were so afraid of the electric lights that had been newly installed in the White House that they always called for the servants to operate the switches.

1893—Hawaiian monarchy is overthrown
—World's Columbian Exposition in Chicago, most splendid ever
1894—First "modern" automobile perfected by Elwood Haynes
1896—Utah enters the Union
1898—U.S. battleship *Maine* blown up in Havana Harbor, Cuba, igniting Spanish-American War
—U.S. Marines invade Cuba, capture Philippines and Puerto Rico
—War success asserts U.S. presence in Caribbean and Pacific
—Hawaii is annexed
—City of New York created by combining five boroughs
—Kensington Runestone discovered in Minnesota
—Mississippi International Exposition held in Omaha, Nebraska
1899—Nome, Alaska, gold rush occurs

World Conflict/World Power (1900-1920)

1900—Chicago River is reversed, creating water route from the Great Lakes to the Gulf of Mexico
—International Ladies' Garment Workers Union founded in New York City
1901—Carlsbad Caverns discovered in New Mexico
—President William McKinley assassinated at Buffalo world's fair; Theodore Roosevelt becomes president

So They Say

In reporting Theodore Roosevelt's 1901 swearing-in ceremony, a New York newspaper reported, "...surrounded by the cabinet and a few distinguished citizens, Mr. Roosevelt took his simple bath, as President of the United States." A typo had changed the "o" in oath to "b." British newspapers carried the story without change.

—Spindletop oil flows in Texas, heralds age of petroleum
1902—Nation's first national forest established, in Wyoming
—Social reforms of Governor Robert M. La Follette in Wisconsin set national pattern
1903—Gold discovered in Fairbanks, Alaska

—Panama Canal Zone comes under U.S. jurisdiction
—Wright Brothers make world's first powered airplane flight
—Louisiana Purchase Exposition held in St. Louis, Missouri
1906—Diamonds discovered in Arkansas
—San Francisco devastated by earthquake and fire
1907—Oklahoma enters the Union
1908—First Model T Ford introduced
1911—First Indianapolis 500 auto race held
—Former President Theodore Roosevelt dedicates Roosevelt Dam in Arizona
—Rebecca Felton, of Georgia, is appointed as first woman U.S. senator
—World's first overland airmail, from Des Moines, Iowa, to Chicago
1912—Georgia is birthplace of Girl Scouts of America
—Women gain right to vote in Oregon and Kansas
—Railroad is built across sea over the Florida Keys, from Miami to Key West
—Arizona and New Mexico become last of the conterminous states
1913—Grand Canyon becomes national park
1914—Panama Canal opens, just as Germany declares war on France
1916—Jeannette Rankin of Montana is first woman elected to Congress
—Virgin Islands purchased from Denmark by the U.S.
1917—The United States joins Allied forces opposing the German alliance in World War I
1918—World War I ends with Allied victory
—Large-scale influenza epidemic ravages the nation
1919—Boston police strike broken by National Guard
1920—World's first commercial broadcasting station established in Pittsburgh
—19th Amendment ratified, giving women right to vote

Peace and Depression (1921-1940)

1921—Great destruction of cotton crops by boll weevil
1922—Lincoln Memorial dedicated

1923—President Warren G. Harding dies; Calvin Coolidge becomes president

---

So They Say

When the laconic President Calvin Coolidge died, columnist Dorothy Parker wrote: "How could they tell?"

1924—George Gershwin's *Rhapsody in Blue* introduces symphonic jazz
—All Native American Indians are made U.S. citizens
—Nellie Tayloe Ross of Wyoming is elected as the first woman governor in the United States

1927—First airplane flight from mainland to Hawaii
—Charles Lindbergh makes first solo flight across the Atlantic

1929—Herbert Hoover inaugurated as president
—Stock market collapse ignites the Great Depression

1931—George Washington Bridge, Empire State Building opened

1932—Winter Olympics are held in the United States for the first time, at Lake Placid
—First woman elected to U.S. Senate, Hattie Caraway of Arkansas

1933—Franklin D. Roosevelt becomes president, begins "100 Days" and New Deal to combat Depression

1934—Nebraska becomes only state with a unicameral legislature

1935—Will Rogers and Wiley Post killed in Alaska plane crash
—Controversial Louisiana politician Huey Long assassinated

1936—Hoover Dam begins operation

1937—Golden Gate Bridge opens in San Francisco
—Dirigible *Hindenburg* explodes at Lakehurst, New Jersey
—Worst Ohio River floods yet

1938—Oregon's Bonneville Dam begins operation

1939—President Roosevelt opens New York World's Fair

1940—Roosevelt elected to unprecedented third term
—Nation's first peacetime draft anticipates war needs

The Nation at War Once More (1941-1945)

1941—Grand Coulee Dam completed in Washington
—U.S. Lend-Lease aid extended to Britain and Soviet Union
—U.S. ships attacked at sea by German submarines
—United States attacked by Japan at Pearl Harbor, declares war

1942—Corregidor falls; Japanese take control of the Philippines
—Americans of Japanese ancestry (Nisei) moved to isolated camps
—American and Philippine prisoners forced on "death march" by Japanese
—Japanese suffer severe naval defeat at Battle of Midway
—Americans land on Guadalcanal Island, take control after bitter battle
—General Dwight Eisenhower lands U.S. forces in North Africa
—First controlled nuclear chain reaction produced at University of Chicago

1943—Allied leaders hold series of meetings at Casablanca, Cairo, and Tehran
—Japanese defeated in Battle of Bismarck Sea with great losses
—U.S. forces free Aleutian Islands
—Allied forces capture Sicily, reach Italian mainland
—U.S. Marines capture "impregnable" Tarawa
—First subway operates in Chicago

1944—50,000 U.S. troops withstand long siege in Casino, Italy
—Eisenhower prepares to attack main German defenses in northern Europe
—American forces capture the Marshall Islands
—American Fifth Army enters Rome
—Vast Allied forces land in Normandy, France (D-Day)
—American forces take Saipan and Marianas
—With slight losses, American forces win Battle of Philippine Sea
—U.S. forces capture Guam in march across the Pacific
—Allied forces enter Paris
—General Douglas MacArthur returns to Philippines, as he promised
—Allies experience severe losses in the Battle of the Bulge
—Allied bombers carry out 40,000 sorties against Germany

1945—Roosevelt, Winston Churchill, and Joseph Stalin meet at Yalta
—Buchenwald extermination camp liberated by U.S. forces
—President Roosevelt dies; Harry S Truman becomes president

So They Say

Harry S Truman had only the initial S as his middle name, without a period. It was the result of a family disagreement on whether his middle name should be Shippe or Solomon, last names from two sides of the family.

—United Nations founded at San Francisco
—Germany surrenders to the Allies unconditionally
—World's first atomic bomb explosion, at Alamogordo, New Mexico
—Dropping of atomic bombs on Hiroshima and Nagasaki brings Japanese surrender

A Cold War World (1946-1959)

1946—In speech at Fulton, Missouri, Churchill coins the phrase "Iron Curtain"
—United States gives the Philippines complete independence
—Mother Frances Xavier Cabrini becomes nation's first Catholic saint
1947—The nation undertakes its responsibilities as a superpower
—United States begins oversight of Trust Territory of the Pacific Islands
—Marshall Plan leads way toward European recovery from war
—Voice of America begins broadcasts to Soviets
—Sound barrier is broken by Charles Yeager
—Jackie Robinson becomes first black in modern major league baseball
1948—Soviets blockade Berlin; U.S./British airlift overcomes the move
1949—Rocket projects begin at Huntsville, Alabama
—United States joins North Atlantic Treaty Organization (NATO)
—Truman announces that Soviets have the atomic bomb

—South Dakota becomes nation's leading gold producer
1950—Truman sends combat troops to Korea
—Wisconsin Senator Joseph McCarthy begins anti-Communism campaign
—Truman assassination attempt fails
—Lava flow from Hawaii's Mauna Loa is largest in modern times
—Ute Indians receive $31,700,000 for lands taken from them
1951—With U.S. help, UN forces capture Seoul, Korea
—Korean War becomes a stalemate
—Atomic-powered electricity operates for first time, in Arco, Idaho
—Ratification of 22nd Amendment limits presidents to two terms of office
1952—White House restoration completed
—First experimental H-bomb exploded at Pacific proving grounds
—Eisenhower elected president
—Puerto Rico becomes a U.S. commonwealth
—Iowa is first state to produce a billion-dollar corn crop
—United Nations moves to New York City headquarters
1953—Eisenhower reaches difficult armistice in Korea
1954—Puerto Rican nationalists fire shots in Congress
—Supreme Court decision *Brown* v. *Board of Education* declares school segregation unconstitutional
—First atomic-powered submarine launched at Groton, Connecticut
—McCarthy censured by Senate; McCarthyism fades
—First Newport jazz festival held in Rhode Island
1955—Polio conquered by new vaccine discovered by Dr. Jonas Salk
—Rosa Parks contests "Jim Crow" segregation in Montgomery, Alabama
—Supreme Court expands desegregation rulings
—Major unions form AFL-CIO
—Air Force Academy opens in Colorado Springs
1957—Eisenhower sends federal troops to enforce court order mandating school desegregation in Little Rock, Arkansas

—First nuclear electric power plant opens in Shippingport, Pennsylvania

—First Soviet satellite brings space race

—Mackinac Bridge is built

1958—*Explorer 1*, first U.S. satellite, launched

—First scheduled jet plane crosses the Atlantic

—American Van Cliburn wins Soviet's Tchaikovsky contest

1959—Alaska and Hawaii become the 49th and 50th states

—St. Lawrence Seaway brings ocean shipping to Great Lakes

—First schools integrated in Virginia

—Widespread earthquake damages Yellowstone National Park

—Soviet Premier Nikita Khrushchev visits United States; first hints of better U.S./Soviet relations

A New World in the Making (1960-1990)

1960—American U-2 reconnaissance plane is shot down over Soviet Union

1961—First American troops arrive in Vietnam

—Freedom Riders challenge Southern segregation practices

—President John F. Kennedy establishes the Peace Corps

—Capitol expansion completed

1962—Astronaut John Glenn makes first U.S. orbital flight

1963—President Kennedy assassinated in Dallas; Lyndon B. Johnson becomes president

—California becomes largest state in population

1964—Reported attack on U.S. destroyers in Gulf of Tonkin; Johnson orders major U.S. involvement in Vietnam

—Landmark Civil Rights Act passed

—Beatles perform first U.S. concert, in New York's Carnegie Hall

—Disastrous Alaska earthquake strikes

—FTC requires health warnings on all cigarette packages

1965—Hurricane Betsy ravages much of the Gulf Coast

—North American Air Defense Command begins operations in Colorado

1966—Gateway Arch dedicated in St. Louis

1967—Thurgood Marshall sworn in as first African-American on Supreme Court

1968—Dr. Martin Luther King, Jr., is shot and killed in Memphis, Tennessee

—Large oil deposits discovered at Prudhoe Bay, Alaska

—Senator Robert F. Kennedy is shot and killed in Los Angeles

1969—Neil Armstrong becomes the first person to walk on the moon

—Harvard scientists discover a single gene, basic unit of heredity

1970—McClellan-Kerr Arkansas River Navigation System begins operations

1971—Spacecraft *Mariner 9* orbits Mars

—John F. Kennedy Center for the Performing Arts opens

1972—President Richard Nixon makes historic trip to China

—First major league baseball strike, lasts for 13 days

1973—U.S. involvement in Vietnam War ends ingloriously, with 50,000 U.S. servicepersons dead

—In *Roe* v. *Wade* decision, Supreme Court rules that abortion is legal

—Congress gives the residents of Washington, DC, the right to elect all local officials

—Senate hearings begin into break-in at Democratic National Committee offices at the Watergate

—Wounded Knee, South Dakota, occupied during Indian protest

1974—Nixon becomes first U.S. president to resign

—Chicago's Sears Tower becomes world's tallest building

1975—Columbia/Snake River navigation system completed

—Elizabeth Ann Seton named first American-born saint

—Ella T. Grasso of Connecticut becomes first woman elected governor without family ties

1976—Bicentennial recognized with extensive national celebrations

—Agreement makes the Mariana Islands a U.S. commonwealth

—Legionnaire's disease identified

1977—First landing of Concorde SST in United States

—Singer Elvis Presley dies

—Trans-Alaska pipeline opens

1978—Hannah Gray becomes president of University of Chicago, first woman to head a major U.S university

1979—Three Mile Island nuclear power plant malfunctions in Pennsylvania

1980—Ronald Reagan is elected president
—First woman graduates from U.S. Military Academy at West Point
—Mt. St. Helens erupts in Washington; ash covers 120 square miles
—Former Beatle John Lennon is shot and killed in New York City

1981—Iran releases 52 Americans held hostage for 444 days
—Reagan is shot and wounded
—First space shuttle is launched
—Sandra Day O'Connor is sworn in as first woman on the Supreme Court

1983—Bomb destroys U.S. Marine headquarters in Beirut, Lebanon, killing 241 servicepersons
—Sally Ride is first U.S. woman in space

1986—Space shuttle *Challenger* explodes; six astronauts and teacher Christa McAuliffe killed
—Congressional hearings begin into Iran/Contra affair

1987—Dow Jones stock index plummets 508 points in one day

1989—U.S. forces invade Panama, overthrow General Manuel Noriega
—Largest oil spill in U.S. history at Prince William Sound, Alaska.
—L. Douglas Wilder of Virginia is first African-American elected governor of a U.S. state since Reconstruction

1990—U.S. forces reach Persian Gulf to defend area against Iraq

Alone at the Top (1991-)

1991—Soviet Union in disarray, separates into individual nations; United States is only remaining "superpower"
—United States and allies defeat Iraq, liberate Kuwait in Gulf War

1992—Riots in Los Angeles follow the acquittal of four policemen on trial for beating a black man
—Hurricane Andrew hits Florida and Gulf states, causing massive destruction
—Carol Moseley-Braun of Illinois is first African-American woman elected to Senate

1993—Midwest suffers one of the most disastrous floods in its history

—Terrorist bomb explodes in New York City's World Trade Center; six people are killed
—Branch Davidian cult headquarters burns at Waco, Texas, during FBI raid; more than 70 cult members die

1994—North American Free Trade Agreement, between U.S., Canada, and Mexico, takes effect
—Earthquake strikes Los Angeles, claiming 61 lives
—Jacqueline Kennedy Onassis dies
—Republicans gain control of both houses of Congress
—Major league baseball players go on strike; World Series canceled

1995—Federal building in Oklahoma City bombed in terrorist attack, killing 168
—Football great O. J. Simpson is acquitted of murder
—An African-American "Million Man March" is held in Washington, DC
—Troops from U.S. and other nations are deployed to help keep peace in Bosnia

1996—Blizzard strikes Northeast
—President Bill Clinton and Congress grapple over federal budget
—TWA flight 800 crashes into Atlantic Ocean, killing all 230 aboard
—Summer Olympics held in Atlanta

1997—Timothy McVeigh convicted in 1995 terrorist bombing of Oklahoma City federal building
—*Pathfinder* mission to Mars collects vast amount of information
—Agreement over a balanced federal budget is reached by President Clinton and Congress
—Three East European nations—Czech Republic, Hungary, and Poland—are invited to join the post-cold-war NATO

1998—Investigation of possible wrongdoing by President Clinton widens amid allegations of sexual misconduct and obstruction of justice

THAT'S INTERESTING

• Until 1579 the Pacific was as peaceful as its name. Then the English terror of the Spaniards, Sir Francis Drake, thrust himself into the Pacific and sailed up the western shore of North America to just above San Francisco. He claimed the land for England in the name of Queen Elizabeth and named the area Nova Albion for New England, because the white cliffs reminded him of Dover in England.

- Every president's family except Washington's has lived in the White House.
- Frances Folsom Cleveland was the only White House bride of a president (June 2, 1886).
- Archie and Quentin Roosevelt, sons of President Theodore Roosevelt, joined the White House police. Quentin's pony received wide fame for riding on the White House elevator.
- Four men could sit in the supersized bathtub installed in the White House for President Taft.
- President Hoover and reporters played Hoover's favorite style of medicine ball each morning at seven.
- Nancy Reagan tasted all the food served to White House guests.
- Gilbert Stuart's 1800 portrait of George Washington has graced the White House longer than any other item of memorabilia.

GENERAL

Independence declared: July 4, 1776
Capital: Washington, DC
Motto: In God We Trust
Bird: Bald eagle
Song: "The Star-Spangled Banner"

THE LAND

Area: 3,717,522 sq. mi.
  Land: 3,536,338 sq. mi.
  Water: 181,184 sq. mi.
    Inland water: 78,641 sq. mi.
    Coastal water: 42,491 sq. mi.
    Great Lakes: 60,052 sq. mi.
Topography: Vast central plain, mountains in west, hills and low mountains in east; rugged mountains and broad river valleys in Alaska; rugged, volcanic topography in Hawaii
Number of counties: 3,092
Geographic center: Butte County, South Dakota, W of Castle Rock, approx. 44°59'N, 103°38'W
Highest point: 20,320 ft. (Mount McKinley, Alaska)
Lowest point: –282 ft. (Death Valley, California)
Coastline: 12,373 mi.

ENVIRONMENT

Hazardous waste sites (1997): 1,206
  Federal sites (1995): 151
  Nonfederal sites (1995): 1,055

LARGEST CITIES, POPULATION, 1996 PERCENTAGE INCREASE, 1990-96

New York, NY, 7,380,906; 0.8%
Los Angeles, CA, 3,553,638; 2.0%
Chicago, IL, 2,721,547; –2.2%
Houston, TX, 1,744,058; 6.5%
Philadelphia, PA, 1,478,002; –6.8%

THE PEOPLE

Population (1997): 267,636,061
  Percent change (1990-97): 7.59%
  Per sq. mi: 71.99
Population (2000 proj.): 276,242,000
  Percent change (1990-2000): 11.07%
Percent in metro. area (1996): 79.68%
Foreign born (1996): 24,600,000
  Percent: 9.3%
Top three ancestries reported:
  German, 23.30%
  Irish, 15.57%
  English, 13.13%
White (1997): 194,400,000, 73%
Black (1997): 33,800,000, 13%
Native American (1997): 2,300,000, 1%
Asian, Pacific Isle (1997): 10,000,000, 4%
Hispanic origin (1997): 29,000,000, 11%
Percent over 5 yrs. old speaking language other than English at home: 13.8%
Percent never married: males, 23.27%; females, 18.37%
Marriages per 1,000 (1996): 10.42
Divorces per 1,000 (1996): 4.6
Percent males (1996): 48.93%; percent females: 51.07%
Under 5 years (1996): 7.34%
18 years and under (1996): 28.79%
65 years and over (1996): 12.76%
Percent increase among the elderly (1995-96): 0.94%
Median age (1997): 34.9

OF VITAL IMPORTANCE

Live births per 1,000 pop. (1996): 14.8
Infant mortality rate per 1,000 births (1996): 7.2
  Rate for whites (1995): 6.3
  Rate for blacks (1995): 15.1
Births to unmarried women, % of total (1996): 32.4%
Births to teenage mothers, % of total (1996): 12.9%

Abortions (1992): 1,528,930
　Rate per 1,000 women 14-44 years old: 25.9
　Percent change (1988-92): –5%
Life expectancy at birth (1997): males, 72.8
　　yrs.; females, 79.5 yrs.
Total death rate per 100,000 pop. (1995):
　　880.0
　Accidents and adverse effects: 35.5
　Alzheimer's disease: 7.8
　Cancer: 204.9
　Cerebrovascular diseases: 60.1
　Chronic liver disease and cirrhosis: 9.6
　Chronic obstructive pulmonary diseases and
　　allied conditions: 39.2
　Diabetes mellitus: 22.6
　Diseases of heart: 280.7
　HIV infection: 16.4
　Homicide: 8.7
　Injury by firearms: 13.7
　Motor vehicle accidents: 16.5
　Pneumonia and influenza: 31.6
　Suicide: 11.9

KEEPING WELL

Active nonfederal physicians per 100,000 pop.
　　(1995): 236
Dentists per 100,000 (1994): 60
Nurses per 100,000 (1995): 809
Hospitals per 100,000 (1995): 1.98
　Admissions per 1,000 (1995): 117.77
　Hospital beds per 1,000 (1995): 3.32
　Occupancy rate per 100 beds (1995):
　　62.83
　Average cost per patient per day (1995):
　　$968
AIDS cases (new, 1996): 66,816; per
　　100,000: 25.2
Persons living with HIV infection not yet
　　AIDS (1996): 76,664
Pop. without health insur. (1996): 15.6%

HOUSEHOLDS

Total households (1996): 98,751,000
　Percent change (1990-96): 7.4%
　Per 1,000 pop. (1996): 372.25
　Percent of householders 65 yrs. and over
　　(1996): 21.65%
　Persons per household (1996): 2.62

LIVING QUARTERS

Total year-round housing units (1993):
　　103,253,000
　Occupied units: 94,724,000
　　Percent of total: 91.7%

Owner-occupied units: 61,252,000
　　Percent of total: 59.3%
Renter-occupied units: 33,472,000
　　Percent of total: 32.4%
Persons in emergency shelters for homeless
　　persons: 178,638, 0.072%
Persons visible in street locations: 49,734,
　　0.0200%
Nursing home population: 1,772,032, 0.71%

CRIME INDEX PER 100,000 (1996)

Total reported: 5,078.9
　Percent change (1995-96): –3.7%
Violent: 634.1
　Percent change (1995-96): –7.4%
Murder and nonnegligent manslaughter: 7.4
Forcible rape: 36.1
Aggravated assault: 388.2
Robbery: 202.4
Property: 4,444.8
　Percent change: –3.2%
Burglary: 943.0
Larceny-theft: 2,975.9
Motor vehicle theft: 525.9

TEACHING AND LEARNING

Literacy rate (age 15 or older; 1994): 96%
Pop. 3 and over enrolled in school (1996):
　　59,490,307
　Percent of pop.: 22.43%
Public elementary & secondary schools (1996-
　　97): 87,125
　Total enrollment (1996): 45,228,526
　　Percent of school-age pop.: 90.89%
　　Percent of total pop.: 17.05%
　Teachers (1996): 2,637,846
　　Percent of pop.: 0.99%
　Pupil/teacher ratio (1995): 17.3
　　Teachers' avg. salary (1996-97): $38,509
　State govt. expenditure per capita (avg.,
　　1992-93): $1,327.16
　　Education as a percent of all state govt.
　　expenditures: 33.3%
　Expenditure per pupil (1994-95): $5,988
Percent of graduates taking SAT (1995): 41%
　Mean SAT verbal scores: 428
　Mean SAT mathematical scores: 482
Percent of graduates taking ACT (1997): 36%
　Mean ACT scores: 21.0
Percent of pop. over 25 completing:
　Less than 9th grade: 10.4%
　High school: 75.2%
　College degree(s): 20.3%

Higher education, institutions (1996): 3,706
Enrollment (1995-96): 14,261,781
Percent increase in enroll. (1990-95): 3.2%
White non-Hispanic (1995): 10,311,243
Percent of enroll.: 72.30%
Total minority enroll. (1995): 3,496,174
Percent of enroll.: 24.51%
Black non-Hispanic (1995): 1,473,672
Percent of enroll.: 10.33%
Hispanic (1995): 1,093,839
Percent of enroll.: 7.67%
Asian/Pacific Islander (1995): 797,359
Percent of enroll.: 5.59%
American Indian/AK native (1995): 131,304
Percent of enroll.: 0.92%
Nonresident alien (1995): 454,364
Percent of enroll.: 3.19%
Female (1995): 7,919,242
Percent of enroll.: 55.53%
Public institutions (1995-96): 1,655
Enrollment: 11,092,374
Percent increase in enrollment (1990-95): 2.3%
Percent of enroll.: 77.78%
Private institutions (1995-96): 2,051
Enrollment: 3,169,407
Percent increase in enrollment (1990-95): 6.6%
Percent of enroll.: 22.22%
Tuition (in state), public 4-year institution (1996-97): $2,986
Tuition (in state), public 2-year institution (1996-97): $1,283
Tuition, private 4-year institution (1996-97): $12,920
Public library systems (1994): 8,921
Books & serial vol. per capita: 2.7
Library visits per capita: 4.1
Circulation per capita: 6.4

LAW ENFORCEMENT AND CORRECTIONS

Police protection and corrections expenditures (1996): $34,497,554,000
Per capita: $130.31
Police per 10,000 pop. (1996): 24.02
Prisoners (1 year or more) per 100,000 pop. (1996): 427
Percent change (1995-96): 4.9%
Percent of inmates that are female: 6.3%
Percent change: 9.1%
Death penalty: In 38 states, by lethal injection, electrocution, hanging, firing squad, or lethal gas

Under sentence of death (January 1998): 3,365
Executed, 1976-97: 434
Executed in 1997: 74

MAKING A LIVING

Personal income per capita (1996): $24,231
Percent increase (1995-96): 3.2%
Disposable personal income per capita (1996): $20,979
Median income of households (1995-96): $35,287
Percent of pop. below poverty level (1995-96): 13.8%

ECONOMY

In civilian labor force (1996): 133,943,000
Percent of total pop.: 50.35%
Percent female: 46.06%
Unemployment rate (1997): 4.9%
Male (1995): 5.58%
Female (1995): 5.61%
Major employer industries (total nonagricultural, 1996):
Construction: 5,407,000, 4.5%
Finance, insurance, & real estate: 6,977,000, 5.8%
Government: 19,461,000, 16.3%
Manufacturing: 18,282,000, 16.3%
Service: 34,359,000, 28.7%
Transportation, communication, & public utilities: 6,316,000, 5.3%
Trade: 28,184,000, 23.6%
New business incorps. (1995): 766,180
Business failures (1995): 71,128
Manufactures (1995):
Value added: $1,707,180,300,000
Per capita: $6,497
Agriculture farm income:
Marketing (1996): $202,338,990,000
Average per farm: $98,032
Average per acre: $209
Leading agricultural products: Cattle, dairy products, corn, soybeans
Average value land & buildings per acre (1997): $942
Percent increase (1996-97): 6%
Government payments (1996): $7,285,541,000
Average per farm: $3,530
Average per acre: $7.51
Value of nonfuel mineral production (1996): $38,200,000,000

Leading mineral products: Coal, copper, lead, molybdenum, phosphates, uranium, bauxite, gold, iron, mercury, nickel, potash, silver, tungsten, zinc

Leading industries: Petroleum, steel, motor vehicles, aerospace, telecommunic., chemicals, electronics, food processing, consumer goods, lumber, mining

Energy consumption per person (1994): 341,400,000 Btu

Retail sales (1996): $2,445,296,000,000
Per household: $24,762
Percent increase (1995-96): 5.2%

Foreign exports, total value (1996): $624,767,000,000
Per capita: $2,355

Gross domestic product per person (1997): $27,607

Public aid recipients (percent of resident pop. 1994): 7.7%

Medicaid recipients as percent of pop. (1995): 13.4%

Medicare recipients per 1,000 pop. (1993): 137.70

TRAVEL AND TRANSPORTATION

Motor vehicle registrations (1996): 206,365,156
Per 1,000 pop.: 778.21

Motorcycle registrations (1996): 3,871,237
Per 1,000 pop.: 18.76

Licensed drivers (1996): 176,634,467
Per 1,000 pop.: 671.90

Public roads & streets (1996):
Total mileage: 3,919,450
Per 1,000 pop.: 14.77
Rural mileage: 3,092,773
Per 1,000 pop.: 11.66
Urban mileage: 826,677
Per 1,000 pop.: 3.12
Interstate mileage: 46,036
Per 1,000 pop.: 0.17

Annual vehicle-mi. of travel per licensed driver (1995): 13,717

Mean travel time for workers age 16+ who work away from home: 22.4 min.

GOVERNMENT

Percent of voting age pop. registered (1996): 74.4%
Percent of voting age pop. voting for president (1996): 49.0%
Percent of voting age pop. voting for U.S. representatives: 45.6%

State legislators, total (1997): 7,424
Women members (1997): 1,590
Percent of legislators: 21%

U.S. Congress: Senate, 100; House of Representatives, 435

U.S. federal budget (fiscal 1997):
Total receipts: $1,579.0 bil.
Per capita: $5,900
Total outlays: $1,601.6 bil.
Per capita: $5,984

Public debt outstanding (end of fiscal 1997): $5,502.4 bil.
Per capita: $20,559

State government revenues (fiscal 1996): $966,298,251,000
Per capita: $3,649.98
Parimutuel & amusement taxes & lotteries, revenue per capita: $121.49

State government expenditures (fiscal 1996): $859,958,632,000
Per capita: $3,248.30

State government debt outstanding (1996): $447,338,625,000
Per capita: $1,689.72

ARTS

Per capita spending by the NEA (1997): $0.30

THE U.S.A. IN THE WORLD

The United States is one of the world's largest countries in area. It is close in size to Canada and China but much smaller than Russia. It ranks a distant third in population, well behind China and India.

With a life expectancy of 76.04 years at birth, Americans can expect shorter lives than people in many other developed countries. Among the "Big Ten" nations listed below, the United States ranks only seventh in life expectancy. It ranks third in birth rate per 1,000 population, behind India and China.

In at least one major respect, the United States ranks first among all nations. It has the world's largest economy by far as measured by gross domestic product.

The following tables compare the United States with the other Group of Seven (G-7) economic giants—Canada, France, Germany, Italy, Japan, and the United Kingdom—plus China, India, and Russia.

Figures for vital statistics and GDP are estimates based on the CIA World Factbook 1997 and may not agree with U.S. figures used elsewhere.

TOTAL AREA
(in square miles)

1. Russia	6,592,800
2. Canada	3,849,674
3. UNITED STATES	3,717,522*
4. China	3,696,100
5. India	1,222,243
6. France	210,026
7. Japan	145,850
8. Germany	137,830
9. Italy	116,341
10. United Kingdom	94,251

*China is often ranked ahead of U.S.; U.S. figure includes inland and coastal water.

POPULATION
(1997 est.)

1. China	1,210,004,956
2. India	967,612,804
3. UNITED STATES	267,636,061
4. Russia	147,987,101
5. Japan	125,716,637
6. Germany	84,068,216
7. United Kingdom	58,610,182
8. France	58,040,230
9. Italy	57,534,088
10. Canada	29,123,194

POPULATION DENSITY
(per square mile, 1997)

1. Japan	862
2. India	792
3. United Kingdom	622
4. Germany	610
5. Italy	495
6. China	327
7. France	276
8. UNITED STATES	72
9. Russia	22
10. Canada	8

BIRTH RATE
(per 1,000 pop., 1997 est.)

1. India	26.2
2. China	16.5
3. UNITED STATES	14.6
4. United Kingdom	12.8
5. Canada	12.4
6. Russia	10.9
7. France	10.8
8. Japan	10.0
9. Italy	9.8
10. Germany	9.5

INFANT MORTALITY RATE
(per 1,000 live births, 1997 est.)

1. India	65.5
2. China	37.9
3. Russia	24.3
4. Italy	6.8
5. UNITED STATES	6.6
6. United Kingdom	6.3
7. France	6.0
8. Germany	5.9
9. Canada	5.7
10. Japan	4.0

LIFE EXPECTANCY
(in yrs. at birth, 1997 est.)

1. Japan	80.5
2. Canada	79.0
3. France	78.6
4. Italy	78.2
5. United Kingdom	76.6
6. Germany	76.1
7. UNITED STATES	76.0
8. China	70.0
9. Russia	63.8
10. India	62.4

ECONOMY
(gross domestic product, 1996 est.)

1. UNITED STATES	$7,610 billion
2. China	$3,390 billion[1]
3. Japan	$2,850 billion
4. Germany	$1,700 billion
5. India	$1,538 billion
6. France	$1,220 billion
7. United Kingdom	$1,190 billion
8. Italy	$1,120 billion
9. Russia	$767 billion
10. Canada	$721 billion

[1]Based on official estimate; could be high.

PER CAPITA GDP
(1996 est.)

1. UNITED STATES	$28,600
2. Canada	$25,000
3. Japan	$22,700
4. France	$20,900
5. Germany	$20,400
United Kingdom	$20,400
7. Italy	$19,600
8. Russia	$5,200
9. China	$2,800[1]
10. India	$1,600

[1]Based on official estimate; could be high.

THE U.S.A. IN THE NEXT MILLENNIUM

The population of the United States is expected to increase greatly in the 21st century. According to Census Bureau projections, the total population is likely to increase to nearly 400,000,000 by the year 2050, with such groups as Hispanics, Asian and Pacific Islanders, and people over 100 years of age growing at the most dramatic rates. People can expect to live longer. Life expectancy at birth is projected to be 79.7 years for men and 84.3 for women by the mid-21st century—one reason why the proportion of older Americans should rise to about one in five.

The following table shows in greater detail what the United States might look like in the next century.

	2000	2010	2030	2050	% CHANGE 2000-2050
Total pop.	274,634,000	297,716,000	346,899,000	393,931,000	43.4
% of pop.	100	100	100	100	—
Under 18	70,782,000	72,511,000	83,443,000	96,117,000	35.8
% of pop.	25.8	24.4	24.1	24.4	—
18-34	63,491,000	68,430,000	74,570,000	85,698,000	35.0
% of pop.	23.1	23.0	21.5	21.8	—
35-64	105,651,000	117,369,000	119,508,000	133,255,000	26.1
% of pop.	38.5	39.4	34.5	33.8	—
65 and over	34,709,000	39,408,000	69,379,000	78,859,000	127.2
% of pop.	12.6	13.2	20.0	20.0	—
100 and over	72,000	131,000	324,000	834,000	1,058.3
% of pop.	0.03	0.04	0.09	0.21	—
Median age	35.7	37.2	38.5	38.1	6.7
Total white pop.	225,532,000	239,588,000	269,046,000	294,615,000	30.6
% of pop.	82.1	80.5	77.6	74.8	—
Total black pop.	35,454,000	40,109,000	50,001,000	60,592,000	70.9
% of pop.	12.9	13.5	14.4	15.4	—
Total American Indian, Eskimo, Aleut pop.	2,402,000	2,754,000	3,515,000	4,371,000	82.0
% of pop.	0.9	0.9	1.0	1.1	—
Total Asian and Pacific Islander pop.	11,245,000	15,265,000	24,337,000	34,352,000	205.5
% of pop.	4.1	5.1	7.0	8.7	—
Total Hispanic pop.	31,366,000	41,139,000	65,570,000	96,508,000	207.7
% of pop.	11.4	13.8	18.9	24.5	—
Life expectancy at birth—male	73.0	74.1	76.9	79.7	9.2
Life expectancy at birth—female	79.7	80.6	82.4	84.3	5.8
No. of households	103,245,963	114,825,428	NA	NA	—
Persons per household	2.59	2.53	NA	NA	—

Note: Percentages may not add, because of independent rounding.

PART II: PORTRAITS OF THE STATES

ALABAMA

"I had no idea Alabama had so much to offer. We have wafted over blue Gulf waters, rustled through venerable historic rooms, lilted across pine-ringed lakes, heard our voices echoed from picturesque mountain tops and resounded through mammoth caverns. We have been transported from the historical lands of the Indians, the Spanish, the French, the English, to the roar of the Space Age, and we had them all and much more in star-studded Alabama."   Anonymous travel writer

True to its nickname, Alabama is the "Heart of Dixie," where the Confederate constitution was formulated, but it is also a state that looks to the future. As a pioneer in the iron and steel industry, Alabama took an early lead in manufacturing in the South. It became a leader in the Space Age—Huntsville, "Rocket City, U.S.A.," is the center for research on rockets and space vehicles. Alabama is also filled with beauty, from forests rising from the red clay soil in the north, through pine forests and rolling grasslands of the south, to the swamps and bayous in the Mobile Delta on the Gulf of Mexico. This football-mad state (the University of Alabama has won many national championships) has become increasingly cosmopolitan.

SUPERLATIVES

• Introduced Mardi Gras to the Western Hemisphere.
• Tuscumbia Railroad, the first west of the Alleghenies.
• The first rocket to put humans on the moon, built in Huntsville.
• First in cast-iron and steel pipe products.
• The only state to possess all the major raw materials needed to make iron and steel.

• World's first electric trolley system—Montgomery, 1886.

MOMENTS IN HISTORY

• In 1540 the Spanish explorer Hernando de Soto and his large party entered Alabama, killing and enslaving the native peoples as they went.
• The Parish of Mobile was organized in 1704.
• The American Revolution had little effect on what is present-day Alabama, but in 1780 the Spanish captured Mobile Bay from the British and held it for Spain during the war.
• Parts of Alabama came to the United States after the Revolution, other parts during the War of 1812.
• On March 27, 1814, Andrew Jackson's victory at the Battle of Horseshoe Bend brought to an end the power of the formidable Creek Confederacy.
• The pioneer smelters built near Russellville in 1818 were forerunners of the state's later leadership in iron and steel.
• The 1830s witnessed the beginning of one of history's saddest episodes as the Five Civilized Tribes were forced to leave their comfortable homes and move west over the "Trail

of Tears." Their valuable property was taken without compensation.

• On January 11, 1861, Alabama seceded from the Union, and on February 4, delegates from six states met at Montgomery and formed the Confederate States of America, with Montgomery as the capital.

• The Confederate flag was designed and first flown in Alabama in 1861.

• Selma, Mobile, Tuscaloosa, and Montgomery fell to Union forces in the Civil War.

So They Say

"Damn the torpedoes—full speed ahead!"

Union Admiral David Farragut, as he moved to capture Mobile Bay—one of the world's most famous battle cries

---

• After the Civil War, Alabama refused to approve the 14th Amendment, and the state suffered many hardships during the Reconstruction period. Federal troops were not withdrawn from Alabama until 1876, and the state then began a slow recovery.

• After the Civil War the condition of the freed slaves did not improve greatly. Then in 1881, Booker T. Washington took over the Tuskegee Institute and was a pioneer in the education of African-Americans.

So They Say

"...progress in the enjoyment of all the privileges that will come to us must be the result of severe and constant struggle rather than of artificial forcing....It is important and right that all privileges of the law be ours, but it is vastly more important that we be prepared for the exercise of those privileges."

George Washington Carver, director of Agricultural Research Dept., Tuskegee Institute

---

• Alabama's first steel was produced in 1888.

• In 1898 an entire battalion of black volunteers joined the state's recruits in the Spanish-American War.

• Alabama was figuratively shaken by a worm in 1910, as the boll weevil threatened the state's vital cotton crop. Although the insect was controlled, peanut growing became important as a substitute.

• In 1932 the judgment of the Alabama Supreme Court was reversed by the U.S. Supreme Court in the famous Scottsboro case, and nine black men were returned for a new trial because their original trial was deemed prejudiced and unfair. Four were later released, and five were convicted.

• In 1933 the Tennessee Valley Authority was established. With its strategic location and pioneer Muscle Shoals dam, Alabama was in an excellent position to benefit from the TVA. Its dams and navigation projects helped to alleviate the severe effects of the Great Depression.

• In 1950, Dr. Werner von Braun brought 120 German rocket scientists to the small town of Huntsville. This started it on its way to becoming the "Rocket Capital of the World."

• In 1955, Rosa Parks contested "Jim Crow" segregation by refusing to move to the back of the bus.

• On January 31, 1958, *Explorer 1* became the West's first satellite; both the rocket and satellite had been developed at the Army Ballistic Missile Agency at Huntsville, under Werner von Braun.

• On May 15, 1972, while campaigning for the Democratic presidential nomination, Governor George Wallace was shot and partially paralyzed; he lost the nomination but was reelected governor in 1974. (He ran again, and won a fourth term, in 1982.)

• A federal district judge in 1991 ordered Alabama's state universities to hire more minority faculty and staff and alter financial and admission policies.

THAT'S INTERESTING

• An important relic discovered in Russell Cave was the skeleton of a prehistoric man. The tip of the spear that killed him was found lying among his bones.

• Mardi Gras was celebrated in Mobile 200 years before it was held in New Orleans.

• The Birmingham Festival of Arts is said to be the world's oldest continuing arts festival.

• Birmingham's Vulcan statue is the largest iron figure ever cast, and one of the few monuments erected to symbolize an industry.

• During the Civil War, John H. Wisdom became known as the Paul Revere of the South, after he galloped the 67 miles between Gadsden, Alabama, and Rome, Georgia, to warn of a Union attack.

• During his 46 years at Tuskegee Institute, black scientist George Washington Carver discovered 300 new uses for the peanut and 175 for the sweet potato, and made many other important contributions toward feeding the modern world.

NOTABLE NATIVES

Henry Louis (Hank) Aaron (Mobile, 1934-), baseball player. Tallulah Brockman Bankhead (Huntsville, 1903-1968), actress. Hugo La-Fayette Black (Harlan, 1886-1971), Supreme Court justice. William Crawford Gorgas (Mobile, 1854-1920), army officer/physician. William Christopher Handy (Florence, 1873-1958), musician/composer. Percy Lavon Julian (Montgomery, 1899-1975), chemist. Helen Adams Keller (Tuscumbia, 1880-1968), author/lecturer. Joe Louis (Lexington, 1914-1981), boxer. Willie Howard Mays, Jr. (Westfield, 1931-), baseball player. Alexander McGillivray (Alabama, 1759?-1793), Indian leader. John Hunt Morgan (Huntsville, 1825-1864), soldier. Jesse Owens (Danville, 1913-1980), athlete.

GENERAL

Admitted to statehood: December 14, 1819
Origin of name: Indian for tribal town, later a tribe (Alabamas or Alibamons) of the Creek confederacy
Capital: Montgomery
Nickname: Cotton State, Heart of Dixie
Motto: *Audemus jura nostra defendere*—We dare defend our rights
Bird: Yellowhammer
Fish: Tarpon (saltwater); largemouth bass (freshwater)
Flower: Camellia
Mineral: Red iron ore (hematite)
Stone: Marble
Song: "Alabama"
Tree: Southern pine

THE LAND

Area: 52,237 sq. mi., 30th
  Land: 50,750 sq. mi., 28th
  Water: 1,487 sq. mi., 20th
    Inland water: 968 sq. mi., 23rd
    Coastal water: 519 sq. mi., 12th
Topography: Coastal plains including Prairie Black Belt give way to hills, broken terrain
Number of counties: 67
Geographic center: Chilton, 12 mi. SW of Clanton
Length: 330 mi.; width: 190 mi.

Highest point: 2,405 ft. (Cheaha Mountain), 35th
Lowest point: sea level (Gulf of Mexico), 3rd
Mean elevation: 500 ft., 40th
Coastline: 53 mi., 17th
Shoreline: 607 mi., 19th

CLIMATE AND ENVIRONMENT

Temp., highest: 112 deg. on Sept. 5, 1925, at Centerville; lowest: –27 deg. on Jan. 30, 1966, at New Market
Monthly average: highest: 91.5 deg., 16th; lowest: 31.0 deg., 42nd; spread (high to low): 60.5 deg., 44th
Hazardous waste sites (1997): 12, 29th
Endangered species: Animals: 49—Southern acornshell, Gray bat, Indiana bat, Alabama cavefish, Black clubshell, Ovate clubshell, Southern clubshell, Cumberlandian combshell, Southern combshell, Upland combshell, Boulder darter, Watercress darter, American peregrine falcon, Fanshell, Triangular kidneyshell, Alabama lampmussel, West Indian manatee, Coosa moccasinshell, Alabama beach mouse, Perdido Key beach mouse, Oyster mussel, Ring pink mussel, Cracking pearlymussel, Cumberland monkeyface pearlymussel, Dromedary pearlymussel, Little-wing pearlymussel, Orange-foot pimple back pearlymussel, Pale lilliput pearlymussel, Pink mucket pearlymussel, Purple cat's paw pearlymussel, Turgid-blossom pearlymussel, White wartyback pearlymussel, Yellow-blossom pearlymussel, Dark pigtoe, Fine-rayed pigtoe, Flat pigtoe, Heavy pigtoe, Rough pigtoe, Shiny pigtoe, Southern pigtoe, Anthony's riversnail, Cahaba shiner, Palezone shiner, Alabama cave shrimp, Tulotoma snail, Stirrupshell, Wood stork, Alabama redbelly turtle, Red-cockaded woodpecker. Plants: 11

MAJOR CITIES
POPULATION, 1996
PERCENTAGE INCREASE, 1990-96

Birmingham, 258,543; –2.6%
Mobile, 202,581; 3.2%
Montgomery, 196,363; 3.2%
Huntsville, 170,424; 6.6%
Tuscaloosa, 82,379; 5.9%

THE PEOPLE

Population (1997): 4,319,154, 23rd
  Percent change (1990-97): 6.90%, 23rd
  Percent of total U.S. pop.: 1.61%, 23rd
  Per sq. mi: 82.39, 25th
Population (2000 proj.): 4,443,500, 22nd
  Percent change (1995-2000): 4.48%, 27th
Percent in metro. area (1996): 67.72%, 32nd
Foreign born: 44,000, 35th
  Percent: 1.1%, 46th
Top three ancestries reported:
  African, 20.77%
  American, 17.00%
  Irish, 15.27%
White (1992): 3,044,000, 73.56%, 44th
Black (1992): 1,053,000, 25.45%, 7th
Native American (1992): 16,000, 0.39%, 28th
Asian, Pacific Isle (1992): 25,000, 0.60%, 46th
Hispanic origin (1992): 27,000, 0.65%, 47th
Percent over 5 yrs. speaking language other than English at home: 2.9%, 46th
Percent males (1996): 48.07%, 49th; percent females: 51.93%, 3rd
Percent never married: 23.9%, 37th
Marriages per 1,000 (1996): 11.08, 8th
Divorces per 1,000 (1996): 6.03, 6th
Median age (1996): 34.9
Under 5 years (1996): 6.98%, 25th
18 years and under (1996): 28.19%, 32nd
65 years and over (1996): 13.04%, 24th
Percent increase among the elderly (1995-96): 0.76%, 25th

OF VITAL IMPORTANCE

Live births per 1,000 pop. (1996): 14.4, 20th
Infant mortality rate per 1,000 live births (1995): 9.8, 3rd
  Rate for whites: 7.1, 12th
  Rate for blacks: 15.2, 19th
Births to unmarried women, % of total (1996): 33.5%, 15th
Births to teenage mothers, % of total (1996): 18.3%, 4th
Abortions (1992): 17,450, 21st
  Rate per 1,000 women 14-44 years old: 18.2, 27th
  Percent change (1988-92): –3%, 18th
Average lifetime (1989-91): 73.54, 48th
Total death rate per 100,000 pop. (1995): 996.1, 9th
  Accidents and adverse effects: 52.5, 4th

Alzheimer's disease: 10.2, 10th
Cancer: 221.4, 14th
Cerebrovascular diseases: 65.2, 22nd
Chronic liver disease and cirrhosis: 8.7, 28th
Chronic obstructive pulmonary diseases and allied conditions: 39.5, 28th
Diabetes mellitus: 27.3, 8th
Diseases of heart: 314.2, 13th
HIV infection: 9.2, 26th
Homicide: 12.5, 7th
Injury by firearms: 21.9, 6th
Motor vehicle accidents: 26.8, 3rd
Pneumonia and influenza: 32.2, 23rd
Suicide: 13.2, 18th

KEEPING WELL

Active nonfederal physicians per 100,000 pop. (1995): 184, 39th
Dentists per 100,000 (1991): 42, 46th
Nurses per 100,000 (1995): 763, 36th
Hospitals per 100,000 (1995): 2.70, 17th
  Admissions per 1,000 (1995): 150.95, 2nd
  Hospital beds per 1,000 (1995): 4.30, 10th
  Occupancy rate per 100 beds (1995): 59.02, 34th
  Average cost per patient per day (1995): $819, 36th
  Average cost per stay (1995): $5,028, 45th
AIDS cases (new, 1996): 607; per 100,000: 14.2, 25th
Persons living with HIV infection, not yet AIDS (1996): 4,065
Other notifiable diseases, per 100,000 pop.:
  Gonorrhea (1995): 345.2, 2nd
  Syphilis (1995): 38.5, 10th
  Tuberculosis (1996): 12.0, 14th
Pop. without health insur. (1996): 12.9%, 29th

HOUSEHOLDS BY TYPE

Total households (1996): 1,624,000, 22nd
  Percent change (1990-96): 7.8%, 21st
  Per 1,000 pop. (1996): 380.06, 27th
  Percent of householders 65 yrs. and over (1996): 22.60%, 18th
  Persons per household (1996): 2.56, 28th
Family households: 1,103,835
  Percent of total: 73.26%, 6th
Nonfamily households: 402,955
  Percent of total: 26.74%, 46th
Pop. living in group quarters: 92,402
  Percent of pop.: 2.29%, 42nd

LIVING QUARTERS

Total housing units: 1,670,379
  Persons per unit: 2.42, 22nd
Occupied housing units: 1,506,790
  Percent of total units: 90.21%, 20th
  Persons per unit: 2.57, 16th
  Percent of units with over 1 person per room: 3.51%, 22nd
Owner-occupied units: 1,061,867
  Percent of total units: 63.57%, 8th
  Percent of occupied units: 70.47%, 6th
  Persons per unit: 2.70, 33rd
  Median value: $53,700, 41st
Renter-occupied units: 444,893
  Percent of total units: 26.63%, 42nd
  Percent of occupied units: 29.53%, 45th
  Persons per unit: 2.44, 14th
  Median contract rent: $229, 48th
  Rental vacancy rate: 9.3%, 19th
Mobile home, trailer & other as a percent of occupied housing units: 15.90%, 12th
Persons in emergency shelters for homeless persons: 1,530, 0.038%, 39th
Persons visible in street locations: 364, 0.0090%, 21st
Nursing home population: 24,031, 0.59%, 38th

CRIME INDEX PER 100,000 (1996)

Total reported: 4,820.1, 25th
  Percent increase: –0.6%, 16th
  Violent: 565.4, 22nd
    Percent increase: –10.6%, 37th
    Murder & nonnegligent manslaughter: 10.4, 7th
    Forcible rape: 32.7, 27th
    Aggravated assault: 355.6, 24th
    Robbery: 166.7, 20th
  Property: 4,254.7, 26th
    Percent increase: 0.9%, 12th
    Burglary: 1,002.1, 16th
    Larceny-theft: 2,886.7, 28th
    Motor vehicle theft: 365.8, 33rd

TEACHING AND LEARNING

Pop. 3 and over enrolled in school (1996): 967,545, 23rd
Percent of pop.: 22.64%, 25th
Public elementary & secondary schools (1996-97): 1,319, 27th
Total enrollment (1996): 741,933, 23rd
  Percent of school age pop.: 95.12%, 9th
  Percent of total pop.: 17.36%, 25th
Teachers (1996): 42,492, 22nd
  Percent of pop.: 0.99%, 34th
Pupil/teacher ratio (1995): 16.9, 21st
Teachers' avg. salary (1996-97): $32,549, 38th
Expenditure per capita (1992-93): $1,060.70, 48th
  Education as % of state govt. expenditures: 32.3%, 39th
Expenditure per pupil (1994-95): $4,405, 47th
  Percent increase (1993-94 & 1994-95): 9.12%, 3rd
Percent at or above grade level, NAEP tests:
  Reading, grade 4 (1994): 23%, 31st
  Math, grade 4 (1996): 48%, 39th
  Math, grade 8 (1996): 45%, 38th
Percent of graduates taking SAT (1995): 8%, 45th
  Mean SAT verbal scores: 491, 12th
  Mean SAT mathematical scores: 538, 14th
Percent of graduates taking ACT (1997): 61%, 20th
  Mean ACT scores: 20.2, 41st
Percent of pop. over 25 completing:
  Less than 9th grade: 13.7%, 8th
  High school: 66.9%, 47th
  College degree(s): 15.7%, 45th
Higher education, institutions (1996): 82, 15th
  Enrollment (1995-96): 225,612, 23rd
    Percent increase in enroll. (1990-95): 3.2%, 25th
  White non-Hispanic (1995): 163,372, 23rd
    Percent of enroll.: 72.41%, 38th
  Total minority enroll. (1995): 57,663, 17th
    Percent of enroll.: 25.56%, 14th
  Black non-Hispanic (1995): 52,311, 12th
    Percent of enroll.: 23.19%, 5th
  Hispanic (1995): 1,718, 35th
    Percent of enroll.: 0.76%, 44th
  Asian/Pacific Islander (1995): 2,326, 34th
    Percent of enroll.: 1.03%, 46th
  American Indian/AK native (1995): 1,308, 27th
    Percent of enroll.: 0.58%, 25th
  Nonresident alien (1995): 4,577, 32nd
    Percent of enroll.: 2.03%, 41st
  Female (1995): 125,835, 23rd
    Percent of enroll.: 55.77%, 30th
  Pub. institutions (1995-96): 53, 10th
    Enrollment: 203,165, 20th
    Percent increase in enrollment (1990-95): 3.7%, 25th
    Percent of enroll.: 90.05%, 9th

Private institutions (1995-96): 29, 20th
  Enrollment: 22,447, 33rd
    Percent increase in enrollment (1990-95): –0.9%, 41st
    Percent of enroll.: 9.95%, 43rd
  Tuition (in state), public 4-year institution (1996-97): $2,363, 31st
  Tuition (in state), public 2-year institution (1996-97): $1,358, 27th
  Tuition, private 4-year institution (1996-97): $8,023, 40th
Public library systems (1994): 207, 16th
  Books & serial vol. per capita: 2.0, 39th
  Library visits per capita: 3.3, 29th
  Circulation per capita: 3.9, 48th

LAW ENFORCEMENT AND CORRECTIONS

Police protection and corrections expenditures (1996): $306,982,000
  Per capita: $71.85, 48th
Police per 10,000 pop. (1996): 21.90, 26th
Prisoners (1 year or more) per 100,000 pop. (1996): 492, 8th
  Percent change (1995-96): 4.9%, 30th
  Percent of inmates that are female: 6.2%, 25th
    Percent change: 4.8%, 36th
Death penalty: yes, by electrocution
  Under sentence (Jan. 1998): 154, 8th
  Executed, 1976-97: 16, 7th
  Executed in 1997: 3, 5th

RELIGION, NUMBER AND PERCENT OF POPULATION

Agnostic: 5,964—0.20%, 42nd
Buddhist: NA
Christian: 2,782,019—93.30%, 5th
Hindu: 2,982—0.10%, 10th
Jewish: 2,982—0.10%, 43rd
Muslim: 5,964—0.20%, 13th
Unitarian: 2,982—0.10%, 31st
Other: 23,854—0.80%, 37th
None: 116,290—3.90%, 44th
Refused to answer: 38,763—1.30%, 45th

MAKING A LIVING

Personal income per capita (1996): $20,055, 40th
  Percent increase (1995-96): 2.8%, 29th
Disposable personal income per capita (1996): $17,785, 41st
Median income of households (average, 1995-96): $28,530, 46th

Percent of pop. below poverty level (1995-96): 17.1%, 7th

ECONOMY

In civilian labor force (1996): 2,088,000
  Percent of total pop.: 63.6%, 42nd
  Percent of total pop. 65 years and over: 9.5% 38th
  Percent of total female pop.: 56.3%, 42nd
Major employer industries (total nonagricultural, 1996):
  Construction: 93,500—5.1%, 18th
  Finance, insurance, & real estate: 81,500—4.5%, 39th
  Government: 341,700—18.7%, 17th
  Manufacturing: 382,600—21.0%, 8th
  Service: 405,500—22.2%, 50th
  Trade: 418,900—23.0%, 35th
  Transportation, communications, public utilities: 90,200—4.9%, 29th
Unemployment rate (1996): 5.1%, 26th
  Male: 4.9%, 28th
  Female: 5.4%, 19th
Total businesses (1995): 96,053, 24th
New business incorps. (1995): 7,686
  Percent of total businesses: 8.00%, 34th
Business failures (1995): 547
  Failures per 10,000 businesses: 56.9, 41st
Agriculture farm income:
  Marketing (1996): $3,173,595,000, 26th
    Average per farm: $70,524, 38th
  Leading products (1997): Broilers, cattle, eggs, greenhouse, cotton, peanuts, pecans, potatoes
  Average value land & build. per acre (1997): $1,480, 20th
    Percent increase (1996-97): 7%, 14th
  Govt. payments (1996): $75,550,000, 26th
    Average per farm: $1,679, 31st
Construction, value of all (1996): $4,793,865,000, 27th
  Per capita: $1,122, 32nd
Manufactures (1995):
  Value added: $29,078,500,000
    Per capita: $6,837, 22nd
  Leading products (1997): Electronics, cast iron and plastic pipe, fabricated steel products, ships, paper products, chemicals, steel, mobile homes, fabrics, poultry processing
Value of nonfuel mineral production (1996): $735,000,000, 17th
Leading mineral products (1996): Coal, petroleum, natural gas, cement, stone, lime, sand/gravel, clays

Energy consumption per person (1994): 446.3 mil. Btu, 7th

Retail sales (1995): $35,946,000,000

Per household: $22,430, 45th

Sales increase (1994-95): 7.0%, 13th

Tourism revenues (1991): $4.5 bil.

Foreign exports, in total value (1996): $5,170,000,000, 26th

Per capita: $1,210, 33rd

Gross state product per person (1994): $21,016, 46th

Public aid recipients (percent of resident pop. 1994): 6.8%, 24th

Medicaid recipients (percent of pop., 1995): 12.7%, 21st

Medicare enrollment per 1,000 pop. (1996): 153, 15th

TRAVEL AND TRANSPORTATION

Motor vehicle registrations (1996): 3,323,683, 22nd

Per 1,000 pop.: 775.26, 30th

Motorcycle registrations (1996): 36,706, 31st

Per 1,000 pop.: 11.04, 46th

Licensed drivers (1996): 3,456,100, 19th

Per 1,000 pop.: 813.93, 1st

Public roads & streets (1996)

Total mileage: 93,340, 17th

Per 1,000 pop.: 121.84, 19th

Rural mileage: 73,224, 19th

Per 1,000 pop.: 17.14, 23rd

Urban mileage: 20,116, 13th

Per 1,000 pop.: 4.71, 2nd

Interstate mileage: 904, 24th

Per 1,000 pop.: 0.21, 24th

Speed limit (max. interstate, autos, mi. per hr., 1997): 70

Annual vehicle-mi. of travel per driver (1996): 16,389, 9th

Mean travel time for workers age 16+ who work away from home: 21.2 min., 20th

GOVERNMENT

Percent of voting age pop. registered (1996): 76.73%, 26th

Percent of voting age pop. voting for president: (1996): 47.7%, 33rd

Percent of voting age pop. voting for U.S. representatives (1996): 45.6%, 33rd

State legislators, total (1997): 140, 28th

Women members (1997): 5

Percent of legislature: 4%, 51st

U.S. Congress, House members (1998): 7

Change (1985-95): 0

Revenues (1996):

State govt.: $12,741,148,000

Per capita: $2,981.78, 45th

Parimutuel & amusement taxes & lotteries, revenue per capita (1995): $1.17, 45th

Expenditures (1996):

State govt.: $12,126,587,000

Per capita: $2,837.96, 35th

Debt outstanding (1996): $3,645,292,000

Per capita: $853.10, 42nd

LAWS AND REGULATIONS

Legal driving age: 16

Marriage age without parental consent: 18

Divorce residence requirement: 6 mo., for qualifications check local statutes

ATTRACTIONS (1997)

Major opera companies: 1

Major symphony orchestras: 1

Major dance companies: 1

Major professional theater companies (non-profit): 1

Per capita spending by the NEA (1997): $0.18, 38th

State Fair in early October at Birmingham

SPORTS AND COMPETITION

NCAA (Division I) football and basketball teams: Alabama State Univ. Hornets, Auburn Univ. Tigers, Jacksonville State Univ. Gamecocks, Samford Univ. Bulldogs, Troy State Univ. Trojans, Univ. of Alabama Crimson Tide, Univ. of Alabama-Birmingham Blazers, Univ. of South Alabama Jaguars (basketball only)

WEBSITES CONTAINING FURTHER INFORMATION

Alabama Dept. of Archives and History	http://sgisrvr.asc.edu/archives/agis.html
AlaWeb	http://alaweb.asc.edu

ALASKA

> "Alaska and its people have been called many things—the greatest, unique, wonderful, a little eccentric, land where railroads disappear, where a volcano blows smoke rings, a lake empties itself on a regular schedule, where the ice barks, and many more."   *All About the U.S.A.*

Vast Alaska could swallow up Texas, California, and Montana, yet it is the third least populous state. It reaches so far to the west that the international date line had to be bent around it to keep all the state in the same day. Although it is generally thought of as a "frozen" land, vegetables and fruit here can grow two or three times their normal size. Alaska is so large and roads are so few that the airplane becomes the "family car." Alaska is a land where railroads sink into the ground, where the ice barks and huge moose sometimes interfere with golf games. Celebrated for its wild grandeur and vast oil resources, Alaska has been called "America's Last Frontier."

SUPERLATIVES

- Largest of all the states, one-fifth as large as all the other states together.
- Only U.S. state extending into the Eastern Hemisphere.
- Mt. McKinley—the highest mountain in North America.
- Nation's largest forest acreage.

MOMENTS IN HISTORY

- Sent by the Russian Czar, Vitus Bering reached Alaska in 1741. Native groups included the Indian, Eskimo, and Aleut, who were decimated by the Russians.
- Russia's trading headquarters were set up at Kodiak in 1784, the first permanent European settlement in present-day Alaska.
- In 1804, Alexander Baranov routed the Sitka Indians and established Sitka, which soon became the highly civilized capital of Alaska.
- As his hold on Alaska weakened, the Russian Czar decided to sell the territory to the United States. Although most Americans thought of Alaska as a barren, frigid waste, on March 30, 1867, the United States bought all of Russian America for $7.2 million.

- In 1880 prospectors discovered a large gold lode near the headwaters of Gold Creek; in less than a year prospectors and settlers rushed in, and the community was named for prospector Joe Juneau.
- In 1896, thousands of American prospectors crossed Alaska over the treacherous passes to reach the gold discoveries of the Canadian Klondike.
- The gold found exposed on the beaches of Nome in 1899 brought prospectors in near-record numbers. As many as 40,000 scratched for the riches.
- On June 6, 1912, the top of Mt. Katmai exploded with a roar heard 750 miles away. The shock has been considered to be the second worst ever recorded.
- On July 15, 1923, at the Tanana River bridge, Alaska's first railroad was dedicated by President Warren G. Harding.
- On August 15, 1935, a pontoon plane crashed, and the "world lost two of its most beloved figures" at a place a few miles from Barrow. Dead were the world-famed humorist/philosopher Will Rogers and noted aviator Wiley Post.

- During World War II, Japanese invaders seized Attu, Kiska, and Agattu islands in 1942, but U.S. forces soon recaptured the Aleutians.
- Alaska became the 49th state on January 3, 1959; it was the first new state in the Union since 1912.
- One of the most disastrous earthquakes ever to hit North America devastated the Anchorage area on March 27, 1964.
- In 1977 the controversial Trans-Alaska pipeline was completed after three years of work, allowing oil to flow from the vast Prudhoe Bay oil field on the Arctic coast.

So They Say

"As soon as she heard the first sounds, she grabbed the kids and ran out of the house. A minute later the yard and the house—everything—fell into that hole."

Dr. Richard Sutherland,
on his wife's experience in
the 1964 earthquake

- The grounding of the *Exxon Valdez* oil tanker in Prince William Sound on March 24, 1989, was one of the nation's worst ecological disasters. A vast oil spill killed unknown numbers of marine and shore animals and birds and affected much of the economy of a vast area. In September 1994, Exxon was ordered to pay $5 billion in damages.

THAT'S INTERESTING

- The state of Rhode Island could fit into Alaska 425 times.
- Self-emptying Lake George is the best known curiosity of its kind. A dam of ice forms each winter and the lake backs up behind it. The pressure of the water causes the dam to burst. The lake empties itself, and the process begins all over.
- To reach Canada's gold, prospectors had to go through Alaska and climb over mountain passes that would have frightened expert mountaineers. Most of the prospectors did not even realize the terrible dangers they faced, but nevertheless, some 22,000 eager gold hunters formed an almost continuous line over Chilkoot Pass.
- During Alaska's statehood celebration, Fairbanks attempted to turn the Chena River into gold, as a symbol of this source of wealth. However, through some chemical mistake, the river turned a lovely green.
- A map maker, unfamiliar with the name of an Alaskan community, wrote "name?" on the map. His draftsman misread the notation and entered the word "Nome" at that location. In doing so, he literally put Nome on the map.

ALASKA NOTABLES

Alexander Baranov (Russia, 1747-1819), trader/public official. **Rex Ellingwood Beach** (Atwood, MI, 1877-1949), author. **Vitus Jonassen Bering** (Denmark, 1681-1741), explorer. **Sheldon Jackson** (Minaville, NY,

1834-1909), missionary. **John Griffith (Jack) London** (San Francisco, CA, 1876-1916), author. **John Muir** (Scotland, 1838-1914), naturalist/explorer/conservationist.

GENERAL

Admitted to statehood: January 3, 1959
Origin of name: Russian version of an Aleutian (Eskimo) word *alakshak,* for "peninsula," "great lands," or "land that is not an island"
Capital: Juneau
Nickname: Last Frontier, Land of Midnight Sun
Motto: North to the future
Bird: Willow ptarmigan
Fish: King salmon
Flower: Forget-me-not
Gem: Jade
Song: "Alaska's Flag"
Tree: Sitka spruce

THE LAND

Area: 615,230 sq. mi., 1st
  Land: 570,374 sq. mi., 1st
  Water: 44,856 sq. mi., 1st
    Inland water: 17,501 sq. mi., 1st
    Coastal water: 27,355 sq. mi., 1st
Topography: Includes Pacific and Arctic mountain systems, central plateau, and Arctic slope. Mt. McKinley, 20,320 ft., is the highest point in North America.
Number of counties: 24 boroughs
Geographic center: lat. 63°50'N, long. 152°W, approx. 60 mi. NW of Mt. McKinley
Length: 1,480 mi.; width: 810 mi.
Highest point: 20,320 ft. (Mt. McKinley), 1st
Lowest point: sea level (Pacific Ocean), 3rd
Mean elevation: 1,900 ft., 15th
Coastline: 6,640 mi., 1st
Shoreline: 33,904 mi., 1st

CLIMATE AND ENVIRONMENT

Temp., highest: 100 deg. on June 27, 1915, at Fort Yukon; lowest: −80 deg. on Jan. 23, 1971, at Prospect Creek Camp
Monthly average: highest: 71.8 deg., 51st; lowest: −21.6 deg., 1st; spread (high to low): 93.4 deg., 1st
Hazardous waste sites (1997): 7, 42nd
Endangered species: Animals: 2—Eskimo curlew, American peregrine falcon. Plants: 1

MAJOR CITIES
POPULATION, 1996
PERCENTAGE INCREASE, 1990-96

Anchorage, 250,505; 10.7%
Fairbanks, 32,960; 6.9%
Juneau, 29,756; 11.2%
College, 11,249; 178.23%
Sitka, 8,588; 10.06%

THE PEOPLE

Population (1997): 609,311, 48th
    Percent change (1990-97): 10.78%, 13th
    Percent of total U.S. pop.: 0.23%, 48th
    Per sq. mi: 0.93, 51st
Population (2000 proj.): 642,500, 48th
    Percent change (1995-2000): 6.37%, 17th
Percent in metro. area (1996): 41.27%, 44th
Foreign born: 25,000, 42nd
    Percent: 4.5%, 19th
Top three ancestries reported:
    German, 23.09%
    English, 14.00%
    Irish, 13.45%
White (1992): 450,000, 76.53%, 42nd
Black (1992): 24,000, 4.08%, 33rd
Native American (1992): 91,000, 15.48%, 1st
Asian, Pacific Isle (1992): 23,000, 3.91%, 6th
Hispanic origin (1992): 20,000, 3.40%, 22nd
Percent over 5 yrs. speaking language other
    than English at home: 12.1%, 15th
Percent males (1996): 52.60%, 1st; percent
    females: 47.40%, 51st
Percent never married: 27.2%, 17th
Marriages per 1,000 (1996): 8.94, 19th
Divorces per 1,000 (1996): 4.66, 19th
Median age (1996): 31.9
Under 5 years (1996): 8.24%, 4th
18 years and under (1996): 33.72%, 2nd
65 years and over (1996): 5.15%, 51st
Percent increase among the elderly (1995-96):
    4.62%, 1st

OF VITAL IMPORTANCE

Live births per 1,000 pop. (1996): 16.7, 5th
Infant mortality rate per 1,000 live births
    (1995): 7.7, 21st
    Rate for whites: 6.1, 32nd
    Rate for blacks: NA
Births to unmarried women, % of total
    (1996): 31.3%, 26th
Births to teenage mothers, % of total (1996):
    11.2%, 33rd
Abortions (1992): 2,370, 47th

Rate per 1,000 women 14-44 years old:
    16.5, 30th
    Percent change (1988-92): –10%, 29th
Average lifetime (1989-91): 74.83, 36th
Total death rate per 100,000 pop. (1995):
    423.0, 51st
    Accidents and adverse effects: 56.2, 2nd
    Alzheimer's disease: NA
    Cancer: 95.1, 51st
    Cerebrovascular diseases: 24.0, 51st
    Chronic liver disease and cirrhosis: 10.1,
        14th
    Chronic obstructive pulmonary diseases and
        allied conditions: 17.7, 51st
    Diabetes mellitus: 9.3, 51st
    Diseases of heart: 90.6, 51st
    HIV infection: 5.0, 39th
    Homicide: 8.9, 18th
    Injury by firearms: 20.2, 8th
    Motor vehicle accidents: 16.1, 30th
    Pneumonia and influenza: 9.1, 51st
    Suicide: 17.1, 6th

KEEPING WELL

Active nonfederal physicians per 100,000 pop.
    (1995): 153, 47th
Dentists per 100,000 (1991): 56, 20th
Nurses per 100,000 (1995): 1,011, 11th
Hospitals per 100,000 (1995): 2.81, 16th
    Admissions per 1,000 (1995): 66.23, 51st
    Hospital beds per 1,000 (1995): 2.15, 49th
    Occupancy rate per 100 beds (1995):
        53.85, 47th
    Average cost per patient per day (1995):
        $1,341, 2nd
    Average cost per stay (1995): $8,282, 3rd
AIDS cases (new, 1996): 36; per 100,000:
    5.9, 42nd
Persons living with HIV infection (1996): NA
    Other notifiable diseases, per 100,000 pop.:
        Gonorrhea (1995): 109.3, 23rd
        Syphilis (1995): 3.3, 38th
        Tuberculosis (1996): 15.8, 3rd
Pop. without health insur. (1996): 13.5%, 24th

HOUSEHOLDS BY TYPE

Total households (1996): 214,000, 50th
    Percent change (1990-96): 13.4%, 10th
    Per 1,000 pop. (1996): 352.55, 48th
    Percent of householders 65 yrs. and over
        (1996): 9.35%, 51st
    Persons per household (1996): 2.76, 5th
Family households: 132,837
    Percent of total: 70.32%, 27th

Nonfamily households: 56,078
Percent of total: 29.68%, 25th
Pop. living in group quarters: 20,701
Percent of pop.: 3.76%, 5th

LIVING QUARTERS

Total housing units: 232,608
Persons per unit: 2.36, 34th
Occupied housing units: 188,915
Percent of total units: 81.22%, 49th
Persons per unit: 2.78, 4th
Percent of units with over 1 person per room: 8.58%, 3rd
Owner-occupied units: 105,989
Percent of total units: 45.57%, 50th
Percent of occupied units: 56.10%, 46th
Persons per unit: 2.97, 3rd
Median value: $94,400, 14th
Renter-occupied units: 82,926
Percent of total units: 35.65%, 8th
Percent of occupied units: 43.90%, 7th
Persons per unit: 2.58, 5th
Median contract rent: $503, 6th
Rental vacancy rate: 8.5%, 24th
Mobile home, trailer & other as a percent of occupied housing units: 13.08%, 22nd
Persons in emergency shelters for homeless persons: 447, 0.081%, 10th
Persons visible in street locations: 79, 0.0144%, 13th
Nursing home population: 1,202, 0.22%, 51st

CRIME INDEX PER 100,000 (1996)

Total reported: 5,450.4, 17th
Percent increase: –5.3%, 34th
Violent: 727.7, 11th
Percent increase: –5.6%, 23rd
Murder & nonnegligent manslaughter: 7.4, 21st
Forcible rape: 65.6, 1st
Aggravated assault: 537.7, 7th
Robbery: 117.0, 31st
Property: 4,722.7, 17th
Percent increase: –5.2%, 35th
Burglary: 843.2, 27th
Larceny-theft: 3,386.7, 16th
Motor vehicle theft: 492.9, 19th

TEACHING AND LEARNING

Pop. 3 and over enrolled in school (1996): 155,363, 48th
Percent of pop.: 25.60%, 5th

Public elementary & secondary schools (1996-97): 495, 43rd
Total enrollment (1996): 126,015, 46th
Percent of school age pop.: 93.34%, 19th
Percent of total pop.: 20.76%, 2nd
Teachers (1996): 7,644, 48th
Percent of pop.: 1.26%, 5th
Pupil/teacher ratio (1995): 17.3, 15th
Teachers' avg. salary (1996-97): $50,647, 1st
Expenditure per capita (1992-93): $2,443.96, 1st
Education as % of state govt. expenditures: 24.3%, 49th
Expenditure per pupil (1994-95): $8,963, 4th
Percent increase (1993-94 & 1994-95): 0.91%, 49th
Percent at or above grade level, NAEP tests:
Reading, grade 4 (1994): NA
Math, grade 4 (1996): 65%, 20th
Math, grade 8 (1996): 68%, 11th
Percent of graduates taking SAT (1995): 47%, 22nd
Mean SAT verbal scores: 445, 28th
Mean SAT mathematical scores: 489, 29th
Percent of graduates taking ACT (1997): 32%, 28th
Mean ACT scores: 21.0, 30th
Percent of pop. over 25 completing:
Less than 9th grade: 5.1%, 50th
High school: 86.6%, 1st
College degree(s): 23.0%, 12th
Higher education, institutions (1996): 9, 49th
Enrollment (1995-96): 29,348, 51st
Percent increase in enroll. (1990-95): –1.6%, 43rd
White non-Hispanic (1995): 23,211, 50th
Percent of enroll.: 79.00%, 30th
Total minority enroll. (1995): 5,534, 42nd
Percent of enroll.: 18.86%, 21st
Black non-Hispanic (1995): 1,004, 43rd
Percent of enroll.: 3.42%, 35th
Hispanic (1995): 796, 42nd
Percent of enroll.: 2.71%, 20th
Asian/Pacific Islander (1995): 879, 44th
Percent of enroll.: 3.00%, 20th
American Indian/AK native (1995): 2,855, 13th
Percent of enroll.: 9.73%, 1st
Nonresident alien (1995): 603, 49th
Percent of enroll.: 2.05%, 40th
Female (1995): 17,480, 50th
Percent of enroll.: 59.56%, 2nd

Pub. institutions (1995-96): 4, 49th
Enrollment: 28,368, 49th
Percent increase in enrollment (1990-95): 2.1%, 28th
Percent of enroll.: 96.66%, 3rd
Private institutions (1995-96): 5, 48th
Enrollment: 980, 50th
Percent increase in enrollment (1990-95): -52.0%, 51st
Percent of enroll.: 3.34%, 49th
Tuition (in state), public 4-year institution (1996-97): $2,552, 27th
Tuition (in state), public 2-year institution (1996-97): $1,850, 14th
Tuition, private 4-year institution (1996-97): $8,108, 39th
Public library systems (1994): 87, 32nd
Books & serial vol. per capita: 3.1, 23rd
Library visits per capita: 3.8, 23rd
Circulation per capita: 6.3, 29th

LAW ENFORCEMENT AND CORRECTIONS

Police protection and corrections expenditures (1996): $203,187,000
Per capita: $334.74, 1st
Police per 10,000 pop. (1996): 18.32, 39th
Prisoners (1 year or more) per 100,000 pop. (1996): 379, 20th
Percent change (1995-96): 13.2%, 8th
Percent of inmates that are female: 7.3%, 10th
Percent change: 10.7%, 22nd
Death penalty: no

RELIGION, NUMBER AND PERCENT OF POPULATION

Agnostic: NA
Buddhist: NA
Christian: NA
Hindu: NA
Jewish: NA
Muslim: NA
Unitarian: NA
Other: NA
None: NA
Refused to answer: NA

MAKING A LIVING

Personal income per capita (1996): $24,558, 20th
Percent increase (1995-96): 0.7%, 49th
Disposable personal income per capita (1996): $21,277, 19th

Median income of households (average, 1995-96): $51,074, 1st
Percent of pop. below poverty level (1995-96): 7.7%, 50th

ECONOMY

In civilian labor force (1996): 316,000
Percent of total pop.: 74.2%, 3rd
Percent of total pop. 65 years and over: NA
Percent of total female pop.: 68.2%, 3rd
Major employer industries (total nonagricultural, 1996):
Construction: 12,500—4.7%, 21st
Finance, insurance, & real estate: 11,700—4.4%, 43rd
Government: 73,100—27.8%, 2nd
Manufacturing: 16,200—6.2%, 47th
Service: 62,400—23.7%, 43rd
Trade: 54,600—20.7%, 48th
Transportation, communications, public utilities: 22,700—8.6%, 1st
Unemployment rate (1996): 7.8%, 3rd
Male: 9.1%, 1st
Female: 6.3%, 9th
Total businesses (1995): 17,264, 50th
New business incorps. (1995): 1,428
Percent of total businesses: 8.27, 32nd
Business failures (1995): 124
Failures per 10,000 businesses: 71.8, 35th
Agriculture farm income:
Marketing (1996): $29,418,000, 50th
Average per farm: $58,836, 44th
Leading products (1997): Barley, oats, hay, silage, potatoes, lettuce
Average value land & build. per acre (1997): NA
Govt. payments (1996): $1,258,000, 47th
Average per farm: $2,516, 24th
Construction, value of all (1996): $983,379,000, 44th
Per capita: $1,620, 9th
Manufactures (1995):
Value added: $1,458,600,000
Per capita: $2,416, 47th
Leading products (1997): Fish products, lumber and pulp, furs
Value of nonfuel mineral production (1996): $523,000,000, 25th
Leading mineral products (1996): Petroleum, natural gas, zinc, lead, gold, sand/gravel, stone
Energy consumption per person (1994): 1,050.8 mil. Btu, 1st

Retail sales (1995): $6,405,000,000
  Per household: $30,198, 4th
  Sales increase (1994-95): 6.0%, 20th
Tourism revenues (1994): $863 mil.
Foreign exports, in total value (1996): $2,879,000,000, 33rd
  Per capita: $4,743, 4th
Gross state product per person (1994): $37,475, 3rd
Public aid recipients (percent of resident pop. 1994): 7.5%, 15th
Medicaid recipients (percent of pop., 1995): 11.3%, 30th
Medicare enrollment per 1,000 pop. (1996): 59, 50th

TRAVEL AND TRANSPORTATION

Motor vehicle registrations (1996): 531,017, 49th
  Per 1,000 pop.: 877.76, 15th
Motorcycle registrations (1996): 13,122, 49th
  Per 1,000 pop.: 24.71, 12th
Licensed drivers (1996): 434,389, 49th
  Per 1,000 pop.: 720.92, 9th
Public roads & streets (1996)
  Total mileage: 13,255, 47th
    Per 1,000 pop.: 121.84, 19th
  Rural mileage: 11,460, 46th
    Per 1,000 pop.: 18.88, 18th
  Urban mileage: 1,795, 49th
    Per 1,000 pop.: 2.96, 32nd
  Interstate mileage: 1,086, 15th
    Per 1,000 pop.: 1.79, 2nd
Speed limit (max. interstate, autos, mi. per hr., 1997): 65
Annual vehicle-mi. of travel per driver (1996): 9,355, 51st
Mean travel time for workers age 16+ who work away from home: 16.7 min., 45th

GOVERNMENT

Percent of voting age pop. registered (1996): 97.60%, 1st
  Percent of voting age pop. voting for president: (1996): 56.9%, 14th
  Percent of voting age pop. voting for U.S. representatives (1996): 55.1%, 15th
State legislators, total (1997): 60, 49th
  Women members (1997): 8
    Percent of legislature: 13%, 45th
U.S. Congress, House members (1998): 1
  Change (1988-98): 0
Revenues (1996):
  State govt.: $8,253,549,000
    Per capita: $13,597.28, 1st
    Parimutuel & amusement taxes & lotteries, revenue per capita (1995): $3.32, 43rd
Expenditures (1996):
  State govt.: $5,629,502,000
    Per capita: $9,274.30, 1st
Debt outstanding (1996): $3,176,601,000
  Per capita: $5,233.28, 3rd

LAWS AND REGULATIONS

Legal driving age: 16
Marriage age without parental consent: 18
Divorce residence requirement: For qualifications check local statutes

ATTRACTIONS (1997)

Major opera companies: 1
Per capita spending by the NEA (1997: $1.01, 4th
State Fair in late August at Palmer

SPORTS AND COMPETITION

NCAA (Division II) basketball teams: Univ. of Alaska-Anchorage Seawolves, Univ. of Alaska-Fairbanks Nanooks

WEBSITES CONTAINING FURTHER INFORMATION

The Alaskan Center	http://alaskan.com
State of Alaska's Home Page	http://www.state.ak.us

ARIZONA

"Land of extremes. Land of contrasts. Land of surprises. Land of contradictions. A land that is never to be fully understood but always to be loved....That is Arizona." Federal Writers' Project, Arizona

The last of the conterminous states to be admitted to the union, Arizona is renowned for its natural wonders, with its magnificent deserts, mountains, and plateaus. The most startling area of the state is, of course, the Grand Canyon, which is one of the Seven Natural Wonders of the World. Long ago, ancient Indian peoples built on Arizona lands great communal cliff dwellings, whose crumbling adobe walls remain as testimony to their culture. The state capital, Phoenix, was founded on Indian ruins and—like its namesake, the mythical bird—grew swiftly out of the remains. In recent years, Arizona has continued to grow spectacularly in population, as its healthful climate and industrious workers have lured both retired persons and industry.

SUPERLATIVES

• The Grand Canyon, one of the world's greatest natural wonders.
• The Arizona trout, found only here.
• Has led the nation in copper production since 1907.
• Leads all states in value of nonfuel mineral production.
• Hoover Dam (partly in Arizona), which impounds the nation's largest artificial body of water.
• The largest tribe on the largest U.S. reservation—Arizona's Navajo Indians.
• World's largest solar telescope, at Kitts Peak National Observatory in Sells.

MOMENTS IN HISTORY

• The Pueblo (Spanish for village) peoples flourished from about 700 A.D through the late 1200s—a striking civilization.
• In 1539, Franciscan friar Marcos de Niza failed to find the fabled wealth of the Seven Cities of Cibola.
• The enormous expedition of Francisco Vásquez de Coronado entered present-day Arizona in 1540 and made many discoveries.
• Garcia Lopez de Cardenas reached the brink of a great gorge one day in 1540, but failed to appreciate the wonders of what is now called the Grand Canyon.

> ### So They Say
> *"...Ours has been the first and will doubtless be the last party of whites to visit this profitless locality."*
>
> **Traveler Joseph Ives, describing the Grand Canyon (1857)**

• Little attention was paid to the area until the arrival of the Jesuits in 1692, led by Father Eusebio Francisco Kino. He baptized thousands, taught them how to raise crops, and explored much of the area.
• In 1752, Tubac, in the Santa Cruz Valley, became the first permanent white settlement in what is now Arizona.
• Arizona continued under Spanish and later Mexican rule until the Mexican War, beginning in 1846. In that war a notable military group, the renowned Mormon volunteer battalion, made the longest infantry march on record.

> ### So They Say
> Lieutenant Colonel Philip St. George Cooke, leader of the Mormon Battalion, "...in the evening [Dec. 18, 1846], camped without water after traveling 30 miles....[Dec. 19] Started again... traveled till a little after dark and still no prospects of water....I was almost choked with thirst and hardly able to stand...passed by many lying on the roadside begging for water. Some of the men finally reached the river..." and brought back water.
>
> **Henry Standage of the Mormon Battalion, in an unpublished journal**

• During the gold rush to California, beginning in 1849, 60,000 persons passed across Arizona, suffering many Indian attacks.
• Gold was discovered north of Fort Yuma in 1858. Soon, Gila City had a population of 1,000, but the boom quickly died.
• In February 1862, Confederate cavalry took over Tucson. Federal troops then occupied Yuma.

• The Battle of Apache Pass, in July 1862, was a major struggle in the Indian wars that took place from the 1860s to the early 1870s. Indians retreated when government troops fired their howitzers.

• During the years 1861 to 1880, travelers and peaceful Indians feared the periodic raids of Chief Geronimo.

• Phoenix originated in 1866 as a hay camp to supply Camp McDowell's fodder. The town grew as soon as Jack Swilling began to restore the prehistoric irrigation canals.

• After several moves the capital was located at Phoenix in 1889.

• In 1911 the Salt River was dammed to make Theodore Roosevelt Lake. It was the first national reclamation project and greatly hastened the state's growth.

• Arizona became the 48th state on February 14, 1912.

• In 1916 the already poor relations with Mexico worsened when Mexican revolutionary Pancho Villa was thwarted as he attempted to enter Nogales from Sonora.

• In 1934, Arizona lost the "water war" when the courts awarded a large share of the Colorado River's water to California.

• In the decades from 1960 to 1990, the population grew amazingly, by more than 250%.

• Governor Evan Mecham was convicted in 1988 by the Arizona Senate on charges of misconduct and removed from office (but was then acquitted of a key criminal charge).

• In 1991 the biosphere, designed as supposedly a complete ecosystem, was sealed for two years in Oracle, beginning a controversial experiment.

• Governor Fife Symington resigned in 1997 after being found guilty of fraud.

THAT'S INTERESTING

• The bed of the Colorado River at the Grand Canyon lies at about the same level as it did millions of years ago. The canyon was formed as the ground continued to rise, and the river continued to carve through it as the force of the water and the sand and boulders cut away at the rising land.

• Arizona has its own 90 deg. share of the only place in the country where four states come together, a point on the map known as the Four Corners.

> ## So They Say
> During the great Pueblo period, grand apartment houses were built with as many as four stories and dozens of rooms. These fantastic structures are found in all parts of Arizona.   **The Enchantment of Arizona**

• The great dome of the White Dove of the Desert mission was formed over a lofty mound of earth, piled up by the Indian converts. Learning that many coins had been buried in the earth beneath the dome, the eager Indians cleared away the entire earthen form to dig up those "riches."

• Because Arizona's conditions seemed ideal for it, Edward F. Beale decided that for desert transport, desert animals should be used, so he imported camels. The great beasts could carry heavy loads and proved useful for a time, but they ultimately proved impractical. Some were abandoned or ran away, and they could occasionally be seen plodding over the sand, but they did not survive.

• Famed Mission San Xavier at Tucson features a carving of a cat. On the opposite side of the mission is a carving of a mouse. According to Indian legend, the world will end when that cat catches the mouse.

• Based on the legend of the phoenix bird, which is burned by fire every 500 years and then rises from its ashes, the new town that rose on the "ashes" of the prehistoric Hohokam settlement was named Phoenix.

> ## So They Say
> "The Casa Grande—a four story building as large as a castle and equal to the finest church in these lands of Sonora."
>
> **Father Eusebio Francisco Kino,
> describing that monument
> to Pueblo culture**

NOTABLE NATIVES

Cesar Estrada Chavez (Yuma, 1927-1993), labor leader. **Cochise** (probably in Arizona, 1812?-1874), Indian leader. **Geronimo** (Arizona, 1829-1909), Indian leader. **Barry Morris Goldwater** (Phoenix, 1909-), public official. **Morris (Mo) King Udall** (St. Johns, 1922-), public official. **Stewart Lee Udall** (St. Johns, 1920-), public official.

GENERAL

Admitted to statehood: February 14, 1912
Origin of name: Spanish version of the Pima
    Indian word for "little spring place," or
    the Aztec word *arizuma*, meaning
    "silver bearing"
Capital: Phoenix
Nickname: Grand Canyon State
Motto: *Ditat Deus*—God enriches
Bird: Cactus wren
Flower: Blossom of the Saguaro cactus
Song: "Arizona"
Tree: Paloverde

THE LAND

Area: 114,006 sq. mi., 6th
    Land: 113,642 sq. mi., 6th
    Water: 364 sq. mi., 45th
    Inland water: 364 sq. mi., 41st
Topography: Colorado plateau in the N,
    containing the Grand Canyon; Mexi-
    can Highlands running diagonally NW
    to SE; Sonoran Desert in the SW
Number of counties: 15
Geographic center: Yavapai, 55 mi. ESE of
    Prescott
Length: 400 mi.; width: 310 mi.
Highest point: 12,633 ft. (Humphreys Peak),
    12th
Lowest point: 70 ft., (Colorado River), 27th
Mean elevation: 4,100 ft., 7th

CLIMATE AND ENVIRONMENT

Temp., highest: 128 deg. on June 29, 1994, at
    Lake Havasu City; lowest: –40 deg. on
    Jan. 7, 1971, at Hawley Lake
Monthly average: highest: 105.0 deg., 1st;
    lowest: 38.1 deg., 49th; spread (high to
    low): 66.9 deg., 30th
Hazardous waste sites (1997): 10, 34th
Endangered species: Animals: 24—Kanab
    ambersnail, Lesser bat, Masked bob-
    white, Bonytail chub, Humpback chub,
    Virgin River chub, Yaqui chub, Ameri-
    can peregrine falcon, Southwestern
    willow flycatcher, Jaguar, Jaguarundi,
    Ocelot, Sonoran pronghorn, Desert
    pupfish, Cactus ferruginous pygmy-
    owl, Yuma clapper rail, Sonoran tiger
    salamander, Colorado squawfish,
    Mount Graham red squirrel, Razorback
    sucker, Gila topminnow, Gila trout,
    Hualapai Mexican vole, Woundfin.
    Plants: 11

MAJOR CITIES POPULATION, 1996 PERCENTAGE INCREASE, 1990-96

Phoenix, 1,159,014; 17.7%
Tucson, 449,002; 9.1%
Mesa, 344,764; 19.2%
Glendale, 182,219; 23.2%
Scottsdale, 179,012; 37.6%

THE PEOPLE

Population (1997): 4,554,966, 21st
    Percent change (1990-97): 24.27%, 2nd
    Percent of total U.S. pop.: 1.70%, 21st
    Per sq. mi: 39.95, 37th
Population (2000 proj.): 4,818,000, 21st
    Percent change (1995-2000): 14.22%, 3rd
Percent in metro. area (1996): 85.05%, 11th
Foreign born: 278,000, 14th
    Percent: 7.6%, 13th
Top three ancestries reported:
    German, 23.96%
    English, 15.99%
    Irish, 14.46%
White: 2,963,186, 80.85%, 33rd
Black: 110,524, 3.02%, 37th
Native American: 203,527, 5.55%, 6th
Asian, Pacific Isle: 55,206, 1.51%, 20th
Other races: 332,785, 9.08%, 4th
Hispanic origin: 688,338, 18.78%, 4th
Percent over 5 yrs. speaking language other
    than English at home: 20.8%, 6th
Percent males (1996): 49.52%, 12th; percent
    females: 50.48%, 40th
Percent never married: 25.5%, 26th
Marriages per 1,000 (1996): 8.86, 20th
Divorces per 1,000 (1996): 5.83, 9th
Median age (1996): 34.4
Under 5 years (1996): 7.97%, 7th
18 years and under (1996): 28.82%, 23rd
65 years and over (1996): 13.23%, 22nd
Percent increase among the elderly (1995-96):
    2.32%, 4th

OF VITAL IMPORTANCE

Live births per 1,000 pop. (1996): 18.0, 2nd
Infant mortality rate per 1,000 live births
    (1995): 7.5, 25th
    Rate for whites: 7.2, 9th
    Rate for blacks: 17.0, 12th
Births to unmarried women, % of total
    (1996): 39.0%, 6th
Births to teenage mothers, % of total (1996):
    15.0%, 14th

Abortions (1992): 20,600, 17th
  Rate per 1,000 women 14-44 years old: 24.1, 16th
  Percent change (1988-92): –16%, 41st
Average lifetime (1989-91): 76.10, 22nd
Total death rate per 100,000 pop. (1995): 837.9, 35th
  Accidents and adverse effects: 47.0, 8th
  Alzheimer's disease: 9.1, 20th
  Cancer: 190.1, 39th
  Cerebrovascular diseases: 51.8, 42nd
  Chronic liver disease and cirrhosis: 13.1, 4th
  Chronic obstructive pulmonary diseases and allied conditions: 48.3, 7th
  Diabetes mellitus: 19.5, 36th
  Diseases of heart: 242.6, 35th
  HIV infection: 11.5, 18th
  Homicide: 12.7, 5th
  Injury by firearms: 23.4, 4th
  Motor vehicle accidents: 23.5, 7th
  Pneumonia and influenza: 27.7, 36th
  Suicide: 19.1, 3rd

KEEPING WELL

Active nonfederal physicians per 100,000 pop. (1995): 198, 31st
Dentists per 100,000 (1991): 50, 33rd
Nurses per 100,000 (1995): 760, 37th
Hospitals per 100,000 (1995): 1.45, 42nd
  Admissions per 1,000 (1995): 101.23, 38th
  Hospital beds per 1,000 (1995): 2.35, 44th
  Occupancy rate per 100 beds (1995): 56.57, 41st
  Average cost per patient per day (1995): $1,191, 7th
  Average cost per stay (1995): $5,613, 32nd
AIDS cases (new, 1996): 594; per 100,000: 13.4, 27th
Persons living with HIV infection, not yet AIDS (1996): 3,070
Other notifiable diseases, per 100,000 pop.:
  Gonorrhea (1995): 91.1, 27th
  Syphilis (1995): 9.8, 27th
  Tuberculosis (1996): 6.4, 20th
Pop. without health insur. (1996): 24.1%, 2nd

HOUSEHOLDS BY TYPE

Total households (1996): 1,687,000, 21st
  Percent change (1990-96): 23.3%, 2nd
  Per 1,000 pop. (1996) 380.98, 24th
  Percent of householders 65 yrs. and over (1996): 21.70%, 26th

Persons per household (1996): 2.59, 23rd
Family households: 940,106
  Percent of total: 68.68%, 41st
Nonfamily households: 428,737
  Percent of total: 31.32%, 11th
Pop. living in group quarters: 80,683
  Percent of pop.: 2.20%, 46th

LIVING QUARTERS

Total housing units: 1,659,430
  Persons per unit: 2.21, 46th
Occupied housing units: 1,368,843
  Percent of total units: 82.49%, 46th
  Persons per unit: 2.59, 15th
  Percent of units with over 1 person per room: 7.42%, 7th
Owner-occupied units: 878,561
  Percent of total units: 52.94%, 44th
  Percent of occupied units: 64.18%, 40th
  Persons per unit: 2.71, 29th
  Median value: $80,100, 20th
Renter-occupied units: 490,282
  Percent of total units: 29.55%, 24th
  Percent of occupied units: 35.82%, 14th
  Persons per unit: 2.46, 12th
  Median contract rent: $370, 18th
  Rental vacancy rate: 15.3%, 1st
Mobile home, trailer & other as a percent of occupied housing units: 20.08%, 4th
Persons in emergency shelters for homeless persons: 2,735, 0.075%, 13th
Persons visible in street locations: 1,897, 0.0518%, 4th
Nursing home population: 14,472, 0.39%, 47th

CRIME INDEX PER 100,000 (1996)

Total reported: 7,067.0, 3rd
  Percent increase: –14.0%, 51st
  Violent: 631.5, 18th
    Percent increase: –11.5%, 45th
    Murder & nonnegligent manslaughter: 8.5, 14th
    Forcible rape: 31.2, 32nd
    Aggravated assault: 424.0, 14th
    Robbery: 167.8, 19th
  Property: 6,435.5, 3rd
    Percent increase: –14.2%, 51st
    Burglary: 1,256.3, 7th
    Larceny-theft: 4,252.5, 4th
    Motor vehicle theft: 926.7, 2nd

TEACHING AND LEARNING

Pop. 3 and over enrolled in school (1996): 1,023,740, 21st
　Percent of pop.: 23.12%, 18th
Public elementary & secondary schools (1996-97): 1,133, 30th
　Total enrollment (1996): 749,759, 22nd
　　Percent of school age pop.: 92.91%, 23rd
　　Percent of total pop.: 16.93%, 30th
　Teachers (1996): 39,315, 25th
　　Percent of pop.: 0.89%, 45th
　Pupil/teacher ratio (1995): 19.6, 6th
　Teachers' avg. salary (1996-97): $33,350, 33rd
　Expenditure per capita (1992-93): $1,303.18, 28th
　　Education as % of state govt. expenditures: 36.1%, 22nd
　Expenditure per pupil (1994-95): $4,778, 41st
　　Percent increase (1993-94 & 1994-95): 3.62%, 30th
Percent at or above grade level, NAEP tests:
　Reading, grade 4 (1994): 24%, 29th
　Math, grade 4 (1996): 57%, 31st
　Math, grade 8 (1996): 57%, 24th
Percent of graduates taking SAT (1995): 27%, 27th
　Mean SAT verbal scores: 448, 25th
　Mean SAT mathematical scores: 496, 26th
Percent of graduates taking ACT (1997): 27%, 30th
　Mean ACT scores: 21.1, 29th
Percent of pop. over 25 completing:
　Less than 9th grade: 9.0%, 29th
　High school: 78.7%, 20th
　College degree(s): 20.3%, 23rd
Higher education, institutions (1996): 45, 28th
　Enrollment (1995-96): 273,981, 19th
　　Percent increase in enroll. (1990-95): 3.7%, 24th
　White non-Hispanic (1995): 200,052, 19th
　　Percent of enroll.: 73.02%, 37th
　Total minority enroll. (1995): 66,658, 15th
　　Percent of enroll.: 24.33%, 16th
　Black non-Hispanic (1995): 8,776, 30th
　　Percent of enroll.: 3.20%, 36th
　Hispanic (1995): 38,691, 6th
　　Percent of enroll.: 14.12%, 4th
　Asian/Pacific Islander (1995): 8,578, 17th
　　Percent of enroll.: 3.13%, 19th
　American Indian/AK native (1995): 10,613, 3rd
　　Percent of enroll.: 3.87%, 7th
　Nonresident alien (1995): 7,271, 19th
　　Percent of enroll.: 2.65%, 26th
　Female (1995): 151,070, 20th
　　Percent of enroll.: 55.14%, 37th
　Pub. institutions (1995-96): 23, 29th
　　Enrollment: 254,530, 12th
　　　Percent increase in enrollment (1990-95): 2.5%, 27th
　　Percent of enroll.: 92.90%, 5th
　Private institutions (1995-96): 22, 29th
　　Enrollment: 19,451, 35th
　　　Percent increase in enrollment (1990-95): 22.1%, 5th
　　Percent of enroll.: 7.10%, 47th
　Tuition (in state), public 4-year institution (1996-97): $2,009, 45th
　Tuition (in state), public 2-year institution (1996-97): $782, 47th
　Tuition, private 4-year institution (1996-97): $7,811, 42nd
Public library systems (1994): 39, 44th
　Books & serial vol. per capita: 2.0, 39th
　Library visits per capita: 4.7, 13th
　Circulation per capita: 6.8, 26th

LAW ENFORCEMENT AND CORRECTIONS

Police protection and corrections expenditures (1996): $619,555,000
　Per capita: $139.92, 15th
Police per 10,000 pop. (1996): 20.40, 32nd
Prisoners (1 year or more) per 100,000 pop. (1996): 481, 9th
　Percent change (1995-96): 6.5%, 22nd
　Percent of inmates that are female: 6.7%, 18th
　　Percent change: 6.1%, 33rd
Death penalty: yes, by lethal gas; lethal injection after 11/15/92
　Under sentence (Jan. 1998): 123, 9th
　Executed, 1976-97: 9, 11th
　Executed in 1997: 2, 8th

RELIGION, NUMBER AND PERCENT OF POPULATION

Agnostic: 29,525—1.10%, 6th
Buddhist: 2,684—0.10%, 17th
Christian: 2,133,867—79.50%, 45th
Hindu: NA
Jewish: 42,946—1.60%, 11th
Muslim: 5,369—0.20%, 13th
Unitarian: 5,368—0.20%, 23rd
Other: 61,735—2.30%, 6th

None: 327,461—12.20%, 6th
Refused to answer: 75,155—2.80%, 12th

MAKING A LIVING

Personal income per capita (1996): $20,989, 37th
Percent increase (1995-96): 5.2%, 8th
Disposable personal income per capita (1996): $18,308, 38th
Median income of households (average, 1995-96): $31,706, 38th
Percent of pop. below poverty level (1995-96): 18.3%, 5th

ECONOMY

In civilian labor force (1996): 2,249,000
Percent of total pop.: 66.4%, 34th
Percent of total pop. 65 years and over: NA
Percent of total female pop.: 58.2%, 39th
Major employer industries (total nonagricultural, 1996):
Construction: 126,500—6.7%, 2nd
Finance, insurance, & real estate: 115,100—6.1%, 11th
Government: 320,600—16.9%, 26th
Manufacturing: 199,500—10.5%, 39th
Service: 561,400—29.6%, 15th
Trade: 466,200—24.6%, 14th
Transportation, communications, public utilities: 92,100—4.9%, 29th
Unemployment rate (1996): 5.5%, 17th
Male: 5.3%, 20th
Female: 5.8%, 15th
Total businesses (1995): 99,583, 22nd
New business incorps. (1995): 10,866
Percent of total businesses: 10.91%, 17th
Business failures (1995): 1,410
Failures per 10,000 businesses: 141.6, 5th
Agriculture farm income:
Marketing (1996): $2,146,417,000, 32nd
Average per farm: $286,189, 2nd
Leading products (1997): Cattle, cotton, lettuce, cauliflower, broccoli, sorghum, barley, corn, wheat, citrus fruits
Average value land & build. per acre (1997): $420, 42nd
Percent increase (1996-97): 5%, 26th
Govt. payments (1996): $57,993,000, 30th
Average per farm: $7,732, 5th
Construction, value of all (1996): $9,790,758,000, 10th
Per capita: $2,211, 2nd

Manufactures (1995):
Value added: $20,911,600,000
Per capita: $4,958, 38th
Leading products (1997): Electronics, printing and publishing, foods, primary and fabricated metals, aircraft and missiles, apparel
Value of nonfuel mineral production (1996): $3,530,000,000, 1st
Leading mineral products (1996): Natural gas, petroleum, coal, copper, sand/gravel, cement, molybdenum, lime
Energy consumption per person (1994): 253.5 mil. Btu, 43rd
Retail sales (1995): $39,322,000,000
Per household: $24,544, 27th
Sales increase (1994-95): 7.7%, 8th
Tourism revenues (1994): $10.5 bil.
Foreign exports, in total value (1996): $10,503,000,000, 17th
Per capita: $2,372, 10th
Gross state product per person (1994): $23,090, 36th
Public aid recipients (percent of resident pop. 1994): 6.5%, 28th
Medicaid recipients (percent of pop., 1995): 11.5%, 29th
Medicare enrollment per 1,000 pop. (1996): 140, 31st

TRAVEL AND TRANSPORTATION

Motor vehicle registrations (1996): 2,982,523, 25th
Per 1,000 pop.: 672.60, 47th
Motorcycle registrations (1996): 71,873, 19th
Per 1,000 pop.: 24.10, 15th
Licensed drivers (1996): 2,626,222, 23rd
Per 1,000 pop.: 610.04, 48th
Public roads & streets (1996)
Total mileage: 54,895, 35th
Per 1,000 pop.: 112.40, 35th
Rural mileage: 38,662, 36th
Per 1,000 pop.: 8.73, 36th
Urban mileage: 16,233, 19th
Per 1,000 pop.: 3.67, 8th
Interstate mileage: 1,169, 13th
Per 1,000 pop.: 0.26, 17th
Speed limit (max. interstate, autos, mi. per hr., 1997): 75
Annual vehicle-mi. of travel per driver (1996): 15,445, 14th
Mean travel time for workers age 16+ who work away from home: 21.6 min., 16th

GOVERNMENT

Percent of voting age pop. registered (1996): 71.37%, 37th

Percent of voting age pop. voting for president: (1996): 45.4%, 43rd

Percent of voting age pop. voting for U.S. representatives (1996): 43.8%, 36th

State legislators, total (1997): 90, 43rd
   Women members (1997): 33
   Percent of legislature: 37%, 3rd

U.S. Congress, House members (1998): 6
   Change (1988-98): 1

Revenues (1996):
   State govt.: $12,594,269,000
   Per capita: $2,844.23, 47th
   Parimutuel & amusement taxes & lotteries, revenue per capita (1995): $64.53, 36th

Expenditures (1996):
   State govt.: $11,898,144,000
   Per capita: $2,687.02, 44th

Debt outstanding (1996): $2,936,004,000
   Per capita: $663.05, 46th

LAWS AND REGULATIONS

Legal driving age: 16
Marriage age without parental consent: 18
Divorce residence requirement: 90 days

ATTRACTIONS (1997)

Major opera companies: 1
Major symphony orchestras: 2
Major dance companies: 1
Major professional theater companies (non-profit): 1

Per capita spending by the NEA (1997): $0.22, 33rd

State Fair in late October-early November at Phoenix

SPORTS AND COMPETITION

NCAA (Division I) football and basketball teams: Arizona State Univ. Sun Devils, Northern Arizona Univ. Lumberjacks, Univ. of Arizona Wildcats

Major league baseball teams: Arizona Diamondbacks (NL West), Bank One Ballpark

NBA basketball teams: Phoenix Suns, America West Arena

WNBA basketball teams: Phoenix Mercury, America West Arena

NFL football teams: Arizona Cardinals (NFC), Sun Devil Stadium

NHL hockey teams: Phoenix Coyotes, America West Arena

WEBSITES CONTAINING FURTHER INFORMATION

Arizona Guide	http://www.arizonaguide.com
State of Arizona Services via World Wide Web	http://www.state.az.us
	http://www.azleg.state.az.us

ARKANSAS

"If I could rest anywhere it would be in Arkansaw, where the men are of the real half-horse, half-alligator breed such as grows nowhere else on the face of the universal earth." Attributed to frontiersman Davy Crockett

Long known as "a state which should be better known," Arkansas was thrust into national prominence and scrutiny in 1992 as its native son Bill Clinton campaigned for and won the presidency of the United States. It is a beautiful state of mountains, valleys, thick forests, and fertile plains, and tourism is one of its most important industries. Millions of travelers come to the state every year—many of them to visit the hot springs in Eureka Springs and Hot Springs. Nearly 99% of the people in this westernmost of the Southern states are native-born Americans.

SUPERLATIVES

- The continent's only diamond mine, located near Murfreesboro.
- Magnet Cove region, claiming to possess the world's greatest mineral variety.
- Pine Bluff—known as the world center of archery bow production.
- The first woman U.S. senator—Hattie Caraway.

MOMENTS IN HISTORY

- In 1541 the large party of Spanish explorer Hernando de Soto moved across the Mississippi into what is now Arkansas and spent the winter at the Indian village of Utiangue on a bluff over the Ouachita River.
- Early explorers found the Quapaw, Osage, and Caddo Indian confederacies.
- The remarkable party of Father Jacques Marquette and Louis Jolliet reached the mouth of the Arkansas River in 1673.
- The French explorer Robert Cavalier, Sieur de La Salle entered present-day Arkansas in 1682.
- Under Henri de Tonty, stragglers from La Salle's party founded Arkansas Post, the first permanent European settlement in the lower Mississippi Valley, and for 80 years the only outpost in a vast region.
- After the United States bought the huge Louisiana Territory from France, U.S. troops took over Arkansas Post in 1804.
- The earthquake that shook the Mississippi Valley in 1811 has been called the strongest ever to strike the continent.

- Despite the opposition to a new slave state, Arkansas became a state on June 15, 1836.
- Fort Smith became a principal outfitting post for travelers to the West, and with the rush of the 1849 gold seekers, it became a rip-roaring frontier settlement.
- Arkansas Governor Henry M. Rector seized Fort Smith, and Arkansas joined the Confederacy in 1861.
- When the Civil War ended in 1865, returning Confederate troops found their farms in ruin, their credit gone, and no mules or plows to put in new crops.
- Arkansas was put under U.S. military rule in 1867.
- After Arkansas adopted a new constitution in 1874, the state returned to civilian rule.
- Until federal Judge Isaac C. Parker took over at Fort Smith in 1875, the region to the west was lawless. For the next 21 years, Parker dispensed stern justice on the frontier.
- Large reserves of bauxite were found in 1887.
- In 1906 diamonds were found near Murfreesboro. This proved to be the only "diamond mine" on the continent.
- In 1919 the state's first oil well was brought in near Stephens; the state has continued to be a major oil and gas producer.
- In the 1957 struggle over school integration, President Dwight Eisenhower sent federal troops to Little Rock to enforce a court integration order.
- Republican Winthrop Rockefeller became governor in 1967, gaining attention as the

second Rockefeller brother to be the governor of a state.

• In November 1992, Governor Bill Clinton was elected as the first U.S. president from Arkansas.

• Major figures involved in the Whitewater Development Corp.—a land deal involving President Clinton in the 1980s—were convicted of fraud and conspiracy in Little Rock in 1996.

THAT'S INTERESTING

• During a battle of Chickasaw versus Quapaw Indians, the Chickasaw ran out of ammunition. The Quawpaw obligingly gave half of their gunpowder to the enemy, and the battle continued.

• The farm of John M. Huddleston was so poor that he was about to give up on it when he discovered the continent's only diamond mine on his property.

• Some Arkansas rivers were so shallow that steamboats were designed to operate in as little as a foot of water.

• Sam Walton founded his Wal-Mart Stores merchandising empire in Bentonville and became one of the nation's richest men.

NOTABLE NATIVES

Johnny Cash (Kingsland, 1932-), singer. **William Jefferson (Bill) Clinton** (Hope, 1946-), U.S. president. **Jay Hanna (Dizzy) Dean** (Lucas, 1911-1974), baseball player. **Orval Faubus** (Combs, 1910-1994), public official. **John Johnson** (Arkansas City, 1918-), publisher. **Scott Joplin** (Texarkana, 1868-1917), musician/composer. **Douglas MacArthur** (Little Rock, 1880-1964), soldier/statesman. **Edward Durell Stone** (Fayetteville, 1902-1978), architect.

GENERAL

Admitted to statehood: June 15, 1836
Origin of name: From the name of the Arkansas Indians, meaning "wind from the south"
Capital: Little Rock
Nickname: Land of Opportunity, Razorback State
Motto: *Regnat Populus*—The people rule
Bird: Mockingbird
Insect: Honeybee
Flower: Apple blossom
Gem: Diamond

Song: "Arkansas"
Tree: Pine

THE LAND

Area: 53,182 sq. mi., 28th
  Land: 52,075 sq. mi., 27th
  Water: 1,107 sq. mi., 27th
    Inland water: 1,107 sq. mi., 18th
Topography: Eastern delta and prairie, southern lowland forests, and the northwestern highland, which includes the Ozark plateaus
Number of counties: 75
Geographic center: Pulaski, 12 mi. NW of Little Rock
Length: 260 mi.; width: 240 mi.
Highest point: 2,753 ft. (Magazine Mountain), 34th
Lowest point: 55 ft. (Ouachita River), 26th
Mean elevation: 650 ft., 36th

CLIMATE AND ENVIRONMENT

Temp., highest: 120 deg. on Aug. 10, 1936, at Ozark; lowest: –29 deg. on Feb. 13, 1905, at Pond
Monthly average: highest: 93.6 deg., 6th; lowest: 26.6 deg., 38th; spread (high to low): 67.0 deg., 28th
Hazardous waste sites (1997): 11, 33rd
Endangered species: Animals: 15—Gray bat, Indiana bat, Ozark big-eared bat, American burying beetle, Cave crayfish (*aculabrum*), Cave crayfish (*zophonastes*), American peregrine falcon, Curtis' pearlymussel, Pink mucket pearlymussel, Fat pocketbook, Speckled pocketbook, Ouachita rock-pocketbook, Pallid sturgeon, Least tern, Red-cockaded woodpecker. Plants: 3

MAJOR CITIES
POPULATION, 1996
PERCENTAGE INCREASE, 1990-96

Little Rock, 175,752; 0.0%
Fort Smith, 75,776; 4.1%
North Little Rock, 60,468; –2.2%
Pine Bluff, 54,165; –5.2%
Jonesboro, 52,656; 13.2%

THE PEOPLE

Population (1997): 2,522,819, 33rd
  Percent change (1990-97): 7.33%, 20th
  Percent of total U.S. pop.: 0.94%, 33rd
  Per sq. mi: 47.44, 36th

Population (2000 proj.): 2,627,000, 33rd
  Percent change (1995-2000): 5.76%, 20th
Percent in metro. area (1996): 45.25%, 40th
Foreign born: 25,000, 42nd
  Percent: 1.1%, 46th
Top three ancestries reported:
  Irish, 19.74%
  German, 17.01%
  African, 13.06%
White (1992): 1,986,000, 82.96%, 35th
Black (1992): 381,000, 15.91%, 13th
Native American (1992): 13,000, 0.54%, 22nd
Asian, Pacific Isle (1992): 14,000, 0.58%, 47th
Hispanic origin (1992): 22,000, 0.92%, 42nd
Percent over 5 yrs. speaking language other than English at home: 2.8%, 48th
Percent males (1996): 48.38%, 40th; percent females: 51.62%, 12th
Percent never married: 20.7%, 51st
Marriages per 1,000 (1996): 14.44, 4th
Divorces per 1,000 (1996): 6.07, 5th
Median age (1996): 35.2
Under 5 years (1996): 7.04%, 21st
18 years and under (1996): 29.26%, 19th
65 years and over (1996): 14.44%, 7th
Percent increase among the elderly (1995-96): 0.34%, 39th

OF VITAL IMPORTANCE

Live births per 1,000 pop. (1996): 14.5, 18th
Infant mortality rate per 1,000 live births (1995): 8.8, 12th
  Rate for whites: 7.2, 9th
  Rate for blacks: 14.3, 25th
Births to unmarried women, % of total (1996): 33.9%, 12th
Births to teenage mothers, % of total (1996): 19.8%, 2nd
Abortions (1992): 7,130, 35th
  Rate per 1,000 women 14-44 years old: 13.5, 38th
  Percent change (1988-92): 16%, 3rd
Average lifetime (1989-91): 74.33, 42nd
Total death rate per 100,000 pop. (1995): 1,075.1, 4th
  Accidents and adverse effects: 48.8, 6th
  Alzheimer's disease: 7.5, 33rd
  Cancer: 244.7, 6th
  Cerebrovascular diseases: 91.5, 1st
  Chronic liver disease and cirrhosis: 8.6, 29th
  Chronic obstructive pulmonary diseases and allied conditions: 45.0, 13th
  Diabetes mellitus: 22.4, 29th
  Diseases of heart: 339.8, 8th
  HIV infection: 6.8, 33rd
  Homicide: 11.6, 8th
  Injury by firearms: 20.5, 7th
  Motor vehicle accidents: 26.3, 5th
  Pneumonia and influenza: 37.9, 8th
  Suicide: 14.5, 15th

KEEPING WELL

Active nonfederal physicians per 100,000 pop. (1995): 171, 42nd
Dentists per 100,000 (1991): 41, 49th
Nurses per 100,000 (1995): 690, 44th
Hospitals per 100,000 (1995): 3.42, 10th
  Admissions per 1,000 (1995): 137.68, 10th
  Hospital beds per 1,000 (1995): 4.07, 14th
  Occupancy rate per 100 beds (1995): 59.41, 32nd
  Average cost per patient per day (1995): $704, 44th
  Average cost per stay (1995): $4,459, 50th
AIDS cases (new, 1996): 269; per 100,000: 10.7, 30th
Persons living with HIV infection, not yet AIDS (1996): 1,463
Other notifiable diseases, per 100,000 pop.:
  Gonorrhea (1995): 226.7, 9th
  Syphilis (1995): 50.1, 4th
  Tuberculosis (1996): 9.0, 15th
Pop. without health insur. (1996): 21.7%, 4th

HOUSEHOLDS BY TYPE

Total households (1996): 951,000, 33rd
  Percent change (1990-96): 6.7%, 29th
  Per 1,000 pop. (1996) 378.88, 28th
  Percent of householders 65 yrs. and over (1996): 24.82%, 7th
  Persons per household (1996): 2.51, 41st
Family households: 651,555
  Percent of total: 73.11%, 7th
Nonfamily households: 239,624
  Percent of total: 26.89%, 45th
Pop. living in group quarters: 58,332
  Percent of pop.: 2.48%, 34th

LIVING QUARTERS

Total housing units: 1,000,667
  Persons per unit: 2.35, 36th
Occupied housing units: 891,179
  Percent of total units: 89.06%, 29th
  Persons per unit: 2.55, 20th
  Percent of units with over 1 person per room: 3.73%, 20th

Owner-occupied units: 619,938
 Percent of total units: 61.95%, 12th
 Percent of occupied units: 69.56%, 14th
 Persons per unit: 2.61, 48th
 Median value: $46,300, 48th
Renter-occupied units: 271,241
 Percent of total units: 27.11%, 38th
 Percent of occupied units: 30.44%, 38th
 Persons per unit: 2.48, 11th
 Median contract rent: $230, 47th
 Rental vacancy rate: 10.4%, 14th
Mobile home, trailer & other as a percent of
 occupied housing units: 15.87%, 13th
Persons in emergency shelters for homeless
 persons: 489, 0.021%, 50th
Persons visible in street locations: 62,
 0.0026%, 43rd
Nursing home population: 21,809, 0.93%, 14th

CRIME INDEX PER 100,000 (1996)

Total reported: 4,699.2, 26th
 Percent increase: 0.2%, 13th
 Violent: 524.3, 25th
  Percent increase: −5.2%, 22nd
  Murder & nonnegligent manslaughter:
   8.7, 12th
  Forcible rape: 41.7, 17th
  Aggravated assault: 359.8, 22nd
  Robbery: 114.1, 33rd
 Property: 4,174.9, 28th
  Percent increase: 0.9%, 13th
  Burglary: 953.2, 21st
  Larceny-theft: 2,908.8, 27th
  Motor vehicle theft: 312.9, 38th

TEACHING AND LEARNING

Pop. 3 and over enrolled in school (1996):
 555,256, 34th
 Percent of pop.: 22.12%, 33rd
Public elementary & secondary schools (1996-
 97): 1,098, 31st
 Total enrollment (1996): 457,076, 34th
  Percent of school age pop.: 94.44%, 13th
  Percent of total pop.: 18.21%, 12th
 Teachers (1996): 29,194, 32nd
  Percent of pop.: 1.16%, 11th
 Pupil/teacher ratio (1995): 17.1, 16th
 Teachers' avg. salary (1996-97): $29,975,
  44th
 Expenditure per capita (1992-93):
  $1,151.93, 43rd
  Education as % of state govt. expendi-
   tures: 38.7%, 7th

Expenditure per pupil (1994-95): $4,459,
 46th
 Percent increase (1993-94 & 1994-95):
  4.18%, 22nd
Percent at or above grade level, NAEP tests:
 Reading, grade 4 (1994): 24%, 29th
 Math, grade 4 (1996): 54%, 34th
 Math, grade 8 (1996): 52%, 32nd
Percent of graduates taking SAT (1995): 6%,
 46th
 Mean SAT verbal scores: 482, 18th
 Mean SAT mathematical scores: 523, 20th
Percent of graduates taking ACT (1997):
 66%, 12th
 Mean ACT scores: 20.3, 39th
Percent of pop. over 25 completing:
 Less than 9th grade: 15.2%, 5th
 High school: 66.3%, 48th
 College degree(s): 13.3%, 50th
Higher education, institutions (1996): 38,
 32nd
 Enrollment (1995-96): 98,180, 36th
  Percent increase in enroll. (1990-95):
   8.6%, 12th
 White non-Hispanic (1995): 78,663, 36th
  Percent of enroll.: 80.12%, 26th
 Total minority enroll. (1995): 17,163,
  34th
  Percent of enroll.: 17.48%, 23rd
 Black non-Hispanic (1995): 14,432, 23rd
  Percent of enroll.: 14.70%, 10th
 Hispanic (1995): 737, 44th
  Percent of enroll.: 0.75%, 45th
 Asian/Pacific Islander (1995): 1,121, 39th
  Percent of enroll.: 1.14%, 44th
 American Indian/AK native (1995): 873,
  34th
  Percent of enroll.: 0.89%, 21st
 Nonresident alien (1995): 2,354, 37th
  Percent of enroll.: 2.40%, 30th
 Female (1995): 56,477, 36th
  Percent of enroll.: 57.52%, 9th
 Pub. institutions (1995-96): 26, 26th
  Enrollment: 87,067, 36th
   Percent increase in enrollment (1990-
    95): 10.7%, 9th
   Percent of enroll.: 88.68%, 10th
 Private institutions (1995-96): 12, 38th
  Enrollment: 11,113, 42nd
   Percent increase in enrollment (1990-
    95): −5.7%, 46th
   Percent of enroll.: 11.32%, 42nd
 Tuition (in state), public 4-year institution
  (1996-97): $2,255, 34th

Tuition (in state), public 2-year institution (1996-97): $941, 44th

Tuition, private 4-year institution (1996-97): $7,012, 48th

Public library systems (1994): 35, 45th

Books & serial vol. per capita: 2.1, 37th

Library visits per capita: 2.3, 41st

Circulation per capita: 4.0, 47th

LAW ENFORCEMENT AND CORRECTIONS

Police protection and corrections expenditures (1996): $223,063,000

Per capita: $88.87, 39th

Police per 10,000 pop. (1996): 19.65, 34th

Prisoners (1 year or more) per 100,000 pop. (1996): 357, 22nd

Percent change (1995-96): –3.0%, 48th

Percent of inmates that are female: 5.8%, 33rd

Percent change: –1.1%, 45th

Death penalty: yes, by electrocution, lethal injection after 7/4/83

Under sentence (Jan. 1998): 33, 20th

Executed, 1976-97: 16, 7th

Executed in 1997: 4, 4th

RELIGION, NUMBER AND PERCENT OF POPULATION

Agnostic: 3,459—0.20%, 42nd

Buddhist: 3,459—0.20%, 11th

Christian: 1,549,716—89.60%, 14th

Hindu: NA

Jewish: 1,730—0.10%, 43rd

Muslim: NA

Unitarian: 3,459—0.20%, 23rd

Other: 12,107—0.70%, 43rd

None: 100,317—5.80%, 35th

Refused to answer: 55,347—3.20%, 6th

MAKING A LIVING

Personal income per capita (1996): $18,928, 48th

Percent increase (1995-96): 3.6%, 19th

Disposable personal income per capita (1996): $16,783, 45th

Median income of households (average, 1995-96): $26,850, 49th

Percent of pop. below poverty level (1995-96): 16.1%, 14th

ECONOMY

In civilian labor force (1996): 1,234,000

Percent of total pop.: 64.7%, 40th

Percent of total pop. 65 years and over: 12.6%, 20th

Percent of total female pop.: 58.4%, 38th

Major employer industries (total nonagricultural, 1996):

Construction: 47,300—4.4%, 30th

Finance, insurance, & real estate: 43,100—4.0%, 47th

Government: 179,300—16.5%, 30th

Manufacturing: 253,500—23.4%, 3rd

Service: 246,500—22.7%, 47th

Trade: 247,400—22.8%, 40th

Transportation, communications, public utilities: 64,900—6.0%, 8th

Unemployment rate (1996): 5.4%, 18th

Male: 5.4%, 17th

Female: 5.4%, 19th

Total businesses (1995): 60,231, 32nd

New business incorps. (1995): 6,298

Percent of total businesses: 10.46%, 18th

Business failures (1995): 737

Failures per 10,000 businesses: 122.4, 10th

Agriculture farm income:

Marketing (1996): $5,886,786,000, 11th

Average per farm: $136,902, 9th

Leading products (1997): Broilers, soybeans, cotton, cattle, rice, tomatoes, grapes, apples, vegetables, peaches, wheat

Average value land & build. per acre (1997): $1,010, 30th

Percent increase (1996-97): 2%, 42nd

Govt. payments (1996): $361,818,000, 6th

Average per farm: $8,414, 3rd

Construction, value of all (1996): $2,795,210,000, 34th

Per capita: $1,114, 34th

Manufactures (1995):

Value added: $18,639,600,000

Per capita: $7,505, 14th

Leading products (1997): Food products, chemicals, lumber, paper, plastics, electric motors, furniture, auto components, airplane parts, apparel, machinery, steel

Value of nonfuel mineral production (1996): $453,000,000, 29th

Leading mineral products (1996): Petroleum, natural gas, stone, bromine, cement, sand/gravel, gemstones

Energy consumption per person (1994): 389.9 mil. Btu, 16th

Retail sales (1995): $20,999,000,000

Per household: $22,100, 46th

Sales increase (1994-95): 10.0%, 4th

Tourism revenues (1995): $3.1 bil.
Foreign exports, in total value (1996): $2,003,000,000, 37th
Per capita: $798, 44th
Gross state product per person (1994): $20,620, 47th
Public aid recipients (percent of resident pop. 1994): 6.6%, 27th
Medicaid recipients (percent of pop., 1995): 14.2%, 14th
Medicare enrollment per 1,000 pop. (1996): 170, 7th

TRAVEL AND TRANSPORTATION

Motor vehicle registrations (1996): 1,633,343, 33rd
Per 1,000 pop.: 651.70, 49th
Motorcycle registrations (1996): 16,490, 45th
Per 1,000 pop.: 10.10, 50th
Licensed drivers (1996): 1,769,012, 32nd
Per 1,000 pop.: 711.94, 13th
Public roads & streets (1996)
Total mileage: 77,746, 26th
Per 1,000 pop.: 130.98, 11th
Rural mileage: 70,048, 23rd
Per 1,000 pop.: 27.91, 11th
Urban mileage: 7,698, 33rd
Per 1,000 pop.: 3.07, 26th
Interstate mileage: 541, 40th
Per 1,000 pop.: 0.22, 21st
Speed limit (max. interstate, autos, mi. per hr., 1997): 70
Annual vehicle-mi. of travel per driver (1996): 15,888, 11th
Mean travel time for workers age 16+ who work away from home: 19.0 min., 38th

GOVERNMENT

Percent of voting age pop. registered (1996): 73.12, 35th

Percent of voting age pop. voting for president: (1996): 47.5%, 34th
Percent of voting age pop. voting for U.S. representatives (1996): 46.4%, 30th
State legislators, total (1997): 135, 31st
Women members (1997): 23
Percent of legislature: 17%, 34th
U.S. Congress, House members (1998): 4
Change (1988-98): 0
Revenues (1996):
State govt.: $8,652,790,000
Per capita: $3,447.33, 26th
Parimutuel & amusement taxes & lotteries, revenue per capita (1995): $4.84, 42nd
Expenditures (1996):
State govt.: $7,050,461,000
Per capita: $2,808.95, 37th
Debt outstanding (1996): $2,142,271,000
Per capita: $853.49, 39

LAWS AND REGULATIONS

Legal driving age: 16
Marriage age without parental consent: 18
Divorce residence requirement: 60 days, for qualifications check local statutes

ATTRACTIONS (1997)

Per capita spending by the NEA (1997): $0.16, 42nd
State Fair in late September–early October at Little Rock

SPORTS AND COMPETITION

NCAA (Division I) basketball and football teams: Arkansas State Univ. Indians, Univ. of Arkansas-Fayetteville Razorbacks, Univ. of Arkansas-Little Rock Trojans (basketball only), Univ. of Arkansas-Pine Bluff Golden Lions

WEBSITES CONTAINING FURTHER INFORMATION

Arkansas Home Page   http://www.state.ar.us

CALIFORNIA

"Not far from the shores there was an island called California, peopled by black women, without a man among them, for they lived in the fashion of Amazons and raided many countries."

Hernando Cortes, Spanish conquistador (1535)

"This is one of the most favored spots of the earth."   John Muir, naturalist

"Why! It is even worth the expense of a trip across the continent."
John D. Rockefeller, Sr., industrialist and philanthropist

The most populous state, California is a land of contrasts, with its high mountains, rocky cliffs, sandy beaches, redwood forests, and barren deserts. This state, with its vast vineyards in the north, its glitter in Hollywood and Beverly Hills in the south, and its tremendous farms and ranches almost everywhere, combines the Old World charm of San Francisco with the unusual lifestyles of Los Angeles to maintain its image as a truly unique part of the country. First in manufacturing, first in agriculture, it also contains some of the largest cities in the nation. If famed naturalist John Muir were alive today, he would be even more convinced that he had been very right when he called California "one of the most favored spots on earth." Millions of visitors have agreed. Despite earthquakes and other traumas, little has occurred to diminish that luster.

So They Say

"California surprises with a geography, climate, vegetation, beasts, birds, fishes even, unlike ours; the land immense; the Pacific sea; Steam brings the near neighborhood of Asia; and South America at your feet; the mountains reaching the altitude of Mont Blanc; the State in its six hundred miles of latitude producing all our Northern fruits, and also the fig, orange and banana....the climate: day after day of uninterrupted sunshine....The whole Country was covered with flowers, and all of them unknown to us except in greenhouses. Every bird that I know at home is represented here, but in gayer plumes."

Writer Ralph Waldo Emerson (1871)

SUPERLATIVES

- First state in population.
- World's largest landlocked harbor—San Francisco Bay.
- Lowest point in the Western Hemisphere—Death Valley, 282 feet below sea level.
- Hottest recorded temperature in the United States—Death Valley, 134 deg. F.
- Most life zones in the nation—six.
- World's most fertile valley.
- Most national sites of any state.
- Largest living tree—General Sherman tree, trunk 101.6 feet in circumference, Sequoia National Park.
- The oldest living thing—a bristlecone pine, approximately 4,600 years old, Inyo National Forest.

MOMENTS IN HISTORY

- In 1535-36, Hernando Cortes reached the boundary of California.
- Nine major tribes were found by the earliest European explorers, beginning around the year 1540.
- In 1540, Hernando de Alarcón may have touched California at the Colorado River.
- Sir Francis Drake explored the coast in 1579 and claimed the area for England's Queen Elizabeth.
- In 1769, Gaspar de Portola and Father Junipero Serra founded the mission of San Diego.
- San Francisco was founded in 1776.
- Sleepy El Pueblo de Nuestra Senora la Reina de Los Angeles de Porciuncula (Los Angeles) was founded in 1781.
- At the missions, Indians became Christianized and, some say, were harshly treated.
- In 1812, Russia established Fort Ross, adding to its Alaskan fur trade.
- In 1825, Mexico took over California, with the capital at Monterey.
- The first overland wagon train to California left Missouri and arrived in the San Joaquin Valley on November 4, 1841.

So They Say

"To this gate I gave the name of Chrysolpylae, or Golden Gate....The form... and its advantages for commerce, Asiatic inclusive, suggested to me the name...".

Explorer John Charles Frémont (1844)

- With the 1848 Treaty of Guadalupe Hidalgo, Mexico gave up California.
- A pea-sized metal pellet from Sutter's Millrace changed the course of history in 1848 when it proved to be gold.

So They Say

"Sir: I have to report to the state department one of the most astonishing excitements...now existing in this country...a placer, a vast tract of land containing gold...."

Staff member Thomas O. Larkin, reporting to President James Buchanan

- News of the gold discovery sparked a record rush to the gold fields. In 1849, thousands of 49ers braved danger and death for riches.
- Congress hesitated to welcome a new free state, but California was at last admitted on September 9, 1850.
- During the Civil War, loyal California's gold helped to support the Union.
- In a last heroic but unsuccessful fight for their rights, the Modoc Indians went to war (1872-73).
- Land booms, growth of agriculture, and the discovery of oil at Bakersfield in 1899 brought people and prosperity.

So They Say

"Of a sudden we had found ourselves staggering and reeling...a sickening swaying of the earth....a great cornice crushed a man as if he were a maggot...."

P. Barrett, San Francisco Examiner, April 19, 1906

- Before the ruins of the earthquake and fire of 1906 had cooled, devastated San Francisco had begun to rebuild.
- In 1916 a Republican dispute gave Woodrow Wilson California's electoral votes, just enough to put him over the top for the White House.

- World War I found California far removed from the conflict, but great numbers of Californians crossed the continent and the sea to serve.
- California was particularly hard hit by the Great Depression. However, despite the Depression, San Francisco's great bridges were opened in 1936-37, and in 1939 the city celebrated with the Golden Gate International Exposition.
- Thought to be a security threat in World War II, Japanese-Americans were sent to relocation camps where they endured many hardships.
- In 1945 the United Nations was founded at San Francisco.
- Big league baseball came to California in 1958 with the Dodgers at Los Angeles and the Giants at San Francisco.
- By 1963, California could claim to be the nation's most populous state.
- In 1969, Richard Nixon became the first Californian to be president of the U.S.
- Los Angeles hosted the financially successful Olympic Summer Games of 1984.
- California's 1980s drought was one of its worst in history; some relief started in 1992.
- Striking just minutes before the start of the third game of the World Series, the 1989 San Francisco earthquake was a major disaster, causing at least 59 deaths and massive property damage.
- In 1992 riots in Los Angeles followed the acquittal of four policemen in the beating of a black man, Rodney King.
- A powerful earthquake shook Los Angeles in January 1994.
- In 1995 world attention was riveted on the notorious murder trial of ex-football star O. J. Simpson, who was found not guilty.
- Heavy rains inundated California in 1995, causing over $700 million in damage.
- In August 1997, Proposition 209, a controversial measure banning racial or gender-based preferences in school admissions and public hiring, went into effect.

THAT'S INTERESTING

- In the Mexican War, the "Paul Revere of the West," John Brown (Lean John), rode horseback from Los Angeles to San Francisco to warn of approaching Mexican troops, making the 500 miles in only five days.

• An 1849 gold rush miner asked Levi Strauss to make a pair of pants. Lacking suitable thread, Strauss stapled the pants at stress points; Levis have been popular ever since.

• Beginning at San Diego in 1769, Father Junipero Serra established nine thriving missions, centers of civilization in the wild; he became known as the "Father of California."

• In the 1849 gold rush, bar owners hired bartenders with large hands. Drinks sold for a pinch of gold dust—the larger the hands, the bigger the pinch.

• The 1916 drought at San Diego was so severe that the city hired the famous rainmaker Charles Hatfield. Shortly after he set up his rainmaking towers, so much rain fell that disastrous floods were caused, and the city refused to pay Hatfield his $10,000 fee.

• Told by a medium that she would never die as long as she kept building her house in San Jose, wealthy widow Sara Winchester kept carpenters busy creating 1,660 rooms, secret passageways, 40 stairways, blind chimneys, and other novel arrangements. Despite spending $5.5 million, she could not forestall her death in 1922.

NOTABLE NATIVES

Joseph Paul (Joe) DiMaggio, Jr. (Martinez, 1914-), baseball player. Robert Lee Frost (San Francisco, 1874-1963), poet. Lillian Moller Gilbreth (Oakland, 1878-1972), consulting engineer. William Randolph Hearst (San Francisco, 1863-1951), publisher. Marilyn Monroe (Los Angeles, 1926-1962), actress. Richard Milhous Nixon (Yorba Linda, 1913-1994), U.S. president. William Saroyan (Fresno, 1908-1981), author. John Ernst Steinbeck (Salinas, 1902-1968), author. Adlai Ewing Stevenson (Los Angeles, 1900-1965), public official. Earl Warren (Los Angeles, 1891-1974), chief justice of the United States. Eldrich (Tiger) Woods (Cypress, 1975-), golfer.

GENERAL

Admitted to statehood: September 9, 1850
Origin of name: Bestowed by the Spanish conquistadors (possibly by Cortes). It was the name of an imaginary island, an earthly paradise, in "Las Serges de Esplandian," a Spanish romance written by Garcí Ordóñez de Montalvo in 1510. Baha California (Lower California, in Mexico) was first visited by the Spanish in 1533. The present U.S. state was called Alta (Upper) California
Capital: Sacramento
Nickname: Golden State
Motto: *Eureka*—I have found it
Animal: California grizzly bear
Bird: California valley quail
Fish: California golden trout
Flower: Golden poppy
Stone: Serpentine
Song: "I Love You, California"
Tree: California redwood

THE LAND

Area: 158,869 sq. mi., 3rd
  Land: 155,973 sq. mi., 3rd
  Water: 2,896 sq. mi., 12th
    Inland water: 2,674 sq. mi., 8th
    Coastal water: 222 sq. mi., 16th
Topography: Long mountainous coastline; central valley; Sierra Nevada on the E; desert basins of the Southern interior; rugged mountains of the N
Number of counties: 58
Geographic center: 38 mi. E of Madera
Length: 770 mi.; width: 250 mi.
Highest point: 14,494 ft. (Mount Whitney), 2nd
Lowest point: –282 ft. (Death Valley), 1st
Mean elevation: 2,900 ft.; 11th
Coastline: 840 mi., 3rd
Shoreline: 3,427 mi., 5th

CLIMATE AND ENVIRONMENT

Temp., highest: 134 deg. on July 10, 1913, at Greenland Ranch; lowest: –45 deg. on Jan. 20, 1937, at Boca
Monthly average: highest: 98.8 deg., 3rd; lowest: 36.8 deg., 48th; spread (high to low): 62.0 deg., 38th
Hazardous waste sites (1997): 91, 3rd
Endangered species: Animals: 58—Mount Hermon June beetle, El Segundo blue butterfly, Lange's metalmark butterfly, Lotis blue butterfly, Mission blue butterfly, Myrtle's silverspot butterfly, Palos Verdes blue butterfly, Quino checkerspot butterfly, San Bruno elfin butterfly, Smith's blue butterfly, Bonytail chub, Mohave tui chub, Owens tui chub, California condor, Shasta crayfish, Conservancy fairy shrimp, Longhorn fairy shrimp, Riverside fairy

shrimp, San Diego fairy shrimp, American peregrine falcon, Delhi Sands flower-loving fly, Southwestern willow flycatcher, San Joaquin kit fox, Tidewater goby, Zayante band-winged grasshopper, Fresno kangaroo rat, Giant kangaroo rat, Morro Bay kangaroo rat, Stephens' kangaroo rat, Tipton kangaroo rat, Blunt-nosed leopard lizard, Point Arena mountain beaver, Pacific pocket mouse, Salt marsh harvest mouse, Brown pelican, Desert pupfish, Owens pupfish, California clapper rail, Light-footed clapper rail, Yuma clapper rail, Desert slender salamander, Santa Cruz long-toed salamander, San Clemente loggerhead shrike, California freshwater shrimp, Laguna Mountains skipper, Morro shoulderband snail, San Francisco garter snake, Colorado squawfish, Unarmored threespine stickleback, Lost river sucker, Modoc sucker, Razorback sucker, Shortnose sucker, Vernal pool tadpole shrimp, California least tern, Arroyo toad, Least bell's vireo, Amargosa vole. Plants: 93

MAJOR CITIES
POPULATION, 1996
PERCENTAGE INCREASE, 1990-96

Los Angeles, 3,553,638; 2.0%
San Diego, 1,171,121; 5.4%
San Jose, 838,744; 7.2%
San Francisco, 735,315; 1.6%
Long Beach, 421,904; −1.7%

THE PEOPLE

Population (1997): 32,268,301, 1st
  Percent change (1990-97): 8.33%, 18th
  Percent of total U.S. pop.: 12.06%, 1st
  Per sq. mi: 197.11, 13th
Population (2000 proj.): 32,472,000, 1st
  Percent change (1995-2000): 2.80%, 38th
Percent in metro. area (1996): 96.65%, 4th
Foreign born: 6,459,000, 1st
  Percent: 21.7%, 1st
Top three ancestries reported:
  Mexican, 17.88%
  German, 16.58%
  English, 12.25%
White (1992): 24,924,000, 80.67%, 38th
Black (1992): 2,381,000, 7.71%, 24th
Native American (1992): 295,000, 0.95%, 16th

Asian, Pacific Isle (1992): 3,295,000, 10.67%, 2nd
Hispanic origin (1992): 8,353,000, 27.04%, 2nd
Percent over 5 yrs. speaking language other than English at home: 31.5%, 2nd
Percent males (1996): 50.08%, 5th; percent females: 49.92%, 47th
Percent never married: 30.1%, 4th
Marriages per 1,000 (1996): 6.87, 44th
Divorces per 1,000 (1996): NA
Median age (1996): 32.7
Under 5 years (1996): 8.67%, 2nd
18 years and under (1996): 30.48%, 10th
65 years and over (1996): 11.03%, 46th
Percent increase among the elderly (1995-96): 1.65%, 11th

OF VITAL IMPORTANCE

Live births per 1,000 pop. (1996): 16.9, 4th
Infant mortality rate per 1,000 live births (1995): 6.3, 41st
  Rate for whites: 5.8, 41st
  Rate for blacks: 14.4, 24th
Births to unmarried women, % of total (1996): 31.6%, 24th
Births to teenage mothers, % of total (1996): 12.0%, 29th
Abortions (1992): 304,230, 1st
  Rate per 1,000 women 14-44 years old: 42.1, 5th
  Percent change (1988-92): −8%, 26th
Average lifetime (1989-91): 75.86, 23rd
Total death rate per 100,000 pop. (1995): 709.8, 47th
  Accidents and adverse effects: 29.3, 43rd
  Alzheimer's disease: 5.4, 48th
  Cancer: 162.8, 46th
  Cerebrovascular diseases: 51.4, 44th
  Chronic liver disease and cirrhosis: 11.3, 8th
  Chronic obstructive pulmonary diseases and allied conditions: 34.2, 41st
  Diabetes mellitus: 16.2, 47th
  Diseases of heart: 216.3, 43rd
  HIV infection: 20.4, 8th
  Homicide: 11.6, 8th
  Injury by firearms: 15.2, 17th
  Motor vehicle accidents: 14.1, 37th
  Pneumonia and influenza: 33.4, 19th
  Suicide: 11.7, 36th

KEEPING WELL

Active nonfederal physicians per 100,000 pop. (1995): 241, 12th

Dentists per 100,000 (1991): 65, 13th
Nurses per 100,000 (1995): 574, 51st
Hospitals per 100,000 (1995): 1.34, 44th
  Admissions per 1,000 (1995): 95.89, 40th
  Hospital beds per 1,000 (1995): 2.37, 43rd
  Occupancy rate per 100 beds (1995):
    60.13, 28th
  Average cost per patient per day (1995):
    $1,315, 4th
  Average cost per stay (1995): $7,111, 7th
AIDS cases (new, 1996): 9,610; per 100,000:
  30.1, 10th
Persons living with HIV infection (1996): NA
Other notifiable diseases, per 100,000 pop.:
  Gonorrhea (1995): 78.5, 29th
  Syphilis (1995): 18.1, 17th
  Tuberculosis (1996): 13.5, 5th
Pop. without health insur. (1996): 20.1%, 6th

HOUSEHOLDS BY TYPE

Total households (1996): 11,101,000, 1st
  Percent change (1990-96): 6.9%, 27th
  Per 1,000 pop. (1996) 348.23, 49th
  Percent of householders 65 yrs. and over
    (1996): 19.39%, 40th
  Persons per household (1996): 2.79, 4th
Family households: 7,139,394
  Percent of total: 68.77%, 40th
Nonfamily households: 3,241,812
  Percent of total: 31.23%, 12th
Pop. living in group quarters: 751,860
  Percent of pop.: 2.53%, 32nd

LIVING QUARTERS

Total housing units: 11,182,882
  Persons per unit: 2.66, 3rd
Occupied housing units: 10,381,206
  Percent of total units: 92.83%, 5th
  Persons per unit: 2.79, 3rd
  Percent of units with over 1 person per
    room: 12.29%, 2nd
Owner-occupied units: 5,773,943
  Percent of total units: 51.63%, 46th
  Percent of occupied units: 55.62%, 47th
  Persons per unit: 2.84, 8th
  Median value: $195,500, 2nd
Renter-occupied units: 4,607,263
  Percent of total units: 41.20%, 4th
  Percent of occupied units: 44.38%, 6th
  Persons per unit: 2.74, 2nd
  Median contract rent: $561, 2nd
  Rental vacancy rate: 5.9%, 46th
Mobile home, trailer & other as a percent of
  occupied housing units: 6.55%, 40th

Persons in emergency shelters for homeless
  persons: 30,806, 0.104%, 5th
Persons visible in street locations: 18,081,
  0.0608%, 2nd
Nursing home population: 148,362, 0.50%,
  45th

CRIME INDEX PER 100,000 (1996)

Total reported: 5,207.8, 20th
  Percent increase: –10.7%, 47th
  Violent: 862.7, 7th
    Percent increase: –10.7%, 38th
    Murder & nonnegligent manslaughter:
      9.1, 10th
    Forcible rape: 32.1, 28th
    Aggravated assault: 525.8, 8th
    Robbery: 295.6, 5th
  Property: 4,345.1, 23rd
    Percent increase: –10.7%, 48th
    Burglary: 979.4, 20th
    Larceny-theft: 2,605.1, 36th
    Motor vehicle theft: 760.6, 3rd

TEACHING AND LEARNING

Pop. 3 and over enrolled in school (1996):
  7,352,354, 1st
  Percent of pop.: 23.06%, 20th
Public elementary & secondary schools (1996-
  97): 7,876, 1st
  Total enrollment (1996): 5,535,312, 1st
    Percent of school age pop.: 90.27%, 34th
    Percent of total pop.: 17.36%, 26th
  Teachers (1996): 228,028, 2nd
    Percent of pop.: 0.72%, 51st
  Pupil/teacher ratio (1995): 24.0, 1st
  Teachers' avg. salary (1996-97): $43,474,
    9th
  Expenditure per capita (1992-93):
    $1,263.19, 30th
    Education as % of state govt. expendi-
      tures: 29.3%, 45th
  Expenditure per pupil (1994-95): $4,992,
    38th
    Percent increase (1993-94 & 1994-95):
      1.44%, 47th
Percent at or above grade level, NAEP tests:
  Reading, grade 4 (1994): 18%, 37th
  Math, grade 4 (1996): 46%, 41st
  Math, grade 8 (1996): 51%, 33rd
Percent of graduates taking SAT (1995): 45%,
  24th
  Mean SAT verbal scores: 417, 45th
  Mean SAT mathematical scores: 485, 30th

Percent of graduates taking ACT (1997): 11%, 38th
　Mean ACT scores: 21.0, 30th
Percent of pop. over 25 completing:
　Less than 9th grade: 11.2%, 16th
　High school: 76.2%, 28th
　College degree(s): 23.4%, 10th
Higher education, institutions (1996): 349, 1st
　Enrollment (1995-96): 1,817,042, 1st
　　Percent increase in enroll. (1990-95): 0.5%, 37th
　　White non-Hispanic (1995): 905,116, 1st
　　Percent of enroll.: 49.81%, 49th
　　Total minority enroll. (1995): 832,127, 1st
　　Percent of enroll.: 45.80%, 2nd
　　Black non-Hispanic (1995): 138,218, 1st
　　Percent of enroll.: 7.61%, 22nd
　　Hispanic (1995): 357,893, 1st
　　Percent of enroll.: 19.70%, 3rd
　　Asian/Pacific Islander (1995): 314,877, 1st
　　Percent of enroll.: 17.33%, 2nd
　　American Indian/AK native (1995): 21,139, 1st
　　Percent of enroll.: 1.16%, 16th
　　Nonresident alien (1995): 79,799, 1st
　　Percent of enroll.: 4.39%, 5th
　　Female (1995): 998,399, 1st
　　Percent of enroll.: 54.95%, 42nd
　Pub. institutions (1995-96): 138, 1st
　　Enrollment: 1,564,230, 1st
　　　Percent increase in enrollment (1990-95): −1.9%, 38th
　　Percent of enroll.: 86.09%, 17th
　Private institutions (1995-96): 211, 2nd
　　Enrollment: 252,812, 3rd
　　　Percent increase in enrollment (1990-95): 18.1%, 8th
　　Percent of enroll.: 13.91%, 35th
　Tuition (in state), public 4-year institution (1996-97): $2,731, 23rd
　Tuition (in state), public 2-year institution (1996-97): $371, 50th
　Tuition, private 4-year institution (1996-97): $14,650, 11th
Public library systems (1994): 170, 19th
　Books & serial vol. per capita: 1.9, 46th
　Library visits per capita: 4.0, 21st
　Circulation per capita: 4.6, 40th

LAW ENFORCEMENT AND CORRECTIONS

Police protection and corrections expenditures (1996): $4,855,524,000
　Per capita: $152.31, 8th

Police per 10,000 pop. (1996): 22.23, 23rd
Prisoners (1 year or more) per 100,000 pop. (1996): 451, 11th
　Percent change (1995-96): 9.6%, 16th
　Percent of inmates that are female: 6.9%, 15th
　　Percent change: 12.8%, 20th
Death penalty: yes, by lethal gas, lethal injection
　Under sentence (Jan. 1998): 477, 1st
　Executed, 1976-97: 4, 18th
　Executed in 1997: 0

RELIGION, NUMBER AND PERCENT OF POPULATION

Agnostic: 264,112—1.20%, 2nd
Buddhist: 154,065—0.70%, 1st
Christian: 16,947,158—77.00%, 48th
Hindu: 22,009—0.10%, 10th
Jewish: 506,214—2.30%, 7th
Muslim: 132,056—0.60%, 2nd
Unitarian: 88,037—0.40%, 8th
Other: 418,177—1.90%, 12th
None: 2,861,209—13.00%, 5th
Refused to answer: 616,260—2.80%, 12th

MAKING A LIVING

Personal income per capita (1996): $25,144, 13th
　Percent increase (1995-96): 3.2%, 23rd
Disposable personal income per capita (1996): $21,760, 12th
Median income of households (average, 1995-96): $38,457, 12th
Percent of pop. below poverty level (1995-96): 16.8%, 10th

ECONOMY

In civilian labor force (1996): 15,596,000
　Percent of total pop.: 65.5%, 38th
　Percent of total pop. 65 years and over: 10.8%, 34th
　Percent of total female pop.: 56.4%, 41st
Major employer industries (total nonagricultural, 1996):
　Construction: 510,500—4.0%, 36th
　Finance, insurance, & real estate: 733,100—5.7%, 17th
　Government: 2,117,000—16.6%, 29th
　Manufacturing: 1,853,200—14.5%, 28th
　Service: 3,916,700—30.7%, 11th
　Trade: 2,973,400—23.3%, 33rd
　Transportation, communications, public utilities: 641,500—5.0%, 26th

Unemployment rate (1996): 7.2%, 5th
  Male: 7.2%, 5th
  Female: 7.2%, 4th
Total businesses (1995): 740,583, 1st
New business incorps. (1995): 41,913
  Percent of total businesses: 5.66%, 49th
Business failures (1995): 16,307
  Failures per 10,000 businesses: 220.2, 1st
Agriculture farm income:
  Marketing (1996): $23,309,526,000, 1st
    Average per farm: $284,263, 3rd
  Leading products (1997): Dairy products, greenhouse, grapes, cattle, cotton, oranges, hay, tomatoe, lettuce, strawberries, almonds, asparagus
  Average value land & build. per acre (1997): $2,510, 9th
    Percent increase (1996-97): 4%, 35th
  Govt. payments (1996): $295,460,000, 9th
    Average per farm: $3,603, 18th
Construction, value of all (1996): $31,734,190,000, 1st
  Per capita: $995, 43rd
Manufactures (1995):
  Value added: $178,358,400,000
    Per capita: $5,646, 32nd
  Leading products (1997): Electronic and electrical equipment, computers, industrial machinery, transportation equipment and instruments, food
Value of nonfuel mineral production (1996): $2,840,000,000, 3rd
Leading mineral products (1996): Petroleum, natural gas, sand/gravel, cement, boron minerals, gold, stone
Energy consumption per person (1994): 240.6 mil. Btu, 49th
Retail sales (1995): $257,662,000,000
  Per household: $23,427, 38th
  Sales increase (1994-95): 4.0%, 29th
Tourism revenues (1996): $58.3 bil.
Foreign exports, in total value (1996): $93,418,000,000, 1st
  Per capita: $2,930, 6th
Gross state product per person (1994): $27,861, 12th
Public aid recipients (percent of resident pop. 1994): 11.7%, 2nd
Medicaid recipients (percent of pop., 1995): 15.9%, 10th
Medicare enrollment per 1,000 pop. (1996): 116, 43rd

TRAVEL AND TRANSPORTATION

Motor vehicle registrations (1996): 25,213,707, 1st
  Per 1,000 pop.: 791.45, 28th
Motorcycle registrations (1996): 526,048, 1st
  Per 1,000 pop.: 20.86, 21st
Licensed drivers (1996): 20,139,586, 1st
  Per 1,000 pop.: 638.03, 43rd
Public roads & streets (1996)
  Total mileage: 170,506, 2nd
    Per 1,000 pop.: 15.35, 48th
  Rural mileage: 87,397, 11th
    Per 1,000 pop.: 2.74, 45th
  Urban mileage: 83,109, 1st
    Per 1,000 pop.: 2.61, 44th
  Interstate mileage: 2,424, 2nd
    Per 1,000 pop.: 0.08, 45th
Speed limit (max. interstate, autos, mi. per hr., 1997): 70
Annual vehicle-mi. of travel per driver (1996): 13,731, 31st
Mean travel time for workers age 16+ who work away from home: 24.6 min., 6th

GOVERNMENT

Percent of voting age pop. registered (1996): 68.62%, 41st
  Percent of voting age pop. voting for president: (1996): 43.3%, 45th
  Percent of voting age pop. voting for U.S. representatives (1996): 41.0%, 41st
State legislators, total (1997): 120, 36th
  Women members (1997): 26
    Percent of legislature: 22%, 25th
U.S. Congress, House members (1998): 52
  Change (1988-98): 7
Revenues (1996):
  State govt.: $123,342,274,000
    Per capita: $3,869.20, 19th
    Parimutuel & amusement taxes & lotteries, revenue per capita (1995): $67.62, 33rd
Expenditures (1996):
  State govt.: $113,361,355,000
    Per capita: $3,556.10, 17th
Debt outstanding (1996): $45,859,003,000
  Per capita: $1,438.58, 23rd

LAWS AND REGULATIONS

Legal driving age: 18, 16 after driver education course
Marriage age without parental consent: 18
Divorce residence requirement: 6 mo., for qualifications check local statutes

ATTRACTIONS (1997)

Major opera companies: 15

Major symphony orchestras: 10

Major dance companies: 13

Major professional theater companies (non-profit): 5

Per capita spending by the NEA (1997): $0.25, 29th

State Fair in late August–early September at Sacramento

SPORTS AND COMPETITION

NCAA (Division I) football and basketball teams: California Polytechnic State Univ. Mustangs, California State Univ.-Fresno Bulldogs, California State Univ.-Fullerton Titans (basketball only), California State Univ.-Northridge Matadors, California State Univ.-Sacramento Hornets, Long Beach State Univ. Forty Niners (basketball only), Loyola Marymount Univ. Lions (basketball only), Pepperdine Univ. Waves (basketball only), Saint Mary's College Gaels, San Diego State Univ. Aztecs, San Jose State Univ. Spartans, Santa Clara Univ. Broncos (basketball only), Stanford Univ. Cardinal, Univ. of California-Berkeley Golden Bears, Univ. of California-Irvine Anteaters (basketball only), Univ. of California-Los Angeles Bruins, Univ. of California-Santa Barbara Gauchos (basketball only), Univ. of the Pacific Tigers (basketball only), Univ.

of San Diego Toreros, Univ. of San Francisco Dons (basketball only), Univ. of Southern California Trojans

Major league baseball teams: San Diego Padres (NL West), Qualcomm Stadium at Jack Murphy Field; Anaheim Angels (AL West), Anaheim Stadium; San Francisco Giants (NL West), 3Com Park at Candlestick Point; Los Angeles Dodgers (NL West), Dodger Stadium; Oakland Athletics (AL West), Oakland Coliseum

Major league soccer teams: Los Angeles Galaxy, Rose Bowl; San Jose Clash, Spartan Stadium

NBA basketball teams: Sacramento Kings, ARCO Arena; Los Angeles Clippers, L.A. Memorial Sports Arena, Arrowhead Pond of Anaheim; Los Angeles Lakers, The Great Western Forum; Golden State Warriors, The New Arena in Oakland

ABL basketball teams: Long Beach StingRays, The Pyramid; San Jose Lasers, San Jose Event Center

WNBA basketball teams: Los Angles Sparks, The Great Western Forum; Sacramento Monarchs, ARCO Arena

NFL football teams: San Francisco 49ers (NFC), 3Com Park at Candlestick Point; Oakland Raiders (AFC), Oakland Coliseum; San Diego Chargers (AFC), Qualcomm Stadium at Jack Murphy Field

NHL hockey teams: Anaheim Mighty Ducks, Arrowhead Pond of Anaheim; San Jose Sharks, San Jose Arena; Los Angeles Kings, The Great Western Forum

WEBSITES CONTAINING FURTHER INFORMATION

California State Home Page	http://www.ca.gov

COLORADO

"Passing through your wonderful mountains and canyons I realize that this state is going to be more and more the playground for the whole republic....You will see this the real Switzerland of America."
President Theodore Roosevelt

"Many claim that Colorado's climate is so good they had to hang somebody in order to start their cemetery."
Anonymous

A skier's paradise, Colorado is the loftiest state in the United States. Its mountain reaches provide some of the nation's most dramatic and beautiful scenery—it was Colorado vistas that inspired the song "America the Beautiful." From those same mountains flow much of the nation's river waters. Colorado is a center for vacationers, with its cool, pleasant summer climate and its winter supply of powdered snow. But it is also the leading manufacturing area in the Rocky Mountain states and a major agricultural and mining state. Indeed, the story of Colorado's rugged gold- and silver-mining boom days has become the theme of two popular musicals—*The Unsinkable Molly Brown* and *The Ballad of Baby Doe*.

SUPERLATIVES

- Highest mean altitude of the states.
- More mountains reaching 14,000 or more feet than any other state.
- Grand Mesa, the world's largest flat-top mountain.
- State where three of the nation's greatest river systems rise.
- Colorado oil shales, thought to contain five times more oil than all the present reserves of the world combined.
- Highest suspension bridge in the world—1,053 feet over the Arkansas River.

MOMENTS IN HISTORY

- The Colorado region was visited by Spanish explorers during the 16th century.
- The first known written record of the Colorado area was left by Diego de Vargas in 1694, as he pursued Indians who had escaped from Taos Pueblo in New Mexico.
- Spain won recognized ownership of the region in 1763.
- In 1803, three years after France acquired eastern Colorado, the United States obtained it as part of the Louisiana Purchase.

- The party of U.S. Lieutenant Zebulon Pike explored present-day Colorado in 1806, discovering the mountain that now bears Pike's name.

So They Say

When Zebulon Pike discovered Pikes Peak, later named for him, that explorer exclaimed that it was so high and massive that it would never be climbed. Not long afterward, the first climbers reached the peak, and it is perhaps the most "climbed" mountain anywhere today. **The Enchantment of Colorado**

- In 1832, William Bent completed the construction of massive Fort Bent, which boasted walls as thick as four feet; this stronghold became the center of trade of a vast Western region.
- Western Colorado, which Mexico won control of in 1821, became U.S. territory in 1848 after the Mexican War.
- Settlers from Mexican lands in 1851 founded San Luis, the oldest continuously occupied community in Colorado.
- In 1858, thousands rushed to the gold at Cherry Creek, spurred by the slogan "Pike's Peak or bust!"
- By June 1858, the "bust" had come. Little easy-to-reach gold had been found, and thousands of disappointed fortune hunters turned back in despair.
- In November 1858, promoter William Larimer and his son William H. H. Larimer came to Cherry Creek and founded Denver, which was named for the current governor of the territory.
- In May 1859, John Gregory made a real gold find; Gregory Gulch was soon to become bustling Central City.
- In 1860, Abe Lee discovered gold in the canyon where the community of Leadville soon developed.

- Retaliating for a ranch massacre, a group of irregulars surprised and massacred a contingent of Indians in 1864 in a slaughter known as the Battle of Sand Creek.
- Enraged over the Sand Creek massacre and other complaints, the Indians attacked, spreading terror. Much of the Indian power was broken in the Battle of Beecher Island, and the last battle with the Indians in Colorado was the Battle of Summit Springs on July 11, 1869. Pawnee Chief Traveling Bear was awarded the Medal of Honor for his support of federal forces in that battle.
- After three tries, Colorado was made a state on August 1, 1876.
- Just as Colorado's gold appeared to be running out, new wealth came from the silver found at Leadville in 1877.
- In 1891 gold brought Cripple Creek to world attention. The overall value of gold taken from the Cripple Creek region has been called second only to that from the Witwatersrand mines in South Africa.
- Women of Colorado won the right to vote in 1893.
- World War I called 43,000 to service from Colorado.
- Royal Gorge was spanned in 1929 by what was, at the time, the world's highest suspension bridge.
- The Great Depression was made even more tragic in the 1930s by the worst drought and dust storms in history.

- Beginning in 1942, nearly 10,000 persons of Japanese-American descent were brought to resettlement camps at Arkansas Valley near Grenada, because of misplaced fears that they might aid Japan during World War II.
- The U.S. Air Force Academy opened in 1955 and moved to its permanent location near Colorado Springs in 1958.
- Deep within Cheyenne Mountain, the North American Air Defense Command headquarters commenced operations in 1965.
- In 1988 the Rocky Flats nuclear weapons plant was closed after three workers were exposed to radiation.
- Demonstrators attacked a bus carrying Ku Klux Klan members from a Klan rally in Denver on the birthday of Martin Luther King Jr., in January 1992.

THAT'S INTERESTING

- At one time giant sequoias grew in Colorado, and their fossil remains now form the Colorado petrified forest west of Colorado Springs. One tree had a circumference of 74 feet.
- Many explanations have been given for the decline of the Pueblo culture. According to one of the most interesting theories, the people ground their grain in stone grinders; fine stone mixed with the meal, and their teeth were ground down until they no longer could eat.
- In 1936 in a unique ceremony, Middle Park officially became a part of the United States. The area supposedly had never been included in any of the cessions of territory to the federal government.
- Mining tycoon Auguste Rische was asked to donate a large chandelier to a church he financed. He refused, saying that he could not play a chandelier, and he thought no one else in the congregation could do so.
- Mrs. James J. (Molly) Brown, socialite wife of a Colorado mining tycoon, survived the sinking of the liner *Titanic* in 1912. She became famous as "the Unsinkable Molly Brown" in the Broadway hit of that name (and later in a hit motion picture). Her home is now a Denver museum.

NOTABLE NATIVES

William Harrison (Jack) Dempsey (Manassa, 1895-1983), boxer. **Douglas Fairbanks** (Denver, 1883-1939), actor. **Byron Raymond White** (Fort Collins, 1917-), Supreme Court justice. **Paul Whiteman** (Denver, 1890-1967), musician/conductor.

GENERAL

Admitted to statehood: August 1, 1876
Origin of name: Spanish, *red*, first applied to
 Colorado River
Capital: Denver
Nickname: Centennial State
Motto: *Nil Sine Numine*—Nothing without
 providence
Animal: Rocky Mountain bighorn sheep
Bird: Lark bunting
Flower: Rocky Mountain columbine
Stone: Aquamarine
Song: "Where the Columbines Grow"
Tree: Colorado blue spruce

THE LAND

Area: 104,100 sq. mi., 8th
 Land: 103,729 sq. mi., 8th
 Water: 371 sq. mi., 43rd
 Inland water: 371 sq. mi., 38th
Topography: Eastern dry high plains; hilly to
 mountainous central plateau; western
 Rocky Mountains of high ranges alter-
 nating with broad valleys and deep,
 narrow canyons.
Number of counties: 63
Geographic center: Park, 30 mi. NW of Pikes
 Peak
Length: 380 mi.; width: 280 mi.
Highest point: 14,433 ft. (Mount Elbert),
 3rd
Lowest point: 3,350 ft. (Arkansas River),
 51st
Mean elevation: 6,800 ft., 1st

CLIMATE AND ENVIRONMENT

Temp., highest: 118 deg. on July 11, 1888, at
 Bennett; lowest: −61 deg. on Feb. 1,
 1985, at Maybell
Monthly average: highest: 92.2 deg., 12th;
 lowest: 14.3 deg., 16th; spread (high to
 low): 77.9 deg., 9th
Hazardous waste sites (1997): 15, 23rd
Endangered species: Animals: 11—
 Uncompahgre fritillary butterfly,
 Bonytail chub, Humpback chub,
 Whooping crane, American peregrine
 falcon, Black-footed ferret, Southwestern willow flycatcher, Colorado squawfish, Razorback sucker, Least tern, Gray
 wolf. Plants: 6

MAJOR CITIES
POPULATION, 1996
PERCENTAGE INCREASE, 1990-96

Denver, 497,840; 6.5%
Colorado Springs, 345,127; 23.1%
Aurora, 252,341; 13.6%
Lakewood, 134,999; 6.7%
Fort Collins, 104,196; 19.1%

THE PEOPLE

Population (1997): 3,892,644, 25th
 Percent change (1990-97): 18.16%, 5th
 Percent of total U.S. pop.: 1.45%, 25th
 Per sq. mi: 37.39, 38th
Population (2000 proj.): 4,161,000, 24th
 Percent change (1995-2000): 11.05%, 5th
Percent in metro. area (1996): 81.18%, 18th
Foreign born: 142,000, 18th
 Percent: 4.3%, 20th
Top three ancestries reported:
 German, 32.30%
 English, 17.67%
 Irish, 16.33%
White (1992): 3,216,000, 92.81%, 15th
Black (1992): 147,000, 4.24%, 32nd
Native American (1992): 33,000, 0.95%,
 16th
Asian, Pacific Isle (1992): 70,000, 2.02%,
 17th
Hispanic origin (1992): 457,000, 13.19%,
 5th
Percent over 5 yrs. speaking language other
 than English at home: 10.5%, 16th
Percent males (1996): 49.61%, 11th; percent
 females: 50.39%, 41st
Percent never married: 25.8%, 24th
Marriages per 1,000 (1996): 9.01, 17th
Divorces per 1,000 (1996): NA
Median age (1996): 35.0
Under 5 years (1996): 7.21%, 15th
18 years and under (1996): 28.91%, 22nd
65 years and over (1996): 10.06%, 48th
Percent increase among the elderly (1995-96):
 1.93%, 5th

OF VITAL IMPORTANCE

Live births per 1,000 pop. (1996): 14.6, 17th
Infant mortality rate per 1,000 live births
 (1995): 6.5, 38th
 Rate for whites: 6.0, 34th
 Rate for blacks: 16.8, 13th
Births to unmarried women, % of total
 (1996): 24.8%, 46th

Births to teenage mothers, % of total (1996): 11.9%, 30th

Abortions (1992): 19,880, 18th
  Rate per 1,000 women 14-44 years old: 23.6, 19th
  Percent change (1988-92): 6%, 9th

Average lifetime (1989-91): 75.96, 6th

Total death rate per 100,000 pop. (1995): 667.6, 48th
  Accidents and adverse effects: 39.8, 22nd
  Alzheimer's disease: 7.5, 33rd
  Cancer: 145.9, 49th
  Cerebrovascular diseases: 42.7, 48th
  Chronic liver disease and cirrhosis: 8.6, 29th
  Chronic obstructive pulmonary diseases and allied conditions: 42.3, 19th
  Diabetes mellitus: 14.3, 49th
  Diseases of heart: 172.1, 49th
  HIV infection: 10.9, 20th
  Homicide: 5.7, 29th
  Injury by firearms: 13.5, 28th
  Motor vehicle accidents: 18.6, 23rd
  Pneumonia and influenza: 25.3, 44th
  Suicide: 17.5, 5th

KEEPING WELL

Active nonfederal physicians per 100,000 pop. (1995): 227, 14th

Dentists per 100,000 (1991): 71, 7th

Nurses per 100,000 (1995): 830, 24th

Hospitals per 100,000 (1995): 1.84, 32nd
  Admissions per 1,000 (1995): 90.74, 45th
  Hospital beds per 1,000 (1995): 2.48, 42nd
  Occupancy rate per 100 beds (1995): 58.06, 37th
  Average cost per patient per day (1995): $1,069, 13th
  Average cost per stay (1995): $6,289, 12th

AIDS cases (new, 1996): 572; per 100,000: 13.7, 26th

Persons living with HIV infection, not yet AIDS (1996): 4,953

Other notifiable diseases, per 100,000 pop.:
  Gonorrhea (1995): 74.8, 30th
  Syphilis (1995): 8.1, 32nd
  Tuberculosis (1996): 2.7, 39th

Pop. without health insur. (1996): 16.6%, 14th

HOUSEHOLDS BY TYPE

Total households (1996): 1,502,000, 24th
  Percent change (1990-96): 17.1%, 5th
  Per 1,000 pop. (1996) 392.89, 3rd

Percent of householders 65 yrs. and over (1996): 16.38%, 50th
  Persons per household (1996): 2.47, 49th

Family households: 854,214
  Percent of total: 66.61%, 49th

Nonfamily households: 428,275
  Percent of total: 33.39%, 3rd

Pop. living in group quarters: 79,472
  Percent of pop.: 2.41%, 37th

LIVING QUARTERS

Total housing units: 1,477,349
  Persons per unit: 2.23, 43rd

Occupied housing units: 1,282,489
  Percent of total units: 86.81%, 38th
  Persons per unit: 2.46, 44th
  Percent of units with over 1 person per room: 2.97%, 25th

Owner-occupied units: 798,277
  Percent of total units: 54.03%, 41st
  Percent of occupied units: 62.24%, 43rd
  Persons per unit: 2.66, 40th
  Median value: $82,700, 18th

Renter-occupied units: 484,212
  Percent of total units: 32.78%, 14th
  Percent of occupied units: 37.76%, 11th
  Persons per unit: 2.25, 39th
  Median contract rent: $362, 20th
  Rental vacancy rate: 11.4%, 10th

Mobile home, trailer & other as a percent of occupied housing units: 7.97%, 32nd

Persons in emergency shelters for homeless persons: 2,554, 0.078%, 11th

Persons visible in street locations: 393, 0.0119%, 14th

Nursing home population: 18,506, 0.56%, 41st

CRIME INDEX PER 100,000 (1996)

Total reported: 5,118.5, 21st
  Percent increase: −5.1%, 32nd
  Violent: 404.5, 34th
    Percent increase: −8.1%, 33rd
    Murder & nonnegligent manslaughter: 4.7, 30th
    Forcible rape: 46.2, 13th
    Aggravated assault: 255.4, 31st
    Robbery: 98.2, 35th
  Property: 4,714.0, 18th
    Percent increase: −4.9%, 34th
    Burglary: 900.8, 23rd
    Larceny-theft: 3,415.5, 15th
    Motor vehicle theft: 397.8, 31st

TEACHING AND LEARNING

Pop. 3 and over enrolled in school (1996): 916,177, 24th
  Percent of pop.: 23.96%, 15th
Public elementary & secondary schools (1996-97): 1,486, 23rd
  Total enrollment (1996): 673,438, 24th
    Percent of school age pop.: 92.51%, 24th
    Percent of total pop.: 17.62%, 20th
  Teachers (1996): 35,900, 28th
    Percent of pop.: 0.94%, 39th
  Pupil/teacher ratio (1995): 18.5, 10th
  Teachers' avg. salary (1996-97): $36,175, 23rd
  Expenditure per capita (1992-93): $1,383.94, 20th
    Education as % of state govt. expenditures: 34.1%, 32nd
  Expenditure per pupil (1994-95): $5,443, 30th
    Percent increase (1993-94 & 1994-95): 6.79%, 6th
Percent at or above grade level, NAEP tests:
  Reading, grade 4 (1994): 28%, 19th
  Math, grade 4 (1996): 67%, 16th
  Math, grade 8 (1996): 67%, 15th
Percent of graduates taking SAT (1995): 29%, 26th
  Mean SAT verbal scores: 462, 23rd
  Mean SAT mathematical scores: 518, 22nd
Percent of graduates taking ACT (1997): 62%, 18th
  Mean ACT scores: 21.5, 16th
Percent of pop. over 25 completing:
  Less than 9th grade: 5.6%, 48th
  High school: 84.4%, 3rd
  College degree(s): 27.0%, 4th
Higher education, institutions (1996): 59, 22nd
  Enrollment (1995-96): 242,739, 22nd
    Percent increase in enroll. (1990-95): 6.9%, 18th
    White non-Hispanic (1995): 195,023, 21st
      Percent of enroll.: 80.34%, 24th
    Total minority enroll. (1995): 42,071, 22nd
      Percent of enroll.: 17.33%, 25th
    Black non-Hispanic (1995): 8,421, 31st
      Percent of enroll.: 3.47%, 34th
    Hispanic (1995): 22,483, 9th
      Percent of enroll.: 9.26%, 7th
    Asian/Pacific Islander (1995): 8,146, 18th
      Percent of enroll.: 3.36%, 17th
    American Indian/AK native (1995): 3,021, 11th
      Percent of enroll.: 1.24%, 15th

Nonresident alien (1995): 5,645, 28th
  Percent of enroll.: 2.33%, 32nd
Female (1995): 131,730, 22nd
  Percent of enroll.: 54.27%, 46th
Pub. institutions (1995-96): 30, 21st
  Enrollment: 210,312, 19th
    Percent increase in enrollment (1990-95): 4.8%, 21st
  Percent of enroll.: 86.64%, 15th
Private institutions (1995-96): 29, 20th
  Enrollment: 32,427, 26th
    Percent increase in enrollment (1990-95): 22.5%, 4th
  Percent of enroll.: 13.36%, 37th
Tuition (in state), public 4-year institution (1996-97): $2,562, 26th
Tuition (in state), public 2-year institution (1996-97): $1,403, 24th
Tuition, private 4-year institution (1996-97): $12,189, 23rd
Public library systems (1994): 120, 24th
  Books & serial vol. per capita: 2.6, 30th
  Library visits per capita: 4.3, 19th
  Circulation per capita: 7.8, 14th

LAW ENFORCEMENT AND CORRECTIONS

Police protection and corrections expenditures (1996): $405,922,000
  Per capita: $106.18, 29th
Police per 10,000 pop. (1996): 23.88, 18th
Prisoners (1 year or more) per 100,000 pop. (1996): 322, 26th
  Percent change (1995-96): 12.4%, 9th
  Percent of inmates that are female: 6.8%, 17th
    Percent change: 18.5%, 12th
Death penalty: yes, by lethal injection
  Under sentence (Jan. 1998): 4, 32nd
  Executed, 1976-97: 1, 25th
  Executed in 1997: 1, 9th

RELIGION, NUMBER AND PERCENT OF POPULATION

Agnostic: 26,764—1.10%, 6th
Buddhist: 2,433—0.10%, 17th
Christian: 1,944,069—79.90%, 43rd
Hindu: 4,866—0.20%, 3rd
Jewish: 43,796—1.80%, 9th
Muslim: NA
Unitarian: 17,032—0.70%, 4th
Other: 48,663—2.00%, 10th
None: 277,377—11.40%, 8th
Refused to answer: 68,128—2.80%, 12th

MAKING A LIVING

Personal income per capita (1996): $25,084, 14th

  Percent increase (1995-96): 4.6%, 10th

Disposable personal income per capita (1996): $21,265, 20th

Median income of households (average, 1995-96): $41,429, 6th

Percent of pop. below poverty level (1995-96): 9.7%, 41st

ECONOMY

In civilian labor force (1996): 2,102,000

  Percent of total pop.: 72.4%, 6th

  Percent of total pop. 65 years and over: NA

  Percent of total female pop.: 65.7%, 11th

Major employer industries (total nonagricultural, 1996):

  Construction: 111,100—5.9%, 8th

  Finance, insurance, & real estate: 117,900—6.2%, 10th

  Government: 308,600—16.3%, 32nd

  Manufacturing: 196,000—10.3%, 41st

  Service: 564,900—29.8%, 13th

  Trade: 464,500—24.5%, 15th

  Transportation, communications, public utilities: 120,300—6.3%, 4th

Unemployment rate (1996): 4.2%, 41st

  Male: 4.4%, 38th

  Female: 4.0%, 44th

Total businesses (1995): 118,192, 21st

New business incorps. (1995): 15,309

  Percent of total businesses: 12.95%, 9th

Business failures (1995): 1,481

  Failures per 10,000 businesses: 125.3, 9th

Agriculture farm income:

  Marketing (1996): $4,229,447,000, 17th

    Average per farm: $172,630, 4th

  Leading products (1997): Cattle, wheat, corn, hay, sugar beets, barley, potatoes, apples, peaches, pears, beans, sorghum, onions, oats, sunflowers, vegetables

  Average value land & build. per acre (1997): $590, 39th

    Percent increase (1996-97): 6%, 20th

  Govt. payments (1996): $176,101,000, 17th

    Average per farm: $7,188, 6th

Construction, value of all (1996): $7,960,610,000, 16th

  Per capita: $2,082, 4th

Manufactures (1995):

  Value added: $18,943,000,000

    Per capita: $5,056, 36th

Leading products (1997): Computer equipment and instruments, foods, machinery, aerospace products

Value of nonfuel mineral production (1996): $528,000,000, 23rd

Leading mineral products (1996): Petroleum, natural gas, coal, sand/gravel, cement, molybdenum, stone, gold

Energy consumption per person (1994): 286.9 mil. Btu, 40th

Retail sales (1995): $36,808,000,000

  Per household: $24,823, 22nd

  Sales increase (1994-95): 3.2%, 34th

Tourism revenues (1992): $6.4 bil.

Foreign exports, in total value (1996): $4,883,000,000, 28th

  Per capita: $1,277, 31st

Gross state product per person (1994): $27,291, 13th

Public aid recipients (percent of resident pop. 1994): 4.7%, 42nd

Medicaid recipients (percent of pop., 1995): 7.8%, 49th

Medicare enrollment per 1,000 pop. (1996): 114, 45th

TRAVEL AND TRANSPORTATION

Motor vehicle registrations (1996): 3,433,287, 21st

  Per 1,000 pop.: 899.67, 10th

Motorcycle registrations (1996): 94,217, 14th

  Per 1,000 pop.: 27.44, 10th

Licensed drivers (1996): 2,727,570, 22nd

  Per 1,000 pop.: 727.83, 7th

Public roads & streets (1996)

  Total mileage: 84,797, 22nd

    Per 1,000 pop.: 122.18, 18th

    Rural mileage: 71,139, 22nd

      Per 1,000 pop.: 18.61, 19th

    Urban mileage: 13,658, 24th

      Per 1,000 pop.: 3.57, 11th

    Interstate mileage: 954, 19th

      Per 1,000 pop.: 0.25, 18th

Speed limit (max. interstate, autos, mi. per hr., 1997): 75

Annual vehicle-mi. of travel per driver (1996): 13,110, 36th

Mean travel time for workers age 16+ who work away from home: 20.7 min., 24th

GOVERNMENT

Percent of voting age pop. registered (1996): 81.98%, 14th

  Percent of voting age pop. voting for president: (1996): 53.1%, 23rd

Percent of voting age pop. voting for U.S. representatives (1996): 51.4%, 22nd
State legislators, total (1997): 100, 42nd
Women members (1997): 34
Percent of legislature: 34%, 4th
U.S. Congress, House members (1998): 6
Change (1988-98): 0
Revenues (1996):
State govt.: $11,865,786,000
Per capita: $3,103.79, 39th
Parimutuel & amusement taxes & lotteries, revenue per capita (1995): $90.60, 25th
Expenditures (1996):
State govt.: $10,311,855,000
Per capita: $2,697.32, 43rd
Debt outstanding (1996): $3,576,722,000
Per capita: $935.58, 38th

LAWS AND REGULATIONS

Legal driving age: 16
Marriage age without parental consent: 18
Divorce residence requirement: 90 days

ATTRACTIONS (1997)

Major opera companies: 3
Major symphony orchestras: 2
Major dance companies: 2
Major professional theater companies (non-profit): 1
Per capita spending by the NEA (1997): $0.37, 19th
State Fair in August at Pueblo

SPORTS AND COMPETITION

NCAA (Division I) football and basketball teams: Colorado State Univ. Rams, U.S. Air Force Academy Falcons, Univ. of Colorado Golden Buffaloes
Major league baseball teams: Colorado Rockies (NL West), Coors Field
Major league soccer teams: Colorado Rapids, Mile High Stadium
NBA basketball teams: Denver Nuggets, McNichols Sports Arena
ABL basketball teams: Colorado Xplosion, Denver Coliseum, McNichols Sports Arena
NFL football teams: Denver Broncos (AFC), Mile High Stadium
NHL hockey teams: Colorado Avalanche, McNichols Sports Arena

WEBSITES CONTAINING FURTHER INFORMATION

State of Colorado Home Page   http://www.state.co.us

CONNECTICUT

"The warm, very warm heart of 'New England at its best,' such a vast abounding arcadia of mountains, broad vales and great rivers and large lakes and white villages embowered in prodigious elms and maples. It is extraordinarily graceful and idyllic."

Henry James, Sr., writer and philosopher

"Nowhere in America do the roots of freedom and democracy go deeper than in Connecticut."

All About the U.S.A.

Although Connecticut is the third smallest of the states geographically, it must rank among the greatest in its contributions to the nation and the world. The state gave the world its "first workable written constitution" and introduced mass production, which paved the way for modern manufacturing. Its inventors and manufacturers introduced a wide variety of inexpensive products. "Yankee pedlars" and the masters of the Yankee clippers carried these products around the nation and the world. Connecticut has long led in the insurance field and in the production of helicopters, jet aircraft engines, submarines, pins and needles, silverware, small firearms, and thread.

SUPERLATIVES

• The first tax-supported library in the United States, at Salisbury.
• Modern manufacturing methods—first developed by Eli Terry and Eli Whitney.
• The first woman to receive a U.S. patent—Mary Kies of South Killingly, for a machine to weave silk and straw.
• America's first cigars, machine-made combs, factory hats, plows, friction matches, and tacks, among many other new products.
• The nation's first commercial telephone exchange, in New Haven.
• America's first trade association, founded by Naugatuck Valley manufacturers.
• First in the value of insurance written.

MOMENTS IN HISTORY

• Adriaen Block, a Dutch explorer, discovered and entered the Connecticut River in 1614.
• In 1633 the Dutch built a fort at present-day Hartford. The British countered with a fortified trading post where Windsor now stands.
• Wethersfield was founded in 1634, becoming the oldest permanent European settlement in Connecticut.

• To counter the threat of Indian attack, a force under Captain John Mason attacked and destroyed the Indian encampment of Pequot in 1637.

So They Say

"The greatness and the violence of the fire... the shrieks and yells of men and women and children....It was a fearful sight to see them frying in the fire and the streams of blood quenching the same."

Clergyman Cotton Mather, describing the destruction of Pequot

• The three towns of Connecticut in 1639 grouped themselves into a commonwealth; they were governed by a covenant known as the Fundamental Orders, sometimes called the first constitution. This document was the first to declare that "the foundation of authority is in the free consent of the people," anticipating the U.S. Constitution.
• The charter granted Connecticut by the English King in 1662 was amazingly liberal. It legalized almost every act previously taken in the Connecticut colony, including the Fundamental Orders.
• In 1687, King James II revoked the Connecticut charter. Royal Governor Sir Edmund Andros attempted to seize the charter, but Joseph Wadsworth stole away with it. Tradition says it was hidden in the hollow of an oak on Samuel Wyllys's property. This "Charter Oak" became a famous landmark.
• In 1770, six years before the Declaration of Independence, Lebanon freemen drafted a declaration of rights, and Old Lyme launched its own "Tea Party" by burning the tea sacks of a traveling peddler.
• During the American Revolution, Connecticut is said to have "furnished more men and money than any other colony except Massachusetts."

- Revolutionary Stonington was attacked in 1775, Danbury was burned and looted in 1777, New Haven in 1779, and Bridgeport and New London in 1781.
- On January 9, 1788, Connecticut became the fifth state, after dropping its claim to extend to the west coast, except for what became the "Western Reserve," now the area of Cleveland, Ohio.
- Connecticut adopted "universal manhood suffrage" in 1845, extending the vote to all men, but not to women.
- Beginning in 1861, the state's quota of Civil War volunteers was met five times over. Of the 57,379 Connecticut men and women serving in the war, more than a third (20,573) were killed or missing in action.
- The nation's first code of law for registering airplanes and licensing pilots was inaugurated in Connecticut in 1911.
- During World War I, Connecticut led all the states in production per person.
- In 1954 the Groton shipyards produced the world's first atomic-powered submarine, the *Nautilus*.
- County government was abolished in Connecticut in 1960, the first such step taken by any state. Local government was transferred to an extension of the existing township system.
- Ella T. Grasso was elected governor in 1975, becoming the first woman in any state to be elected governor without having been preceded by her husband.
- Three years of recession in the state by 1992 had resulted in high unemployment and declining budgets. Defense contractors were hardest hit. However, the subsequent recovery was remarkable.

THAT'S INTERESTING

- Early Hartford, described as a Puritan theocracy, was known for its strict religious law. Its "blue laws" called for the death penalty for any son who cursed or struck his parents. Elder Malbone once flogged his daughter Martha on the green for going on a date with a young gentleman.
- The great charter of 1662 extended Connecticut west even to the Pacific Ocean.
- The village of Moodus has experienced "supernatural" noises, rumbles, groans, and screeches. The explanation takes away much of the mystery. The village lies at the junction

of many fault lines, and the sounds come from the joints as they settle.
- During the American Revolution, Lime Rock metalworkers forged a huge chain that was stretched across the Hudson River to keep British ships from sailing up that strategic waterway. Each link was three feet long.
- During the American Revolution, at the age of 15, Samuel Smedley of Fairfield became a captain of a privateer ship. By war's end he had captured more enemy prize ships than any other captain, surpassing even the small U.S. Navy.

> ### So They Say
>
> "There is little hope of conquering an enemy whose very schoolboys are capable of valor equaling that of trained veterans of naval warfare."
>
> Comment of a captured British sea captain

- Connecticut's Charter Oak gained such fame that it became fashionable to own a product supposedly made from its trunk. It was said that Charter Oak products included walking sticks, dog collars, needle cases, three-legged stools, dinner tables, tenpin alleys, toothpicks, and enough alleged Charter Oak to build a plank road from Hartford to Salt Lake City.
- An excited colonial lady watched a procession of shabbily dressed soldiers riding off to the French and Indian War. Elizabeth Fitch was horrified that they had no uniform, so she made each man put a feather in his cap. An American colonel was so intrigued by the men's "dandy" appearance that he composed a song that is still loved today—"Yankee Doodle Dandy."

NOTABLE NATIVES

Ethan Allen (Litchfield, 1738-1789), Revolutionary soldier. **Phineas Taylor Barnum** (Bethel, 1810-1891), showman. **John Brown** (Torrington, 1800-1859), abolitionist. **Samuel Colt** (Hartford, 1814-1862), inventor. **John Fitch** (Hartford County, 1743-1798), inventor. **Charles Goodyear** (New Haven, 1800-1860), inventor/manufacturer. **Nathan Hale** (Coventry, 1755-1776), soldier. **Katharine Hepburn** (Hartford, 1907-), actress. **Elias Howe**

(Spencer, 1819-1867), inventor. **Collis Potter Huntington** (Harwinton, 1821-1900), railroad builder. **John Pierpont Morgan** (Hartford, 1837-1913), financier. **Ralph Nader** (Winsted, 1934-), consumer advocate. **Harriet Beecher Stowe** (Litchfield, 1811-1896), author. **Eli Terry** (East Windsor, 1772-1852), clock manufacturer. **John Trumbull** (Lebanon, 1756-1843), artist. **Jonathan Trumbull** (Lebanon, 1710-1785), public official. **Noah Webster** (West Hartford, 1758-1843), lexicographer. **Emma Hart Willard** (Berlin, 1787-1870), educator.

GENERAL

Admitted to statehood: January 9, 1788
Origin of name: From Mohican and other Algonquin words meaning "long river place"
Capital: Hartford
Nickname: Constitution State, Nutmeg State
Motto: *Qui Transtulit Sustinet*—He who transplanted still sustains
Animal: Sperm whale
Bird: American robin
Insect: Praying mantis
Flower: Mountain laurel
Mineral: Garnet
Song: "Yankee Doodle"
Tree: White oak

THE LAND

Area: 5,544 sq. mi., 48th
  Land: 4,845 sq. mi., 48th
  Water: 699 sq. mi., 36th
    Inland water: 161 sq. mi., 47th
    Coastal water: 538 sq. mi., 11th
Topography: Western upland, the Berkshires, in the NW, highest elevations; narrow central lowland; hilly eastern upland drained by rivers
Number of counties: 8
Geographic center: Hartford, at East Berlin
Length: 110 mi.; width: 70 mi.
Highest point: 2,380 ft. (Mount Frissell), 36th
Lowest point: sea level (Long Island Sound), 3rd
Mean elevation: 500 ft., 41st
Coastline: 0 mi., 24th
Shoreline: 618 mi., 18th

CLIMATE AND ENVIRONMENT

Temp., highest: 106 deg. on July 15, 1995, at Danbury; lowest: –32 deg. on Feb. 16, 1943, at Falls Village
Monthly average: highest: 84.8 deg., 39th; lowest: 16.7 deg., 22nd; spread (high to low): 68.1 deg., 27th
Hazardous waste sites (1997): 14, 26th
Endangered species: Animals: 3—American peregrine falcon, Dwarf wedge mussel, Roseate tern. Plants: 1

MAJOR CITIES POPULATION, 1996 PERCENTAGE INCREASE, 1990-96

Bridgeport, 137,990; –2.6%
Hartford, 133,086; –4.8%
New Haven, 124,665; –4.5%
Stamford, 110,056; 1.9%
Waterbury, 106,412; –2.3%

THE PEOPLE

Population (1997): 3,269,858, 28th
  Percent change (1990-97): –0.53%, 49th
  Percent of total U.S. pop.: 1.22%, 28th
  Per sq. mi: 589.80, 4th
Population (2000 proj.): 3,285,000, 29th
  Percent change (1995-2000): 0.31%, 49th
Percent in metro. area (1996): 91.30%, 9th
Foreign born: 279,000, 13th
  Percent: 8.5%, 11th
Top three ancestries reported:
  Italian, 19.11%
  Irish, 18.68%
  English, 14.09%
White (1992): 2,926,000, 89.23%, 23rd
Black (1992): 288,000, 8.78%, 22nd
Native American (1992): 7,000, 0.21%, 45th
Asian, Pacific Isle (1992): 58,000, 1.77%, 19th
Hispanic origin (1992): 228,000, 6.95%, 12th
Percent over 5 yrs. speaking language other than English at home: 15.2%, 10th
Percent males (1996): 48.61%, 33rd; percent females: 51.39%, 19th
Percent never married: 29.0%, 9th
Marriages per 1,000 (1996): 6.54, 46th
Divorces per 1,000 (1996): 3.22, 40th
Median age (1996): 36.2
Under 5 years (1996): 6.82%, 34th
18 years and under (1996): 26.68%, 45th
65 years and over (1996): 14.35%, 9th

Percent increase among the elderly (1995-96): 0.50%, 35th

OF VITAL IMPORTANCE

Live births per 1,000 pop. (1996): 13.5, 38th

Infant mortality rate per 1,000 live births (1995): 7.2, 31st
Rate for whites: 6.5, 21st
Rate for blacks: 12.6, 31st

Births to unmarried women, % of total (1996): 31.3%, 26th

Births to teenage mothers, % of total (1996): 8.2%, 48th

Abortions (1992): 19,720, 19th
Rate per 1,000 women 14-44 years old: 26.2, 13th
Percent change (1988-92): −16%, 41st

Average lifetime (1989-91): 76.91, 8th

Total death rate per 100,000 pop. (1995): 899.5, 28th
Accidents and adverse effects: 32.9, 38th
Alzheimer's disease: 7.3, 37th
Cancer: 215.6, 19th
Cerebrovascular diseases: 57.2, 32nd
Chronic liver disease and cirrhosis: 9.9, 17th
Chronic obstructive pulmonary diseases and allied conditions: 35.5, 39th
Diabetes mellitus: 18.1, 41st
Diseases of heart: 298.9, 21st
HIV infection: 18.4, 9th
Homicide: 4.6, 38th
Injury by firearms: 7.8, 45th
Motor vehicle accidents: 10.7, 47th
Pneumonia and influenza: 33.9, 16th
Suicide: 9.9, 44th

KEEPING WELL

Active nonfederal physicians per 100,000 pop. (1995): 334, 5th

Dentists per 100,000 (1991): 80, 2nd

Nurses per 100,000 (1995): 1,032, 9th

Hospitals per 100,000 (1995): 1.04, 50th
Admissions per 1,000 (1995): 103.21, 37th
Hospital beds per 1,000 (1995): 2.29, 46th
Occupancy rate per 100 beds (1995): 73.33, 4th
Average cost per patient per day (1995): $1,264, 5th
Average cost per stay (1995): $7,358, 5th

AIDS cases (new, 1996): 1,112; per 100,000: 34.0, 7th

Persons living with HIV infection (1996): NA

Other notifiable diseases, per 100,000 pop.:
Gonorrhea (1995): 123.8, 21st
Syphilis (1995): 8.3, 30th
Tuberculosis (1996): 4.2, 31st

Pop. without health insur. (1996): 11.0%, 41st

HOUSEHOLDS BY TYPE

Total households (1996): 1,231,000, 29th
Percent change (1990-96): 0.0%, 49th
Per 1,000 pop. (1996) 375.99, 34th
Percent of householders 65 yrs. and over (1996): 23.31%, 10th
Persons per household (1996): 2.65, 13th

Family households: 864,493
Percent of total: 70.26%, 28th

Nonfamily households: 365,986
Percent of total: 29.74%, 24th

Pop. living in group quarters: 101,167
Percent of pop.: 3.08%, 14th

LIVING QUARTERS

Total housing units: 1,320,850
Persons per unit: 2.49, 9th

Occupied housing units: 1,230,479
Percent of total units: 93.16%, 3rd
Persons per unit: 2.52, 26th
Percent of units with over 1 person per room: 2.29%, 38th

Owner-occupied units: 807,481
Percent of total units: 61.13%, 18th
Percent of occupied units: 65.62%, 34th
Persons per unit: 2.74, 22nd
Median value: $177,800, 3rd

Renter-occupied units: 422,998
Percent of total units: 32.02%, 15th
Percent of occupied units: 34.38%, 19th
Persons per unit: 2.30, 32nd
Median contract rent: $510, 4th
Rental vacancy rate: 6.9%, 42nd

Mobile home, trailer & other as a percent of occupied housing units: 2.52%, 48th

Persons in emergency shelters for homeless persons: 4,194, 0.128%, 3rd

Persons visible in street locations: 221, 0.0067%, 25th

Nursing home population: 30,962, 0.94%, 12th

CRIME INDEX PER 100,000 (1996)

Total reported: 4,227.7, 36th
Percent increase: −6.1%, 38th

Violent: 412.0, 33rd
  Percent increase: 1.5%, 6th
  Murder & nonnegligent manslaughter:
    4.8, 28th
  Forcible rape: 23.1, 46th
  Aggravated assault: 214.6, 36th
  Robbery: 169.6, 18th
Property: 3,815.6, 35th
  Percent increase: −6.9%, 39th
  Burglary: 842.2, 28th
  Larceny-theft: 2,484.1, 39th
  Motor vehicle theft: 489.4, 21st

TEACHING AND LEARNING

Pop. 3 and over enrolled in school (1996):
    680,749, 29th
  Percent of pop.: 20.79%, 48th
Public elementary & secondary schools (1996-
    97): 1,045, 33rd
  Total enrollment (1996): 523,054, 29th
    Percent of school age pop.: 90.97%, 28th
    Percent of total pop.: 15.98%, 42nd
  Teachers (1996): 36,800, 27th
    Percent of pop.: 1.12%, 18th
  Pupil/teacher ratio (1995): 14.4, 46th
  Teachers' avg. salary (1996-97): $50,426, 2nd
  Expenditure per capita (1992-93):
    $1,448.21, 15th
    Education as % of state govt. expendi-
      tures: 30.1%, 41st
    Expenditure per pupil (1994-95): $8,817,
      5th
    Percent increase (1993-94 & 1994-95):
      4.06%, 26th
Percent at or above grade level, NAEP tests:
  Reading, grade 4 (1994): 38%, 2nd
  Math, grade 4 (1996): 75%, 2nd
  Math, grade 8 (1996): 70%, 9th
Percent of graduates taking SAT (1995): 81%,
    1st
  Mean SAT verbal scores: 431, 32nd
  Mean SAT mathematical scores: 477, 36th
Percent of graduates taking ACT (1997): 3%,
    47th
  Mean ACT scores: 21.7, 10th
Percent of pop. over 25 completing:
  Less than 9th grade: 8.4%, 34th
  High school: 79.2%, 17th
  College degree(s): 27.2%, 3rd
Higher education, institutions (1996): 42,
    31st
  Enrollment (1995-96): 157,695, 31st
    Percent increase in enroll. (1990-95):
      −6.5%, 51st

White non-Hispanic (1995): 126,335,
    32nd
  Percent of enroll.: 80.11%, 27th
Total minority enroll. (1995): 25,763, 30th
  Percent of enroll.: 16.34%, 28th
Black non-Hispanic (1995): 11,879, 27th
  Percent of enroll.: 7.53%, 23rd
Hispanic (1995): 7,735, 16th
  Percent of enroll.: 4.91%, 11th
Asian/Pacific Islander (1995): 5,610, 23rd
  Percent of enroll.: 3.56%, 14th
American Indian/AK native (1995): 539,
    41st
  Percent of enroll.: 0.34%, 43rd
Nonresident alien (1995): 5,597, 29th
  Percent of enroll.: 3.55%, 11th
Female (1995): 89,195, 31st
  Percent of enroll.: 56.56%, 17th
Pub. institutions (1995-96): 19, 34th
  Enrollment: 100,539, 33rd
    Percent increase in enrollment (1990-
      95): −8.2%, 49th
    Percent of enroll.: 63.76%, 44th
Private institutions (1995-96): 23, 26th
  Enrollment: 57,156, 18th
    Percent increase in enrollment (1990-
      95): −3.2%, 45th
    Percent of enroll.: 36.24%, 8th
Tuition (in state), public 4-year institution
    (1996-97): $4,105, 7th
Tuition (in state), public 2-year institution
    (1996-97): $1,722, 18th
Tuition, private 4-year institution (1996-
    97): $17,495, 1st
Public library systems (1994): 194, 18th
  Books & serial vol. per capita: 4.3, 7th
  Library visits per capita: 6.3, 1st
  Circulation per capita: 8.1, 11th

LAW ENFORCEMENT AND CORRECTIONS

Police protection and corrections expenditures
    (1996): $570,894,000
  Per capita: $174.38, 4th
Police per 10,000 pop. (1996): 26.90, 9th
Prisoners (1 year or more) per 100,000 pop.
    (1996): 314, 28th
  Percent change (1995-96): −1.1%, 47th
  Percent of inmates that are female: 7.5%,
    4th
    Percent change: 16.2%, 13th
Death penalty: yes, by lethal injection
  Under sentence (Jan. 1998): 5, 31st
  Executed, 1976-97: 0

RELIGION, NUMBER AND PERCENT OF POPULATION

Agnostic: 12,688—0.50%, 27th
Buddhist: 5,075—0.20%, 11th
Christian: 2,167,055—85.40%, 29th
Hindu: 2,538—0.10%, 10th
Jewish: 60,901—2.40%, 6th
Muslim: 2,538—0.10%, 22nd
Unitarian: 7,613—0.30%, 15th
Other: 32,988—1.30%, 24th
None: 147,177—5.80%, 35th
Refused to answer: 98,964—3.90%, 3rd

MAKING A LIVING

Personal income per capita (1996): $33,189, 2nd
Percent increase (1995-96): 2.2%, 40th
Disposable personal income per capita (1996): $27,706, 2nd
Median income of households (average, 1995-96): $41,775, 5th
Percent of pop. below poverty level (1995-96): 10.7%, 37th

ECONOMY

In civilian labor force (1996): 1,720,000
    Percent of total pop.: 68.2%, 27th
    Percent of total pop. 65 years and over: NA
    Percent of total female pop.: 62.5%, 18th
Major employer industries (total nonagricultural, 1996):
    Construction: 51,600—3.3%, 46th
    Finance, insurance, & real estate: 130,600—8.3%, 3rd
    Government: 223,600—14.1%, 44th
    Manufacturing: 275,200—17.4%, 17th
    Service: 481,400—30.4%, 12th
    Trade: 346,700—21.9%, 46th
    Transportation, communications, public utilities: 73,100—4.6%, 38th
Unemployment rate (1996): 5.7%, 14th
    Male: 5.7%, 15th
    Female: 5.7%, 18th
Total businesses (1995): 91,189, 26th
New business incorps. (1995): 4,830
    Percent of total businesses: 5.30%, 50th
Business failures (1995): 485
    Failures per 10,000 businesses: 53.2, 44th
Agriculture farm income:
    Marketing (1996): $489,113,000, 42nd
    Average per farm: $128,714, 13th
    Leading products (1997): Greenhouse, Christmas trees, mushrooms, vegetables, corn, tobacco, apples

Average value land & build. per acre (1997): $7,500, 3rd
    Percent increase (1996-97): 10%, 2nd
Govt. payments (1996): $1,791,000, 45th
    Average per farm: $471, 44th
Construction, value of all (1996): $3,423,652,000, 32nd
    Per capita: $1,046, 38th
Manufactures (1995):
    Value added: $24,988,200,000
    Per capita: $7,631, 12th
    Leading products (1997): Aircraft engines and parts, submarines, helicopters, medical instruments, machinery & computer equipment, electronics & electrical equipment, pharmaceuticals
Value of nonfuel mineral production (1996): $103,000,000, 44th
Leading mineral products (1996): Stone, sand/gravel, stone, clays, gemstones
Energy consumption per person (1994): 243.4 mil. Btu, 47th
Retail sales (1995): $31,844,000,000
    Per household: $25,847, 12th
    Sales increase (1994-95): −1.2%, 50th
Tourism revenues (1993): $3.9 bil.
Foreign exports, in total value (1996): $6,100,000,000, 24th
    Per capita: $1,863, 18th
Gross state product per person (1994): $33,722, 4th
Public aid recipients (percent of resident pop. 1994): 6.4%, 30th
Medicaid recipients (percent of pop., 1995): 11.6%, 28th
Medicare enrollment per 1,000 pop. (1996): 155, 12th

TRAVEL AND TRANSPORTATION

Motor vehicle registrations (1996): 2,608,831, 30th
    Per 1,000 pop.: 798.47, 27th
Motorcycle registrations (1996): 48,328, 27th
Licensed drivers (1996): 2,349,051, 28th
    Per 1,000 pop.: 718.20, 10th
    Per 1,000 pop.: 18.52, 30th
Public roads & streets (1996)
    Total mileage: 20,600, 44th
        Per 1,000 pop.: 16.29, 43rd
    Rural mileage: 8,920, 47th
        Per 1,000 pop.: 2.72, 46th
    Urban mileage: 11,680, 26th
        Per 1,000 pop.: 3.57, 11th

Interstate mileage: 344, 45th
  Per 1,000 pop.: 0.11, 41st
Speed limit (max. interstate, autos, mi. per hr., 1997): 55
Annual vehicle-mi. of travel per driver (1996): 12,004, 40th
Mean travel time for workers age 16+ who work away from home: 21.1 min., 22nd

GOVERNMENT

Percent of voting age pop. registered (1996): 75.89%, 28th
  Percent of voting age pop. voting for president: (1996): 56.4%, 15th
  Percent of voting age pop. voting for U.S. representatives (1996): 52.4%, 15th
State legislators, total (1997): 187, 9th
  Women members (1997): 52
  Percent of legislature: 28%, 11th
U.S. Congress, House members (1998): 6
  Change (1988-98): 0
Revenues (1996):
  State govt.: $14,349,487,000
  Per capita: $4,382.86, 12th
  Parimutuel & amusement taxes & lotteries, revenue per capita (1995): $244.28, 5th
Expenditures (1996):
  State govt.: $13,529,622,000
  Per capita: $4,132.44, 6th

Debt outstanding (1996): $16,415,336,000
  Per capita: $5,013.85, 4th

LAWS AND REGULATIONS

Legal driving age: 18, 16 if completed driver education course
Marriage age without parental consent: 18
Divorce residence requirement: 1 yr., for qualifications check local statutes

ATTRACTIONS (1997)

Major opera companies: 2
Major symphony orchestras: 2
Major dance companies: 2
Major professional theater companies (non-profit): 3
Per capita spending by the NEA (1997): $0.39, 18th

SPORTS AND COMPETITION

NCAA (Division I) football and basketball teams: Central Connecticut State Blue Devils, Fairfield Univ. Stags, Univ. of Connecticut Huskies, Univ. of Hartford Hawks (basketball only), Yale Univ. Elis/Bulldogs
ABL basketball teams: New England Blizzard, Hartford Civic Center, Springfield Civic Center (MA)

WEBSITES CONTAINING FURTHER INFORMATION

| Connecticut Government Information Home Page | http://www.state.ct.us |
| The Connecticut Homepage | http://www.connecticut.com |

DELAWARE

"Delaware is like a diamond, diminutive, but having within it inherent value."
John Lofland, poet and author

The distinguished history of the second smallest state geographically extends over more than 300 years. Delaware is proud to be known as the "First State," the first to accept the new U.S. Constitution. It was the only colony to have been claimed by Sweden, Holland, and England. The lotus plants found here have led some specialists to believe that the region may have been visited by early Egyptian explorers. Swedish settlers here introduced the log cabin to American shores, and the nation's first regularly operated steam railroad was started here. Today, Delaware is both a farming and an industrial region and leads the nation in the production of chemicals. More corporations are headquartered in Delaware than in any other state as a result of its corporate laws.

SUPERLATIVES

• The European-style log cabin, introduced to the United States in Delaware.
• The nation's first regularly operated steam railroad, beginning operations out of New Castle in 1831.
• At one time the nation's flour industry center, with the price of wheat set in Wilmington.

MOMENTS IN HISTORY

• Henry Hudson sailed his storied ship, the *Half Moon*, up Delaware Bay in 1609, becoming the first European known to have visited the area.
• In 1613 another explorer, Cornelius Jacobsen Mey, explored and traded in the area.

• Dutch leader Peter Minuit, employed by Sweden, brought settlers in two ships to what is now Wilmington in 1638.
• In 1655, New Amsterdam Governor Peter Stuyvesant brought a large fleet to the area, captured all of New Sweden for the Dutch, and ended Swedish rule in America.
• In 1682, William Penn, new proprietor of Delaware and Pennsylvania, sailed up the Delaware River past flourishing Christina on his way to his new capital, Philadelphia. Delaware would be governed from there until it became a British crown colony in 1704.
• In 1739, Willington—the name the British had given to Swedish Christina after they took it over—was renamed Wilmington. Spurred by a talented and ambitious group of settlers, the community began to flourish.
• In 1776, although he was seriously ill, Caesar Rodney, a member of the Continental Congress, made a famous ride from Wilmington to Philadelphia in order to cast the deciding vote for the Declaration of Independence.
• On August 27, 1776, Delaware's First Regiment played a key role in the important Battle of Long Island.
• Delaware gained distinction as the "First State" when it ratified the U.S. Constitution on December 7, 1787.
• During the War of 1812, Delaware's Captain Thomas Macdonough's victory in the Battle of Lake Champlain became a turning point of that conflict.

So They Say

He "...did there trade with the inhabitants; said trade consisting of sables, Furs, Robes and other skins.... He hath found the said Country full of trees, to wit: Oaks, hickory and pines; which trees were, in some places covered with vines...in the said country, Bucks and does, turkeys and partridges...."

Explorer Cornelius Hendrickson,
on the exploration of
Cornelius Jacobsen Mey

So They Say

"Sir: The Almighty has been pleased to grant us a signal victory on Lake Champlain in the capture of one frigate, one brig, and two sloops of war of the enemy."

Captain Thomas Macdonough
reporting to his commander,
modestly neglecting to mention
that he had brought the entire
British fleet into his hands

• In the Civil War's Battle of Antietam on September 17, 1862, almost half of the Delaware men who took part were killed.

• During the great storm of 1889, 40 ships were destroyed off Lewes and 70 lives were lost.

• The disastrous Pocomoke Swamp fire of 1930 burned the underlying peat for eight months.

• A 1978 order of the U.S. Supreme Court permitted the busing of children from Wilmington to the suburbs to promote racial integration. The decision was a landmark for the establishment of this practice.

• In 1992, Delaware carried out its first execution since 1946, as convicted murderer Steve Brian Pennell was put to death.

THAT'S INTERESTING

• Johan Prinz, capable governor of New Sweden from 1643 to 1653, was the "greatest" of all colonial governors. He weighed 400 pounds and was called the "Big Tub."

• When a ship carrying peas wrecked on a sandbar, the peas grew and collected so much sand that a new island formed, now Pea Patch Island.

• One of the most curious exhibits to be found at the Delaware Historical Society is a cigar store white man, a carving of George Washington.

NOTABLE NATIVES

James Asheton Bayard (Wilmington, 1799-1880), public official. **Henry Seidel Canby** (Wilmington, 1878-1961), author/publisher. **Annie Jump Cannon** (Dover, 1863-1941), astronomer. **John Middleton Clayton** (Dagsborough, 1796-1856), jurist/statesman. **Alfred Irenee Du Pont** (near Wilmington, 1864-1965), industrialist/philanthropist. **Henry Du Pont** (Wilmington, 1812-1889), industrialist/philanthropist. **Henry Algernon Du Pont** (near Wilmington, 1838-1926), public official/industrialist. **Pierre Samuel Du Pont** (Wilmington, 1870-1954), industrialist. **Jacob Jones** (near Smyrna, 1768-1850), naval officer. **Thomas Macdonough** (Macdonough, 1783-1825), naval officer. **John Phillips Marquand** (Wilmington, 1893-1960), author. **Howard Pyle** (Wilmington, 1853-1911), author/artist. **Caesar Rodney** (near Dover, 1728-1784), patriot/statesman.

GENERAL

Admitted to statehood: December 7, 1787
Origin of name: Named for Lord De La Warr, early governor of Virginia; the name was first applied to the river, then to the Indian tribe (Lenni-Lenape) and to the state
Capital: Dover
Nickname: Diamond State, First State, Blue Hen State
Motto: Liberty and independence
Bird: Blue hen chicken
Insect: Lady Bug
Fish: Weakfish
Flower: Peach blossom
Mineral: Sillimanite
Song: "Our Delaware"
Tree: American holly

THE LAND

Area: 2,397 sq. mi., 49th
    Land: 1,955 sq. mi., 49th
    Water: 442 sq. mi., 41st
        Inland water: 71 sq. mi., 49th
        Coastal water: 371 sq. mi., 15th
Topography: Piedmont plateau in the northern tip, sloping to a near sea-level coastal plain
Number of counties: 3
Geographic center: Kent, 11 mi. S of Dover
Length: 100 mi.; width: 30 mi.
Highest point: 442 ft. (Ebright Road), 49th
Lowest point: sea level (Atlantic Ocean), 3rd
Mean elevation: 60 ft., 51st
Coastline: 28 mi., 21st
Shoreline: 381 mi., 21st

CLIMATE AND ENVIRONMENT

Temp., highest: 110 deg. on July 21, 1930, at Millsboro; lowest: −17 deg. on Jan. 17, 1893, at Millsboro
Monthly average: highest: 85.6 deg., 35th; lowest: 23.2 deg., 32nd; spread (high to low): 62.4 deg., 36th
Hazardous waste sites (1997): 17, 20th
Endangered species: Animals: 2—American peregrine falcon, Delmarva Peninsula fox squirrel. Plants: 1

MAJOR CITIES
POPULATION, 1996
PERCENTAGE INCREASE, 1990-96

Wilmington, 69,490; 2.9%
Dover, 30,414; 10.1%
Newark, 27,870; 5.3%
Milford, 6,557; 8.7%
Seaford, 6,400; 12.5%

THE PEOPLE

Population (1997): 731,581, 46th
  Percent change (1990-97): 9.82%, 16th
  Percent of total U.S. pop.: 0.27%, 46th
  Per sq. mi: 293.93, 8th
Population (2000 proj.): 763,000, 46th
  Percent change (1995-2000): 6.42%, 16th
Percent in metro. area (1996): 81.90%, 17th
Foreign born: 22,000, 44th
  Percent: 3.3%, 24th
Top three ancestries reported:
  Irish, 20.87%
  German, 20.72%
  English, 18.47%
White (1992): 557,000, 80.61%, 39th
Black (1992): 121,000, 17.51%, 10th
Native American (1992): 2,000, 0.29%, 34th
Asian, Pacific Isle (1992): 11,000, 1.59%, 21st
Hispanic origin (1992): 18,000, 2.60%, 27th
Percent over 5 yrs. speaking language other than English at home: 6.9%, 27th
Percent males (1996): 48.74%, 28th; percent females: 51.26%, 24th
Percent never married: 27.6%, 12th
Marriages per 1,000 (1996): 7.17, 40th
Divorces per 1,000 (1996): 4.62, 21st
Median age (1996): 35.0
Under 5 years (1996): 6.93%, 28th
18 years and under (1996): 26.87%, 43rd
65 years and over (1996): 12.76%, 26th
Percent increase among the elderly (1995-96): 1.86%, 7th

OF VITAL IMPORTANCE

Live births per 1,000 pop. (1996): 14.1, 26th
Infant mortality rate per 1,000 live births (1995): 7.5, 25th
  Rate for whites: 6.0, 34th
  Rate for blacks: 13.1, 29th
Births to unmarried women, % of total (1996): 35.5%, 10th
Births to teenage mothers, % of total (1996): 13.7%, 19th
Abortions (1992): 5,730, 39th
  Rate per 1,000 women 14-44 years old: 35.2, 6th
  Percent change (1988-92): −1%, 15th
Average lifetime (1989-91): 74.76, 38th
Total death rate per 100,000 pop. (1995): 875.9, 33rd
  Accidents and adverse effects: 37.1, 26th
  Alzheimer's disease: 5.7, 46th
  Cancer: 227.3, 12th

Cerebrovascular diseases: 47.8, 45th
Chronic liver disease and cirrhosis: 8.4, 33rd
Chronic obstructive pulmonary diseases and allied conditions: 36.0, 38th
Diabetes mellitus: 26.9, 10th
Diseases of heart: 276.1, 30th
HIV infection: 22.7, 6th
Homicide: 5.9, 28th
Injury by firearms: 8.4, 44th
Motor vehicle accidents: 17.6, 25th
Pneumonia and influenza: 29.1, 30th
Suicide: 11.2, 41st

KEEPING WELL

Active nonfederal physicians per 100,000 pop. (1995): 217, 22nd
Dentists per 100,000 (1991): 45, 42nd
Nurses per 100,000 (1995): 1,067, 7th
Hospitals per 100,000 (1995): 1.12, 48th
  Admissions per 1,000 (1995): 112.97, 28th
  Hospital beds per 1,000 (1995): 2.65, 39th
  Occupancy rate per 100 beds (1995): 78.95, 3rd
  Average cost per patient per day (1995): $1,058, 17th
  Average cost per stay (1995): $7,298, 6th
AIDS cases (new, 1996): 285; per 100,000: 39.3, 6th
Persons living with HIV infection (1996): NA
Other notifiable diseases, per 100,000 pop.:
  Gonorrhea (1995): 306.9, 5th
  Syphilis (1995): 18.0, 18th
  Tuberculosis (1996): 5.9, 23rd
Pop. without health insur. (1996): 13.4%, 27th

HOUSEHOLDS BY TYPE

Total households (1996): 276,000, 45th
  Percent change (1990-96): 11.4%, 12th
  Per 1,000 pop. (1996) 380.69, 25th
  Percent of householders 65 yrs. and over (1996): 21.01%, 33rd
  Persons per household (1996): 2.82, 3rd
Family households: 175,867
  Percent of total: 71.06%, 22nd
Nonfamily households: 71,630
  Percent of total: 28.94%, 30th
Pop. living in group quarters: 20,071
  Percent of pop.: 3.01%, 17th

LIVING QUARTERS

Total housing units: 289,919
  Persons per unit: 2.30, 40th

Occupied housing units: 247,497
  Percent of total units: 85.37%, 42nd
  Persons per unit: 2.55, 20th
  Percent of units with over 1 person per room: 2.27%, 39th
Owner-occupied units: 173,813
  Percent of total units: 59.95%, 23rd
  Percent of occupied units: 70.23%, 9th
  Persons per unit: 2.71, 29th
  Median value: $100,100, 11th
Renter-occupied units: 73,684
  Percent of total units: 25.42%, 47th
  Percent of occupied units: 29.77%, 43rd
  Persons per unit: 2.38, 22nd
  Median contract rent: $425, 12th
  Rental vacancy rate: 7.8%, 33rd
Mobile home, trailer & other as a percent of occupied housing units: 14.98%, 14th
Persons in emergency shelters for homeless persons: 313, 0.047%, 25th
Persons visible in street locations: 19, 0.0029%, 38th
Nursing home population: 4,596, 0.69%, 29th

CRIME INDEX PER 100,000 (1996)

Total reported: 4,894.9, 24th
  Percent increase: −5.1%, 32nd
  Violent: 668.3, 13th
    Percent increase: −7.8%, 31st
    Murder & nonnegligent manslaughter: 4.3, 32nd
    Forcible rape: 62.6, 3rd
    Aggravated assault: 421.5, 15th
    Robbery: 179.9, 13th
  Property: 4,226.6, 27th
    Percent increase: −4.7%, 32nd
    Burglary: 804.1, 31st
    Larceny-theft: 2,988.3, 25th
    Motor vehicle theft: 434.2, 25th

TEACHING AND LEARNING

Pop. 3 and over enrolled in school (1996): 154,856, 49th
  Percent of pop.: 21.36%, 43rd
Public elementary & secondary schools (1996-97): 181, 51st
  Total enrollment (1996): 110,549, 48th
    Percent of school age pop.: 87.74%, 44th
    Percent of total pop.: 15.25%, 49th
  Teachers (1996): 6,642, 50th
    Percent of pop.: 0.92%, 42nd
  Pupil/teacher ratio (1995): 16.8, 23rd

  Teachers' avg. salary (1996-97): $41,436, 12th
  Expenditure per capita (1992-93): $1,656.86, 4th
    Education as % of state govt. expenditures: 37.9%, 9th
  Expenditure per pupil (1994-95): $7,030, 10th
    Percent increase (1993-94 & 1994-95): 6.18%, 9th
Percent at or above grade level, NAEP tests:
  Reading, grade 4 (1994): 23%, 31st
  Math, grade 4 (1996): 54%, 34th
  Math, grade 8 (1996): 55%, 28th
Percent of graduates taking SAT (1995): 68%, 8th
  Mean SAT verbal scores: 429, 35th
  Mean SAT mathematical scores: 468, 43rd
Percent of graduates taking ACT (1997): 3%, 47th
  Mean ACT scores: 21.0, 30th
Percent of pop. over 25 completing:
  Less than 9th grade: 7.2%, 43rd
  High school: 77.5%, 23rd
  College degree(s): 21.4%, 17th
Higher education, institutions (1996): 9, 49th
  Enrollment (1995-96): 44,307, 45th
    Percent increase in enroll. (1990-95): 5.5%, 22nd
  White non-Hispanic (1995): 35,299, 46th
    Percent of enroll.: 79.67%, 29th
  Total minority enroll. (1995): 8,071, 41st
    Percent of enroll.: 18.22%, 22nd
  Black non-Hispanic (1995): 6,018, 33rd
    Percent of enroll.: 13.58%, 12th
  Hispanic (1995): 793, 43rd
    Percent of enroll.: 1.79%, 32nd
  Asian/Pacific Islander (1995): 1,064, 40th
    Percent of enroll.: 2.40%, 24th
  American Indian/AK native (1995): 196, 51st
    Percent of enroll.: 0.44%, 30th
  Nonresident alien (1995): 937, 47th
    Percent of enroll.: 2.11%, 39th
  Female (1995): 25,444, 45th
    Percent of enroll.: 57.43%, 11th
  Pub. institutions (1995-96): 5, 48th
    Enrollment: 36,204, 45th
      Percent increase in enrollment (1990-95): 5.7%, 20th
    Percent of enroll.: 81.71%, 29th
  Private institutions (1995-96): 4, 49th
    Enrollment: 8,103, 44th
      Percent increase in enrollment (1990-95): 4.5%, 27th
    Percent of enroll.: 18.29%, 23rd

Tuition (in state), public 4-year institution (1996-97): $4,180, 6th

Tuition (in state), public 2-year institution (1996-97): $1,330, 28th

Tuition, private 4-year institution (1996-97): $7,674, 44th

Public library systems (1994): 29, 46th
Books & serial vol. per capita: 1.9, 46th
Library visits per capita: 3.3, 29th
Circulation per capita: 4.3, 44th

LAW ENFORCEMENT AND CORRECTIONS

Police protection and corrections expenditures (1996): $160,996,000
Per capita: $222.06, 2nd

Police per 10,000 pop. (1996): 28.82, 6th

Prisoners (1 year or more) per 100,000 pop. (1996): 428, 14th
Percent change (1995-96): 4.7%, 31st
Percent of inmates that are female: 7.4%, 6th
Percent change: 6.2%, 32nd

Death penalty: yes, by Hanging, lethal injection
Under sentence (Jan. 1998): 15, 26th
Executed, 1976-97: 8, 13th
Executed in 1997: 0

RELIGION, NUMBER AND PERCENT OF POPULATION

Agnostic: NA
Buddhist: NA
Christian: 429,414—85.40%, 29th
Hindu: NA
Jewish: 7,040—1.40%, 14th
Muslim: NA
Unitarian: NA
Other: 1,509—0.30%, 48th
None: 36,204—7.20%, 20th
Refused to answer: 28,661—5.70%, 1st

MAKING A LIVING

Personal income per capita (1996): $27,622, 6th
Percent increase (1995-96): 4.0%, 15th

Disposable personal income per capita (1996): $23,654, 6th

Median income of households (average, 1995-96): $37,634, 16th

Percent of pop. below poverty level (1995-96): 9.5%, 43rd

ECONOMY

In civilian labor force (1996): 382,000
Percent of total pop.: 68.5%, 23rd
Percent of total pop. 65 years and over: 11.4%, 30th
Percent of total female pop.: 63.7%, 11th

Major employer industries (total nonagricultural, 1996):
Construction: 20,500—5.4%, 12th
Finance, insurance, & real estate: 43,500—11.5%, 1st
Government: 52,600—14.0%, 46th
Manufacturing: 58,100—15.4%, 24th
Service: 102,200—27.1%, 26th
Trade: 84,100—22.3%, 44th
Transportation, communications, public utilities: 15,700—4.2%, 46th

Unemployment rate (1996): 5.2%, 23rd
Male: 5.8%, 13th
Female: 4.5%, 38th

Total businesses (1995): 20,991, 46th

New business incorps. (1995): 50,094
Percent of total businesses: 238.65%, 1st

Business failures (1995): 45
Failures per 10,000 businesses: 21.4, 51st

Agriculture farm income:
Marketing (1996): $757,036,000, 39th
Average per farm: $302,814, 1st
Leading products (1997): Broilers, soybeans, corn, greenhouse, potatoes, mushrooms, lima beans, peas, barley, cucumbers, wheat, grain sorghum
Average value land & build. per acre (1997): $3,170, 6th
Percent increase (1996-97): 9%, 5th
Govt. payments (1996): $4,888,000, 39th
Average per farm: $1,955, 29th

Construction, value of all (1996): $799,621,000, 47th
Per capita: $1,103, 36th

Manufactures (1995):
Value added: $5,665,700,000
Per capita: $7,900, 11th
Leading products (1997): Nylon, apparel, luggage, foods, automobiles, processed meats and vegetables, railroad and aircraft equipment

Value of nonfuel mineral production (1996): $10,700,000, 50th

Leading mineral products (1996): Sand/gravel, magnesium compounds, gemstones

Energy consumption per person (1994): 374.9 mil. Btu, 19th

Retail sales (1995): $7,545,000,000
Per household: $28,048, 5th
Sales increase (1994-95): 14.7%, 2nd

Tourism revenues (1995): $836 mil.

Foreign exports, in total value (1996): $1,594,000,000, 39th
Per capita: $2,199, 11th

Gross state product per person (1994): $37,796, 2nd

Public aid recipients (percent of resident pop. 1994): 5.2%, 38th

Medicaid recipients (percent of pop., 1995): 11.0%, 32nd

Medicare enrollment per 1,000 pop. (1996): 143, 27th

TRAVEL AND TRANSPORTATION

Motor vehicle registrations (1996): 593,007, 47th
Per 1,000 pop.: 819.66, 23rd

Motorcycle registrations (1996): 9,985, 50th
Per 1,000 pop.: 16.84, 32nd

Licensed drivers (1996): 524,992, 45th
Per 1,000 pop.: 732.16, 6th

Public roads & streets (1996)
Total mileage: 5,715, 49th
Per 1,000 pop.: 17.88, 42nd
Rural mileage: 3,733, 48th
Per 1,000 pop.: 5.15, 41st
Urban mileage: 1,982, 45th
Per 1,000 pop.: 2.73, 41st
Interstate mileage: 0, 49th
Per 1,000 pop.: 0.00, 49th

Speed limit (max. interstate, autos, mi. per hr., 1997): 65

Annual vehicle-mi. of travel per driver (1996): 14,484, 26th

Mean travel time for workers age 16+ who work away from home: 20.0 min., 30th

GOVERNMENT

Percent of voting age pop. registered (1996): 76.95%, 25th
Percent of voting age pop. voting for president: (1996): 49.5%, 28th
Percent of voting age pop. voting for U.S. representatives (1996): 48.8%, 24th

State legislators, total (1997): 62, 48th
Women members (1997): 15
Percent of legislature: 24%, 18th

U.S. Congress, House members (1998): 1
Change (1988-98): 0

Revenues (1996):
State govt.: $3,618,697,000
Per capita: $4,991.31, 4th
Parimutuel & amusement taxes & lotteries, revenue per capita (1995): $152.30, 12th

Expenditures (1996):
State govt.: $3,248,174,000
Per capita: $4,480.24, 4th

Debt outstanding (1996): $4,278,539,000
Per capita: $5,901.43, 1st

LAWS AND REGULATIONS

Legal driving age: 18, 16 if complete driver education course

Marriage age without parental consent: 18

Divorce residence requirement: 6 mo.

ATTRACTIONS (1997)

Major opera companies: 1

Major symphony orchestras: 1

Per capita spending by the NEA (1997): $0.74, 9th

State Fair in end of July at Harrington

SPORTS AND COMPETITION

NCAA (Division I) football and basketball teams: Delaware State Univ. Hornets, Univ. of Delaware Fightin' Blue Hens

WEBSITES CONTAINING FURTHER INFORMATION

| State of Delaware | http://www.state.de.us |

DISTRICT OF COLUMBIA

"I went to Washington the other day...and I felt that the sun in all its course could not look down upon a better sight than that majestic home of the Republic that had taught the world its best lessons in liberty."   Henry W. Grady, journalist and author

The city of Washington and the District of Columbia—"the District," as residents call it—are one and the same. The site was selected by Congress as the nation's capital, and over the years the District has brought together the nation's most famous statesmen and politicians. The city of Washington has been a target in wartime. It was burned by the British in the War of 1812, and its capture was threatened in the Civil War. Events that affect the nation and the world have occurred with regularity in its legislative, executive, and judicial halls. Washington has been the center of national mourning, where martyred presidents were honored. The grandeur of its buildings and monuments and the glamour of its world figures attract tourists from home and abroad. Washington has become an international metropolis in every sense of the word. With its increasing world importance has come an increasing awareness, closer to home, of the District's citizens and their welfare.

MOMENTS IN HISTORY

• In 1790 a bill was passed to locate a new capital on the Potomac River along the Virginia-Maryland border.

• The cornerstone of the Capitol was laid in 1793 by George Washington, who was a skilled mason.

• In 1800 the federal government moved to Washington, with 300 clerks, 138 members of Congress, and justices of the Supreme Court and the Circuit Court all crowded into the unfinished Capitol. The East Room of the uncompleted president's house was used by Mrs. John Adams for drying the family laundry.

• The British burned Washington during the War of 1812, and first lady Dolley Madison escaped carrying only a portrait of Washington, some official papers, and a few valuables.

• The French architect Pierre L'Enfant designed the basic plan for the new city, though the plan was only imperfectly followed after a dispute led to his dismissal in 1792.

> ### So They Say
> "Mrs. Madison's drawing room was often filled with gallants immaculate in sheer ruffles and small [tight] clothes...dainty belles in frills, flounces and furbelows."
>
> **Contemporary account of Dolley Madison's social accomplishments**

• The Marquis de Lafayette visited Washington in 1824 and received a gift of the "incredible sum" of $200,000. He was the first foreign dignitary ever to address the full Congress.

> ### So They Say
> "I was delighted with the whole aspect of Washington; light, cheerful, and airy, it reminded me of our fashionable watering-places....From the base of the hill on which the capitol stands extends a street of most magnificent width, planted on each side with trees, and ornamented by many splendid shops. This street, which is called Pennsylvania Avenue, is above a mile in length, and at the end of it is the handsome mansion of the President...."
>
> **British travel writer Frances Trollope (1832)**

• In the 1840s about one-third of the District's territory was returned to Virginia.

• Washington might have been captured by the Confederates if they had followed up on their victory after the first Battle of Bull Run on July 21, 1861.

• Abraham Lincoln was shot at Ford's Theater on the evening of April 14, 1865, and died the next day. Washington mourned its leader, martyred on the threshold of Civil War victory.

• President James Garfield died on September 19, 1881, after having been shot in a Washington rail station.

• Protesting unemployment, Jacob Coxey in 1894 "invaded" Washington with 300 followers. Accused of walking on the grass, Coxey was arrested, and his followers were dispersed.

> ### So They Say
>
> "One evening Calvin Coolidge took a short walk around the White House with Senator Selden P. Spencer of Missouri. As they were returning, Spencer pointed to the Executive Mansion and said facetiously: 'I wonder who lives there.' 'Nobody,' said Silent Cal glumly. 'They just come and go.'"
>
> **Biographer Paul F. Boller, Jr.**

• In March 1952, a total restoration of the White House was finished.

• Residents of Washington were given the right to vote for president and vice president with the ratification of the 23rd Amendment in 1961.

• Under a new home rule charter, Washington's mayor and city council took office in 1975.

• In 1990, Mayor Marion S. Barry was sentenced to jail for six months for cocaine possession. Four years later he was returned to office.

• The White House came under attack in 1994 when a gunman sprayed the north side with rifle bullets and a pilot crashed a small plane on the South Lawn.

• In 1995 the "Million Man March" descended on Washington; traffic was barred in front of the White House.

• In 1997, Eleanor Roosevelt became the first presidential wife honored with a statue at her husband's memorial; Fala, Franklin Roosevelt's dog, was also the first dog to be so honored.

THAT'S INTERESTING

• Roosevelt Island in the Potomac River at Theodore Roosevelt Memorial Bridge "grows" about 20 acres every hundred years, as new land forms around the brush and branches that have floated down the river.

• In the competition for the design of the Capitol, one plan called for the structure to be topped by the statue of an enormous rooster.

• House Speaker Joe Cannon gave Congress one of its cherished traditions when he commanded that his famous bean soup be served every day in the Capitol. It has been on the menu since 1907.

> ### So They Say
>
> Washington has a reputation for unpleasant climate that it may not deserve. "With blue skies, soft winds, and rich landscapes, only an ingrate would complain of the few admittedly difficult months."
>
> **Federal Writers' Project,
> District of Columbia**

• Sudden rises of temperature in the Washington Monument cause the moisture to condense, so that "rain" falls inside.

• The only woman whose portrait appeared on a currency note was Martha Washington. The wife of the first president was on the $1 silver certificate of 1886 and 1891, and on the back of the $1 silver certificate in 1896.

• William Howard Taft was the biggest man ever to occupy the White House. He weighed between 300 and 350 pounds. A special bathtub had to be installed for him.

NOTABLE NATIVES

Edward Albee (1928-), playwright. **Pat Buchanan** (1938-), political commentator. **Al Gore, Jr.** (1948-), U.S. vice president. **Marjorie Kinnan Rawlings** (1896-1953), author.

GENERAL

Origin of District name: For Christopher Columbus

Origin of city name: For George Washington; originally called Federal City

Nickname: Nation's Capital, America's First City

Motto: *Justitia Omnibus*—Justice for all

Bird: Wood thrush

Flower: American beauty rose

Tree: Scarlet oak

THE LAND

Area: 68 sq. mi., 51st

  Land: 61 sq. mi., 51st

  Water: 7 sq. mi., 51st

    Inland water: 7 sq. mi., 51st

Topography: Low hills rise toward N away from the Potomac River and slope to the S.

Geographic center: Near 4th and L Streets NW

Highest point: 410 ft. (Tenleytown at Reno Reservoir), 50th
Lowest point: 1 ft. (Potomac River), 25th
Mean elevation: 150 ft., 48th
Hazardous waste sites (1997): 0, 50th

CLIMATE AND ENVIRONMENT

Temp., highest: 106 deg. on July 20, 1930; lowest: –15 deg. on Feb. 11, 1988
Monthly average: highest: 87.9 deg., 24th; lowest: 27.5 deg., 40th; spread (high to low): 60.4 deg., 45th
Endangered species: Animals: 2—Hay's spring amphipod, American peregrine falcon. Plants: 0

THE PEOPLE

Population (1997): 528,964, 50th
  Percent change (1990-97): –12.84%, 51st
  Percent of total U.S. pop.: 0.20%, 50th
  Per sq. mi: 7,778.88, 1st
Population (2000 proj.): 526,500, 50th
  Percent change (1995-2000): –4.96%, 51st
Percent in metro. area (1996): 100.00%, 1st
Foreign born: 59,000, 31st
  Percent: 9.7%, 6th
Top three ancestries reported:
  African, 51.89%
  German, 6.43%
  Irish, 5.60%
White (1992): 185,000, 31.62%, 51st
Black (1992): 384,000, 65.64%, 1st
Native American (1992): 1,000, 0.17%, 48th
Asian, Pacific Isle (1992): 16,000, 2.74%, 11th
Hispanic origin (1992): 35,000, 5.98%, 13th
Percent over 5 yrs. speaking language other than English at home: 12.5%, 14th
Percent males (1996): 46.83%, 51st; percent females: 53.17%, 1st
Percent never married: 47.6%, 1st
Marriages per 1,000 (1996): 6.19, 48th
Divorces per 1,000 (1996): NA
Median age (1996): 35.6
Under 5 years (1996): 6.17%, 48th
18 years and under (1996): 22.20%, 51st
65 years and over (1996): 13.89%, 12th
Percent increase among the elderly (1995-96): –0.98%, 51st

OF VITAL IMPORTANCE

Live births per 1,000 pop. (1996): 15.3, 13th
Infant mortality rate per 1,000 live births (1995): 16.2, 1st

Rate for whites: NA
Rate for blacks: 19.6, 2nd
Births to unmarried women, % of total (1996): 66.0%, 1st
Births to teenage mothers, % of total (1996): 16.8%, 8th
Abortions (1992): 21,320, 16th
  Rate per 1,000 women 14-44 years old: 138.4, 1st
  Percent change (1988-92): –15%, 38th
Average lifetime (1989-91): 67.99, 51st
Total death rate per 100,000 pop. (1995): 1,244.2, 1st
  Accidents and adverse effects: 34.8, 33rd
  Alzheimer's disease: 8.1, 28th
  Cancer: 267.2, 1st
  Cerebrovascular diseases: 66.8, 21st
  Chronic liver disease and cirrhosis: 16.8, 1st
  Chronic obstructive pulmonary diseases and allied conditions: 24.2, 48th
  Diabetes mellitus: 39.5, 1st
  Diseases of heart: 302.4, 20th
  HIV infection: 117.8, 1st
  Homicide: 56.8, 1st
  Injury by firearms: 48.5, 1st
  Motor vehicle accidents: 12.3, 44th
  Pneumonia and influenza: 39.9, 6th
  Suicide: 7.0, 51st

KEEPING WELL

Active nonfederal physicians per 100,000 pop. (1995): 662, 1st
Dentists per 100,000 (1991): 122, 1st
Nurses per 100,000 (1995): 1,699, 1st
  Average cost per stay (1995): $8,632, 1st
Hospitals per 100,000 (1995): 2.17, 26th
  Admissions per 1,000 (1995): 277.98, 1st
  Hospital beds per 1,000 (1995): 6.86, 1st
  Occupancy rate per 100 beds (1995): 71.05, 7th
  Average cost per patient per day (1995): $1,346, 1st
AIDS cases (new, 1996): 1,262; per 100,000: 232.3, 1st
Persons living with HIV infection (1996): NA
Other notifiable diseases, per 100,000 pop.:
  Gonorrhea (1995): NA
  Syphilis (1995): NA
  Tuberculosis (1996): 25.6, 1st
Pop. without health insur. (1996): 14.8%, 22nd

HOUSEHOLDS BY TYPE

Total households (1996): 231,000, 48th
  Percent change (1990-96): –7.3%, 51st
  Per 1,000 pop. (1996) 425.41, 1st
  Percent of householders 65 yrs. and over (1996): 21.65%, 27th
  Persons per household (1996): 2.24, 51st
Family households: 122,087
  Percent of total: 48.91%, 51st
Nonfamily households: 127,547
  Percent of total: 51.09%, 1st
Pop. living in group quarters: 41,717
  Percent of pop.: 6.87%, 1st

LIVING QUARTERS

Total housing units: 278,489
  Persons per unit: 2.18, 48th
Occupied housing units: 249,634
  Percent of total units: 89.64%, 25th
  Persons per unit: 2.31, 51st
  Percent of units with over 1 person per room: 8.25%, 4th
Owner-occupied units: 97,108
  Percent of total units: 34.87%, 51st
  Percent of occupied units: 38.90%, 51st
  Persons per unit: 2.50, 50th
  Median value: $123,900, 9th
Renter-occupied units: 152,526
  Percent of total units: 54.77%, 1st
  Percent of occupied units: 61.10%, 1st
  Persons per unit: 2.12, 50th
  Median contract rent: $441, 10th
  Rental vacancy rate: 7.9%, 30th
Mobile home, trailer & other as a percent of occupied housing units: 1.14%, 51st
Persons in emergency shelters for homeless persons: 4,682, 0.771%, 1st
Persons visible in street locations: 131, 0.0216%, 7th
Nursing home population: 7,008, 1.15%, 5th

CRIME INDEX PER 100,000 (1996)

Total reported: 11,896.7, 1st
  Percent increase: –2.3%, 24th
  Violent: 2,469.8, 1st
    Percent increase: –7.2%, 29th
    Murder & nonnegligent manslaughter: 73.1, 1st
    Forcible rape: 47.9, 10th
    Aggravated assault: 1,162.1, 1st
    Robbery: 1,186.7, 1st
  Property: 9,426.9, 1st
    Percent increase: –0.9%, 21st

Burglary: 1,809.9, 1st
Larceny-theft: 5,779.9, 1st
Motor vehicle theft: 1,837.0, 1st

TEACHING AND LEARNING

Pop. 3 and over enrolled in school (1996): 156,436, 47th
  Percent of pop.: 28.81%, 2nd
Public elementary & secondary schools (1996-97): 186, 50th
  Total enrollment (1996): 79,159, 51st
    Percent of school age pop.: 105.55%, 1st
    Percent of total pop.: 14.58%, 51st
  Teachers (1996): 5,398, 51st
    Percent of pop.: 0.99%, 34th
  Pupil/teacher ratio (1995): 15.0, 40th
  Teachers' avg. salary (1996-97): $45,012, 6th
  Expenditure per capita (1992-93): $1,244.05, 32nd
    Education as % of state govt. expenditures: 16.1%, 51st
  Expenditure per pupil (1994-95): $9,335, 3rd
    Percent increase (1993-94 & 1994-95): –8.30%, 51st
Percent at or above grade level, NAEP tests:
  Reading, grade 4 (1994): NA
  Math, grade 4 (1996): 20%, 44th
  Math, grade 8 (1996): 20%, 41st
Percent of graduates taking SAT (1995): 53%, 18th
  Mean SAT verbal scores: 412, 47th
  Mean SAT mathematical scores: 445, 50th
Percent of graduates taking ACT (1997): 5%, 45th
  Mean ACT scores: 17.2, 51st
Percent of pop. over 25 completing:
  Less than 9th grade: 9.6%, 23rd
  High school: 73.1%, 39th
  College degree(s): 33.3%, 1st
Higher education, institutions (1996): 18, 43rd
  Enrollment (1995-96): 77,277, 38th
    Percent increase in enroll. (1990-95): –2.9%, 45th
  White non-Hispanic (1995): 37,346, 43rd
    Percent of enroll.: 48.33%, 50th
  Total minority enroll. (1995): 31,906, 27th
    Percent of enroll.: 41.29%, 4th
  Black non-Hispanic (1995): 24,429, 20th
    Percent of enroll.: 31.61%, 1st
  Hispanic (1995): 3,015, 30th
    Percent of enroll.: 3.90%, 14th

Asian/Pacific Islander (1995): 4,248, 25th
   Percent of enroll.: 5.50%, 9th
American Indian/AK native (1995): 214, 49th
   Percent of enroll.: 0.28%, 46th
Nonresident alien (1995): 8,025, 16th
   Percent of enroll.: 10.38%, 1st
Female (1995): 42,764, 38th
   Percent of enroll.: 55.34%, 34th
Pub. institutions (1995-96): 1, 51st
   Enrollment: 9,663, 51st
     Percent increase in enrollment (1990-95): –19%, 51st
   Percent of enroll.: 12.50%, 51st
Private institutions (1995-96): 17, 32nd
   Enrollment: 67,614, 12th
     Percent increase in enrollment (1990-95): 0.1%, 38th
   Percent of enroll.: 87.50%, 1st
Tuition (in state), public 4-year institution (1996-97): $1,502, 51st
Tuition (in state), public 2-year institution (1996-97): NA
Tuition, private 4-year institution (1996-97): $15,457, 7th
Public library systems (1994): 1, 50th
   Books & serial vol. per capita: 3.6, 15th
   Library visits per capita: 3.5, 26th
   Circulation per capita: 3.1, 50th

LAW ENFORCEMENT, COURTS, AND PRISONS

Police protection, corrections, judicial and legal functions expenditures (1992): $719,000,000
   Per capita: $1,229, 1st
Police per 10,000 pop. (1996): 66.89, 1st
Prisoners (1 year or more) per 100,000 pop. (1996): 1,609, 1st
   Percent change (1995-96): –4.2%, 49th
   Percent of inmates that are female: 4.6%, 45th
   Percent change: –12.6%, 50th
Death penalty: no

RELIGION, NUMBER AND PERCENT OF POPULATION

Agnostic: 2,449—0.50%, 27th
Buddhist: 1,469—0.30%, 8th
Christian: 417,806—85.30%, 31st
Hindu: NA
Jewish: 11,266—2.30%, 7th
Muslim: 2,939—0.60%, 2nd
Unitarian: NA

Other: 12,245—2.50%, 4th
None: 30,858—6.30%, 30th
Refused to answer: 10,776—2.20%, 23rd

MAKING A LIVING

Personal income per capita (1996): $34,932, 1st
   Percent increase (1995-96): 0.6%, 50th
Disposable personal income per capita (1996): $29,567, 1st
Median income of households (average, 1995-96): $31,811, 36th
Percent of pop. below poverty level (1995-96): 23.2%, 2nd

ECONOMY

In civilian labor force (1996): 272,000
   Percent of total pop.: 63.6%, 42nd
   Percent of total pop. 65 years and over: 12.2%, 23rd
   Percent of total female pop.: 60.1%, 32nd
Major employer industries (total nonagricultural, 1996):
   Construction: 8,500—1.4%, 50th
   Finance, insurance, & real estate: 28,400—4.6%, 35th
   Government: 241,400—38.7%, 1st
   Manufacturing: 13,100—2.1%, 51st
   Service: 262,500—42.1%, 2nd
   Trade: 49,700—8.0%, 51st
   Transportation, communications, public utilities: 19,300—3.1%, 51st
Unemployment rate (1996): 8.5%, 1st
   Male: 8.7%, 2nd
   Female: 8.4%, 1st
Total businesses (1995): 19,451, 49th
New business incorps. (1995): 2,256
   Percent of total businesses: 11.60%, 15th
Business failures (1995): 155
   Failures per 10,000 businesses: 79.7, 26th
Agriculture farm income:
   Marketing (1996): NA
Construction, value of all (1996): $1,162,103,000, 42nd
   Per capita: $2,139, 3rd
Manufactures (1995):
   Value added: $1,636,400,000
     Per capita: $2,952, 44th
Value of nonfuel mineral production: NA
Energy consumption per person (1994): 310.3 mil. Btu, 37th
Retail sales (1995): $3,760,000,000
   Per household: $16,405, 51st
   Sales increase (1994-95): –0.1%, 48th

Tourism revenues (1994): $3.48 bil.

Foreign exports, in total value (1996): $305,000,000, 50th
Per capita: $561, 48th

Gross state product per person (1994): $84,234, 1st

Public aid recipients (percent of resident pop. 1994): 16.6%, 1st

Medicaid recipients (percent of pop., 1995): 25.0%, 2nd

Medicare enrollment per 1,000 pop. (1996): 142, 28th

TRAVEL AND TRANSPORTATION

Motor vehicle registrations (1996): 237,415, 51st
Per 1,000 pop.: 440.25, 51st

Motorcycle registrations (1996): 1,600, 51st
Per 1,000 pop.: 6.74, 51st

Licensed drivers (1996): 338,549, 51st
Per 1,000 pop.: 610.52, 47th

Public roads & streets (1996)
Total mileage: 1,413, 51st
Per 1,000 pop.: 12.60, 51st
Rural mileage: 0, 51st
Per 1,000 pop.: 0.00, 51st
Urban mileage: 1,413, 50th
Per 1,000 pop.: 2.60, 45th
Interstate mileage: 0, 49th
Per 1,000 pop.: 0.00, 49th

Speed limit (max. interstate, autos, mi. per hr., 1997): NA

Annual vehicle-mi. of travel per driver (1996): 9,945, 50th

Mean travel time for workers age 16+ who work away from home: 27.1 min., 2nd

GOVERNMENT

Percent of voting age pop. registered (1996): 85.64%, 9th

Percent of voting age pop. voting for president: (1996): 42.7%, 46th

Percent of voting age pop. voting for U.S. representatives (1996): NA

U.S. Congress, House members (1998): 1 delegate, voting only in committee

District legislators, total (1997): 13, 51st

LAWS AND REGULATIONS

Legal driving age: 18
Marriage age without parental consent: 18
Divorce residence requirement: 6 mo.
Women members: 7
Percent of legislature: 54%, 1st

ATTRACTIONS (1997)

Major opera companies: 2
Major symphony orchestras: 2
Major dance companies: 2
Major professional theater companies (non-profit): 2
Per capita spending by the NEA (1997): $4.84, 1st

SPORTS AND COMPETITION

NCAA (Division I) football and basketball teams: American Univ. Eagles (basketball only), George Washington Univ. Colonials (basketball only), Georgetown Univ. Hoyas, Howard Univ. Bison

Major league soccer teams: D.C. United, RFK Stadium

NBA basketball teams: Washington Wizards, MCI Center

WNBA basketball teams: Washington Mystics, MCI Center

NFL football teams: Washington Redskins (NFC), Jack Kent Cooke Stadium (MD)

NHL hockey teams: Washington Capitals, MCI Center

WEBSITES CONTAINING FURTHER INFORMATION

| The Washington DC City Pages | http://dcpages.ari.net |

FLORIDA

"Florida has perhaps more variety of tourist attractions, both natural and manmade, than any other area of its size anywhere."   *All About the U.S.A.*

"Florida is today to the United States what the United States was to Europe 100 years ago—a melting pot, a frontier, a place to improve your health or your luck."   Budd Schulberg, author

Florida boasts the nation's oldest European settlement in continuous occupation. A land of sunshine and flowers, Florida has become one of the world's tourist magnets, with Walt Disney World leading the way. The state's gleaming beaches, crystal springs, sophisticated cities, and other recreational opportunities have made it a leading center for retired persons as well as tourists. The quality of its labor and its moderate climate have brought rapidly increasing numbers of industries and businesses. To winter-weary northerners, Florida is an Eden where they might still find Ponce de León's legendary Fountain of Youth. The state has come to increasing recognition of its responsibilities in public safety and in its relationship with a host of newcomers, including many refugees from Cuba, Haiti, and other countries.

SUPERLATIVES

• St. Augustine—the oldest continuously occupied European settlement in North America.
• Pan American started flights from Key West to Cuba, bringing commercial aviation to the United States.
• The nation's principal launching pad for space flights, on Cape Canaveral.
• First in the United States in citrus production.
• Walt Disney World in Orlando, luring more visitors than any other single attraction anywhere.
• More than a fourth of all the country's major springs.

MOMENTS IN HISTORY

• Juan Ponce de León sighted present-day Florida on March 27, 1513. Although others knew of the area before, he is generally recognized its "discoverer."
• A 1502 map by Alberto Cantino clearly shows the distinctive Florida outline, but it apparently was not known to Ponce de León.

• Panfilo de Narvaez and his large force entered Tampa Bay in 1528. Only four of his 400 men survived the ensuing hurricanes and other disasters.
• The huge expedition of Hernando de Soto landed at present-day Tampa on May 30, 1539. His letter to the King of Spain is thought to be the first letter mailed from what is today the United States.

So They Say
"...a country of rivers, havens and islands of such surpassing fruitfulness as cannot by the tongue be expressed."

Explorer Jean Ribaut, describing the St. Johns River area (1562)

• Pedro Menéndez de Aviles entered a harbor on the Florida peninsula on St. Augustine's feast day. The place he founded there in 1565 took the saint's name, and St. Augustine remains the oldest continuing settlement in the country.
• Englishman Sir Francis Drake captured St. Augustine in 1586 and burned it to the ground, but the Spanish rebuilt the town.
• In 1763 the English returned and captured Cuba from Spain. The British then traded Cuba back to Spain for Florida.
• Florida remained faithful to Britain during the American Revolution, but Spain gave the British the Bahamas and Gibraltar in return for Florida.
• Spain ceded Florida to the United States in 1819, with final ratification two years later. On July 17, 1821, Andrew Jackson received the transfer of Florida from Spain to the United States. The Stars and Stripes then flew over Castillo de San Marcos at St. Augustine, which had never been captured in battle.
• A costly war with the Seminole Indians broke out in the mid-1830s, as the United States sought to "remove" the Seminoles from Florida. It is said that this was the only Indian war never won by the United States, and the $20 million cost was enormous for the time.

• Florida became a state on March 3, 1845, a move delayed by the reluctance of Congress to admit another slave state.

• When the issue of slavery finally led to the Civil War, Florida joined the Confederacy on January 10, 1861.

• Union forces lost the Battle of Olustee on February 20, 1864, the largest battle of the war on Florida soil.

• Florida forces repelled a Union attack on Tallahassee in the Battle of Natural Bridge on March 6, 1865.

So They Say

"From boys of fourteen to men of seventy, from the humble woodsmen to the highest civil dignitaries, all came to the defense of their country."

General William Miller,
on the Battle of Natural Bridge

• Much of Florida's wealth was destroyed by the Civil War, but new development began in earnest in 1881 when Hamilton Disston paid the state $1 million for 4 million acres of state land.

• Florida became the main point of embarkation for troops and supplies in the Spanish-American War in 1898, expanding business there.

So They Say

"...It is the dream of my life to see this wilderness [Miami] turned into prosperous country and where this tangled mass of vines, brush, trees and rocks now are, to see homes, surrounded by beautiful grassy lawns."

Julia D. Tuttle, an associate of
Henry Flagler (1890)

• Florida promoter Henry Flagler built a railroad from Miami to Key West, going "out to sea" on a series of bridges built from island to island in the Florida Keys. The first train reached Key West in 1912.

• The great Florida land boom that began in 1919 was the largest in the country to that time. Carl Fisher founded Miami Beach in that year, and other promoters brought hosts of investors to the state.

• The hurricane of 1926 brought 16 hours of destruction to the Miami area.

• In February 1933 at Miami, President-elect Franklin D. Roosevelt escaped an assassination attempt, but Mayor Anton Cermak of Chicago was fatally shot in the attack.

• In 1962, John Glenn soared into space from Cape Canaveral, becoming the first American in orbit.

• The early 1980s posed great problems for the state in accommodating the Cuban boat people, refugees from the troubles of their homeland.

• On January 28, 1986, the space shuttle *Challenger* exploded after liftoff from Cape Canaveral, killing the seven persons aboard, including Christa McAuliffe, the first teacher in space.

• In August 1992, Hurricane Andrew devastated southern Florida, claiming more than 60 lives and causing damage estimated as high as $30 billion.

THAT'S INTERESTING

• During the Seminole War, Seminole leader Coacoochee went to a council wearing Shakespearean costume, which he found in the baggage he had captured from a theatrical company.

• During the hurricane of 1926, the barometer at Miami reached the country's record low, causing hundreds to faint from lack of oxygen.

• When a British captain's ear was cut off in a war between Spain and England, the conflict, which was waged in Florida, became known as the War of Jenkins's Ear.

• The demand was so great for Florida property during the great land boom that investors paid up to $25,000 for lots that had not yet been dredged up from the ocean.

• Florida attractions, combined—including the Everglades, Disney World, and the Florida Keys with their one-of-a-kind highway—are said to offer more variety than any other area of similar size worldwide.

FLORIDA NOTABLES

John James Audubon (Haiti, 1785-1851), ornithologist/artist. **Jacqueline Cochran** (Pensacola, 1910?-1980), aviator/business leader. **Henry Morrison Flagler** (Hopewell, NY, 1830-1913), capitalist/promoter. **John Gorrie** (Charleston, SC, 1803-1855), physician/inventor. **Edmund Kirby-Smith** (St. Augustine, 1824-1893), army officer. **Osceola** (in Georgia, 1804?-1838), Indian leader.

GENERAL

Admitted to statehood: March 3, 1845
Origin of name: Named by Ponce de León on
    Pascua Florida, "Flowery Easter," on
    Easter Sunday, 1513
Capital: Tallahassee
Nickname: Sunshine State
Motto: In God we trust
Bird: Mockingbird
Flower: Orange blossom
Gem: Moonstone
Song: "Swanee River" (Old Folks at Home)
Tree: Sabal palmetto palm

THE LAND

Area: 59,928 sq. mi., 23rd
    Land: 53,937 sq. mi., 26th
    Water: 5,991 sq. mi., 7th
        Inland water: 4,683 sq. mi., 4th
        Coastal water: 1,308 sq. mi., 6th
Topography: Land is flat or rolling to highest
    point, in the NW
Number of counties: 67
Geographic center: Hernando, 12 mi. NNW
    of Brooksville
Length: 500 mi.; width: 160 mi.
Highest point: 345 ft. (in Walton County),
    51st
Lowest point: sea level (Atlantic Ocean), 3rd
Mean elevation: 100 ft., 49th
Coastline: 1,350 mi., 2nd
Shoreline: 8,426 mi., 2nd

CLIMATE AND ENVIRONMENT

Temp., highest: 109 deg. on June 29, 1931, at
    Monticello; lowest: –2 deg. on Feb. 13,
    1899, at Tallahassee
Monthly average: highest: 91.7 deg., 15th;
    lowest: 39.9 deg., 50th; spread (high to
    low): 51.8 deg., 49th
Hazardous waste sites (1997): 52, 6th
Endangered species: Animals: 24—Gray bat,
    Schaus swallowtail butterfly, American
    crocodile, Okaloosa darter, Key deer,
    American peregrine falcon, Everglade
    snail kite, West Indian manatee, Anas-
    tasia Island beach mouse, Choctawa-
    hatchee beach mouse, Key Largo cotton
    mouse, Perdido Key beach mouse,
    Florida panther, Lower Keys rabbit,
    Rice rat, Cape Sable seaside sparrow,
    Florida grasshopper sparrow, Wood
    stork, Green sea turtle, Hawksbill sea
    turtle, Leatherback sea turtle, Florida

salt marsh vole, Red-cockaded woodpecker, Key Largo woodrat. Plants: 44

MAJOR CITIES
POPULATION, 1996
PERCENTAGE INCREASE, 1990-96

Jacksonville, 679,792; 7.0%
Miami, 365,127; 1.8%
Tampa, 285,206; 1.9%
St. Petersburg, 235,988; –1.8%
Hialeah, 204,684; 8.9%

THE PEOPLE

Population (1997): 14,653,945, 4th
    Percent change (1990-97): 13.26%, 11th
    Percent of total U.S. pop.: 5.48%, 4th
    Per sq. mi: 222.85, 11th
Population (2000 proj.): 15,241,500, 4th
    Percent change (1995-2000): 7.59%, 15th
Percent in metro. area (1996): 92.92%, 5th
Foreign born: 1,663,000, 3rd
    Percent: 12.9%, 4th
Top three ancestries reported:
    German, 18.63%
    Irish, 14.68%
    English, 14.27%
White (1992): 11,354,000, 84.21%, 31st
Black (1992): 1,903,000, 14.11%, 16th
Native American (1992): 41,000, 0.30%,
    33rd
Asian, Pacific Isle (1992): 184,000, 1.36%,
    23rd
Hispanic origin (1992): 1,733,000, 12.85%,
    7th
Percent over 5 yrs. speaking language other
    than English at home: 17.3%, 8th
Percent males (1996): 48.57%, 36th; percent
    females: 51.43%, 16th
Percent never married: 22.6%, 44th
Marriages per 1,000 (1996): 10.41, 10th
Divorces per 1,000 (1996): 5.57, 11th
Median age (1996): 37.6
Under 5 years (1996): 6.74%, 36th
18 years and under (1996): 26.09%, 49th
65 years and over (1996): 18.45%, 1st
Percent increase among the elderly (1995-96):
    1.20%, 20th

OF VITAL IMPORTANCE

Live births per 1,000 pop. (1996): 13.2, 39th
Infant mortality rate per 1,000 live births
    (1995): 7.5, 25th
    Rate for whites: 6.0, 34th
    Rate for blacks: 13.0, 30th

Births to unmarried women, % of total (1996): 36.0%, 9th
Births to teenage mothers, % of total (1996): 13.4%, 21st
Abortions (1992): 84,680, 4th
  Rate per 1,000 women 14-44 years old: 30.0, 8th
  Percent change (1988-92): −5%, 20th
Average lifetime (1989-91): 75.84, 24th
Total death rate per 100,000 pop. (1995): 1,081.3, 3rd
  Accidents and adverse effects: 38.1, 24th
  Alzheimer's disease: 9.8, 15th
  Cancer: 263.5, 2nd
  Cerebrovascular diseases: 69.9, 13th
  Chronic liver disease and cirrhosis: 13.0, 5th
  Chronic obstructive pulmonary diseases and allied conditions: 52.9, 5th
  Diabetes mellitus: 26.0, 12th
  Diseases of heart: 351.6, 4th
  HIV infection: 30.8, 3rd
  Homicide: 8.8, 21st
  Injury by firearms: 15.2, 17th
  Motor vehicle accidents: 19.8, 20th
  Pneumonia and influenza: 27.2, 40th
  Suicide: 15.3, 10th

KEEPING WELL

Active nonfederal physicians per 100,000 pop. (1995): 220, 19th
Dentists per 100,000 (1991): 51, 31st
Nurses per 100,000 (1995): 1,699, 1st
Hospitals per 100,000 (1995): 1.50, 41st
  Admissions per 1,000 (1995): 125.09, 16th
  Hospital beds per 1,000 (1995): 3.51, 23rd
  Occupancy rate per 100 beds (1995): 59.15, 33rd
  Average cost per patient per day (1995): $1,004, 19th
  Average cost per stay (1995): $6,040, 21st
AIDS cases (new, 1996): 7,330; per 100,000: 50.9, 3rd
Persons living with HIV infection (1996): NA
Other notifiable diseases, per 100,000 pop.:
  Gonorrhea (1995): 147.4, 19th
  Syphilis (1995): 24.5, 13th
  Tuberculosis (1996): 9.8, 10th
Pop. without health insur. (1996): 18.9%, 7th

HOUSEHOLDS BY TYPE

Total households (1996): 5,684,000, 4th
  Percent change (1990-96): 10.0%, 16th

Per 1,000 pop. (1996) 394.72, 2nd
Percent of householders 65 yrs. and over (1996): 28.85%, 1st
Persons per household (1996): 2.45, 50th
Family households: 3,511,825
  Percent of total: 68.39%, 44th
Nonfamily households: 1,623,044
  Percent of total: 31.61%, 8th
Pop. living in group quarters: 307,461
  Percent of pop.: 2.38%, 39th

LIVING QUARTERS

Total housing units: 6,100,262
  Persons per unit: 2.12, 49th
Occupied housing units: 5,134,869
  Percent of total units: 84.17%, 44th
  Persons per unit: 2.44, 48th
  Percent of units with over 1 person per room: 5.79%, 12th
Owner-occupied units: 3,452,160
  Percent of total units: 56.59%, 36th
  Percent of occupied units: 67.23%, 27th
  Persons per unit: 2.49, 51st
  Median value: $77,100, 21st
Renter-occupied units: 1,682,709
  Percent of total units: 27.58%, 35th
  Percent of occupied units: 32.77%, 25th
  Persons per unit: 2.39, 18th
  Median contract rent: $402, 15th
  Rental vacancy rate: 12.4%, 6th
Mobile home, trailer & other as a percent of occupied housing units: 15.99%, 11th
Persons in emergency shelters for homeless persons: 7,110, 0.055%, 20th
Persons visible in street locations: 3,189, 0.0246%, 6th
Nursing home population: 80,298, 0.62%, 33rd

CRIME INDEX PER 100,000 (1996)

Total reported: 7,497.4, 2nd
  Percent increase: −2.7%, 27th
  Violent: 1,051.0, 2nd
    Percent increase: −1.9%, 14th
    Murder & nonnegligent manslaughter: 7.5, 18th
    Forcible rape: 52.1, 6th
    Aggravated assault: 702.2, 3rd
    Robbery: 289.2, 6th
  Property: 6,446.3, 2nd
    Percent increase: −2.8%, 27th
    Burglary: 1,521.2, 2nd

Larceny-theft: 4,204.5, 5th
Motor vehicle theft: 720.6, 4th

TEACHING AND LEARNING

Pop. 3 and over enrolled in school (1996): 2,877,586, 4th
Percent of pop.: 19.98%, 50th
Public elementary & secondary schools (1996-97): 2,760, 8th
Total enrollment (1996): 2,240,283, 4th
Percent of school age pop.: 90.81%, 31st
Percent of total pop.: 15.56%, 44th
Teachers (1996): 120,450, 4th
Percent of pop.: 0.84%, 49th
Pupil/teacher ratio (1995): 18.9, 9th
Teachers' avg. salary (1996-97): $33,881, 30th
Expenditure per capita (1992-93): $1,087.70, 47th
Education as % of state govt. expenditures: 29.5%, 44th
Expenditure per pupil (1994-95): $5,718, 27th
Percent increase (1993-94 & 1994-95): 3.66%, 29th
Percent at or above grade level, NAEP tests:
Reading, grade 4 (1994): 23%, 31st
Math, grade 4 (1996): 55%, 33rd
Math, grade 8 (1996): 54%, 29th
Percent of graduates taking SAT (1995): 48%, 20th
Mean SAT verbal scores: 420, 40th
Mean SAT mathematical scores: 469, 41st
Percent of graduates taking ACT (1997): 36%, 27th
Mean ACT scores: 20.7, 35th
Percent of pop. over 25 completing:
Less than 9th grade: 9.5%, 24th
High school: 74.4%, 37th
College degree(s): 18.3%, 30th
Higher education, institutions (1996): 114, 10th
Enrollment (1995-96): 637,303, 5th
Percent increase in enroll. (1990-95): 8.4%, 15th
White non-Hispanic (1995): 426,419, 8th
Percent of enroll.: 66.91%, 43rd
Total minority enroll. (1995): 191,314, 4th
Percent of enroll.: 30.02%, 8th
Black non-Hispanic (1995): 83,432, 5th
Percent of enroll.: 13.09%, 13th
Hispanic (1995): 86,064, 4th
Percent of enroll.: 13.50%, 5th
Asian/Pacific Islander (1995): 18,927, 10th
Percent of enroll.: 2.97%, 21st

American Indian/AK native (1995): 2,891, 12th
Percent of enroll.: 0.45%, 29th
Nonresident alien (1995): 19,570, 5th
Percent of enroll.: 3.07%, 18th
Female (1995): 359,511, 5th
Percent of enroll.: 56.41%, 19th
Pub. institutions (1995-96): 38, 13th
Enrollment: 530,607, 4th
Percent increase in enrollment (1990-95): 8.5%, 15th
Percent of enroll.: 83.26%, 23rd
Private institutions (1995-96): 76, 7th
Enrollment: 106,696, 8th
Percent increase in enrollment (1990-95): 7.8%, 20th
Percent of enroll.: 16.74%, 29th
Tuition (in state), public 4-year institution (1996-97): $1,789, 50th
Tuition (in state), public 2-year institution (1996-97): $1,151, 35th
Tuition, private 4-year institution (1996-97): $11,099, 26th
Public library systems (1994): 97, 29th
Books & serial vol. per capita: 1.7, 49th
Library visits per capita: NA
Circulation per capita: 5.1, 36th

LAW ENFORCEMENT AND CORRECTIONS

Police protection and corrections expenditures (1996): $1,942,357,000
Per capita: $134.89, 18th
Police per 10,000 pop. (1996): 24.15, 15th
Prisoners (1 year or more) per 100,000 pop. (1996): 439, 13th
Percent change (1995-96): –0.2%, 46th
Percent of inmates that are female: 5.2%, 40th
Percent change: –9.8%, 49th
Death penalty: yes, by electrocution
Under sentence (Jan. 1998): 389, 3rd
Executed, 1976-97: 39, 3rd
Executed in 1997: 1, 9th

RELIGION, NUMBER AND PERCENT OF POPULATION

Agnostic: 100,717—1.00%, 10th
Buddhist: 10,072—0.10%, 17th
Christian: 8,480,362—84.20%, 38th
Hindu: 10,072—0.10%, 10th
Jewish: 362,581—3.60%, 3rd
Muslim: 10,072—0.10%, 22nd
Unitarian: 30,215—0.30%, 15th

Other: 130,932—1.30%, 24th
None: 725,162—7.20%, 20th
Refused to answer: 211,506—2.10%, 28th

MAKING A LIVING

Personal income per capita (1996): $24,104, 21st
Percent increase (1995-96): 4.1%, 14th
Disposable personal income per capita (1996): $21,185, 21st
Median income of households (average, 1995-96): $30,632, 41st
Percent of pop. below poverty level (1995-96): 15.2%, 17th

ECONOMY

In civilian labor force (1996): 6,938,000
Percent of total pop.: 62.0%, 49th
Percent of total pop. 65 years and over: 10.1%, 37th
Percent of total female pop.: 54.8%, 48th
Major employer industries (total nonagricultural, 1996):
Construction: 323,500—5.2%, 17th
Finance, insurance, & real estate: 393,800—6.4%, 7th
Government: 929,200—15.0%, 39th
Manufacturing: 490,400—7.9%, 42nd
Service: 2,117,600—34.3%, 4th
Trade: 1,606,900—26.0%, 2nd
Transportation, communications, public utilities: 314,100—5.1%, 22nd
Unemployment rate (1996): 5.1%, 26th
Male: 4.8%, 34th
Female: 5.4%, 19th
Total businesses (1995): 398,232, 4th
New business incorps. (1995): 98,066
Percent of total businesses: 24.63%, 3rd
Business failures (1995): 2,904
Failures per 10,000 businesses: 72.9, 33rd
Agriculture farm income:
Marketing (1996): $6,130,658,000, 9th
Average per farm: $153,266, 8th
Leading products (1997): Greenhouse, citrus fruits, vegetables, potatoes, melons, strawberries, cane/sugar
Average value land & build. per acre (1997): $2,300, 10th
Percent increase (1996-97): 0%, 48th
Govt. payments (1996): $22,872,000, 36th
Average per farm: $572, 43rd
Construction, value of all (1996): $22,314,402,000, 3rd
Per capita: $1,550, 12th

Manufactures (1995):
Value added: $37,933,600,000
Per capita: $2,678, 45th
Leading products (1997): Electric and electronic equipment, transportation equipment, foods, printing & publishing, chemicals, instruments
Value of nonfuel mineral production (1996): $1,540,000,000, 8th
Leading mineral products (1996): Phosphate rock, petroleum, stone, cement, sand/gravel, clays
Energy consumption per person (1994): 242.3 mil. Btu, 48th
Retail sales (1995): $145,665,000,000
Per household: $25,688, 14th
Sales increase (1994-95): 5.7%, 21st
Tourism revenues (1994): $33.39 bil.
Foreign exports, in total value (1996): $20,744,000,000, 9th
Per capita: $1,441, 29th
Gross state product per person (1994): $22,779, 39th
Public aid recipients (percent of resident pop. 1994): 6.8%, 24th
Medicaid recipients (percent of pop., 1995): 12.2%, 24th
Medicare enrollment per 1,000 pop. (1996): 186, 3rd

TRAVEL AND TRANSPORTATION

Motor vehicle registrations (1996): 10,888,596, 3rd
Per 1,000 pop.: 755.16, 36th
Motorcycle registrations (1996): 203,334, 3rd
Per 1,000 pop.: 18.67, 29th
Licensed drivers (1996): 11,024,064, 3rd
Per 1,000 pop.: 777.21, 5th
Public roads & streets (1996)
Total mileage: 114,422, 10th
Per 1,000 pop.: 17.95, 41st
Rural mileage: 66,083, 26th
Per 1,000 pop.: 4.59, 42nd
Urban mileage: 48,339, 3rd
Per 1,000 pop.: 3.36, 13th
Interstate mileage: 1,471, 7th
Per 1,000 pop.: 0.10, 42nd
Speed limit (max. interstate, autos, mi. per hr., 1997): 70
Annual vehicle-mi. of travel per driver (1996): 11,404, 45th
Mean travel time for workers age 16+ who work away from home: 21.8 min., 15th

GOVERNMENT

Percent of voting age pop. registered (1996): 73.15%, 34th
Percent of voting age pop. voting for president: (1996): 48.0%, 32nd
Percent of voting age pop. voting for U.S. representatives (1996): 42.5%, 39th
State legislators, total (1997): 160, 18th
  Women members (1997): 37
    Percent of legislature: 23%, 19th
U.S. Congress, House members (1998): 23
  Change (1988-98): 4
Revenues (1996):
  State govt.: $41,679,890,000
    Per capita: $2,894.44, 46th
    Parimutuel & amusement taxes & lotteries, revenue per capita (1995): $156.12, 10th
Expenditures (1996):
  State govt.: $36,454,217,000
    Per capita: $2,531.54, 48th
Debt outstanding (1996): $15,514,762,000
  Per capita: $1,077.41, 35th

LAWS AND REGULATIONS

Legal driving age: 16
Marriage age without parental consent: 18
Divorce residence requirement: 6 mo.

ATTRACTIONS (1997)

Major opera companies: 4
Major symphony orchestras: 7
Major dance companies: 3
Major professional theater companies (non-profit): 1

Per capita spending by the NEA (1997): $0.08, 51st
State Fair in early to mid-February at Tampa

SPORTS AND COMPETITION

NCAA (Division I) football and basketball teams: Bethune-Cookman College Wildcats, Florida A&M Univ. Rattlers, Florida Atlantic Univ. Owls (basketball only), Florida International Univ. Golden Panthers (basketball only), Jacksonville Univ. Dolphins (basketball only), Florida State Univ. Seminoles, Stetson Univ. Hatters (basketball only), Univ. of Central Florida Golden Knights, Univ. of Florida Gators, Univ. of Miami Hurricanes, Univ. of South Florida Bulls (basketball only)
Major league baseball teams: Florida Marlins (NL East), Pro Player Stadium; Tampa Bay Devil Rays (AL East), Houlihan's Stadium
Major league soccer teams: Miami Fusion, Lockhart Stadium; Tampa Bay Mutiny, Tampa Stadium
NBA basketball teams: Orlando Magic, Orlando Arena; Miami Heat, Miami Arena
NFL football teams: Jacksonville Jaguars (AFC), ALLTEL Stadium; Miami Dolphins (AFC), Pro Player Stadium; Tampa Bay Buccaneers (NFC), Houlihan' Stadium
NHL hockey teams: Florida Panthers, Miami Arena; Tampa Bay Lightning, Ice Palace

WEBSITES CONTAINING FURTHER INFORMATION

Florida Government Services Direct   http://www.state.fl.us

GEORGIA

> "...the transportation, manufacturing, and marketing hub of the Deep South...the charm of the South as symbolized by Greek porticos, Doric columns, and romantic traditions. Here is a land where modern fortresses [Air Force bases] are not far from communities where sacred harp singing is still carried on...a land of forested mountains, deep lakes, and clear mountain streams, contrasted with miles of sunny beaches and sun-drenched isles, with still further contrast in the misty swamps where alligators splash and exotic tropical birds preen their elaborate plumage."
>
> President Jimmy Carter

Today the commercial leader of its region, Georgia was the only colony to be founded as a refuge for poor and deserving people. Invented in Georgia, the cotton gin revolutionized the South. The state ranks first in the production of peanuts and pecans, lima beans, and pimiento peppers. It leads the nation in production of fine china clays. Savannah is the nation's foremost cotton port and is often called "the nation's most beautiful city." Atlanta has become the leading transportation center of the Southeast. Georgia gave Coca-Cola to the world, and Atlanta native Margaret Mitchell was the author of one of the world's best-known novels, *Gone With the Wind*. During the mid-1990s, much attention was focused on the 1996 Summer Olympics, hosted by Atlanta.

SUPERLATIVES

- First steamship to cross the Atlantic—the *City of Savannah* sailing from Georgia.
- Site of the first U.S. gold rush, at Dahlonga.
- Home of the cotton gin.
- First U.S. source of aluminum.

MOMENTS IN HISTORY

- In 1540 the great expedition of Hernando de Soto entered what is now Georgia. The visit left a never-forgiven legacy of cruelty to the Indians.
- Beginning in 1565, Spaniard Pedro Menéndez de Aviles established forts and missions in the area.
- English and French pirates plagued the Spanish settlements beginning in 1670.
- The pirate Blackbeard made his headquarters on Blackbeard Island in 1716, becoming a de facto lord of the area.
- On February 12, 1733, James Oglethorpe first arrived at present-day Savannah to claim and settle the land he called Georgia in honor

of the King of England. He and 125 colonists pitched their tents and founded the last of the original 13 British colonies.

So They Say

The Georgia charter provided a grant for "...the land lying between the Savannah and Altamaha rivers and westward from the sources to the South Sea" for the purpose of "settling poor persons of London."

- In 1736, Oglethorpe arrived again with a large group of colonists, in "the Great Embarkation." They laid out the city, including the neat pattern of square parks that still distinguish Savannah.
- When the Spanish attempted to take the colony, Oglethorpe's forces won the Battle of Bloody Marsh on July 7, 1742. This small struggle has been called "one of the decisive battles of world history" because it kept the Spanish from pressing their claims northward on the coast.
- In 1752, Georgia became a crown colony.
- During the Revolution, the British captured Savannah in a surprise attack on December 29, 1778.
- On July 11, 1782, Savannah was recaptured by American General Anthony Wayne, and the Revolution was over in Georgia.
- Georgia unanimously ratified the U.S. Constitution and became the fourth state on January 2, 1788.
- After the War of 1812, Georgia entered its "Golden Age of Prosperity."
- In 1838 the Indians remaining in Georgia were forced from their lands and sent west over the "Trail of Tears."
- On January 19, 1861, Georgia joined the Confederacy.
- During the Civil War one of the most important Union aims was to take the state.

After many unsuccessful efforts, Union General William Tecumseh Sherman, "marching through Georgia," captured and burned Atlanta and left almost complete destruction in his subsequent path to the sea, capturing Savannah on December 22, 1864.

So They Say

"From all this ruin and devastation a new city [Atlanta, 1866] is springing up with marvellous rapidity. The narrow and irregular and numerous streets are alive from morning till night with drays and carts and hand-barrows and wagons...with hauling teams and shouting men with loads of lumber and loads of brick and loads of sand—with piles of furniture and hundreds of packed boxes, with mortar, rubbish removers and house-builders, with a never-ending throng of pushing and crowding and scrambling and eager and excited and enterprising men, all bent on building and trading and swift fortune-making."

Reporter Sidney Andrews

• After a harsh Reconstruction period, Georgia was readmitted to the Union in 1870.

• More than 3,000 Georgia men volunteered to serve in the Spanish-American War in 1898.

• Although Atlanta suffered a disastrous fire in 1917, the area remained a major military training center during World War I.

• In 1924 a young polio victim visited Warm Springs. He was so pleased with the relief he received in the warm waters that he often returned to his cottage there. When Franklin D. Roosevelt became president, the small community gained great fame.

• Georgia once again became a center of activity during World War II, and the state drew world attention with the death of President Roosevelt at Warm Springs on April 12, 1945.

• Jimmy Carter was inaugurated in 1977, the first U.S. president from the state.

• Thirty people died, 16 in Americus, when a tropical storm brought heavy rains and flooding in 1994.

THAT'S INTERESTING

• Rivalry between Indian tribes did not always lead to war. Some disputes between Cherokee and Creek groups were settled by a ball game.

• In the 1740s, Mary Jones was the skillful and successful captain of Fort Wimberley during a Spanish attack.

• The sculpture created by Gutzon Borglum on the side of Stone Mountain was so grand that Borglum once hosted 20 guests at breakfast on the shoulder of the Robert E. Lee carving. The work was later destroyed to make way for a smaller monument.

NOTABLE NATIVES

James Nathaniel (Jim) Brown (Saint Simons Island, 1936-), football player. Asa Griggs Candler (near Villa Rica, 1851-1929), business leader/philanthropist. James Earl (Jimmy) Carter (Plains, 1924-), U.S. president. Tyrus Raymond (Ty) Cobb (Narrows, 1886-1961), baseball player. John Charles Frémont (Savannah, 1813-1890), soldier. Joel Chandler Harris (Eatonton, 1848-1908), journalist/author. Robert Tyre (Bobby) Jones (Atlanta, 1902-1971), golfer. Martin Luther King, Jr. (Atlanta, 1929-1968), religious leader/social reformer. Sidney Lanier (Macon, 1842-1881), poet/critic. Crawford Williamson Long (Danielsville, 1815-1878), surgeon. Carson Smith McCullers (Columbus, 1917-1967), author. Margaret Mitchell (Atlanta, 1900-1949), author. Jack Roosevelt (Jackie) Robinson (Cairo, 1919-1972), baseball player. Alexander Hamilton Stephens (Wilkes County, later Taliaferro County, 1812-1883), statesman.

So They Say

"Jimmy Carter failed as President because, like [Gerald] Ford, he never figured out how to exercise authority. He seemed more interested in examining his conscience, in ensuring his own worthiness before God...than in exercising power." Writer Max Lerner

---

GENERAL

Admitted to statehood: January 2, 1788
Origin of name: For King George II of England by James Oglethorpe, colonial administrator, 1732
Capital: Atlanta

Nickname: Empire State of the South, Peach State
Motto: Wisdom, justice, and moderation
Bird: Brown thrasher
Fish: Largemouth bass
Flower: Cherokee rose
Song: "Georgia on My Mind"
Tree: Live oak

THE LAND

Area: 58,977 sq. mi., 24th
  Land: 57,919 sq. mi., 21st
  Water: 1,058 sq. mi., 29th
    Inland water: 1,011 sq. mi., 20th
    Coastal water: 47 sq. mi., 18th
Topography: Most southerly of the Blue Ridge Mtns. cover NE and N central; central piedmont extends to the fall line of rivers; coastal plain levels to the coast flatlands.
Number of counties: 159
Geographic center: Twiggs, 18 mi. SE of Macon
Length: 300 mi.; width: 230 mi.
Highest point: 4,784 ft. (Brasstown Bald), 25th
Lowest point: sea level (Atlantic Ocean), 3rd
Mean elevation: 600 ft., 37th
Coastline: 100 mi., 16th
Shoreline: 2,344 mi., 12th

CLIMATE AND ENVIRONMENT

Temp., highest: 112 deg. on July 24, 1952, at Louisville; lowest: –17 deg. on Jan. 27, 1940, at CCC Camp F-16
Monthly average: highest: 92.2 deg., 12th; lowest: 32.6 deg., 44th; spread (high to low): 59.6 deg., 46th
Hazardous waste sites (1997): 15, 23rd
Endangered species: Animals: 16—Southern acornshell, Gray bat, Indiana bat, Ovate clubshell, Southern clubshell, Upland combshell, Amber darter, Etowah darter, American peregrine falcon, Triangular kidneyshell, Conasauga logperch, West Indian manatee, Coosa moccasinshell, Southern pigtoe, Wood stork, Red-cockaded woodpecker. Plants: 16

MAJOR CITIES
POPULATION, 1996
PERCENTAGE INCREASE, 1990-96

Atlanta, 401,907; 2.0%
Columbus, 182,828; 2.3%
Savannah, 136,262; –1.1%
Macon, 113,352; 5.6%
Albany, 78,591; –0.27%

THE PEOPLE

Population (1997): 7,486,242, 10th
  Percent change (1990-97): 15.56%, 6th
  Percent of total U.S. pop.: 2.80%, 10th
  Per sq. mi: 125.94, 18th
Population (2000 proj.): 7,884,000, 10th
  Percent change (1995-2000): 9.48%, 7th
Percent in metro. area (1996): 68.51%, 28th
Foreign born: 173,000, 16th
  Percent: 2.7%, 29th
Top three ancestries reported:
  African, 21.94%
  Irish, 14.99%
  English, 13.74%
White (1992): 4,811,000, 71.03%, 45th
Black (1992): 1,856,000, 27.40%, 5th
Native American (1992): 15,000, 0.22%, 39th
Asian, Pacific Isle (1992): 92,000, 1.36%, 23rd
Hispanic origin (1992): 124,000, 1.83%, 33rd
Percent over 5 yrs. speaking language other than English at home: 4.8%, 39th
Percent males (1996): 48.73%, 29th; percent females: 51.27%, 21st
Percent never married: 26.2%, 22nd
Marriages per 1,000 (1996): 8.17, 28th
Divorces per 1,000 (1996): 4.88, 15th
Median age (1996): 33.3
Under 5 years (1996): 7.66%, 11th
18 years and under (1996): 29.42%, 16th
65 years and over (1996): 9.92%, 49th
Percent increase among the elderly (1995-96): 1.40%, 16th

OF VITAL IMPORTANCE

Live births per 1,000 pop. (1996): 15.6, 9th
Infant mortality rate per 1,000 live births (1995): 9.4, 7th
  Rate for whites: 6.5, 21st
  Rate for blacks: 15.1, 20th
Births to unmarried women, % of total (1996): 35.0%, 11th
Births to teenage mothers, % of total (1996): 15.9%, 13th
Abortions (1992): 39,680, 11th
  Rate per 1,000 women 14-44 years old: 24.0, 17th
  Percent change (1988-92): 2%, 10th

Average lifetime (1989-91): 73.61, 47th
Total death rate per 100,000 pop. (1995): 810.8, 39th
  Accidents and adverse effects: 41.1, 18th
  Alzheimer's disease: 7.1, 38th
  Cancer: 177.3, 43rd
  Cerebrovascular diseases: 56.2, 35th
  Chronic liver disease and cirrhosis: 8.1, 37th
  Chronic obstructive pulmonary diseases and allied conditions: 34.2, 42nd
  Diabetes mellitus: 16.7, 46th
  Diseases of heart: 242.4, 36th
  HIV infection: 22.0, 7th
  Homicide: 10.3, 13th
  Injury by firearms: 16.4, 13th
  Motor vehicle accidents: 21.4, 14th
  Pneumonia and influenza: 27.6, 37th
  Suicide: 11.5, 37th

KEEPING WELL

Active nonfederal physicians per 100,000 pop. (1995): 196, 33rd
Dentists per 100,000 (1991): 46, 41st
Nurses per 100,000 (1995): 818, 27th
Hospitals per 100,000 (1995): 2.22, 24th
  Admissions per 1,000 (1995): 119.29, 22nd
  Hospital beds per 1,000 (1995): 3.62, 21st
  Occupancy rate per 100 beds (1995): 60.54, 26th
  Average cost per patient per day (1995): $836, 34th
  Average cost per stay (1995): $5,618, 31st
AIDS cases (new, 1996): 2,411; per 100,000: 32.8, 9th
Persons living with HIV infection (1996): NA
Other notifiable diseases, per 100,000 pop.:
  Gonorrhea (1995): 292.0, 6th
  Syphilis (1995): 51.1, 3rd
  Tuberculosis (1996): 10.7, 7th
Pop. without health insur. (1996): 17.8%, 9th

HOUSEHOLDS BY TYPE

Total households (1996): 2,723,000, 11th
  Percent change (1990-96): 15.1%, 6th
  Per 1,000 pop. (1996) 370.33, 39th
  Percent of householders 65 yrs. and over (1996): 17.08%, 49th
  Persons per household (1996): 2.65, 13th
Family households: 1,713,072
  Percent of total: 72.38%, 12th
Nonfamily households: 653,543
  Percent of total: 27.62%, 40th

Pop. living in group quarters: 173,633
  Percent of pop.: 2.68%, 29th

LIVING QUARTERS

Total housing units: 2,638,418
  Persons per unit: 2.46, 14th
Occupied housing units: 2,366,615
  Percent of total units: 89.70%, 24th
  Persons per unit: 2.63, 11th
  Percent of units with over 1 person per room: 4.05%, 16th
Owner-occupied units: 1,536,759
  Percent of total units: 58.25%, 30th
  Percent of occupied units: 64.93%, 37th
  Persons per unit: 2.76, 20th
  Median value: $71,300, 23rd
Renter-occupied units: 829,856
  Percent of total units: 31.45%, 17th
  Percent of occupied units: 35.07%, 17th
  Persons per unit: 2.49, 10th
  Median contract rent: $344, 23rd
  Rental vacancy rate: 12.2%, 7th
Mobile home, trailer & other as a percent of occupied housing units: 13.85%, 18th
Persons in emergency shelters for homeless persons: 3,930, 0.061%, 17th
Persons visible in street locations: 450, 0.0069%, 24th
Nursing home population: 36,549, 0.56%, 41st

CRIME INDEX PER 100,000 (1996)

Total reported: 6,309.7, 7th
  Percent increase: 5.1%, 2nd
  Violent: 638.7, 16th
    Percent increase: −2.8%, 15th
    Murder & nonnegligent manslaughter: 8.6, 13th
    Forcible rape: 32.1, 28th
    Aggravated assault: 392.8, 18th
    Robbery: 205.4, 11th
  Property: 5,671.0, 7th
    Percent increase: 6.1%, 2nd
    Burglary: 1,114.8, 12th
    Larceny-theft: 3,927.7, 8th
    Motor vehicle theft: 628.5, 10th

TEACHING AND LEARNING

Pop. 3 and over enrolled in school (1996): 1,635,951, 9th
  Percent of pop.: 22.25%, 29th
Public elementary & secondary schools (1996-97): 1,763, 19th
  Total enrollment (1996): 1,321,239, 9th

Percent of school age pop.: 94.31%, 14th
Percent of total pop.: 17.97%, 15th
Teachers (1996): 81,683, 10th
Percent of pop.: 1.11%, 19th
Pupil/teacher ratio (1995): 16.5, 27th
Teachers' avg. salary (1996-97): $36,042, 24th
Expenditure per capita (1992-93): $1,157.24, 42nd
Education as % of state govt. expenditures: 33%, 37th
Expenditure per pupil (1994-95): $5,193, 35th
Percent increase (1993-94 & 1994-95): 5.66%, 12th
Percent at or above grade level, NAEP tests:
Reading, grade 4 (1994): 26%, 23rd
Math, grade 4 (1996): 53%, 36th
Math, grade 8 (1996): 51%, 33rd
Percent of graduates taking SAT (1995): 65%, 11th
Mean SAT verbal scores: 406, 50th
Mean SAT mathematical scores: 448, 49th
Percent of graduates taking ACT (1997): 16%, 33rd
Mean ACT scores: 20.2, 41st
Percent of pop. over 25 completing:
Less than 9th grade: 12.0%, 13th
High school: 70.9%, 42nd
College degree(s): 19.3%, 26th
Higher education, institutions (1996): 120, 8th
Enrollment (1995-96): 314,712, 13th
Percent increase in enroll. (1990-95): 25.0%, 1st
White non-Hispanic (1995): 215,506, 18th
Percent of enroll.: 68.48%, 41st
Total minority enroll. (1995): 91,064, 8th
Percent of enroll.: 28.94%, 11th
Black non-Hispanic (1995): 77,418, 6th
Percent of enroll.: 24.60%, 4th
Hispanic (1995): 4,659, 23rd
Percent of enroll.: 1.48%, 35th
Asian/Pacific Islander (1995): 8,143, 19th
Percent of enroll.: 2.59%, 23rd
American Indian/AK native (1995): 844, 36th
Percent of enroll.: 0.27%, 49th
Nonresident alien (1995): 8,142, 15th
Percent of enroll.: 2.59%, 27th
Female (1995): 179,830, 13th
Percent of enroll.: 57.14%, 13th
Pub. institutions (1995-96): 73, 5th
Enrollment: 248,682, 13th
Percent increase in enrollment (1990-95): 26.6%, 2nd

Percent of enroll.: 79.02%, 34th
Private institutions (1995-96): 47, 14th
Enrollment: 66,030, 13th
Percent increase in enrollment (1990-95): 19.2%, 7th
Percent of enroll.: 20.98%, 18th
Tuition (in state), public 4-year institution (1996-97): $2,244, 35th
Tuition (in state), public 2-year institution (1996-97): $1,110, 37th
Tuition, private 4-year institution (1996-97): $10,973, 27th
Public library systems (1994): 54, 40th
Books & serial vol. per capita: 1.8, 48th
Library visits per capita: 2.8, 37th
Circulation per capita: 4.4, 42nd

LAW ENFORCEMENT AND CORRECTIONS

Police protection and corrections expenditures (1996): $966,600,000
Per capita: $131.46, 19th
Police per 10,000 pop. (1996): 29.97, 5th
Prisoners (1 year or more) per 100,000 pop. (1996): 462, 10th
Percent change (1995-96): 0.5%, 44th
Percent of inmates that are female: 6.4%, 22nd
Percent change: 10.0%, 24th
Death penalty: yes, by electrocution
Under sentence (Jan. 1998): 113, 11th
Executed, 1976-97: 22, 6th
Executed in 1997: 0

RELIGION, NUMBER AND PERCENT OF POPULATION

Agnostic: 14,253—0.30%, 37th
Buddhist: 4,751—0.10%, 17th
Christian: 4,328,082—91.10%, 7th
Hindu: 9,502—0.20%, 3rd
Jewish: 23,755—0.50%, 27th
Muslim: 14,253—0.30%, 9th
Unitarian: 4,751—0.10%, 31st
Other: 66,513—1.40%, 20th
None: 218,542—4.60%, 43rd
Refused to answer: 66,513—1.40%, 44th

MAKING A LIVING

Personal income per capita (1996): $22,709, 27th
Percent increase (1995-96): 4.4%, 12th
Disposable personal income per capita (1996) $19,664, 28th

Median income of households (average, 1995-96): $33,801, 31st

Percent of pop. below poverty level (1995-96): 13.5%, 18th

ECONOMY

In civilian labor force (1996): 3,753,000
  Percent of total pop.: 67.8%, 28th
  Percent of total pop. 65 years and over: 11.5%, 27th
  Percent of total female pop.: 60.2%, 31st
Major employer industries (total nonagricultural, 1996):
  Construction: 164,700—4.7%, 21st
  Finance, insurance, & real estate: 180,400—5.1%, 26th
  Government: 569,100—16.1%, 33rd
  Manufacturing: 584,700—16.6%, 20th
  Service: 903,100—25.6%, 39th
  Trade: 896,600—25.4%, 6th
  Transportation, communications, public utilities: 221,900—6.3%, 4th
Unemployment rate (1996): 4.6%, 34th
  Male: 4.0%, 42nd
  Female: 5.3%, 25th
Total businesses (1995): 179,006, 11th
New business incorps. (1995): 26,990
  Percent of total businesses: 15.08%, 6th
Business failures (1995): 1,481
  Failures per 10,000 businesses: 82.7, 23rd
Agriculture farm income:
  Marketing (1996): $5,687,046,000, 12th
    Average per farm: $132,257, 11th
  Leading products (1997): Broilers, peanuts, cattle, eggs, cotton, corn, tobacco, hay, soybeans
  Average value land & build. per acre (1997): $1,430, 22nd
    Percent increase (1996-97): 5%, 26th
  Govt. payments (1996): $114,524,000, 22nd
    Average per farm: $2,663, 23rd
Construction, value of all (1996): $12,302,301,000, 8th
  Per capita: $1,673, 8th
Manufactures (1995):
  Value added: $50,219,600,000
    Per capita: $6,974, 19th
  Leading products (1997): Textiles, apparel, pulp & paper products
Value of nonfuel mineral production (1996): $1,720,000,000, 6th
Leading mineral products (1996): Clays, stone, cement, sand/gravel
Energy consumption per person (1994): 336.9 mil. Btu, 28th

Retail sales (1995): $65,389,000,000
  Per household: $24,643, 25th
  Sales increase (1994-95): 7.4%, 11th
Tourism revenues (1995): $13.5 bil.
Foreign exports, in total value (1996): $10,982,000,000, 16th
  Per capita: $1,493, 27th
Gross state product per person (1994): $25,944, 19th
Public aid recipients (percent of resident pop. 1994): 8.2%, 13th
Medicaid recipients (percent of pop., 1995): 15.9%, 10th
Medicare enrollment per 1,000 pop. (1996): 116, 43rd

TRAVEL AND TRANSPORTATION

Motor vehicle registrations (1996): 6,282,672, 9th
  Per 1,000 pop.: 856.62, 18th
Motorcycle registrations (1996): 73,492, 18th
  Per 1,000 pop.: 11.70, 43rd
Licensed drivers (1996): 4,840,495, 11th
  Per 1,000 pop.: 671.48, 34th
100,000 pop. (1995): 23.62, 12th
Public roads & streets (1996)
  Total mileage: 111,746, 14th
    Per 1,000 pop.: 115.20, 30th
  Rural mileage: 85,091, 13th
    Per 1,000 pop.: 11.57, 29th
  Urban mileage: 26,655, 9th
    Per 1,000 pop.: 3.62, 9th
  Interstate mileage: 1,241, 8th
    Per 1,000 pop.: 0.17, 32nd
Speed limit (max. interstate, autos, mi. per hr., 1997): 70
Annual vehicle-mi. of travel per driver (1996): 17,947, 4th
Mean travel time for workers age 16+ who work away from home: 22.7 min., 9th

GOVERNMENT

Percent of voting age pop. registered (1996): 70.34%, 39th
  Percent of voting age pop. voting for president: (1996): 42.6%, 47th
  Percent of voting age pop. voting for U.S. representatives (1996): 40.1%, 43re
State legislators, total (1997): 236, 3rd
  Women members (1997): 39
  Percent of legislature: 17%, 35th
U.S. Congress, House members (1998): 11
  Change (1988-98): 1

Revenues (1996):
   State govt.: $22,408,977,000
      Per capita: $3,047.60, 42nd
      Parimutuel & amusement taxes & lotter-
      ies, revenue per capita (1995): $179.64,
      9th
Expenditures (1996):
   State govt.: $20,013,038,000
      Per capita: $2,721.75, 40th
Debt outstanding (1996): $6,199,913,000
   Per capita: $843.18, 42nd

LAWS AND REGULATIONS

Legal driving age: 16
Marriage age without parental consent: 18
Divorce residence requirement: 6 mo.

ATTRACTIONS (1997)

Major opera companies: 2
Major symphony orchestras: 2
Major dance companies: 1

Major professional theater companies (non-
   profit): 1
Per capita spending by the NEA (1997):
   $0.25, 30th

SPORTS AND COMPETITION

NCAA (Division I) football and basketball
   teams: Georgia Southern Univ. Eagles,
   Georgia   State   Univ.   Panthers
   (basketball only), Georgia Institute of
   Technology Yellow Jackets, Mercer
   Univ. Bears (basketball only), Univ. of
   Georgia Bulldogs
Major league baseball teams: Atlanta Braves (NL
   East), Turner Field
NBA basketball teams: Atlanta Hawks, Geor-
   gia Dome, Alexander Memorial Coli-
   seum
ABL basketball teams: Atlanta Glory, More-
   house Olympic Arena
NFL football teams: Atlanta Falcons (NFC),
   Georgia Dome

WEBSITES CONTAINING FURTHER INFORMATION

| State of Georgia Home Page Go Network | http://www.state.ga.us |
| Georgia On My Mind Online | http://www.gomm.com/cgi-ole/gomm.exe |

H A W A I I

"Hawaii rests like a water lily on the swelling bosom of the Pacific. The heaven is tranquil above our heads, and the sun keeps his jealous eye upon us every day while his rays are so tempered that they never wither prematurely what they have warmed into life."   King Kamehameha I

"The loveliest fleet of islands that lies anchored in any ocean....No other land could so longingly and bewitchingly haunt me, sleeping and waking, through half a lifetime, as that one has done."

Mark Twain, author

In some ways Hawaii is the nation's most unusual state. It is the only state ever to have been governed directly by monarchs recognized by international law. The nation's only island state, it forms the world's longest island chain. The only tropical state, it has a climate that "sweetens one's bones," as Robert Louis Stevenson described it. Consequently, the language of Hawaii has no word for weather. Among Hawaii's natural wonders is stupendous Waimea Canyon, which rivals that of the Colorado River. The island chain was the home of unique prehistoric peoples who left mysterious evidence of their culture. They were followed by native peoples noted for their wisdom, strength, bravery, and loyalty. With the greatest ethnic and racial diversity of any state, Hawaii maintains constant vigil over the rights of its many peoples.

SUPERLATIVES

- World's bulkiest mountain—Mauna Loa.
- "The wettest place on earth"—Mt. Waialeale.
- Only state that has an official native language.
- King Kalakaua, the first reigning monarch ever to visit the United States (1874).
- World's most diverse population mix.
- Leader in pineapple production.
- World's most active volcano—the crater of Kilauea on Mauna Loa.

MOMENTS IN HISTORY

- As early as 500 B.C., expert navigators arrived at Hawaii in their double-hulled canoes, bringing evidence of their Indo-Malay culture.
- In 1778 native Hawaiians were astonished to see two "floating islands" carrying strange white-skinned men. Captain James Cook had arrived at Kauai, and he named the archipelago the Sandwich Islands.

- On the Big Island (Hawaii), Cook was killed in 1789 in revenge for the many injustices he and his men had committed against the islanders.
- In 1795, King Kamehameha I conquered Oahu; he soon extended his rule across the islands, acquiring the title of "the Great."
- The first American missionaries arrived in 1820 aboard the *Thaddeus*, in a move that was to transform the islands.

So They Say

"It is no small thing to say of the missionaries...that in less than 40 years they have taught this whole people to read and to write, to cipher, and to sew. They have given them an alphabet, grammar, and dictionary, preserved their language... given [them] a literature, and translated into it the Bible and works of devotion, science, and entertainment...."

Richard Henry Dana, lawyer and author

- During the reign of Kamehameha III, in 1840, the feudal system was changed into a constitutional monarchy.
- The new constitution of 1852 created a two-house legislature and courts of law. Religious freedom was guaranteed.
- Queen Liliuokalani, the last Hawaiian monarch, was overthrown and a temporary republic set up in 1893.
- In 1898 the Hawaiian republic transferred sovereignty to the United States by a treaty accepted on both sides.
- In 1900, Hawaii became a U.S. territory, with all residents becoming U.S. citizens.
- In 1903 the first Hawaiian pineapple was packed, and the islands' commerce increased so rapidly that many Asian immigrants were brought in as workers.

- Hawaiian isolation became a thing of the past after the first flight arrived from the mainland in 1927, and radio-telephone communication came in 1931.
- The Japanese bombing of Pearl Harbor on December 7, 1941, was a "day of infamy" never to be forgotten. Hawaii then became the principal Pacific fortress of the war, the greatest arsenal the world had ever known.
- The 1950 lava flow from the Mauna Loa eruption was considered to have been the largest in historic times.
- The first proposal for Hawaiian statehood was made during the time of Kamehameha II. Statehood finally occurred on August 21, 1959, and the United States had its 50th state.
- In the 1990s a growing movement sought to gain some form of sovereignty for part-native Hawaiians.

THAT'S INTERESTING

- As many as 100 people often crowded into a single Polynesian double-hulled canoe as the seaworthy ships sailed the thousands of stormy ocean miles from the South Pacific to populate Hawaii.
- When the Hawaiians killed Captain Cook in 1789, they prepared his body as they would have their own great chief, removing the flesh from the bones before burial.
- Hawaiian kings were noted for their great size and strength. Kamehameha I once moved a 4,500-pound stone. His Queen, Kaahumanu, weighed 300 pounds.

NOTABLE NATIVES

Samuel Chapman Armstrong (Maui, 1839-1893), educator. **Sanford Ballard Dole** (Honolulu, 1844-1926), public official. **Luther Halsey Gulick** (Honolulu, 1865-1918), educator. **Don Ho** (Kakaaho, Oahu, 1930-), singer. **Daniel K. Inouye** (Honolulu, 1924-), public official. **Kamehameha I** (Hawaii Island, 1758?-1819), king of Hawaii. **Kamehameha II** (Hawaii Island, 1796?-1824), king of Hawaii. **Kamehameha III** (Oahu, 1813-1854), king of Hawaii. **Kamehameha IV** (Oahu, 1834-1863), king of Hawaii. **Kamehameha V** (Oahu, 1830-1872), king of Hawaii. **Liliuokalani** (Oahu, 1838-1917), queen of Hawaii.

GENERAL

Admitted to statehood: August 21, 1959
Origin of name: Possibly derived from native word for homeland, *Hawaiki* or *Owyhyhee*

Capital: Honolulu
Nickname: Aloha State
Motto: *Ua Mau Ke Ea O Ka Aina I Ka Pono*—The life of the land is perpetuated in righteousness
Bird: Nene (Hawaiian goose)
Flower: Red hibiscus
Song: "Hawaii Ponoi"
Tree: Kukui (candlenut)

THE LAND

Area: 6,459 sq. mi., 47th
  Land: 6,423 sq. mi., 47th
  Water: 36 sq. mi., 50th
    Inland water: 36 sq. mi., 50th
Topography: Eight main islands, which are the tops of a chain of submerged volcanic mountains; active volcanoes: Mauna Loa, Kilauea
Number of counties: 5
Geographic center: Hawaii, 20°15'N, 156°20'W, off Maui Island
Length: 1600 mi.
Highest point: 13,796 ft. (Mauna Kea), 6th
Lowest point: sea level (Pacific Ocean), 3rd
Mean elevation: 3,030 ft., 10th
Coastline: 750 mi., 4th
Shoreline: 1,052 mi., 17th

CLIMATE AND ENVIRONMENT

Temp., highest: 100 deg. on April 27, 1931, at Pahala; lowest: 12 deg. on May 17, 1979, at Mauna Kea
Monthly average: highest: 87.1 deg., 26th; lowest: 65.3 deg., 51st; spread (high to low): 21.8 deg., 51st
Hazardous waste sites (1997): 4, 45th
Endangered species: Animals: 32—Hawaiian hoary bat, Hawaiian coot, Hawaiian creeper, Molokai creeper, Oahu creeper, Hawaiian crow, Hawaiian duck, Laysan duck, Laysan finch, Nihoa finch, Hawaiian goose, Hawaiian hawk, Crested honeycreeper, Nihoa millerbird, Hawaiian common moorhen, Nukupu'u, Palila, Maui parrotbill, Hawaiian dark-rumped petrel, Po'ouli, Oahu tree snail, Hawaiian stilt, Large Kauai thrush, Molokai thrush, Small Kauai thrush, Hawksbill sea turtle, Hawaii 'Akepa, Maui 'Akepa, Kauai 'Akialoa, 'Akiapola'au, Kauai 'O'o, 'O'u. Plants: 253

MAJOR CITIES
POPULATION, 1996
PERCENTAGE INCREASE, 1990-96

Honolulu, 423,475; 12.3%
Other cities: NA

THE PEOPLE

Population (1997): 1,186,602, 41st
  Percent change (1990-97): 7.07%, 22nd
  Percent of total U.S. pop.: 0.44%, 41st
  Per sq. mi: 108.54, 21st
Population (2000 proj.): 1,247,500, 41st
  Percent change (1995-2000): 5.10%, 22nd
Percent in metro. area (1996): 73.65%, 23rd
Foreign born: 163,000, 17th
  Percent: 14.7%, 3rd
Top three ancestries reported:
  Japanese, 23.65%
  Filipino, 15.88%
  Hawaiian, 14.17%
White (1992): 387,000, 33.48%, 50th
Black (1992): 29,000, 2.51%, 38th
Native American (1992): 6,000, 0.52%, 23rd
Asian, Pacific Isle (1992): 733,000, 63.41%, 1st
Hispanic origin (1992): 90,000, 7.79%, 11th
Percent over 5 yrs. speaking language other than English at home: 24.8%, 4th
Percent males (1996): 50.46%, 3rd; percent females: 49.54%, 49th
Percent never married: 29.8%, 5th
Marriages per 1,000 (1996): 16.45, 2nd
Divorces per 1,000 (1996): 4.06, 28th
Median age (1996): 35.1
Under 5 years (1996): 7.74%, 9th
18 years and under (1996): 28.74%, 25th
65 years and over (1996): 12.89%, 25th
Percent increase among the elderly (1995-96): 2.49%, 3rd

OF VITAL IMPORTANCE

Live births per 1,000 pop. (1996): 15.5, 11th
Infant mortality rate per 1,000 live births (1995): 5.8, 47th
  Rate for whites: NA
  Rate for blacks: NA
Births to unmarried women, % of total (1996): 30.2%, 30th
Births to teenage mothers, % of total (1996): 10.3%, 40th
Abortions (1992): 12,190, 30th
  Rate per 1,000 women 14-44 years old: 46.0, 3rd

Percent change (1988-92): 7%, 7th
Average lifetime (1989-91): 78.21, 1st
Total death rate per 100,000 pop. (1995): 643.1, 49th
  Accidents and adverse effects: 27.6, 46th
  Alzheimer's disease: 4.0, 49th
  Cancer: 156.4, 48th
  Cerebrovascular diseases: 51.5, 43rd
  Chronic liver disease and cirrhosis: 6.3, 47th
  Chronic obstructive pulmonary diseases and allied conditions: 20.4, 50th
  Diabetes mellitus: 14.2, 50th
  Diseases of heart: 196.0, 48th
  HIV infection: 10.4, 22nd
  Homicide: 4.9, 34th
  Injury by firearms: 6.3, 48th
  Motor vehicle accidents: 12.0, 45th
  Pneumonia and influenza: 26.7, 43rd
  Suicide: 12.0, 28th

KEEPING WELL

Active nonfederal physicians per 100,000 pop. (1995): 248, 10th
Dentists per 100,000 (1991): 78, 4th
Nurses per 100,000 (1995): 733, 40th
Hospitals per 100,000 (1995): 1.77, 34th
  Admissions per 1,000 (1995): 81.72, 50th
  Hospital beds per 1,000 (1995): 2.53, 40th
  Occupancy rate per 100 beds (1995): 80.00, 1st
  Average cost per patient per day (1995): $956, 25th
  Average cost per stay (1995): $8,445, 2nd
AIDS cases (new, 1996): 198; per 100,000: 16.7, 19th
Persons living with HIV infection (1996): NA
Other notifiable diseases, per 100,000 pop.:
  Gonorrhea (1995): 47.4, 38th
  Syphilis (1995): 2.1, 41st
  Tuberculosis (1996): 16.9, 2nd
Pop. without health insur. (1996): 8.6%, 50th

HOUSEHOLDS BY TYPE

Total households (1996): 389,000, 42nd
  Percent change (1990-96): 9.0%, 19th
  Per 1,000 pop. (1996) 328.55, 50th
  Percent of householders 65 yrs. and over (1996): 22.37%, 21st
  Persons per household (1996): 2.97, 2nd
Family households: 263,456
  Percent of total: 73.95%, 3rd

Nonfamily households: 92,811
  Percent of total: 26.05%, 49th
Pop. living in group quarters: 37,632
  Percent of pop.: 3.40%, 9th

LIVING QUARTERS

Total housing units: 389,810
  Persons per unit: 2.84, 2nd
Occupied housing units: 356,267
  Percent of total units: 91.40%, 14th
  Persons per unit: 2.99, 2nd
  Percent of units with over 1 person per room: 15.92%, 1st
Owner-occupied units: 191,911
  Percent of total units: 49.23%, 47th
  Percent of occupied units: 53.87%, 49th
  Persons per unit: 3.19, 2nd
  Median value: $245,300, 1st
Renter-occupied units: 164,356
  Percent of total units: 42.16%, 3rd
  Percent of occupied units: 46.13%, 3rd
  Persons per unit: 2.78, 1st
  Median contract rent: $599, 1st
  Rental vacancy rate: 5.4%, 48th
Mobile home, trailer & other as a percent of occupied housing units: 1.71%, 50th
Persons in emergency shelters for homeless persons: 854, 0.077%, 12th
Persons visible in street locations: 1,071, 0.0966%, 1st
Nursing home population: 3,225, 0.29%, 50th

CRIME INDEX PER 100,000 (1996)

Total reported: 6,584.5, 6th
  Percent increase: –8.5%, 42nd
  Violent: 280.6, 40th
    Percent increase: –5.1%, 21st
    Murder & nonnegligent manslaughter: 3.4, 40th
    Forcible rape: 27.5, 37th
    Aggravated assault: 114.0, 46th
    Robbery: 135.6, 24th
  Property: 6,304.0, 4th
    Percent increase: –8.7%, 46th
    Burglary: 1,079.5, 13th
    Larceny-theft: 4,620.0, 2nd
    Motor vehicle theft: 604.5, 11th

TEACHING AND LEARNING

Pop. 3 and over enrolled in school (1996): 251,683, 42nd
  Percent of pop.: 21.26%, 46th

Public elementary & secondary schools (1996-97): 246, 49th
  Total enrollment (1996): 188,485, 42nd
    Percent of school age pop.: 87.67%, 46th
    Percent of total pop.: 15.92%, 43rd
  Teachers (1996): 10,675, 42nd
    Percent of pop.: 0.90%, 44th
  Pupil/teacher ratio (1995): 17.8, 11th
  Teachers' avg. salary (1996-97): $35,842, 25th
  Expenditure per capita (1992-93): $1,234.67, 35th
    Education as % of state govt. expenditures: 22.7%, 50th
  Expenditure per pupil (1994-95): $6,078, 20th
    Percent increase (1993-94 & 1994-95): 3.38%, 32nd
Percent at or above grade level, NAEP tests:
  Reading, grade 4 (1994): 19%, 36th
  Math, grade 4 (1996): 53%, 36th
  Math, grade 8 (1996): 51%, 33rd
Percent of graduates taking SAT (1995): 57%, 17th
  Mean SAT verbal scores: 407, 49th
  Mean SAT mathematical scores: 482, 33rd
Percent of graduates taking ACT (1997): 17%, 32nd
  Mean ACT scores: 21.6, 13th
Percent of pop. over 25 completing:
  Less than 9th grade: 10.1%, 21st
  High school: 80.1%, 13th
  College degree(s): 22.9%, 14th
Higher education, institutions (1996): 17, 44th
  Enrollment (1995-96): 63,198, 42nd
    Percent increase in enroll. (1990-95): 12.0%, 6th
  White non-Hispanic (1995): 16,781, 51st
    Percent of enroll.: 26.55%, 51st
  Total minority enroll. (1995): 40,643, 23rd
    Percent of enroll.: 64.31%, 1st
  Black non-Hispanic (1995): 1,238, 41st
    Percent of enroll.: 1.96%, 41st
  Hispanic (1995): 1,362, 38th
    Percent of enroll.: 2.16%, 27th
  Asian/Pacific Islander (1995): 37,787, 5th
    Percent of enroll.: 59.79%, 1st
  American Indian/AK native (1995): 256, 48th
    Percent of enroll.: 0.41%, 31st
  Nonresident alien (1995): 5,774, 26th
    Percent of enroll.: 9.14%, 2nd
  Female (1995): 34,993, 42nd
    Percent of enroll.: 55.37%, 33rd

Pub. institutions (1995-96): 10, 41st
  Enrollment: 50,198, 39th
    Percent increase in enrollment (1990-95): 9.8%, 12th
  Percent of enroll.: 79.43%, 33rd
Private institutions (1995-96): 7, 44th
  Enrollment: 13,000, 39th
    Percent increase in enrollment (1990-95): 21.4%, 6th
  Percent of enroll.: 20.57%, 19th
Tuition (in state), public 4-year institution (1996-97): $2,298, 32nd
Tuition (in state), public 2-year institution (1996-97): $789, 45th
Tuition, private 4-year institution (1996-97): $6,492, 49th
Public library systems (1994): 1, 50th
  Books & serial vol. per capita: 2.3, 34th
  Library visits per capita: 2.9, 35th
  Circulation per capita: 5.7, 34th

LAW ENFORCEMENT AND CORRECTIONS

Police protection and corrections expenditures (1996): $114,615,000
  Per capita: $96.80, 35th
Police per 10,000 pop. (1996): 21.88, 27th
Prisoners (1 year or more) per 100,000 pop. (1996): 249, 37th
  Percent change (1995-96): 14.1%, 6th
  Percent of inmates that are female: 9.6%, 2nd
    Percent change: 23.4%, 9th
Death penalty: no

RELIGION, NUMBER AND PERCENT OF POPULATION

Agnostic: NA
Buddhist: NA
Christian: NA
Hindu: NA
Jewish: NA
Muslim: NA
Unitarian: NA
Other: NA
None: NA
Refused to answer: NA

MAKING A LIVING

Personal income per capita (1996): $25,159, 12th
  Percent increase (1995-96): 0.0%, 51st
Disposable personal income per capita (1996): $21,776, 11th

Median income of households (average, 1995-96): $42,944, 4th
Percent of pop. below poverty level (1995-96): 11.2%, 32nd

ECONOMY

In civilian labor force (1996): 591,000
  Percent of total pop.: 68.3%, 26th
  Percent of total pop. 65 years and over: 14.2%, 12th
  Percent of total female pop.: 61.9%, 20th
Major employer industries (total nonagricultural, 1996):
  Construction: NA—NA, NA
  Finance, insurance, & real estate: 36,800—7.0%, 4th
  Government: 110,100—20.8%, 7th
  Manufacturing: 16,600—3.1%, 50th
  Service: 166,100—31.4%, 8th
  Trade: 135,300—25.6%, 5th
  Transportation, communications, public utilities: 40,900—7.7%, 2nd
Unemployment rate (1996): 6.4%, 8th
  Male: 6.9%, 6th
  Female: 5.8%, 15th
Total businesses (1995): 29,942, 42nd
New business incorps. (1995): 3,792
  Percent of total businesses: 12.66%, 11th
Business failures (1995): 270
  Failures per 10,000 businesses: 90.2, 19th
Agriculture farm income:
  Marketing (1996): $482,589,000, 44th
    Average per farm: $104,911, 22nd
  Leading products (1997): Sugar, pineapples, greenhouse, nuts, fruits, coffee, vegetables
  Average value land & build. per acre (1997): NA
  Govt. payments (1996): $580,000, 49th
    Average per farm: $126, 50th
Construction, value of all (1996): $1,805,439,000, 39th
  Per capita: $1,525, 14th
Manufactures (1995):
  Value added: $1,488,500,000
    Per capita: $1,254, 51st
  Leading products (1997): Sugar, canned pineapple, apparel, foods, printing and publishing
Value of nonfuel mineral production (1996): $112,000,000, 43rd
Leading mineral products (1996): Stone, cement, sand/gravel, gemstones
Energy consumption per person (1994): 220.3 mil. Btu, 50th

Retail sales (1995): $12,806,000,000
  Per household: $32,912, 2nd
  Sales increase (1994-95): 1.0%, 46th
Tourism revenues (1995): $11.6 bil.
Foreign exports, in total value (1996):
  $284,000,000, 51st
  Per capita: $240, 51st
Gross state product per person (1994):
  $31,155, 8th
Public aid recipients (percent of resident pop.
  1994): 6.9%, 23rd
Medicaid recipients (percent of pop., 1995):
  4.4%, 51st
Medicare enrollment per 1,000 pop. (1996):
  130, 36th

TRAVEL AND TRANSPORTATION

Motor vehicle registrations (1996): 785,917,
  43rd
  Per 1,000 pop.: 664.37, 48th
Motorcycle registrations (1996): 25,114, 37th
  Per 1,000 pop.: 31.96, 7th
Licensed drivers (1996): 732,508, 42nd
  Per 1,000 pop.: 621.19, 45th
Public roads & streets (1996)
  Total mileage: 4,142, 50th
    Per 1,000 pop.: 13.50, 50th
  Rural mileage: 2,291, 49th
    Per 1,000 pop.: 1.94, 48th
  Urban mileage: 1,851, 47th
    Per 1,000 pop.: 1.56, 51st
  Interstate mileage: 0, 49th
    Per 1,000 pop.: 0.00, 49th
Speed limit (max. interstate, autos, mi. per
  hr., 1997): 55
Annual vehicle-mi. of travel per driver (1996):
  10,948, 48th
Mean travel time for workers age 16+ who
  work away from home: 23.8 min., 8th

GOVERNMENT

Percent of voting age pop. registered (1996):
  61.23%, 48th
  Percent of voting age pop. voting for presi-
    dent: (1996): 40.8%, 50th
  Percent of voting age pop. voting for U.S.
    representatives (1996): 40.0%, 44th
State legislators, total (1997): 76, 46th
  Women members (1997): 12
    Percent of legislature: 16%, 38th
U.S. Congress, House members (1998): 2
  Change (1988-98): 0
Revenues (1996):
  State govt.: $6,383,347,000
    Per capita: $5,391.34, 2nd
    Parimutuel & amusement taxes & lotter-
      ies, revenue per capita (1995): NA
Expenditures (1996):
  State govt.: $5,946,676,000
    Per capita: $5,022.53, 2nd
Debt outstanding (1996): $5,116,982,000
  Per capita: $4,321.78, 6th

LAWS AND REGULATIONS

Legal driving age: 15
Marriage age without parental consent: 18
Divorce residence requirement: 6 mo.

ATTRACTIONS (1997)

Major opera companies: 1
Per capita spending by the NEA (1997):
  $0.58, 12th
State Fair in June at Honolulu

SPORTS AND COMPETITION

NCAA (Division I) football and basketball
  teams: Univ. of Hawaii-Manoa Rain-
  bows

WEBSITES CONTAINING FURTHER INFORMATION

Hawaii State Government Home Page   http://www.hawaii.gov

IDAHO

"Dice 'em, hash 'em, boil 'em, mash 'em! Idaho, Idaho, Idaho!"

An Idaho football cheer

Idaho is a land of dramatic natural features, with towering, snow-capped mountain ranges, swirling white rapids, deep canyons, and peaceful lakes that deserve to be ranked among the world's most beautiful. The Snake River rushes through Hells Canyon, which is deeper than the Grand Canyon. Idaho's Shoshone Falls, on the Snake River, are higher than Niagara Falls. Known the world round for its potatoes, the state also possesses vast and unique mineral resources and forest reserves. Idahoans believe they live in a state where life is still unmatched for serenity and harmony, despite some recent social concerns.

SUPERLATIVES

- The tiny Malad River, said to be the shortest river in the world.
- Largest prehistoric art work in the United States, near Nampa.
- Hells Canyon—the deepest gorge in North America.
- World's largest stands of white pine.
- World's largest reserves of phosphate.
- First in silver production.
- Two-thirds of all U.S. processed potatoes produced.

MOMENTS IN HISTORY

- The great exploration of Meriwether Lewis and William Clark provided the first record of the area as the explorers crossed it in 1805.
- Waiting for the snows to melt on their return journey home in 1806, Lewis and Clark performed many different kindnesses for the Indians.
- Representing the Hudson Bay Company, noted explorer David Thompson set up the first trading post in present-day Idaho in 1809, Kullyspell House on Pend Oreille Lake.
- In 1810, Andrew Henry built Fort Henry, the first American trading post in the Pacific Northwest, but it was later abandoned.
- In 1818-19, Donald Mackenzie firmly established the Idaho fur trade and began what became the great annual fur "rendezvous," attracting some of the most rowdy gatherings of the West.

> ## So They Say
> "I have again to repeat to you the advice which I before gave you not to come with a small party to the American rendezvous. There are here a great collection of scoundrels."
> **Pioneer Nathaniel Wyeth**

- Fort Hall on the Snake River was built by Nathaniel Wyeth in 1834 and sold two years later to Dr. John McLaughlin, "ruler" of the Hudson Bay Company in the region.
- In 1834 the first missionaries arrived, and at Fort Hall the Reverend Jason Lee conducted the first Christian religious service in present-day Idaho.
- The Reverend and Mrs. Henry H. Spalding established Lapwai Mission in Nez Percé country near Lewiston in 1836. He served his Indian congregation until his death in 1874.
- By the mid-1840s, a stream of settlers was crossing over the Oregon Trail, and many turned off to settle in present-day Idaho.
- Beginning in 1849, more thousands crossed the region on their way to California gold.
- Indian wars followed until 1855, when the tribes agreed to move to other tracts.
- Franklin, the first permanent European-style town in Idaho, was founded by the Mormons in 1860.
- Also in 1860, gold discoveries led to a boom, and the town that sprang up at the site was named for E. D. Pierce, a pioneer gold prospector.
- On June 17, 1877, the longtime friendship between the Nez Percé and the whites ended in the Battle of White Bird Canyon, during which the government forces lost a third of their men. Then, under the superb leadership of Chief Joseph, the Nez Percé tribe began its bitter flight from its ancestral lands.
- With the defeat of the Sheepeater tribe in 1879, Indian wars ended in Idaho.
- The 1870s brought rich gold strikes.
- Even greater was the strike of 1883 in silver, lead, and zinc in the Coeur d'Alene district.
- Idaho became a state on July 3, 1890.

• A particularly bitter miners' strike took place in 1899.

• In December 1905, Frank Steunenberg, governor at the time of the miners' strike, was killed in a bomb explosion; his murder trial gained international prominence.

• Craters of the Moon National Monument became a reality in 1924.

• Development of Sun Valley began in 1936.

• The world's first usable atomic-powered electricity was generated in 1951 at the National Reactor Testing Station.

• More than 460 miles from the sea, remote inland Lewiston became an "ocean port" with the opening of the Snake River Navigation Project in 1975.

• The collapse of the Teton Dam in June 1976 caused vast property damage, particularly to the cattle industry.

• The grasshopper infestation of 1985 devastated the state's farmlands.

THAT'S INTERESTING

• Thirsty travelers on the brink of Hells Canyon could look down on the waters of the Snake River but had no way to get down to drink.

• Wood River is known as the Upside Down River. At one place it flows through a gorge 4 feet wide and 104 feet deep. At another point the gorge is 104 feet wide and the river 4 feet deep.

• The Craters of the Moon were named because the fantastic surface of the area was thought to resemble the moon when viewed through a telescope. There are spectacular lava flows, cinder cones, and other volcanic creations resulting from lava flows over a period of 15,000 years.

• A unique Idaho attraction is Thousand Springs. Each spring spouts out from the side of a single cliff.

IDAHO NOTABLES

William Edgar Borah (Fairfield, IL, 1865-1940), public official/political leader. **William Dudley (Big Bill) Haywood** (Salt Lake City, UT, 1869-1928), labor leader. **Chief Joseph** (Wallowa Valley, near Idaho/Oregon/Washington border, 1840?-1904), Indian leader. **Ezra Loomis Pound** (Hailey, 1885-1972), poet. **Sacajawea** (Eastern Idaho or western Montana, 1787?-1812?), Indian guide.

GENERAL

Admitted to statehood: July 3, 1890

Origin of name: A coined name with an invented Indian meaning, "gem of the mountains"; was originally suggested for the Pikes Peak mining territory (Colorado), then applied to the new mining territory of the Pacific Northwest. Another theory suggests Idaho may be a Kiowa Apache term for the Comanche

Capital: Boise

Nickname: Gem State

Motto: *Esto Perpetua*—It is perpetual

Bird: Mountain bluebird

Flower: Syringa

Gem: Star garnet

Song: "Here We Have Idaho"

Tree: White pine

THE LAND

Area: 83,574 sq. mi., 14th

  Land: 82,751 sq. mi., 11th

    Water: 823 sq. mi., 31st

      Inland water: 823 sq. mi., 25th

Topography: Snake River plains in the S; central region of mountains, canyons, gorges (Hells Canyon, 7,900 ft., deepest in North America); subalpine northern region

Number of counties: 44

Geographic center: Custer, SW of Challis

Length: 570 mi.; width: 300 mi.

Highest point: 12,662 ft. (Borah Peak), 11th

Lowest point: 710 ft. (Snake River), 44th

Mean elevation: 5,000 ft., 6th

CLIMATE AND ENVIRONMENT

Temp., highest: 118 deg. on July 28, 1934, at Orofino; lowest: –60 deg. on Jan. 18, 1943, at Island Park Dam

Monthly average: highest: 90.6 deg., 18th; lowest: 15.1 deg., 17th; spread (high to low): 75.5 deg., 14th

Hazardous waste sites (1997): 7, 42nd

Endangered species: Animals: 10—Woodland caribou, Whooping crane, American peregrine falcon, Banbury springs limpet, Snake River physa snail, Utah valvata snail, Bruneau hot springsnail, Idaho springsnail, White sturgeon, Gray wolf. Plants: 0

MAJOR CITIES
POPULATION, 1996
PERCENTAGE INCREASE, 1990-96

Boise City, 152,737; 20.6%
Pocatello, 51,344; 11.3%
Idaho Falls, 48,079; 9.3%
Nampa, 37,558; 32.4%
Twin Falls, 31,989; 15.8%

THE PEOPLE

Population (1997): 1,210,232, 40th
    Percent change (1990-97): 20.21%, 3rd
    Percent of total U.S. pop.: 0.45%, 40th
    Per sq. mi: 14.48, 45th
Population (2000 proj.): 1,339,500, 39th
    Percent change (1995-2000): 15.18%, 2nd
Percent in metro. area (1996): 31.33%, 49th
Foreign born: 29,000, 40th
    Percent: 2.9%, 28th
Top three ancestries reported:
    English, 28.90%
    German, 27.71%
    Irish, 14.10%
White (1992): 1,036,000, 97.19%, 4th
Black (1992): 4,000, 0.38%, 49th
Native American (1992): 15,000, 1.41%, 12th
Asian, Pacific Isle (1992): 11,000, 1.03%, 31st
Hispanic origin (1992): 59,000, 5.53%, 15th
Percent over 5 yrs. speaking language other than English at home: 6.4%, 30th
Percent males (1996): 50.00%, 6th; percent females: 50.00%, 46th
Percent never married: 21.2%, 49th
Marriages per 1,000 (1996): 12.59, 5th
Divorces per 1,000 (1996): 5.90, 7th
Median age (1996): 33.0
Under 5 years (1996): 7.74%, 9th
18 years and under (1996): 32.87%, 3rd
65 years and over (1996): 11.35%, 42nd
Percent increase among the elderly (1995-96): 1.38%, 17th

OF VITAL IMPORTANCE

Live births per 1,000 pop. (1996): 16.0, 7th
Infant mortality rate per 1,000 live births (1995): 6.1, 43rd
    Rate for whites: 5.8, 41st
    Rate for blacks: NA
Births to unmarried women, % of total (1996): 21.3%, 50th
Births to teenage mothers, % of total (1996): 13.5%, 20th

Abortions (1992): 1,710, 48th
    Rate per 1,000 women 14-44 years old: 7.2, 49th
    Percent change (1988-92): −12%, 32nd
Average lifetime (1989-91): 76.88, 10th
Total death rate per 100,000 pop. (1995): 732.1, 46th
    Accidents and adverse effects: 45.2, 9th
    Alzheimer's disease: 7.7, 31st
    Cancer: 172.4, 44th
    Cerebrovascular diseases: 54.8, 38th
    Chronic liver disease and cirrhosis: 7.5, 40th
    Chronic obstructive pulmonary diseases and allied conditions: 38.2, 31st
    Diabetes mellitus: 17.7, 43rd
    Diseases of heart: 212.3, 44th
    HIV infection: 3.7, 45th
    Homicide: 4.0, 40th
    Injury by firearms: 15.0, 21st
    Motor vehicle accidents: 22.7, 9th
    Pneumonia and influenza: 27.5, 39th
    Suicide: 16.0, 8th

KEEPING WELL

Active nonfederal physicians per 100,000 pop. (1995): 137, 50th
Dentists per 100,000 (1991): 54, 24th
Nurses per 100,000 (1995): 766, 35th
Hospitals per 100,000 (1995): 3.53, 9th
    Admissions per 1,000 (1995): 89.42, 47th
    Hospital beds per 1,000 (1995): 2.92, 36th
    Occupancy rate per 100 beds (1995): 61.76, 21st
    Average cost per patient per day (1995): $719, 42nd
    Average cost per stay (1995): $4,686, 49th
AIDS cases (new, 1996): 39; per 100,000: 3.3, 48th
Persons living with HIV infection, not yet AIDS (1996): 223
Other notifiable diseases, per 100,000 pop.:
    Gonorrhea (1995): 12.8, 44th
    Syphilis (1995): 1.0, 45th
    Tuberculosis (1996): 1.3, 48th
Pop. without health insur. (1996): 16.5%, 15th

HOUSEHOLDS BY TYPE

Total households (1996): 430,000, 41st
    Percent change (1990-96): 19.1%, 3rd
    Per 1,000 pop. (1996) 361.65, 43rd
    Percent of householders 65 yrs. and over (1996): 20.00%, 37th
    Persons per household (1996): 2.68, 9th

Family households: 263,194
  Percent of total: 72.96%, 8th
Nonfamily households: 97,529
  Percent of total: 27.04%, 44th
Pop. living in group quarters: 21,490
  Percent of pop.: 2.13%, 47th

LIVING QUARTERS

Total housing units: 413,327
  Persons per unit: 2.44, 17th
Occupied housing units: 360,723
  Percent of total units: 87.27%, 36th
  Persons per unit: 2.67, 9th
  Percent of units with over 1 person per room: 4.21%, 14th
Owner-occupied units: 252,734
  Percent of total units: 61.15%, 17th
  Percent of occupied units: 70.06%, 10th
  Persons per unit: 2.82, 10th
  Median value: $58,200, 38th
Renter-occupied units: 107,989
  Percent of total units: 26.13%, 43rd
  Percent of occupied units: 29.94%, 42nd
  Persons per unit: 2.51, 9th
  Median contract rent: $261, 41st
  Rental vacancy rate: 7.3%, 38th
Mobile home, trailer & other as a percent of occupied housing units: 16.70%, 8th
Persons in emergency shelters for homeless persons: 461, 0.046%, 27th
Persons visible in street locations: 19, 0.0019%, 45th
Nursing home population: 6,318, 0.63%, 32nd

CRIME INDEX PER 100,000 (1996)

Total reported: 4,012.5, 38th
  Percent increase: −8.8%, 44th
  Violent: 267.2, 42nd
    Percent increase: −17.0%, 50th
    Murder & nonnegligent manslaughter: 3.6, 38th
    Forcible rape: 26.3, 42nd
    Aggravated assault: 217.0, 35th
    Robbery: 20.3, 48th
  Property: 3,745.3, 37th
    Percent increase: −8.2%, 43rd
    Burglary: 709.1, 37th
    Larceny-theft: 2,848.8, 31st
    Motor vehicle theft: 187.5, 45th

TEACHING AND LEARNING

Pop. 3 and over enrolled in school (1996): 304,818, 39th
  Percent of pop.: 25.64%, 4th
Public elementary & secondary schools (1996-97): 618, 41st
  Total enrollment (1996): 245,252, 39th
    Percent of school age pop.: 95.06%, 10th
    Percent of total pop.: 20.63%, 3rd
  Teachers (1996): 13,059, 40th
    Percent of pop.: 1.10%, 21st
  Pupil/teacher ratio (1995): 19.0, 8th
  Teachers' avg. salary (1996-97): $31,818, 39th
  Expenditure per capita (1992-93): $1,165.61, 41st
    Education as % of state govt. expenditures: 37%, 17th
  Expenditure per pupil (1994-95): $4,210, 49th
    Percent increase (1993-94 & 1994-95): 9.52%, 2nd
Percent at or above grade level, NAEP tests:
  Reading, grade 4 (1994): NA
  Math, grade 4 (1996): NA
  Math, grade 8 (1996): NA
Percent of graduates taking SAT (1995): 15%, 31st
  Mean SAT verbal scores: 468, 22nd
  Mean SAT mathematical scores: 511, 24th
Percent of graduates taking ACT (1997): 62%, 18th
  Mean ACT scores: 21.4, 19th
Percent of pop. over 25 completing:
  Less than 9th grade: 7.4%, 42nd
  High school: 79.7%, 16th
  College degree(s): 17.7%, 35th
Higher education, institutions (1996): 12, 46th
  Enrollment (1995-96): 59,566, 43rd
    Percent increase in enroll. (1990-95): 14.8%, 5th
  White non-Hispanic (1995): 54,535, 40th
    Percent of enroll.: 91.55%, 5th
  Total minority enroll. (1995): 3,740, 45th
    Percent of enroll.: 6.28%, 47th
  Black non-Hispanic (1995): 390, 47th
    Percent of enroll.: 0.65%, 49th
  Hispanic (1995): 1,683, 36th
    Percent of enroll.: 2.83%, 19th
  Asian/Pacific Islander (1995): 874, 46th
    Percent of enroll.: 1.47%, 40th
  American Indian/AK native (1995): 793, 37th

Percent of enroll.: 1.33%, 14th
Nonresident alien (1995): 1,291, 43rd
  Percent of enroll.: 2.17%, 38th
Female (1995): 32,847, 44th
  Percent of enroll.: 55.14%, 37th
Pub. institutions (1995-96): 6, 45th
  Enrollment: 48,986, 40th
    Percent increase in enrollment (1990-95): 18.6%, 3rd
  Percent of enroll.: 82.24%, 27th
Private institutions (1995-96): 6, 46th
  Enrollment: 10,580, 43rd
    Percent increase in enrollment (1990-95): 0.1%, 38th
  Percent of enroll.: 17.76%, 25th
Tuition (in state), public 4-year institution (1996-97): $1,973, 46th
Tuition (in state), public 2-year institution (1996-97): $1,045, 41st
Tuition, private 4-year institution (1996-97): $12,256, 22nd
Public library systems (1994): 107, 28th
  Books & serial vol. per capita: 3.3, 20th
  Library visits per capita: 4.9, 10th
  Circulation per capita: 7.9, 13th

LAW ENFORCEMENT AND CORRECTIONS

Police protection and corrections expenditures (1996): $127,995,000
  Per capita: $107.65, 28th
Police per 10,000 pop. (1996): 17.88, 41st
Prisoners (1 year or more) per 100,000 pop. (1996): 319, 27th
  Percent change (1995-96): 15.2%, 3rd
  Percent of inmates that are female: 7.1%, 12th
  Percent change: 28.8%, 6th
Death penalty: yes, by firing squad, lethal injection
  Under sentence (Jan. 1998): 19, 23rd
  Executed, 1976-97: 1, 25th
  Executed in 1997: 0

RELIGION, NUMBER AND PERCENT OF POPULATION

Agnostic: 7,682—1.10%, 6th
Buddhist: 1,397—0.20%, 11th
Christian: 571,944—81.90%, 41st
Hindu: NA
Jewish: NA
Muslim: NA
Unitarian: 2,793—0.40%, 8th
Other: 9,777—1.40%, 20th

None: 83,103—11.90%, 7th
Refused to answer: 21,649—3.10%, 7th

MAKING A LIVING

Personal income per capita (1996): $19,539, 44th
  Percent increase (1995-96): 3.9%, 17th
Disposable personal income per capita (1996): $16,722, 46th
Median income of households (average, 1995-96): $34,175, 29th
Percent of pop. below poverty level (1995-96): 13.2%, 19th

ECONOMY

In civilian labor force (1996): 619,000
  Percent of total pop.: 70.4%, 14th
  Percent of total pop. 65 years and over: 13.3%, 18th
  Percent of total female pop.: 62.9%, 16th
Major employer industries (total nonagricultural, 1996):
  Construction: 30,400—6.2%, 5th
  Finance, insurance, & real estate: 25,300—5.1%, 26th
  Government: 97,700—19.8%, 13th
  Manufacturing: 72,600—14.7%, 26th
  Service: 114,900—23.3%, 44th
  Trade: 125,100—25.4%, 6th
  Transportation, communications, public utilities: 23,200—4.7%, 35th
Unemployment rate (1996): 5.2%, 23rd
  Male: 5.1%, 24th
  Female: 5.4%, 19th
Total businesses (1995): 32,972, 41st
New business incorps. (1995): 2,622
  Percent of total businesses: 7.95%, 35th
Business failures (1995): 388
  Failures per 10,000 businesses: 117.7, 13th
Agriculture farm income:
  Marketing (1996): $3,409,945,000, 25th
    Average per farm: $154,998, 7th
  Leading products (1997): Cattle, potatoes, dairy products, wheat, peas, beans, sugar beets, alfalfa seed, lentils, hops, barley, plums and prunes, mint, onions, corn, cherries, apples, hay
  Average value land & build. per acre (1997): $960, 34th
    Percent increase (1996-97): 6%, 20th
  Govt. payments (1996): $116,009,000, 21st
    Average per farm: $5,273, 10th
Construction, value of all (1996): $1,877,973,000, 37th
  Per capita: $1,579, 10th

Manufactures (1995):
  Value added: $7,931,900,000
    Per capita: $6,819, 23rd
  Leading products (1997): Processed foods, lumber and wood products, chemical products, primary metals, fabricated metal products, machinery, electronic parts, computer equipment
Value of nonfuel mineral production (1996): $411,000,000, 32nd
Leading mineral products (1996): Gold, phosphate rock, molybdenum, sand/gravel, silver
Energy consumption per person (1994): 389.0 mil. Btu, 17th
Retail sales (1995): $10,766,000,000
  Per household: $25,308, 18th
  Sales increase (1994-95): 2.6%, 39th
Tourism revenues (1994): $1.4 bil.
Foreign exports, in total value (1996): $1,571,000,000, 40th
  Per capita: $1,321, 30th
Gross state product per person (1994): $21,345, 43rd
Public aid recipients (percent of resident pop. 1994): 3.4%, 51st
Medicaid recipients (percent of pop., 1995): 9.9%, 41st
Medicare enrollment per 1,000 pop. (1996): 54, 51st

TRAVEL AND TRANSPORTATION

Motor vehicle registrations (1996): 1,061,125, 40th
  Per 1,000 pop.: 893.51, 13th
Motorcycle registrations (1996): 34,034, 33rd
  Per 1,000 pop.: 32.07, 6th
Licensed drivers (1996): 805,911, 41st
  Per 1,000 pop.: 691.11, 27th
Public roads & streets (1996)
  Total mileage: 59,674, 33rd
    Per 1,000 pop.: 150.18, 7th
  Rural mileage: 55,901, 30th
    Per 1,000 pop.: 47.01, 7th
  Urban mileage: 3,773, 39th
    Per 1,000 pop.: 3.17, 22nd

Interstate mileage: 611, 35th
  Per 1,000 pop.: 0.51, 8th
Speed limit (max. interstate, autos, mi. per hr., 1997): 75
Annual vehicle-mi. of travel per driver (1996): 15,812, 12th
Mean travel time for workers age 16+ who work away from home: 17.3 min., 43rd

GOVERNMENT

Percent of voting age pop. registered (1996): 81.64%, 17th
  Percent of voting age pop. voting for president: (1996): 58.2%, 7th
  Percent of voting age pop. voting for U.S. representatives (1996): 58.5%, 6th
State legislators, total (1997): 105, 39th
  Women members (1997): 24
    Percent of legislature: 23%, 20
U.S. Congress, House members (1998): 2
  Change (1988-98): 0
Revenues (1996):
  State govt.: $4,383,680,000
    Per capita: $3,686.86, 22nd
    Parimutuel & amusement taxes & lotteries, revenue per capita (1995): $77.26, 29th
Expenditures (1996):
  State govt.: $3,501,298,000
    Per capita: $2,944.74, 32nd
Debt outstanding (1996): $1,453,555,000
    Per capita: $1,222.50, 32nd

LAWS AND REGULATIONS

Legal driving age: 17
Marriage age without parental consent: 18
Divorce residence requirement: 6 wks.

ATTRACTIONS (1997)

Per capita spending by the NEA (1997): $0.35, 21st
State Fair in late August at Boise and early September at Blackfoot

SPORTS AND COMPETITION

NCAA (Division I) football and basketball teams: Boise State Univ. Broncos, Idaho State Univ. Bengals, Univ. of Idaho Vandals

WEBSITES CONTAINING FURTHER INFORMATION

State of Idaho Home Page   http://www.state.id.us

ILLINOIS

"Illinois is perhaps the most American of all the states. It's the U.S.A. in capsule....The capacity for greatness is as limitless as the sweep of the undulating corn fields." — Clyde Brion Davis, journalist and author

The Land of Lincoln nourished the future president and gave him his start toward world fame. The state is rich in archaeological treasures, including the unique Piasa bird and the largest primitive earthworks anywhere. Because of its central location and access to both the Mississippi and the Great Lakes, Illinois has the world's greatest concentration of transportation facilities by land, water, and air. The Chicago area ranks as the nation's major center of manufacture, and the state often leads the nation in production of foodstuffs, particularly corn and soybeans. Some of the world's tallest buildings rise above a Chicago skyline that contains many architectural masterpieces and has been praised as the world's most beautiful. The concentration of attractions on the northern section of Chicago's Michigan Avenue has given it the nickname of the "Magnificent Mile."

So They Say

"The first great school of American skyscraper construction, the 'Chicago School,' was marked not only by its new uses of steel, but just as much by its pioneer use of glass....."

Historian Daniel J. Boorstin

SUPERLATIVES

- World center of transportation.
- One of the world's busiest airports—Chicago's O'Hare.
- World's first skyscraper.
- Tallest building in the United States—Sears Tower, Chicago.
- A principal center of printing.
- Pioneer in commercial television.
- Leader in mail order sales.
- Leader in exports.

MOMENTS IN HISTORY

- The expedition of Louis Jolliet and Father Jacques Marquette brought the first Europeans to Illinois in 1673.

So They Say

"Most beautiful and suitable for settlement...a settler would not there spend ten years in cutting down and burning trees; on the very day of his arrival, he could put his plow into the ground. Thus he would easily find in the country his food and clothing." — Louis Jolliet

- French priests founded Cahokia in 1699—oldest European settlement in the state.
- After the French surrendered North America, their flag at Fort de Chartres in 1765 was the last to be lowered on the continent.
- From 1765 to 1778, British rule was weak, and Illinois became a lawless "wild west."
- During the Revolution, American General George Rogers Clark and 175 men captured Kaskaskia on July 4, 1778.
- In 1809 the Territory of Illinois was created, with popular Ninian Edwards as its governor.

So They Say

"We will enter upon a state government with better prospects than any state ever did—the best soil in the world, a mild climate, a large state with the most ample funds to educate every child in the state."

Nathaniel Pope, Illinois territorial delegate to Congress

- During the War of 1812, tiny Fort Dearborn (Chicago) was ordered evacuated, and the people were massacred by the Potawatomi Indians.
- On December 3, 1818, Illinois became the 21st state.
- When Chief Black Hawk of the Sauk and Fox tried to reclaim the tribal lands in 1832, the Black Hawk War began. His forces won the small Battle of Stillman's Run in April, but he was later defeated in Wisconsin.
- Chicago was incorporated in 1837 with a population of 4,000.

• Nauvoo was the largest city in Illinois when Joseph Smith, the Mormon leader, was killed there in 1844. The Mormons left for the West, and Nauvoo became a ghost town.

• By 1845 the Galena area had become the nation's leading supplier of lead, and Galena had become the largest city in the state. The mining boom had almost died out by 1850.

• In 1858, Abraham Lincoln and Stephen Douglas engaged in a series of debates that gave Lincoln national prominence.

• In 1861, President-elect Lincoln left Springfield for the last time.

• On February 14, 1865, only days after Lee had surrendered at Appomattox, victorious President Lincoln was shot; he died the next day. His body was returned to a sorrowing Springfield.

• Galena's Ulysses S. Grant was elected president in 1868 and reelected in 1872.

• The great Chicago fire of 1871 destroyed much of the city, but rebuilding began before the ashes had died down.

• In 1893 the magnificent World's Columbian Exposition at Chicago dazzled visitors from around the world.

• In one of the great engineering feats of all time, in 1900, the Chicago River was reversed to dispose of sewage and to create a water route from the Great Lakes to the Gulf of Mexico.

So They Say

As the Marquette/Jolliet party rested near present Chicago, Marquette proposed the theory that creating a short canal at their campsite on the watershed would provide a waterway to connect Lake Michigan with the Gulf of Mexico. Centuries later this brilliant theory became a reality. **The Enchantment of Illinois**

• The first baseball game in American League history was played in Chicago in 1901.

• On December 2, 1942, the power of the atom was mastered at the University of Chicago, when the first nuclear chain reaction was produced.

• Riots at the Democratic National Convention at Chicago in 1968 brought the city notoriety.

• Sears Tower opened in 1974, at the time the world's tallest building.

• In 1978, Hannah Gray became the first woman president of a major U.S. university, the University of Chicago.

• On November 25, 1987, Harold Washington, Chicago's first black mayor, died of a heart attack at his desk.

• Carol Moseley-Braun was elected to the U.S. Senate in 1992, the first African-American woman elected to that body.

• In 1992, violent natural gas explosions ripped up city streets, destroyed 18 buildings, and killed two people; and the business district was flooded after workers accidentally breached a tunnel beneath the Chicago River.

• More than 500 people died in Chicago as a result of record heat in July 1995.

THAT'S INTERESTING

• One of the most mysterious of all prehistoric remains is the huge figure of a monster, known as the Piasa Bird, painted high on the bluff near Alton. Its origin has never been determined.

• Lincoln, Illinois, was the only town named for Abraham Lincoln during his lifetime. Invited to dedicate the town, he christened it with watermelon juice and provided watermelon for the crowd.

• When a gang of counterfeiters tried to steal Abraham Lincoln's body from his tomb in Springfield in exchange for a jailed member's freedom, quick Secret Service work foiled the bizarre ransom attempt.

• When young Ronald Reagan was a lifeguard at Lowell Park Riverside beach near Dixon, he saved 77 people from drowning, and the town put up a plaque in his honor.

NOTABLE NATIVES

Jane Addams (Cedarville, 1860-1935), social reformer. **Jack Benny** (Chicago, 1894-1974), comedian. **Black Hawk** (near Rockford, 1767-1838), Indian leader. **William Jennings Bryan** (Salem, 1860-1925), political leader. **Hillary Rodham Clinton** (Chicago, 1947-), U.S. first lady. **Everett McKinley Dirksen** (Pekin, 1896-1969), public official. **Walter Elias Disney** (Chicago, 1901-1966), animator/producer. **Charles Edgar Duryea** (near Canton, 1861-1938), inventor. **Wyatt Berry Stapp Earp** (Monmouth, 1848-1929), frontiersman. **Betty Naomi Goldstein Friedan** (Peoria, 1921-), author/social reformer. **Benjamin David (Benny) Goodman** (Chicago, 1909-1986), musician. **Hugh Hefner**

(Chicago, 1926-), publisher. **Ernest Miller Hemingway** (Oak Park, 1899-1961), author. **James Butler (Wild Bill) Hickock** (Troy Grove, 1837-1876), scout/frontiersman. **Harriet Monroe** (Chicago, 1860-1936), editor/poet. **Ronald Wilson Reagan** (Tampico, 1911-), U.S. president. **Carl August Sandburg** (Galesburg, 1878-1967), poet. **Charles Rudolph Walgreen** (Knox County, 1873-1939), pharmacist/merchant. **Florenz Ziegfeld** (Chicago, 1869-1932), theatrical producer.

GENERAL

Admitted to statehood: December 3, 1818
Origin of name: French for the *Illini* or "land of *Illini*," Algonquin word meaning men or warriors
Capital: Springfield
Nickname: Prairie State
Motto: State sovereignty, national union
Slogan: Land of Lincoln
Animal: White-tailed deer
Bird: Cardinal
Insect: Monarch butterfly
Fish: Bluegill
Flower: Native violet
Mineral: Fluorite
Song: "Illinois"
Tree: White oak

THE LAND

Area: 57,918 sq. mi., 25th
  Land: 55,593 sq. mi., 24th
  Water: 2,325 sq. mi., 17th
    Inland water: 750 sq. mi., 29th
    Great Lakes: 1,575 sq. mi., 6th
Topography: Prairies and fertile plains throughout; open hills in the southern region
Number of counties: 102
Geographic center: Logan, 28 mi. NE of Springfield
Length: 390 mi.; width: 210 mi.
Highest point: 1,235 ft. (Charles Mound), 45th
Lowest point: 279 ft. (Mississippi River), 33rd
Mean elevation: 600 ft., 38th

CLIMATE AND ENVIRONMENT

Temp., highest: 117 deg. on July 14, 1954, at East St. Louis; lowest: –35 deg. on Jan. 22, 1930, and on Feb. 3, 1996, at Mount Carroll

Monthly average: highest: 87.1 deg., 26th; lowest: 9.8 deg., 11th; spread (high to low): 77.3 deg., 11th
Hazardous waste sites (1997): 38, 9th
Endangered species: Animals: 13—Gray bat, Indiana bat, Karner blue butterfly, Hine's emerald dragonfly, American peregrine falcon, Fanshell, Higgins' eye pearlymussel, Orange-foot pimple back pearlymussel, Pink mucket pearlymussel, Fat pocketbook, Iowa pleistocene snail, Pallid sturgeon, Least tern. Plants: 1

MAJOR CITIES POPULATION, 1996 PERCENTAGE INCREASE, 1990-96

Chicago, 2,721,547; –2.2%
Rockford, 143,531; 1.2%
Aurora, 116,405; 16.8%
Springfield, 112,921; 7.1%
Peoria, 112,306; –1.1%

THE PEOPLE

Population (1997): 11,895,849, 6th
  Percent change (1990-97): 4.07%, 38th
  Percent of total U.S. pop.: 4.44%, 6th
  Per sq. mi: 205.39, 12th
Population (2000 proj.): 12,060,000, 6th
  Percent change (1995-2000): 1.94%, 41st
Percent in metro. area (1996): 84.11%, 14th
Foreign born: 952,000, 6th
  Percent: 8.3%, 12th
Top three ancestries reported:
  German, 29.10%
  Irish, 16.28%
  African, 12.47%
White (1992): 9,511,000, 81.90%, 36th
Black (1992): 1,756,000, 15.12%, 14th
Native American (1992): 25,000, 0.22%, 39th
Asian, Pacific Isle (1992): 322,000, 2.77%, 10th
Hispanic origin (1992): 975,000, 8.40%, 10th
Percent over 5 yrs. speaking language other than English at home: 14.2%, 12th
Percent males (1996): 48.83%, 26th; percent females: 51.17%, 26th
Percent never married: 28.8%, 10th
Marriages per 1,000 (1996): 7.61, 36th
Divorces per 1,000 (1996): 3.41, 35th
Median age (1996): 34.3
Under 5 years (1996): 7.76%, 8th
18 years and under (1996): 29.37%, 18th

65 years and over (1996): 12.54%, 30th
Percent increase among the elderly (1995-96): 0.15%, 45th

OF VITAL IMPORTANCE

Live births per 1,000 pop. (1996): 15.6, 9th
Infant mortality rate per 1,000 live births (1995): 9.4, 7th
  Rate for whites: 7.2, 9th
  Rate for blacks: 18.7, 3rd
Births to unmarried women, % of total (1996): 33.7%, 14th
Births to teenage mothers, % of total (1996): 12.7%, 26th
Abortions (1992): 68,420, 5th
  Rate per 1,000 women 14-44 years old: 25.4, 14th
  Percent change (1988-92): –4%, 19th
Average lifetime (1989-91): 74.90, 35th
Total death rate per 100,000 pop. (1995): 916.9, 23rd
  Accidents and adverse effects: 33.9, 35th
  Alzheimer's disease: 8.8, 23rd
  Cancer: 212.2, 26th
  Cerebrovascular diseases: 63.3, 25th
  Chronic liver disease and cirrhosis: 10.0, 15th
  Chronic obstructive pulmonary diseases and allied conditions: 38.0, 32nd
  Diabetes mellitus: 22.5, 27th
  Diseases of heart: 304.4, 17th
  HIV infection: 12.1, 17th
  Homicide: 11.0, 12th
  Injury by firearms: 12.3, 31st
  Motor vehicle accidents: 14.7, 34th
  Pneumonia and influenza: 32.6, 22nd
  Suicide: 9.5, 46th

KEEPING WELL

Active nonfederal physicians per 100,000 pop. (1995): 244, 11th
Dentists per 100,000 (1991): 67, 10th
Nurses per 100,000 (1995): 595, 49th
Hospitals per 100,000 (1995): 1.75, 35th
  Admissions per 1,000 (1995): 122.74, 19th
  Hospital beds per 1,000 (1995): 3.55, 22nd
  Occupancy rate per 100 beds (1995): 59.76, 30th
  Average cost per patient per day (1995): $1,050, 18th
  Average cost per stay (1995): $6,584, 10th
AIDS cases (new, 1996): 2,199; per 100,000: 18.6, 16th
Persons living with HIV infection (1996): NA

Other notifiable diseases, per 100,000 pop.:
  Gonorrhea (1995): 183.8, 14th
  Syphilis (1995): 30.8, 11th
  Tuberculosis (1996): 8.9, 16th
Pop. without health insur. (1996): 11.3%, 39th

HOUSEHOLDS BY TYPE

Total households (1996): 4,352,000, 6th
  Percent change (1990-96): 3.6%, 42nd
  Per 1,000 pop. (1996) 367.35, 41st
  Percent of householders 65 yrs. and over (1996): 21.65%, 27th
  Persons per household (1996): 2.65, 13th
Family households: 2,924,880
  Percent of total: 69.60%, 34th
Nonfamily households: 1,277,360
  Percent of total: 30.40%, 17th
Pop. living in group quarters: 286,956
  Percent of pop.: 2.51%, 33rd

LIVING QUARTERS

Total housing units: 4,506,275
  Persons per unit: 2.54, 5th
Occupied housing units: 4,202,240
  Percent of total units: 93.25%, 2nd
  Persons per unit: 2.59, 14th
  Percent of units with over 1 person per room: 3.97%, 17th
Owner-occupied units: 2,699,182
  Percent of total units: 59.90%, 24th
  Percent of occupied units: 64.23%, 39th
  Persons per unit: 2.81, 12th
  Median value: $80,900, 19th
Renter-occupied units: 1,503,058
  Percent of total units: 33.35%, 13th
  Percent of occupied units: 35.77%, 15th
  Persons per unit: 2.37, 24th
  Median contract rent: $369, 19th
  Rental vacancy rate: 8.0%, 29th
Mobile home, trailer & other as a percent of occupied housing units: 4.50%, 44th
Persons in emergency shelters for homeless persons: 7,481, 0.065%, 16th
Persons visible in street locations: 1,755, 0.0154%, 12th
Nursing home population: 93,662, 0.82%, 20th

CRIME INDEX PER 100,000 (1996)

Total reported: 5,315.8, 19th
  Percent increase: –2.6%, 26th

Violent: 886.2, 6th
  Percent increase: –11.0%, 39th
  Murder & nonnegligent manslaughter:
    10.0, 8th
  Forcible rape: 34.2, 25th
  Aggravated assault: 562.6, 6th
  Robbery: 279.4, 7th
Property: 4,429.6, 22nd
  Percent increase: –0.7%, 20th
  Burglary: 913.2, 22nd
  Larceny-theft: 3,026.2, 24th
  Motor vehicle theft: 490.2, 20th

TEACHING AND LEARNING

Pop. 3 and over enrolled in school (1996):
  2,679,153, 5th
Percent of pop.: 22.61%, 26th
Public elementary & secondary schools (1996-
  97): 4,142, 4th
  Total enrollment (1996): 1,961,299, 5th
    Percent of school age pop.: 87.52%, 47th
    Percent of total pop.: 16.56%, 36th
  Teachers (1996): 115,859, 5th
    Percent of pop.: 0.98%, 36th
  Pupil/teacher ratio (1995): 17.1, 16th
  Teachers' avg. salary (1996-97): $42,679,
    11th
  Expenditure   per   capita   (1992-93):
    $1,241.48, 33rd
    Education as % of state govt. expendi-
      tures: 33.8%, 33rd
  Expenditure per pupil (1994-95): $6,136,
    18th
    Percent increase (1993-94 & 1994-95):
      4.12%, 23rd
Percent at or above grade level, NAEP tests:
  Reading, grade 4 (1994): NA
  Math, grade 4 (1996): NA
  Math, grade 8 (1996): NA
Percent of graduates taking SAT (1995): 13%,
  32nd
  Mean SAT verbal scores: 488, 14th
  Mean SAT mathematical scores: 560, 7th
Percent of graduates taking ACT (1997):
  69%, 8th
  Mean ACT scores: 21.2, 27th
Percent of pop. over 25 completing:
  Less than 9th grade: 10.3%, 19th
  High school: 76.2%, 29th
  College degree(s): 21.0%, 20th
Higher education, institutions (1996): 169,
  5th
  Enrollment (1995-96): 717,854, 4th
    Percent increase in enroll. (1990-95):
      –1.6%, 43rd

White non-Hispanic (1995): 509,044, 5th
  Percent of enroll.: 70.91%, 39th
Total minority enroll. (1995): 190,803, 5th
  Percent of enroll.: 26.58%, 13th
Black non-Hispanic (1995): 90,674, 4th
  Percent of enroll.: 12.63%, 15th
Hispanic (1995): 58,244, 5th
  Percent of enroll.: 8.11%, 9th
Asian/Pacific Islander (1995): 39,477, 4th
  Percent of enroll.: 5.50%, 9th
American Indian/AK native (1995): 2,408,
  19th
  Percent of enroll.: 0.34%, 43rd
Nonresident alien (1995): 18,007, 6th
  Percent of enroll.: 2.51%, 29th
Female (1995): 401,562, 4th
  Percent of enroll.: 55.94%, 25th
Pub. institutions (1995-96): 61, 8th
  Enrollment: 530,248, 5th
    Percent increase in enrollment (1990-
      95): –3.8%, 41st
    Percent of enroll.: 73.87%, 40th
Private institutions (1995-96): 108, 4th
  Enrollment: 187,606, 5th
    Percent increase in enrollment (1990-
      95): 5.4%, 24th
    Percent of enroll.: 26.13%, 12th
Tuition (in state), public 4-year institution
  (1996-97): $3,525, 16th
Tuition (in state), public 2-year institution
  (1996-97): $1,290, 29th
Tuition, private 4-year institution (1996-
  97): $12,424, 20th
Public library systems (1994): 606, 2nd
  Books & serial vol. per capita: 3.4, 18th
  Library visits per capita: 5.3, 5th
  Circulation per capita: 7.5, 18th

LAW ENFORCEMENT AND CORRECTIONS

Police protection and corrections expenditures
  (1996): $1,167,743,000
  Per capita: $98.57, 34th
Police per 10,000 pop. (1996): 27.45, 7th
Prisoners (1 year or more) per 100,000 pop.
  (1996): 327, 25th
  Percent change (1995-96): 3.2%, 37th
  Percent of inmates that are female: 5.8%,
    33rd
  Percent change: 2.4%, 41st
Death penalty: yes, by lethal injection
  Under sentence (Jan. 1998): 165, 7th
  Executed, 1976-97: 11, 10th
  Executed in 1997: 2, 7th

RELIGION, NUMBER AND PERCENT OF POPULATION

Agnostic: 50,905—0.60%, 19th
Buddhist: 8,484—0.10%, 17th
Christian: 7,262,506—85.60%, 27th
Hindu: 16,969—0.20%, 3rd
Jewish: 127,264—1.50%, 13th
Muslim: 33,937—0.40%, 5th
Unitarian: 33,937—0.40%, 8th
Other: 118,779—1.40%, 20th
None: 593,897—7.00%, 23rd
Refused to answer: 237,559—2.80%, 12th

MAKING A LIVING

Personal income per capita (1996): $26,598, 8th
  Percent increase (1995-96): 3.4%, 21st
Disposable personal income per capita (1996): $22,778, 9th
Median income of households (average, 1995-96): $39,375, 11th
Percent of pop. below poverty level (1995-96): 12.3%, 22nd

ECONOMY

In civilian labor force (1996): 6,100,000
  Percent of total pop.: 68.5%, 23rd
  Percent of total pop. 65 years and over: 14.3%, 11th
  Percent of total female pop.: 60.7%, 29th
Major employer industries (total nonagricultural, 1996):
  Construction: 220,800—3.9%, 39th
  Finance, insurance, & real estate: 385,700—6.8%, 6th
  Government: 810,300—14.3%, 42nd
  Manufacturing: 972,000—17.1%, 18th
  Service: 1,640,000—28.9%, 18th
  Trade: 1,303,800—23.0%, 35th
  Transportation, communications, public utilities: 331,000—5.8%, 13th
Unemployment rate (1996): 5.3%, 20th
  Male: 5.3%, 20th
  Female: 5.2%, 26th
Total businesses (1995): 293,694, 5th
New business incorps. (1995): 34,495
  Percent of total businesses: 11.75%, 14th
Business failures (1995): 1,696
  Failures per 10,000 businesses: 57.7, 40th
Agriculture farm income:
  Marketing (1996): $9,049,998,000, 5th
    Average per farm: $119,079, 16th
  Leading products (1997): Corn, soybeans, hogs, cattle, wheat, sorghum, hay

Average value land & build. per acre (1997): $2,210, 11th
  Percent increase (1996-97): 7%, 14th
Govt. payments (1996): $386,767,000, 5th
  Average per farm: $5,089, 12th
Construction, value of all (1996): $12,567,052,000, 6th
  Per capita: $1,061, 37th
Manufactures (1995):
  Value added: $93,762,800,000
    Per capita: $7,926, 10th
  Leading products (1997): Machinery, electric and electronic equipment, primary and fabricated metals, chemical products, printing and publishing, food and food products
Value of nonfuel mineral production (1996): $817,000,000, 16th
Leading mineral products (1996): Coal, petroleum, stone, cement, sand/gravel, clays
Energy consumption per person (1994): 315.3 mil. Btu, 34th
Retail sales (1995): $104,528,000,000
  Per household: $24,093, 33rd
  Sales increase (1994-95): 4.6%, 26th
Tourism revenues (1995): $17 bil.
Foreign exports, in total value (1996): $24,176,000,000, 6th
  Per capita: $2,041, 13th
Gross state product per person (1994): $28,324, 11th
Public aid recipients (percent of resident pop. 1994): 8.3%, 12th
Medicaid recipients (percent of pop., 1995): 13.2% 19th
Medicare enrollment per 1,000 pop. (1996): 1,364, 1st

TRAVEL AND TRANSPORTATION

Motor vehicle registrations (1996): 8,816,876, 6th
  Per 1,000 pop.: 744.33, 38th
Motorcycle registrations (1996): 171,091, 5th
  Per 1,000 pop.: 19.40, 25th
Licensed drivers (1996): 7,210,972, 7th
  Per 1,000 pop.: 611.60, 46th
Public roads & streets (1996)
  Total mileage: 137,577, 3rd
    Per 1,000 pop.: 111.61, 37th
  Rural mileage: 101,888, 6th
    Per 1,000 pop.: 8.60, 37th
  Urban mileage: 35,689, 5th
    Per 1,000 pop.: 3.01, 30th

Interstate mileage: 2,163, 3rd
  Per 1,000 pop.: 0.18, 31st
Speed limit (max. interstate, autos, mi. per
  hr., 1997): 65
Annual vehicle-mi. of travel per driver (1996):
  12,712, 37th
Mean travel time for workers age 16+ who
  work away from home: 25.1 min., 5th

GOVERNMENT

Percent of voting age pop. registered (1996):
  76.12%, 27th
  Percent of voting age pop. voting for presi-
    dent: (1996): 49.2%, 29th
  Percent of voting age pop. voting for U.S.
    representatives (1996): 47.1%, 27th
State legislators, total (1997): 177, 13th
  Women members (1997): 46
    Percent of legislature: 26%, 14th
U.S. Congress, House members (1998): 20
  Change (1988-98): –2
Revenues (1996):
  State govt.: $36,990,605,000
    Per capita: $3,122.36, 37th
    Parimutuel & amusement taxes & lotter-
      ies, revenue per capita (1995): $151.26,
      13th
Expenditures (1996):
  State govt.: $34,111,276,000
    Per capita: $2,879.32, 34th
Debt outstanding (1996): $22,676,430,000
  Per capita: $1,914.11, 13th

LAWS AND REGULATIONS

Legal driving age: 18, 16 if completed driver
  education course
Marriage age without parental consent: 18
Divorce residence requirement: 90 days

ATTRACTIONS (1997)

Major opera companies: 3
Major symphony orchestras: 4
Major dance companies: 6
Major professional theater companies (non-
  profit): 2
Per capita spending by the NEA (1997):
  $0.23, 32nd
State Fair in early August at Springfield and
  late August at DuQuoin

SPORTS AND COMPETITION

NCAA (Division I) football and basketball
  teams: Bradley Univ. Braves (basketball
  only), Chicago State Univ. Cougars
  (basketball only), DePaul Univ. Blue
  Demons (basketball only), Eastern Illi-
  nois Univ. Panthers, Illinois State Univ.
  Redbirds, Loyola Univ. Ramblers
  (basketball only), Northeastern Illinois
  Univ. Golden Eagles (basketball only),
  Northern Illinois Univ. Huskies,
  Northwestern Univ. Wildcats, Southern
  Illinois Univ. Salukis, Univ. of Illinois-
  Champaign Fighting Illini, Univ. of Illi-
  nois-Chicago Flames (basketball only),
  Western Illinois Univ. Leathernecks
Major league baseball teams: Chicago White Sox
  (AL Central), Comiskey Park; Chicago
  Cubs (NL Central), Wrigley Field
Major league soccer teams: Chicago Fire,
  Soldier Field
NBA basketball teams: Chicago Bulls, United
  Center
NFL football teams: Chicago Bears (NFC),
  Soldier Field
NHL hockey teams: Chicago Blackhawks,
  United Center

WEBSITES CONTAINING FURTHER INFORMATION

State of Illinois   http://www.state.il.us

INDIANA

"Blest Indiana....Find here the best retreat on earth."   John Finley, explorer

The Hoosier State provided a natural route between Canada and Louisiana for French explorers, trappers, and traders. Captured by the United States in the Revolution and secured by the War of 1812, Indiana soon greeted large numbers of settlers who came floating down the Ohio River in flatboats. The area has nurtured an extraordinary number of notables, including Indian leaders, future presidents, and four vice presidents, plus an impressive number of literary figures, musicians, inventors, industrialists, and other personalities. The state also enjoys frequent leadership in sports, particularly in basketball.

SUPERLATIVES

- Wabash—first electrically lighted city.
- The first U.S. industrial union, founded by Eugene V. Debs at Terre Haute.
- National leader in production of musical instruments.
- Produces 80% of the nation's dimensional limestone.

MOMENTS IN HISTORY

- In 1673, Robert Cavelier, Sieur de La Salle, entered the St. Joseph River near present-day Benton Harbor, the first recorded European visit.
- Records are unclear, but it is thought that Vincennes took shape between 1727 and 1732, when French fur trappers and traders plied their trade.
- In 1749, Pierre Joseph, Celeron de Bienville, led a colorful expedition down the Ohio River. He buried a series of lead plates along the way as evidence of French ownership of the region.
- In 1763 the British took over.
- During the American Revolution in 1779, American General George Rogers Clark, with only a handful of men, captured Vincennes and its hated leader, Henry Hamilton.

So They Say

"The capture of Vincennes by George Rogers Clark has been called...one of the most heroic episodes in U.S. history...one of the greatest exploits of American arms."   **Anonymous**

- The Northwest Ordinance of 1787 paved the way for settlement in Indiana.
- Alarmed at the prospect of losing their lands, the Indians took up arms. But Revolutionary hero General "Mad Anthony" Wayne overcame Indian resistance and in 1795 forced the Indian leaders to sign a treaty giving up much of the region.
- On November 7, 1811, territorial Governor William Henry Harrison decisively defeated the Indian confederation led by Chief Tecumseh and his brother, The Prophet—at their Prophetstown headquarters near present-day Lafayette, in the Battle of Tippecanoe.
- Indiana became the 19th state on December 11, 1816.
- Many Indiana cities became "stations" on the Underground Railroad in the years before the Civil War. More than 2,000 slaves found refuge at Levi Coffin's house in Fountain City on their way to freedom in Canada.
- The Civil War reached Indiana in 1863 when Confederate raider John Hunt Morgan swept through the state.
- The worst-yet Ohio River floods in history occurred in 1937.
- Burns Harbor opened for shipping in 1970, giving Indiana a much-needed major Great Lakes shipping port.

THAT'S INTERESTING

- The British governor of Indiana, Henry Hamilton, was known as the "Hair Buyer" because he encouraged Indians friendly to the British to take American scalps, for which they were paid.
- Indiana's Lost River travels 22 miles underground.
- Indiana General Ambrose Burnside's bushy whiskers were originally called "burnsides" after him, and now are known as "sideburns."

NOTABLE NATIVES

George Ade (Kentland, 1866-1944), humorist/playwright. **Charles Austin Beard** (near Knightstown, 1874-1948), **political scientist/historian**. **Albert Jeremiah Beveridge** (Highland County, 1862-1927), public official/historian. **Larry Joe Bird** (West Baden,

1956-), basketball player. **Ambrose Everett Burnside** (Liberty, 1824-1881), soldier/public official. **Theodore Dreiser** (Terre Haute, 1871-1945), author. **Edward Eggleston** (Vevay, 1837-1902), religious leader/historian. **John Milton Hay** (Salem, 1838-1905), diplomat/author. **James (Jimmy) Riddle Hoffa** (Brazil, 1913-1975?), labor leader. **Robert Staughton Lind** (New Albany, 1892-1970), sociologist. **Thomas Riley Marshall** (North Manchester, 1854-1925), U.S. vice president. **John Tinney McCutcheon** (Tippecanoe County, 1870-1949), cartoonist. **Oliver Perry Morton** (Salisbury, 1823-1877), public official. **Cole Porter** (Peru, 1893-1964), lyricist/composer. **Gene Stratton Porter** (Wabash County, 1863-1924), author. **Ernest Taylor (Ernie) Pyle** (Dana, 1900-1945), journalist. **James Danforth (Dan) Quayle** (Indianapolis, 1947-), U.S. vice president. **James Whitcomb Riley** (Greenfield, 1849-1916), poet. **Newton Booth Tarkington** (Indianapolis, 1869-1946), author. **Lewis (Lew) Wallace** (Brookville, 1827-1905), soldier/diplomat/author. **Wendell L. Willkie** (Elwood, 1892-1944), industrialist/political leader. **Wilbur Wright** (Millville, 1867-1912), inventor/aviator.

GENERAL

Admitted to statehood: December 11, 1816
Origin of name: From the Latin for "land of the Indians"
Capital: Indianapolis
Nickname: Hoosier State
Motto: The crossroads of America
Bird: Cardinal
Flower: Peony
Stone: Limestone
Song: "On the Banks of the Wabash, Far Away"
Tree: Tulip poplar

THE LAND

Area: 36,420 sq. mi., 38th
   Land: 35,870 sq. mi., 38th
   Water: 550 sq. mi., 38th
      Inland water: 315 sq. mi., 42nd
      Great Lakes: 235 sq. mi., 8th
Topography: Hilly southern region; fertile rolling plains of central region; flat, heavily glaciated N; dunes along Lake Michigan shore
Number of counties: 92

Geographic center: Boone, 14 mi. NNW of Indianapolis
Length: 270 mi.; width: 140 mi.
Highest point: 1,257 ft. (Franklin Township), 44th
Lowest point: 320 ft. (Ohio River), 35th
Mean elevation: 700 ft., 34th

CLIMATE AND ENVIRONMENT

Temp., highest: 116 deg. on July 14, 1936, at Collegeville; lowest: –36 deg. on Jan. 19, 1994, at New Whiteland
Monthly average: highest: 88.8 deg., 21st; lowest: 15.8 deg., 21st; spread (high to low): 73.0 deg., 19th
Hazardous waste sites (1997): 28, 12th
Endangered species: Animals: 19—Gray bat, Indiana bat, Karner blue butterfly, Mitchell's satyr butterfly, Clubshell, American peregrine falcon, Fanshell, Ring pink mussel, Cracking pearlymussel, Orange-foot pimple back pearlymussel, Pink mucket pearlymussel, Tubercled-blossom pearlymussel, White cat's paw pearlymussel, White wartyback pearlymussel, Rough pigtoe, Piping plover, Fat pocketbook, Northern riffleshell, Least tern. Plants: 1

MAJOR CITIES
POPULATION, 1996
PERCENTAGE INCREASE, 1990-96

Indianapolis, 746,737; 2.1%
Fort Wayne, 184,783; –3.7%
Evansville, 123,456; –2.2%
Gary, 110,975; –4.9%
South Bend, 102,100; –3.2%

THE PEOPLE

Population (1997): 5,864,108, 14th
   Percent change (1990-97): 5.77%, 28th
   Percent of total U.S. pop.: 2.19%, 14th
   Per sq. mi: 161.01, 14th
Population (2000 proj.): 6,052,500, 14th
   Percent change (1995-2000): 4.30%, 29th
Percent in metro. area (1996): 71.69%, 24th
Foreign born: 94,000, 25th
   Percent: 1.7%, 37th
Top three ancestries reported:
   German, 37.61%
   Irish, 17.41%
   English, 13.83%
White (1992): 5,153,000, 91.07%, 21st
Black (1992): 450,000, 7.95%, 23rd

Native American (1992): 13,000, 0.23%, 38th

Asian, Pacific Isle (1992): 42,000, 0.74%, 38th

Hispanic origin (1992): 106,000, 1.87%, 32nd

Percent over 5 yrs. speaking language other than English at home: 4.8%, 39th

Percent males (1996): 48.73%, 29th; percent females: 51.27%, 21st

Percent never married: 24.3%, 35th

Marriages per 1,000 (1996): 8.42, 23rd

Divorces per 1,000 (1996): NA

Median age (1996): 34.8

Under 5 years (1996): 7.07%, 20th

18 years and under (1996): 28.59%, 27th

65 years and over (1996): 12.58%, 28th

Percent increase among the elderly (1995-96): 0.54%, 32nd

OF VITAL IMPORTANCE

Live births per 1,000 pop. (1996): 14.3, 22nd

Infant mortality rate per 1,000 live births (1995): 8.4, 14th
  Rate for whites: 7.3, 6th
  Rate for blacks: 17.5, 9th

Births to unmarried women, % of total (1996): 32.6%, 21st

Births to teenage mothers, % of total (1996): 14.5%, 16th

Abortions (1992): 15,840, 24th
  Rate per 1,000 women 14-44 years old: 12.0, 42nd
  Percent change (1988-92): 01%, 12th

Average lifetime (1989-91): 75.39, 27th

Total death rate per 100,000 pop. (1995): 918.2, 22nd
  Accidents and adverse effects: 38.0, 25th
  Alzheimer's disease: 9.4, 16th
  Cancer: 216.3, 18th
  Cerebrovascular diseases: 68.9, 16th
  Chronic liver disease and cirrhosis: 6.9, 42nd
  Chronic obstructive pulmonary diseases and allied conditions: 41.3, 24th
  Diabetes mellitus: 24.8, 15th
  Diseases of heart: 294.3, 24th
  HIV infection: 6.7, 34th
  Homicide: 7.8, 23rd
  Injury by firearms: 14.3, 26th
  Motor vehicle accidents: 17.1, 28th
  Pneumonia and influenza: 31.6, 26th
  Suicide: 12.0, 28th

KEEPING WELL

Active nonfederal physicians per 100,000 pop. (1995): 180, 41st

Dentists per 100,000 (1991): 48, 35th

Nurses per 100,000 (1995): 866, 21st

Hospitals per 100,000 (1995): 1.98, 30th
  Admissions per 1,000 (1995): 120.45, 20th
  Hospital beds per 1,000 (1995): 3.34, 26th
  Occupancy rate per 100 beds (1995): 58.25, 36th
  Average cost per patient per day (1995): $963, 22nd
  Average cost per stay (1995): $5,610, 34th

AIDS cases (new, 1996): 596; per 100,000: 10.2, 33rd

Persons living with HIV infection, not yet AIDS (1996): 2,720

Other notifiable diseases, per 100,000 pop.:
  Gonorrhea (1995): 153.0, 18th
  Syphilis (1995): 15.2, 22nd
  Tuberculosis (1996): 3.5, 33rd

Pop. without health insur. (1996): 10.6%, 42nd

HOUSEHOLDS BY TYPE

Total households (1996): 2,209,000, 14th
  Percent change (1990-96): 6.9%, 27th
  Per 1,000 pop. (1996) 378.19, 30th
  Percent of householders 65 yrs. and over (1996): 21.37%, 30th
  Persons per household (1996): 2.57, 26th

Family households: 1,480,351
  Percent of total: 71.68%, 16th

Nonfamily households: 585,004
  Percent of total: 28.32%, 36th

Pop. living in group quarters: 161,992
  Percent of pop.: 2.92%, 22nd

LIVING QUARTERS

Total housing units: 2,246,046
  Persons per unit: 2.47, 12th

Occupied housing units: 2,065,355
  Percent of total: 91.96%, 9th
  Persons per unit: 2.52, 28th
  Percent of units with over 1 person per room: 2.20%, 40th

Owner-occupied units: 1,450,898
  Percent of total units: 64.60%, 3rd
  Percent of occupied units: 70.25%, 8th
  Persons per unit: 2.73, 26th
  Median value: $53,900, 40th

Renter-occupied units: 614,457
  Percent of total units: 27.36%, 37th
  Percent of occupied units: 29.75%, 44th

Persons per unit: 2.30, 32nd
Median contract rent: $291, 32nd
Rental vacancy rate: 8.3%, 26th
Mobile home, trailer & other as a percent of occupied housing units: 8.53%, 30th
Persons in emergency shelters for homeless persons: 2,251, 0.041%, 33rd
Persons visible in street locations: 268, 0.0048%, 29th
Nursing home population: 50,845, 0.92%, 16th

CRIME INDEX PER 100,000 (1996)

Total reported: 4,498.2, 29th
Percent increase: −2.9%, 28th
Violent: 537.0, 23rd
Percent increase: 2.3%, 5th
Murder & nonnegligent manslaughter: 7.2, 23rd
Forcible rape: 34.1, 26th
Aggravated assault: 371.6, 21st
Robbery: 124.1, 27th
Property: 3,961.2, 34th
Percent increase: −3.5%, 29th
Burglary: 783.8, 33rd
Larceny-theft: 2,752.6, 34th
Motor vehicle theft: 424.9, 28th

TEACHING AND LEARNING

Pop. 3 and over enrolled in school (1996): 1,274,225, 14th
Percent of pop.: 21.82%, 37th
Public elementary & secondary schools (1996-97): 1,924, 15th
Total enrollment (1996): 984,610, 13th
Percent of school age pop.: 90.41%, 33rd
Percent of total pop.: 16.86%, 31st
Teachers (1996): 56,412, 15th
Percent of pop.: 0.97%, 37th
Pupil/teacher ratio (1995): 17.5, 13th
Teachers' avg. salary (1996-97): $38,575, 17th
Expenditure per capita (1992-93): $1,308.98, 26th
Education as % of state govt. expenditures: 37.5%, 14th
Expenditure per pupil (1994-95): $5,826, 25th
Percent increase (1993-94 & 1994-95): 3.48%, 31st
Percent at or above grade level, NAEP tests:
Reading, grade 4 (1994): 33%, 10th

Math, grade 4 (1996): 72%, 7th
Math, grade 8 (1996): 68%, 11th
Percent of graduates taking SAT (1995): 58%, 15th
Mean SAT verbal scores: 415, 46th
Mean SAT mathematical scores: 467, 45th
Percent of graduates taking ACT (1997): 19%, 31st
Mean ACT scores: 21.2, 27th
Percent of pop. over 25 completing:
Less than 9th grade: 8.5%, 33rd
High school: 75.6%, 31st
College degree(s): 15.6%, 46th
Higher education, institutions (1996): 78, 16th
Enrollment (1995-96): 289,615, 16th
Percent increase in enroll. (1990-95): 1.7%, 31st
White non-Hispanic (1995): 250,483, 13th
Percent of enroll.: 86.49%, 16th
Total minority enroll. (1995): 30,578, 28th
Percent of enroll.: 10.56%, 37th
Black non-Hispanic (1995): 17,980, 22nd
Percent of enroll.: 6.21%, 26th
Hispanic (1995): 6,277, 19th
Percent of enroll.: 2.17%, 26th
Asian/Pacific Islander (1995): 5,233, 24th
Percent of enroll.: 1.81%, 36th
American Indian/AK native (1995): 1,088, 29th
Percent of enroll.: 0.38%, 36th
Nonresident alien (1995): 8,554, 13th
Percent of enroll.: 2.95%, 19th
Female (1995): 157,376, 17th
Percent of enroll.: 54.34%, 45th
Pub. institutions (1995-96): 28, 25th
Enrollment: 224,795, 16th
Percent increase in enrollment (1990-95): 0.4%, 35th
Percent of enroll.: 77.62%, 36th
Private institutions (1995-96): 50, 12th
Enrollment: 64,820, 14th
Percent increase in enrollment (1990-95): 6.5%, 23rd
Percent of enroll.: 22.38%, 16th
Tuition (in state), public 4-year institution (1996-97): $3,200, 20th
Tuition (in state), public 2-year institution (1996-97): $2,331, 7th
Tuition, private 4-year institution (1996-97): $13,268, 16th
Public library systems (1994): 238, 13th
Books & serial vol. per capita: 3.7, 14th
Library visits per capita: 5.7, 2nd
Circulation per capita: 9.6, 3rd

LAW ENFORCEMENT AND CORRECTIONS

Police protection and corrections expenditures (1996): $523,285,000
 Per capita: $89.59, 38th
Police per 10,000 pop. (1996): 17.35, 43rd
Prisoners (1 year or more) per 100,000 pop. (1996): 287, 33rd
 Percent change (1995-96): 4.7%, 31st
 Percent of inmates that are female: 5.9%, 31st
 Percent change: 13.0%, 19th
Death penalty: yes, by lethal injection
 Under sentence (Jan. 1998): 46, 18th
 Executed, 1976-97: 5, 16th
 Executed in 1997: 1, 9th

RELIGION, NUMBER AND PERCENT OF POPULATION

Agnostic: 12,265—0.30%, 37th
Buddhist: 4,088—0.10%, 17th
Christian: 3,577,171—87.50%, 21st
Hindu: NA
Jewish: 12,265—0.30%, 35th
Muslim: 4,089—0.10%, 22nd
Unitarian: 4,088—0.10%, 31st
Other: 77,676—1.90%, 12th
None: 302,526—7.40%, 17th
Refused to answer: 94,029—2.30%, 21st

MAKING A LIVING

Personal income per capita (1996): $22,440, 30th
 Percent increase (1995-96): 3.1%, 26th
Disposable personal income per capita (1996): $19,433, 31st
Median income of households (average, 1995-96): $34,759, 26th
Percent of pop. below poverty level (1995-96): 8.6%, 47th

ECONOMY

In civilian labor force (1996): 3,072,000
 Percent of total pop.: 69.2%, 18th
 Percent of total pop. 65 years and over: 11.0%, 33rd
 Percent of total female pop.: 61.9%, 20th
Major employer industries (total nonagricultural, 1996):
 Construction: 132,100—4.7%, 21st
 Finance, insurance, & real estate: 134,800—4.8%, 32nd
 Government: 393,700—14.0%, 46th

Manufacturing: 673,700—24.0%, 1st
Service: 652,900—23.2%, 45th
Trade: 680,000—24.2%, 19th
Transportation, communications, public utilities: 139,400—5.0%, 26th
Unemployment rate (1996): 4.1%, 43rd
 Male: 3.9%, 43rd
 Female: 4.4%, 41st
Total businesses (1995): 141,253, 15th
New business incorps. (1995): 12,451
 Percent of total businesses: 8.81%, 26th
Business failures (1995): 798
 Failures per 10,000 businesses: 56.5, 42nd
Agriculture farm income:
 Marketing (1996): $5,558,099,000, 14th
 Average per farm: $91,116, 25th
 Leading products (1997): Corn, soybeans, hogs, cattle, wheat, greenhouse, vegetables, popcorn, fruit, hay, tobacco, mint
 Average value land & build. per acre (1997): $1,970, 15th
 Percent increase (1996-97): 9%, 5th
 Govt. payments (1996): $213,703,000, 14th
 Average per farm: $3,503, 19th
Construction, value of all (1996): $8,931,472,000, 13th
 Per capita: $1,529, 13th
Manufactures (1995):
 Value added: $60,991,800,000
 Per capita: $10,510, 1st
 Leading products (1997): Primary metals, transportation equipment, motor vehicles and equipment, industrial machinery equipment, electric and electronic equipment
Value of nonfuel mineral production (1996): $617,000,000, 21st
Leading mineral products (1996): Coal, petroleum, stone, cement, sand/gravel, lime
Energy consumption per person (1994): 439.3 mil. Btu, 10th
Retail sales (1995): $53,056,000,000
 Per household: $24,264, 32nd
 Sales increase (1994-95): 7.3%, 12th
Tourism revenues (1993): $4.4 bil.
Foreign exports, in total value (1996): $10,984,000,000, 15th
 Per capita: $1,881, 17th
Gross state product per person (1994): $24,024, 32nd

Public aid recipients (percent of resident pop. 1994): 5.2%, 38th

Medicaid recipients (percent of pop., 1995): 9.6%, 43rd

Medicare enrollment per 1,000 pop. (1996): 70, 49th

TRAVEL AND TRANSPORTATION

Motor vehicle registrations (1996): 5,215,572, 13th
Per 1,000 pop.: 894.90, 12th

Motorcycle registrations (1996): 96,518, 13th
Per 1,000 pop.: 18.51, 31st

Licensed drivers (1996): 3,706,182, 16th
Per 1,000 pop.: 639.33, 42nd

Public roads & streets (1996)
Total mileage: 92,970, 18th
Per 1,000 pop.: 115.92, 28th
Rural mileage: 73,326, 18th
Per 1,000 pop.: 12.55, 28th
Urban mileage: 19,644, 14th
Per 1,000 pop.: 3.36, 13th
Interstate mileage: 1,172, 12th
Per 1,000 pop.: 0.20, 26th

Speed limit (max. interstate, autos, mi. per hr., 1997): 65

Annual vehicle-mi. of travel per driver (1996): 17,877, 5th

Mean travel time for workers age 16+ who work away from home: 20.4 min., 29th

GOVERNMENT

Percent of voting age pop. registered (1996): 79.75%, 21st
Percent of voting age pop. voting for president: (1996): 48.9%, 31st
Percent of voting age pop. voting for U.S. representatives (1996): 47.7%, 26th

State legislators, total (1997): 150, 19th
Women members (1997): 28
Percent of legislature: 19%, 29th

U.S. Congress, House members (1998): 10
Change (1988-98): 0

Revenues (1996):
State govt.: $16,549,937,000
Per capita: $2,833.41, 48th
Parimutuel & amusement taxes & lotteries, revenue per capita (1995): $97.62, 23rd

Expenditures (1996):
State govt.: $15,367,687,000
Per capita: $2,631.00, 46th

Debt outstanding (1996): $6,116,873,000
Per capita: $1,047.23, 36th

LAWS AND REGULATIONS

Legal driving age: 18, 16 if completed driver education course

Marriage age without parental consent: 18

Divorce residence requirement: 6 mo., for qualifications check local statutes

ATTRACTIONS (1997)

Major opera companies: 1

Major symphony orchestras: 2

Major dance companies: 1

Per capita spending by the NEA (1997): $0.10, 49th

State Fair in mid-August at Indianapolis

SPORTS AND COMPETITION

NCAA (Division I) football and basketball teams: Ball State Univ. Cardinals, Butler Univ. Bulldogs, Indiana State Univ. Sycamores, Indiana Univ.-Bloomington Hoosiers, Purdue Univ. Boilermakers, Univ. of Evansville Aces, Univ. of Notre Dame Fighting Irish, Valparaiso Univ. Crusaders

NBA basketball teams: Indiana Pacers, Market Square Arena

NFL football teams: Indianapolis Colts (AFC), RCA Dome

WEBSITES CONTAINING FURTHER INFORMATION

Access Indiana Information Network   http://www.state.in.us

IOWA

> "The people who have lived on the land between the two great rivers have fought, struggled, labored, laughed, and grown in wealth and culture through the years. No other similar area has produced so much to feed the world—Iowa, an often neglected treasure!"
>
> Allan Carpenter, native of Waterloo, Iowa

Many think of Iowa as a land of huge farms and small cities populated by people right out of Meredith Willson's *The Music Man*. True, it is one of the greatest farming states in the country, producing about one-fifth of the nation's corn supply and containing about a quarter of the country's richest farmlands. But it is also a leader in manufacturing cereals, tractors, and washing machines. Iowa also has one of the finest writing programs in the country (at the University of Iowa), and among Iowa's notables are many authors and artists, including Grant Wood. The state capital is known as the "Hartford of the West" because of its many insurance company headquarters. The state is experiencing rapidly increasing growth in the manufacturing and service industries.

SUPERLATIVES

- Birthplace of Herbert Hoover, first U.S. president born west of the Mississippi River.
- The first state ever to produce a billion-dollar harvest from a single crop.
- Produced the first "traction machine" (tractor).
- World's largest tractor plant, at Waterloo.
- The mechanical washing machine, first manufactured in Iowa.

MOMENTS IN HISTORY

- In 1673, European explorers first glimpsed present-day Iowa as Father Jacques Marquette and Louis Jolliet marveled at the Iowa bluffs above the Mississippi River.

So They Say

"The Indians treated the exploring party [Marquette and Jolliet] with great respect, preparing a huge feast of dog meat and other delicacies. The hosts, as a sign of honor, insisted on placing the food in the mouths of the guests, much to the visitors' discomfort."

The Palimpsest (historical magazine)

- The French claimed the region, and explorer Joseph Des Noyelles fought a little-known battle with the Fox and Sauk Indians in 1735, at the junction of the Raccoon and Des Moines rivers.
- In 1762, France turned over to Spain its claims west of the Mississippi, including Iowa.
- In 1788, Julian Dubuque settled at Catfish Creek on the Mississippi, founding the community of Dubuque, where he mined the plentiful lead of the region.
- In 1800, Spain secretly returned the Louisiana Territory to France. The Louisiana Purchase of 1803 brought Iowa to the United States.
- In 1819 the first steamer, the *Western Engineer*, reached the area of Council Bluffs on the Missouri River.
- On December 28, 1846, Iowa became the first free state in the old Louisiana Territory.
- Progress continued rapidly with the first state fair, at Fairfield in 1854, at the University of Iowa at Iowa City in 1855, and at the new capital at Des Moines in 1856.
- In 1856 the bridge between Davenport and Rock Island was the first to span the mighty Mississippi River.
- Notorious abolitionist John Brown headquartered for a time at Tabor as he helped slaves escape to freedom over the Underground Railroad.
- In 1869, Council Bluffs became the eastern terminus of the Central Pacific Railroad.
- In 1889, Grinnell College and the University of Iowa played the first intercollegiate football game west of the Mississippi.
- In the 1890s, Independence became famous as a center for trotting races.
- The 1980s brought increasing problems to Iowa farmers, with rising costs, falling prices and values, and overextended debt, but the 1990s brought an upturn.
- In 1994, Representative Fred Grandy (remembered for his role as "Gopher" on the television show *The Loveboat*) failed in his bid for the Iowa governorship.

- On November 19, 1997, a 29-year-old seamstress from Carlisle, Bobbi McCaughey, gave birth to septuplets, the first time in the United States that so many infants in a multiple birth were born alive.

THAT'S INTERESTING

- The honey trees of a region disputed between Iowa and Missouri were so prized that the two states almost came to blows in a territorial dispute called the Honey War.
- Iowa's Civil War Greybeard Regiment, made up of men over the legal age of 45, was the only one of its kind ever authorized.
- James "Tama Jim" Wilson of Traer holds the all-time record for service in any cabinet office—16 years as secretary of agriculture.
- Early European visitors to Iowa thought the land was worthless, but over the years the incredible richness of the soil probably has provided the richest treasure of any state. Iowa possesses one-fourth of all the grade A land in the United States, and from this treasure comes a far greater production of food than from any similar region in the world.

NOTABLE NATIVES

Adrian Constantine (Cap) Anson (Marshalltown, 1851-1922), baseball player/manager. William Frederick (Buffalo Bill) Cody (Scott County, 1846-1917), frontiersman/showman. Robert William Andrew Feller (Van Meter, 1918-   ), baseball player. George Horace Gallup (Jefferson, 1901-1984), statistician/public opinion analyst. James Norman Hall (Colfax, 1887-1951), author. Herbert Clark Hoover (West Branch, 1874-1964), U.S. president. MacKinlay Kantor (Webster City, 1904-1977), author. Glenn Miller (Clarinda, 1904-1944), bandleader. Lillian Russell (Clinton, 1861-1922), singer/actress. William Ashley (Billy) Sunday (Ames, 1862-1935), evangelist. James Alfred Van Allen (Mount Pleasant, 1914-   ), astrophysicist. Henry Agard Wallace (Adair County, 1888-1965), U.S. vice president. John Wayne (Winterset, 1907-1979), actor. Margaret Wilson (Traer, 1882-1976), author. Grant Wood (near Anamosa, 1892-1942), artist.

GENERAL

Admitted to statehood: December 28, 1846
Origin of name: Indian word variously translated as "one who puts to sleep" or "beautiful land"

Capital: Des Moines
Nickname: Hawkeye State
Motto: Our liberties we prize and our rights we will maintain
Bird: Eastern goldfinch
Flower: Wild rose
Stone: Geode
Song: "Song of Iowa"
Tree: Oak

THE LAND

Area: 56,276 sq. mi., 26th
    Land: 55,875 sq. mi., 23rd
    Water: 401 sq. mi., 42nd
    Inland water: 401 sq. mi., 36th
Topography: Watershed from NW to SE; soil especially rich and land level in the N central counties
Number of counties: 99
Geographic center: Story, 5 mi. NE of Ames
Length: 310 mi.; width: 200 mi.
Highest point: 1,670 ft. (Sec. 29, T100N, R41W, Osceola County), 42nd
Lowest point: 480 ft. (Mississippi River), 38th
Mean elevation: 1,100 ft., 22nd

CLIMATE AND ENVIRONMENT

Temp., highest: 118 deg. on July 20, 1934, at Keokuk; lowest: −47 deg. on Jan. 12, 1912, at Washta, and on Feb. 3, 1996, at Elkader
Monthly average: highest: 86.2 deg., 32nd; lowest: 6.3 deg., 6th; spread (high to low): 79.9 deg., 7th
Hazardous waste sites (1997): 16, 21st
Endangered species: Animals: 6—Indiana bat, American peregrine falcon, Higgins' eye pearlymussel, Iowa pleistocene snail, Pallid sturgeon, Least tern. Plants: 0

MAJOR CITIES
POPULATION, 1996
PERCENTAGE INCREASE, 1990-96

Des Moines, 193,422; 0.1%
Cedar Rapids, 113,482; 4.3%
Davenport, 97,010; 1.8%
Sioux City, 83,791; 4.1%
Waterloo, 65,022; −2.2%

THE PEOPLE

Population (1997): 2,852,423, 30th
    Percent change (1990-97): 2.72%, 42nd
    Percent of total U.S. pop.: 1.07%, 30th
    Per sq. mi: 50.69, 34th

Population (2000 proj.): 2,895,500, 30th
  Percent change (1995-2000): 1.88%, 42nd
Percent in metro. area (1996): 44.33%, 41st
Foreign born: 43,000, 36th
  Percent: 1.6%, 41st
Top three ancestries reported:
  German, 50.23%
  Irish, 18.98%
  English, 14.01%
White (1992): 2,714,000, 96.82%, 5th
Black (1992): 52,000, 1.86%, 41st
Native American (1992): 8,000, 0.29%, 34th
Asian, Pacific Isle (1992): 29,000, 1.03%, 31st
Hispanic origin (1992): 37,000, 1.32%, 37th
Percent over 5 yrs. speaking language other than English at home: 3.9%, 42nd
Percent males (1996): 48.73%, 29th; percent females: 51.27%, 21st
Percent never married: 23.7%, 39th
Marriages per 1,000 (1996): 8.36, 25th
Divorces per 1,000 (1996): 3.47, 34th
Median age (1996): 36.1
Under 5 years (1996): 6.40%, 44th
18 years and under (1996): 28.21%, 31st
65 years and over (1996): 15.17%, 5th
Percent increase among the elderly (1995-96): −0.09%, 50th

OF VITAL IMPORTANCE

Live births per 1,000 pop. (1996): 13.0, 42nd
Infant mortality rate per 1,000 live births (1995): 8.2, 17th
  Rate for whites: 7.8, 3rd
  Rate for blacks: 21.2, 1st
Births to unmarried women, % of total (1996): 26.3%, 43rd
Births to teenage mothers, % of total (1996): 11.0%, 34th
Abortions (1992): 6,970, 37th
  Rate per 1,000 women 14-44 years old: 11.4, 44th
  Percent change (1988-92): −22%, 47th
Average lifetime (1989-91): 77.29, 5th
Total death rate per 100,000 pop. (1995): 986.0, 10th
  Accidents and adverse effects: 41.1, 18th
  Alzheimer's disease: 11.8, 5th
  Cancer: 219.1, 16th
  Cerebrovascular diseases: 77.5, 4th
  Chronic liver disease and cirrhosis: 5.4, 50th
  Chronic obstructive pulmonary diseases and allied conditions: 48.3, 7th

Diabetes mellitus: 22.4, 29th
Diseases of heart: 332.0, 10th
HIV infection: 3.1, 47th
Homicide: 2.3, 45th
Injury by firearms: 7.7, 47th
Motor vehicle accidents: 19.2, 21st
Pneumonia and influenza: 42.8, 2nd
Suicide: 11.8, 33rd

KEEPING WELL

Active nonfederal physicians per 100,000 pop. (1995): 166, 43rd
Dentists per 100,000 (1991): 54, 24th
Nurses per 100,000 (1995): 784, 34th
Hospitals per 100,000 (1995): 4.08, 7th
  Admissions per 1,000 (1995): 127.02, 15th
  Hospital beds per 1,000 (1995): 4.43, 7th
  Occupancy rate per 100 beds (1995): 56.35, 43rd
  Average cost per patient per day (1995): $702, 45th
  Average cost per stay (1995): $5,049, 44th
AIDS cases (new, 1996): 112; per 100,000: 3.9, 46th
Persons living with HIV infection (1996): NA
Other notifiable diseases, per 100,000 pop.:
  Gonorrhea (1995): 60.6, 35th
  Syphilis (1995): 6.0, 33rd
  Tuberculosis (1996): 2.5, 42nd
Pop. without health insur. (1996): 11.6%, 34th

HOUSEHOLDS BY TYPE

Total households (1996): 1,103,000, 30th
  Percent change (1990-96): 3.6%, 42nd
  Per 1,000 pop. (1996) 386.75, 8th
  Percent of householders 65 yrs. and over (1996): 24.93%, 5th
  Persons per household (1996): 2.51, 41st
Family households: 740,819
  Percent of total: 69.60%, 35th
Nonfamily households: 323,506
  Percent of total: 30.40%, 18th
Pop. living in group quarters: 99,520
  Percent of pop.: 3.58%, 7th

LIVING QUARTERS

Total housing units: 1,143,669
  Persons per unit: 2.43, 19th
Occupied housing units: 1,064,325
  Percent of total units: 93.06%, 4th
  Persons per unit: 2.44, 48th
  Percent of units with over 1 person per room: 1.50%, 51st

Owner-occupied units: 745,377
  Percent of total units: 65.17%, 2nd
  Percent of occupied units: 70.03%, 11th
  Persons per unit: 2.63, 44th
  Median value: $15,900, 51st
Renter-occupied units: 318,948
  Percent of total units: 27.89%, 31st
  Percent of occupied units: 29.97%, 41st
  Persons per unit: 2.25, 39th
  Median contract rent: $216, 50th
  Rental vacancy rate: 6.4%, 45th
Mobile home, trailer & other as a percent of
  occupied housing units: 6.43%, 41st
Persons in emergency shelters for homeless
  persons: 989, 0.036%, 43rd
Persons visible in street locations: 148,
  0.0053%, 27th
Nursing home population: 36,455, 1.31%, 2nd

CRIME INDEX PER 100,000 (1996)

Total reported: 3,648.9, 43rd
  Percent increase: −11.0%, 48th
  Violent: 272.5, 41st
    Percent increase: −23.1%, 51st
    Murder & nonnegligent manslaughter:
      1.9, 48th
    Forcible rape: 19.7, 50th
    Aggravated assault: 205.9, 37th
    Robbery: 45.1, 42nd
  Property: 3,376.4, 42nd
    Percent increase: −9.9%, 47th
    Burglary: 664.6, 41st
    Larceny-theft: 2,520.8, 38th
    Motor vehicle theft: 191.1, 43rd

TEACHING AND LEARNING

Pop. 3 and over enrolled in school (1996):
  678,346, 30th
  Percent of pop.: 23.78%, 17th
Public elementary & secondary schools (1996-
  97): 1,556, 21st
  Total enrollment (1996): 504,511, 30th
    Percent of school age pop.: 93.95%, 16th
    Percent of total pop.: 17.69%, 18th
  Teachers (1996): 32,549, 29th
    Percent of pop.: 1.14%, 14th
  Pupil/teacher ratio (1995): 15.5, 36th
  Teachers' avg. salary (1996-97): $33,275,
    34th
  Expenditure per capita (1992-93): $1,448.41,
    14th
    Education as % of state govt. expendi-
      tures: 37.8%, 11th

Expenditure per pupil (1994-95): $5,483,
  29th
  Percent increase (1993-94 & 1994-95):
    3.69%, 28th
Percent at or above grade level, NAEP tests:
  Reading, grade 4 (1994): 35%, 6th
  Math, grade 4 (1996): 74%, 5th
  Math, grade 8 (1996): 78%, 1st
Percent of graduates taking SAT (1995): 5%,
  47th
  Mean SAT verbal scores: 516, 1st
  Mean SAT mathematical scores: 583, 2nd
Percent of graduates taking ACT (1997):
  64%, 15th
  Mean ACT scores: 22.1, 5th
Percent of pop. over 25 completing:
  Less than 9th grade: 9.2%, 28th
  High school: 80.1%, 14th
  College degree(s): 16.9%, 41st
Higher education, institutions (1996): 59,
  22nd
  Enrollment (1995-96): 173,835, 29th
    Percent increase in enroll. (1990-95):
      1.9%, 30th
  White non-Hispanic (1995): 154,375, 25th
    Percent of enroll.: 88.81%, 11th
  Total minority enroll. (1995): 12,419, 37th
    Percent of enroll.: 7.14%, 45th
  Black non-Hispanic (1995): 4,878, 34th
    Percent of enroll.: 2.81%, 39th
  Hispanic (1995): 2,792, 31st
    Percent of enroll.: 1.61%, 33rd
  Asian/Pacific Islander (1995): 4,034, 29th
    Percent of enroll.: 2.32%, 25th
  American Indian/AK native (1995): 715,
    39th
    Percent of enroll.: 0.41%, 31st
  Nonresident alien (1995): 7,041, 20th
    Percent of enroll.: 4.05%, 7th
  Female (1995): 95,804, 29th
    Percent of enroll.: 55.11%, 39th
  Pub. institutions (1995-96): 20, 32nd
    Enrollment: 122,396, 30th
      Percent increase in enrollment (1990-
        95): 3.9%, 24th
      Percent of enroll.: 70.41%, 41st
  Private institutions (1995-96): 39, 17th
    Enrollment: 51,439, 21st
      Percent increase in enrollment (1990-
        95): -2.4%, 44th
      Percent of enroll.: 29.59%, 11th
Tuition (in state), public 4-year institution
  (1996-97): $2,655, 25th
Tuition (in state), public 2-year institution
  (1996-97): $1,840, 15th

Tuition, private 4-year institution (1996-97): $12,394, 21st

Public library systems (1994): 518, 3rd
　Books & serial vol. per capita: 3.9, 11th
　Library visits per capita: 5.2, 6th
　Circulation per capita: 8.9, 8th

LAW ENFORCEMENT AND CORRECTIONS

Police protection and corrections expenditures (1996): $245,084,000
　Per capita: $85.94, 42nd
Police per 10,000 pop. (1996): 16.51, 45th
Prisoners (1 year or more) per 100,000 pop. (1996): 222, 42nd
　Percent change (1995-96): 7.4%, 19th
　Percent of inmates that are female: 7.4%, 6th
　　Percent change: 10.6%, 23rd
Death penalty: no

RELIGION, NUMBER AND PERCENT OF POPULATION

Agnostic: 22,637—1.10%, 6th
Buddhist: NA
Christian: 1,837,682—89.30%, 15th
Hindu: 2,058—0.10%, 10th
Jewish: NA
Muslim: NA
Unitarian: 2,058—0.10%, 31st
Other: 41,158—2.00%, 10th
None: 121,415—5.90%, 34th
Refused to answer: 30,868—1.50%, 42nd

MAKING A LIVING

Personal income per capita (1996): $22,560, 29th
　Percent increase (1995-96): 6.0%, 5th
Disposable personal income per capita (1996): $19,723, 27th
Median income of households (average, 1995-96): $34,888, 24th
Percent of pop. below poverty level (1995-96): 10.9%, 35th

ECONOMY

In civilian labor force (1996): 1,599,000
　Percent of total pop.: 73.6%, 5th
　Percent of total pop. 65 years and over: 16.4%, 4th
　Percent of total female pop.: 68.1%, 4th
Major employer industries (total nonagricultural, 1996):
　Construction: 58,500—4.2%, 34th

Finance, insurance, & real estate: 77,600—5.6%, 20th
Government: 231,600—16.8%, 27th
Manufacturing: 247,400—17.9%, 14th
Service: 359,100—26.0%, 36th
Trade: 341,100—24.7%, 12th
Transportation, communications, public utilities: 62,900—4.6%, 38th
Unemployment rate (1996): 3.8%, 46th
　Male: 3.5%, 47th
　Female: 4.1%, 43rd
Total businesses (1995): 78,464, 30th
New business incorps. (1995): 5,925
　Percent of total businesses: 7.55%, 40th
Business failures (1995): 573
　Failures per 10,000 businesses: 73.0, 32nd
Agriculture farm income:
　Marketing (1996): $12,852,687,000, 3rd
　　Average per farm: $131,150, 12th
　Leading products (1997): Hogs, corn, cattle, soybeans, oats, hay
　Average value land & build. per acre (1997): $1,570, 18th
　　Percent increase (1996-97): 9%, 5th
　Govt. payments (1996): $501,694,000, 3rd
　　Average per farm: $5,119.00, 11th
Construction, value of all (1996): $2,795,137,000, 35th
　Per capita: $980, 44th
Manufactures (1995):
　Value added: $26,215,200,000
　　Per capita: $9,225, 5th
　Leading products (1997): Processed food products, tires, farm machinery, electronic products, appliances, household furniture, chemicals, fertilizers, auto accessories
Value of nonfuel mineral production (1996): $486,000,000, 28th
Leading mineral products (1996): Stone, cement, sand/gravel, gypsum, lime
Energy consumption per person (1994): 365.5 mil. Btu, 21st
Retail sales (1995): $26,968,000,000
　Per household: $24,536, 28th
　Sales increase (1994-95): 5.6%, 23rd
Tourism revenues (1995): $2.3 bil.
Foreign exports, in total value (1996): $4,400,000,000, 29th
　Per capita: $1,543, 25th
Gross state product per person (1994): $24,140, 30th
Public aid recipients (percent of resident pop. 1994): 5.4%, 36th

Medicaid recipients (percent of pop., 1995): 10.7%, 33rd

Medicare enrollment per 1,000 pop. (1996): 81, 48th

TRAVEL AND TRANSPORTATION

Motor vehicle registrations (1996): 2,869,445, 26th

Per 1,000 pop.: 1,007.52, 5th

Motorcycle registrations (1996): 131,851, 10th

Per 1,000 pop.: 45.95, 2nd

Licensed drivers (1996): 1,905,450, 30th

Per 1,000 pop.: 670.21, 35th

Public roads & streets (1996)

Total mileage: 112,708, 11th

Per 1,000 pop.: 139.52, 8th

Rural mileage: 103,359, 5th

Per 1,000 pop.: 36.24, 8th

Urban mileage: 9,349, 31st

Per 1,000 pop.: 3.28, 17th

Interstate mileage: 781, 28th

Per 1,000 pop.: 0.27, 16th

Speed limit (max. interstate, autos, mi. per hr., 1997): 65

Annual vehicle-mi. of travel per driver (1996): 13,745, 30th

Mean travel time for workers age 16+ who work away from home: 16.2 min., 46th

GOVERNMENT

Percent of voting age pop. registered (1996): 83.09%, 12th

Percent of voting age pop. voting for president: (1996): 57.7%, 9th

Percent of voting age pop. voting for U.S. representatives (1996): 56.1%, 10th

State legislators, total (1997): 150, 19th

Women members (1997): 31

Percent of legislature: 21%, 28th

U.S. Congress, House members (1998): 5

Change (1988-98): −1

Revenues (1996):

State govt.: $9,244,859,000

Per capita: $3,241.54, 32nd

Parimutuel & amusement taxes & lotteries, revenue per capita (1995): $75.69, 30th

Expenditures (1996):

State govt.: $8,853,150,000

Per capita: $3,104.19, 26th

Debt outstanding (1996): $2,064,507,000

Per capita: $723.88, 45th

LAWS AND REGULATIONS

Legal driving age: 18, 16 if completed driver education course

Marriage age without parental consent: 18

Divorce residence requirement: 1 yr., for qualifications check local statutes

ATTRACTIONS (1997)

Major opera companies: 1

Major symphony orchestras: 2

Per capita spending by the NEA (1997): $0.21, 35th

State Fair in mid-August at Des Moines

SPORTS AND COMPETITION

NCAA (Division I) football and basketball teams: Drake Univ. Bulldogs, Iowa State Univ. Cyclones, Univ. of Iowa Hawkeyes, Univ. of Northern Iowa Panthers (basketball only)

WEBSITES CONTAINING FURTHER INFORMATION

| State of Iowa Home Page | http://www.state.ia.us |
| Iowa Virtual Tourist | http://www.jeonet.com/tourist |

KANSAS

"There is no monument under heaven on which I would rather have my name inscribed than on this goodly state of Kansas."

Henry Ward Beecher, clergyman

Kansas is known as a world breadbasket and Hutchinson as a world grain center. At the same time, the state is also famous for aviation manufacture, with Wichita a major leader in private aircraft production. Kansas's historic trails were critical in the opening of the West. Dodge City, "the cowboy capital of the world," was once the world's largest cattle-market town—a dusty, brawling crossroads that was home to Wyatt Earp, Bat Masterson, and Wild Bill Hickock. Perhaps unexpectedly, this prairie state is also a world center of psychiatric study and practice, thanks to the Menninger family of Topeka. William Allen White's pioneer leadership as a Kansas newspaper editor anticipated many features of present-day journalism.

SUPERLATIVES

• Geographic center of the 48 conterminous states—in Smith County, Kansas.
• The world's greatest salt deposits, located at Hutchinson.
• Largest primary hard wheat market in the world.
• Long a major transportation crossroads of the nation.
• World leader in the manufacture of personal aircraft.

MOMENTS IN HISTORY

• In 1541, Spanish explorer Francisco Vásquez de Coronado came overland from Mexico, reaching what is now Junction City before turning back.
• In 1719, French explorer Claude du Tisne crossed the southeastern border of present-day Kansas, but aside from a few other explorers, the region remained Indian country in the early days.
• Explorer Zebulon Pike crossed the length of Kansas in 1806. At a "grand council" with the Pawnees, he raised the U.S. flag for the first time in Kansas territory.
• In 1822, Captain William H. Becknell pioneered the Santa Fe Trail, and before long thousands of wagons used the trail, crossing 500 miles of Kansas to carry on very profitable trade with New Mexico.

• In 1824, Benton Pixley established a mission to the Osage Indians in present Neosho County, and in the years that followed, the Kansas plains were dotted with mission stations of many denominations.
• Fort Leavenworth was established in 1827.
• In 1854, Kansas was opened to settlement by the Kansas-Nebraska Act. This act permitted the residents of the territory to decide whether the territory would be free or slave, setting the stage for a frantic period when both sides came to blows over slavery, and Kansas became "Bleeding Kansas."
• The population grew, and Kansas became a free state on January 29, 1861.
• During the Civil War, Confederate raiders made many attacks on Kansas communities. The notorious raider William Clarke Quantrill raided Lawrence on August 21, 1863; he burned some 200 buildings, and killed 150 civilians there.
• In the Battle of Mine Creek on October 25, 1864, Union forces were victorious, and the threat of Confederate invasion was ended.
• In 1867 the first cattle were driven up the Chisholm Trail to Abilene, where the railroad had arrived.
• As the railroad moved west, other communities became the principal cow towns including famed Dodge City, which was established in 1872.
• In 1887, Susanna Salter was elected mayor of Argonia; she was said to be the first woman mayor in the United States.
• During World War I, thousands of Kansas acres were plowed for the first time to provide food. Later, during the drought of the 1930s, dirt from these fields was carried up into terrible dust storms.

- During 1951, Kansas experienced great floods, with damage amounting to about $2.5 billion.
- Kansas's adopted son, Dwight David Eisenhower—who grew up on a farm in Abilene—won the 1952 and 1956 presidential elections.
- In 1954 the U.S. Supreme Court struck down the segregation policies of the Topeka school system in a far-reaching decision.
- In 1987, former Governor Alf Landon celebrated his 100th birthday, but within a few weeks of the celebration Kansas lost its beloved centenarian.
- The largest remaining stretch of virgin Kansas prairie was plowed under in 1990.
- Kansas elected its first woman governor, Joan Finney, in 1991.

THAT'S INTERESTING

- The legendary lawmen of Dodge City, such as Bat Masterson and Wyatt Earp, were not always so heroic. On one occasion, Earp was said to have "amateurishly loaded all six chambers of his revolver and blasted a hole through his coat."
- Pioneering the Santa Fe Trail, the Becknell party almost died of thirst on the dry bed of the Cimarron River until they discovered by accident that the river was "flowing" beneath the sand.
- With the slaughter of the buffalo, the scattered bones became so valuable that they were collected by the tons, and Dodge City bankers and businesses accepted them as legal tender.

NOTABLE NATIVES

Gwendolyn Elizabeth Brooks (Topeka, 1917-), poet. **Walter Percy Chrysler** (Wamego, 1875-1940), automobile manufacturer. **John Steuart Curry** (Jefferson County, 1897-1946), artist. **Charles Curtis** (Topeka, 1860-1936), U.S. vice president. **Robert Joseph Dole** (Russell, 1923-). **Amelia Mary Earhart** (Atchison, 1897-1937), aviator. **William Inge** (Independence, 1913-1973), playwright. **Emmett Kelly** (Sedan, 1898-1979), clown. **Edgar Lee Masters** (Garnett, 1869-1950), poet/biographer. **Karl Menninger** (Topeka, 1893-1990), psychiatrist. **Alfred Damon Runyon** (Manhattan, 1884-1946), journalist/author. **William Allen White** (Emporia, 1868-1944), editor/writer.

GENERAL

Admitted to statehood: January 29, 1861
Origin of name: Sioux word for "south wind people"
Capital: Topeka
Nickname: Sunflower State, Jayhawk State
Motto: *Ad Astra per Aspera*—To the stars through difficulties
Animal: American buffalo
Bird: Western meadowlark
Insect: Honeybee
Flower: Wild native sunflower
Song: "Home on the Range"
Tree: Cottonwood

THE LAND

Area: 82,282 sq. mi., 15th
  Land: 81,823 sq. mi., 13th
  Water: 459 sq. mi., 40th
    Inland water: 459 sq. mi., 34th
Topography: Hilly Osage plains in the E; central region level prairie and hills; high plains in the W
Number of counties: 105
Geographic center: Barton, 15 mi. NE of Great Bend
Length: 400 mi.; width: 210 mi.
Highest point: 4,039 ft. (Mount Sunflower), 28th
Lowest point: 679 ft. (Verdigris River), 43rd
Mean elevation: 2,000 ft., 14th

CLIMATE AND ENVIRONMENT

Temp., highest: 121 deg. on July 24, 1936, near Alton; lowest: −40 deg. on Feb. 13, 1905, at Lebanon
Monthly average: highest: 92.9 deg., 9th; lowest: 15.7 deg., 20th; spread (high to low): 77.2 deg., 12th
Hazardous waste sites (1997): 10, 34th
Endangered species: Animals: 9—Gray bat, Indiana bat, Whooping crane, Eskimo curlew, American peregrine falcon, Black-footed ferret, Pallid sturgeon, Least tern, Black-capped vireo. Plants: 0

MAJOR CITIES
POPULATION, 1996
PERCENTAGE INCREASE, 1990-96

Wichita, 320,395; 5.4%
Kansas City, 142,654; −5.9%
Overland Park, 131,053; 17.2%
Topeka, 119,658; −0.2%
Olathe, 78,666; 24.1%

THE PEOPLE

Population (1997): 2,594,840, 32nd
  Percent change (1990-97): 4.73%, 36th
  Percent of total U.S. pop.: 0.97%, 32nd
  Per sq. mi: 31.54, 41st
Population (2000 proj.): 2,671,500, 32nd
  Percent change (1995-2000): 4.15%, 30th
Percent in metro. area (1996): 55.42%, 37th
Foreign born: 63,000, 30th
  Percent: 2.5%, 31st
Top three ancestries reported:
  German, 39.06%
  Irish, 17.59%
  English, 16.38%
White (1992): 2,306,000, 91.69%, 18th
Black (1992): 150,000, 5.96%, 28th
Native American (1992): 23,000, 0.91%, 18th
Asian, Pacific Isle (1992): 36,000, 1.43%, 22nd
Hispanic origin (1992): 101,000, 4.02%, 21st
Percent over 5 yrs. speaking language other than English at home: 5.7%, 33rd
Percent males (1996): 49.23%, 20th; percent females: 50.77%, 32nd
Percent never married: 22.7%, 43rd
Marriages per 1,000 (1996): 8.01, 30th
Divorces per 1,000 (1996): 4.54, 22nd
Median age (1996): 34.7
Under 5 years (1996): 7.04%, 21st
18 years and under (1996): 29.68%, 12th
65 years and over (1996): 13.68%, 16th
Percent increase among the elderly (1995-96): 0.09%, 48th

OF VITAL IMPORTANCE

Live births per 1,000 pop. (1996): 15.4, 12th
Infant mortality rate per 1,000 live births (1995): 7.0, 34th
  Rate for whites: 6.2, 26th
  Rate for blacks: 17.6, 6th
Births to unmarried women, % of total (1996): 26.9%, 41st
Births to teenage mothers, % of total (1996): 13.1%, 25th
Abortions (1992): 12,570, 29th
  Rate per 1,000 women 14-44 years old: 22.4, 22nd
  Percent change (1988-92): 11%, 4th
Average lifetime (1989-91): 76.76, 13th
Total death rate per 100,000 pop. (1995): 933.0, 17th
  Accidents and adverse effects: 38.7, 23rd

Alzheimer's disease: 9.4, 16th
Cancer: 205.9, 30th
Cerebrovascular diseases: 70.6, 12th
Chronic liver disease and cirrhosis: 6.4, 45th
Chronic obstructive pulmonary diseases and allied conditions: 44.9, 14th
Diabetes mellitus: 22.5, 27th
Diseases of heart: 297.7, 22nd
HIV infection: 5.6, 36th
Homicide: 6.3, 27th
Injury by firearms: 12.7, 30th
Motor vehicle accidents: 17.6, 25th
Pneumonia and influenza: 34.2, 15th
Suicide: 11.3, 39th

KEEPING WELL

Active nonfederal physicians per 100,000 pop. (1995): 195, 35th
Dentists per 100,000 (1991): 51, 31st
Nurses per 100,000 (1995): 814, 29th
Hospitals per 100,000 (1995): 5.15, 6th
  Admissions per 1,000 (1995): 113.45, 27th
  Hospital beds per 1,000 (1995): 4.21, 11th
  Occupancy rate per 100 beds (1995): 52.78, 49th
  Average cost per patient per day (1995): $732, 41st
  Average cost per stay (1995): $5,308, 41st
AIDS cases (new, 1996): 239; per 100,000: 9.3, 36th
Persons living with HIV infection (1996): NA
Other notifiable diseases, per 100,000 pop.:
  Gonorrhea (1995): 109.0, 24th
  Syphilis (1995): 5.9, 34th
  Tuberculosis (1996): 2.9, 36th
Pop. without health insur. (1996): 11.4%, 36th

HOUSEHOLDS BY TYPE

Total households (1996): 982,000, 31st
  Percent change (1990-96): 3.9%, 39th
  Per 1,000 pop. (1996) 381.80, 20th
  Percent of householders 65 yrs. and over (1996): 22.81%, 15th
  Persons per household (1996): 2.54, 33rd
Family households: 658,600
  Percent of total: 69.71%, 32nd
Nonfamily households: 286,126
  Percent of total: 30.29%, 20th
Pop. living in group quarters: 82,765
  Percent of pop.: 3.34%, 13th

LIVING QUARTERS

Total housing units: 1,044,112
  Persons per unit: 2.37, 32nd
  Occupied housing units: 944,726
  Percent of total units: 90.48%, 19th
  Persons per unit: 2.48, 38th
  Percent of units with over 1 person per
    room: 2.51%, 36th
Owner-occupied units: 641,762
  Percent of total units: 61.46%, 14th
  Percent of occupied units: 67.93%, 22nd
  Persons per unit: 2.64, 43rd
  Median value: $52,200, 42nd
Renter-occupied units: 302,964
  Percent of total units: 29.02%, 27th
  Percent of occupied units: 32.07%, 30th
  Persons per unit: 2.31, 30th
  Median contract rent: $285, 33rd
  Rental vacancy rate: 11.1%, 12th
Mobile home, trailer & other as a percent
  of occupied housing units: 8.30%,
  31st
Persons in emergency shelters for homeless
  persons: 940, 0.038%, 39th
Persons visible in street locations: 158,
  0.0064%, 26th
Nursing home population: 26,155, 1.06%, 7th

CRIME INDEX PER 100,000 (1996)

Total reported: 4,681.7, 27th
  Percent increase: –4.2%, 31st
  Violent: 413.8, 32nd
    Percent increase: –1.6%, 12th
    Murder & nonnegligent manslaughter:
      6.6, 25th
    Forcible rape: 42.6, 15th
    Aggravated assault: 268.3, 28th
    Robbery: 96.3, 37th
  Property: 4,268.0, 25th
    Percent increase: –4.4%, 31st
    Burglary: 981.3, 19th
    Larceny-theft: 3,038.3, 23rd
    Motor vehicle theft: 248.4, 42nd

TEACHING AND LEARNING

Pop. 3 and over enrolled in school (1996):
  642,783, 31st
Percent of pop.: 24.99%, 7th
Public elementary & secondary schools (1996-
  97): 1,487, 22nd
  Total enrollment (1996): 465,140, 33rd
    Percent of school age pop.: 91.74%, 26th
    Percent of total pop.: 18.08%, 14th

Teachers (1996): 30,750, 30th
  Percent of pop.: 1.20%, 8th
Pupil/teacher ratio (1995): 15.1, 39th
Teachers' avg. salary (1996-97): $35,837,
  26th
Expenditure per capita (1992-93):
  $1,428.26, 17th
  Education as % of state govt. expendi-
    tures: 40.1%, 3rd
Expenditure per pupil (1994-95): $5,817,
  26th
  Percent increase (1993-94 & 1994-95):
    2.79%, 35th
Percent at or above grade level, NAEP tests:
  Reading, grade 4 (1994): NA
  Math, grade 4 (1996): NA
  Math, grade 8 (1996): NA
Percent of graduates taking SAT (1995): 9%,
  38th
  Mean SAT verbal scores: 503, 6th
  Mean SAT mathematical scores: 557, 8th
Percent of graduates taking ACT (1997):
  74%, 5th
  Mean ACT scores: 21.7, 10th
Percent of pop. over 25 completing:
  Less than 9th grade: 7.7%, 41st
  High school: 81.3%, 10th
  College degree(s): 21.1%, 19th
Higher education, institutions (1996): 54, 26th
  Enrollment (1995-96): 177,643, 27th
    Percent increase in enroll. (1990-95):
      8.5%, 13th
    White non-Hispanic (1995): 149,727, 26th
      Percent of enroll.: 84.29%, 19th
    Total minority enroll. (1995): 21,926, 32nd
      Percent of enroll.: 12.34%, 34th
    Black non-Hispanic (1995): 9,419, 29th
      Percent of enroll.: 5.30%, 29th
    Hispanic (1995): 5,856, 21st
      Percent of enroll.: 3.30%, 18th
    Asian/Pacific Islander (1995): 4,043, 28th
      Percent of enroll.: 2.28%, 26th
    American Indian/AK native (1995): 2,608,
      15th
      Percent of enroll.: 1.47%, 13th
    Nonresident alien (1995): 5,990, 24th
      Percent of enroll.: 3.37%, 15th
    Female (1995): 98,803, 27th
      Percent of enroll.: 55.62%, 32nd
  Pub. institutions (1995-96): 31, 19th
    Enrollment: 160,449, 25th
      Percent increase in enrollment (1990-
        95): 7.6%, 17th
      Percent of enroll.: 90.32%, 7th

Private institutions (1995-96): 23, 26th
　Enrollment: 17,194, 37th
　　Percent increase in enrollment (1990-95): 17.6%, 10th
　Percent of enroll.: 9.68%, 45th
　Tuition (in state), public 4-year institution (1996-97): $2,223, 38th
　Tuition (in state), public 2-year institution (1996-97): $1,244, 32nd
　Tuition, private 4-year institution (1996-97): $9,180, 37th
Public library systems (1994): 324, 9th
　Books & serial vol. per capita: 4.4, 5th
　Library visits per capita: 5.1, 8th
　Circulation per capita: 9.2, 6th

LAW ENFORCEMENT AND CORRECTIONS

Police protection and corrections expenditures (1996): $235,528,000
　Per capita: $91.58, 36th
Police per 10,000 pop. (1996): 24.87, 13th
Prisoners (1 year or more) per 100,000 pop. (1996): 301, 31st
　Percent change (1995-96): 10.0%, 14th
　Percent of inmates that are female: 6.1%, 27th
　　Percent change: 6.0%, 34th
Death penalty: yes, by lethal injection
　Under sentence (Jan. 1998): 0
　Executed, 1976-97: 0

RELIGION, NUMBER AND PERCENT OF POPULATION

Agnostic: 10,896—0.60%, 19th
Buddhist: 5,448—0.30%, 8th
Christian: 1,632,548—89.90%, 12th
Hindu: 1,816.0—0.10%, 10th
Jewish: 5,448—0.30%, 35th
Muslim: 1,816—0.10%, 22nd
Unitarian: 7,264—0.40%, 8th
Other: 16,344—0.90%, 35th
None: 103,510—5.70%, 37th
Refused to answer: 30,871—1.70%, 35th

MAKING A LIVING

Personal income per capita (1996): $23,281, 23rd
　Percent increase (1995-96): 4.6%, 10th
Disposable personal income per capita (1996): $20,225, 23rd
Median income of households (average, 1995-96): $31,911, 35th

Percent of pop. below poverty level (1995-96): 11%, 34th

ECONOMY

In civilian labor force (1996): 1,340,000
　Percent of total pop.: 70.1%, 16th
　Percent of total pop. 65 years and over: 18.8%, 1st
　Percent of total female pop.: 63.2%, 15th
Major employer industries (total nonagricultural, 1996):
　Construction: 56,800—4.6%, 25th
　Finance, insurance, & real estate: 58,600—4.8%, 32nd
　Government: 235,100—19.1%, 14th
　Manufacturing: 196,100—16.0%, 23rd
　Service: 300,600—24.5%, 41st
　Trade: 303,300—24.7%, 12th
　Transportation, communications, public utilities: 69,800—5.7%, 15th
Unemployment rate (1996): 4.5%, 37th
　Male: 4.1%, 41st
　Female: 5.0%, 27th
Total businesses (1995): 70,894, 31st
New business incorps. (1995): 4,475
　Percent of total businesses: 6.31%, 45th
Business failures (1995): 947
　Failures per 10,000 businesses: 133.6, 7th
Agriculture farm income:
　Marketing (1996): $7,869,209,000, 7th
　　Average per farm: $119,230, 15th
　Leading products (1997): Cattle, wheat, corn, soybeans, sorghum, hay, and sunflowers
　Average value land & build. per acre (1997): $575, 40th
　　Percent increase (1996-97): 4%, 35th
　Govt. payments (1996): $555,139,000, 2nd
　　Average per farm: $8,411, 4th
Construction, value of all (1996): $3,772,052,000, 29th
　Per capita: $1,466, 17th
Manufactures (1995):
　Value added: $17,742,600,000
　　Per capita: $6,916, 20th
　Leading products (1997): Transportation equipment, machinery & computer equipment, food and food products, printing and publishing products
Value of nonfuel mineral production (1996): $524,000,000, 24th
Leading mineral products (1996): Petroleum, natural gas, cement, helium, stone, salt, sand/gravel

Energy consumption per person (1994): 420.2 mil. Btu, 13th

Retail sales (1995): $22,943,000,000
  Per household: $23,371, 39th
  Sales increase (1994-95): 1.9%, 43rd

Tourism revenues (1991): $2.1 bil.

Foreign exports, in total value (1996): $3,784,000,000, 30th
  Per capita: $1,471, 28th

Gross state product per person (1994): $24,180, 29th

Public aid recipients (percent of resident pop. 1994): 4.7%, 42nd

Medicaid recipients (percent of pop., 1995): 10.0, 40th

Medicare enrollment per 1,000 pop. (1996): 150, 17th

TRAVEL AND TRANSPORTATION

Motor vehicle registrations (1996): 2,109,814, 32nd
  Per 1,000 pop.: 818.03, 24th

Motorcycle registrations (1996): 48,835, 26th
  Per 1,000 pop.: 23.15, 16th

Licensed drivers (1996): 1,770,786, 31st
  Per 1,000 pop.: 690.74, 28th

Public roads & streets (1996)
  Total mileage: 133,386, 4th
    Per 1,000 pop.: 151.86, 6th
  Rural mileage: 123,629, 2nd
    Per 1,000 pop.: 48.06, 6th
  Urban mileage: 9,757, 30th
    Per 1,000 pop.: 3.79, 6th
  Interstate mileage: 872, 26th
    Per 1,000 pop.: 0.34, 11th

Speed limit (max. interstate, autos, mi. per hr., 1997): 70

Annual vehicle-mi. of travel per driver (1996): 14,507, 25th

Mean travel time for workers age 16+ who work away from home: 17.2 min., 44th

GOVERNMENT

Percent of voting age pop. registered (1996): 75.72%, 29th
  Percent of voting age pop. voting for president: (1996): 56.8%, 14th
  Percent of voting age pop. voting for U.S. representatives (1996): 55.3%, 13th

State legislators, total (1997): 165, 17th
  Women members (1997): 49
    Percent of legislature: 30%, 8th

U.S. Congress, House members (1998): 4
  Change (1988-98): –1

Revenues (1996):
  State govt.: $7,864,247,000
    Per capita: $3,057.64, 41st
    Parimutuel & amusement taxes & lotteries, revenue per capita (1995): $66.16, 34th

Expenditures (1996):
  State govt.: $7,275,754,000
    Per capita: $2,828.83, 36th

Debt outstanding (1996): $1,161,470,000
  Per capita: $451.58, 49th

LAWS AND REGULATIONS

Legal driving age: 16

Marriage age without parental consent: 18

Divorce residence requirement: 60 days

ATTRACTIONS (1997)

Major symphony orchestras: 1

Per capita spending by the NEA (1997): $0.20, 36th

State Fair mid-September at Hutchinson

SPORTS AND COMPETITION

NCAA (Division I) football and basketball teams: Kansas State Univ. Wildcats, Univ. of Kansas Jayhawks, Wichita State Univ. Shockers (basketball only)

WEBSITES CONTAINING FURTHER INFORMATION

| Kansas Home Page | http://www.state.ks.us |

KENTUCKY

The sun shines bright on my old Kentucky·home,
My old Kentucky home far away.   Stephen Collins Foster (1853)

"I gained the summit of a commanding ridge . . . with astonishing delight, beheld the ample plains, the beauteous tracts below. . .the famous Ohio River, that rolled in silent dignity, marking the western boundary of Kentucky with inconceivable grandeur."   Daniel Boone, frontiersman

The Bluegrass State is famed for its fine horses, the renowned Kentucky Derby, its bourbon, and its fine tobacco, but it deserves greater fame for the extraordinary personalities who have been associated with it and for a state park system that has been called "the finest in the nation." Louisville's symphony is renowned as a leader in first performances of classical music, and the baseball world could not survive without "Louisville Slugger" bats. Among the numerous natural attractions, Mammoth Cave contains three rivers, two lakes, and one "sea." Millions around the world sing of the joys of "My Old Kentucky Home." When statesman Henry Clay stood at Cumberland Gap, he said, "I am listening to the tread of the coming millions," and they have indeed followed in his footsteps.

SUPERLATIVES

- Kentucky's Cave Region—world unique.
- First in pedigreed horses.
- World's largest loose-leaf tobacco market.
- First in fine grass seed.
- World's largest producer of bourbon.
- First in bituminous coal production.
- First daily newspaper published west of the Alleghenies.

MOMENTS IN HISTORY

- The first recorded exploration of Kentucky was made by Virginia Colonel Abram Wood in 1654.
- By 1690 most of the native Indian people had been driven from the region by the Iroquois. Then a few scattered groups of Native Americans returned.
- The whole vast region west of the Allegheny Mountains was claimed by France, and around 1729, Lower Shawneetown was begun by French traders and groups of Delaware, Shawnee, and Mingo tribes. It was abandoned before the French and Indian War.
- The British did not recognize French claims, and in 1750, Dr. Thomas Walker explored the region for the British Loyal Land Company of Virginia.
- In 1751 explorer Christopher Gist traveled the Ohio River country and visited Lower Shawneetown, as noted in his journal.
- The British were triumphant in the French and Indian War in 1763.
- In 1769, John Findley and Daniel Boone crossed the pass now known as the Cumberland Gap.

So They Say

"...returned to my family, being determined to reside in Kentucky which I esteemed a second paradise."
Daniel Boone (1771)

- James Harrod and a group of 31 settlers founded present-day Harrodsburg in 1774. It became the state's oldest permanent European settlement.
- After leading a party over "Boone's Trace" on April 5, 1775, Boone and 30 men began to build Fort Boonesborough.
- As the Revolutionary War approached, the British stirred up Indians against the settlers, and in July 1776, Indians attacked Boonesborough and captured Daniel Boone's daughter and two other young women. They were rescued by a party led by Boone.
- Indian attacks continued after the Revolution, but settlement grew and on June 1, 1792, Kentucky became the first state to be carved from the great wilderness west.
- In 1799 a hunter tracking a wounded animal discovered Mammoth Cave.
- The terrible earthquake of 1811 shook western Kentucky, but progress came that year with the arrival of the first steamboat on the Ohio River.
- The state was bitterly divided over slavery during the Civil War. By 1862, Union forces

controlled the state, but costly guerrilla warfare continued. At war's end in 1865, 90,000 from Kentucky had served in Union forces; 45,000 had fought for the Confederacy.

- The nation's first great suspension bridge, across the Ohio River between Covington and Cincinnati, Ohio, was completed in 1867.
- The Kentucky Derby began at Louisville in 1875.
- In 1900, William Goebel, candidate for governor, was murdered; the mystery of his death was never solved.
- In 1937 the Ohio River floods were the worst yet in the river's history.
- A terrible supper club fire at Southgate in 1977 took 164 lives.

THAT'S INTERESTING

- Prehistoric bones were not so highly regarded in 1773, when explorer James Douglas used the ribs of mastodons for tent poles.
- Because Mammoth Cave has a constant 54 deg. temperature, it "breathes" in when the outside temperature is high and "exhales" when the temperature is lower.
- The horse industry is big business in Kentucky. Almost every type of fine horse is raised, shown, sold, and raced in the state. Horse auctions attract eager buyers who often spend millions for the individual animals. However, one of the most famous horses of all, Man o' War, was bought for only $5,000.

NOTABLE NATIVES

Muhammad Ali (Louisville, 1942-), boxer. Alben William Barkley (Graves County, 1877-1956), U.S. vice president. Louis Dembitz Brandeis (Louisville, 1856-1941), Supreme Court justice. Christopher (Kit) Carson (Madison County, 1809-1868), trapper/soldier. Jefferson Davis (Fairview, 1808-1889), president of the Confederate States of America. Abraham Lincoln (near Hodgenville, 1809-1865), U.S. president. Carry Amelia Moore Nation (Gerrard County, 1846-1911), social reformer. Frederick Moore Vinson (Louisa, 1890-1953), chief justice of the United States. Whitney Moore Young, Jr. (Lincoln Ridge, 1921-1971), social reformer.

GENERAL

Admitted to statehood: June 1, 1792
Origin of name: Indian word variously translated as "dark and bloody ground," "meadowland," "land of tomorrow"

Capital: Frankfort
Nickname: Bluegrass State
Motto: United we stand, divided we fall
Bird: Cardinal
Fish: Bass
Flower: Goldenrod
Song: "My Old Kentucky Home"
Tree: Tulip poplar

THE LAND

Area: 40,411 sq. mi., 37th
   Land: 39,732 sq. mi., 36th
   Water: 679 sq. mi., 37th
    Inland water: 679 sq. mi., 32nd
Topography: Mountainous in E; rounded hills of the Knobs in the N; Bluegrass, heart of state; wooded rocky hillsides of the Pennyroyal; western coal field; the fertile Purchase in the SW
Number of counties: 120
Geographic center: Marion, 3 mi. NNW of Lebanon
Length: 380 mi.; width: 140 mi.
Highest point: 4,139 ft. (Black Mountain), 27th
Lowest point: 257 ft. (Mississippi River), 32nd
Mean elevation: 750 ft., 33rd

CLIMATE AND ENVIRONMENT

Temp., highest: 114 deg. on July 28, 1930, at Greensburg; lowest: -37 deg. on Jan. 19, 1994, at Shelbyville
Monthly average: highest: 87.6 deg., 25th; lowest: 23.1 deg., 31st; spread (high to low): 64.5 deg., 32nd
Hazardous waste sites (1997): 16, 21st
Endangered species: Animals: 31—Gray bat, Indiana bat, Virginia big-eared bat, Clubshell, Cumberlandian combshell, Relict darter, Cumberland elktoe, American peregrine falcon, Fanshell, Oyster mussel, Ring pink mussel, Winged mapleleaf mussel, Cracking pearlymussel, Cumberland bean pearlymussel, Dromedary pearlymussel, Little-wing pearlymussel, Orange-foot pimple back pearlymussel, Pink mucket pearlymussel, Purple cat's paw pearlymussel, Tubercled-blossom pearlymussel, White wartyback pearlymussel, Rough pigtoe, Fat pocketbook, Rough rabbitsfoot, Northern riffleshell, Tan riffleshell, Palezone shiner, Kentucky cave shrimp, Pallid sturgeon, Least tern, Red-cockaded woodpecker. Plants: 4

MAJOR CITIES
POPULATION, 1996
PERCENTAGE INCREASE, 1990-96

Louisville, 260,689; –3.3%
Lexington-Fayette, 239,942; 6.5%
Owensboro, 54,350; 1.4%
Bowling Green, 44,208; 6.0%
Covington, 40,971; –6.1%

THE PEOPLE

Population (1997): 3,908,124, 24th
Percent change (1990-97): 6.00%, 27th
Percent of total U.S. pop.: 1.46%, 24th
Per sq. mi: 96.71, 23rd
Population (2000 proj.): 3,992,500, 25th
Percent change (1995-2000): 3.43%, 34th
Percent in metro. area (1996): 48.23%, 39th
Foreign born: 34,000, 39th
Percent: 0.9%, 49th
Top three ancestries reported:
German, 21.64%
Irish, 18.88%
American, 15.89%
White (1992): 3,460,000, 92.17%, 17th
Black (1992): 269,000, 7.17%, 26th
Native American (1992): 6,000, 0.16%, 49th
Asian, Pacific Isle (1992): 20,000, 0.53%, 50th
Hispanic origin (1992): 23,000, 0.61%, 49th
Percent over 5 yrs. speaking language other than English at home: 2.5%, 51st
Percent males (1996): 48.58%, 35th; percent females: 51.42%, 17th
Percent never married: 22.6%, 44th
Marriages per 1,000 (1996): 11.15, 7th
Divorces per 1,000 (1996): 5.46, 12th
Median age (1996): 35.1
Under 5 years (1996): 6.71%, 38th
Under 18 years (1996): 28.01%, 34th
65 years & older (1996) 12.60%, 27th:
Percent increase among the elderly (1995-96): 0.57%, 30th

OF VITAL IMPORTANCE

Live births per 1,000 pop. (1996): 13.6, 36th
Infant mortality rate per 1,000 live births (1995): 7.6, 24th
Rate for whites: 7.4, 5th
Rate for blacks: 10.7, 33rd
Births to unmarried women, % of total (1996): 29.8%, 31st
Births to teenage mothers, % of total (1996): 17.0%, 7th

Abortions (1992): 10,000, 32nd
Rate per 1,000 women 14-44 years old: 11.4, 44th
Percent change (1988-92): –12%, 32nd
Average lifetime (1989-91): 74.37, 41st
Total death rate per 100,000 pop. (1995): 963.7, 13th
Accidents and adverse effects: 44.2, 13th
Alzheimer's disease: 10.2, 10th
Cancer: 229.2, 11th
Cerebrovascular diseases: 63.9, 24th
Chronic liver disease and cirrhosis: 9.0, 27th
Chronic obstructive pulmonary diseases and allied conditions: 48.1, 9th
Diabetes mellitus: 25.1, 14th
Diseases of heart: 315.8, 12th
HIV infection: 5.6, 36th
Homicide: 6.5, 25th
Injury by firearms: 14.5, 23rd
Motor vehicle accidents: 22.0, 13th
Pneumonia and influenza: 37.7, 9th
Suicide: 12.4, 25th

KEEPING WELL

Active nonfederal physicians per 100,000 pop. (1995): 193, 36th
Dentists per 100,000 (1991): 54, 24th
Nurses per 100,000 (1995): 756, 38th
Hospitals per 100,000 (1995): 2.69, 18th
Admissions per 1,000 (1995): 138.34, 9th
Hospital beds per 1,000 (1995): 3.91, 18th
Occupancy rate per 100 beds (1995): 59.60, 31st
Average cost per patient per day (1995): $795, 37th
Average cost per stay (1995): $4,838, 47th
AIDS cases (new, 1996): 401; per 100,000: 10.3, 32nd
Persons living with HIV infection (1996): NA
Other notifiable diseases, per 100,000 pop.:
Gonorrhea (1995): 123.1, 22nd
Syphilis (1995): 13.0, 23rd
Tuberculosis (1996): 6.7, 19th
Pop. without health insur. (1996): 15.4%, 18th

HOUSEHOLDS BY TYPE

Total households (1996): 1,478,000, 25th
Percent change (1990-96): 7.1%, 24th
Per 1,000 pop. (1996) 380.54, 26th
Percent of householders 65 yrs. and over (1996): 21.79%, 25th
Persons per household (1996): 2.55, 31st

Family households: 1,015,998
  Percent of total: 73.63%, 5th
Nonfamily households: 363,784
  Percent of total: 26.37%, 47th
Pop. living in group quarters: 101,176
  Percent of pop.: 2.75%, 25th

LIVING QUARTERS

Total housing units: 1,506,845
  Persons per unit: 2.45, 16th
Occupied housing units: 1,379,782
  Percent of total units: 91.57%, 12th
  Persons per unit: 2.54, 22nd
  Percent of units with over 1 person per
    room: 2.60%, 33rd
Owner-occupied units: 960,469
  Percent of total units: 63.74%, 7th
  Percent of occupied units: 69.61%, 13th
  Persons per unit: 2.69, 35th
  Median value: $50,500, 44th
Renter-occupied units: 419,313
  Percent of total units: 27.83%, 33rd
  Percent of occupied units: 30.39%, 39th
  Persons per unit: 2.39, 18th
  Median contract rent: $250, 45th
  Rental vacancy rate: 8.2%, 27th
Mobile home, trailer & other as a percent of
    occupied housing units: 14.46%, 17th
Persons in emergency shelters for homeless
    persons: 1,284, 0.035%, 44th
Persons visible in street locations: 118,
    0.0032%, 35th
Nursing home population: 27,874, 0.76%, 22nd

CRIME INDEX PER 100,000
(1996)

Total reported: 3,166.3, 46th
  Percent increase: −5.5%, 35th
  Violent: 320.5, 39th
    Percent increase: −12.1%, 46th
    Murder & nonnegligent manslaughter:
      5.9, 26th
    Forcible rape: 31.7, 30th
    Aggravated assault: 189.2, 40th
    Robbery: 93.8, 38th
  Property: 2,845.8, 47th
    Percent increase: −4.7%, 33rd
    Burglary: 688.4, 39th
    Larceny-theft: 1,896.3, 50th
    Motor vehicle theft: 261.1, 40th

TEACHING AND LEARNING

Pop. 3 and over enrolled in school (1996):
    841,929, 25th
  Percent of pop.: 21.68%, 39th

Public elementary & secondary schools (1996-
    97): 1,402, 26th
  Total enrollment (1996): 663,071, 25th
    Percent of school age pop.: 93.39%, 18th
    Percent of total pop.: 17.07%, 29th
  Teachers (1996): 39,235, 26th
    Percent of pop.: 1.01%, 31st
  Pupil/teacher ratio (1995): 16.9, 21st
  Teachers' avg. salary (1996-97): $33,950, 29th
  Expenditure per capita (1992-93):
    $1,100.46, 46th
    Education as % of state govt. expendi-
      tures: 33.6%, 35th
  Expenditure per pupil (1994-95): $5,217, 34th
    Percent increase (1993-94 & 1994-95):
      2.15%, 42nd
Percent at or above grade level, NAEP tests:
  Reading, grade 4 (1994): 26%, 23rd
  Math, grade 4 (1996): 60%, 28th
  Math, grade 8 (1996): 56%, 26th
Percent of graduates taking SAT (1995): 11%,
    34th
  Mean SAT verbal scores: 477, 19th
  Mean SAT mathematical scores: 522, 21st
Percent of graduates taking ACT (1997):
    65%, 14th
  Mean ACT scores: 20.1, 44th
Percent of pop. over 25 completing:
  Less than 9th grade: 19.0%, 1st
  High school: 64.6%, 50th
  College degree(s): 13.6%, 49th
Higher education, institutions (1996): 61,
    20th
  Enrollment (1995-96): 178,858, 26th
    Percent increase in enroll. (1990-95):
      0.6%, 35th
    White non-Hispanic (1995): 159,762,
      24th
      Percent of enroll.: 89.32%, 9th
    Total minority enroll. (1995): 15,977, 35th
      Percent of enroll.: 8.93%, 39th
    Black non-Hispanic (1995): 12,089, 26th
      Percent of enroll.: 6.76%, 25th
    Hispanic (1995): 1,150, 40th
      Percent of enroll.: 0.64%, 46th
    Asian/Pacific Islander (1995): 2,083, 37th
      Percent of enroll.: 1.16%, 43rd
    American Indian/AK native (1995): 655,
      40th
      Percent of enroll.: 0.37%, 39th
    Nonresident alien (1995): 3,119, 33rd
      Percent of enroll.: 1.74%, 46th
    Female (1995): 104,604, 25th
      Percent of enroll.: 58.48%, 3rd
  Pub. institutions (1995-96): 22, 30th

Enrollment: 148,808, 27th
Percent increase in enrollment (1990-95): 1.2%, 30th
Percent of enroll.: 83.20%, 24th
Private institutions (1995-96): 39, 17th
Enrollment: 30,050, 27th
Percent increase in enrollment (1990-95): -2.3%, 43rd
Percent of enroll.: 16.80%, 28th
Tuition (in state), public 4-year institution (1996-97): $2,241, 36th
Tuition (in state), public 2-year institution (1996-97): $1,211, 34th
Tuition, private 4-year institution (1996-97): $8,134, 38th
Public library systems (1994): 116, 25th
Books & serial vol. per capita: 2.0, 39th
Library visits per capita: 2.6, 38th
Circulation per capita: 5.1, 36th

LAW ENFORCEMENT AND CORRECTIONS

Police protection and corrections expenditures (1996): $341,092,000
Per capita: $87.82, 40th
Police per 10,000 pop. (1996): 18.01, 40th
Prisoners (1 year or more) per 100,000 pop. (1996): 331, 24th
Percent change (1995-96): 7.0%, 20th
Percent of inmates that are female: 6.4%, 22nd
Percent change: 11.7%, 21st
Death penalty: yes, by electrocution
Under sentence (Jan. 1998): 30, 21st
Executed, 1976-97: 1, 25th
Executed in 1997: 1, 9th

RELIGION, NUMBER AND PERCENT OF POPULATION

Agnostic: 8,194—0.30%, 37th
Buddhist: 2,731—0.10%, 17th
Christian: 2,452,619—89.80%, 13th
Hindu: NA
Jewish: 5,462—0.20%, 40th
Muslim: NA
Unitarian: 5,462—0.20%, 23rd
Other: 32,774—1.20%, 29th
None: 177,528—6.50%, 25th
Refused to answer: 46,430—1.70%, 35th

MAKING A LIVING

Personal income per capita (1996): $19,687, 43rd
Percent increase (1995-96): 2.8%, 29th

Disposable personal income per capita (1996): $17,192, 43rd
Median income of households (average, 1995-96): $31,552, 39th
Percent of pop. below poverty level (1995-96): 15.9%, 15th

ECONOMY

In civilian labor force (1996): 1,867,000
Percent of total pop.: 62.5%, 46th
Percent of total pop. 65 years and over: 11.5%, 27th
Percent of total female pop.: 56.1%, 43rd
Major employer industries (total nonagricultural, 1996):
Construction: 76,900—4.6%, 25th
Finance, insurance, & real estate: 67,600—4.0%, 47th
Government: 289,600—17.3%, 24th
Manufacturing: 311,600—18.6%, 13th
Service: 408,300—24.4%, 42nd
Trade: 400,900—24.0%, 22nd
Transportation, communications, public utilities: 93,300—5.6%, 18th
Unemployment rate (1996): 5.6%, 15th
Male: 5.4%, 17th
Female: 5.9%, 13th
Total businesses (1995): 85,123, 28th
New business incorps. (1995): 7,764
Percent of total businesses: 9.12%, 23rd
Business failures (1995): 659
Failures per 10,000 businesses: 77.4, 29th
Agriculture farm income:
Marketing (1996): $3,550,232,000, 22nd
Average per farm: $40,344, 48th
Leading products (1997): Tobacco, cattle, horses, dairy products, corn, soybeans
Average value land & build. per acre (1997): $1,450, 21st
Percent increase (1996-97): 5%, 26th
Govt. payments (1996): $74,542,000, 27th
Average per farm: $847, 38th
Construction, value of all (1996): $4,693,285,000, 28th
Per capita: $1,208, 26th
Manufactures (1995):
Value added: $33,632,000,000
Per capita: $8,712, 7th
Leading products (1997): Industrial machinery, transportation equipment, food products, rubber & plastic products, apparel, printing and publishing
Value of nonfuel mineral production (1996): $453,000,000, 29th

Leading mineral products (1996): Coal, petroleum, stone, lime, cement, sand/gravel, clays

Energy consumption per person (1994): 445.5 mil. Btu, 8th

Retail sales (1995): $33,020,000,000
Per household: $22,663, 44th
Sales increase (1994-95): 6.6%, 18th

Tourism revenues (1995): $7.1 bil.

Foreign exports, in total value (1996): $6,385,000,000, 23rd
Per capita: $1,644, 23rd

Gross state product per person (1994): $22,600, 40th

Public aid recipients (percent of resident pop. 1994): 9.3%, 7th

Medicaid recipients (percent of pop., 1995): 16.6%, 9th

Medicare enrollment per 1,000 pop. (1996): 154, 14th

TRAVEL AND TRANSPORTATION

Motor vehicle registrations (1996): 2,695,985, 29th
Per 1,000 pop.: 694.47, 45th

Motorcycle registrations (1996): 36,603, 32nd
Per 1,000 pop.: 13.58, 38th

Licensed drivers (1996): 2,535,463, 27th
Per 1,000 pop.: 657.39, 40th

Public roads & streets (1996)
Total mileage: 73,158, 28th
Per 1,000 pop.: 118.84, 24th
Rural mileage: 62,875, 28th
Per 1,000 pop.: 16.19, 24th
Urban mileage: 10,283, 28th
Per 1,000 pop.: 2.65, 42nd
Interstate mileage: 762, 30th
Per 1,000 pop.: 0.20, 26th

Speed limit (max. interstate, autos, mi. per hr., 1997): 65

Annual vehicle-mi. of travel per driver (1996): 16,593, 6th

Mean travel time for workers age 16+ who work away from home: 20.7 min., 24th

GOVERNMENT

Percent of voting age pop. registered (1996): 81.83%, 15th
Percent of voting age pop. voting for president: (1996): 47.5%, 34th
Percent of voting age pop. voting for U.S. representatives (1996): 42.3%, 40th

State legislators, total (1997): 138, 30th
Women members (1997): 13
Percent of legislature: 9%, 50

U.S. Congress, House members (1998): 6
Change (1988-98): –1

Revenues (1996):
State govt.: $13,788,272,000
Per capita: $3,550.02, 24th
Parimutuel & amusement taxes & lotteries, revenue per capita (1995): $129.92, 17th

Expenditures (1996):
State govt.: $11,842,386,000
Per capita: $3,049.02, 29th

Debt outstanding (1996): $7,030,482,000
Per capita: $1,810.11, 16th

LAWS AND REGULATIONS

Legal driving age: 16
Marriage age without parental consent: 18
Divorce residence requirement: 180 days

ATTRACTIONS (1997)

Major opera companies: 1
Major symphony orchestras: 1
Major dance companies: 1
Major professional theater companies (nonprofit): 1
Per capita spending by the NEA (1997): $0.24, 31st
State Fair in mid-August at Louisville

SPORTS AND COMPETITION

NCAA (Division I) football and basketball teams: Eastern Kentucky Univ. Colonels, Morehead State Univ. Eagles, Murray State Univ. Racers, Univ. of Kentucky Wildcats, Univ. of Louisville Cardinals, Western Kentucky Univ. Hilltoppers

WEBSITES CONTAINING FURTHER INFORMATION

Commonwealth of Kentucky Homepage	http://www.state.sy.us
Kentucky Atlas & Gazetteer	http://www.uky.edu/KentuckyAtlas/kentucky-atlas.html

LOUISIANA

"But where is that favored Land?—It is in this great continent.—It is, reader, in Louisiana that these bounties of nature are in the greatest perfection."　　　John James Audubon, ornithologist and artist

Louisiana is the home of the famous Mardi Gras held in New Orleans, that charming old city with its rich French heritage. Many people from southern Louisiana are descended from the French settlers who left the Acadia region of eastern Canada. Louisiana is one of the nation's busiest commercial areas. Shipping is important, as are fishing, petroleum production, and farming. White-columned mansions, built before the Civil War, symbolize Louisiana's past glory. Louisiana has been called "an unparalleled combination of beauty, historic charm, and bountiful resources." New Orleans continues to flourish as a major tourist center.

SUPERLATIVES

- Claimed at one time by more nations than any other state.
- Birthplace of jazz.
- Nation's leading port.
- Four major deep-water harbors.
- Largest U.S. iron ore reserves.
- First in sulfur production.
- First in production of fur pelts.

MOMENTS IN HISTORY

- In 1519, Spanish explorer Alonso de Pineda claimed to have reached the mouth of the Mississippi, calling it Rio del Espiritu Santo (River of the Holy Spirit).
- Despite Pineda's claims, Hernando de Soto is generally thought of as the Mississippi's discoverer, in his 1541-42 expedition to the region.
- Few visitors touched the present state until 1682, when Robert Cavalier, Sieur de La Salle, claimed the entire Mississippi watershed for France and named it for King Louis XIV.
- In 1699, explorations of the brothers Pierre Le Moyne, Sieur d'Iberville, and the Sieur de Bienville strengthened French claims, and France made Louisiana a crown colony that year.
- Juchereau de St. Denis founded what is now Natchitoches in 1714; it was the first permanent European settlement in Louisiana.
- Bienville founded New Orleans in 1718.
- In 1743, Marquis de Vaudreuil became governor of French Louisiana.

So They Say

"His administration...was for Louisiana...what the reign of Louis XIV had been for France.... He loved to keep up a miniature court, a distant imitation of that of Versailles...old people were fond of talking of the exquisitely refined manner, the magnificent balls, the splendidly uniformed troops...and many other unparalleled things they had seen in the day of the great Marquis."

Historian Charles Gayarre, on the Marquis de Vaudreuil

- In 1762, King Louis XV gave his cousin Charles II of Spain all the land west of the Mississippi, to keep it out of British hands.
- In 1768, colonists of Louisiana rebelled against Spanish rule and governed an independent republic for almost a year.
- Spanish rule was reestablished in 1769.
- On Good Friday 1788, much of the city of New Orleans was destroyed by fire.
- The Treaty of San Ildefonso in 1801 returned Louisiana to France.
- On November 30, 1803, the United States took over the Cabildo (capitol) at New Orleans, after buying the entire Louisiana Territory from France in one of history's best real estate deals.
- Spain continued to claim eastern Louisiana, but it was taken by the United States in 1810.
- Louisiana became the 18th state on April 30, 1812.
- On January 8, 1815, Andrew Jackson scored a sweeping victory at the Battle of New Orleans. He had not heard that the War of 1812 had already ended.
- One of the states most dependent on slavery, Louisiana moved quickly to join the Confederacy on January 26, 1861.
- On April 29, 1862, Union Admiral David Farragut captured New Orleans.
- When Confederate General Edmund Kirby-Smith surrendered at Shreveport on June 2, 1865, his was the last major army of the South to lay down arms.

- In 1892, New Orleans was hit by a general strike, the first in the nation.
- In 1901 the state's first oil flowed from a "monster" well near Jennings.
- In 1915, New Orleans jazz spread to Chicago and was soon popularized around the world.
- Huey Long was elected governor in 1928 and soon became one of the nation's best-known and most powerful politicians.
- In 1935, Long—by then a U.S. senator—was assassinated on the steps of the state capitol.
- In the mid-1990s, New Orleans retained its longtime position as the nation's busiest port.

THAT'S INTERESTING

- The Indians painted a conspicuous tree bright red as a marker. The French called this tree "baton rouge" (red stick), giving the Louisiana capital its name.
- In August 1997, Louisiana instituted "covenant marriage," an optional form of marriage that requires special premarital counseling and is more restrictive than other marriage in grounds allowed for divorce.

NOTABLE NATIVES

Louis Daniel Armstrong (New Orleans, 1900-1971), musician. **Pierre Gustave Toutant Beauregard** (New Orleans, 1818-1893), soldier. **Truman Capote** (New Orleans, 1924-1984), author. **Louis Moreau Gottschalk** (New Orleans, 1829-1869), musician/composer. **Lillian Hellman** (New Orleans, 1905-1984), playwright. **Mahalia Jackson** (New Orleans, 1911-1972), gospel singer. **Huddie (Leadbelly) Ledbetter** (near Shreveport, 1888?-1949), folk singer/composer. **Huey Pierce Long** (Winnfield, 1893-1935), public official. **Edward Douglass White** (Lafourche Parish, 1845-1921), Supreme Court justice.

GENERAL

Admitted to statehood: April 30, 1812
Origin of name: Part of territory called Louisiana by Sieur de La Salle for French King Louis XIV
Capital: Baton Rouge
Nickname: Pelican State
Motto: Union, justice, and confidence
Bird: Eastern (Louisiana) brown pelican

Insect: Honeybee
Flower: Magnolia bloom
Song: "Give Me Louisiana" and "You Are My Sunshine"
Tree: Bald cypress

THE LAND

Area: 49,650 sq. mi., 31st
  Land: 43,566 sq. mi., 33rd
  Water: 6,084 sq. mi., 6th
    Inland water: 4,153 sq. mi., 5th
    Coastal water: 1,931 sq. mi., 3rd
Topography: Lowlands of the marshes and Mississippi River flood plain; Red River Valley lowlands; upland hills in the Florida parishes
Number of counties: 64 parishes
Geographic center: Avoyelles, 3 mi. SE of Marksville
Length: 380 mi.; width: 130 mi.
Highest point: 535 ft. (Driskill Mountain), 48th
Lowest point: –8 ft. (New Orleans), 2nd
Mean elevation: 100 ft., 50th
Coastline: 397 mi., 5th
Shoreline: 7,721 mi., 3rd

CLIMATE AND ENVIRONMENT

Temp., highest: 114 deg. on Aug. 10, 1936, at Plain Dealing; lowest: –16 deg. on Feb. 13, 1899, at Minden
Monthly average: highest: 93.3 deg., 7th; lowest: 36.2 deg., 47th; spread (high to low): 57.1 deg., 48th
Hazardous waste sites (1997): 14, 26th
Endangered species: Animals: 8—American peregrine falcon, West Indian manatee, Pink mucket pearlymussel, Brown pelican, Pallid sturgeon, Least tern, Black-capped bireo, Red-cockaded woodpecker. Plants: 3

MAJOR CITIES
POPULATION, 1996
PERCENTAGE INCREASE, 1990-96

New Orleans, 476,625; –4.1%
Baton Rouge, 215,882; –1.7%
Shreveport, 191,558; –3.5%
Lafayette, 104,899; 3.0%
Kenner, 72,345; 0.4%

THE PEOPLE

Population (1997): 4,351,769, 22nd
  Percent change (1990-97): 3.08%, 41st

Percent of total U.S. pop.: 1.63%, 22nd
Per sq. mi: 83.94, 24th
Population (2000 proj.): 4,435,000, 23rd
Percent change (1995-2000): 2.14%, 40th
Percent in metro. area (1996): 75.18%, 22nd
Foreign born: 87,000, 26th
Percent: 2.1%, 34th
Top three ancestries reported:
African, 26.00%
French, 13.03%
Irish, 12.27%
White (1992): 2,876,000, 67.21%, 48th
Black (1992): 1,337,000, 31.25%, 3rd
Native American (1992): 19,000, 0.44%, 25th
Asian, Pacific Isle (1992): 47,000, 1.10%, 30th
Hispanic origin (1992): 98,000, 2.29%, 28th
Percent over 5 yrs. speaking language other than English at home: 10.1%, 17th
Percent males (1996): 48.21%, 45th; percent females: 51.79%, 7th
Percent never married: 27.4%, 14th
Marriages per 1,000 (1996): 8.95, 18th
Divorces per 1,000 (1996): NA
Median age (1996): 33.0
Under 5 years (1996): 7.56%, 13th
18 years and under (1996): 31.62%, 5th
65 years and over (1996): 11.41%, 40th
Percent increase among the elderly (1995-96): 0.67%, 27th

OF VITAL IMPORTANCE

Live births per 1,000 pop. (1996): 15.2, 15th
Infant mortality rate per 1,000 live births (1995): 9.8, 3rd
Rate for whites: 6.2, 26th
Rate for blacks: 15.3, 16th
Births to unmarried women, % of total (1996): 43.4%, 3rd
Births to teenage mothers, % of total (1996): 18.9%, 3rd
Abortions (1992): 13,600, 26th
Rate per 1,000 women 14-44 years old: 13.4, 39th
Percent change (1988-92): –18%, 45th
Average lifetime (1989-91): 73.05, 49th
Total death rate per 100,000 pop. (1995): 914.4, 24th
Accidents and adverse effects: 42.4, 17th
Alzheimer's disease: 8.4, 27th
Cancer: 214.3, 23rd
Cerebrovascular diseases: 58.6, 30th
Chronic liver disease and cirrhosis: 8.1, 37th

Chronic obstructive pulmonary diseases and allied conditions: 32.7, 46th
Diabetes mellitus: 34.4, 2nd
Diseases of heart: 279.4, 27th
HIV infection: 16.8, 10th
Homicide: 17.6, 2nd
Injury by firearms: 25.0, 3rd
Motor vehicle accidents: 21.0, 16th
Pneumonia and influenza: 23.7, 48th
Suicide: 12.5, 23rd

KEEPING WELL

Active nonfederal physicians per 100,000 pop. (1995): 222, 18th
Dentists per 100,000 (1991): 47, 38th
Nurses per 100,000 (1995): 724, 41st
Hospitals per 100,000 (1995): 2.99, 15th
Admissions per 1,000 (1995): 143.25, 6th
Hospital beds per 1,000 (1995): 4.40, 9th
Occupancy rate per 100 beds (1995): 56.02, 44th
Average cost per patient per day (1995): $902, 30th
Average cost per stay (1995): $5,612, 33rd
AIDS cases (new, 1996): 1,470; per 100,000: 33.8, 8th
Persons living with HIV infection, not yet AIDS (1996): 4,699
Other notifiable diseases, per 100,000 pop.:
Gonorrhea (1995): 214.0, 10th
Syphilis (1995): 84.6, 2nd
Tuberculosis (1996): 9.7, 11th
Pop. without health insur. (1996): 20.9%, 5th

HOUSEHOLDS BY TYPE

Total households (1996): 1,572,000, 23rd
Percent change (1990-96): 4.8%, 34th
Per 1,000 pop. (1996) 361.30, 45th
Percent of householders 65 yrs. and over (1996): 20.61%, 36th
Persons per household (1996): 2.67, 10th
Family households: 1,089,882
Percent of total: 72.69%, 10th
Nonfamily households: 409,387
Percent of total: 27.31%, 42nd
Pop. living in group quarters: 112,578
Percent of pop.: 2.67%, 30th

LIVING QUARTERS

Total housing units: 1,716,241
Persons per unit: 2.46, 13th
Occupied housing units: 1,499,269
Percent of total units: 87.36%, 35th
Persons per unit: 2.70, 6th

Percent of units with over 1 person per room: 5.95%, 10th

Owner-occupied units: 987,919
Percent of total units: 57.56%, 33rd
Percent of occupied units: 65.89%, 33rd
Persons per unit: 2.83, 9th
Median value: $58,500, 36th

Renter-occupied units: 511,250
Percent of total units: 29.79%, 23rd
Percent of occupied units: 34.10%, 20th
Persons per unit: 2.57, 6th
Median contract rent: $260, 42nd
Rental vacancy rate: 12.5%, 5th

Mobile home, trailer & other as a percent of occupied housing units: 14.51%, 16th

Persons in emergency shelters for homeless persons: 1,559, 0.037%, 42nd

Persons visible in street locations: 184, 0.0044%, 31st

Nursing home population: 32,072, 0.76%, 22nd

CRIME INDEX PER 100,000 (1996)

Total reported: 6,838.8, 4th
Percent increase: 2.4%, 6th
Violent: 929.1, 5th
Percent increase: –7.8%, 31st
Murder & nonnegligent manslaughter: 17.5, 2nd
Forcible rape: 41.5, 18th
Aggravated assault: 593.5, 5th
Robbery: 276.6, 8th
Property: 5,909.7, 5th
Percent increase: 4.3%, 3rd
Burglary: 1,295.8, 5th
Larceny-theft: 3,982.3, 7th
Motor vehicle theft: 631.6, 9th

TEACHING AND LEARNING

Pop. 3 and over enrolled in school (1996): 981,505, 22nd
Percent of pop.: 22.56%, 27th
Public elementary & secondary schools (1996-97): 1,470, 24th
Total enrollment (1996): 777,570, 21st
Percent of school age pop.: 85.82%, 50th
Percent of total pop.: 17.87%, 17th
Teachers (1996): 48,047, 18th
Percent of pop.: 1.10%, 21st
Pupil/teacher ratio (1995): 16.6, 26th
Teachers' avg. salary (1996-97): $28,347, 48th
Expenditure per capita (1992-93): $1,150.41, 44th

Education as % of state govt. expenditures: 29.9%, 42nd
Expenditure per pupil (1994-95): $4,761, 44th
Percent increase (1993-94 & 1994-95): 5.36%, 13th

Percent at or above grade level, NAEP tests:
Reading, grade 4 (1994): 15%, 39
Math, grade 4 (1996): 44%, 42
Math, grade 8 (1996): 38%, 39

Percent of graduates taking SAT (1995): 9%, 38th
Mean SAT verbal scores: 486, 15th
Mean SAT mathematical scores: 535, 17th
Percent of graduates taking ACT (1997): 80%, 2nd
Mean ACT scores: 19.4, 47th

Percent of pop. over 25 completing:
Less than 9th grade: 14.7%, 7th
High school: 68.3%, 44th
College degree(s): 16.1%, 43rd

Higher education, institutions (1996): 36, 33rd
Enrollment (1995-96): 203,935, 24th
Percent increase in enroll. (1990-95): 9.1%, 10th
White non-Hispanic (1995): 135,074, 29th
Percent of enroll.: 66.23%, 45th
Total minority enroll. (1995): 62,880, 16th
Percent of enroll.: 30.83%, 7th
Black non-Hispanic (1995): 53,002, 11th
Percent of enroll.: 25.99%, 3rd
Hispanic (1995): 4,634, 25th
Percent of enroll.: 2.27%, 24th
Asian/Pacific Islander (1995): 4,120, 26th
Percent of enroll.: 2.02%, 31st
American Indian/AK native (1995): 1,124, 28th
Percent of enroll.: 0.55%, 26th
Nonresident alien (1995): 5,981, 25th
Percent of enroll.: 2.93%, 21st
Female (1995): 117,823, 24th
Percent of enroll.: 57.77%, 7th
Pub. institutions (1995-96): 20, 32nd
Enrollment: 174,873, 24th
Percent increase in enrollment (1990-95): 10.5%, 10th
Percent of enroll.: 85.75%, 19th
Private institutions (1995-96): 16, 34th
Enrollment: 29,062, 28th
Percent increase in enrollment (1990-95): 1.8%, 35th
Percent of enroll.: 14.25%, 33rd

Tuition (in state), public 4-year institution (1996-97): $2,230, 37th

Tuition (in state), public 2-year institution (1996-97): $1,054, 38th

Tuition, private 4-year institution (1996-97): $13,002, 17th

Public library systems (1994): 65, 39th

Books & serial vol. per capita: 2.2, 35th

Library visits per capita: 2.3, 41st

Circulation per capita: 4.4, 42nd

LAW ENFORCEMENT AND CORRECTIONS

Police protection and corrections expenditures (1996): $550,563,000

Per capita: $126.54, 22nd

Police per 10,000 pop. (1996): 32.71, 4th

Prisoners (1 year or more) per 100,000 pop. (1996): 615, 3rd

Percent change (1995-96): 6.3%, 26th

Percent of inmates that are female: 5.8%, 33rd

Percent change: 9.7%, 25th

Death penalty: yes, by lethal injection

Under sentence (Jan. 1998): 72, 15th

Executed, 1976-97: 24, 5th

Executed in 1997: 1, 9th

RELIGION, NUMBER AND PERCENT OF POPULATION

Agnostic: NA

Buddhist: 2,993—0.10%, 17th

Christian: 2,834,091—94.70%, 1st

Hindu: NA

Jewish: 5,985—0.20%, 40th

Muslim: 2,993—0.10%, 22nd

Unitarian: NA

Other: 23,942—0.80%, 37th

None: 86,788—2.90%, 46th

Refused to answer: 35,912—1.20%, 46th

MAKING A LIVING

Personal income per capita (1996): $19,824, 41st

Percent increase (1995-96): 2.5%, 35th

Disposable personal income per capita (1996): $17,786, 40th

Median income of households (average, 1995-96): $29,518, 44th

Percent of pop. below poverty level (1995-96): 20.1%, 4th

ECONOMY

In civilian labor force (1996): 1,997,000

Percent of total pop.: 62.1%, 48th

Percent of total pop. 65 years and over: NA

Percent of total female pop.: 55.2%, 46th

Major employer industries (total nonagricultural, 1996):

Construction: 112,700—6.2%, 5th

Finance, insurance, & real estate: 82,800—4.6%, 35th

Government: 361,300—20.0%, 9th

Manufacturing: 188,300—10.4%, 40th

Service: 485,800—26.8%, 30th

Trade: 422,600—23.3%, 33rd

Transportation, communications, public utilities: 108,300—6.0%, 8th

Unemployment rate (1996): 6.7%, 6th

Male: 5.6%, 16th

Female: 8.0%, 2nd

Total businesses (1995): 98,063, 23rd

New business incorps. (1995): 11,082

Percent of total businesses: 11.30%, 16th

Business failures (1995): 456

Failures per 10,000 businesses: 46.5, 48th

Agriculture farm income:

Marketing (1996): $2,342,068,000, 31st

Average per farm: $86,743, 28th

Leading products (1997): Cotton, sugar, cattle, soybeans, rice, corn, sweet potatoes, pecans, sorghum, aquaculture

Average value land & build. per acre (1997): $1,230, 27th

Percent increase (1996-97): 5%, 26th

Govt. payments (1996): $176,471,000, 16th

Average per farm: $6,536, 9th

Construction, value of all (1996): $4,874,998,000, 26th

Per capita: $1,121, 33rd

Manufactures (1995):

Value added: $30,404,600,000

Per capita: $7,002, 18th

Leading products (1997): Chemical products, foods, transportation equipment, electronic equipment, petroleum products, lumber, wood, paper

Value of nonfuel mineral production (1996): $428,000,000, 31st

Leading mineral products (1996): Petroleum, natural gas, salt, sulfur, sand/gravel, stone

Energy consumption per person (1994): 884.5 mil. Btu, 2nd

Retail sales (1995): $37,668,000,000
  Per household: $24,271, 31st
  Sales increase (1994-95): 6.3%, 19th
Tourism revenues (1992): $5.2 bil.
Foreign exports, in total value (1996): $21,667,000,000, 8th
  Per capita: $4,980, 2nd
Gross state product per person (1994): $23,430, 35th
Public aid recipients (percent of resident pop. 1994): 9.7%, 5th
Medicaid recipients (percent of pop., 1995): 18.1%, 5th
Medicare enrollment per 1,000 pop. (1996): 135, 35th

TRAVEL AND TRANSPORTATION

Motor vehicle registrations (1996): 3,318,205, 23rd
  Per 1,000 pop.: 764.42, 35th
Motorcycle registrations (1996): 37,072, 30th
  Per 1,000 pop.: 11.17, 45th
Licensed drivers (1996): 2,593,509, 24th
  Per 1,000 pop.: 597.85, 50th
Public roads & streets (1996)
  Total mileage: 60,667, 32nd
    Per 1,000 pop.: 113.94, 32nd
    Rural mileage: 46,702, 34th
      Per 1,000 pop.: 10.73, 32nd
    Urban mileage: 13,965, 22nd
      Per 1,000 pop.: 3.21, 19th
    Interstate mileage: 893, 25th
      Per 1,000 pop.: 0.21, 24th
Speed limit (max. interstate, autos, mi. per hr., 1997): 70
Annual vehicle-mi. of travel per driver (1996): 14,517, 24th
Mean travel time for workers age 16+ who work away from home: 22.3 min., 11th

GOVERNMENT

Percent of voting age pop. registered (1996): 81.74, 16th
  Percent of voting age pop. voting for president: (1996): 56.9%, 12th
  Percent of voting age pop. voting for U.S. representatives (1996): 15.1%, 48th

State legislators, total (1997): 144, 27th
  Women members (1997): 16
    Percent of legislature: 11%, 47th
U.S. Congress, House members (1998): 7
  Change (1988-98): –1
Revenues (1996):
  State govt.: $14,296,187,000
    Per capita: $3,285.72, 30th
    Parimutuel & amusement taxes & lotteries, revenue per capita (1995): $66.07, 35th
Expenditures (1996):
  State govt.: $14,029,815,000
    Per capita: $3,224.50, 22nd
Debt outstanding (1996): $7,452,387,000
  Per capita: $1,712.80, 18th

LAWS AND REGULATIONS

Legal driving age: 17, 15 if completed driver education course
Marriage age without parental consent: 18
Divorce residence requirement: 6 mo., for qualifications check local statutes

ATTRACTIONS (1997)

Major opera companies: 1
Major symphony orchestras: 2
Per capita spending by the NEA (1997): $0.20, 37th
State Fair in October at Shreveport

SPORTS AND COMPETITION

NCAA (Division I) football and basketball teams: Centenary College Gentlemen (basketball only), Grambling State Univ. Tigers, Louisiana State Univ. Fighting Tigers, Louisiana Tech Univ. Bulldogs, McNeese State Univ. Cowboys, Nicholls State Univ. Colonels, Northeast Louisiana Univ. Indians, Northwestern State Univ. Demons, Southeastern Louisiana Univ. Lions (basketball only), Southern Univ. Jaguars, Tulane Univ. Green Wave, Univ. of New Orleans Privateers (basketball only), Univ. of Southwestern Louisiana Ragin' Cajuns
NFL football teams: New Orleans Saints (NFC), Louisiana Superdome

WEBSITES CONTAINING FURTHER INFORMATION

| Info Louisiana: Main Page | http://www.state.la.us |

MAINE

"Did you ever see a place that looks like it was built just to enjoy? Well this whole state of Maine looks that way." — Will Rogers, humorist

Potatoes, lobsters, and submarines make an unusual combination, but Maine has been famous for all of these. The seacoast of "hundred-harbor Maine," with its lighthouses, sandy beaches, quiet fishing villages, and thousands of off-shore islands, is one of the world's most notable for its beauty. It is also noted for tremendous catches of fish, many outstanding ports, and shipbuilding—boasting the first ship built in the Western Hemisphere. Although not primarily farming land, Maine has farms that are world famous for the wonderful white potatoes grown there. The lack of natural resources has been overcome by courage, ingenuity, and persistence.

SUPERLATIVES

- World's highest tides.
- First ship launched in the Western Hemisphere—the *Virginia*, in 1607.
- First atomic submarine, the *Swordfish*, built in Maine.
- Leader in canoe manufacture.
- Holds clipper ship sailing record.
- First sawmill in the United States.
- Produces one-fourth of all U.S. feldspar.
- Leader in lobster catch.
- World's first steel sailing vessel.

MOMENTS IN HISTORY

- In 1604, Pierre du Guast of France landed at Dochet Island and began a place he called St. Croix.
- In 1607 the primeval forests of Maine provided timber, the 120 settlers at the mouth of the Kennebec River provided the labor, and the *Virginia*, the first ship ever to be launched in the hemisphere, went down the primitive ways.
- Henry Hudson visited Maine in 1609, robbing friendly Indians who had been kind to him.
- In 1613 the devoted Jesuits established the first monastery mission east of California in Maine.
- Captain John Smith visited present-day Maine in 1614.
- In 1622, Maine's first permanent European settlement, Monhegan, was established.
- During King Philip's War, Saco was attacked on September 18, 1675, and a long period of war with the Indians continued.

- Peace came to Maine in 1760 in a treaty made with the Indians during the French and Indian War.
- The British King had claimed most of the area's best trees for masts. In 1775, when an armed British ship, the *Margaretta*, attempted to take the trees, the people of Machiasport rose up under Foster and Jeremiah O'Brien, captured the boat, and killed the commander. This engagement has been called the first naval battle of the Revolution, and it took place just five days before the Battle of Bunker Hill.
- During the Revolution, the coastal towns of Maine endured much destruction, but the British were not able to remove the needed mast trees for their navy.
- Maine suffered again during the War of 1812. Bangor was captured, and Britain seized sizable portions of Maine.
- Based on an ancient map by explorer Samuel de Champlain, the border with Canada was decided in Maine's favor in 1815, keeping much of present-day eastern Maine in U.S. hands.
- Maine became the 23rd state on March 15, 1820.
- Another boundary dispute was settled by the Webster-Ashburton Treaty of 1842, with Canada receiving a substantial area claimed by the United States.
- Portland suffered a destructive fire in 1866.

So They Say

"I have been in Portland since the fire. Desolation, desolation, desolation! It reminds me of Pompeii."

Poet Henry Wadsworth Longfellow

- In 1948, Margaret Chase Smith became the first Republican woman elected to the U.S. Senate.
- Schoolgirl Samantha Smith of Maine gained world fame in 1983 when she wrote a letter to Soviet leader Yuri Andropov expressing her fear of nuclear war, and then visited the Soviet Union at his invitation. She died tragically on August 25, 1985, in a private plane crash.

THAT'S INTERESTING

• The first European settlers in Maine brought timber in their ships to build houses and were astonished that their new home had its own magnificent forests.

• Because Cushnoc Island in the Kennebec River at Augusta was a navigation hazard, the people there hitched 200 oxen to the island, but they failed to move it an inch.

• Thanksgiving in Maine predated the Pilgrims. The Etchimin Indians celebrated for two weeks in autumn. Their feasts included turkey, cranberries, popcorn, and other familiar delicacies.

• Samuel Francis Smith of Waterville gave the nation "America" ("My Country, 'Tis of Thee"), which many believe should be the national anthem.

NOTABLE NATIVES

Cyrus H. K. Curtis (Portland, 1850-1933), publisher. **Dorothea Lynde Dix** (Hampden, 1802-1887), educator/social reformer. **Melville Weston Fuller** (Augusta, 1833-1910), chief justice of the United States. **Hannibal Hamlin** (Paris Hill, 1809-1891), U.S. vice president. **Stephen King** (Portland, 1947-), author. **Henry Wadsworth Longfellow** (Portland, 1807-1882), poet. **Hiram Stevens Maxim** (near Sangerville, 1840-1916), inventor. **Edna St. Vincent Millay** (Rockland, 1892-1950), poet. **Lillian Nordica** (Farmington, 1857-1914), opera singer. **John Knowles Paine** (Portland, 1839-1906), composer/educator. **Sir William Phips** (Maine frontier, 1651-1695), colonial governor. **Thomas Brackett Reed** (Portland, 1839-1902), public official. **Kenneth Lewis Roberts** (Kennebunkport, 1885-1957), author. **Edwin Arlington Robinson** (Head Tide, 1869-1935), poet. **Nelson Aldrich Rockefeller** (Bar Harbor, 1908-1979), public official/U.S. vice president. **Margaret Chase Smith** (Skowhegan, 1897-1995), public official. **Nathaniel Parker Willis** (Portland, 1806-1867), poet.

GENERAL

Admitted to statehood: March 15, 1820

Origin of name: From Maine, ancient French province. Also descriptive, referring to the mainland as distinct from the many coastal islands

Capital: Augusta

Nickname: Pine Tree State

Motto: *Dirigo*—I direct

Animal: Moose

Bird: Chickadee

Insect: Honeybee

Fish: Landlocked salmon

Flower: White pine cone and tassel

Gem: Tourmaline

Song: "State of Maine Song"

Tree: Eastern white pine

THE LAND

Area: 33,741 sq. mi., 39th
  Land: 30,865 sq. mi., 39th
  Water: 2,876 sq. mi., 13th
    Inland water: 2,263 sq. mi., 9th
    Coastal water: 613 sq. mi., 9th

Topography: Appalachian Mountains extend through state; western borders have rugged terrain; long sand beaches on southern coast; northern coast mainly rocky promontories, peninsulas, fjords

Number of counties: 16

Geographic center: Piscataquis, N of Dover

Length: 320 mi.; width: 190 mi.

Highest point: 5,267 ft. (Mount Katahdin), 22nd

Lowest point: sea level (Atlantic Ocean), 3rd

Mean elevation: 600 ft., 39th

Coastline: 228 mi., 9th

Shoreline: 3,478 mi., 4th

CLIMATE AND ENVIRONMENT

Temp., highest: 105 deg. on July 10, 1911, at North Bridgton; lowest: –48 deg. on Jan. 19, 1925, at Van Buren

Monthly average: highest: 78.9 deg., 50th; lowest: 11.9 deg., 12th; spread (high to low): 67.0 deg., 28th

Hazardous waste sites (1997): 12, 29th

Endangered species: Animals: 2—American peregrine falcon, Roseate tern. Plants: 1

MAJOR CITIES
POPULATION, 1996
PERCENTAGE INCREASE, 1990-96

Portland, 63,123; –1.6%

Lewiston, 36,830; –7.4%

Bangor, 31,649; –4.6%

Auburn, 22,997; –5.4%

South Portland, 22,985; –0.8%

THE PEOPLE

Population (1997): 1,242,051, 39th
  Percent change (1990-97): 1.15%, 45th

Percent of total U.S. pop.: 0.46%, 39th
Per sq. mi: 35.10, 39th
Population (2000 proj.): 1,254,500, 40th
Percent change (1995-2000): 1.09%, 46th
Percent in metro. area (1996): 40.04%, 45th
Foreign born: 36,000, 38th
Percent: 3.0%, 27th
Top three ancestries reported:
English, 30.29%
French, 18.24%
Irish, 17.67%
White (1992): 1,217,000, 98.46%, 2nd
Black (1992): 5,000, 0.40%, 48th
Native American (1992): 6,000, 0.49%, 24th
Asian, Pacific Isle (1992): 8,000, 0.65%, 42nd
Hispanic origin (1992): 7,000, 0.57%, 50th
Percent over 5 yrs. speaking language other than English at home: 9.2%, 18th
Percent males (1996): 48.84%, 25th; percent females: 51.16%, 27th
Percent never married: 24.0%, 36th
Marriages per 1,000 (1996): NA
Divorces per 1,000 (1996): NA
Median age (1996): 36.6
Under 5 years (1996): 5.75%, 51st
18 years and under (1996): 26.79%, 44th
65 years and over (1996): 13.95%, 11th
Percent increase among the elderly (1995-96): 0.52%, 34th

OF VITAL IMPORTANCE

Live births per 1,000 pop. (1996): 11.1, 51st
Infant mortality rate per 1,000 live births (1995): 6.5, 38th
Rate for whites: 6.3, 24th
Rate for blacks: NA
Births to unmarried women, % of total (1996): 28.7%, 35th
Births to teenage mothers, % of total (1996): 9.7%, 43rd
Abortions (1992): 4,200, 41st
Rate per 1,000 women 14-44 years old: 14.7, 34th
Percent change (1988-92): –9%, 28th
Average lifetime (1989-91): 76.35, 19th
Total death rate per 100,000 pop. (1995): 946.8, 16th
Accidents and adverse effects: 32.1, 42nd
Alzheimer's disease: 14.2, 2nd
Cancer: 242.9, 7th
Cerebrovascular diseases: 59.9, 29th
Chronic liver disease and cirrhosis: 9.4, 21st
Chronic obstructive pulmonary diseases and allied conditions: 54.3, 4th
Diabetes mellitus: 25.4, 13th
Diseases of heart: 293.9, 25th
HIV infection: 6.1, 35th
Homicide: 1.7, 46th
Injury by firearms: 8.8, 42nd
Motor vehicle accidents: 14.7, 34th
Pneumonia and influenza: 27.6, 37th
Suicide: 13.0, 19th

KEEPING WELL

Active nonfederal physicians per 100,000 pop. (1995): 198, 31st
Dentists per 100,000 (1991): 47, 38th
Nurses per 100,000 (1995): 1,059, 8th
Hospitals per 100,000 (1995): 3.14, 13th
Admissions per 1,000 (1995): 114.42, 25th
Hospital beds per 1,000 (1995): 3.22, 28th
Occupancy rate per 100 beds (1995): 65.00, 15th
Average cost per patient per day (1995): $915, 27th
Average cost per stay (1995): $6,083, 20th
AIDS cases (new, 1996): 50; per 100,000: 4.0, 45th
Persons living with HIV infection (1996): NA
Other notifiable diseases, per 100,000 pop.:
Gonorrhea (1995): 7.6, 48th
Syphilis (1995): 0.3, 48th
Tuberculosis (1996): 1.7, 46th
Pop. without health insur. (1996): 12.1%, 32nd

HOUSEHOLDS BY TYPE

Total households (1996): 483,000, 39th
Percent change (1990-96): 3.8%, 40th
Per 1,000 pop. (1996) 388.58, 6th
Percent of householders 65 yrs. and over (1996): 22.57%, 19th
Persons per household (1996): 2.54, 33rd
Family households: 328,685
Percent of total: 70.64%, 26th
Nonfamily households: 136,627
Percent of total: 29.36%, 26th
Pop. living in group quarters: 37,169
Percent of pop.: 3.03%, 16th

LIVING QUARTERS

Total housing units: 587,045
Persons per unit: 2.09, 50th
Occupied housing units: 465,312
Percent of total units: 79.26%, 50th
Persons per unit: 2.46, 44th
Percent of units with over 1 person per room: 1.72%, 48th

Owner-occupied units: 327,888
  Percent of total units: 55.85%, 38th
  Percent of occupied units: 70.47%, 6th
  Persons per unit: 2.71, 29th
  Median value: $87,400, 17th
Renter-occupied units: 137,424
  Percent of total units: 23.41%, 50th
  Percent of occupied units: 29.53%, 45th
  Persons per unit: 2.20, 47th
  Median contract rent: $358, 21st
  Rental vacancy rate: 8.4%, 25th
Mobile home, trailer & other as a percent of
  occupied housing units: 14.62%, 15th
Persons in emergency shelters for homeless
  persons: 419, 0.034%, 45th
Persons visible in street locations: 7, 0.0006%,
  51st
Nursing home population: 9,855, 0.80%, 21st

CRIME INDEX PER 100,000 (1996)

Total reported: 3,394.1, 44th
  Percent increase: 3.3%, 3rd
  Violent: 124.9, 48th
    Percent increase: –4.9%, 19th
    Murder & nonnegligent manslaughter:
      2.0, 47th
    Forcible rape: 20.9, 49th
    Aggravated assault: 78.5, 48th
    Robbery: 23.5, 46th
  Property: 3,269.2, 43rd
    Percent increase: 3.7%, 4th
    Burglary: 748.4, 35th
    Larceny-theft: 2,377.9, 41st
    Motor vehicle theft: 142.9, 49th

TEACHING AND LEARNING

Pop. 3 and over enrolled in school (1996):
  275,107, 40th
  Percent of pop.: 22.13%, 32nd
Public elementary & secondary schools (1996-
  97): 726, 39th
  Total enrollment (1996): 218,560, 40th
    Percent of school age pop.: 95.86%, 8th
    Percent of total pop.: 17.58%, 22nd
  Teachers (1996): 14,458, 39th
    Percent of pop.: 1.16%, 12th
  Pupil/teacher ratio (1995): 13.9, 49th
  Teachers' avg. salary (1996-97): $33,800,
    31st
Expenditure   per   capita   (1992-93):
  $1,303.65, 27th
  Education as % of state govt. expendi-
    tures: 33.7%, 34th

Expenditure per pupil (1994-95): $6,428,
  15th
  Percent increase (1993-94 & 1994-95):
    5.92%, 10th
Percent at or above grade level, NAEP tests:
  Reading, grade 4 (1994): 41%, 1st
  Math, grade 4 (1996): 75%, 2nd
  Math, grade 8 (1996): 77%, 2nd
Percent of graduates taking SAT (1995): 68%,
  8th
  Mean SAT verbal scores: 427, 38th
  Mean SAT mathematical scores: 469,
    41st
Percent of graduates taking ACT (1997): 2%,
  50th
  Mean ACT scores: 21.5, 16th
Percent of pop. over 25 completing:
  Less than 9th grade: 8.8%, 30th
  High school: 78.8%, 18th
  College degree(s): 18.8%, 29th
Higher education, institutions (1996): 33,
  36th
  Enrollment (1995-96): 56,547, 44th
    Percent increase in enroll. (1990-95):
      –1.1%, 42nd
    White non-Hispanic (1995): 53,241, 41st
    Percent of enroll.: 94.15%, 1st
    Total minority enroll. (1995): 2,712, 49th
    Percent of enroll.: 4.80%, 51st
    Black non-Hispanic (1995): 620, 45th
    Percent of enroll.: 1.10%, 45th
    Hispanic (1995): 359, 49th
    Percent of enroll.: 0.63%, 47th
    Asian/Pacific Islander (1995): 875, 45th
    Percent of enroll.: 1.55%, 39th
    American Indian/AK native (1995): 858,
      35th
    Percent of enroll.: 1.52%, 11th
    Nonresident alien (1995): 594, 50th
    Percent of enroll.: 1.05%, 51st
    Female (1995): 33,937, 43rd
    Percent of enroll.: 60.02%, 1st
  Pub. institutions (1995-96): 14, 39th
    Enrollment: 38,195, 42nd
      Percent increase in enrollment (1990-
        95): –8.0%, 48th
    Percent of enroll.: 67.55%, 42nd
  Private institutions (1995-96): 19, 30th
    Enrollment: 18,352, 36th
      Percent increase in enrollment (1990-
        95): 17%, 11th
    Percent of enroll.: 32.45%, 10th
  Tuition (in state), public 4-year institution
    (1996-97): $3,639, 14th

Tuition (in state), public 2-year institution (1996-97): $2,558, 3rd

Tuition, private 4-year institution (1996-97): $16,802, 3rd

Public library systems (1994): 232, 14th

Books & serial vol. per capita: 4.9, 1st

Library visits per capita: NA

Circulation per capita: 7.6, 17th

LAW ENFORCEMENT AND CORRECTIONS

Police protection and corrections expenditures (1996): $98,060,000

Per capita: $78.89, 46th

Police per 10,000 pop. (1996): 16.31, 49th

Prisoners (1 year or more) per 100,000 pop. (1996): 112, 49th

Percent change (1995-96): 5.7%, 28th

Percent of inmates that are female: 2.6%, 51st

Percent change: 8.3%, 26th

Death penalty: no

RELIGION, NUMBER AND PERCENT OF POPULATION

Agnostic: 8,270—0.90%, 14th

Buddhist: 919—0.10%, 17th

Christian: 780,168—84.90%, 35th

Hindu: 919—0.10%, 10th

Jewish: 3,676—0.40%, 31st

Muslim: NA

Unitarian: 5,514—0.60%, 5th

Other: 7,351—0.80%, 37th

None: 91,893—10.00%, 11th

Refused to answer: 20,216—2.20%, 23rd

MAKING A LIVING

Personal income per capita (1996): $20,826, 38th

Percent increase (1995-96): 1.7%, 47th

Disposable personal income per capita (1996): $18,219, 39th

Median income of households (average, 1995-96): $34,777, 25th

Percent of pop. below poverty level (1995-96): 11.2%, 32nd

ECONOMY

In civilian labor force (1996): 669,000

Percent of total pop.: 69.0%, 20th

Percent of total pop. 65 years and over: 12.0%, 24th

Percent of total female pop.: 63.5%, 13th

Major employer industries (total nonagricultural, 1996):

Construction: 23,000—4.3%, 33rd

Finance, insurance, & real estate: 26,700—4.9%, 31st

Government: 93,100—17.2%, 25th

Manufacturing: 88,100—16.3%, 21st

Service: 150,400—27.9%, 20th

Trade: 136,200—25.2%, 8th

Transportation, communications, public utilities: 22,400—4.1%, 47th

Unemployment rate (1996): 5.1%, 26th

Male: 5.4%, 17th

Female: 4.8%, 30th

Total businesses (1995): 36,298, 39th

New business incorps. (1995): 2,805

Percent of total businesses: 7.73%, 38th

Business failures (1995): 317

Failures per 10,000 businesses: 87.3, 20th

Agriculture farm income:

Marketing (1996): $485,111,000, 43rd

Average per farm: $65,556, 41st

Leading products (1997): Eggs, potatoes, dairy products, aquaculture

Average value land & build. per acre (1997): $1,300, 25th

Percent increase (1996-97): 1%, 44th

Govt. payments (1996): $4,638,000, 40th

Average per farm: $627, 42nd

Construction, value of all (1996): $983,416,000, 43rd

Per capita: $791, 47th

Manufactures (1995):

Value added: $7,030,300,000

Per capita: $5,663, 31st

Leading products (1997): Paper and wood products, transportation equipment

Value of nonfuel mineral production (1996): $73,100,000, 45th

Leading mineral products (1996): Sand/gravel, cement, stone, peat

Energy consumption per person (1994): 441.3 mil. Btu, 9th

Retail sales (1995): $11,568,000,000

Per household: $24,349, 29th

Sales increase (1994-95): –1.0%, 49th

Tourism revenues (1995): $3 bil.

Foreign exports, in total value (1996): $1,380,000,000, 42nd

Per capita: $1,110, 37th

Gross state product per person (1994): $21,020, 45th

Public aid recipients (percent of resident pop. 1994): 7.4%, 17th

Medicaid recipients (percent of pop., 1995): 12.4%, 22nd

Medicare enrollment per 1,000 pop. (1996): 165, 8th

TRAVEL AND TRANSPORTATION

Motor vehicle registrations (1996): 958,659, 42nd
  Per 1,000 pop.: 774.01, 31st
Motorcycle registrations (1996): 26,768, 36th
  Per 1,000 pop.: 27.92, 9th
Licensed drivers (1996): 864,447, 40th
  Per 1,000 pop.: 697.94, 22nd
Public roads & streets (1996)
  Total mileage: 22,577, 43rd
    Per 1,000 pop.: 118.16, 25th
    Rural mileage: 19,962, 40th
    Per 1,000 pop.: 16.06, 25th
    Urban mileage: 2,615, 42nd
    Per 1,000 pop.: 2.10, 49th
    Interstate mileage: 368, 44th
    Per 1,000 pop.: 0.30, 12th
Speed limit (max. interstate, autos, mi. per hr., 1997): 65
Annual vehicle-mi. of travel per driver (1996): 14,672, 23rd
Mean travel time for workers age 16+ who work away from home: 19.0 min., 38th

GOVERNMENT

Percent of voting age pop. registered (1996): NA
  Percent of voting age pop. voting for president: (1996): 64.5%, 1st

Percent of voting age pop. voting for U.S. representatives (1996): 63.9%, 1st
State legislators, total (1997): 186, 10th
  Women members (1997): 48
    Percent of legislature: 26%, 15th
U.S. Congress, House members (1998): 2
  Change (1988-98): 0
Revenues (1996):
  State govt.: $4,266,881,000
    Per capita: $3,432.73, 27th
    Parimutuel & amusement taxes & lotteries, revenue per capita (1995): $126.41, 18th
Expenditures (1996):
  State govt.: $4,239,839,000
    Per capita: $3,410.97, 19th
Debt outstanding (1996): $3,159,694,000
    Per capita: $2,541.99, 11th

LAWS AND REGULATIONS

Legal driving age: 17, 16 if completed driver education course
Marriage age without parental consent: 18
Divorce residence requirement: 6 mo., for qualifications check local statutes

ATTRACTIONS (1997)

Major symphony orchestras: 1
Per capita spending by the NEA (1997): $0.54, 14th
State Fair in mid-August at Skowhegan

SPORTS AND COMPETITION

NCAA (Division I) football and basketball teams: Univ. of Maine Black Bears

WEBSITES CONTAINING FURTHER INFORMATION

Maine Map of WWW Resources	http://www.destek.net/Maps/ME.html
Maine State Government (WWW) Home Page	http://www.state.me.us

MARYLAND

"...a delightsome land!"   Captain John Smith, explorer

"America in miniature—a small state, it offers a large part of the variety of attractions found in the United States as a whole."
Theodore McKeldin, governor of Maryland (1951-59)

C hesapeake Bay, which divides Maryland into two parts, furnishes the state with several excellent harbors as well as fine seafood, especially crabs. The defense of Fort McHenry in the War of 1812 inspired the national anthem, "The Star-Spangled Banner," and some experts believe that the success there indeed "preserved us a nation," as the anthem proclaims. Maryland was given to the lords Baltimore for the annual rent of two Indian arrows a year plus complete loyalty to the King. Although Maryland was a slave-holding southern state, it remained loyal to the Union during the Civil War. Among its many contributions, it donated the site of the national capital. The state continues to benefit from its location, with increasing government and commercial activities making it a growing population magnet.

SUPERLATIVES

- Narrowest width of any state—1 mile wide, near Hancock.
- Most navigable rivers of any state.
- One of the foremost sources of marine fossils.
- First military highway in the United States.
- First railway locomotive in the United States.
- World's first telegraph line: Baltimore—Washington, D.C.
- First U.S. manufacture of umbrellas.

MOMENTS IN HISTORY

- In 1524, Giovanni de Verrazano described an estuary believed to be Chincoteague Bay.
- The first recorded European visit to what is now Maryland was made by Captain John Smith in 1608.
- William Claiborne's trading post on Kent Island in 1631 became the first permanent European settlement in Maryland.
- Cecilius Calvert, the second Lord Baltimore, arrived on November 22, 1633, to take possession of his great grant.

> ### So They Say
> "Smyth Fales...abundance of fish, lying so thick with their heads above the waters, as for want of nets...we attempted to catch them with a frying pan...neither better fish, more plentyous nor more varietie for small fish had any of us ever seen in any place, but they could not be catched with frying pans." **Captain John Smith**

- In 1649, Maryland colonists pioneered one of the real acts of progress. For the first time in world history, they provided by law for religious freedom for all Christians.
- Conflicting claims made for unsettled times during the Cromwell period, but in 1660 the new King, Charles II, affirmed the Baltimore lords' titles.
- In 1692 a royal governor took over the Maryland colony.
- The capital was moved to newly incorporated Annapolis in 1694.
- Baltimore was founded in 1729, and the colony's boundaries with Pennsylvania and Maryland were settled that year.
- Fort Mt. Pleasant was begun in 1754 by a youthful George Washington, to discourage French claims in the western area.
- In 1774, Maryland had its own "tea party" protesting the mother country's tax on tea, and delegates were chosen for the Continental Congress.
- On August 27, 1776, Maryland troops played a key role in the Battle of Long Island, saving Washington's forces from destruction.
- During the Revolution the Maryland Navy also had a key role, and in 1778, Count Casimir Pulaski organized his independent "legion" of fighting men at Baltimore.
- Because of mob action at Philadelphia, the capital of the infant United States was moved to Annapolis on November 26, 1783.
- In Annapolis, the Revolutionary War officially came to an end when the Congress

ratified the Treaty of Paris. Annapolis thus became the first peacetime capital of the United States.

• Maryland became the seventh state on April 28, 1788.

• In 1791, Maryland made a notable gift to the United States—the 70 square miles of territory that then became the District of Columbia. Also, $72,000 was included for buildings, a much more significant amount then than today.

• During the War of 1812, the bells of Baltimore warned that a British fleet was approaching. The fleet attacked Fort McHenry with advanced weapons, including new rockets. The British defeat outside of Baltimore was a turning point in the war.

So They Say

"Sir—I have the honor of informing you that the enemy...appears to be retiring. We have a force hanging on their rear....P.S. The enemy's vessels in the Patapsco are all under way going down the river."

U.S. Commander Samuel Smith
at the Battle of Baltimore

• Baltimore became a center of the slave trade, but there also was much opposition to slavery, especially in the west.

• When the Civil War came, President Abraham Lincoln placed Maryland under military control.

• The Battle of Antietam Creek near Sharpsburg on September 17, 1862, is known as the most costly single day of battle in the country, with some 23,000 dead or wounded.

• In 1872 the Radical Republicans held their national convention at Baltimore.

• In 1889 the Johns Hopkins Hospital opened.

• A disastrous fire swept Baltimore in 1904, bringing fire companies from as far away as New York City.

• In 1927, Maryland created the nation's first permanent interracial commission.

• In 1992 the state required some form of public service to qualify for high school graduation.

• In 1992, in a controversial move, the city of Baltimore became the first U.S. city to contract with a private firm to manage a group of city schools.

THAT'S INTERESTING

• Near the town of Hancock, Maryland is only about 1 mile wide, the narrowest width of any state.

• There is much to be said for the argument that a Maryland man was the first president of the United States. When the Articles of Confederation were adopted, the governing body was a "congress," presided over by a "president." The Articles stated, "The stile of this confederacy shall be the United States of America." John Hanson of Maryland was elected as "President of the United States in Congress Assembled."

• The British attack on Fort McHenry during the War of 1812, with its "rockets' red glare," inspired onlooker Francis Scott Key to write the poem that is now the national anthem.

• One of the king's colonial grants was known as the Thumb Grant, because the grantee was given as much land as his thumb could cover on a map.

• Maryland is the only state to have developed a distinct breed of dog—the Chesapeake Bay retriever.

• Baltimore is sometimes known as the "Monumental City." The first major monument ever made to honor George Washington was begun at Baltimore in 1815 and finished in 1829.

NOTABLE NATIVES

Benjamin Banneker (Ellicott, 1731-1806), mathematician. Anna Ellis Carroll (Pocomoke City, 1815-1893), political scientist. Charles Carroll (Annapolis, 1737-1832), Revolutionary leader/public official. Samuel Chase (Somerset County, 1741-1811), Supreme Court justice. Stephen Decatur (Sineppuxent, 1779-1820), naval officer. John Dickinson (Talbot County, 1732-1808), colonial figure/public official. Frederick Douglass (Tuckahoe, 1817-1895), social reformer. John Hanson (Charles County, 1721-1783), president under the Articles of Confederation. Billie Holiday (Baltimore, 1915-1959), singer. Francis Scott Key (Carroll County, 1779-1843), lawyer/poet. Thurgood Marshall (Baltimore, 1908-1993), Supreme Court justice. Henry Louis Mencken (Baltimore, 1880-1956), journalist/editor/critic. Charles Willson Peale (Queen Anne's County, 1741-1827), artist/naturalist. Anne Newport Royall (Maryland, 1769-1854), author. **James Rumsey** (Cecil County, 1743-1792), inventor. **George Herman (Babe) Ruth** (Baltimore, 1895-1948), baseball player. **Upton Beall Sinclair** (Baltimore, 1878-1968), author/social reformer. **Roger Brooke Taney** (Calvert County, 1777-1864), chief justice of the United States. **Harriet Tubman** (Dorchester County, 1820?-1913), abolitionist. **Leon Uris** (Baltimore, 1924-), author. **Mason Locke (Parson) Weems** (Anne Arundel County, 1759-1825), author.

GENERAL

Admitted to statehood: April 28, 1788
Origin of name: For Queen Henrietta Maria, wife of Charles I of England
Capital: Annapolis
Nickname: Old Line State, Free State, Pine Tree State, Lumber State
Motto: *Fatti Maschii, Parole Femine*—Manly deeds, womanly words
Bird: Baltimore oriole
Insect: Baltimore checkerspot butterfly
Fish: Striped bass, or rockfish
Flower: Black-eyed Susan
Song: "Maryland, My Maryland"
Tree: White oak

THE LAND

Area: 12,297 sq. mi., 42nd
    Land: 9,775 sq. mi., 42nd
    Water: 2,522 sq. mi., 16th
        Inland water: 680 sq. mi., 31st
        Coastal water: 1,842 sq. mi., 4th
Topography: Eastern Shore of coastal plain and Maryland Main of coastal plain, piedmont plateau, and the Blue Ridge, separated by Chesapeake Bay
Number of counties: 23
Geographic center: Prince Georges, 4.5 mi. NW of Davidsonville
Length: 250 mi.; width: 90 mi.
Highest point: 3,360 ft. (Backbone Mountain), 32nd
Lowest point: sea level (Atlantic Ocean), 3rd
Mean elevation: 350 ft., 43rd
Coastline: 31 mi., 20th
Shoreline: 3,190 mi., 9th

CLIMATE AND ENVIRONMENT

Temp., highest: 109 deg. on July 10, 1936, at Cumberland and Frederick; lowest: –40 deg. on Jan. 13, 1912, at Oakland

Monthly average: highest: 87.1 deg., 26th; lowest: 24.3 deg., 35th; spread (high to low): 62.8 deg., 35th
Hazardous waste sites (1997): 15, 23rd
Endangered species: Animals: 5—Indiana bat, Maryland darter, American peregrine falcon, Dwarf wedge mussel, Delmarva Peninsula fox squirrel. Plants: 4

MAJOR CITIES
POPULATION, 1996
PERCENTAGE INCREASE, 1990-96

Baltimore, 675,401; –8.2%
Frederick, 46,227; 15.0%
Rockville, 46,019; 2.7%
Gaithersburg, 45,361; 14.3%
Bowie, 40,181; 6.7%

THE PEOPLE

Population (1997): 5,094,289, 19th
    Percent change (1990-97): 6.56%, 24th
    Percent of total U.S. pop.: 1.90%, 19th
    Per sq. mi: 410.60, 6th
Population (2000 proj.): 5,268,000, 19th
    Percent change (1995-2000): 4.48%, 28th
Percent in metro. area (1996): 92.76%, 6th
Foreign born: 313,000, 11th
    Percent: 6.6%, 14th
Top three ancestries reported:
    German, 25.48%
    African, 20.20%
    Irish, 16.08%
White (1992): 3,482,000, 70.82%, 46th
Black (1992): 1,262,000, 25.67%, 6th
Native American (1992): 14,000, 0.28%, 36th
Asian, Pacific Isle (1992): 160,000, 3.25%, 8th
Hispanic origin (1992): 143,000, 2.91%, 24th
Percent over 5 yrs. speaking language other than English at home: 8.9%, 20th
Percent males (1996): 48.69%, 32nd; percent females: 51.31%, 20th
Percent never married: 29.1%, 7th
Marriages per 1,000 (1996): 8.24, 27th
Divorces per 1,000 (1996): 3.22, 40th
Median age (1996): 34.9
Under 5 years (1996): 7.14%, 17th
18 years and under (1996): 27.80%, 36th
65 years and over (1996): 11.39%, 41st
Percent increase among the elderly (1995-96): 1.27%, 19th

OF VITAL IMPORTANCE

Live births per 1,000 pop. (1996): 13.7, 32nd
Infant mortality rate per 1,000 live births (1995): 8.9, 11th
  Rate for whites: 6.0, 34th
  Rate for blacks: 15.3, 16th
Births to unmarried women, % of total (1996): 33.4%, 16th
Births to teenage mothers, % of total (1996): 10.3%, 40th
Abortions (1992): 31,260, 15th
  Rate per 1,000 women 14-44 years old: 26.4, 12th
  Percent change (1988-92): –8%, 26th
Average lifetime (1989-91): 74.79, 37th
Total death rate per 100,000 pop. (1995): 829.8, 36th
  Accidents and adverse effects: 27.6, 46th
  Alzheimer's disease: 6.8, 40th
  Cancer: 201.9, 34th
  Cerebrovascular diseases: 52.5, 40th
  Chronic liver disease and cirrhosis: 8.4, 33rd
  Chronic obstructive pulmonary diseases and allied conditions: 31.6, 47th
  Diabetes mellitus: 27.0, 9th
  Diseases of heart: 236.4, 39th
  HIV infection: 25.6, 5th
  Homicide: 12.7, 5th
  Injury by firearms: 15.1, 20th
  Motor vehicle accidents: 13.5, 40th
  Pneumonia and influenza: 26.9, 42nd
  Suicide: 10.1, 43rd

KEEPING WELL

Active nonfederal physicians per 100,000 pop. (1995): 349, 4th
Dentists per 100,000 (1991): 71, 7th
Nurses per 100,000 (1995): 854, 22nd
Hospitals per 100,000 (1995): 0.99, 51st
  Admissions per 1,000 (1995): 113.84, 26th
  Hospital beds per 1,000 (1995): 2.50, 41st
  Occupancy rate per 100 beds (1995): 68.78, 10th
  Average cost per patient per day (1995): $1,064, 14th
  Average cost per stay (1995): $5,899, 24th
AIDS cases (new, 1996): 2,253; per 100,000: 44.4, 5th
Persons living with HIV infection (1996): NA
Other notifiable diseases, per 100,000 pop.:
  Gonorrhea (1995): 257.5, 8th
  Syphilis (1995): 29.2, 12th
  Tuberculosis (1996): 6.3, 21st

Pop. without health insur. (1996): 11.4%, 36th

HOUSEHOLDS BY TYPE

Total households (1996): 1,871,000, 19th
  Percent change (1990-96): 7.0%, 25th
  Per 1,000 pop. (1996) 368.89, 40th
  Percent of householders 65 yrs. and over (1996): 19.03%, 42nd
  Persons per household (1996): 2.70, 7th
Family households: 1,245,814
  Percent of total: 71.23%, 19th
Nonfamily households: 503,177
  Percent of total: 28.77%, 33rd
Pop. living in group quarters: 113,856
  Percent of pop.: 2.38%, 38th

LIVING QUARTERS

Total housing units: 1,891,917
  Persons per unit: 2.53, 6th
Occupied housing units: 1,748,991
  Percent of total units: 92.45%, 6th
  Persons per unit: 2.62, 12th
  Percent of units with over 1 person per room: 3.04%, 24th
Owner-occupied units: 1,137,296
  Percent of total units: 60.11%, 22nd
  Percent of occupied units: 65.03%, 36th
  Persons per unit: 2.79, 15th
  Median value: $116,500, 10th
Renter-occupied units: 661,695
  Percent of total units: 34.97%, 9th
  Percent of occupied units: 37.83%, 10th
  Persons per unit: 2.45, 13th
  Median contract rent: $473, 8th
  Rental vacancy rate: 6.8%, 44th
Mobile home, trailer & other as a percent of occupied housing units: 3.20%, 45th
Persons in emergency shelters for homeless persons: 2,507, 0.052%, 22nd
Persons visible in street locations: 523, 0.0109%, 17th
Nursing home population: 26,884, 0.56%, 41st

CRIME INDEX PER 100,000 (1996)

Total reported: 6,061.9, 9th
  Percent increase: –3.7%, 30th
  Violent: 931.2, 4th
    Percent increase: –5.6%, 23rd
    Murder & nonnegligent manslaughter: 11.6, 4th
    Forcible rape: 37.6, 22nd

Aggravated assault: 488.8, 10th
Robbery: 393.2, 2nd
Property: 5,130.7, 13th
Percent increase: –3.3%, 28th
Burglary: 992.3, 17th
Larceny-theft: 3,427.0, 14th
Motor vehicle theft: 711.4, 5th

TEACHING AND LEARNING

Pop. 3 and over enrolled in school (1996): 1,085,257, 20th
Percent of pop.: 21.40%, 41st
Public elementary & secondary schools (1996-97): 1,276, 28th
Total enrollment (1996): 818,947, 20th
Percent of school age pop.: 88.34%, 40th
Percent of total pop.: 16.15%, 41st
Teachers (1996): 47,005, 21st
Percent of pop.: 0.93%, 41st
Pupil/teacher ratio (1995): 16.8, 23rd
Teachers' avg. salary (1996-97): $41,148, 13th
Expenditure per capita (1992-93): $1,335.17, 24th
Education as % of state govt. expenditures: 35.9%, 24th
Expenditure per pupil (1994-95): $7,245, 8th
Percent increase (1993-94 & 1994-95): 4.12%, 24th
Percent at or above grade level, NAEP tests:
Reading, grade 4 (1994): 26%, 23rd
Math, grade 4 (1996): 59%, 29th
Math, grade 8 (1996): 57%, 24th
Percent of graduates taking SAT (1995): 64%, 13th
Mean SAT verbal scores: 430, 33rd
Mean SAT mathematical scores: 479, 34th
Percent of graduates taking ACT (1997): 11%, 38th
Mean ACT scores: 20.7, 35th
Percent of pop. over 25 completing:
Less than 9th grade: 7.9%, 38th
High school: 78.4%, 22nd
College degree(s): 26.5%, 5th
Higher education, institutions (1996): 57, 25th
Enrollment (1995-96): 266,310, 20th
Percent increase in enroll. (1990-95): 2.5%, 28th
White non-Hispanic (1995): 177,612, 22nd
Percent of enroll.: 66.69%, 44th

Total minority enroll. (1995): 79,438, 12th
Percent of enroll.: 29.83%, 9th
Black non-Hispanic (1995): 57,579, 9th
Percent of enroll.: 21.62%, 7th
Hispanic (1995): 6,209, 20th
Percent of enroll.: 2.33%, 22nd
Asian/Pacific Islander (1995): 14,590, 13th
Percent of enroll.: 5.48%, 11th
American Indian/AK native (1995): 1,060, 31st
Percent of enroll.: 0.40%, 34th
Nonresident alien (1995): 9,260, 11th
Percent of enroll.: 3.48%, 12th
Female (1995): 154,413, 19th
Percent of enroll.: 57.98%, 5th
Pub. institutions (1995-96): 33, 15th
Enrollment: 222,857, 17th
Percent increase in enrollment (1990-95): 0.9%, 33rd
Percent of enroll.: 83.68%, 22nd
Private institutions (1995-96): 24, 25th
Enrollment: 43,453, 22nd
Percent increase in enrollment (1990-95): 11.7%, 16th
Percent of enroll.: 16.32%, 30th
Tuition (in state), public 4-year institution (1996-97): $3,848, 11th
Tuition (in state), public 2-year institution (1996-97): $2,103, 10th
Tuition, private 4-year institution (1996-97): $15,365, 8th
Public library systems (1994): 24, 47th
Books & serial vol. per capita: 2.7, 28th
Library visits per capita: 4.5, 17th
Circulation per capita: 9.1, 7th

LAW ENFORCEMENT AND CORRECTIONS

Police protection and corrections expenditures (1996): $1,017,567,000
Per capita: $200.63, 3rd
Police per 10,000 pop. (1996): 27.05, 8th
Prisoners (1 year or more) per 100,000 pop. (1996): 412, 16th
Percent change (1995-96): 2.6%, 41st
Percent of inmates that are female: 4.8%, 43rd
Percent change: –2.2%, 48th
Death penalty: yes, by lethal gas, lethal injection after 3/25/94
Under sentence (Jan. 1998): 17, 24th
Executed, 1976-97: 2, 21st
Executed in 1997: 1, 9th

RELIGION, NUMBER AND PERCENT OF POPULATION

Agnostic: 25,335—0.70%, 17th
Buddhist: 3,619—0.10%, 17th
Christian: 3,069,105—84.80%, 36th
Hindu: 7,239—0.20%, 3rd
Jewish: 101,338—2.80%, 5th
Muslim: 7,239—0.20%, 13th
Unitarian: 10,858—0.30%, 15th
Other: 50,669—1.40%, 20th
None: 260,584—7.20%, 20th
Refused to answer: 83,242—2.30%, 21st

MAKING A LIVING

Personal income per capita (1996): $27,221, 7th
Percent increase (1995-96): 1.8%, 45th
Disposable personal income per capita (1996): $23,158, 8th
Median income of households (average, 1995-96): $43,123, 3rd
Percent of pop. below poverty level (1995-96): 10.2%, 39th

ECONOMY

In civilian labor force (1996): 2,786,000
Percent of total pop.: 72.0%, 8th
Percent of total pop. 65 years and over: 15.3%, 6th
Percent of total female pop.: 66.8%, 6th
Major employer industries (total nonagricultural, 1996):
Construction: 130,300—5.9%, 8th
Finance, insurance, & real estate: 128,200—5.8%, 14th
Government: 421,600—19.1%, 14th
Manufacturing: 173,900—7.9%, 42nd
Service: 715,200—32.4%, 7th
Trade: 529,100—24.0%, 22nd
Transportation, communications, public utilities: 106,500—4.8%, 33rd
Unemployment rate (1996): 4.9%, 31st
Male: 4.9%, 28th
Female: 4.9%, 29th
Total businesses (1995): 122,350, 20th
New business incorps. (1995): 18,014
Percent of total businesses: 14.72%, 7th
Business failures (1995): 1,804
Failures per 10,000 businesses: 147.4, 4th
Agriculture farm income:
Marketing (1996): $1,533,770,000, 36th
Average per farm: $111,954, 21st
Leading products (1997): Broilers, greenhouse, dairy products, soybeans, corn

Average value land & build. per acre (1997): $4,000, 5th
Percent increase (1996-97): 5%, 26th
Govt. payments (1996): $17,647,000, 38th
Average per farm: $1,288, 34th
Construction, value of all (1996): $6,470,321,000, 20th
Per capita: $1,276, 23rd
Manufactures (1995):
Value added: $17,147,800,000
Per capita: $3,401, 43rd
Leading products (1997): Electric and electronic equipment, food and food products, chemicals and allied products
Value of nonfuel mineral production (1996): $324,000,000, 36th
Leading mineral products (1996): Coal, stone, cement, sand/gravel
Energy consumption per person (1994): 256.6 mil. Btu, 42nd
Retail sales (1995): $45,644,000,000
Per household: $24,552, 26th
Sales increase (1994-95): 3.3%, 31st
Tourism revenues (1995): $5.8 bil.
Foreign exports, in total value (1996): $5,019,000,000, 27th
Per capita: $990, 41st
Gross state product per person (1994): $26,507, 17th
Public aid recipients (percent of resident pop. 1994): 5.9%, 34th
Medicaid recipients (percent of pop., 1995): 8.2%, 47th
Medicare enrollment per 1,000 pop. (1996): 121, 42nd

TRAVEL AND TRANSPORTATION

Motor vehicle registrations (1996): 3,634,579, 20th
Per 1,000 pop.: 718.25, 40th
Motorcycle registrations (1996): 37,936, 29th
Per 1,000 pop.: 10.44, 48th
Licensed drivers (1996): 3,344,125, 20th
Per 1,000 pop.: 663.66, 36th
Public roads & streets (1996)
Total mileage: 29,680, 42nd
Per 1,000 pop.: 15.85, 46th
Rural mileage: 15,781, 41st
Per 1,000 pop.: 3.11, 44th
Urban mileage: 13,899, 23rd
Per 1,000 pop.: 2.74, 40th
Interstate mileage: 482, 41st
Per 1,000 pop.: 0.10, 42nd
Speed limit (max. interstate, autos, mi. per hr., 1997): 65

Annual vehicle-mi. of travel per driver (1996): 13,675, 32nd

Mean travel time for workers age 16+ who work away from home: 27.0 min., 3rd

GOVERNMENT

Percent of voting age pop. registered (1996): 67.75%, 43rd

Percent of voting age pop. voting for president: (1996): 46.7%, 38th

Percent of voting age pop. voting for U.S. representatives (1996): 43.0%, 38th

State legislators, total (1997): 188, 8th

Women members (1997): 55

Percent of legislature: 29%, 10th

U.S. Congress, House members (1998): 8

Change (1988-98): 0

Revenues (1996):

State govt.: $16,041,152,000

Per capita: $3,162.69, 36th

Parimutuel & amusement taxes & lotteries, revenue per capita (1995): $197.12, 7th

Expenditures (1996):

State govt.: $15,554,009,000

Per capita: $3,066.64, 28th

Debt outstanding (1996): $9,690,915,000

Per capita: $1,910.67, 14th

LAWS AND REGULATIONS

Legal driving age: 18, 16 if completed driver education course

Marriage age without parental consent: 18

Divorce residence requirement: For qualifications check local statutes

ATTRACTIONS (1997)

Major opera companies: 1

Major symphony orchestras: 1

Major professional theater companies (nonprofit): 1

Per capita spending by the NEA (1997): $3.93, 2nd

State Fair in late August–early September at Timonium

SPORTS AND COMPETITION

NCAA (Division I) football and basketball teams: Coppin State College Eagles (basketball only), Loyola College Greyhounds (basketball only), Morgan State Univ. Bears (basketball only), Mount St. Mary's College Mountaineers (basketball only), Towson Univ. Tigers, U.S. Naval Academy Midshipmen, Univ. of Maryland-Baltimore County Retrievers (basketball only), Univ. of Maryland-College Park Terps, Univ. of Maryland-Eastern Shore Hawks (basketball only)

Major league baseball teams: Baltimore Orioles (AL East), Oriole Park at Camden Yards

NBA basketball teams: Washington Wizards, USAir Arena

NFL football teams: Baltimore Ravens (AFC), Memorial Stadium

WEBSITES CONTAINING FURTHER INFORMATION

Maryland Government—the Maryland Electronic Capital	http://www.gov.state.md.us
Maryland State Archives Homepage	http://www.mdarchives.state.md.us

MASSACHUSETTS

"A spirit that's as American as apple pie. For the spirit of Massachusetts truly is the spirit of America."   Governor Michael S. Dukakis

"Massachusetts—the cornerstone of a nation!"

Henry Wadsworth Longfellow, poet

Even though it is the 44th state in terms of area, the commonwealth of Massachusetts has always been a national leader. The first printing press, regularly published newspaper, college, and secondary school in the country were established here. Massachusetts has also given the nation four presidents. It has long been one of the top manufacturing states. The historic city of Boston is a major seaport and airline terminal, and the many universities in and around Boston make this area one of the world's greatest educational, research, and cultural centers. The Revolutionary War really began in Massachusetts with the Boston Massacre, the Boston Tea Party, the battles of Lexington and Concord, and the Battle of Bunker Hill. The state has been home to more than its share of writers and statesmen. The city of Boston continues its progress in political diversity.

SUPERLATIVES

- The Mayflower Compact, model for future governments.
- First popular U.S. election.
- Institution of the town meeting.
- First Thanksgiving, 1621.
- Gave birth to the American Revolution.
- Birthplace of the iron/steel industry.
- First U.S. public school.
- Home of Harvard University, the oldest American college/university.
- Oldest U.S. private secondary school, the Mather School in Boston.
- Oldest boys' boarding school, Phillips Academy in Andover.
- First pipe organ in America.

MOMENTS IN HISTORY

- On his voyage of 1497-98, John Cabot made the first record of European presence in what is now Massachusetts.
- In 1602, Bartholomew Gosnold noted so many codfish in the area that he named the nearby land Cape Cod.
- Church of England dissenters landed at Cape Cod near present-day Provincetown on November 11, 1620, to become the Pilgrims in this new land. A month later they reached their new home and named it Plymouth.
- In April 1621, the Pilgrims and the Wampanoag chief Massasoit made a treaty regarding the settlement, kept by the chief for the rest of his life.
- In the fall of 1621, the Pilgrims and their Indian friends celebrated what became known as the first Thanksgiving.
- The Royal Charter of 1629 provided the foundation for democratic government in the Massachusetts Bay Colony.
- Boston was founded by a Puritan group in 1630.
- Only six years later, Harvard was founded.
- Beginning in 1662, trouble with the Indian leaders brought on a protracted period of conflict.
- The terrible witchcraft hysteria reached its darkest period about 1692 with the trials at Salem, as a result of which 19 accused witches were hanged and one was crushed to death.
- By the mid-1700s, the colony prospered with fishing and trade in lumber, carried by ships built locally and manned by local sailors.
- Increasing laws and regulations imposed on the colony by Britain brought growing resistance. On March 5, 1770, British troops fired on a Boston mob and five died in the Boston Massacre.

So They Say

By the rude bridge that arched the flood,
Their flag to April's breeze unfurled,
Here once the embattled farmers stood
And fired the shot heard round the world.   Ralph Waldo Emerson

---

- Protesting the British tax on tea, Bostonians dressed as Indians boarded a tea ship and threw its cargo into the harbor in December 1773—the famed Boston Tea Party.
- Alerted by Paul Revere and others, patriots in April 1775 harried British troops in the

region of Lexington and Concord. The patriots' shots "heard round the world" heralded the coming Revolution.

- On June 17, 1775, one of the first Revolutionary struggles took place on Breed's Hill; it was mistakenly called the Battle of Bunker Hill.
- The British laid siege to Boston but on March 17, 1776, were forced to withdraw, in the first great American victory of the war.
- Massachusetts became a state on February 6, 1788.
- In 1796, John Adams of Massachusetts was elected president. The famed Adams family also contributed his son, John Quincy Adams, to the presidency in 1824.
- As early as 1832, an antislavery society was founded in Boston.

- The Civil War called 160,000 to service from Massachusetts. The 54th Massachusetts Regiment was the first black regiment recruited in the North.
- His handling of the Boston police strike of 1919 brought national fame to Governor Calvin Coolidge, who in 1923 became the third president from Massachusetts. (He was actually born in Vermont but lived in the Bay State.)
- In 1961, Massachusetts celebrated the inauguration of its fourth U.S. president, John Fitzgerald Kennedy, but all too soon mourned his assassination, in 1963.
- In 1986, Harvard University celebrated its 350th anniversary.

- For the first time in 116 years, Old Ironsides, the oldest U.S. commissioned warship afloat, left harbor under its own power in 1997.

THAT'S INTERESTING

- Chief Massasoit brought 94 of his people to the first Thanksgiving, but they also brought much food. The men played games, while five Pilgrim women and a few girls labored over the feast of venison, geese, turkey, clam chowder, oysters, lobsters, fish,. dried fruits and berries, corn biscuits, Indian pudding, and probably popcorn balls.
- The first cargo ship sent out by the colony was seized by the French as a prize of war.
- Several religious movements were founded in the Bay State. Mary Baker Eddy founded the Church of Christ Scientist in 1879. Following the lead of William Ellery Channing, the American Unitarian Association was organized in 1825. Dwight L. Moody established his evangelistic headquarters at Northfield in the late 1870s.

NOTABLE NATIVES

John Adams (Braintree, later Quincy, 1735-1826), U.S. president. **John Quincy Adams** (Braintree, later Quincy, 1767-1848), U.S. president. **Susan Brownwell Anthony** (Adams, 1820-1906), social reformer. **Clara Harlow Barton** (Oxford, 1821-1912), founder of the American Red Cross. **Katharine Lee Bates** (Falmouth, 1859-1929), educator/author. **William Cullen Bryant** (Cummington, 1794-1878), poet/editor. **Charles Bulfinch** (Boston, 1763-1844), architect. **Luther Burbank** (Lancaster, 1849-1926), horticulturist. **Bette Davis** (Lowell, 1908-1989), actress. **Emily Elizabeth Dickinson** (Amherst, 1830-1886), poet. **Ralph Waldo Emerson** (Boston, 1803-1882), poet/essayist. **Benjamin Franklin** (Boston, 1706-1790), public official/diplomat/scientist. **Edward Everett Hale** (Boston, 1822-1909), religious leader. **John Hancock** (Braintree, 1737-1793), merchant/public official. **Nathaniel Hawthorne** (Salem, 1804-1864), author. **Oliver Wendell Holmes** (Cambridge, 1809-1894), physician/author/educator. **Oliver Wendell Holmes** (Boston, 1841-1935), Supreme Court justice. **Winslow Homer** (Boston, 1836-1910), artist. **Elias Howe** (Spencer, 1819-1867), inventor. **Helen Maria Hunt Jackson** (Amherst, 1830-1885), author. **James Jackson Jarves** (Boston, 1818-1888), art critic/collector. **William LeBaron Jenney** (Fairhaven, 1832-1907), architect. **John Fitzgerald Kennedy** (Brookline, 1917-1963), U.S. president. **Jack Lemmon** (Boston, 1925-), actor. **Henry Cabot Lodge** (Boston, 1850-1924), author/public official. **Horace Mann** (Franklin, 1796-1859), educator. **Dwight Lyman Moody** (Northfield, 1837-1899), evangelist. **Samuel Finley Breese Morse** (Charlestown, 1791-1872), artist/inventor. **George Peabody** (South Danvers, 1795-1869), merchant/philanthropist. **Frances Perkins** (Boston, 1862-1965), social worker/public official. **Edgar Allan Poe** (Boston, 1809-1849), writer. **Paul Revere** (Boston, 1735-1818), patriot/silversmith. **Henry David Thoreau** (Concord, 1817-1862), philosopher/naturalist. **James Abbott McNeill Whistler** (Lowell, 1834-1903), artist. **Eli Whitney** (Westboro, 1765-1825), inventor. **John Greenleaf Whittier** (Haverhill, 1807-1892), poet/abolitionist.

GENERAL

Admitted to statehood: February 6, 1788
Origin of name: From Indian tribe named after "large hill place" identified by Captain John Smith as being near Milton, Massachusetts
Capital: Boston
Nickname: Bay State, Old Colony State
Motto: *Ense Petit Placidam Sub Libertate Quietem*—By the sword we seek peace, but peace only under liberty
Animal: Morgan horse
Bird: Chickadee
Insect: Ladybug
Fish: Cod
Flower: Mayflower, or trailing arbutus
Gem: Rhodonite
Mineral: Babingtonite
Song: "All Hail to Massachusetts"
Tree: American elm

THE LAND

Area: 9,241 sq. mi., 45th
 Land: 7,838 sq. mi., 45th
 Water: 1,403 sq. mi., 21st
  Inland water: 424 sq. mi., 35th
  Coastal water: 979 sq. mi., 7th
Topography: Jagged indented coast from Rhode Island around Cape Cod; flat land yields to stony upland pastures near central region and gentle hill country in W; except in W, land is rocky, sandy, and not fertile.
Number of counties: 14
Geographic center: Worcester, N part of city
Length: 190 mi.; width: 50 mi.
Highest point: 3,487 ft. (Mount Greylock), 31st
Lowest point: sea level (Atlantic Ocean), 3rd
Mean elevation: 500 ft., 42nd
Coastline: 192 mi., 10th
Shoreline: 1,519 mi., 15th

CLIMATE AND ENVIRONMENT

Temp., highest: 107 deg. on Aug. 2, 1975, at Chester and New Bedford; lowest: –35 deg. on Jan. 12, 1981, at Chester
Monthly average: highest: 81.8 deg., 47th; lowest: 15.6 deg., 19th; spread (high to low): 66.2 deg., 31st
Hazardous waste sites (1997): 30, 11th
Endangered species: Animals: 6—American burying beetle, American peregrine falcon, Dwarf wedge mussel, Piping plover, Roseate tern, Plymouth redbelly turtle. Plants: 2

MAJOR CITIES
POPULATION, 1996
PERCENTAGE INCREASE, 1990-96

Boston, 558,394; –2.8%
Worcester, 166,350; –2.0%
Springfield, 149,948; –4.5%
Lowell, 100,973; –2.4%
New Bedford, 96,903; –3.0%

THE PEOPLE

Population (1997): 6,117,520, 13th
 Percent change (1990-97): 1.68%, 43rd
 Percent of total U.S. pop.: 2.29%, 13th
 Per sq. mi: 579.59, 5th
Population (2000 proj.): 6,211,500, 13th
 Percent change (1995-2000): 2.26%, 39th
Percent in metro. area (1996): 98.49%, 3rd
Foreign born: 574,000, 7th
 Percent: 9.5%, 7th
Top three ancestries reported:
 Irish, 26.11%
 English, 15.31%
 Italian, 14.03%
White (1992): 5,469,000, 91.26%, 20th
Black (1992): 347,000, 5.79%, 29th
Native American (1992): 13,000, 0.22%, 39th
Asian, Pacific Isle (1992): 163,000, 2.72%, 13th

Hispanic origin (1992): 314,000, 5.24%, 16th

Percent over 5 yrs. speaking language other than English at home: 15.2%, 10th

Percent males (1996): 48.27%, 43rd; percent females: 51.73%, 8th

Percent never married: 32.8%, 2nd

Marriages per 1,000 (1996): 6.66, 45th

Divorces per 1,000 (1996): 2.03, 44th

Median age (1996): 35.6

Under 5 years (1996): 6.44%, 43rd

18 years and under (1996): 25.68%, 50th

65 years and over (1996): 14.10%, 10th

Percent increase among the elderly (1995-96): 0.30%, 40th

OF VITAL IMPORTANCE

Live births per 1,000 pop. (1996): 13.2, 39th

Infant mortality rate per 1,000 live births (1995): 5.2, 51st

Rate for whites: 4.7, 49th

Rate for blacks: 9.0, 34th

Births to unmarried women, % of total (1996): 25.6%, 44th

Births to teenage mothers, % of total (1996): 7.3%, 51st

Abortions (1992): 40,660, 10th

Rate per 1,000 women 14-44 years old: 28.4, 10th

Percent change (1988-92): –6%, 22nd

Average lifetime (1989-91): 76.72, 14th

Total death rate per 100,000 pop. (1995): 913.4, 25th

Accidents and adverse effects: 20.1, 51st

Alzheimer's disease: 11.3, 8th

Cancer: 231.9, 8th

Cerebrovascular diseases: 57.0, 34th

Chronic liver disease and cirrhosis: 9.4, 21st

Chronic obstructive pulmonary diseases and allied conditions: 38.8, 29th

Diabetes mellitus: 21.8, 32nd

Diseases of heart: 275.8, 31st

HIV infection: 15.5, 11th

Homicide: 3.7, 43rd

Injury by firearms: 4.6, 51st

Motor vehicle accidents: 8.0, 51st

Pneumonia and influenza: 44.8, 1st

Suicide: 8.1, 48th

KEEPING WELL

Active nonfederal physicians per 100,000 pop. (1995): 387, 2nd

Dentists per 100,000 (1991): 76, 6th

Nurses per 100,000 (1995): 1,195, 3rd

Hospitals per 100,000 (1995): 1.58, 40th

Admissions per 1,000 (1995): 123.64, 17th

Hospital beds per 1,000 (1995): 3.11, 30th

Occupancy rate per 100 beds (1995): 69.84, 8th

Average cost per patient per day (1995): $1,157, 8th

Average cost per stay (1995): $7,099, 8th

AIDS cases (new, 1996): 1,307; per 100,000: 21.5, 14th

Persons living with HIV infection (1996): NA

Other notifiable diseases, per 100,000 pop.:

Gonorrhea (1995): 43.8, 40th

Syphilis (1995): 8.4, 29th

Tuberculosis (1996): 4.3, 30th

Pop. without health insur. (1996): 12.4%, 31st

HOUSEHOLDS BY TYPE

Total households (1996): 2,322,000, 13th

Percent change (1990-96): 3.3%, 45th

Per 1,000 pop. (1996) 381.16, 22nd

Percent of householders 65 yrs. and over (1996): 23.08%, 13th

Persons per household (1996): 2.61, 20th

Family households: 1,514,746

Percent of total: 67.41%, 48th

Nonfamily households: 732,364

Percent of total: 32.59%, 4th

Pop. living in group quarters: 214,307

Percent of pop.: 3.56%, 8th

LIVING QUARTERS

Total housing units: 2,472,711

Persons per unit: 2.43, 18th

Occupied housing units: 2,247,110

Percent of total units: 90.88%, 17th

Persons per unit: 2.53, 23rd

Percent of units with over 1 person per room: 2.52%, 35th

Owner-occupied units: 1,331,493

Percent of total units: 53.85%, 42nd

Percent of occupied units: 59.25%, 45th

Persons per unit: 2.82, 10th

Median value: $162,800, 4th

Renter-occupied units: 915,617

Percent of total units: 37.03%, 6th

Percent of occupied units: 40.75%, 8th

Persons per unit: 2.24, 42nd

Median contract rent: $506, 5th

Rental vacancy rate: 6.9%, 42nd

Mobile home, trailer & other as a percent of occupied housing units: 2.27% 49th

Persons in emergency shelters for homeless persons: 6,207, 0.103%, 6th

Persons visible in street locations: 674, 0.0112%, 15th

Nursing home population: 55,662, 0.93%, 14th

CRIME INDEX PER 100,000 (1996)

Total reported: 3,837.1, 41st
  Percent increase: –11.6%, 49th
  Violent: 642.2, 15th
    Percent increase: –6.5%, 28th
    Murder & nonnegligent manslaughter: 2.6, 44th
    Forcible rape: 29.0, 35th
    Aggravated assault: 482.9, 11th
    Robbery: 127.7, 26th
  Property: 3,194.9, 44th
    Percent increase: –12.6%, 49th
    Burglary: 704.1, 38th
    Larceny-theft: 1,962.6, 49th
    Motor vehicle theft: 528.2, 16th

TEACHING AND LEARNING

Pop. 3 and over enrolled in school (1996): 1,350,588, 13th
  Percent of pop.: 22.17%, 31st
Public elementary & secondary schools (1996-97): 1,850, 17th
  Total enrollment (1996): 936,794, 15th
    Percent of school age pop.: 90.86%, 29th
    Percent of total pop.: 15.38%, 46th
  Teachers (1996): 65,863, 13th
    Percent of pop.: 1.08%, 24th
  Pupil/teacher ratio (1995): 14.6, 43rd
  Teachers' avg. salary (1996-97): $43,806, 8th
  Expenditure per capita (1992-93): $1,106.92, 45th
    Education as % of state govt. expenditures: 25.8%, 48th
  Expenditure per pupil (1994-95): $7,287, 7th
    Percent increase (1993-94 & 1994-95): 4.71%, 19th
Percent at or above grade level, NAEP tests:
  Reading, grade 4 (1994): 36%, 4th
  Math, grade 4 (1996): 71%, 8th
  Math, grade 8 (1996): 68%, 11th
Percent of graduates taking SAT (1995): 80%, 2nd
  Mean SAT verbal scores: 430, 33rd

Mean SAT mathematical scores: 477, 36th
Percent of graduates taking ACT (1997): 6%, 43rd
  Mean ACT scores: 21.6, 13th
Percent of pop. over 25 completing:
  Less than 9th grade: 8.0%, 36th
  High school: 80.0%, 15th
  College degree(s): 27.2%, 2nd
Higher education, institutions (1996): 116, 9th
  Enrollment (1995-96): 413,794, 9th
    Percent increase in enroll. (1990-95): –1.0%, 41st
    White non-Hispanic (1995): 322,092, 9th
      Percent of enroll.: 77.84%, 31st
    Total minority enroll. (1995): 67,405, 14th
      Percent of enroll.: 16.29%, 29th
    Black non-Hispanic (1995): 23,079, 21st
      Percent of enroll.: 5.58%, 27th
    Hispanic (1995): 18,102, 10th
      Percent of enroll.: 4.37%, 12th
    Asian/Pacific Islander (1995): 24,513, 6th
      Percent of enroll.: 5.92%, 6th
    American Indian/AK native (1995): 1,711, 22nd
      Percent of enroll.: 0.41%, 31st
    Nonresident alien (1995): 24,297, 4th
      Percent of enroll.: 5.87%, 3rd
    Female (1995): 233,062, 9th
      Percent of enroll.: 56.32%, 22nd
  Pub. institutions (1995-96): 32, 18th
    Enrollment: 176,777, 23rd
      Percent increase in enrollment (1990-95): –5.0%, 45th
      Percent of enroll.: 42.72%, 50th
  Private institutions (1995-96): 84, 6th
    Enrollment: 237,017, 4th
      Percent increase in enrollment (1990-95): 2.3%, 33rd
      Percent of enroll.: 57.28%, 2nd
  Tuition (in state), public 4-year institution (1996-97): $4,266, 5th
  Tuition (in state), public 2-year institution (1996-97): $2,342, 6th
  Tuition, private 4-year institution (1996-97): $17,248, 2nd
Public library systems (1994): 373, 8th
  Books & serial vol. per capita: 4.7, 3rd
  Library visits per capita: NA
  Circulation per capita: 6.9, 25th

LAW ENFORCEMENT AND CORRECTIONS

Police protection and corrections expenditures (1996): $1,016,198,000
  Per capita: $166.81, 6th

Police per 10,000 pop. (1996): 26.41, 10th
Prisoners (1 year or more) per 100,000 pop. (1996): 302, 30th
Percent change (1995-96): 5.3%, 29th
Percent of inmates that are female: 6.3%, 24th
Percent change: 13.9%, 18th
Death penalty: no

RELIGION, NUMBER AND PERCENT OF POPULATION

Agnostic: 46,634—1.00%, 10th
Buddhist: 18,653—0.40%, 5th
Christian: 3,837,937—82.30%, 40th
Hindu: 4,663—0.10%, 10th
Jewish: 163,217—3.50%, 4th
Muslim: 18,653—0.40%, 5th
Unitarian: 37,307—0.80%, 3rd
Other: 51,297—1.10%, 32nd
None: 340,425—7.30%, 19th
Refused to answer: 144,564—3.10%, 7th

MAKING A LIVING

Personal income per capita (1996): $29,439, 4th
Percent increase (1995-96): 3.2%, 23rd
Disposable personal income per capita (1996): $24,720, 4th
Median income of households (average, 1995-96): $39,604, 10th
Percent of pop. below poverty level (1995-96): 10.6%, 38th

ECONOMY

In civilian labor force (1996): 3,189,000
Percent of total pop.: 67.5%, 29th
Percent of total pop. 65 years and over: 11.2%, 31st
Percent of total female pop.: 61.5%, 23rd
Major employer industries (total nonagricultural, 1996):
Construction: 93,900—3.1%, 48th
Finance, insurance, & real estate: 208,600—6.9%, 5th
Government: 400,200—13.2%, 50th
Manufacturing: 444,100—14.6%, 27th
Service: 1,062,600—35.0%, 3rd
Trade: 696,500—22.9%, 37th
Transportation, communications, public utilities: 129,200—4.3%, 45th
Unemployment rate (1996): 4.3%, 39th
Male: 4.9%, 28th
Female: 3.7%, 45th
Total businesses (1995): 160,350, 13th

New business incorps. (1995): 13,479
Percent of total businesses: 8.41%, 31st
Business failures (1995): 1,927
Failures per 10,000 businesses: 120.2, 12th
Agriculture farm income:
Marketing (1996): $477,698,000, 45th
Average per farm: $78,311, 32nd
Leading products (1997): Greenhouse, cranberries, dairy products, eggs, vegetables
Average value land & build. per acre (1997): $6,200, 4th
Percent increase (1996-97): 11%, 1st
Govt. payments (1996): $1,548,000, 46th
Average per farm: $254, 47th
Construction, value of all (1996): $7,674,078,000, 17th
Per capita: $1,260, 24th
Manufactures (1995):
Value added: $41,900,700,000
Per capita: $6,899, 21st
Leading products (1997): Electric and electronic equipment, instruments, industrial machinery and equipment, printing and publishing, fabricated metal products
Value of nonfuel mineral production (1996): $191,000,000, 39th
Leading mineral products (1996): Sand/gravel, stone, lime, clays
Energy consumption per person (1994): 246.2 mil. Btu, 46th
Retail sales (1995): $53,873,000,000
Per household: $23,652, 36th
Sales increase (1994-95): 2.7%, 38th
Tourism revenues (1994): $9.2 bil.
Foreign exports, in total value (1996): $14,524,000,000, 11th
Per capita: $2,384, 9th
Gross state product per person (1994): $30,822, 9th
Public aid recipients (percent of resident pop. 1994): 7.5%, 15th
Medicaid recipients (percent of pop., 1995): 12.0%, 25th
Medicare enrollment per 1,000 pop. (1996): 155, 12th

TRAVEL AND TRANSPORTATION

Motor vehicle registrations (1996): 4,702,389, 15th
Per 1,000 pop.: 772.73, 32nd
Motorcycle registrations (1996): 90,844, 16th
Per 1,000 pop.: 19.32, 26th
Licensed drivers (1996): 4,211,029, 13th
Per 1,000 pop.: 693.62, 24th

Public roads & streets (1996)
  Total mileage: 34,725, 40th
    Per 1,000 pop.: 15.70, 47th
    Rural mileage: 12,050, 44th
    Per 1,000 pop.: 1.98, 47th
    Urban mileage: 22,675, 11th
    Per 1,000 pop.: 3.72, 7th
    Interstate mileage: 565, 37th
    Per 1,000 pop.: 0.09, 44th
Speed limit (max. interstate, autos, mi. per hr., 1997): 65
Annual vehicle-mi. of travel per driver (1996): 11,471, 44th
Mean travel time for workers age 16+ who work away from home: 22.7 min., 9th

GOVERNMENT

Percent of voting age pop. registered (1996): 74.41%, 32nd
  Percent of voting age pop. voting for president: (1996): 55.3%, 18th
  Percent of voting age pop. voting for U.S. representatives (1996): 52.1%, 21st
State legislators, total (1997): 200, 6th
  Women members (1997): 45
    Percent of legislature: 23%, 21st
U.S. Congress, House members (1998): 10
  Change (1988-98): −1
Revenues (1996):
  State govt.: $25,196,723,000
    Per capita: $4,136.03, 14th
    Parimutuel & amusement taxes & lotteries, revenue per capita (1995): $437.09, 1st
Expenditures (1996):
  State govt.: $24,949,729,000
    Per capita: $4,095.49, 8th

Debt outstanding (1996): $29,294,682,000
  Per capita: $4,808.71, 5th

LAWS AND REGULATIONS

Legal driving age: 18
Marriage age without parental consent: 18
Divorce residence requirement: 1 yr., for qualifications check local statutes

ATTRACTIONS (1997)

Major opera companies: 3
Major symphony orchestras: 2
Major dance companies: 1
Major professional theater companies (non-profit): 2
Per capita spending by the NEA (1997): $0.50, 16th

SPORTS AND COMPETITION

NCAA (Division I) football and basketball teams: Boston College Eagles, Boston Univ. Terriers, Harvard Univ. Crimson, College of the Holy Cross Crusaders, Northeastern Univ. Huskies, Univ. of Massachusetts-Amherst Minutemen
Major league baseball teams: Boston Red Sox (AL East), Fenway Park
Major league soccer teams: New England Revolution, Foxboro Stadium
NBA basketball teams: Boston Celtics, Fleet-Center
ABL basketball teams: New England Blizzard, Springfield Civic Center, Hartford Civic Center (CT)
NFL football teams: New England Patriots (AFC), Foxboro Stadium
NHL hockey teams: Boston Bruins, FleetCenter

WEBSITES CONTAINING FURTHER INFORMATION

Commonwealth of Massachusetts—MAGNet	http://www.state.ma.us
Massachusetts Office of Travel and Tourism	http://www.mass-vacation.com

MICHIGAN

"Michigan, handsome as a well made woman, and dressed and jewelled. It seemed to me that the earth was generous and outgoing here in the heartland, and, perhaps its people took a cue from it."
John Steinbeck, novelist

Michigan extends as far east as parts of South Carolina. Parts of Canada, the "northern" neighbor, actually lie south of northern Michigan. Michigan is the only state that is divided into two peninsulas—Upper and Lower. The Upper Peninsula is sparsely populated and quite rural, whereas the Lower Peninsula contains all the large cities and most of the industry and agriculture. Michigan is a state in which almost half its area is fresh water. Michigan had the imagination to create a capital in the wilderness and the courage to elect the youngest governor to serve anywhere in the United States. The world automobile industry was established there, and Michigan still leads the United States in auto production. Detroit continues to work toward improvement in its response to social problems.

SUPERLATIVES

- Longest siege in Indian warfare—175 days, by Chief Pontiac.
- First in U.S. automobile production.
- World's busiest ship canal.
- Detroit River carries the world's greatest tonnage.
- Most million-ton ports in the United States.
- Greatest variety of trees in the United States.
- Largest copper reserve in the United States.
- First university established by a state.

MOMENTS IN HISTORY

- Coming from French Canada, Etienne Brulé reached present-day Michigan during his journeys of 1618-22.
- In 1668, Father Jacques Marquette and Father Claude Dablon founded the first permanent European settlement in what is now Michigan—Sault Sainte Marie, at the Soo.
- In 1679, Robert Cavalier, Sieur de La Salle, constructed the first French fort in lower Michigan, where St. Joseph now stands.
- Detroit was begun in 1701 by Antoine de la Mothe, Sieur de Cadillac; it became the first major city founded in the Midwest.

- In 1760, Major Robert Rogers and his Royal English Rangers captured Detroit without a struggle, ending French rule.
- Angered by British mistreatment, Chief Pontiac laid siege to Detroit in 1763. Lasting for 175 days, it was the longest siege in Indian warfare, but he failed to take the city.
- The Treaty of Paris in 1783 gave Michigan to the young United States, but the British continued to occupy most of the area until General "Mad Anthony" Wayne asserted American control, confirmed by the Jay Treaty of 1795.
- In 1805 much of Detroit was destroyed by fire.
- During the War of 1812, the British retook Detroit, but the Americans returned in September 1813.
- The cholera epidemic of 1832 took many lives, including that of the beloved priest Father Gabriel Richard.

So They Say

"Father Gabriel Richard...might be seen clothed in the robes of his high calling, pale and emaciated...going from house to house...encouraging the well, and administering spiritual consolation to the sick and dying." **Anonymous**

- Michigan became the 26th U.S. state on January 26, 1837.
- In 1840 the rich copper lands in the Upper Peninsula were discovered.
- A Republican party was created at Jackson on July 6, 1854, and later the same year Michigan became the first state to elect a Republican governor.
- By strange coincidence a terrible fire roared through Holland and other areas of Michigan on the same day of the great Chicago fire, October 8, 1871.
- Around the turn of the century, Detroit began its rise as the principal center of automobile production.
- In 1957, Big Mac, the bridge, linked the Upper and Lower peninsulas of the state for the first time.

- The riots of 1967 destroyed much of the inner city of Detroit.
- During the 1980s, Michigan auto industries began to encounter stiff competition from Japanese automobiles.
- In 1992 scientists announced that the largest living thing in the world was a fungus, *Armillaria bulbosa*, growing beneath 37 acres near Crystal Falls. (However, an organism in Washington State was later claimed to be larger.)

THAT'S INTERESTING

- Michigan history took a peculiar turn when Mormon leader James Strang proclaimed himself King of Beaver Island. He was assassinated in 1856, and mainland forces took over the Mormon properties.
- Disguised as a man, Sarah Emma Edmonds fought through four major Civil War campaigns before her identity was discovered.

NOTABLE NATIVES

Avery Brundage (Detroit, 1887-1975), businessman/sportsman. **Ralph Johnson Bunche** (Detroit, 1904-1971), diplomat. **Thomas Edmund Dewey** (Owosso, 1902-1971), public official. **Edna Ferber** (Kalamazoo, 1887-1968), author. **Henry Ford** (near Dearborn, 1863-1947), industrialist/philanthropist. **Will Keith Kellogg** (Battle Creek, 1860-1951), businessman. **Ring Lardner** (Niles, 1885-1933), journalist/author. **Charles Augustus Lindbergh** (Detroit, 1902-1974), aviator. **Theodore Roethke** (Saginaw, 1908-1963), poet. **Glenn Theodore Seaborg** (Ishpeming, 1912-), chemist.

GENERAL

Admitted to statehood: January 26, 1837
Origin of name: From Chippewa words *mici gama*, meaning "great water," after the lake of the same name
Capital: Lansing
Nickname: Wolverine State, Great Lakes State, Water Wonderland
Motto: *Si Quaeris Peninsulam Amoenam Circumspice*—If you seek a pleasant peninsula, look about you
Bird: Robin
Fish: Brook trout
Flower: Apple blossom
Gem: Isle Royal greenstone
Stone: Petoskey stone

Song: "Michigan, My Michigan"
Tree: White pine

THE LAND

Area: 96,705 sq. mi., 11th
  Land: 56,809 sq. mi., 22nd
  Water: 39,896 sq. mi., 2nd
    Inland water: 1,704 sq. mi., 13th
    Great Lakes: 38,192 sq. mi., 1st
Topography: Low rolling hills give way to northern tableland of hilly belts in Lower Peninsula; Upper Peninsula is level in E, with swampy areas; western region is higher and more rugged.
Number of counties: 83
Geographic center: Wexford, 5 mi. NNW of Cadillac
Length: 490 mi.; width: 240 mi.
Highest point: 1,979 ft. (Mount Arvon), 38th
Lowest point: 572 ft. (Lake Erie), 40th
Mean elevation: 900 ft., 29th

CLIMATE AND ENVIRONMENT

Temp., highest: 112 deg. on July 13, 1936, at Mio; lowest: -51 deg. on Feb. 9, 1934, at Vanderbilt
Monthly average: highest: 83.1 deg., 43rd; lowest: 14.0 deg., 15th; spread (high to low): 69.1 deg., 24th
Hazardous waste sites (1997): 72, 5th
Endangered species: Animals: 11—Indiana bat, American burying beetle, Hungerford's crawling water beetle, Karner blue butterfly, Mitchell's satyr butterfly, Clubshell, American peregrine falcon, Piping plover, Northern rifleshell, Kirtland's warbler, Gray wolf. Plants: 1

MAJOR CITIES
POPULATION, 1996
PERCENTAGE INCREASE, 1990-96

Detroit, 1,000,272; -2.7%
Grand Rapids, 188,242; -0.5%
Warren, 138,078; -4.7%
Flint, 134,881; -4.3%
Lansing, 125,736; -1.2%

THE PEOPLE

Population (1997): 9,773,892, 8th
  Percent change (1990-97): 5.15%, 34th
  Percent of total U.S. pop.: 3.65%, 8th
  Per sq. mi: 100.96, 22nd
Population (2000 proj.): 9,695,000, 8th
  Percent change (1995-2000): 1.53%, 44th

Percent in metro. area (1996): 82.45%, 16th
Foreign born: 355,000, 9th
  Percent: 3.8%, 21st
Top three ancestries reported:
  German, 28.68%
  Irish, 14.20%
  English, 14.15%
White (1992): 7,920,000, 83.95%, 32nd
Black (1992): 1,337,000, 14.17%, 15th
Native American (1992): 58,000, 0.61%, 20th
Asian, Pacific Isle (1992): 119,000, 1.26%, 26th
Hispanic origin (1992): 215,000, 2.28%, 29th
Percent over 5 yrs. speaking language other than English at home: 6.6%, 28th
Percent males (1996): 48.75%, 27th; percent females: 51.25%, 25th
Percent never married: 27.8%, 11th
Marriages per 1,000 (1996): 7.20, 39th
Divorces per 1,000 (1996): 4.03, 29th
Median age (1996): 34.6
Under 5 years (1996): 7.04%, 21st
18 years and under (1996): 29.25%, 20th
65 years and over (1996): 12.44%, 32nd
Percent increase among the elderly (1995-96): 0.76%, 25th

OF VITAL IMPORTANCE

Live births per 1,000 pop. (1996): 14.3, 22nd
Infant mortality rate per 1,000 live births (1995): 8.3, 15th
  Rate for whites: 6.2, 26th
  Rate for blacks: 17.3, 11th
Births to unmarried women, % of total (1996): 33.8%, 13th
Births to teenage mothers, % of total (1996): 12.2%, 28th
Abortions (1992): 55,580, 6th
  Rate per 1,000 women 14-44 years old: 25.2, 15th
  Percent change (1988-92): −11%, 30th
Average lifetime (1989-91): 75.04, 34th
Total death rate per 100,000 pop. (1995): 876.1, 32nd
  Accidents and adverse effects: 33.2, 37th
  Alzheimer's disease: 6.2, 44th
  Cancer: 203.5, 32nd
  Cerebrovascular diseases: 61.4, 26th
  Chronic liver disease and cirrhosis: 10.4, 11th
  Chronic obstructive pulmonary diseases and allied conditions: 37.5, 35th

  Diabetes mellitus: 23.4, 22nd
  Diseases of heart: 294.8, 23rd
  HIV infection: 8.4, 30th
  Homicide: 9.9, 15th
  Injury by firearms: 13.5, 28th
  Motor vehicle accidents: 17.0, 29th
  Pneumonia and influenza: 31.2, 27th
  Suicide: 10.3, 42nd

KEEPING WELL

Active nonfederal physicians per 100,000 pop. (1995): 210, 27th
Dentists per 100,000 (1991): 62, 16th
Nurses per 100,000 (1995): 820, 25th
Hospitals per 100,000 (1995): 1.75, 35th
  Admissions per 1,000 (1995): 117.29, 23rd
  Hospital beds per 1,000 (1995): 3.10, 31st
  Occupancy rate per 100 beds (1995): 65.20, 14th
  Average cost per patient per day (1995): $994, 20th
  Average cost per stay (1995): $6,218, 15th
AIDS cases (new, 1996): 965; per 100,000: 10.1, 34th
Persons living with HIV infection, not yet AIDS (1996): 3,110
Other notifiable diseases, per 100,000 pop.:
  Gonorrhea (1995): 190.8, 13th
  Syphilis (1995): 12.6, 25th
  Tuberculosis (1996): 4.6, 29th
Pop. without health insur. (1996): 8.9%, 49th

HOUSEHOLDS BY TYPE

Total households (1996): 3,576,000, 8th
  Percent change (1990-96): 4.6%, 36th
  Per 1,000 pop. (1996) 372.73, 36th
  Percent of householders 65 yrs. and over (1996): 21.39%, 29th
  Persons per household (1996): 2.66, 11th
Family households: 2,439,171
  Percent of total: 71.33%, 18th
Nonfamily households: 980,160
  Percent of total: 28.67%, 34th
Pop. living in group quarters: 211,692
  Percent of pop.: 2.28%, 43rd

LIVING QUARTERS

Total housing units: 3,847,926
  Persons per unit: 2.42, 23rd
Occupied housing units: 3,419,331
  Percent of total units: 88.86%, 30th
  Persons per unit: 2.56, 19th
  Percent of units with over 1 person per room: 2.65%, 32nd

Owner-occupied units: 2,427,643
  Percent of total units: 63.09%, 9th
  Percent of occupied units: 71.00%, 4th
  Persons per unit: 2.80, 13th
  Median value: $60,600, 33rd
Renter-occupied units: 991,688
  Percent of total units: 25.77%, 45th
  Percent of occupied units: 29.00%, 48th
  Persons per unit: 2.31, 30th
  Median contract rent: $343, 25th
  Rental vacancy rate: 7.2%, 40th
Mobile home, trailer & other as a percent of
  occupied housing units: 6.69%, 39th
Persons in emergency shelters for homeless
  persons: 3,784, 0.041%, 33rd
Persons visible in street locations: 262,
  0.0028%, 41st
Nursing home population: 57,622, 0.62%, 33rd

CRIME INDEX PER 100,000 (1996)

Total reported: 5,117.5, 22nd
  Percent increase: −1.3%, 19th
  Violent: 635.3, 17th
    Percent increase: −7.6%, 30th
    Murder & nonnegligent manslaughter:
      7.5, 18th
    Forcible rape: 57.0, 4th
    Aggravated assault: 394.6, 17th
    Robbery: 176.2, 14th
  Property: 4,482.2, 21st
    Percent increase: −0.3%, 18th
    Burglary: 895.4, 24th
    Larceny-theft: 2,886.3, 29th
    Motor vehicle theft: 700.5, 6th

TEACHING AND LEARNING

Pop. 3 and over enrolled in school (1996):
  2,210,439, 8th
Percent of pop.: 23.04%, 21st
Public elementary & secondary schools (1996-
  97): 3,748, 6th
  Total enrollment (1996): 1,662,100, 8th
    Percent of school age pop.: 89.12%, 37th
    Percent of total pop.: 17.32%, 27th
  Teachers (1996): 84,200, 9th
    Percent of pop.: 0.88%, 46th
  Pupil/teacher ratio (1995): 19.7, 5th
  Teachers' avg. salary (1996-97): $44,251,
    7th
  Expenditure per capita (1992-93):
    $1,562.94, 9th
    Education as % of state govt. expendi-
      tures: 39.4%, 4th

Expenditure per pupil (1994-95): $6,994,
  11th
  Percent increase (1993-94 & 1994-95):
    5.05%, 15th
Percent at or above grade level, NAEP tests:
  Reading, grade 4 (1994): NA
  Math, grade 4 (1996): 68%, 13th
  Math, grade 8 (1996): 67%, 15th
Percent of graduates taking SAT (1995): 11%,
  34th
  Mean SAT verbal scores: 484, 17th
  Mean SAT mathematical scores: 549, 11th
Percent of graduates taking ACT (1997):
  68%, 10th
  Mean ACT scores: 21.3, 23rd
Percent of pop. over 25 completing:
  Less than 9th grade: 7.8%, 40th
  High school: 76.8%, 25th
  College degree(s): 17.4%, 37th
Higher education, institutions (1996): 109, 11th
  Enrollment (1995-96): 548,339, 7th
    Percent increase in enroll. (1990-95):
      −3.8%, 49th
    White non-Hispanic (1995): 440,026, 7th
      Percent of enroll.: 80.25%, 25th
    Total minority enroll. (1995): 91,310, 7th
      Percent of enroll.: 16.65%, 27th
    Black non-Hispanic (1995): 59,893, 8th
      Percent of enroll.: 10.92%, 17th
    Hispanic (1995): 11,593, 11th
      Percent of enroll.: 2.11%, 28th
    Asian/Pacific Islander (1995): 15,320, 12th
      Percent of enroll.: 2.79%, 22nd
    American Indian/AK native (1995): 4,504,
      7th
      Percent of enroll.: 0.82%, 22nd
    Nonresident alien (1995): 17,003, 7th
      Percent of enroll.: 3.10%, 17th
    Female (1995): 307,179, 7th
      Percent of enroll.: 56.02%, 23rd
  Pub. institutions (1995-96): 45, 11th
    Enrollment: 462,390, 6th
      Percent increase in enrollment (1990-
        95): −5.1%, 47th
      Percent of enroll.: 84.33%, 21st
  Private institutions (1995-96): 64, 10th
    Enrollment: 85,949, 10th
      Percent increase in enrollment (1990-
        95): 4.3%, 29th
      Percent of enroll.: 15.67%, 31st
  Tuition (in state), public 4-year institution
    (1996-97): $3,986, 8th
  Tuition (in state), public 2-year institution
    (1996-97): $1,578, 20th

Tuition, private 4-year institution (1996-97): $9,683, 34th

Public library systems (1994): 380, 7th
Books & serial vol. per capita: 2.9, 25th
Library visits per capita: 3.8, 23rd
Circulation per capita: 5.4, 35th

LAW ENFORCEMENT AND CORRECTIONS

Police protection and corrections expenditures (1996): $1,469,964,000
Per capita: $153.22, 7th

Police per 10,000 pop. (1996): 20.87, 31st

Prisoners (1 year or more) per 100,000 pop. (1996): 440, 12th
Percent change (1995-96): 3.0%, 38th
Percent of inmates that are female: 4.5%, 46th
Percent change: 4.2%, 38th

Death penalty: no

RELIGION, NUMBER AND PERCENT OF POPULATION

Agnostic: 34,183—0.50%, 27th
Buddhist: 6,837—0.10%, 17th
Christian: 5,790,543—84.70%, 37th
Hindu: 13,673—0.20%, 3rd
Jewish: 54,692—0.80%, 20th
Muslim: 20,510—0.30%, 9th
Unitarian: 20,510—0.30%, 15th
Other: 157,240—2.30%, 6th
None: 594,778—8.70%, 13th
Refused to answer: 143,567—2.10%, 28th

MAKING A LIVING

Personal income per capita (1996): $24,810, 17th
Percent increase (1995-96): 2.1%, 41st

Disposable personal income per capita (1996): $21,376, 18th

Median income of households (average, 1995-96): $38,364, 13th

Percent of pop. below poverty level (1995-96): 11.7%, 27th

ECONOMY

In civilian labor force (1996): 4,807,000
Percent of total pop.: 66.3%, 35th
Percent of total pop. 65 years and over: 9.5%, 38th
Percent of total female pop.: 58.6%, 36th

Major employer industries (total nonagricultural, 1996):
Construction: 167,700—3.9%, 39th

Finance, insurance, & real estate: 201,100—4.6%, 35th
Government: 643,300—14.8%, 40th
Manufacturing: 966,900—22.3%, 6th
Service: 1,165,400—26.8%, 30th
Trade: 1,024,700—23.6%, 26th
Transportation, communications, public utilities: 168,400—3.9%, 48th

Unemployment rate (1996): 4.9%, 31st
Male: 5.1%, 24th
Female: 4.6%, 32nd

Total businesses (1995): 226,973, 8th

New business incorps. (1995): 31,254
Percent of total businesses: 13.77%, 8th

Business failures (1995): 1,681
Failures per 10,000 businesses: 74.1, 31st

Agriculture farm income:
Marketing (1996): $3,642,927,000, 20th
Average per farm: $68,734, 39th
Leading products (1997): Dairy products, corn, soybeans, wheat, dry beans, hay, potatoes, corn, apples, cherries, sugar beets, blueberries, cucumbers
Average value land & build. per acre (1997): $1,600, 17th
Percent increase (1996-97): 9%, 5th
Govt. payments (1996): $109,585,000, 23rd
Average per farm: $2,068, 26th

Construction, value of all (1996): $10,784,198,000, 9th
Per capita: $1,124, 31st

Manufactures (1995):
Value added: $87,397,500,000
Per capita: $9,152, 6th
Leading products (1997): Automobiles, transportation equipment, machinery, fabricated metals, food products, plastics, office furniture

Value of nonfuel mineral production (1996): $1,510,000,000, 9th

Leading mineral products (1996): Petroleum, iron ore, natural gas, cement, sand/gravel, magneium compounds, stone, salt

Energy consumption per person (1994): 325.6 mil. Btu, 30th

Retail sales (1995): $91,524,000,000
Per household: $25,867, 11th
Sales increase (1994-95): 4.1%, 28th

Tourism revenues (1995): $8 bil.

Foreign exports, in total value (1996): $27,553,000,000, 4th
Per capita: $2,872, 7th

Gross state product per person (1994): $25,314, 23rd

Public aid recipients (percent of resident pop. 1994): 9.1%, 8th

Medicaid recipients (percent of pop., 1995): 12.3%, 23rd

Medicare enrollment per 1,000 pop. (1996): 142, 28th

TRAVEL AND TRANSPORTATION

Motor vehicle registrations (1996): 8,010,396, 8th
  Per 1,000 pop.: 823.19, 22nd

Motorcycle registrations (1996): 149,971, 7th
  Per 1,000 pop.: 18.72, 28th

Licensed drivers (1996): 6,658,750, 8th
  Per 1,000 pop.: 698.13, 20th

Public roads & streets (1996)
  Total mileage: 117,620, 8th
    Per 1,000 pop.: 112.26, 36th
  Rural mileage: 89,478, 9th
    Per 1,000 pop.: 9.33, 35th
  Urban mileage: 28,142, 8th
    Per 1,000 pop.: 2.93, 33rd
  Interstate mileage: 1,239, 9th
    Per 1,000 pop.: 0.13, 39th

Speed limit (max. interstate, autos, mi. per hr., 1997): 70

Annual vehicle-mi. of travel per driver (1996): 13,431, 34th

Mean travel time for workers age 16+ who work away from home: 21.2 min., 20th

GOVERNMENT

Percent of voting age pop. registered (1996): 94.42%, 2nd
  Percent of voting age pop. voting for president: (1996): 54.5%, 20th
  Percent of voting age pop. voting for U.S. representatives (1996): 52.3%, 20th

State legislators, total (1997): 148, 24th
  Women members (1997): 34
  Percent of legislature: 23%, 22nd

U.S. Congress, House members (1998): 16
  Change (1988-98): –2

Revenues (1996):
  State govt.: $38,047,205,000
    Per capita: $3,965.73, 16th
    Parimutuel & amusement taxes & lotteries, revenue per capita (1995): $133.19, 16th

Expenditures (1996):
  State govt.: $35,079,667,000
    Per capita: $3,656.42, 15th

Debt outstanding (1996): $13,667,509,000
  Per capita: $1,424.59, 24th

LAWS AND REGULATIONS

Legal driving age: 18, 16 if completed driver education course

Marriage age without parental consent: 18

Divorce residence requirement: 180 days, for qualifications check local statutes

ATTRACTIONS (1997)

Major opera companies: 2

Major symphony orchestras: 3

Major dance companies: 1

Per capita spending by the NEA (1997): $0.10, 50th

State Fair in mid-August at Escanaba for the Upper Peninsula and late-August–early September at Detroit

SPORTS AND COMPETITION

NCAA (Division I) football and basketball teams: Central Michigan Univ. Chippewas, Eastern Michigan Univ. Eagles, Michigan State Univ. Spartans, Univ. of Detroit Titans (basketball only), Univ. of Michigan Wolverines, Western Michigan Univ. Broncos

Major league baseball teams: Detroit Tigers (AL East), Tiger Stadium

NBA basketball teams: Detroit Pistons, The Palace of Auburn Hills

WNBA basketball teams: Detroit Shock, The Palace of Auburn Hills

NFL football teams: Detroit Lions (NFC), Pontiac Silverdome

NHL hockey teams: Detroit Red Wings, Joe Louis Arena

WEBSITES CONTAINING FURTHER INFORMATION

RING!OnLine	
Michigan's Internet SuperStation	http://www.ring.com/michigan.html

MINNESOTA

"Minnesotans are just different, that's all...with the wind chill hovering at fifty-seven below...there were all these Minnesotans running around outdoors, happy as lambs in the spring."

Charles Kuralt, broadcaster

Minnesota modestly boasts of its 10,000 lakes, but in reality there are more than 15,000. Its history is said by some experts to hark back to Viking explorers in the 1300s, and the state has long been a haven for Scandinavian immigrants. Almost 3 million cattle graze on its rich pastures. The state makes more butter than any other, and it is a leading milk and cheese producer. It cherishes a world-renowned facility for medical care and research, the Mayo Clinic, and its state university system ranks among the largest and best. It is a principal world center of milling concerns. Today, the Twin Cities of Minneapolis and St. Paul are a leading center of music, theater, and shopping. Enhancing the attraction of the Twin Cities is the nation's largest shopping mall.

SUPERLATIVES

- Source of the Mississippi River.
- Only state with source of three main river systems (Mississippi, St. Lawrence, Red River of the North).
- Principal U.S. source of manganese.
- Lady's slipper, unique among the state flowers.
- Pioneer in open-pit mining.
- Pioneer in overland bus travel.

MOMENTS IN HISTORY

- Some experts believe that European explorers reached Minnesota in the 1300s. This belief is based on artifacts such as a carving called the Kensington Runestone, found near Kensington. But other experts call it a hoax.

So They Say

"We had a camp by two islands. We were out fishing one day. When we returned home, we found ten men red of blood and dead...Save us from evil."

From a translation of the Kensington Runestone

- The first authenticated record of European visitors was made by explorer Daniel Greysolon, Sieur de Lhut (Duluth), in 1679.

- Beginning in 1727, French trading posts were established, and in 1763 the British took control from the French.
- The Northwest Ordinance of 1787 included most of eastern Minnesota, and the Louisiana Purchase of 1803 brought most of western Minnesota under U.S. control.
- In 1805, Zebulon Pike raised the U.S. flag over Minnesota for the first time, but the British paid little attention to U.S. claims.
- The War of 1812 finally settled the ownership of Minnesota.
- In 1820, Colonel Josiah Snelling started the fort bearing his name, erected at the site where the Minnesota and Mississippi rivers join together.
- In 1832, Henry R. Schoolcraft discovered the long-sought source of the Mississippi River and named it Lake Itasca.
- In 1838 both St. Paul and Minneapolis were begun separately.
- Most of Minnesota's northern boundary was established by the Webster-Ashburton Treaty of 1842.
- On May 11, 1858, Minnesota became the 32nd state, with Henry H. Sibley as the first governor.
- In 1862 the Sioux Indians went on a rampage. The warfare finally was put down by Henry H. Sibley, who took approximately 2,000 prisoners.
- The boundary line of the Lake of the Woods, extending into Canada, was not settled until 1873.
- The capitol was dedicated in 1905 and boasts the world's largest unsupported marble dome.
- The election of 1936 brought a dramatic victory to the Farmer-Labor party.
- The opening of the St. Lawrence Seaway in 1959 brought ocean traffic to the great port of Duluth.
- From 1965 to 1969, beloved Minnesota political figure Hubert Humphrey served as vice president under Lyndon B. Johnson. From 1977 to 1981, Minnesota's Walter Mondale was vice president under Jimmy Carter.

- In 1993, Minneapolis elected its first African-American mayor, Sharon Sayles Belton, a Democrat.

THAT'S INTERESTING

- There are so many lakes in Minnesota that novel names are scarce. There are 91 Long Lakes, and other bodies of water also have identical names.
- The Falls of St. Anthony have "traveled." Their waters have continued to cut into the soft limestone, causing them to move upstream about 4 miles since their discovery.
- The red-colored stone of Pipestone National Monument is found nowhere else. It was a sacred place to the Indians, who carved their peace pipes from its soft redstone.

NOTABLE NATIVES

Warren Earl Burger (St. Paul, 1907-1995), chief justice of the United States. William Orville Douglas (Maine, 1898-1980), Supreme Court justice. Bob Dylan (Robert Zimmerman) (Duluth, 1941-   ), singer/songwriter. Francis Scott Fitzgerald (St. Paul, 1896-1940), author. James Earle Fraser (Winona, 1876-1953), sculptor. Judy Garland (Grand Rapids, 1922-1969), actress/singer. Jean Paul Getty (Minneapolis, 1892-1976), businessman. Garrison Keillor (Anoka, 1942-), humorist. Sinclair Lewis (Sauk Centre, 1885-1951), author. Charles Horace Mayo (Rochester, 1865-1939), physician. William James Mayo (Le Sueur, 1861-1939), physician. Charles Monroe Schulz (Minneapolis, 1922-), cartoonist. Harold Edward Stassen (West St. Paul, 1907-) public official. DeWitt Wallace (St. Paul, 1889-1981), editor/publisher.

GENERAL

Admitted to statehood: May 11, 1858
Origin of name: From Dakota Sioux word meaning "cloudy water" or "sky-tinted water" of the Minnesota River
Capital: St. Paul
Nickname: North Star State, Gopher State
Motto: L'Etoile du Nord—The star of the North
Bird: Common loon
Fish: Walleye
Flower: Pink and white lady's slipper
Gem: Lake Superior agate
Song: "Hail! Minnesota"
Tree: Red (Norway) pine

THE LAND

Area: 86,943 sq. mi., 12th
   Land: 79,617 sq. mi., 14th
   Water: 7,326 sq. mi., 4th
      Inland water: 4,780 sq. mi., 3rd
      Great Lakes: 2,546 sq. mi., 5th
Topography: Central hill and lake region covering approximately half the state; to the NE, rocky ridges and deep lakes; to the NW, flat plain; to the S, rolling plains and deep river valleys
Number of counties: 87
Geographic center: Crow Wing, 10 mi. SW of Brainerd
Length: 400 mi.; width: 250 mi.
Highest point: 2,301 ft. (Eagle Mountain), 37th
Lowest point: 602 ft. (Lake Superior), 42nd
Mean elevation: 1,200 ft., 21st

CLIMATE AND ENVIRONMENT

Temp., highest: 114 deg. on July 6, 1936, at Moorhead; lowest: -60 deg. on Feb. 2, 1996, at Tower
Monthly average: highest: 83.4 deg., 42nd; lowest: −2.9 deg., 3rd; spread (high to low): 86.3 deg., 3rd
Hazardous waste sites (1997): 28, 12th
Endangered species: Animals: 5—Karner blue butterfly, American peregrine falcon, Winged mapleleaf mussel, Higgins' eye pearlymussel, Piping plover. Plants: 1

MAJOR CITIES
POPULATION, 1996
PERCENTAGE INCREASE, 1990-96

Minneapolis, 358,785; −2.6%
St. Paul, 259,606; −4.6%
Bloomington, 86,664; 0.4%
Duluth, 83,699; −2.1%
Rochester, 75,638; 6.9%

THE PEOPLE

Population (1997): 4,685,549, 20th
   Percent change (1990-97): 7.08%, 21st
   Percent of total U.S. pop.: 1.75%, 20th
   Per sq. mi: 53.89, 33rd
Population (2000 proj.): 4,826,000, 20th
   Percent change (1995-2000): 4.69%, 24th
Percent in metro. area (1996): 69.72%, 26th
Foreign born: 113,000, 22nd
   Percent: 2.6%, 30th

Top three ancestries reported:
  German, 46.18%
  Norwegian, 17.30%
  Irish, 13.12%
White (1992): 4,215,000, 94.34%, 11th
Black (1992): 109,000, 2.44%, 39th
Native American (1992): 53,000, 1.19%, 15th
Asian, Pacific Isle (1992): 91,000, 2.04%, 16th
Hispanic origin (1992): 62,000, 1.39%, 35th
Percent over 5 yrs. speaking language other than English at home: 5.6%, 35th
Percent males (1996): 49.34%, 16th; percent females: 50.66%, 36th
Percent never married: 27.4%, 14th
Marriages per 1,000 (1996): 7.12, 41st
Divorces per 1,000 (1996): 3.27, 38th
Median age (1996): 34.6
Under 5 years (1996): 6.86%, 33rd
18 years and under (1996): 29.57%, 15th
65 years and over (1996): 12.39%, 33rd
Percent increase among the elderly (1995-96): 0.48%, 36th

Of Vital Importance

Live births per 1,000 pop. (1996): 13.7, 32nd
Infant mortality rate per 1,000 live births (1995): 6.7, 36th
  Rate for whites: 6.0, 34th
  Rate for blacks: 17.6, 6th
Births to unmarried women, % of total (1996): 24.4%, 48th
Births to teenage mothers, % of total (1996): 8.5%, 47th
Abortions (1992): 16,180, 22nd
  Rate per 1,000 women 14-44 years old: 15.6, 33rd
  Percent change (1988-92): –14%, 36th
Average lifetime (1989-91): 77.76, 2nd
Total death rate per 100,000 pop. (1995): 813.7, 38th
  Accidents and adverse effects: 36.1, 27th
  Alzheimer's disease: 10.5, 9th
  Cancer: 188.6, 40th
  Cerebrovascular diseases: 67.8, 20th
  Chronic liver disease and cirrhosis: 6.7, 44th
  Chronic obstructive pulmonary diseases and allied conditions: 36.3, 37th
  Diabetes mellitus: 18.7, 40th
  Diseases of heart: 225.2, 41st
  HIV infection: 5.6, 36th
  Homicide: 3.8, 42nd

  Injury by firearms: 8.5, 43rd
  Motor vehicle accidents: 14.4, 36th
  Pneumonia and influenza: 32.8, 21st
  Suicide: 11.3, 39th

Keeping Well

Active nonfederal physicians per 100,000 pop. (1995): 239, 13th
Dentists per 100,000 (1991): 66, 11th
Nurses per 100,000 (1995): 955, 13th
Hospitals per 100,000 (1995): 3.08, 14th
  Admissions per 1,000 (1995): 107.59, 34th
  Hospital beds per 1,000 (1995): 3.77, 19th
  Occupancy rate per 100 beds (1995): 64.94, 16th
  Average cost per patient per day (1995): $736, 40th
  Average cost per stay (1995): $6,241, 13th
AIDS cases (new, 1996): 304; per 100,000: 6.5, 40th
Persons living with HIV infection, not yet AIDS (1996): 2,033
Other notifiable diseases, per 100,000 pop.:
  Gonorrhea (1995): 61.9, 34th
  Syphilis (1995): 4.1, 35th
  Tuberculosis (1996): 2.8, 38th
Pop. without health insur. (1996): 10.2%, 43rd

Households by Type

Total households (1996): 1,763,000, 20th
  Percent change (1990-96): 7.0%, 25th
  Per 1,000 pop. (1996) 378.49, 29th
  Percent of householders 65 yrs. and over (1996): 20.76%, 35th
  Persons per household (1996): 2.58, 24th
Family households: 1,130,683
  Percent of total: 68.62%, 42nd
Nonfamily households: 517,170
  Percent of total: 31.38%, 10th
Pop. living in group quarters: 117,621
  Percent of pop.: 2.69%, 28th

Living Quarters

Total housing units: 1,848,445
  Persons per unit: 2.37, 33rd
Occupied housing units: 1,647,853
  Percent of total units: 89.15%, 28th
  Persons per unit: 2.43, 50th
  Percent of units with over 1 person per room: 2.07%, 42nd
Owner-occupied units: 1,183,673
  Percent of total units: 64.04%, 6th

Percent of occupied units: 71.83%, 2nd
Persons per unit: 2.78, 17th
Median value: $74,000, 22nd
Renter-occupied units: 464,180
Percent of total units: 25.11%, 48th
Percent of occupied units: 28.17%, 50th
Persons per unit: 2.08, 51st
Median contract rent: $348, 22nd
Rental vacancy rate: 7.9%, 30th
Mobile home, trailer & other as a percent of occupied housing units: 6.77%, 38th
Persons in emergency shelters for homeless persons: 2,253, 0.051%, 23rd
Persons visible in street locations: 138, 0.0032%, 35th
Nursing home population: 47,051, 1.08%, 6th

CRIME INDEX PER 100,000 (1996)

Total reported: 4,463.1, 31st
Percent increase: –0.8%, 18th
Violent: 338.8, 37th
Percent increase: –4.9%, 19th
Murder & nonnegligent manslaughter: 3.6, 38th
Forcible rape: 50.0, 8th
Aggravated assault: 169.7, 42nd
Robbery: 115.6, 32nd
Property: 4,124.3, 29th
Percent increase: –0.4%, 19th
Burglary: 762.5, 34th
Larceny-theft: 2,977.1, 26th
Motor vehicle theft: 384.8, 32nd

TEACHING AND LEARNING

Pop. 3 and over enrolled in school (1996): 1,117,516, 19th
Percent of pop.: 23.99%, 14th
Public elementary & secondary schools (1996-97): 2,157, 11th
Total enrollment (1996): 836,700, 19th
Percent of school age pop.: 89.87%, 36th
Percent of total pop.: 17.96%, 16th
Teachers (1996): 47,600, 19th
Percent of pop.: 1.02%, 29th
Pupil/teacher ratio (1995): 17.8, 11th
Teachers' avg. salary (1996-97): $37,975, 18th
Expenditure per capita (1992-93): $1,592.45, 7th
Education as % of state govt. expenditures: 33.2%, 36th
Expenditure per pupil (1994-95): $6,000, 21st

Percent increase (1993-94 & 1994-95): 4.90%, 17th
Percent at or above grade level, NAEP tests:
Reading, grade 4 (1994): 33%, 10th
Math, grade 4 (1996): 76%, 1st
Math, grade 8 (1996): 75%, 5th
Percent of graduates taking SAT (1995): 9%, 38th
Mean SAT verbal scores: 506, 4th
Mean SAT mathematical scores: 579, 3rd
Percent of graduates taking ACT (1997): 60%, 21st
Mean ACT scores: 22.1, 5th
Percent of pop. over 25 completing:
Less than 9th grade: 8.6%, 32nd
High school: 82.4%, 6th
College degree(s): 21.8%, 16th
Higher education, institutions (1996): 106, 12th
Enrollment (1995-96): 280,816, 18th
Percent increase in enroll. (1990-95): 10.6%, 7th
White non-Hispanic (1995): 250,123, 14th
Percent of enroll.: 89.07%, 10th
Total minority enroll. (1995): 24,305, 31st
Percent of enroll.: 8.66%, 41st
Black non-Hispanic (1995): 7,975, 32nd
Percent of enroll.: 2.84%, 38th
Hispanic (1995): 3,985, 28th
Percent of enroll.: 1.42%, 38th
Asian/Pacific Islander (1995): 9,514, 16th
Percent of enroll.: 3.39%, 16th
American Indian/AK native (1995): 2,831, 14th
Percent of enroll.: 1.01%, 20th
Nonresident alien (1995): 6,388, 22nd
Percent of enroll.: 2.27%, 34th
Female (1995): 154,517, 18th
Percent of enroll.: 55.02%, 40th
Pub. institutions (1995-96): 62, 7th
Enrollment: 217,249, 18th
Percent increase in enrollment (1990-95): 9.1%, 13th
Percent of enroll.: 77.36%, 37th
Private institutions (1995-96): 44, 16th
Enrollment: 63,567, 15th
Percent increase in enrollment (1990-95): 16.5%, 13th
Percent of enroll.: 22.64%, 15th
Tuition (in state), public 4-year institution (1996-97): $3,539, 15th
Tuition (in state), public 2-year institution (1996-97): $2,219, 9th

Tuition, private 4-year institution (1996-97): $13,633, 15th
Public library systems (1994): 132, 22nd
Books & serial vol. per capita: 2.8, 26th
Library visits per capita: 4.6, 16th
Circulation per capita: 9.4, 5th

LAW ENFORCEMENT AND CORRECTIONS

Police protection and corrections expenditures (1996): $390,793,000
Per capita: $83.90, 43rd
Police per 10,000 pop. (1996): 16.33, 48th
Prisoners (1 year or more) per 100,000 pop. (1996): 110, 50th
Percent change (1995-96): 6.4%, 25th
Percent of inmates that are female: 4.5%, 46th
Percent change: 7.8%, 28th
Death penalty: no

RELIGION, NUMBER AND PERCENT OF POPULATION

Agnostic: 19,250—0.60%, 19th
Buddhist: 3,208—0.10%, 17th
Christian: 2,865,026—89.30%, 15th
Hindu: 3,208—0.10%, 10th
Jewish: 25,667—0.80%, 20th
Muslim: 3,208—0.10%, 22nd
Unitarian: 12,833—0.40%, 8th
Other: 25,667—0.80%, 37th
None: 179,666—5.60%, 38th
Refused to answer: 70,583—2.20%, 23rd

MAKING A LIVING

Personal income per capita (1996): $25,580, 10th
Percent increase (1995-96): 5.6%, 6th
Disposable personal income per capita (1996): $21,597, 15th
Median income of households (average, 1995-96): $40,022, 8th
Percent of pop. below poverty level (1995-96): 9.5%, 43rd

ECONOMY

In civilian labor force (1996): 2,609,000
Percent of total pop.: 74.7%, 1st
Percent of total pop. 65 years and over: 14.1%, 13th
Percent of total female pop.: 68.7%, 2nd
Major employer industries (total nonagricultural, 1996):
Construction: 88,800—3.7%, 42nd

Finance, insurance, & real estate: 142,500—5.9%, 13th
Government: 379,900—15.6%, 35th
Manufacturing: 428,300—17.6%, 15th
Service: 671,800—27.6%, 22nd
Trade: 592,800—24.4%, 18th
Transportation, communications, public utilities: 119,700—4.9%, 29th
Unemployment rate (1996): 4.0%, 45th
Male: 4.8%, 34th
Female: 3.1%, 50th
Total businesses (1995): 125,927, 18th
New business incorps. (1995): 12,203
Percent of total businesses: 9.69%, 21st
Business failures (1995): 903
Failures per 10,000 businesses: 71.7, 36th
Agriculture farm income:
Marketing (1996): $8,808,931,000, 6th
Average per farm: $101,252, 23rd
Leading products (1997): Dairy products, cattle, hogs, corn, soybeans, wheat, sugar beets, hay, barley, potatoes, sunflowers
Average value land & build. per acre (1997): $1,040, 29th
Percent increase (1996-97): 7%, 14th
Govt. payments (1996): $348,804,000, 8th
Average per farm: $4,009, 16th
Construction, value of all (1996): $5,420,761,000, 24th
Per capita: $1,164, 27th
Manufactures (1995):
Value added: $32,553,400,000
Per capita: $7,062, 16th
Leading products (1997): Food, chemical & paper products, industrial machinery, electric & electronic equipment, computers, printing and publishing, scientific & medical instruments, fabricated metal products, forest products
Value of nonfuel mineral production (1996): $1,800,000,000, 4th
Leading mineral products (1996): Iron ore, sand/gravel, stone
Energy consumption per person (1994): 342.1 mil. Btu, 26th
Retail sales (1995): $44,277,000,000
Per household: $25,371, 17th
Sales increase (1994-95): 5.1%, 25th
Tourism revenues (1994): $7 bil.
Foreign exports, in total value (1996): $8,992,000,000, 19th
Per capita: $1,931, 15th

Gross state product per person (1994): $27,290, 14th

Public aid recipients (percent of resident pop. 1994): 5.4%, 36th

Medicaid recipients (percent of pop., 1995): 10.3%, 35th

Medicare enrollment per 1,000 pop. (1996): 137, 33rd

TRAVEL AND TRANSPORTATION

Motor vehicle registrations (1996): 3,860,894, 19th
  Per 1,000 pop.: 830.55, 21st

Motorcycle registrations (1996): 116,189, 11th
  Per 1,000 pop.: 30.09, 8th

Licensed drivers (1996): 2,761,121, 21st
  Per 1,000 pop.: 598.34, 49th

Public roads & streets (1996)
  Total mileage: 130,613, 5th
    Per 1,000 pop.: 128.04, 13th
  Rural mileage: 115,232, 3rd
    Per 1,000 pop.: 24.74, 13th
  Urban mileage: 15,381, 21st
    Per 1,000 pop.: 3.30, 15th
  Interstate mileage: 913, 22nd
    Per 1,000 pop.: 0.20, 26th

Speed limit (max. interstate, autos, mi. per hr., 1997): 70

Annual vehicle-mi. of travel per driver (1996): 15,711, 13th

Mean travel time for workers age 16+ who work away from home: 19.1 min., 36th

GOVERNMENT

Percent of voting age pop. registered (1996): 89.65%, 4th
  Percent of voting age pop. voting for president: (1996): 64.3%, 2nd
  Percent of voting age pop. voting for U.S. representatives (1996): 62.8%, 2nd

State legislators, total (1997): 201, 5th
  Women members (1997): 61
    Percent of legislature: 30%, 9th

U.S. Congress, House members (1998): 8
  Change (1988-98): 0

Revenues (1996):
  State govt.: $20,525,269,000
    Per capita: $4,406.46, 11th
    Parimutuel & amusement taxes & lotteries, revenue per capita (1995): $83.14, 28th

Expenditures (1996):
  State govt.: $17,325,287,000
    Per capita: $3,719.47, 13th

Debt outstanding (1996): $4,858,281,000
  Per capita: $1,043.00, 37th

LAWS AND REGULATIONS

Legal driving age: 18, 16 if completed driver education course

Marriage age without parental consent: 18

Divorce residence requirement: 180 days

ATTRACTIONS (1997)

Major symphony orchestras: 2

Major dance companies: 2

Major professional theater companies (non-profit): 2

Per capita spending by the NEA (1997): $0.58, 13th

State Fair in late August–early September at St. Paul

SPORTS AND COMPETITION

NCAA (Division I) football and basketball teams: Univ. of Minnesota-Twin Cities Golden Gophers

Major league baseball teams: Minnesota Twins (AL Central), Hubert H. Humphrey Metrodome

NBA basketball teams: Minnesota Timberwolves, Target Center

NFL football teams: Minnesota Vikings (NFC), Hubert H. Humphrey Metrodome

WEBSITES CONTAINING FURTHER INFORMATION

State of Minnesota—North Star Options   http://www.state.mn.us

MISSISSIPPI

"By far the most prominent feature of the geography is the mighty river called Meact Chassipi by the Indians, roughly translated as 'ancient father of water.' For 400 miles along the state's western boundary, the mighty Mississippi River swells and courses, ebbs and flows, gleams and glistens, twists and turns."

The Enchantment of Mississippi

Mississippi is a land where a beetle (the boll weevil) changed the way of life. Before the Civil War the planters of Mississippi, with their "Little Cotton Kingdoms" and mansions, enjoyed the brilliant plantation culture, which was based on slave labor. During that war the state suffered greatly; it suffered still more during the brutal period of Reconstruction. At one time, Mississippi was the home of one of the largest Indian populations, but the Indians, known for their civilized lifestyle, were forced to leave their property to travel west over the "Trail of Tears." As the native state of some of the nation's best-known authors, composers, and playwrights, Mississippi has a well-earned reputation for culture, combined with a notable blending of rural and cosmopolitan backgrounds.

SUPERLATIVES

• First European settlement in the southern Mississippi Valley — Ocean Springs.
• One of the earliest and best reforestation programs.
• Natchez, boasting more than 500 pre-Civil War mansions.
• Biloxi, which has had a record eight flags flying over it.
• Celebrated the first "Decoration Day," now Memorial Day.
• First U.S. state-operated university for women, at Columbus.
• Pioneer in state system of junior colleges.

MOMENTS IN HISTORY

• In 1540, Hernando de Soto and his expedition entered present-day Mississippi near where Columbus now stands, and his party may have been the first Europeans to see the Mississippi River. Their cruelty to the Indians was well-known.
• In 1682, Robert Cavelier, Sieur de La Salle, claimed the vast region drained by the Mississippi for the King of France.
• The first European settlement in the entire Mississippi Valley—Fort Maurepas, now

Ocean Springs—was founded in 1699 by Pierre Le Moyne, Sieur d'Iberville.
• In 1720 at the command of King Louis XV, John Law was sent with 200 settlers to the Pascagoula area. Although other settlers arrived, Law's "Mississippi Bubble" burst, almost bringing France to financial collapse.
• After years of Indian attacks, in 1736, French forces under the Sieur de Bienville were defeated by the Chickasaw, hastening the French decline in North America.
• With the French withdrawal in 1763, the British made their headquarters at present-day Natchez, and most of the area now Mississippi became part of British West Florida. During the American Revolution, the Spanish attacked the area, and by 1781 they had seized British West Florida.
• After a long dispute with Spain over the ownership of the region, in 1798, Spanish forces left the upper area, and Congress created the Mississippi Territory.
• On December 10, 1817, Mississippi was admitted as the 20th state.
• By 1832 the last of the Indian tribes had their substantial property seized. Forced to leave the state, they trudged in desperation over the "Trail of Tears" on their way to western lands.
• The great plantations of Mississippi depended on their slave labor, and on January 9, 1861, Mississippi became the second state to secede from the Union.
• The 47-day siege of Vicksburg during the Civil War ended on July 4, 1863, and the

---

So They Say

"For five days 10,000 men worked hard with a will in that work of destruction with axes, crowbars, sledges, clawbars, and fire, and I have no hesitation in pronouncing the work well done. Meridian...no longer exists."

General William Tecumseh Sherman,
on the destruction of Meridian

battle for that city was one of the most crucial of the entire conflict. The Union success, under General Ulysses S. Grant, cut the Confederacy in two and opened the entire Mississippi to Union forces.

- Civil War battles raged across the state, ending with the Battle of Tupelo in early 1865. The state lost 60,000 soldiers.
- Mississippi was readmitted to the Union in 1870, but the terrible hardships of Reconstruction endured until about 1875.
- An epidemic of yellow fever swept the state in 1878, and thousands died.
- In 1904, James K. Vardaman became governor with the support of small farmers and others, ending the control of the plantation "planter class."
- The Mississippi River floods of 1927 were the worst in memory.
- During World War II, more Mississippians won the Medal of Honor than those of any other state.
- In 1967 the space age came to the state with the opening of what became the National Space Technology Laboratories.

THAT'S INTERESTING

- Warfare among Indian nations consisted mostly of ambushes and surprise attacks. Sometimes these surprises were so successful that almost an entire Indian nation would be wiped out.
- The mother-daughter combination of Maria and Miranda Younghans staffed the Biloxi lighthouse for a total of 62 years.
- Mississippi is the only state whose state flower is the blossom of the state tree.

NOTABLE NATIVES

Theodore Bilbo (near Poplarville, 1877-1947), public official. William Cuthbert Faulkner (New Albany, 1897-1962), author. James Earl Jones (Arkabutla, 1931-), actor. Elvis Aaron Presley (Tupelo, 1935-1977), singer. Leontyne Price (Laurel, 1927-), opera singer. William Grant Still (Woodville, 1895-1978), composer. Eudora Welty (Jackson, 1909-), author. Tennessee Williams (Columbus, 1911-1983), playwright.

GENERAL

Admitted to statehood: December 10, 1817
Origin of name: Probably Chippewa; *mici*

zibi, "great river" or "gathering-in of all the waters"
Capital: Jackson
Nickname: Magnolia State
Motto: *Virtute et Armis*—By valor and arms
Bird: Mockingbird
Flower: Magnolia
Song: "Go, Mississippi"
Tree: Magnolia

THE LAND

Area: 48,286 sq. mi., 32nd
  Land: 46,914 sq. mi., 31st
  Water: 1,372 sq. mi., 22nd
    Inland water: 781 sq. mi., 27th
    Coastal water: 591 sq. mi., 10th
Topography: Low, fertile delta between Yazoo and Mississippi rivers; loess bluffs stretching around delta border; sandy gulf coastal terraces followed by piney woods and prairie; rugged, high sandy hills in extreme NE, followed by black prairie belt, Pontotoc Ridge, and flatwoods into the N central highlands
Number of counties: 82
Geographic center: Leake, 9 mi. WNW of Carthage
Length: 340 mi.; width: 170 mi.
Highest point: 806 ft. (Woodall Mountain), 47th
Lowest point: sea level (Gulf of Mexico), 3rd
Mean elevation: 300 ft., 45th
Coastline: 44 mi., 18th
Shoreline: 359 mi., 22nd

CLIMATE AND ENVIRONMENT

Temp., highest: 115 deg. on July 29, 1930, at Holly Springs; lowest: –19 deg. on Jan. 30, 1966, at Corinth
Monthly average: highest: 92.5 deg., 11th; lowest: 34.9 deg., 46th; spread (high to low): 57.6 deg., 47th
Hazardous waste sites (1997): 1, 48th
Endangered species: Animals: 16—Indiana bat, Black clubshell, Ovate clubshell, Southern clubshell, Southern combshell, Mississippi sandhill crane, American peregrine falcon, West Indian manatee, Brown pelican, Flat pigtoe, Heavy pigtoe, Fat pocketbook, Stirrupshell, Pallid sturgeon, Least tern, Red-cockaded woodpecker. Plants: 2

MAJOR CITIES
POPULATION, 1996
PERCENTAGE INCREASE, 1990-96

Jackson, 192,923; –4.5%
Gulfport, 64,829; 1.2%
Biloxi, 48,414; 4.5%
Hattiesburg, 47,803; 5.5%
Greenville, 42,933; –5.1%

THE PEOPLE

Population (1997): 2,730,501, 31st
    Percent change (1990-97): 6.02%, 26th
    Percent of total U.S. pop.: 1.02%, 31st
    Per sq. mi: 56.38, 32nd
Population (2000 proj.): 2,821,000, 31st
    Percent change (1995-2000): 4.60%, 26th
Percent in metro. area (1996): 31.37%, 48th
Foreign born: 20,000, 45th
    Percent: 0.8%, 51st
Top three ancestries reported:
    African, 30.10%
    Irish, 15.26%
    American, 12.31%
White (1992): 1,655,000, 63.29%, 49th
Black (1992): 937,000, 35.83%, 2nd
Native American (1992): 9,000, 0.34%, 32nd
Asian, Pacific Isle (1992): 14,000, 0.54%, 49th
Hispanic origin (1992): 17,000, 0.65%, 47th
Percent over 5 yrs. speaking language other than English at home: 2.8%, 48th
Percent males (1996): 48.03%, 50th; percent females: 51.97%, 2nd
Percent never married: 26.7%, 20th
Marriages per 1,000 (1996): 7.86, 33rd
Divorces per 1,000 (1996): 5.78, 10th
Median age (1996): 32.9
Under 5 years (1996): 7.57%, 12th
18 years and under (1996): 31.17%, 7th
65 years and over (1996): 12.27%, 34th
Percent increase among the elderly (1995-96): 0.37%, 38th

OF VITAL IMPORTANCE

Live births per 1,000 pop. (1996): 15.3, 13th
Infant mortality rate per 1,000 live births (1995): 10.5, 2nd
    Rate for whites: 7.0, 13th
    Rate for blacks: 14.7, 22nd
Births to unmarried women, % of total (1996): 45.1%, 2nd
Births to teenage mothers, % of total (1996): 21.3%, 1st

Abortions (1992): 7,550, 34th
    Rate per 1,000 women 14-44 years old: 12.4, 41st
    Percent change (1988-92): 48%, 1st
Average lifetime (1989-91): 73.03, 50th
Total death rate per 100,000 pop. (1995): 1,002.0, 8th
    Accidents and adverse effects: 59.6, 1st
    Alzheimer's disease: 6.2, 44th
    Cancer: 213.1, 25th
    Cerebrovascular diseases: 69.3, 15th
    Chronic liver disease and cirrhosis: 8.6, 29th
    Chronic obstructive pulmonary diseases and allied conditions: 37.9, 33rd
    Diabetes mellitus: 18.1, 41st
    Diseases of heart: 356.0, 3rd
    HIV infection: 9.5, 25th
    Homicide: 15.9, 3rd
    Injury by firearms: 22.4, 5th
    Motor vehicle accidents: 33.5, 1st
    Pneumonia and influenza: 35.3, 14th
    Suicide: 11.8, 33rd

KEEPING WELL

Active nonfederal physicians per 100,000 pop. (1995): 138, 49th
Dentists per 100,000 (1991): 38, 51st
Nurses per 100,000 (1995): 709, 42nd
Hospitals per 100,000 (1995): 3.60, 8th
    Admissions per 1,000 (1995): 143.86, 5th
    Hospital beds per 1,000 (1995): 4.67, 6th
    Occupancy rate per 100 beds (1995): 61.11, 23rd
    Average cost per patient per day (1995): $584, 47th
    Average cost per stay (1995): $4,265, 51st
AIDS cases (new, 1996): 450; per 100,000: 16.6, 20th
Persons living with HIV infection, not yet AIDS (1996): 3,273
Other notifiable diseases, per 100,000 pop.:
    Gonorrhea (1995): 352.6, 1st
    Syphilis (1995): 168.7, 1st
    Tuberculosis (1996): 9.2, 14th
Pop. without health insur. (1996): 18.5%, 8th

HOUSEHOLDS BY TYPE

Total households (1996): 979,000, 32nd
    Percent change (1990-96): 7.4%, 23rd
    Per 1,000 pop. (1996) 360.46, 46th
    Percent of householders 65 yrs. and over (1996): 22.68%, 16th
    Persons per household (1996): 2.66, 11th

Family households: 674,378
Percent of total: 74.00%, 2nd
Nonfamily households: 236,996
Percent of total: 26.00%, 50th
Pop. living in group quarters: 69,717
Percent of pop.: 2.71%, 27th

LIVING QUARTERS

Total housing units: 1,010,423
Persons per unit: 2.55, 4th
Occupied housing units: 911,374
Percent of total units: 90.20%, 21st
Persons per unit: 2.72, 5th
Percent of units with over 1 person per
room: 5.80%, 11th
Owner-occupied units: 651,587
Percent of total units: 64.49%, 4th
Percent of occupied units: 71.50%, 3rd
Persons per unit: 2.78, 17th
Median value: $45,600, 49th
Renter-occupied units: 259,787
Percent of total units: 25.71%, 46th
Percent of occupied units: 28.50%, 49th
Persons per unit: 2.65, 4th
Median contract rent: $215, 51st
Rental vacancy rate: 9.5%, 18th
Mobile home, trailer & other as a percent of
occupied housing units: 16.38%, 9th
Persons in emergency shelters for homeless
persons: 383, 0.015%, 51st
Persons visible in street locations: 83,
0.0032%, 35th
Nursing home population: 15,803, 0.61%, 35th

CRIME INDEX PER 100,000 (1996)

Total reported: 4,522.9, 28th
Percent increase: 0.2%, 13th
Violent: 488.3, 26th
Percent increase: –2.9%, 16th
Murder & nonnegligent manslaughter:
11.1, 6th
Forcible rape: 36.1, 23rd
Aggravated assault: 306.8, 26th
Robbery: 134.2, 25th
Property: 4,034.6, 30th
Percent increase: 0.6%, 16th
Burglary: 1,132.4, 11th
Larceny-theft: 2,551.5, 37th
Motor vehicle theft: 350.8, 34th

TEACHING AND LEARNING

Pop. 3 and over enrolled in school (1996):
626,858, 32nd
Percent of pop.: 23.08%, 19th

Public elementary & secondary schools (1996-
97): 1,011, 34th
Total enrollment (1996): 504,168, 31st
Percent of school age pop.: 91.33%, 27th
Percent of total pop.: 18.56%, 10th
Teachers (1996): 29,237, 31st
Percent of pop.: 1.08%, 24th
Pupil/teacher ratio (1995): 17.5, 13th
Teachers' avg. salary (1996-97): $27,720,
49th
Expenditure per capita (1992-93):
$1,052.79, 49th
Education as % of state govt. expendi-
tures: 35%, 28th
Expenditure per pupil (1994-95): $4,080,
50th
Percent increase (1993-94 & 1994-95):
11.48%, 1st
Percent at or above grade level, NAEP tests:
Reading, grade 4 (1994): 18%, 37th
Math, grade 4 (1996): 42%, 43rd
Math, grade 8 (1996): 36%, 40th
Percent of graduates taking SAT (1995): 4%,
50th
Mean SAT verbal scores: 496, 9th
Mean SAT mathematical scores: 540, 13th
Percent of graduates taking ACT (1997):
79%, 3rd
Mean ACT scores: 18.7, 50th
Percent of pop. over 25 completing:
Less than 9th grade: 15.6%, 4th
High school: 64.3%, 51st
College degree(s): 14.7%, 48th
Higher education, institutions (1996): 46,
27th
Enrollment (1995-96): 122,690, 33rd
Percent increase in enroll. (1990-95):
–0.2%, 39th
White non-Hispanic (1995): 82,685, 34th
Percent of enroll.: 67.39%, 42nd
Total minority enroll. (1995): 38,027,
25th
Percent of enroll.: 30.99%, 6th
Black non-Hispanic (1995): 35,884, 18th
Percent of enroll.: 29.25%, 2nd
Hispanic (1995): 654, 45th
Percent of enroll.: 0.53%, 50th
Asian/Pacific Islander (1995): 1,051, 41st
Percent of enroll.: 0.86%, 47th
American Indian/AK native (1995): 438,
44th
Percent of enroll.: 0.36%, 41st
Nonresident alien (1995): 1,978, 38th
Percent of enroll.: 1.61%, 48th

Female (1995): 70,081, 33rd
  Percent of enroll.: 57.12%, 14th
Pub. institutions (1995-96): 31, 19th
  Enrollment: 110,600, 31st
    Percent increase in enrollment (1990-95): 1.4%, 29th
  Percent of enroll.: 90.15%, 8th
Private institutions (1995-96): 15, 37th
  Enrollment: 12,090, 40th
    Percent increase in enrollment (1990-95): –12.7%, 50th
  Percent of enroll.: 9.85%, 44th
Tuition (in state), public 4-year institution (1996-97): $2,497, 28th
Tuition (in state), public 2-year institution (1996-97): $952, 43rd
Tuition, private 4-year institution (1996-97): $7,226, 47th
Public library systems (1994): 47, 42nd
  Books & serial vol. per capita: 2.0, 39th
  Library visits per capita: 2.5, 39th
  Circulation per capita: 3.1, 50th

LAW ENFORCEMENT AND CORRECTIONS

Police protection and corrections expenditures (1996): $282,796,000
  Per capita: $104.13, 31st
Police per 10,000 pop. (1996): 18.80, 38th
Prisoners (1 year or more) per 100,000 pop. (1996): 498, 7th
  Percent change (1995-96): 10.8%, 12th
  Percent of inmates that are female: 6.6%, 20th
    Percent change: 19.0%, 11th
Death penalty: yes, by lethal gas, lethal injection after 7/1/84
  Under sentence (Jan. 1998): 63, 17th
  Executed, 1976-97: 4, 18th
  Executed in 1997: 0

RELIGION, NUMBER AND PERCENT OF POPULATION

Agnostic: 9,132—0.50%, 27th
Buddhist: NA
Christian: 1,720,521—94.20%, 3rd
Hindu: NA
Jewish: 10,959—0.60%, 25th
Muslim: NA
Unitarian: NA
Other: 23,744—1.30%, 24th
None: 51,141—2.80%, 47th
Refused to answer: 10,959—0.60%, 49th

MAKING A LIVING

Personal income per capita (1996): $17,471, 51st
  Percent increase (1995-96): 3.3%, 22nd
Disposable personal income per capita (1996): $15,911, 51st
Median income of households (average, 1995-96): $27,000, 48th
Percent of pop. below poverty level (1995-96): 22.1%, 3rd

ECONOMY

In civilian labor force (1996): 1,262,000
  Percent of total pop.: 62.3%, 47th
  Percent of total pop. 65 years and over: 9.4%, 40th
  Percent of total female pop.: 54.7%, 49th
Major employer industries (total nonagricultural, 1996):
  Construction: 48,700—4.5%, 28th
  Finance, insurance, & real estate: 40,900—3.8%, 50th
  Government: 217,900—20.0%, 9th
  Manufacturing: 245,700—22.5%, 5th
  Service: 246,600—22.6%, 48th
  Trade: 232,600—21.3%, 47th
  Transportation, communications, public utilities: 52,700—4.8%, 33rd
Unemployment rate (1996): 6.1%, 11th
  Male: 5.2%, 23rd
  Female: 7.2%, 4th
Total businesses (1995): 57,095, 33rd
New business incorps. (1995): 4,680
  Percent of total businesses: 8.20%, 33rd
Business failures (1995): 232
  Failures per 10,000 businesses: 40.6, 50th
Agriculture farm income:
  Marketing (1996): $3,462,784,000, 24th
    Average per farm: $78,700, 31st
  Leading products (1997): Broilers, cotton, soybeans, rice
  Average value land & build. per acre (1997): $950, 35th
    Percent increase (1996-97): 4%, 35th
  Govt. payments (1996): $184,925,000, 15th
    Average per farm: $4,203, 15th
Construction, value of all (1996): $3,562,977,000, 31st
  Per capita: $1,312, 20th
Manufactures (1995):
  Value added: $17,442,500,000
    Per capita: $6,467, 24th
  Leading products (1997): Apparel, furniture, lumber and wood products, foods

and food products, electrical machinery, transportation equipment

Value of nonfuel mineral production (1996): $140,000,000, 42nd

Leading mineral products (1996): Petroleum, natural gas, sand/gravel, clays, cement, stone

Energy consumption per person (1994): 398.0 mil. Btu, 14th

Retail sales (1995): $19,109,000,000
  Per household: $19,763, 49th
  Sales increase (1994-95): 8.5%, 6th

Tourism revenues (1996): $4.4 bil.

Foreign exports, in total value (1996): $2,623,000,000, 34th
  Per capita: $966, 42nd

Gross state product per person (1994): $18,953, 51st

Public aid recipients (percent of resident pop. 1994): 10.9%, 3rd

Medicaid recipients (percent of pop., 1995): 19.3%, 4th

Medicare enrollment per 1,000 pop. (1996): 149, 20th

TRAVEL AND TRANSPORTATION

Motor vehicle registrations (1996): 2,181,727, 31st
  Per 1,000 pop.: 804.84, 26th

Motorcycle registrations (1996): 30,162, 35th
  Per 1,000 pop.: 13.82, 37th

Licensed drivers (1996): 1,693,159, 33rd
  Per 1,000 pop.: 627.98, 44th

Public roads & streets (1996)
  Total mileage: 73,202, 27th
    Per 1,000 pop.: 126.95, 14th
  Rural mileage: 65,281, 27th
    Per 1,000 pop.: 24.03, 14th
  Urban mileage: 7,921, 32nd
    Per 1,000 pop.: 2.92, 34th
  Interstate mileage: 685, 33rd
    Per 1,000 pop.: 0.25, 18th

Speed limit (max. interstate, autos, mi. per hr., 1997): 70

Annual vehicle-mi. of travel per driver (1996): 17,976, 3rd

Mean travel time for workers age 16+ who work away from home: 20.6 min., 27th

GOVERNMENT

Percent of voting age pop. registered (1996): 87.24%, 5th
  Percent of voting age pop. voting for president: (1996): 45.6%, 42nd
  Percent of voting age pop. voting for U.S. representatives (1996): 46.1%, 31st

State legislators, total (1997): 174, 14th
  Women members (1997): 19
    Percent of legislature: 11%, 48th

U.S. Congress, House members (1998): 5
  Change (1988-98): 0

Revenues (1996):
  State govt.: $8,864,863,000
    Per capita: $3,263.94, 31st
    Parimutuel & amusement taxes & lotteries, revenue per capita (1995): $70.99, 32nd

Expenditures (1996):
  State govt.: $8,216,867,000
    Per capita: $3,025.36, 30th

Debt outstanding (1996): $2,232,015,000
  Per capita: $821.80, 43rd

LAWS AND REGULATIONS

Legal driving age: 16

Marriage age without parental consent: consult statutes

Divorce residence requirement: 6 mo.

ATTRACTIONS (1997)

Major symphony orchestras: 1

Per capita spending by the NEA (1997): $0.18, 39th

State Fair early October at Jackson

SPORTS AND COMPETITION

NCAA (Division I) football and basketball teams: Alcorn State Univ. Braves, Jackson State Univ. Tigers, Mississippi State Univ. Bulldogs, Mississippi Valley State Univ. Delta Devils, Univ. of Mississippi Rebels, Univ. of Southern Mississippi Golden Eagles

WEBSITES CONTAINING FURTHER INFORMATION

| State of Mississippi | http://www.state.ms.us |

MISSOURI

"I come from a state that raises corn and cotton and cockleburs and Democrats, and frothy eloquence neither convinces nor satisfies me. I am from Missouri. You have got to show me."

Representative Willard D. Vandiver (1899)

Missouri is the "Show Me" state, a nickname that stands for intelligent skepticism. The name came into being when Missouri Congressman Willard Duncan Vandiver, in an 1899 speech in Philadelphia, said, "Frothy eloquence neither convinces nor satisfies me. I am from Missouri. You have got to show me." Missouri is a center of transportation. The nation's two greatest rivers, the Mississippi on the eastern border and the Missouri winding through the state, lend themselves to shipping. Fifteen major railroads and many transcontinental airlines service Missouri. The state is sometimes called "the Mother of the West" because it supplied so many of the pioneers who moved on to settle the land between the Missouri and the Pacific Ocean. In recent years, both St. Louis and Kansas City have led the way toward making improvements in infrastructure and other aspects of city life.

SUPERLATIVES

• Nation's tallest monument, the Gateway Arch in St. Louis.
• The University of Missouri—the first state university west of the Mississippi and the first college in the world to grant a journalism degree.
• First in U.S. production of lead.
• Center of U.S. barite mining.
• World's largest shoe manufacturing center, St. Louis.
• First newspaper published west of the Mississippi.
• Home of the Missouri mule.
• First Pony Express run, starting from St. Joseph.
• World's first all-steel railroad bridge.

MOMENTS IN HISTORY

• Father Jacques Marquette and Louis Jolliet floated down the Mississippi in 1673 and found the mouth of the Missouri.
• In 1682, Robert Cavalier, Sieur de La Salle, claimed the entire Mississippi Valley watershed in the name of France.

• In 1735, Ste. Genevieve was founded, the first permanent European settlement in what is now Missouri.
• St. Louis was begun in March 1764 by René Auguste Chouteau.

So They Say

"...the first boat reached the mouth of the gully at the head of which were the marked trees....I put the men to work....They commenced the shed, and the little cabins for the men were built in the vicinity."

René Auguste Chouteau, on the founding of St. Louis

• After France relinquished the area to Spain in 1764, settlers flocked to St. Louis, and the fur trade flourished.
• In 1780, 50 defenders of St. Louis held off more than 1,000 Indians and 24 white traders, keeping the vital Mississippi open to the United States.
• Spain returned the Louisiana territory to France. Then the entire Louisiana territory was bought by the United States from the French in 1803.
• On May 14, 1804, the great Lewis and Clark expedition left St. Louis to explore the country's new territory.
• On December 16, 1811, the area for hundreds of miles around New Madrid was rocked by what has been called the strongest earthquake in North American history.
• Indian wars occurred between 1811 and 1815, but Missouri defenders held out.
• In 1819 the *Western Engineer* was the first steamboat to sail up the Missouri River.
• Missouri was admitted as a slave state on August 10, 1821, after an agreement known as the Missouri Compromise.
• After William H. Becknell blazed the Santa Fe Trail in 1822, fortunes were made in the New Mexico trade.
• In 1831, Mormon leader Joseph Smith and his followers arrived. They founded the towns of Salem and Far West, becoming so powerful that they were persecuted and fled

the state. Far West was destroyed, and its site is now a field; the town of Salem remains.

- The University of Missouri was founded in Columbia in 1839.
- By the 1840s, thousands of immigrants began their trips to the far west from various Missouri cities, principally St. Louis, the "Gateway to the West."

So They Say

"It is a singular though very natural feature in the society of these distant settlements [St. Louis] that it is mainly composed of adventurous persons in the prime of life, and has very few grey heads among it."

Charles Dickens (1842)

- In the conflict over slavery, many from Missouri moved to Kansas in an effort to make it a slave state. They fought with free-state settlers until about 1858.
- Missouri refused to join the Confederacy in the Civil War, and many bloody battles were fought there for this critical state. The last major conflict, the Battle of Westport, was won by the Union on October 13, 1864. But Missouri was the center of raids by Confederate guerrillas.

So They Say

"The guerrilla warfare...was a war of terror, surprise, sabotage, and arson...a total war,...cold-blooded...hit-and-run."

Anonymous

- By the war's end, Missouri counted 1,100 battles and skirmishes.
- On January 11, 1865, Missouri became the first slave state to free its slaves.
- Former guerrillas turned into bandits, robbed banks, held up trains, and plagued the Midwest until about 1882.
- A border dispute between Missouri and Iowa was settled by the U.S. Supreme Court in 1896.
- In 1904, St. Louis held the Louisiana Purchase Exposition, a great world's fair, celebrating that historic event just over a hundred years later.
- A Missouri native, General John J. Pershing, led the U.S. expeditionary force during World War I.

- On the death of President Franklin D. Roosevelt, Missouri's Harry S Truman became president on April 12, 1945.
- World War II ended in the Pacific when the Japanese signed the surrender on the battleship *Missouri* on September 2, 1945.
- In 1946, Winston Churchill coined the phrase "Iron Curtain" at Fulton.
- The Gateway Arch was dedicated in St. Louis in 1966.
- In 1992 the bones of Missouri native William Clarke Quantrill, the Confederate guerilla, were returned from Ohio and buried in Higginsville.
- In 1995 the National Football League approved the move of the Los Angeles Rams to St. Louis.

THAT'S INTERESTING

- From the first steamboat on the Missouri River, smoke poured out of a stack made like a dragon's head to frighten the Indians.
- St. Louis is perhaps the only major city to have been founded by a 14-year-old boy—Réne Auguste Chouteau, acting at the request of his patron, Pierre Laclede Liguest.
- The ice cream cone is said by some to have originated at the St. Louis world's fair of 1904.

So They Say

"In the old French portion of the town [St. Louis], the thoroughfares are narrow and crooked, and some of the houses are very quaint and picturesque; being built of wood, with tumbledown galleries before the windows, approachable by stairs or rather ladders from the street. There are queer little barbers' shops and drinking houses too, in this quarter....Some of these ancient habitations, with high garret gable-windows...have a kind of French shrug about them...and appear to hold their heads askew."   Charles Dickens (1842)

NOTABLE NATIVES

Josephine Baker (St. Louis, 1906-1975), entertainer. **Thomas Hart Benton** (Neosho, 1889-1975), artist. **Omar Nelson Bradley** (Clark, 1893-1981), soldier. **Dale Carnegie** (Maryville, 1888-1935), author/teacher of public speaking. **George Washington Carver** (near Diamond Grove, 1864?-1943), agronomist/chemist. **Winston Churchill** (St. Louis, 1871-1947), author. **Samuel Langhorne Clemens (Mark Twain)** (Florida, 1835-1910), humorist/author. **Walter Leland Cronkite, Jr.** (St. Joseph, 1916-), journalist/commentator. **Thomas Stearns (T. S.) Eliot** (St. Louis, 1888-1965), poet/critic. **Eugene Field** (St. Louis, 1850-1895), author/poet. **James William Fulbright** (Sumner, 1905-1995), public official. **James Langston Hughes** (Joplin, 1902-1967), author. **James Cash Penney** (Hamilton, 1875-1971), merchant. **John Joseph Pershing** (Laclede, 1860-1948), soldier. **Ginger Rogers (Virginia McMath)** (Independence, 1911-1995), actress/dancer. **Harry S Truman** (Lamar, 1884-1972), U.S. president.

So They Say

"It is often said that...[Harry Truman] was an ordinary man who made a good president—but that isn't true. Truman had a modest background, but he was an extraordinary man, a member of Thomas Jefferson's 'Natural Aristocracy' of virtue and talent."   **Writer Max Lerner**

GENERAL

Admitted to statehood: August 10, 1821
Origin of name: Algonquin Indian tribe named after Missouri River, meaning "muddy water"
Capital: Jefferson City
Nickname: Show Me State
Motto: *Salus Populi Suprema Lex Esto*—The welfare of the people shall be the supreme law
Bird: Eastern bluebird
Flower: Hawthorn blossom
Mineral: Galena (lead)
Stone: Mozarkite
Song: "Missouri Waltz"
Tree: Flowering dogwood

THE LAND

Area: 69,709 sq. mi., 21st
  Land: 68,896 sq. mi., 18th
  Water: 811 sq. mi., 32nd
    Inland water: 811 sq. mi., 26th
Topography: Rolling hills, open, fertile plains, and well-watered prairie N of the Missouri River; S of the river land is rough and hilly with deep, narrow valleys; alluvial plain in the SE; low elevation in the W
Number of counties: 114
Geographic center: Miller, 20 mi. SW of Jefferson City
Length: 300 mi.; width: 240 mi.
Highest point: 1,772 ft. (Taum Sauk Mountain), 41st
Lowest point: 230 ft. (St. Francis River), 30th
Mean elevation: 800 ft., 32nd

CLIMATE AND ENVIRONMENT

Temp., highest: 118 deg. on July 14, 1954, at Warsaw and Union; lowest: –40 deg. on Feb. 13, 1905, at Warsaw
Monthly average: highest: 90.5 deg., 19th; lowest: 19.4 deg., 24th; spread (high to low): 71.1 deg., 21st
Hazardous waste sites (1997): 22, 18th
Endangered species: Animals: 10—Gray bat, Indiana bat, Ozark big-eared bat, American peregrine falcon, Curtis' pearlymussel, Higgins' eye pearlymussel, Pink mucket pearlymussel, Fat pocketbook, Pallid sturgeon, Least tern. Plants: 3

MAJOR CITIES
POPULATION, 1996
PERCENTAGE INCREASE, 1990-96

Kansas City, 441,259; 1.5%
St. Louis, 351,565; –11.4%
Springfield, 143,407; 2.1%
Independence, 110,303; –1.8%
Columbia, 76,756; 11.0%

THE PEOPLE

Population (1997): 5,402,058, 16th
  Percent change (1990-97): 5.57%, 32nd
  Percent of total U.S. pop.: 2.02%, 16th
  Per sq. mi: 77.49, 28th
Population (2000 proj.): 5,543,500, 17th
  Percent change (1995-2000): 4.12%, 31st
Percent in metro. area (1996): 67.99%, 29th
Foreign born: 84,000, 27th
  Percent: 1.6%, 41st
Top three ancestries reported:
  German, 36.02%
  Irish, 20.29%
  English, 14.52%
White (1992): 4,558,000, 87.81%, 27th
Black (1992): 565,000, 10.88%, 20th
Native American (1992): 20,000, 0.39%, 28th

Asian, Pacific Isle (1992): 48,000, 0.92%, 35th
Hispanic origin (1992): 66,000, 1.27%, 38th
Percent over 5 yrs. speaking language other than English at home: 3.8%, 44th
Percent males (1996): 48.47%, 38th; percent females: 51.53%, 14th
Percent never married: 23.9%, 37th
Marriages per 1,000 (1996): 8.60, 21st
Divorces per 1,000 (1996): 4.90, 13th
Median age (1996): 35.2
Under 5 years (1996): 6.89%, 31st
18 years and under (1996): 28.82%, 23rd
65 years and over (1996): 13.85%, 13th
Percent increase among the elderly (1995-96): 0.18%, 43rd

OF VITAL IMPORTANCE

Live births per 1,000 pop. (1996): 13.8, 30th
Infant mortality rate per 1,000 live births (1995): 7.4, 28th
  Rate for whites: 6.4, 23rd
  Rate for blacks: 13.8, 27th
Births to unmarried women, % of total (1996): 33.1%, 18th
Births to teenage mothers, % of total (1996): 14.1%, 18th
Abortions (1992): 13,510, 27th
  Rate per 1,000 women 14-44 years old: 11.6, 43rd
  Percent change (1988-92): −29%, 51st
Average lifetime (1989-91): 75.25, 30th
Total death rate per 100,000 pop. (1995): 1,021.9, 6th
  Accidents and adverse effects: 43.5, 15th
  Alzheimer's disease: 8.7, 25th
  Cancer: 230.7, 10th
  Cerebrovascular diseases: 72.9, 8th
  Chronic liver disease and cirrhosis: 7.9, 39th
  Chronic obstructive pulmonary diseases and allied conditions: 46.1, 11th
  Diabetes mellitus: 23.4, 22nd
  Diseases of heart: 345.3, 6th
  HIV infection: 8.8, 29th
  Homicide: 8.9, 18th
  Injury by firearms: 15.8, 16th
  Motor vehicle accidents: 20.6, 18th
  Pneumonia and influenza: 41.6, 4th
  Suicide: 13.5, 17th

KEEPING WELL

Active nonfederal physicians per 100,000 pop. (1995): 218, 21st

Dentists per 100,000 (1991): 53, 29th
Nurses per 100,000 (1995): 940, 14th
Hospitals per 100,000 (1995): 2.37, 23rd
  Admissions per 1,000 (1995): 134.11, 12th
  Hospital beds per 1,000 (1995): 4.11, 13th
  Occupancy rate per 100 beds (1995): 57.53, 38th
  Average cost per patient per day (1995): $967, 21st
  Average cost per stay (1995): $6,228; 14th
AIDS cases (new, 1996): 858; per 100,000: 16.0, 21st
Persons living with HIV infection, not yet AIDS (1996): 3,393
Other notifiable diseases, per 100,000 pop.:
  Gonorrhea (1995): 212.8, 11th
  Syphilis (1995): 23.9, 15th
  Tuberculosis (1996): 4.2, 31st
Pop. without health insur. (1996): 13.2%, 28th

HOUSEHOLDS BY TYPE

Total households (1996): 2,052,000, 16th
  Percent change (1990-96): 4.6%, 36th
  Per 1,000 pop. (1996) 382.91, 15th
  Percent of householders 65 yrs. and over (1996): 23.29%, 12th
  Persons per household (1996): 2.51, 41st
Family households: 1,368,334
  Percent of total: 69.77%, 31st
Nonfamily households: 592,872
  Percent of total: 30.23%, 21st
Pop. living in group quarters: 145,397
  Percent of pop.: 2.84%, 24th

LIVING QUARTERS

Total housing units: 2,199,129
  Persons per unit: 2.33, 37th
Occupied housing units: 1,961,206
  Percent of total units: 89.18%, 27th
  Persons per unit: 2.46, 44th
  Percent of units with over 1 person per room: 2.46%, 37th
Owner-occupied units: 1,348,746
  Percent of total units: 61.33%, 15th
  Percent of occupied units: 68.77%, 16th
  Persons per unit: 2.67, 38th
  Median value: $59,800, 34th
Renter-occupied units: 612,460
  Percent of total units: 27.85%, 32nd
  Percent of occupied units: 31.23%, 36th
  Persons per unit: 2.24, 42nd
  Median contract rent: $282, 35th
  Rental vacancy rate: 10.7%, 13th

Mobile home, trailer & other as a percent of occupied housing units: 9.28%, 29th

Persons in emergency shelters for homeless persons: 2,276, 0.044%, 29th

Persons visible in street locations: 215, 0.0042%, 33rd

Nursing home population: 52,060, 1.02%, 9th

CRIME INDEX PER 100,000 (1996)

Total reported: 5,084.0, 23rd
  Percent increase: −0.7%, 17th
  Violent: 590.9, 20th
    Percent increase: −11.0%, 39th
    Murder & nonnegligent manslaughter: 8.1, 16th
    Forcible rape: 29.2, 33rd
    Aggravated assault: 383.1, 20th
    Robbery: 170.6, 17th
      Percent increase: −16.4%, 48th
  Property: 4,493.0, 20th
    Percent increase: 0.8%, 14th
    Burglary: 894.2, 25th
    Larceny-theft: 3,151.1, 21st
    Motor vehicle theft: 447.7, 24th

TEACHING AND LEARNING

Pop. 3 and over enrolled in school (1996): 1,174,863, 17th
  Percent of pop.: 21.92%, 35th
Public elementary & secondary schools (1996-97): 2,256, 10th
  Total enrollment (1996): 883,327, 18th
    Percent of school age pop.: 86.01%, 49th
    Percent of total pop.: 16.48%, 37th
  Teachers (1996): 59,222, 14th
    Percent of pop.: 1.11%, 19th
  Pupil/teacher ratio (1995): 15.4, 38th
  Teachers' avg. salary (1996-97): $34,342, 28th
  Expenditure per capita (1992-93): $1,052.79, 50th
    Education as % of state govt. expenditures: 36.2%, 21st
  Expenditure per pupil (1994-95): $5,383, 31st
    Percent increase (1993-94 & 1994-95): 5.26%, 14th
Percent at or above grade level, NAEP tests:
  Reading, grade 4 (1994): 31%, 15th
  Math, grade 4 (1996): 66%, 19th
  Math, grade 8 (1996): 64%, 19th

Percent of graduates taking SAT (1995): 9%, 38th
  Mean SAT verbal scores: 495, 10th
  Mean SAT mathematical scores: 550, 10th
Percent of graduates taking ACT (1997): 64%, 15th
  Mean ACT scores: 21.5, 15th
Percent of pop. over 25 completing:
  Less than 9th grade: 11.6%, 14th
  High school: 73.9%, 38th
  College degree(s): 17.8%, 34th
Higher education, institutions (1996): 101, 13th
  Enrollment (1995-96): 291,536, 15th
    Percent increase in enroll. (1990-95): 0.6%, 35th
  White non-Hispanic (1995): 246,071, 15th
    Percent of enroll.: 84.41%, 18th
  Total minority enroll. (1995): 38,051, 24th
    Percent of enroll.: 13.05%, 32nd
  Black non-Hispanic (1995): 25,493, 19th
    Percent of enroll.: 8.74%, 20th
  Hispanic (1995): 4,653, 24th
    Percent of enroll.: 1.60%, 34th
  Asian/Pacific Islander (1995): 6,405, 22nd
    Percent of enroll.: 2.20%, 28th
  American Indian/AK native (1995): 1,500, 24th
    Percent of enroll.: 0.51%, 27th
  Nonresident alien (1995): 7,414, 18th
    Percent of enroll.: 2.54%, 28th
  Female (1995): 164,276, 15th
    Percent of enroll.: 56.35%, 21st
  Pub. institutions (1995-96): 30, 21st
    Enrollment: 189,993, 22nd
      Percent increase in enrollment (1990-95): −5.0%, 45th
    Percent of enroll.: 65.17%, 43rd
  Private institutions (1995-96): 71, 9th
    Enrollment: 101,543, 9th
      Percent increase in enrollment (1990-95): 13.1%, 14th
    Percent of enroll.: 34.83%, 9th
  Tuition (in state), public 4-year institution (1996-97): $3,230, 18th
  Tuition (in state), public 2-year institution (1996-97): $1,283, 30th
  Tuition, private 4-year institution (1996-97): $10,169, 32nd
Public library systems (1994): 147, 20th
  Books & serial vol. per capita: 4.0, 10th
  Library visits per capita: 4.3, 19th
  Circulation per capita: 7.8, 14th

LAW ENFORCEMENT AND CORRECTIONS

Police protection and corrections expenditures (1996): $442,133,000

Per capita: $82.51, 45th

Police per 10,000 pop. (1996): 21.16, 30th

Prisoners (1 year or more) per 100,000 pop. (1996): 409, 17th

Percent change (1995-96): 15.0%, 4th

Percent of inmates that are female: 6.7%, 18th

Percent change: 24.7%, 8th

Death penalty: yes, by lethal gas, lethal injection

Under sentence (Jan. 1998): 91, 13th

Executed, 1976-97: 29, 4th

Executed in 1997: 6, 3rd

RELIGION, NUMBER AND PERCENT OF POPULATION

Agnostic: 15,209—0.40%, 34th

Buddhist: 3,802—0.10%, 17th

Christian: 3,372,593—88.70%, 17th

Hindu: NA

Jewish: 22,814—0.60%, 25th

Muslim: NA

Unitarian: 7,605—0.20%, 23rd

Other: 49,429—1.30%, 24th

None: 247,146—6.50%, 25th

Refused to answer: 83,650—2.20%, 23rd

MAKING A LIVING

Personal income per capita (1996): $22,864, 26th

Percent increase (1995-96): 3.2%, 23rd

Disposable personal income per capita (1996): $19,906, 25th

Median income of households (average, 1995-96): $35,059, 22nd

Percent of pop. below poverty level (1995-96): 9.5%, 43rd

ECONOMY

In civilian labor force (1996): 2,898,000

Percent of total pop.: 71.8%, 10th

Percent of total pop. 65 years and over: 13.7%, 14th

Percent of total female pop.: 66.3%, 9th

Major employer industries (total nonagricultural, 1996):

Construction: 115,500—4.5%, 28th

Finance, insurance, & real estate: 149,800—5.8%, 14th

Government: 399,700—15.6%, 35th

Manufacturing: 414,000—16.1%, 22nd

Service: 707,900—27.6%, 22nd

Trade: 612,800—23.9%, 24th

Transportation, communications, public utilities: 159,700—6.2%, 6th

Unemployment rate (1996): 4.6%, 34th

Male: 4.9%, 28th

Female: 4.3%, 42nd

Total businesses (1995): 139,980, 16th

New business incorps. (1995): 10,743

Percent of total businesses: 7.67%, 39th

Business failures (1995): 1,109

Failures per 10,000 businesses: 79.2, 28th

Agriculture farm income:

Marketing (1996): $4,950,421,000, 16th

Average per farm: $47,600, 47th

Leading products (1997): Cattle, soybeans, hogs, corn, wheat, hay

Average value land & build. per acre (1997): $1,010, 30th

Percent increase (1996-97): 7%, 14th

Govt. payments (1996): $289,279,000, 10th

Average per farm: $2,782, 21st

Construction, value of all (1996): $6,042,038,000, 21st

Per capita: $1,128, 30th

Manufactures (1995):

Value added: $39,736,700,000

Per capita: $7,464, 15th

Leading products (1997): Transportation equipment, food & food products, electric & electronic equipment, chemicals

Value of nonfuel mineral production (1996): $1,250,000,000, 10th

Leading mineral products (1996): Lead, stone, cement, lime, zinc

Energy consumption per person (1994): 305.6 mil. Btu, 38th

Retail sales (1995): $52,511,000,000

Per household: $25,589, 15th

Sales increase (1994-95): 7.6%, 9th

Tourism revenues (1993): $5 bil.

Foreign exports, in total value (1996): $5,404,000,000, 25th

Per capita: $1,008, 39th

Gross state product per person (1994): $24,294, 28th

Public aid recipients (percent of resident pop. 1994): 7.1%, 20th

Medicaid recipients (percent of pop., 1995): 13.1%, 20th

Medicare enrollment per 1,000 pop. (1996): 157, 11th

TRAVEL AND TRANSPORTATION

Motor vehicle registrations (1996): 4,350,440, 17th
  Per 1,000 pop.: 811.09, 25th
Motorcycle registrations (1996): 54,118, 24th
  Per 1,000 pop.: 12.44, 41st
Licensed drivers (1996): 3,587,086, 18th
  Per 1,000 pop.: 674.35, 33rd
Public roads & streets (1996)
  Total mileage: 122,748, 6th
      Per 1,000 pop.: 122.91, 17th
      Rural mileage: 106,333, 4th
      Per 1,000 pop.: 19.84, 17th
      Urban mileage: 16,415, 18th
      Per 1,000 pop.: 3.06, 27th
      Interstate mileage: 1,178, 11th
      Per 1,000 pop.: 0.22, 21st
Speed limit (max. interstate, autos, mi. per hr., 1997): 70
Annual vehicle-mi. of travel per driver (1996): 16,313, 10th
Mean travel time for workers age 16+ who work away from home: 21.6 min., 16th

GOVERNMENT

Percent of voting age pop. registered (1996): 83.68%, 11th
  Percent of voting age pop. voting for president: (1996): 54.2%, 22nd
  Percent of voting age pop. voting for U.S. representatives (1996): 53.2%, 16th
State legislators, total (1997): 197, 7th
  Women members (1997): 44
    Percent of legislature: 22%, 26th
U.S. Congress, House members (1998): 9
  Change (1988-98): 0
Revenues (1996):
  State govt.: $17,050,787,000
    Per capita: $3,181.71, 35th
    Parimutuel & amusement taxes & lotteries, revenue per capita (1995): $84.32, 27th

Expenditures (1996):
  State govt.: $12,841,102,000
    Per capita: $2,396.18, 50th
Debt outstanding (1996): $7,128,377,000
    Per capita: $1,330.17, 26th

LAWS AND REGULATIONS

Legal driving age: 16
Marriage age without parental consent: 18
Divorce residence requirement: 90 days

ATTRACTIONS (1997)

Major opera companies: 2
Major symphony orchestras: 2
Major dance companies: 1
Major professional theater companies (non profit): 1
Per capita spending by the NEA (1997): $0.34, 22nd
State Fair in the 3rd week in August at Sedalia

SPORTS AND COMPETITION

NCAA (Division I) football and basketball teams: St. Louis Univ. Billikens (basketball only), Southeast Missouri State Univ. Indians, Southwest Missouri State Univ. Bears, Univ. of Missouri-Columbia Tigers (basketball only), Univ. of Missouri-Kansas City Kangaroos (basketball only)
Major league baseball teams: St. Louis Cardinals (NL Central), Busch Stadium; Kansas City Royals (AL Central), Kauffman Stadium
Major league soccer teams: Kansas City Wizards, Arrowhead Stadium
NFL football teams: Kansas City Chiefs (AFC), Arrowhead Stadium; St. Louis Rams (NFC), Trans World Dome
NHL hockey teams: St. Louis Blues, Kiel Center

WEBSITES CONTAINING FURTHER INFORMATION

| Missouri State Government Home Page | http://www.state.mo.us |

MONTANA

"I am in love with Montana. Montana seems to me to be what a small boy would think Texas is like from hearing Texans."

John Steinbeck, novelist

Montana is "Big Sky Country," a land of tall, rugged mountains in the west and broad plains in the east. The mountains have produced a great wealth of gold and silver, and some of the peaks in Glacier National Park are so steep and remote that they have never been climbed. On the prairies, huge herds of cattle graze. Montana's history recounts one of the nation's most memorable events, the Battle of Little Bighorn. Tourists feel close to the old frontier days in Montana when they visit the mountains, the battlefields, the old gold-mining camps, and the vast, lonely plains. The Indians knew the area as the Shining Land, and, despite some societal problems, the name still fits.

SUPERLATIVES

- "Birthplace" of the Missouri River.
- Site of Custer's Last Stand.
- First woman in U.S. House—Jeannette Rankin, 1917.

So They Say

"You cannot afford not to vote. You represent the womanhood of the country in the American Congress."

"I cannot vote for war...I vote No."

Representatives Joseph Cannon and Jeannette Rankin, on her vote against World War I

MOMENTS IN HISTORY

- The La Vérendrye brothers, Francis and Louis Joseph, are said to have reached Montana in 1742, before any other Europeans.
- James Mackay paid a visit to the region about 1795 and named the Yellowstone River.
- Little was known about the area until the great exploration of Meriwether Lewis and William Clark reached what is now Montana in 1805.
- On July 25, 1805, Lewis and Clark made a dramatic discovery. After much searching and discussion they concluded that the place where three rivers met was the long-sought "ultimate source of the Missouri River."

- On their way back to St. Louis, Lewis and Clark again entered and passed through what is now Montana on June 29, 1806.
- Many traders took advantage of the explorers' discoveries. In 1807, Manuel Lisa built a trading post fort where the Yellowstone and Big Horn rivers meet.
- The first steamboat reached Fort Union in 1832.
- By means of infected blankets, the white "civilization" deliberately brought a terrible and deadly smallpox epidemic to the Indians in 1837.
- St. Mary's Mission was founded in 1842.
- The main beaver trapping period lasted until about 1843.
- In 1858, John Mullan began the Mullan Road, which became the first wagon road over the northern Rockies.
- The mid-1850s found some disappointed miners from the California gold fields coming to Montana in search of possible rich finds there.
- John White made the first real gold discovery in July 1862, and Camp Bannack reached a population of 500 within a few days. A number of other gold discoveries were made as time went on.
- Butte was founded in 1864, after it started as a gold camp.
- Montana territory was created on May 26, 1864.
- The best known battle with the Indians in the nation's history took place at the Little Bighorn River on June 25, 1876. Civil War hero George Armstrong Custer led his troops into a massacre, and he and his entire force were killed. One horse was the lone survivor of the Custer forces.

So They Say

"Every man kept fighting to the last. There were no cowards on either side....Long Hair [Custer] was not scalped. He was a great chief. My people did not want his scalp." **Chief Sitting Bull**

- Another Indian battle with an entirely different ending occurred on August 7, 1877. Brave

and brilliant Chief Joseph of the Nez Percé tribe surrendered after the Battle of Big Hole Prairie.
• The Northern Pacific Railroad arrived on July 5, 1881.
• Statehood was achieved on November 8, 1889.
• The United States and Canada cooperated to create the International Peace Park in 1932, with Glacier National Park (established in 1910) as the U.S. portion.
• On August 17, 1959, a severe earthquake caused damage over a wide area. A mountain-side collapsed across the Madison River, creating Earthquake Lake.
• The state adopted a new constitution in 1978.
• In 1992 the House of Representatives voted to shelter 1.5 million acres of Montana wilderness from development.
• In 1996 accused Unabomber terrorist Theodore Kaczynski was seized in Montana.

THAT'S INTERESTING

• On the present site of Helena, a little party of gold miners agreed that they had reached their "last chance" to find wealth. Then they made a strike on what is now the city's main street, Last Chance Gulch.
• By the time Montana territory was created in 1864, many newcomers moved into homes visitors might have considered to be mounds of earth. In many places sod was the only available building material, and spring bloom would burst all over such houses.
• In 1867, Montana's territorial governor, Francis Meagher, a hero of the Civil War, boarded a Missouri River steamboat at Fort Benton, went to his stateroom, and was never seen again.

NOTABLE NATIVES

Gary Cooper (Helena, 1901-1961), actor. **Chet Huntley** (Cardwell, 1911-1974), journalist/commentator. **Myrna Loy** (Radersburg, 1905-1993), actress. **Jeannette Rankin** (near Missoula, 1880-1973), social reformer/public official. **Sacajawea** (in either western Montana or eastern Idaho, 1787?-1812?), Indian guide. **Washakie** (in what is now Montana, 1804?-1900), Indian leader.

GENERAL

Admitted to statehood: November 8, 1889
Origin of name: Latin or Spanish for "mountainous"

Capital: Helena
Nickname: Treasure State
Motto: *Oro y Plata*—Gold and silver
Bird: Western meadowlark
Flower: Bitterroot
Stone: Sapphire, agate
Song: "Montana"
Tree: Ponderosa pine

THE LAND

Area: 147,046 sq. mi., 4th
    Land: 145,556 sq. mi., 4th
    Water: 1,490 sq. mi., 19th
        Inland water: 1,490 sq. mi., 15th
Topography: Rocky Mountains in western third of the state; eastern two-thirds gently rolling northern Great Plains
Number of counties: 56
Geographic center: Fergus, 11 mi. W of Lewistown
Length: 630 mi.; width: 280 mi.
Highest point: 12,799 ft. (Granite Peak), 10th
Lowest point: 1,800 ft., (Kootenai River), 47th
Mean elevation: 3,400 ft., 8th

CLIMATE AND ENVIRONMENT

Temp., highest: 117 deg. on July 5, 1937, at Medicine Lake; lowest: –70 deg. on Jan. 20, 1954, at Rogers Pass
Monthly average: highest: 86.6 deg., 30th; lowest: 8.1 deg., 8th; spread (high to low): 78.5 deg., 8th
Hazardous waste sites (1997): 8, 40th
Endangered species: Animals: 8—Whooping crane, Eskimo curlew, American peregrine falcon, Black-footed ferret, Pallid sturgeon, White sturgeon, Least tern, Gray wolf. Plants: 0

MAJOR CITIES
POPULATION, 1996
PERCENTAGE INCREASE, 1990-96

Billings, 91,195; 12.4%
Great Falls, 57,758; 4.8%
Missoula, 51,204; 19.3%
Butte-Silver Bow, 34,051; 2.1%
Bozeman, 28,522; 25.9%

THE PEOPLE

Population (1997): 878,810, 44th
    Percent change (1990-97): 9.98%, 15th

Percent of total U.S. pop.: 0.33%, 44th
Per sq. mi: 5.98, 49th
Population (2000 proj.): 943,500, 44th
Percent change (1995-2000): 8.45%, 9th
Percent in metro. area (1996): 23.55%, 51st
Foreign born: 14,000, 48th
Percent: 1.7%, 37th
Top three ancestries reported:
German, 35.67%
Irish, 17.40%
English, 17.15%
White (1992): 766,000, 93.19%, 13th
Black (1992): 3,000, 0.36%, 50th
Native American (1992): 49,000, 5.96%, 5th
Asian, Pacific Isle (1992): 5,000, 0.61%, 45th
Hispanic origin (1992): 13,000, 1.58%, 34th
Percent over 5 yrs. speaking language other than English at home: 5.0%, 37th
Percent males (1996): 49.82%, 8th; percent females: 50.18%, 43rd
Percent never married: 22.3%, 46th
Marriages per 1,000 (1996): 7.53, 37th
Divorces per 1,000 (1996): 4.83, 16th
Median age (1996): 36.5
Under 5 years (1996): 6.40%, 44th
18 years and under (1996): 29.63%, 14th
65 years and over (1996): 13.19%, 23rd
Percent increase among the elderly (1995-96): 1.19%, 21st

OF VITAL IMPORTANCE

Live births per 1,000 pop. (1996): 12.2, 48th
Infant mortality rate per 1,000 live births (1995): 7.0, 34th
Rate for whites: 7.0, 13th
Rate for blacks: NA
Births to unmarried women, % of total (1996): 27.8%, 37th
Births to teenage mothers, % of total (1996): 12.5%, 27th
Abortions (1992): 3,300, 44th
Rate per 1,000 women 14-44 years old: 18.2, 27th
Percent change (1988-92): 11%, 4th
Average lifetime (1989-91): 76.23, 20th
Total death rate per 100,000 pop. (1995): 876.6, 31st
Accidents and adverse effects: 43.7, 14th
Alzheimer's disease: 14.5, 1st
Cancer: 203.4, 33rd
Cerebrovascular diseases: 68.3, 18th
Chronic liver disease and cirrhosis: 9.5, 20th
Chronic obstructive pulmonary diseases and allied conditions: 55.2, 3rd

Diabetes mellitus: 24.1, 21st
Diseases of heart: 230.3, 40th
HIV infection: 2.6, 49th
Homicide: 5.4, 32nd
Injury by firearms: 18.5, 10th
Motor vehicle accidents: 22.4, 10th
Pneumonia and influenza: 36.8, 10th
Suicide: 23.1, 2nd

KEEPING WELL

Active nonfederal physicians per 100,000 pop. (1995): 181, 40th
Dentists per 100,000 (1991): 56, 20th
Nurses per 100,000 (1995): 751, 39th
Hospitals per 100,000 (1995): 6.32, 3rd
Admissions per 1,000 (1995): 110.34, 32nd
Hospital beds per 1,000 (1995): 4.83, 4th
Occupancy rate per 100 beds (1995): 64.29, 18th
Average cost per patient per day (1995): $493, 50th
Average cost per stay (1995): $5,184, 43rd
AIDS cases (new, 1996): 34; per 100,000: 3.9, 47th
Persons living with HIV infection (1996): NA
Other notifiable diseases, per 100,000 pop.:
Gonorrhea (1995): 7.5, 49th
Syphilis (1995): 1.5, 44th
Tuberculosis (1996): 2.2, 43rd
Pop. without health insur. (1996): 13.6%, 23rd

HOUSEHOLDS BY TYPE

Total households (1996): 341,000, 44th
Percent change (1990-96): 11.3%, 13th
Per 1,000 pop. (1996) 387.94, 7th
Percent of householders 65 yrs. and over (1996): 21.99%, 23rd
Persons per household (1996): 2.50, 46th
Family households: 211,666
Percent of total: 69.14%, 36th
Nonfamily households: 94,497
Percent of total: 30.86%, 16th
Pop. living in group quarters: 23,747
Percent of pop.: 2.97%, 20th

LIVING QUARTERS

Total housing units: 361,155
Persons per unit: 2.21, 45th
Occupied housing units: 306,163
Percent of total units: 84.77%, 43rd
Persons per unit: 2.47, 42nd
Percent of units with over 1 person per room: 2.90%, 27th

Owner-occupied units: 205,899
  Percent of total units: 57.01%, 35th
  Percent of occupied units: 67.25%, 26th
  Persons per unit: 2.65, 42nd
  Median value: $56,600, 39th
Renter-occupied units: 100,264
  Percent of total units: 27.76%, 34th
  Percent of occupied units: 32.75%, 26th
  Persons per unit: 2.28, 35th
  Median contract rent: $251, 44th
  Rental vacancy rate: 9.6%, 16th
Mobile home, trailer & other as a percent of
    occupied housing units: 19.13%, 5th
Persons in emergency shelters for homeless
    persons: 445, 0.056%, 19th
Persons visible in street locations: 17,
    0.0021%, 44th
Nursing home population: 7,764, 0.97%, 11th

CRIME INDEX PER 100,000 (1996)

Total reported: 4,493.6, 30th
  Percent increase: –6.3%, 39th
  Violent: 161.0, 47th
    Percent increase: –6.1%, 27th
    Murder & nonnegligent manslaughter:
      3.9, 36th
    Forcible rape: 27.1, 38th
    Aggravated assault: 100.3, 47th
    Robbery: 29.7, 44th
  Property: 4,332.7, 24th
    Percent increase: –6.3%, 38th
    Burglary: 558.4, 46th
    Larceny-theft: 3,518.5, 11th
    Motor vehicle theft: 255.7, 41st

TEACHING AND LEARNING

Pop. 3 and over enrolled in school (1996):
    209,583, 44th
  Percent of pop.: 23.84%, 16th
Public elementary & secondary schools (1996-
    97): 894, 35th
  Total enrollment (1996): 166,909, 43rd
    Percent of school age pop.: 94.30%, 15th
    Percent of total pop.: 18.99%, 8th
  Teachers (1996): 10,110, 44th
    Percent of pop.: 1.15%, 13th
  Pupil/teacher ratio (1995): 16.4, 28th
  Teachers' avg. salary (1996-97): $29,950,
    45th
  Expenditure per capita (1992-93):
    $1,366.02, 21st
    Education as % of state govt. expendi-
      tures: 36.9%, 18th

Expenditure per pupil (1994-95): $5,692,
    28th
  Percent increase (1993-94 & 1994-95):
    1.68%, 46th
Percent at or above grade level, NAEP tests:
  Reading, grade 4 (1994): 35%, 6th
  Math, grade 4 (1996): 71%, 8th
  Math, grade 8 (1996): 75%, 5th
Percent of graduates taking SAT (1995): 21%,
    29th
  Mean SAT verbal scores: 473, 21st
  Mean SAT mathematical scores: 536, 15th
Percent of graduates taking ACT (1997):
    55%, 25th
  Mean ACT scores: 21.9, 7th
Percent of pop. over 25 completing:
  Less than 9th grade: 8.1%, 35th
  High school: 81.0%, 11th
  College degree(s): 19.8%, 25th
Higher education, institutions (1996): 28,
    38th
  Enrollment (1995-96): 42,674, 46th
    Percent increase in enroll. (1990-95):
      18.9%, 4th
    White non-Hispanic (1995): 36,924,
      44th
      Percent of enroll.: 86.53%, 15th
    Total minority enroll. (1995): 4,729, 44th
      Percent of enroll.: 11.08%, 36th
    Black non-Hispanic (1995): 146, 51st
      Percent of enroll.: 0.34%, 51st
    Hispanic (1995): 484, 46th
      Percent of enroll.: 1.13%, 41st
    Asian/Pacific Islander (1995): 337, 48th
      Percent of enroll.: 0.79%, 48th
    American Indian/AK native (1995): 3,762,
      10th
      Percent of enroll.: 8.82%, 2nd
    Nonresident alien (1995): 1,021, 45th
      Percent of enroll.: 2.39%, 31st
    Female (1995): 22,716, 46th
      Percent of enroll.: 53.23%, 49th
  Pub. institutions (1995-96): 19, 34th
    Enrollment: 37,435, 43rd
      Percent increase in enrollment (1990-
        95): 17.5%, 4th
      Percent of enroll.: 87.72%, 12th
  Private institutions (1995-96): 9, 42nd
    Enrollment: 5,239, 46th
      Percent increase in enrollment (1990-
        95): 30.6%, 3rd
      Percent of enroll.: 12.28%, 40th
  Tuition (in state), public 4-year institution
    (1996-97): $2,488, 29th

Tuition (in state), public 2-year institution (1996-97): $1,600, 19th

Tuition, private 4-year institution (1996-97): $8,022, 41st

Public library systems (1994): 82, 33rd

Books & serial vol. per capita: 3.1, 23rd

Library visits per capita: 3.5, 26th

Circulation per capita: 6.0, 31st

LAW ENFORCEMENT AND CORRECTIONS

Police protection and corrections expenditures (1996): $96,413,000

Per capita: $109.69, 27th

Police per 10,000 pop. (1996): 16.61, 44th

Prisoners (1 year or more) per 100,000 pop. (1996): 235, 38th

Percent change (1995-96): 3.7%, 34th

Percent of inmates that are female: 5.6%, 36th

Percent change: 4.5%, 37th

Death penalty: yes, by lethal injection

Under sentence (Jan. 1998): 7, 30th

Executed, 1976-97: 1, 25th

Executed in 1997: 0

RELIGION, NUMBER AND PERCENT OF POPULATION

Agnostic: 3,462—0.60%, 19th

Buddhist: NA

Christian: 490,417—85.00%, 33rd

Hindu: NA

Jewish: NA

Muslim: NA

Unitarian: 1,731—0.30%, 15th

Other: 6,924—1.20%, 29th

None: 58,850—10.20%, 10th

Refused to answer: 15,578—2.70%, 16th

MAKING A LIVING

Personal income per capita (1996): $19,047, 47th

Percent increase (1995-96): 2.0%, 43rd

Disposable personal income per capita (1996): $16,656, 48th

Median income of households (average, 1995-96): $28,631, 45th

Percent of pop. below poverty level (1995-96): 16.2%, 13th

ECONOMY

In civilian labor force (1996): 447,000

Percent of total pop.: 66.6%, 33rd

Percent of total pop. 65 years and over: 14.4%, 10th

Percent of total female pop.: 60.6%, 30th

Major employer industries (total nonagricultural, 1996):

Construction: 17,000—4.7%, 21st

Finance, insurance, & real estate: 16,000—4.5%, 39th

Government: 76,600—21.3%, 6th

Manufacturing: 23,800—6.6%, 45th

Service: 101,800—28.4%, 19th

Trade: 97,700—27.2%, 1st

Transportation, communications, public utilities: 20,700—5.8%, 13th

Unemployment rate (1996): 5.3%, 20th

Male: 5.9%, 10th

Female: 4.6%, 32nd

Total businesses (1995): 29,109, 43rd

New business incorps. (1995): 1,767

Percent of total businesses: 6.07%, 48th

Business failures (1995): 152

Failures per 10,000 businesses: 52.2, 46th

Agriculture farm income:

Marketing (1996): $2,027,226,000, 33rd

Average per farm: $92,147, 24th

Leading products (1997): Cattle, wheat, barley, hay, sugar beets, oats

Average value land & build. per acre (1997): $305, 46th

Percent increase (1996-97): 6%, 20th

Govt. payments (1996): $240,874,000, 11th

Average per farm: $10,949, 2nd

Construction, value of all (1996): $916,046,000, 45th

Per capita: $1,042, 39th

Manufactures (1995):

Value added: $1,779,000,000

Per capita: $2,044, 49th

Leading products (1997): Food products, wood and paper products, primary metals, printing and publishing, petroleum and coal products

Value of nonfuel mineral production (1996): $523,000,000, 25th

Leading mineral products (1996): Petroleum, coal, natural gas, gold, copper, cement, zinc, sand/gravel

Energy consumption per person (1994): 430.8 mil. Btu, 11th

Retail sales (1995): $7,831,000,000

Per household: $23,182, 41st

Sales increase (1994-95): 3.2%, 34th

Tourism revenues (1996): $1.3 bil.

Foreign exports, in total value (1996): $440,000,000, 49th

Per capita: $500, 50th

Gross state product per person (1994): $19,698, 49th

Public aid recipients (percent of resident pop. 1994): 5.6%, 35th

Medicaid recipients (percent of pop., 1995): 11.3%, 30th

Medicare enrollment per 1,000 pop. (1996): 150, 17th

TRAVEL AND TRANSPORTATION

Motor vehicle registrations (1996): 973,074, 41st
    Per 1,000 pop.: 1,109.95, 2nd
Motorcycle registrations (1996): 20,868, 41st
    Per 1,000 pop.: 21.45, 19th
Licensed drivers (1996): 573,749, 44th
    Per 1,000 pop.: 659.22, 37th
Public roads & streets (1996)
    Total mileage: 69,809, 29th
       Per 1,000 pop.: 179.39, 3rd
    Rural mileage: 67,389, 25th
       Per 1,000 pop.: 76.63, 3rd
    Urban mileage: 2,420, 43rd
       Per 1,000 pop.: 2.75, 38th
    Interstate mileage: 1,190, 10th
       Per 1,000 pop.: 1.35, 3rd
Speed limit (max. interstate, autos, mi. per hr., 1997): No fixed limit
Annual vehicle-mi. of travel per driver (1996): 16,464, 7th
Mean travel time for workers age 16+ who work away from home: 14.8 min., 49th

GOVERNMENT

Percent of voting age pop. registered (1996): 90.05%, 3rd

Percent of voting age pop. voting for president: (1996): 62.9%, 3rd

Percent of voting age pop. voting for U.S. representatives (1996): 62.4%, 3rd

State legislators, total (1997): 150, 21st
    Women members (1997): 35
       Percent of legislature: 23%, 23rd

U.S. Congress, House members (1998): 1
Change (1988-98): -1

Revenues (1996):
    State govt.: $3,475,665,000
       Per capita: $3,954.11, 17th
       Parimutuel & amusement taxes & lotteries, revenue per capita (1995): $35.68, 38th

Expenditures (1996):
    State govt.: $3,136,205,000
       Per capita: $3,567.92, 16th

Debt outstanding (1996): $2,244,202,000
    Per capita: $2,553.13, 10th

LAWS AND REGULATIONS

Legal driving age: 16, 15 if completed driver education course

Marriage age without parental consent: 18

Divorce residence requirement: 90 days

ATTRACTIONS (1997)

Per capita spending by the NEA (1997): $0.68, 10th

State Fair in late July-early August at Great Falls

SPORTS AND COMPETITION

NCAA (Division I) football and basketball teams: Montana State Univ. Bobcats, Univ. of Montana Grizzlies

WEBSITES CONTAINING FURTHER INFORMATION

Montana Online: Homepage for the State of Montana	http://www.mt.gov
MontanaWeb!	http://search.MontanaWeb.com

NEBRASKA

"For more than a century the wide Platte Valley has been the high-road to the American West. But Nebraska is more than a mere pathway...a land where the West that was wild continues to mingle with evidences of the most modern civilization...great cattle herds, nuclear reactors power modern industry...superhighways...replacing the ruts of the Oregon trail....Up-to-date cities have grown from the tracks of the Mormon wagons...some of the finest museums, music and other cultural attractions anywhere." *Enchantment of America—Nebraska*

Once referred to as part of "the great American desert," Nebraska was changed into a land of vast farms through the spirit and determination of its early settlers. In the west are wheat fields as far as the eye can see. In the north-central region, huge herds of beef cattle graze on enormous ranches. In the east, corn, grain, sorghum, and other crops are grown. Nebraska is the only state to bear a nickname based on a college football team—the University of Nebraska Cornhuskers. Football at the university is so popular that on Saturdays when there is a home game, the stadium in Lincoln becomes "the third largest city in the state," after Omaha and Lincoln. Athletic prowess is balanced by notable civic and cultural institutions.

SUPERLATIVES

• Nation's first Homestead grant claimed by a Nebraskan, 1862.
• Capitol ranked among world's ten greatest buildings.
• First in alfalfa and other hays.
• World's largest concentration of meat packing and processing.
• Headquarters of many insurance companies.

MOMENTS IN HISTORY

• In 1699 a Navajo group returned to the Spanish Southwest, probably from the South Platte valley, and they carried trophies indicating that there were French settlers there.
• In an effort to drive the French out, Pedro de Villasur in 1720 attacked them and was killed somewhere along the Platte River.
• After the region came to the United States in 1803 as part of the Louisiana Purchase, the explorers Meriwether Lewis and William Clark reached the mouth of the Platte on July 21, 1804.
• Lewis and Clark made their last camp in Nebraska on September 7, 1804, and contin-

ued up the Missouri River. They returned back down the river in 1806.
• The American fur trader Manuel Lisa followed the explorers and set up a fur trading operation in 1807.
• Bellevue was founded in 1823 by Peter Sarpy as an American Fur Company post, and it proved to be the first permanent European settlement in what is now Nebraska.
• Nebraska soon became a highway to the West, and more than 6,000 Mormon faithful crossed the Nebraska plains in the winter of 1846-47 on their way to the "promised land" of Utah.
• The next major crossing of the state came with the almost endless procession of 49ers hurrying to the California gold fields, beginning in 1849.

So They Say

"The onlookers witnessed sights ranging from the laughable to the alarming. In one place six men were assisted ashore by hanging to the tail of a mule, with a rider on him....The line of wagons stretched for two miles...busy as it ordinarily [is] in St. Louis...."

Emigrant's journal of a 49er party crossing the Platte River

• In 1862, Daniel Freeman of Beatrice was the nation's first recipient of land granted under the unique Homestead Act, which took effect on January 1, 1863.
• President Andrew Johnson vetoed the Nebraska statehood bill of 1866, but Congress overrode his veto, and Nebraska became a state on March 1, 1867.
• On May 6, 1877, famed Chief Crazy Horse surrendered with 1,000 of his followers near Camp Robinson. On September 7, 1877, he was killed because he was said to have resisted his captors.
• President William McKinley opened the

Mississippi International Exposition at Omaha in 1898.

- In 1934, Nebraska became unique among the states when it installed its unicameral (one-house) legislature, consisting only of a Senate.
- By 1997, Omaha had become the home of more than 20 insurance companies.

THAT'S INTERESTING

- Boosters of Omaha as state capital, rather than Lincoln, claimed the capital had been stolen from them. Armed bands roamed the streets to keep the capital records in Omaha. The records had to be moved secretly at night.
- On the first Arbor Day, the founder of the event, J. Sterling Morton, was unable to take part because the 800 tree seedlings he had ordered were not delivered. However, he already had planted thousands of trees on almost treeless Nebraska.
- The only national forest to have a large part planted by human hands began when Dr. Charles Bessey persuaded Theodore Roosevelt to establish an area to research planting of forests on the great plains. From no trees at all, that preserve spread to become the Nebraska National Forest.

NOTABLE NATIVES

Fred Astaire (Omaha, 1899-1987), dancer/actor. **Marlon Brando** (Omaha, 1924-), actor. **Henry Fonda** (Grand Island, 1905-1982), actor. **Gerald Rudolph Ford** (Omaha, 1913-), U.S. president. **Howard Hanson** (Wahoo, 1896-1981), composer/conductor. **Harold Lloyd** (Burchard, 1893-1971), actor/producer. **Malcolm X** (Omaha, 1925-1965), religious leader/reformer. **Roscoe Pound** (Lincoln, 1870-1964), educator/legal scholar. **Red Cloud** (in north-central Nebraska, 1822-1909), Indian leader.

GENERAL

Admitted to statehood: March 1, 1867
Origin of name: From Omaha or Otos Indian word meaning "broad water" or "flat river," describing the Platte River
Capital: Lincoln
Nickname: Cornhusker State, Tree Planters State
Motto: Equality before the law
Bird: Western meadowlark
Insect: Honeybee
Flower: Goldenrod

Gem: Blue chalcedony (agate)
Stone: Prairie agate
Song: "Beautiful Nebraska"
Tree: Cottonwood

THE LAND

Area: 77,359 sq. mi., 16th
 Land: 76,878 sq. mi., 15th
 Water: 481 sq. mi., 39th
  Inland water: 481 sq. mi., 33rd
Topography: Till plains of the central lowland in the eastern third rising to the Great Plains and hill country of the N central and NW
Number of counties: 93
Geographic center: Custer, 10 mi. NW of Broken Bow
Length: 430 mi.; width: 210 mi.
Highest point: 5,424 ft. (Johnson Township), 20th
Lowest point: 480 ft. (Missouri River), 38th
Mean elevation: 2,600 ft., 12th

CLIMATE AND ENVIRONMENT

Temp., highest: 118 deg. on July 24, 1936, at Minden; lowest: –47 deg. on Feb. 12, 1899, at Camp Clarke
Monthly average: highest: 89.5 deg., 20th; lowest: 8.9 deg., 9th; spread (high to low): 80.6 deg., 6th
Hazardous waste sites (1997): 10, 34th
Endangered species: Animals: 7—American burying beetle, Whooping crane, Eskimo curlew, American peregrine falcon, Black-footed ferret, Pallid sturgeon, Least tern. Plants: 1

MAJOR CITIES
POPULATION, 1996
PERCENTAGE INCREASE, 1990-96

Omaha, 364,253; 6.2%
Lincoln, 209,192; 9.0%
Bellevue, 42,807; 9.1%
Grand Island, 41,177; 4.3%
Kearney, 27,314; 12.0%

THE PEOPLE

Population (1997): 1,656,870, 38th
 Percent change (1990-97): 4.97%, 35th
 Percent of total U.S. pop.: 0.62%, 38th
 Per sq. mi: 21.42, 43rd
Population (2000 proj.): 1,702,500, 38th
 Percent change (1995-2000): 4.00%, 32nd
Percent in metro. area (1996): 51.27%, 38th

Foreign born: 28,000, 41st
    Percent: 1.8%, 36th
Top three ancestries reported:
    German, 50.38%
    Irish, 17.24%
    English, 13.24%
White (1992): 1,513,000, 94.50%, 9th
Black (1992): 60,000, 3.75%, 34th
Native American (1992): 13,000, 0.81%, 20th
Asian, Pacific Isle (1992): 15,000, 0.94%, 33rd
Hispanic origin (1992): 42,000, 2.62%, 26th
Percent over 5 yrs. speaking language other than English at home: 4.8%, 39th
Percent males (1996): 48.98%, 23rd; percent females: 51.02%, 29th
Percent never married: 24.4%, 33rd
Marriages per 1,000 (1996): 7.72, 35th
Divorces per 1,000 (1996): 3.69, 32nd
Median age (1996): 34.9
Under 5 years (1996): 6.92%, 29th
18 years and under (1996): 29.79%, 11th
65 years and over (1996): 13.84%, 14th
Percent increase among the elderly (1995-96): 0.14%, 46th

OF VITAL IMPORTANCE

Live births per 1,000 pop. (1996): 14.1, 26th
Infant mortality rate per 1,000 live births (1995): 7.4, 28th
    Rate for whites: 7.3, 6th
    Rate for blacks: NA
Births to unmarried women, % of total (1996): 24.7%, 47th
Births to teenage mothers, % of total (1996): 10.6%, 36th
Abortions (1992): 5,580, 40th
    Rate per 1,000 women 14-44 years old: 15.7, 32nd
    Percent change (1988-92): −11%, 30th
Average lifetime (1989-91): 76.92, 7th
Total death rate per 100,000 pop. (1995): 932.6, 18th
    Accidents and adverse effects: 35.2, 31st
    Alzheimer's disease: 11.6, 6th
    Cancer: 206.2, 29th
    Cerebrovascular diseases: 71.2, 11th
    Chronic liver disease and cirrhosis: 5.9, 49th
    Chronic obstructive pulmonary diseases and allied conditions: 44.6, 15th
    Diabetes mellitus: 17.5, 45th
    Diseases of heart: 312.0, 15th

HIV infection: 3.7, 45th
Homicide: 4.1, 39th
Injury by firearms: 10.3, 37th
Motor vehicle accidents: 15.5, 32nd
Pneumonia and influenza: 39.8, 7th
Suicide: 11.4, 38th

KEEPING WELL

Active nonfederal physicians per 100,000 pop. (1995): 199, 29th
Dentists per 100,000 (1991): 64, 15th
Nurses per 100,000 (1995): 940, 14th
Hospitals per 100,000 (1995): 5.56, 4th
    Admissions per 1,000 (1995): 111.79, 30th
    Hospital beds per 1,000 (1995): 4.83, 4th
    Occupancy rate per 100 beds (1995): 56.96, 39th
    Average cost per patient per day (1995): $661, 46th
    Average cost per stay (1995): $5,880, 26th
AIDS cases (new, 1996): 100; per 100,000: 6.1, 41st
Persons living with HIV infection, not yet AIDS (1996): 266
Other notifiable diseases, per 100,000 pop.:
    Gonorrhea (1995): 69.2, 32nd
    Syphilis (1995): 2.1, 41st
    Tuberculosis (1996): 1.3, 48th
Pop. without health insur. (1996): 11.4%, 36th

HOUSEHOLDS BY TYPE

Total households (1996): 631,000, 36th
    Percent change (1990-96): 4.8%, 34th
    Per 1,000 pop. (1996) 381.96, 17th
    Percent of householders 65 yrs. and over (1996): 23.30%, 11th
    Persons per household (1996): 2.54, 33rd
Family households: 415,427
    Percent of total: 68.97%, 38th
Nonfamily households: 186,936
    Percent of total: 31.03%, 14th
Pop. living in group quarters: 47,553
    Percent of pop.: 3.01%, 18th

LIVING QUARTERS

Total housing units: 660,621
    Persons per unit: 2.39, 28th
Occupied housing units: 602,363
    Percent of total units: 91.18%, 15th
    Persons per unit: 2.48, 38th
    Percent of units with over 1 person per room: 1.75%, 47th
Owner-occupied units: 400,394
    Percent of total units: 60.61%, 21st

Percent of occupied units: 66.47%, 30th
Persons per unit: 2.68, 36th
Median value: $50,400, 45th
Renter-occupied units: 201,969
  Percent of total units: 30.57%, 19th
  Percent of occupied units: 33.53%, 23rd
  Persons per unit: 2.27, 36th
  Median contract rent: $282, 35th
  Rental vacancy rate: 7.7%, 34th
Mobile home, trailer & other as a percent of occupied housing units: 6.98%, 37th
Persons in emergency shelters for homeless persons: 764, 0.048%, 24th
Persons visible in street locations: 20, 0.0013%, 49th
Nursing home population: 19,171, 1.21%, 4th

CRIME INDEX PER 100,000 (1996)

Total reported: 4,436.6, 33rd
  Percent increase: –2.4%, 25th
  Violent: 434.7, 28th
    Percent increase: 13.8%, 1st
    Murder & nonnegligent manslaughter: 2.9, 43rd
    Forcible rape: 27.1, 38th
    Aggravated assault: 341.1, 25th
    Robbery: 63.7, 41st
  Property: 4,001.8, 33rd
    Percent increase: –3.9%, 30th
    Burglary: 614.5, 43rd
    Larceny-theft: 3,045.7, 22nd
    Motor vehicle theft: 341.6, 36th

TEACHING AND LEARNING

Pop. 3 and over enrolled in school (1996): 407,839, 36th
  Percent of pop.: 24.69%, 9th
Public elementary & secondary schools (1996-97): 1,411, 25th
  Total enrollment (1996): 292,121, 37th
    Percent of school age pop.: 88.79%, 38th
    Percent of total pop.: 17.68%, 19th
  Teachers (1996): 20,109, 36th
    Percent of pop.: 1.22%, 6th
  Pupil/teacher ratio (1995): 14.5, 45th
  Teachers' avg. salary (1996-97): $31,768, 40th
  Expenditure per capita (1992-93): $1,473.44, 13th
    Education as % of state govt. expenditures: 40.8%, 2nd

Expenditure per pupil (1994-95): $5,935, 22nd
  Percent increase (1993-94 & 1994-95): 5.03%, 16th
Percent at or above grade level, NAEP tests:
  Reading, grade 4 (1994): 34%, 9th
  Math, grade 4 (1996): 70%, 10th
  Math, grade 8 (1996): 76%, 4th
Percent of graduates taking SAT (1995): 9%, 38th
  Mean SAT verbal scores: 494, 11th
  Mean SAT mathematical scores: 556, 9th
Percent of graduates taking ACT (1997): 73%, 6th
  Mean ACT scores: 21.7, 10th
Percent of pop. over 25 completing:
  Less than 9th grade: 8.0%, 36th
  High school: 81.8%, 8th
  College degree(s): 18.9%, 27th
Higher education, institutions (1996): 35, 34th
  Enrollment (1995-96): 115,718, 34th
    Percent increase in enroll. (1990-95): 2.6%, 27th
  White non-Hispanic (1995): 104,352, 33rd
    Percent of enroll.: 90.18%, 7th
  Total minority enroll. (1995): 8,784, 39th
    Percent of enroll.: 7.59%, 42nd
  Black non-Hispanic (1995): 3,408, 36th
    Percent of enroll.: 2.95%, 37th
  Hispanic (1995): 2,268, 34th
    Percent of enroll.: 1.96%, 30th
  Asian/Pacific Islander (1995): 2,216, 36th
    Percent of enroll.: 1.92%, 34th
  American Indian/AK native (1995): 892, 33rd
    Percent of enroll.: 0.77%, 24th
  Nonresident alien (1995): 2,582, 35th
    Percent of enroll.: 2.23%, 36th
  Female (1995): 63,266, 34th
    Percent of enroll.: 54.67%, 43rd
  Pub. institutions (1995-96): 18, 36th
    Enrollment: 95,599, 35th
      Percent increase in enrollment (1990-95): 1%, 31st
    Percent of enroll.: 82.61%, 25th
  Private institutions (1995-96): 17, 32nd
    Enrollment: 20,119, 34th
      Percent increase in enrollment (1990-95): 10.4%, 17th
    Percent of enroll.: 17.39%, 27th
  Tuition (in state), public 4-year institution (1996-97): $2,269, 33rd
  Tuition (in state), public 2-year institution (1996-97): $1,224, 33rd

Tuition, private 4-year institution (1996-97): $9,859, 33rd

Public library systems (1994): 269, 11th
Books & serial vol. per capita: 3.8, 12th
Library visits per capita: NA
Circulation per capita: 7.8, 14th

LAW ENFORCEMENT AND CORRECTIONS

Police protection and corrections expenditures (1996): $136,396,000
Per capita: $82.56, 44th
Police per 10,000 pop. (1996): 18.83, 37th
Prisoners (1 year or more) per 100,000 pop. (1996): 194, 44th
Percent change (1995-96): 6.9%, 21st
Percent of inmates that are female: 7.0%, 13th
Percent change: 8.1%, 27th
Death penalty: yes, by electrocution
Under sentence (Jan. 1998): 9, 29th
Executed, 1976-97: 3, 20th
Executed in 1997: 1, 9th

RELIGION, NUMBER AND PERCENT OF POPULATION

Agnostic: 1,149—0.10%, 47th
Buddhist: 1,149—0.10%, 17th
Christian: 1,016,046—88.40%, 18th
Hindu: 2,299—0.20%, 3rd
Jewish: 5,747—0.50%, 27th
Muslim: NA
Unitarian: 5,747—0.50%, 6th
Other: 17,241—1.50%, 18th
None: 80,456—7.00%, 23rd
Refused to answer: 19,539—1.70%, 35th

MAKING A LIVING

Personal income per capita (1996): $23,047, 25th
Percent increase (1995-96): 6.1%, 4th
Disposable personal income per capita (1996): $20,180, 24th
Median income of households (average, 1995-96): $33,958, 30th
Percent of pop. below poverty level (1995-96): 9.9%, 40th

ECONOMY

In civilian labor force (1996): 913,000
Percent of total pop.: 74.2%, 3rd
Percent of total pop. 65 years and over: 17.8% 3rd
Percent of total female pop.: 67.7%, 5th

Major employer industries (total nonagricultural, 1996):
Construction: 36,700—4.4%, 30th
Finance, insurance, & real estate: 53,100—6.4%, 7th
Government: 151,500—18.2%, 19th
Manufacturing: 113,700—13.6%, 31st
Service: 220,400—26.4%, 34th
Trade: 207,500—24.9%, 10th
Transportation, communications, public utilities: 50,300—6.0%, 8th
Unemployment rate (1996): 2.9%, 51st
Male: 2.7%, 51st
Female: 3.2%, 47th
Total businesses (1995): 47,128, 34th
New business incorps. (1995): 3,360
Percent of total businesses: 7.13%, 41st
Business failures (1995): 323
Failures per 10,000 businesses: 68.5, 38th
Agriculture farm income:
Marketing (1996): $9,454,041,000, 4th
Average per farm: $168,822, 5th
Leading products (1997): Cattle, corn, hogs, soybeans, sorghum, hay, wheat, dry beans, oats, potatoes, sugar beets
Average value land & build. per acre (1997): $680, 37th
Percent increase (1996-97): 8%, 10th
Govt. payments (1996): $388,819,000, 4th
Average per farm: $6,943, 8th
Construction, value of all (1996): $1,869,209,000, 38th
Per capita: $1,131, 29th
Manufactures (1995):
Value added: $9,360,600,000
Per capita: $5,718, 30th
Leading products (1997): Processed foods, industrial machinery, printed materials, electric and electronic equipment, primary and fabricated metal products, transportation equipment
Value of nonfuel mineral production (1996): $147,000,000, 41st
Leading mineral products (1996): Petroleum, cement, sand/gravel, stone, clays
Energy consumption per person (1994): 344.8 mil. Btu, 25th
Retail sales (1995): $15,731,000,000
Per household: $25,073, 19th
Sales increase (1994-95): 3.3%, 31st
Tourism revenues (1995): $2 bil.
Foreign exports, in total value (1996): $1,907,000,000, 38th
Per capita: $1,154, 36th

Gross state product per person (1994): $25,484, 22nd

Public aid recipients (percent of resident pop. 1994): 4.0%, 46th

Medicaid recipients (percent of pop., 1995): 10.3%, 35th

Medicare enrollment per 1,000 pop. (1996): 152, 16th

TRAVEL AND TRANSPORTATION

Motor vehicle registrations (1996): 1,478,558, 35th

Per 1,000 pop.: 896.80, 11th

Motorcycle registrations (1996): 18,596, 42nd

Per 1,000 pop.: 12.58, 40th

Licensed drivers (1996): 1,151,764, 37th

Per 1,000 pop.: 702.63, 16th

Public roads & streets (1996)

Total mileage: 92,805, 19th

Per 1,000 pop.: 156.17, 5th

Rural mileage: 87,684, 10th

Per 1,000 pop.: 53.07, 5th

Urban mileage: 5,121, 37th

Per 1,000 pop.: 3.10, 24th

Interstate mileage: 480, 42nd

Per 1,000 pop.: 0.29, 14th

Speed limit (max. interstate, autos, mi. per hr., 1997): 75

Annual vehicle-mi. of travel per driver (1996): 14,000 28th

Mean travel time for workers age 16+ who work away from home: 15.8 min., 47th

GOVERNMENT

Percent of voting age pop. registered (1996): 83.82%, 10th

Percent of voting age pop. voting for president: (1996): 56.1%, 17th

Percent of voting age pop. voting for U.S. representatives (1996): 54.8%, 15th

State legislators, total (1997): 49, 50th

Women members (1997): 13

Percent of legislature: 27%, 12th

U.S. Congress, House members (1998): 3

Change (1988-98): 0

Revenues (1996):

State govt.: $4,998,908,000

Per capita: $3,025.97, 43rd

Parimutuel & amusement taxes & lotteries, revenue per capita (1995): $55.61, 37th

Expenditures (1996):

State govt.: $4,489,725,000

Per capita: $2,717.75, 41st

Debt outstanding (1996): $1,401,777,000

Per capita: $848.53, 41st

LAWS AND REGULATIONS

Legal driving age: 16

Marriage age without parental consent: 19

Divorce residence requirement: 1 yr., for qualifications check local statutes

ATTRACTIONS (1997)

Major opera companies: 1

Major symphony orchestras: 1

Major dance companies: 1

Per capita spending by the NEA (1997): $0.30, 24th

State Fair in late August–early September at Lincoln

SPORTS AND COMPETITION

NCAA (Division I) football and basketball teams: Creighton Univ. Bluejays (basketball only), Univ. of Nebraska Cornhuskers

WEBSITES CONTAINING FURTHER INFORMATION

Nebraska State Government	http://www.state.ne.us
Nebraska Travel & Tourism Office	http://www.ded.state.ne.us/tourism.html

NEVADA

"I had previously seen some beautiful valleys, but I place none of these ahead of Carson."
                                    Horace Greeley, journalist

Every year, Nevada has enough tourists coming to the state to outnumber the population of several states. Some come only for the gambling—it is home to the world's most popular gambling and entertainment center—but many come for the vast tracts of beautiful deserts, plains, and mountains. Nevada is a cattle- and sheep-raising state, and most of the grains grown there are used to feed livestock. Hoover Dam, on the Colorado River, created Lake Mead, one of the world's largest artificial lakes. All of this has come from the desert lands where no European was known until 1826. As the 1990s progressed, the "splendor" of Las Vegas assumed even more striking proportions, accompanied by growth of pleasant new suburbs and increasing opportunities for newcomers.

SUPERLATIVES

- Home of two world-famed entertainment centers.
- Kept the Union solvent in the Civil War.
- Major world supplier of turquoise.
- World center of rare opals.
- World's largest open-pit copper mine.
- First large-scale reclamation program in the United States.
- Claims first use of skis in the United States.

MOMENTS IN HISTORY

- Father Silvestre Vélez de Escalante may have visited the Nevada region in 1775, but records of European exploration do not begin until 1826, with the exploration of Peter Skene Ogden.
- Walker Pass and Walker Lake are named for Joseph Walker, who brought an expedition in 1833.
- More complete records on Nevada were made by John C. Frémont, who came to the area in 1843-44 with his guide, the famed Kit Carson.
- In 1846 the Donner party was blocked by heavy snow in what is now Donner Pass, and only about half of the party of 87 survived to reach California.
- Beginning in 1849, thousands of 49ers crossed the bleak country, and by fall of 1850 at least 60,000 had passed through in covered wagons, on muleback and horseback, and even on foot.
- In 1859, one of the world's richest silver discoveries was made in the region that became known as the Comstock, and Virginia City sprang up almost overnight.
- In 1862, Samuel Clemens of later fame arrived at Virginia City and took the name Mark Twain while working on the *Territorial Enterprise,* poking fun at almost everyone.
- By 1863, Virginia City had become the second most important city in the West, with luxurious homes, four banks, an opera house, six churches, 110 saloons, and the only elevator between Chicago and the west coast.
- During the Civil War, the wealth of Nevada silver was critically important in keeping the North solvent.

- On October 31, 1864, at the urging of President Abraham Lincoln, Nevada became a state.
- New mineral finds occurred at Eureka in 1864 and Hamilton in 1869, but the wealth of the Comstock dwindled, and by 1880, Virginia City had become a sleepy village.
- In 1869 the transcontinental railroad was completed.
- The 1897 heavyweight championship boxing bout held at Carson City brought world attention to the state. Bob Fitzsimmons defeated James J. Corbett.
- New mineral booms occurred at Tonopah and Goldfield in 1906. Goldfield soon became a ghost town, but Tonopah continued.
- In 1931 gambling was made legal, laying the foundations for the future reputation of the state.
- Hoover Dam was finished in 1936.
- In 1951 the Atomic Energy Commission established the Nevada Proving Ground.

• In the late 1970s, Nevada ranchers launched what was called the "Sagebrush Rebellion," in an effort to reduce federal control of ranch lands.

• The census of 1990 revealed Nevada as the state with the largest percentage growth of population.

THAT'S INTERESTING

• In order to meet a deadline for statehood, the entire constitution of Nevada was sent to Washington by telegram at a cost of $3,400.

• Dat-So-La-Lee was born in Nevada and grew up without the benefit of any formal education. She lived all her 96 years in a remote land, but she nevertheless became the greatest master of the Indian art of basketmaking. Some of her finest baskets took more than a year to make, all showing absolutely true perspective.

• When early miners came to the famed Comstock Lode, they complained bitterly that the gold was contaminated by a gooey blue clay. Only later did they discover that this clay actually offered the wonderful wealth of the Comstock—the silver that helped the North win the Civil War.

NEVADA NOTABLES

Henry Tompkins Paige Comstock (Canada, 1820-1870), trapper/prospector. **Dat-So-La-Lee** (Washoe tribal lands, 1829?-1925), artist/weaver. **James Graham Fair** (Ireland, 1831-1894), mining leader/public official. **George Hearst** (Sullivan, MO, 1820-1891), businessman/public official. **John William Mackay** (Ireland, 1831-1902), mining leader/businessman. **James Warren Nye** (DeRuyter, NY, 1814-1876), public official. **William Morris Stewart** (Galen, NY, 1827-1909), lawyer/public official. **Sarah Winnemucca** (Humboldt Lake, 1844?-1891), Indian guide/author.

GENERAL

Admitted to statehood: October 31, 1864
Origin of name: Spanish for "snow-clad"
Capital: Carson City
Nickname: Silver State, Sagebrush State, Battle Born State
Motto: All for our country
Bird: Mountain bluebird
Flower: Sagebrush
Song: "Home Means Nevada"
Tree: Single-leaf piñon

THE LAND

Area: 110,567 sq. mi., 7th
  Land: 109,806 sq. mi., 7th
  Water: 761 sq. mi., 34th
    Inland water: 761 sq. mi., 28th
Topography: Rugged N-S mountain ranges; southern area is within the Mojave Desert with the Colorado River Canyon
Number of counties: 16
Geographic center: Lander, located 26 mi. SE of Austin
Length: 490 mi.; width: 320 mi.
Highest point: 13,140 ft. (Boundary Peak), 9th
Lowest point: 479 ft. (Colorado River), 37th
Mean elevation: 5,500 ft., 5th

CLIMATE AND ENVIRONMENT

Temp., highest: 125 deg. on June 29, 1994, at Laughlin; lowest: –50 deg. on Jan. 8, 1937, at San Jacinto
Monthly average: highest: 104.5 deg., 2nd; lowest: 19.5 deg., 25th; spread (high to low): 85.0 deg., 4th
Hazardous waste sites (1997): 1, 48th
Endangered species: Animals: 18—Bonytail chub, Pahranagat roundtail chub, Virgin River chub, Cui-ui, Ash meadows speckled dace, Clover Valley speckled dace, Independence Valley speckled dace, Moapa dace, American peregrine falcon, Poolfish, Ash meadows amargosa pupfish, Devils hole pupfish, Warm Springs pupfish, White River spinedace, Hiko White River springfish, White River springfish, Razorback sucker, Woundfin. Plants: 2

MAJOR CITIES
POPULATION, 1996
PERCENTAGE INCREASE, 1990-96

Las Vegas, 376,906; 46.0%
Reno, 155,499; 16.2%
Henderson, 122,339; 88.4%
North Las Vegas, 78,659; 64.4%
Sparks, 59,496; 11.5%

THE PEOPLE

Population (1997): 1,676,809, 37th
  Percent change (1990-97): 39.54%, 1st
  Percent of total U.S. pop.: 0.63%, 37th
  Per sq. mi: 15.17, 44th

Population (2000 proj.): 1,867,000, 35th
  Percent change (1995-2000): 22.03%, 1st
Percent in metro. area (1996): 85.68%, 10th
Foreign born: 105,000, 23rd
  Percent: 8.7%, 10th
Top three ancestries reported:
  German, 23.29%
  English, 17.22%
  Irish, 16.64%
White (1992): 1,173,000, 87.80%, 28th
Black (1992): 92,000, 6.89%, 27th
Native American (1992): 23,000, 1.72%, 10th
Asian, Pacific Isle (1992): 48,000, 3.59%, 7th
Hispanic origin (1992): 149,000, 11.15%, 8th
Percent over 5 yrs. speaking language other than English at home: 13.2%, 13th
Percent males (1996): 50.99%, 2nd; percent females: 49.01%, 50th
Percent never married: 23.7%, 39th
Marriages per 1,000 (1996): 88.09, 1st
Divorces per 1,000 (1996): 9.94, 1st
Median age (1996): 34.8
Under 5 years (1996): 8.06%, 5th
18 years and under (1996): 28.40%, 28th
65 years and over (1996): 11.44%, 39th
Percent increase among the elderly (1995-96): 4.49%, 2nd

OF VITAL IMPORTANCE

Live births per 1,000 pop. (1996): 16.2, 6th
Infant mortality rate per 1,000 live births (1995): 5.7, 48th
  Rate for whites: 5.5, 45th
  Rate for blacks: NA
Births to unmarried women, % of total (1996): 42.7%, 4th
Births to teenage mothers, % of total (1996): 13.3%, 22nd
Abortions (1992): 13,300, 28th
  Rate per 1,000 women 14-44 years old: 44.2, 4th
  Ratio per 1,000 live births: 591, 4th
  Percent change (1988-92): 10%, 6th
Average lifetime (1989-91): 74.18, 45th
Total death rate per 100,000 pop. (1995): 818.6, 37th
  Accidents and adverse effects: 36.0, 28th
  Alzheimer's disease: 5.6, 47th
  Cancer: 194.5, 37th
  Cerebrovascular diseases: 46.4, 46th
  Chronic liver disease and cirrhosis: 14.0, 3rd

Chronic obstructive pulmonary diseases and allied conditions: 52.0, 6th
  Diabetes mellitus: 15.4, 48th
  Diseases of heart: 246.9, 34th
  HIV infection: 13.2, 15th
  Homicide: 11.2, 10th
  Injury by firearms: 26.0, 2nd
  Motor vehicle accidents: 19.9, 19th
  Pneumonia and influenza: 24.2, 46th
  Suicide: 25.8, 1st

KEEPING WELL

Active nonfederal physicians per 100,000 pop. (1995): 157, 46th
Dentists per 100,000 (1991): 43, 44th
Nurses per 100,000 (1995): 611, 48th
Hospitals per 100,000 (1995): 1.31, 45th
  Admissions per 1,000 (1995): 97.39, 39th
  Hospital beds per 1,000 (1995): 2.35, 44th
  Occupancy rate per 100 beds (1995): 61.11, 23rd
  Average cost per patient per day (1995): $1,072, 12th
  Average cost per stay (1995): $6,014, 22nd
AIDS cases (new, 1996): 427; per 100,000: 26.6, 11th
Persons living with HIV infection, not yet AIDS (1996): 2,099
Other notifiable diseases, per 100,000 pop.:
  Gonorrhea (1995): 80.8, 28th
  Syphilis (1995): 12.7, 24th
  Tuberculosis (1996): 8.5, 17th
Pop. without health insur. (1996): 15.6%, 17th

HOUSEHOLDS BY TYPE

Total households (1996): 619,000, 37th
  Percent change (1990-96): 32.8%, 1st
  Per 1,000 pop. (1996) 386.15, 10th
  Percent of householders 65 yrs. and over (1996): 18.58%, 46th
  Persons per household (1996): 2.53, 37th
Family households: 307,400
  Percent of total: 65.92%, 50th
Nonfamily households: 158,897
  Percent of total: 34.08%, 2nd
Pop. living in group quarters: 24,200
  Percent of pop.: 2.01%, 49th

LIVING QUARTERS

Total housing units: 518,858
  Persons per unit: 2.32, 38th
Occupied housing units: 466,297
  Percent of total units: 89.87%, 22nd

Persons per unit: 2.51, 29th

Percent of units with over 1 person per room: 6.41%, 9th

Owner-occupied units: 255,388

Percent of total units: 49.22%, 48th

Percent of occupied units: 54.77%, 48th

Persons per unit: 2.67, 38th

Median value: $95,700, 12th

Renter-occupied units: 210,909

Percent of total units: 40.65%, 5th

Percent of occupied units: 45.23%, 5th

Persons per unit: 2.35, 25th

Median contract rent: $445, 9th

Rental vacancy rate: 9.1%, 21st

Mobile home, trailer & other as a percent of occupied housing units: 16.22%, 10th

Persons in emergency shelters for homeless persons: 1,013, 0.084%, 9th

Persons visible in street locations: 436, 0.0363%, 5th

Nursing home population: 3,605, 0.30%, 49th

CRIME INDEX PER 100,000 (1996)

Total reported: 5,992.0, 11th

Percent increase: –8.9%, 45th

Violent: 811.3, 9th

Percent increase: –14.2%, 48th

Murder & nonnegligent manslaughter: 13.7, 3rd

Forcible rape: 53.4, 5th

Aggravated assault: 436.6, 13th

Robbery: 307.6, 4th

Property: 5,180.7, 12th

Percent increase: –8.0%, 42nd

Burglary: 1,220.1, 9th

Larceny-theft: 3,262.3, 18th

Motor vehicle theft: 698.3, 7th

TEACHING AND LEARNING

Pop. 3 and over enrolled in school (1996): 349,957, 38th

Percent of pop.: 21.83%, 36th

Public elementary & secondary schools (1996-97): 423, 45th

Total enrollment (1996): 282,131, 38th

Percent of school age pop.: 96.29%, 6th

Percent of total pop.: 17.60%, 21st

Teachers (1996): 14,723, 38th

Percent of pop.: 0.92%, 42nd

Pupil/teacher ratio (1995): 19.1, 7th

Teachers' avg. salary (1996-97): $37,340, 20th

Expenditure per capita (1992-93): $1,170.67, 40th

Education as % of state govt. expenditures: 29.1%, 46th

Expenditure per pupil (1994-95): $5,160, 36th

Percent increase (1993-94 & 1994-95): 2.14%, 43rd

Percent at or above grade level, NAEP tests:

Reading, grade 4 (1994): 36%, 4th

Math, grade 4 (1996): 57%, 31st

Math, grade 8 (1996): NA

Percent of graduates taking SAT (1995): 30%, 25th

Mean SAT verbal scores: 434, 31st

Mean SAT mathematical scores: 483, 32nd

Percent of graduates taking ACT (1997): 39%, 26th

Mean ACT scores: 21.3, 23rd

Percent of pop. over 25 completing:

Less than 9th grade: 6.0%, 46th

High school: 78.8%, 19th

College degree(s): 15.3%, 47th

Higher education, institutions (1996): 10, 48th

Enrollment (1995-96): 67,826, 40th

Percent increase in enroll. (1990-95): 9.9%, 8th

White non-Hispanic (1995): 51,988, 42nd

Percent of enroll.: 76.65%, 32nd

Total minority enroll. (1995): 13,929, 36th

Percent of enroll.: 20.54%, 19th

Black non-Hispanic (1995): 3,715, 35th

Percent of enroll.: 5.48%, 28th

Hispanic (1995): 5,135, 22nd

Percent of enroll.: 7.57%, 10th

Asian/Pacific Islander (1995): 4,004, 30th

Percent of enroll.: 5.90%, 7th

American Indian/AK native (1995): 1,075, 30th

Percent of enroll.: 1.58%, 9th

Nonresident alien (1995): 1,909, 39th

Percent of enroll.: 2.81%, 22nd

Female (1995): 37,843, 40th

Percent of enroll.: 55.79%, 28th

Pub. institutions (1995-96): 6, 45th

Enrollment: 66,683, 38th

Percent increase in enrollment (1990-95): 8.9%, 14th

Percent of enroll.: 98.31%, 1st

Private institutions (1995-96): 4, 49th

Enrollment: 1,143, 49th

Percent increase in enrollment (1990-95): 135.2%, 2nd

Percent of enroll.: 1.69%, 51st

Tuition (in state), public 4-year institution (1996-97): $1,814, 49th

Tuition (in state), public 2-year institution (1996-97): $1,002, 42nd

Tuition, private 4-year institution (1996-97): $7,780, 43rd

Public library systems (1994): 23, 48th

Books & serial vol. per capita: 2.0, 39th

Library visits per capita: 3.1, 32nd

Circulation per capita: 4.8, 38th

LAW ENFORCEMENT AND CORRECTIONS

Police protection and corrections expenditures (1996): $189,936,000

Per capita: $118.49, 25th

Police per 10,000 pop. (1996): 24.58, 14th

Prisoners (1 year or more) per 100,000 pop. (1996): 502, 6th

Percent change (1995-96): 6.5%, 22nd

Percent of inmates that are female: 7.4%, 6th

Percent change: 14.5%, 17th

Death penalty: yes, by lethal injection, Hanging

Under sentence (Jan. 1998): 87, 14th

Executed, 1976-97: 6, 15th

Executed in 1997: 0

RELIGION, NUMBER AND PERCENT OF POPULATION

Agnostic: 8,144—0.90%, 14th

Buddhist: 3,620—0.40%, 5th

Christian: 773,677—85.50%, 28th

Hindu: NA

Jewish: 8,144—0.90%, 18th

Muslim: NA

Unitarian: 8,144—0.90%, 2nd

Other: 11,764—1.30%, 24th

None: 73,296—8.10%, 14th

Refused to answer: 18,098—2.00%, 30th

MAKING A LIVING

Personal income per capita (1996): $25,451, 11th

Percent increase (1995-96): 6.9%, 3rd

Disposable personal income per capita (1996): $21,805, 10th

Median income of households (average, 1995-96): $37,845, 15th

Percent of pop. below poverty level (1995-96): 9.6%, 42nd

ECONOMY

In civilian labor force (1996): 844,000

Percent of total pop.: 69.1%, 19th

Percent of total pop. 65 years and over: 13.4%, 17th

Percent of total female pop.: 60.8%, 26th

Major employer industries (total nonagricultural, 1996):

Construction: 74,800—8.9%, 1st

Finance, insurance, & real estate: 37,800—4.5%, 39th

Government: 101,200—12.0%, 51st

Manufacturing: 38,600—4.6%, 49th

Service: 363,500—43.1%, 1st

Trade: 167,700—20.1%, 50th

Transportation, communications, public utilities: 42,300—5.0%, 26th

Unemployment rate (1996): 5.4%, 18th

Male: 4.8%, 34th

Female: 6.2%, 10th

Total businesses (1995): 37,219, 38th

New business incorps. (1995): 18,926

Percent of total businesses: 50.85%, 2nd

Business failures (1995): 453

Failures per 10,000 businesses: 121.7, 11th

Agriculture farm income:

Marketing (1996): $286,002,000, 47th

Average per farm: $114,401, 18th

Leading products (1997): Cattle, hay, dairy products, potatoes, alfalfa seed, onions, garlic, barley, wheat

Average value land & build. per acre (1997): $350, 44th

Percent increase (1996-97): 5%, 26th

Govt. payments (1996): $2,605,000, 44th

Average per farm: $1,042, 36th

Construction, value of all (1996): $7,034,658,000, 19th

Per capita: $4,388, 1st

Manufactures (1995):

Value added: $2,991,100,000

Per capita: $1,955, 50th

Leading products (1997): Food products, plastics, chemicals, aerospace products, lawn and garden irrigation equipment, seismic and machinery-monitoring devices

Value of nonfuel mineral production (1996): $3,230,000,000, 2nd

Leading mineral products (1996): Gold, silver, sand/gravel, copper, diatomite

Energy consumption per person (1994): 351.8 mil. Btu, 24th

Retail sales (1995): $16,678,000,000
Per household: $26,900, 7th
Sales increase (1994-95): 11.9%, 3rd
Tourism revenues (1995): $27.5 bil.
Foreign exports, in total value (1996): $1,268,000,000, 43rd
Per capita: $791, 45th
Gross state product per person (1994): $30,170, 10th
Public aid recipients (percent of resident pop. 1994): 3.8%, 48th
Medicaid recipients (percent of pop., 1995): 6.9%, 50th
Medicare enrollment per 1,000 pop. (1996): 128, 37th

TRAVEL AND TRANSPORTATION

Motor vehicle registrations (1996): 1,095,676, 39th
Per 1,000 pop.: 684.45, 46th
Motorcycle registrations (1996): 22,471, 40th
Per 1,000 pop.: 20.51, 23rd
Licensed drivers (1996): 1,044,609, 38th
Per 1,000 pop.: 681.20, 29th
Public roads & streets (1996)
Total mileage: 45,039, 36th
Per 1,000 pop.: 128.09, 12th
Rural mileage: 39,741, 35th
Per 1,000 pop.: 24.79, 12th
Urban mileage: 5,298, 36th
Per 1,000 pop.: 3.30, 15th
Interstate mileage: 563, 38th
Per 1,000 pop.: 0.35, 10th
Speed limit (max. interstate, autos, mi. per hr., 1997): 75
Annual vehicle-mi. of travel per driver (1996): 12,677, 38th
Mean travel time for workers age 16+ who work away from home: 19.8 min., 31st

GOVERNMENT

Percent of voting age pop. registered (1996): 64.20%, 47th
Percent of voting age pop. voting for president: (1996): 39.3%, 51st
Percent of voting age pop. voting for U.S. representatives (1996): 38.1%, 47th
State legislators, total (1997): 63, 46th
Women members (1997): 20
Percent of legislature: 32%, 5th
U.S. Congress, House members (1998): 2
Change (1988-98): 0
Revenues (1996):
State govt.: $5,997,387,000
Per capita: $3,741.35, 21st
Parimutuel & amusement taxes & lotteries, revenue per capita (1995): $293.55, 3rd
Expenditures (1996):
State govt.: $4,831,342,000
Per capita: $3,013.94, 31st
Debt outstanding (1996): $2,258,523,000
Per capita: $1,408.94, 25th

LAWS AND REGULATIONS

Legal driving age: 16
Marriage age without parental consent: 18
Divorce residence requirement: 6 wks.

ATTRACTIONS (1997)

Major opera companies: 1
Major dance companies: 1
Per capita spending by the NEA (1997): $0.27, 25th
State Fair in late August–early September at Reno

SPORTS AND COMPETITION

NCAA (Division I) football and basketball teams: Univ. of Nevada-Las Vegas Runnin' Rebels, Univ. of Nevada-Reno Wolf Pack

WEBSITES CONTAINING FURTHER INFORMATION

| State of Nevada Home Page | http://www.state.nv.us |

NEW HAMPSHIRE

"Up in the mountains of New Hampshire God Almighty has hung out a sign to show that there he makes men."

Attributed to statesman Daniel Webster

New Hampshire was one of the leaders on the road to independence. The state adopted a constitution six months before the Declaration of Independence was signed. New Hampshire offers year-round tourist attractions. In the summer, visitors flock to the rugged mountains, the blue lakes, the sandy beaches, and the quiet villages. In the fall, the state is a riot of color as the leaves turn. In the winter, skiers arrive from all over the East. New Hampshire might well be nicknamed "the Preparedness State," because it has seemed to be ready for any emergency and quick to respond to opportunities. The state's early and important presidential primary attracts public attention every four years.

SUPERLATIVES

- Top of Mt. Washington said to be the windiest place on earth,
- Alpine zone unique in eastern United States.
- Home of the Concord stagecoach.
- Produced the world's first machine-made watches.
- Nation's first regular stage run, between Portsmouth and Boston.
- Cog railroad system pioneered on Mt. Washington.

MOMENTS IN HISTORY

- Martin Pring in 1603 and Samuel de Champlain in 1605 both ventured up the Piscataqua River.
- Portsmouth and Dover, each founded in 1623, are usually said to be the oldest permanent European settlements in what is now New Hampshire.
- In 1627 the great Indian leader Passaconaway (Child of the Bear) united about 17 Indian groups in the Penacook Confederacy.
- In 1642 the New Hampshire region came under Massachusetts rule.
- In 1649, Hampton became the first community in America to establish tax-funded education for both sexes.

> ### So They Say
>
> "The Great Spirit...whispers me now— Tell your people, Peace, peace, is the only hope of your race...these forests shall fall by the axe—the pale faces shall live upon your hunting grounds, and make their village upon your fishing places!...We are few and powerless before them.' "
> **Chief Passaconaway**

- Indian leader King Philip responded to growing white intrusion with raids beginning in 1675, and the French and Indian War led to more frightful raids on settlements.
- Meanwhile, New Hampshire separated from Massachusetts in 1679 and became a royal colony in 1680.
- In 1764 the King placed the western boundary along the west bank of the Connecticut River, where it remains.
- On January 5, 1776, an independent provisional government was set up, the first in the 13 colonies. The new government voted for independence 10 days later.
- In a sense, New Hampshire "created" the new nation by becoming the ninth state on June 21, 1788, meeting the requirement for nine states to ratify the Constitution.
- In the case of New Hampshire against Dartmouth College in 1819, the U.S. Supreme Court held for the college in a landmark decision upholding private property.
- The Webster-Ashburton Treaty of 1842 (negotiated by the state's native Daniel Webster) finally decided the boundary between the state and Canada.
- The only native president from the state, Franklin Pierce, took that office in 1853.
- After 13 years of work, in 1869, Enos M. Clough of Sunapee developed a successful horseless carriage, but the city fathers made him give it up because of the noise it made.
- In 1907 the MacDowell Colony was the first artists' colony to be founded in the United States. It continues to be the largest.
- In 1961, Alan Shepard of East Derry became the first American in space.
- A boundary dispute with Maine was decided by the U.S. Supreme Court in 1976, giving most of the coastal waters to Maine.

- The tragic 1986 destruction of the space shuttle *Challenger* had particular meaning for the state in the loss of New Hampshire school teacher Christa McAuliffe.

THAT'S INTERESTING

- One of the world's notable natural features is the Old Man of the Mountain. This granite profile looms 48 feet from chin to forehead. In 1915 the Old Man was falling apart. His forehead was slipping, which meant it probably would break off his nose. He was saved by a "surgeon" named Geddes, who drilled holes in the granite and inserted special anchors to hold the features in place.
- New Hampshire's state House is the largest of all the states, with a total of 400 members.

NOTABLE NATIVES

Lewis Cass (Exeter, 1782-1866), public official. **Salmon Portland Chase** (Cornish, 1808-1873), chief justice of the United States. **Jonas Chickering** (Mason Village, 1798-1853), piano manufacturer. **Ralph Adams Cram** (Hampton Falls, 1863-1942), architect. **John Adams Dix** (Boscawen, 1798-1879), soldier/public official. **Mary Morse Baker Eddy** (Bow, 1821-1910), religious leader. **Sam Walter Foss** (Candia, 1858-1911), poet/journalist. **Daniel Chester French** (Exeter, 1850-1931), sculptor. **Horace Greeley** (Amherst, 1811-1872), reformer/political leader. **John Parker Hale** (Rochester, 1806-1873), public official. **Sarah Josepha Buell Hale** (Newport, 1788-1879), editor/author. **John Irving** (Exeter, 1942-), author. **Thaddeus Sobieski Coulincourt Lowe** (Riverton, 1832-1913), aeronaut/inventor. **Franklin Pierce** (Hillsboro, 1804-1869), U.S. president. **Alan Barlett Shepard, Jr.** (East Derry, 1923-), astronaut. **John Stark** (Londonderry, 1728-1822), Revolutionary soldier. **John Sullivan** (Somersworth, 1740-1795), Revolutionary soldier/public official. **Daniel Webster** (Salisbury, 1782-1852), lawyer/public official. **Benning Wentworth** (Portsmouth, 1696-1770), merchant/public official. **John Wentworth** (Portsmouth, 1737-1820), merchant/public official. **John (Long John) Wentworth** (Sandwich, 1815-1888), editor/public official. **Paul Wentworth** (probably in New Hampshire, ?-1793), British spy. **Henry Wilson** (Farmington, 1812-1875), U.S. vice president.

GENERAL

Admitted to statehood: June 21, 1788
Origin of name: Named 1629 by Captain John Mason of Plymouth Council for his home county in England
Capital: Concord
Nickname: Granite State
Motto: Live free or die
Bird: Purple finch
Flower: Purple lilac
Song: "Old New Hampshire," "New Hampshire, My New Hampshire," "New Hampshire Hills"
Tree: Paper (white) birch

THE LAND

Area: 9,283 sq. mi., 44th
　Land: 8,969 sq. mi., 44th
　Water: 314 sq. mi., 46th
　Inland water: 314 sq. mi., 43rd
Topography: Low, rolling coast followed by countless hills and mountains rising out of a central plateau
Number of counties: 10
Geographic center: Belknap, 3 mi. E of Ashland
Length: 190 mi.; width: 70 mi.
Highest point: 6,288 ft. (Mount Washington), 18th
Lowest point: sea level (Atlantic Ocean), 3rd
Mean elevation: 1,000 ft., 25th
Coastline: 13 mi., 22nd
Shoreline: 131 mi., 23rd

CLIMATE AND ENVIRONMENT

Temp., highest: 106 deg. on July 4, 1911, at Nashua; lowest: –46 deg. on Jan. 28, 1925, at Pittsburg
Monthly average: highest: 82.6 deg., 45th; lowest: 9.0 deg., 10th; spread (high to low): 73.6 deg., 16th
Hazardous waste sites (1997): 18, 19th
Endangered species: Animals: 3—Karner blue butterfly, American peregrine falcon, Dwarf wedge mussel. Plants: 3

MAJOR CITIES
POPULATION, 1996
PERCENTAGE INCREASE, 1990-96

Manchester, 100,967; 1.6%
Nashua, 81,094; 1.8%
Concord, 37,021; 2.8%
Rochester, 27,704; 4.0%
Dover, 25,766; 2.9%

THE PEOPLE

Population (1997): 1,172,709, 42nd
  Percent change (1990-97): 5.72%, 30th
  Percent of total U.S. pop.: 0.44%, 41st
  Per sq. mi: 125.41, 19th
Population (2000 proj.): 1,220,500, 42nd
  Percent change (1995-2000): 6.32%, 18th
Percent in metro. area (1996): 62.32%, 34th
Foreign born: 41,000, 37th
  Percent: 3.7%, 22nd
Top three ancestries reported:
  English, 23.99%
  Irish, 20.92%
  French, 18.49%
White (1992): 1,096,000, 98.30%, 3rd
Black (1992): 7,000, 0.63%, 45th
Native American (1992): 2,000, 0.18%, 47th
Asian, Pacific Isle (1992): 10,000, 0.90%, 36th
Hispanic origin (1992): 12,000, 1.08%, 40th
Percent over 5 yrs. speaking language other than English at home: 8.7%, 21st
Percent males (1996): 49.24%, 19th; percent females: 50.76%, 33rd
Percent never married: 25.5%, 26th
Marriages per 1,000 (1996): 8.36, 25th
Divorces per 1,000 (1996): 4.30, 24th
Median age (1996): 35.1
Under 5 years (1996): 6.58%, 39th
18 years and under (1996): 27.87%, 35th
65 years and over (1996): 12.01%, 37th
Percent increase among the elderly (1995-96): 1.34%, 18th

OF VITAL IMPORTANCE

Live births per 1,000 pop. (1996): 12.5, 46th
Infant mortality rate per 1,000 live births (1995): 5.5, 49th
  Rate for whites: 5.5, 45th
  Rate for blacks: NA
Births to unmarried women, % of total (1996): 23.4%, 49th
Births to teenage mothers, % of total (1996): 7.4%, 50th
Abortions (1992): 3,890, 43rd
  Rate per 1,000 women 14-44 years old: 14.6, 35th
  Percent change (1988-92): –17%, 44th
Average lifetime (1989-91): 76.72, 14th
Total death rate per 100,000 pop. (1995): 803.6, 40th
  Accidents and adverse effects: 25.0, 49th

Alzheimer's disease: 10.1, 13th
Cancer: 205.2, 31st
Cerebrovascular diseases: 55.2, 37th
Chronic liver disease and cirrhosis: 8.4, 33rd
Chronic obstructive pulmonary diseases and allied conditions: 41.5, 22nd
Diabetes mellitus: 22.6, 26th
Diseases of heart: 256.9, 33rd
HIV infection: 4.1, 44th
Homicide: NA
Injury by firearms: 7.8, 45th
Motor vehicle accidents: 11.8, 46th
Pneumonia and influenza: 19.0, 50th
Suicide: 11.9, 30th

KEEPING WELL

Active nonfederal physicians per 100,000 pop. (1995): 214, 23rd
Dentists per 100,000 (1991): 59, 19th
Nurses per 100,000 (1995): 993, 12th
Hospitals per 100,000 (1995): 2.53, 19th
  Admissions per 1,000 (1995): 95.82, 41st
  Hospital beds per 1,000 (1995): 2.96, 35th
  Occupancy rate per 100 beds (1995): 61.76, 21st
  Average cost per patient per day (1995): $915, 27th
  Average cost per stay (1995): $6,188, 17th
AIDS cases (new, 1996): 93; per 100,000: 8.0, 38th
Persons living with HIV infection (1996): NA
Other notifiable diseases, per 100,000 pop.:
  Gonorrhea (1995): 10.3, 47th
  Syphilis (1995): 2.8, 39th
  Tuberculosis (1996): 1.8, 45th
Pop. without health insur. (1996): 9.5%, 46th

HOUSEHOLDS BY TYPE

Total households (1996): 439,000, 40th
  Percent change (1990-96): 6.7%, 29th
  Per 1,000 pop. (1996) 377.80, 31st
  Percent of householders 65 yrs. and over (1996): 19.36%, 41st
  Persons per household (1996): 2.62, 19th
Family households: 292,601
  Percent of total: 71.16%, 20th
Nonfamily households: 118,585
  Percent of total: 28.84%, 32nd
Pop. living in group quarters: 32,151
  Percent of pop.: 2.90%, 23rd

LIVING QUARTERS

Total housing units: 503,904
  Persons per unit: 2.20, 47th
Occupied housing units: 411,186
  Percent of total units: 81.60%, 47th
  Persons per unit: 2.52, 26th
  Percent of units with over 1 person per room: 1.61%, 50th
Owner-occupied units: 280,372
  Percent of total units: 55.64%, 39th
  Percent of occupied units: 68.19%, 17th
  Persons per unit: 2.80, 13th
  Median value: $129,400, 8th
Renter-occupied units: 130,814
  Percent of total units: 25.96%, 44th
  Percent of occupied units: 31.81%, 35th
  Persons per unit: 2.24, 42nd
  Median contract rent: $479, 7th
  Rental vacancy rate: 11.8%, 8th
Mobile home, trailer & other as a percent of occupied housing units: 10.20%, 28th
Persons in emergency shelters for homeless persons: 377, 0.034%, 45th
Persons visible in street locations: 8, 0.0007%, 50th
Nursing home population: 8,202, 0.74%, 24th

CRIME INDEX PER 100,000 (1996)

Total reported: 2,823.5, 49th
  Percent increase: 6.3%, 1st
  Violent: 118.2, 50th
    Percent increase: 3.2%, 2nd
    Murder & nonnegligent manslaughter: 1.7, 50th
    Forcible rape: 34.8, 24th
    Aggravated assault: 54.4, 50th
    Robbery: 27.3, 45th
  Property: 2,705.3, 49th
    Percent increase: 6.5%, 1st
    Burglary: 435.7, 50th
    Larceny-theft: 2,118.0, 45th
    Motor vehicle theft: 151.6, 47th

TEACHING AND LEARNING

Pop. 3 and over enrolled in school (1996): 258,908, 41st
  Percent of pop.: 22.28%, 28th
Public elementary & secondary schools (1996-97): 460, 44th
  Total enrollment (1996): 194,581, 41st
    Percent of school age pop.: 88.45%, 39th
    Percent of total pop.: 16.75%, 33rd

Teachers (1996): 12,394, 41st
  Percent of pop.: 1.07%, 26th
Pupil/teacher ratio (1995): 15.7, 33rd
Teachers' avg. salary (1996-97): $36,867, 22nd
Expenditure per capita (1992-93): $1,227.49, 36th
  Education as % of state govt. expenditures: 32.4%, 38th
Expenditure per pupil (1994-95): $5,859, 24th
  Percent increase (1993-94 & 1994-95): 2.38%, 38th
Percent at or above grade level, NAEP tests:
  Reading, grade 4 (1994): NA
  Math, grade 4 (1996): NA
  Math, grade 8 (1996): NA
Percent of graduates taking SAT (1995): 70%, 4th
  Mean SAT verbal scores: 444, 29th
  Mean SAT mathematical scores: 491, 28th
Percent of graduates taking ACT (1997): 4%, 46th
  Mean ACT scores: 22.3, 2nd
Percent of pop. over 25 completing:
  Less than 9th grade: 6.7%, 44th
  High school: 82.2%, 7th
  College degree(s): 24.4%, 8th
Higher education, institutions (1996): 30, 37th
  Enrollment (1995-96): 64,327, 41st
    Percent increase in enroll. (1990-95): 8.1%, 16th
  White non-Hispanic (1995): 59,885, 38th
    Percent of enroll.: 93.09%, 2nd
  Total minority enroll. (1995): 3,280, 46th
    Percent of enroll.: 5.10%, 50th
  Black non-Hispanic (1995): 1,056, 42nd
    Percent of enroll.: 1.64%, 43rd
  Hispanic (1995): 950, 41st
    Percent of enroll.: 1.48%, 35th
  Asian/Pacific Islander (1995): 1,017, 42nd
    Percent of enroll.: 1.58%, 38th
  American Indian/AK native (1995): 257, 47th
    Percent of enroll.: 0.40%, 34th
  Nonresident alien (1995): 1,162, 44th
    Percent of enroll.: 1.81%, 44th
  Female (1995): 36,950, 41st
    Percent of enroll.: 57.44%, 10th
  Pub. institutions (1995-96): 12, 40th
    Enrollment: 36,069, 46th
      Percent increase in enrollment (1990-95): 12.1%, 7th

Percent of enroll.: 56.07%, 47th
Private institutions (1995-96): 18, 31st
Enrollment: 28,258, 29th
Percent increase in enrollment (1990-95): 3.3%, 30th
Percent of enroll.: 43.93%, 5th
Tuition (in state), public 4-year institution (1996-97): $4,644, 3rd
Tuition (in state), public 2-year institution (1996-97): $2,784, 2nd
Tuition, private 4-year institution (1996-97): $15,863, 5th
Public library systems (1994): 229, 15th
Books & serial vol. per capita: 4.4, 5th
Library visits per capita: 4.8, 12th
Circulation per capita: 7.5, 18th

LAW ENFORCEMENT AND CORRECTIONS

Police protection and corrections expenditures (1996): $88,467,000
Per capita: $76.13, 47th
Police per 10,000 pop. (1996): 21.92, 25th
Prisoners (1 year or more) per 100,000 pop. (1996): 177, 46th
Percent change (1995-96): 2.8%, 39th
Percent of inmates that are female: 5.1%, 42nd
Percent change: –0.9%, 44th
Death penalty: yes, by lethal injection
Under sentence (Jan. 1998): 0
Executed, 1976-97: 0

RELIGION, NUMBER AND PERCENT OF POPULATION

Agnostic: 9,966—1.20%, 2nd
Buddhist: 4,153—0.50%, 2nd
Christian: 650,279—78.30%, 46th
Hindu: NA
Jewish: 8,305—1.00%, 17th
Muslim: 1,661—0.20%, 13th
Unitarian: 1,661—0.20%, 23rd
Other: 22,423—2.70%, 2nd
None: 111,287—13.40%, 4th
Refused to answer: 20,762—2.50%, 18th

MAKING A LIVING

Personal income per capita (1996): $26,520, 9th
Percent increase (1995-96): 2.9%, 28th
Disposable personal income per capita (1996): $23,329, 7th
Median income of households (average, 1995-96): $39,868, 9th

Percent of pop. below poverty level (1995-96): 5.9%, 51st

ECONOMY

In civilian labor force (1996): 624,000
Percent of total pop.: 70.2%, 15th
Percent of total pop. 65 years and over: 13.6%, 15th
Percent of total female pop.: 62.9%, 16th
Major employer industries (total nonagricultural, 1996):
Construction: 20,800—3.7%, 42nd
Finance, insurance, & real estate: 28,200—5.0%, 29th
Government: 78,900—14.1%, 44th
Manufacturing: 104,600—18.7%, 11th
Service: 162,400—29.0%, 17th
Trade: 144,900—25.9%, 4th
Transportation, communications, public utilities: 19,500—3.5%, 49th
Unemployment rate (1996): 4.2%, 41st
Male: 3.9%, 43rd
Female: 4.5%, 38th
Total businesses (1995): 34,647, 40th
New business incorps. (1995): 3,095
Percent of total businesses: 8.93%, 24th
Business failures (1995): 389
Failures per 10,000 businesses: 112.3, 14th
Agriculture farm income:
Marketing (1996): $160,907,000, 48th
Average per farm: $67,045, 40th
Leading products (1997): Dairy products, greenhouse, hay, vegetables, fruit, maple syrup & sugar products
Average value land & build. per acre (1997): $2,600, 8th
Percent increase (1996-97): 1%, 44th
Govt. payments (1996): $1,093,000, 48th
Average per farm: $455, 45th
Construction, value of all (1996): $1,211,543,000, 41st
Per capita: $1,042, 39th
Manufactures (1995):
Value added: $8,658,500,000
Per capita: $7,541, 13th
Leading products (1997): Machinery, electric and electronic products, plastics, fabricated metal products
Value of nonfuel mineral production (1996): $43,900,000, 47th
Leading mineral products (1996): Sand/gravel, stone, clays, gemstones

Energy consumption per person (1994): 251.4 mil. Btu, 44th

Retail sales (1995): $12,997,000,000
 Per household: $30,240, 3rd
 Sales increase (1994-95): 1.8%, 44th

Tourism revenues (1996): $2.7 bil.

Foreign exports, in total value (1996): $1,481,000,000, 41st
 Per capita: $1,274, 32nd

Gross state product per person (1994): $25,855, 20th

Public aid recipients (percent of resident pop. 1994): 3.5%, 50th

Medicaid recipients (percent of pop., 1995): 8.4%, 46th

Medicare enrollment per 1,000 pop. (1996): 137, 33rd

TRAVEL AND TRANSPORTATION

Motor vehicle registrations (1996): 1,112,113, 38th
 Per 1,000 pop.: 958.54, 6th

Motorcycle registrations (1996): 51,890, 25th
 Per 1,000 pop.: 46.66, 1st

Licensed drivers (1996): 901,104, 39th
 Per 1,000 pop.: 784.77, 3rd

Public roads & streets (1996)
 Total mileage: 15,106, 45th
  Per 1,000 pop.: 112.99, 34th
  Rural mileage: 12,190, 43rd
  Per 1,000 pop.: 10.49, 33rd
  Urban mileage: 2,916, 41st
  Per 1,000 pop.: 2.51, 46th
  Interstate mileage: 224, 47th
  Per 1,000 pop.: 0.19, 30th

Speed limit (max. interstate, autos, mi. per hr., 1997): 65

Annual vehicle-mi. of travel per driver (1996): 12,002, 41st

Mean travel time for workers age 16+ who work away from home: 21.9 min., 14th

GOVERNMENT

Percent of voting age pop. registered (1996): 86.66%, 6th
 Percent of voting age pop. voting for president: (1996): 58.0%, 8th
 Percent of voting age pop. voting for U.S. representatives (1996): 57.1%, 8th

State legislators, total (1997): 424, 1st
 Women members (1997): 132
  Percent of legislature: 31%, 7th

U.S. Congress, House members (1998): 2
 Change (1988-98): 0

Revenues (1996):
 State govt.: $3,560,835,000
  Per capita: $3,064.40, 40th
  Parimutuel & amusement taxes & lotteries, revenue per capita (1995): $122.99, 21st

Expenditures (1996):
 State govt.: $3,240,034,000
  Per capita: $2,788.33, 39th

Debt outstanding (1996): $5,832,969,000
 Per capita: $5,019.77, 3rd

LAWS AND REGULATIONS

Legal driving age: 18, 16 if completed driver education course

Marriage age without parental consent: 18

Divorce residence requirement: 1 yr., for qualifications check local statutes

ATTRACTIONS (1997)

Major opera companies: 1

Per capita spending by the NEA (1997): $0.51, 15th

SPORTS AND COMPETITION

NCAA (Division I) football and basketball teams: Dartmouth College Big Green, Univ. of New Hampshire Wildcats

WEBSITES CONTAINING FURTHER INFORMATION

| The New Hampshire State Government Online Information Center | http://www.state.nh.us |

NEW JERSEY

New Jersey gave the world both football and baseball, as well as Thomas Nast's Democratic donkey, the Republican elephant, and Santa Claus. It was the home to at least three of the most important inventors in American history. It was here that Thomas A. Edison invented the electric light bulb, Samuel F. B. Morse the electric telegraph, and John P. Holland the submarine. Washington's famed crossing of the Delaware brought his forces to the Jersey shore. The state became the "pathway of the Revolution" and suffered through four major battles. New Jersey leads the nation in many areas of manufacture and science and has long proven it is more than a convenient route from North to South.

SUPERLATIVES

- Claims greatest variety of manufactured products.
- Major glass manufacturing center.
- Leader in flag manufacture.
- Chemistry industry leader.
- The national jewelry center—Newark.
- Leader in scientific/industrial research.
- World's first four-lane highway, constructed between Elizabeth and Newark.
- First U.S. charter for a railroad.

MOMENTS IN HISTORY

- Explorers John Cabot in 1497 and Giovanni de Verrazano in 1524 sailed past what is now the Jersey shore.
- The first record of a European on New Jersey soil belongs to Henry Hudson, in 1609.

> ### So They Say
> "This is a very good Land to fall with, and a pleasant land to see."   **Henry Hudson**

- By 1618 the Dutch had set up a trading post at Bergen.
- New Sweden was organized on the lower Delaware in 1638.
- Johan Printz ("Big Tub"), a 7-foot giant of 400 pounds, took control of the Swedish settlement in 1643.
- In 1664, England took over the colony, and the city of Elizabeth was founded.

- New Jersey became a crown colony in 1702, under the governor of New York.
- In 1738, New Jersey got its own government.
- William Franklin, son of Benjamin Franklin, became governor in 1763.
- Dissatisfaction with the crown led to the little-known New Jersey "tea party" on December 22, 1774.
- After the Declaration of Independence, a provincial Congress took control and arrested Governor Franklin.
- After the Revolution reached New Jersey, the state endured four major battles and 90 minor skirmishes, becoming known as the "pathway of the Revolution."
- General George Washington and his armies crossed and recrossed New Jersey four times.
- Washington made his famed crossing of the Delaware River to the Jersey shore, and his victory at the Battle of Trenton at Christmas time, 1776, gave hope to the American cause.

> ### So They Say
> "Our hopes were blasted by that unhappy affair at Trenton."
> **Anonymous British officer**

- By the close of the Revolution, 17,000 New Jersey men had fought for the new country, and New Jersey became known as the Garden State for supplying war provisions.
- In 1783, Princeton was the temporary capital of the new country.
- New Jersey became the third state on December 18, 1787.
- In 1846 the New Jersey legislature passed a law to free all slaves in the state, but since the slaves were still made to serve their former masters as apprentices, their "freedom" was questionable.
- The first organized baseball game was played at Hoboken in 1846.
- Divided over slavery, New Jersey nevertheless was important in the Underground Railroad. After the Civil War broke out, the New Jersey Brigade in May 1861 became the first to reach Washington, DC's defenses.
- By war's end, 88,000 from New Jersey had been in service. Because of overcrowding

and disease, thousands of Confederate prisoners died at the prison camp at Fort Delaware.

So They Say

"...a thousand ill, 20 deaths a day from dysentery....Thus a Christian nation treats the captives of the sword."

Anonymous federal inspector
at Fort Delaware

• The nation's first intercollegiate football game was played at New Brunswick in 1869 between Rutgers and Princeton. Rutgers won.

• Opposition to the power of big business brought reforms in the period 1911-13, under Governor Woodrow Wilson.

• Spurred by the inventions of Thomas Edison in New Jersey, the state reigned as motion picture capital of the world until about 1916.

• During World War I, the state led in shipbuilding and production of artillery shells, and Hoboken became the major embarkation point of the war.

• The Miss America contest began at Atlantic City in 1921.

• The great George Washington Bridge was opened in 1931, and Bergen County became "the bedroom of New York."

• The days of the passenger dirigible came to an end at Lakehurst with the spectacular destruction of the *Hindenburg* in 1937.

• In World War II, New Jersey was predominant in production of airplane engines and warships, among other war matériel. Camp Kilmer was a major debarkation center.

• During the 1940s and 1950s, a series of hurricanes—including Diane, Donna, and Hazel—took many lives and destroyed hundreds of millions of dollars' worth of property.

• The great Meadowlands development opened in 1976 with games of major league teams.

• The 1980s were notable for the resumption of large-scale gambling at Atlantic City.

• In 1991, New Jersey terminated ocean dumping.

THAT'S INTERESTING

• Johan Printz, governor of New Sweden, was so heavy (400 pounds) that the gangplank almost collapsed when he arrived at his colony. The Indians called him "Big Tub."

• When American Revolutionary heroine Molly Pitcher's husband was killed, she fought in his place at his cannon.

• The first derby in the country was run at Passaic in 1864.

• One William Campbell, a non-Indian, founded a wampum mint near Hackensack; it operated until 1889.

• Colonel John Stevens of Hoboken operated an experimental railroad track of 630 feet near there.

• Standard Time was devised in 1883 by William F. Allen of South Orange.

NOTABLE NATIVES

William (Count) Basie (Red Bank, 1904-1984), musician. **William Joseph Brennan, Jr.** (Newark, 1906-1997), Supreme Court justice. **Aaron Burr** (Newark, 1756-1836), public official/political leader. **Grover Cleveland** (Caldwell, 1837-1908), U.S. president. **James Fenimore Cooper** (Burlington, 1789-1851), author. **Stephen Crane** (Newark, 1871-1900), author. **Alfred Joyce Kilmer** (New Brunswick, 1886-1918), poet. **James Lawrence** (Burlington, 1781-1813), naval officer. **Mary Ludwig Hays McCauley (Molly Pitcher)** (Trenton, 1754-1832), Revolutionary heroine. **Jack Nicholson** (Neptune, 1937-), actor. **Dorothy Parker** (West End, 1893-1967), author. **Zebulon Montgomery Pike** (Trenton, 1779-1813), soldier/explorer. **Paul Bustill Robeson** (Princeton, 1898-1976), singer/actor. **Philip Milton Roth** (Newark, 1933-), author. **Francis Albert (Frank) Sinatra** (Hoboken, 1915-), singer/actor. **Amos Alonzo Stagg** (West Orange, 1862-1965), football coach. **Robert Field Stockman** (Princeton, 1834-1902), naval officer. **Meryl Streep** (Summit, 1949-), actress. **Albert Payson Terhune** (Newark, 1872-1942), author. **William Henry Vanderbilt** (New Brunswick, 1821-1865), financier. **William Carlos Williams** (Rutherford, 1883-1963), poet/physician.

So They Say

After President Grover Cleveland secretly underwent an operation at sea to repair a cancerous jaw, he lost almost half his mouth and could not speak; he was fitted with an artificial rubber jaw. Almost immediately he addressed a session of Congress with perfect diction. The situation was not revealed until much later.

GENERAL

Admitted to statehood: December 18, 1787
Origin of name: The Duke of York, 1664, gave a patent to John Berkeley and Sir George Carteret to be called Nova Caesaria, or New Jersey, after England's Isle of Jersey
Capital: Trenton
Nickname: Garden State
Motto: Liberty and prosperity
Animal: Horse
Bird: Eastern goldfinch
Insect: Honeybee
Flower: Purple violet
Song: "New Jersey Loyalty" (unofficial)
Tree: Red oak

THE LAND

Area: 8,215 sq. mi., 46th
  Land: 7,419 sq. mi., 46th
  Water: 796 sq. mi., 33rd
    Inland water: 371 sq. mi., 39th
    Coastal water: 425 sq. mi., 13th
Topography: Appalachian Valley in the NW has highest elevation; Appalachian Highlands, flat-topped NE-SW mountain ranges; piedmont plateau, low plains broken by high ridges; coastal plain, covering three-fifths of state in SE, gradually rises to gentle slopes.
Number of counties: 21
Geographic center: Mercer, 5 mi. SE of Trenton
Length: 150 mi.; width: 70 mi.
Highest point: 1,803 ft. (High Point), 40th
Lowest point: sea level (Atlantic Ocean), 3rd
Mean elevation: 250 ft., 46th
Coastline: 130 mi., 13th
Shoreline: 1,792 mi., 14th

CLIMATE AND ENVIRONMENT

Temp., highest: 110 deg. on July 10, 1936, at Runyon; lowest: –34 deg. on Jan. 5, 1904, at River Vale
Monthly average: highest: 85.6 deg., 35th; lowest: 24.2 deg., 34th; spread (high to low): 61.4 deg., 41st
Hazardous waste sites (1997): 106, 1st
Endangered species: Animals: 3—Indiana bat, American peregrine falcon, Roseate tern. Plants: 1

MAJOR CITIES
POPULATION, 1996
PERCENTAGE INCREASE, 1990-96

Newark, 268,510; –2.4%
Jersey City, 229,039; 0.2%
Paterson, 150,270; 6.7%
Elizabeth, 110,149; 0.1%
Trenton, 85,437; –3.7%

THE PEOPLE

Population (1997): 8,052,849, 9th
  Percent change (1990-97): 3.94%, 39th
  Percent of total U.S. pop.: 3.01%, 9th
  Per sq. mi: 923.28, 2nd
Population (2000 proj.): 8,181,500, 9th
  Percent change (1995-2000): 2.98%, 35th
Percent in metro. area (1996): 100.00%, 1st
Foreign born: 967,000, 5th
  Percent: 12.5%, 5th
Top three ancestries reported:
  Italian, 18.85%
  Irish, 18.31%
  German, 18.21%
White (1992): 6,385,000, 81.65%, 37th
Black (1992): 1,101,000, 14.08%, 17th
Native American (1992): 17,000, 0.22%, 39th
Asian, Pacific Isle (1992): 317,000, 4.05%, 5th
Hispanic origin (1992): 807,000, 10.32%, 9th
Percent over 5 yrs. speaking language other than English at home: 19.5%, 7th
Percent males (1996): 48.52%, 37th; percent females: 51.48%, 15th
Percent never married: 29.1%, 7th
Marriages per 1,000 (1996): 6.47, 47th
Divorces per 1,000 (1996): 3.14, 43rd
Median age (1996): 36.0
Under 5 years (1996): 7.20%, 16th
18 years and under (1996): 27.32%, 41st
65 years and over (1996): 13.77%, 15th
Percent increase among the elderly (1995-96): 0.67%, 27th

OF VITAL IMPORTANCE

Live births per 1,000 pop. (1996): 14.3, 22nd
Infant mortality rate per 1,000 live births (1995): 6.6, 37th
  Rate for whites: 5.3, 47th
  Rate for blacks: 13.3, 28th
Births to unmarried women, % of total (1996): 27.9%, 36th

Births to teenage mothers, % of total (1996): 7.7%, 49th

Abortions (1992): 55,320, 7th

Rate per 1,000 women 14-44 years old: 31.0, 7th

Percent change (1988-92): –12%, 32nd

Average lifetime (1989-91): 75.42, 26th

Total death rate per 100,000 pop. (1995): 932.5, 19th

Accidents and adverse effects: 29.1, 44th

Alzheimer's disease: 6.6, 41st

Cancer: 231.9, 8th

Cerebrovascular diseases: 53.4, 39th

Chronic liver disease and cirrhosis: 10.6, 10th

Chronic obstructive pulmonary diseases and allied conditions: 34.5, 40th

Diabetes mellitus: 30.1, 4th

Diseases of heart: 303.3, 19th

HIV infection: 30.7, 4th

Homicide: 5.4, 32nd

Injury by firearms: 5.9, 50th

Motor vehicle accidents: 10.6, 48th

Pneumonia and influenza: 31.7, 25th

Suicide: 7.3, 50th

KEEPING WELL

Active nonfederal physicians per 100,000 pop. (1995): 276, 7th

Dentists per 100,000 (1991): 78, 4th

Nurses per 100,000 (1995): 850, 23rd

Hospitals per 100,000 (1995): 1.16, 47th

Admissions per 1,000 (1995): 134.42, 11th

Hospital beds per 1,000 (1995): 3.76, 20th

Occupancy rate per 100 beds (1995): 71.57, 6th

Average cost per patient per day (1995): $962, 24th

Average cost per stay (1995): $7,007, 9th

AIDS cases (new, 1996): 3,613; per 100,000: 45.2, 4th

Persons living with HIV infection, not yet AIDS (1996): 10,701

Other notifiable diseases, per 100,000 pop.:

Gonorrhea (1995): 72.8, 31st

Syphilis (1995): 18.8, 16th

Tuberculosis (1996): 10.3, 8th

Pop. without health insur. (1996): 16.7%, 13th

HOUSEHOLDS BY TYPE

Total households (1996): 2,889,000, 9th

Percent change (1990-96): 3.4%, 44th

Per 1,000 pop. (1996) 361.67, 42nd

Percent of householders 65 yrs. and over (1996): 23.33%, 9th

Persons per household (1996): 2.75, 6th

Family households: 2,021,346

Percent of total: 72.33%, 13th

Nonfamily households: 773,365

Percent of total: 27.67%, 39th

Pop. living in group quarters: 171,368

Percent of pop.: 2.22%, 45th

LIVING QUARTERS

Total housing units: 3,075,310

Persons per unit: 2.51, 7th

Occupied housing units: 2,794,711

Percent of total units: 90.88%, 17th

Persons per unit: 2.64, 10th

Percent of units with over 1 person per room: 3.89%, 18th

Owner-occupied units: 1,813,381

Percent of total units: 58.97%, 26th

Percent of occupied units: 64.89%, 38th

Persons per unit: 2.87, 4th

Median value: $162,300, 5th

Renter-occupied units: 981,330

Percent of total units: 31.91%, 16th

Percent of occupied units: 35.11%, 16th

Persons per unit: 2.40, 17th

Median contract rent: $521, 3rd

Rental vacancy rate: 7.4%, 37th

Mobile home, trailer & other as a percent of occupied housing units: 2.74%, 46th

Persons in emergency shelters for homeless persons: 7,470, 0.097%, 7th

Persons visible in street locations: 1,639, 0.0212%, 8th

Nursing home population: 47,054, 0.61%, 35th

CRIME INDEX PER 100,000 (1996)

Total reported: 4,332.9, 34th

Percent increase: –7.9%, 41st

Violent: 531.5, 24th

Percent increase: –11.4%, 43rd

Murder & nonnegligent manslaughter: 4.2, 33rd

Forcible rape: 24.7, 44th

Aggravated assault: 266.7, 29th

Robbery: 235.8, 9th

Property: 3,801.4, 36th

Percent increase: –7.4%, 41st

Burglary: 791.9, 32nd

Larceny-theft: 2,428.2, 40th
Motor vehicle theft: 581.3, 13th

TEACHING AND LEARNING

Pop. 3 and over enrolled in school (1996): 1,554,844, 11th
  Percent of pop.: 19.46%, 51st
Public elementary & secondary schools (1996-97): 2,279, 9th
  Total enrollment (1996): 1,221,013, 10th
    Percent of school age pop.: 86.29%, 48th
    Percent of total pop.: 15.29%, 47th
  Teachers (1996): 90,703, 8th
    Percent of pop.: 1.14%, 14th
  Pupil/teacher ratio (1995): 13.8, 50th
  Teachers' avg. salary (1996-97): $49,349, 4th
  Expenditure per capita (1992-93): $1,607.71, 6th
    Education as % of state govt. expenditures: 34.8%, 29th
  Expenditure per pupil (1994-95): $9,774, 1st
    Percent increase (1993-94 & 1994-95): 1.00%, 48th
Percent at or above grade level, NAEP tests:
  Reading, grade 4 (1994): 33%, 10th
  Math, grade 4 (1996): 38%, 13th
  Math, grade 8 (1996): NA
Percent of graduates taking SAT (1995): 70%, 4th
  Mean SAT verbal scores: 420, 40th
  Mean SAT mathematical scores: 478, 35th
Percent of graduates taking ACT (1997): 3%, 47th
  Mean ACT scores: 20.8, 34th
Percent of pop. over 25 completing:
  Less than 9th grade: 9.4%, 26th
  High school: 76.7%, 26th
  College degree(s): 24.9%, 6th
Higher education, institutions (1996): 61, 20th
  Enrollment (1995-96): 333,831, 12th
    Percent increase in enroll. (1990-95): 2.9%, 26th
  White non-Hispanic (1995): 230,349, 16th
    Percent of enroll.: 69.00%, 40th
  Total minority enroll. (1995): 92,089, 6th
    Percent of enroll.: 27.59%, 12th
  Black non-Hispanic (1995): 39,273, 15th
    Percent of enroll.: 11.76%, 16th
  Hispanic (1995): 30,764, 8th
    Percent of enroll.: 9.22%, 8th
  Asian/Pacific Islander (1995): 21,105, 8th
    Percent of enroll.: 6.32%, 5th

  American Indian/AK native (1995): 947, 32nd
    Percent of enroll.: 0.28%, 46th
  Nonresident alien (1995): 11,393, 10th
    Percent of enroll.: 3.41%, 13th
  Female (1995): 188,192, 12th
    Percent of enroll.: 56.37%, 20th
  Pub. institutions (1995-96): 33, 15th
    Enrollment: 271,069, 11th
      Percent increase in enrollment (1990-95): 3.6%, 26th
    Percent of enroll.: 81.20%, 31st
  Private institutions (1995-96): 28, 22nd
    Enrollment: 62,762, 17th
      Percent increase in enrollment (1990-95): 0.1%, 38th
    Percent of enroll.: 18.80%, 21st
  Tuition (in state), public 4-year institution (1996-97): $4,269, 4th
  Tuition (in state), public 2-year institution (1996-97): $1,947, 12th
  Tuition, private 4-year institution (1996-97): $14,388, 13th
Public library systems (1994): 309, 10th
  Books & serial vol. per capita: 3.8, 12th
  Library visits per capita: 4.7, 13th
  Circulation per capita: 5.8, 33rd

LAW ENFORCEMENT AND CORRECTIONS

Police protection and corrections expenditures (1996): $1,133,265,000
  Per capita: $141.87, 13th
Police per 10,000 pop. (1996): 36.67, 3rd
Prisoners (1 year or more) per 100,000 pop. (1996): 343, 23rd
  Percent change (1995-96): 1.6%, 43rd
  Percent of inmates that are female: 4.7%, 44th
    Percent change: −2.0%, 47th
Death penalty: yes, by lethal injection
  Under sentence (Jan. 1998): 15, 25th
  Executed, 1976-97: 0

RELIGION, NUMBER AND PERCENT OF POPULATION

Agnostic: 35,584—0.60%, 19th
Buddhist: 5,931—0.10%, 17th
Christian: 5,041,117—85.00%, 33rd
Hindu: 17,792—0.30%, 2nd
Jewish: 255,021—4.30%, 2nd
Muslim: 35,584—0.60%, 2nd
Unitarian: 5,931—0.10%, 31st

Other: 47,446—0.80%, 37th
None: 326,190—5.50%, 39th
Refused to answer: 160,130—2.70%, 16th

MAKING A LIVING

Personal income per capita (1996): $31,053, 3rd
Percent increase (1995-96): 2.4%, 38th
Disposable personal income per capita (1996): $26,570, 3rd
Median income of households (average, 1995-96): $46,345, 2nd
Percent of pop. below poverty level (1995-96): 8.5%, 48th

ECONOMY

In civilian labor force (1996): 4,124,000
Percent of total pop.: 67.2%, 31st
Percent of total pop. 65 years and over: 12.8%, 19th
Percent of total female pop.: 59.5%, 34th
Major employer industries (total nonagricultural, 1996):
Construction: 123,400—3.4%, 45th
Finance, insurance, & real estate: 231,600—6.4%, 7th
Government: 566,800—15.6%, 35th
Manufacturing: 485,300—13.3%, 33rd
Service: 1,121,800—30.8%, 10th
Trade: 855,300—23.5%, 28th
Transportation, communications, public utilities: 254,000—7.0%, 3rd
Unemployment rate (1996): 6.2%, 9th
Male: 6.0%, 8th
Female: 6.4%, 8th
Total businesses (1995): 220,991, 9th
New business incorps. (1995): 37,861
Percent of total businesses: 17.13%, 4th
Business failures (1995): 2,779
Failures per 10,000 businesses: 125.8, 8th
Agriculture farm income:
Marketing (1996): $800,958,000, 38th
Average per farm: $87,061, 27th
Leading products (1997): Greenhouse, dairy products, eggs, blueberries, tomatoes, peaches, peppers, cranberries, soybeans
Average value land & build. per acre (1997): $8,290, 1st
Percent increase (1996-97): 1%, 44th
Govt. payments (1996): $3,258,000, 43rd
Average per farm: $354, 46th
Construction, value of all (1996): $7,123,588,000, 18th
Per capita: $892, 46th

Manufactures (1995):
Value added: $48,260,400,000
Per capita: $6,074, 26th
Leading products (1997): Chemicals, electric and electronic equipment, nonelectrical machinery, fabricated metals
Value of nonfuel mineral production (1996): $222,000,000, 38th
Leading mineral products (1996): Stone, sand/gravel, greensand marl, peat
Energy consumption per person (1994): 322.3 mil. Btu, 31st
Retail sales (1995): $74,425,000,000
Per household: $25,979, 9th
Sales increase (1994-95): 2.9%, 37th
Tourism revenues (1996): $24.6 bil.
Foreign exports, in total value (1996): $13,119,000,000, 13th
Per capita: $1,642, 24th
Gross state product per person (1994): $32,255, 6th
Public aid recipients (percent of resident pop. 1994): 6.0%, 33rd
Medicaid recipients (percent of pop., 1995): 9.9%, 41st
Medicare enrollment per 1,000 pop. (1996): 147, 23rd

TRAVEL AND TRANSPORTATION

Motor vehicle registrations (1996): 5,821,536, 10th
Per 1,000 pop.: 727.52, 39th
Motorcycle registrations (1996): 91,995, 15th
Per 1,000 pop.: 15.80, 35th
Licensed drivers (1996): 5,403,671, 9th
Per 1,000 pop.: 679.75, 30th
Public roads & streets (1996)
Total mileage: 35,924, 38th
Per 1,000 pop.: 14.50, 49th
Rural mileage: 11,683, 45th
Per 1,000 pop.: 1.46, 49th
Urban mileage: 24,241, 10th
Per 1,000 pop.: 3.03, 29th
Interstate mileage: 422, 43rd
Per 1,000 pop.: 0.05, 48th
Speed limit (max. interstate, autos, mi. per hr., 1997): 55
Annual vehicle-mi. of travel per driver (1996): 11,362, 46th
Mean travel time for workers age 16+ who work away from home: 25.3 min., 4th

GOVERNMENT

Percent of voting age pop. registered (1996): 71.61%, 36th

Percent of voting age pop. voting for president: (1996): 51.2%, 25th

Percent of voting age pop. voting for U.S. representatives (1996): 47.0%, 28th

State legislators, total (1997): 120, 36th

Women members (1997): 18

Percent of legislature: 15%, 40

U.S. Congress, House members (1998): 13

Change (1988-98): –1

Revenues (1996):

State govt.: $35,857,209,000

Per capita: $4,488.88, 9th

Parimutuel & amusement taxes & lotteries, revenue per capita (1995): $225.62, 6th

Expenditures (1996):

State govt.: $32,314,887,000

Per capita: $4,045.43, 9th

Debt outstanding (1996): $25,601,576,000

Per capita: $3,205.00, 8th

LAWS AND REGULATIONS

Legal driving age: 17

Marriage age without parental consent: 18

Divorce residence requirement: 1 yr., for qualifications check local statutes

ATTRACTIONS (1997)

Major opera companies: 3

Major symphony orchestras: 1

Major dance companies: 1

Major professional theater companies (non-profit): 1

Per capita spending by the NEA (1997): $0.13, 47th

State Fair in August at Cherry Hill

SPORTS AND COMPETITION

NCAA (Division I) football and basketball teams: Fairleigh Dickinson Univ. Knights (basketball only), Monmouth Univ. Hawks, Princeton Univ. Tigers, Rider Univ. Broncs (basketball only), Seton Hall Univ. Pirates (basketball only), St. Peter's College Peacocks, State Univ. of N.J.-Rutgers Scarlet Knights

Major league soccer teams: NY/NJ Metro-Stars, Giants Stadium

NBA basketball teams: New Jersey Nets, Continental Airlines Arena

NFL football teams: New York Jets (AFC), Giants Stadium; New York Giants (NFC), Giants Stadium

NHL hockey teams: New Jersey Devils, Continental Airlines Arena

WEBSITES CONTAINING FURTHER INFORMATION

State of New Jersey   http://www.state.nj.us

NEW MEXICO

"I think New Mexico was the greatest experience from the outside world that I ever had. It certainly changed me forever....The moment I saw the brilliant, proud morning shine high over the deserts of Santa Fe, something stood still in my soul....For a greatness of beauty I have never experienced anything like New Mexico....Just day itself is tremendous there."   D. H. Lawrence, novelist

Early explorers failed to find the fabled seven cities of gold in New Mexico, but the prehistoric cities of the Pueblo peoples far outshone the mythical ones. Among their more important contributions, these gave the state the nation's oldest "cooperative apartments." By contrast with its ancient history, New Mexico is the state where the atomic age became a reality. This land of sunshine is governed from the nation's oldest state capital, where visitors from around the world can experience superlative grand opera. Visitors can follow the course of the country's oldest highway, take in the unique sights of Taos Pueblo and the other pueblos, and enjoy the Indian festivals held around the state. The remarkable attraction of the state for authors, artists, and musicians have long been evident.

SUPERLATIVES

- Oldest capital city in the United States—Santa Fe.
- Oldest highway in the United States—the King's Highway.
- Yucca, the only commercially valuable state flower.
- First in production of potash.
- Leads in dry ice production from carbon dioxide wells.
- Birthplace of the U.S. livestock industry.

MOMENTS IN HISTORY

- The Pueblo people are among the most remarkable and most studied of prehistoric Americans. They developed substantial cities of stone masonry—their "skyscrapers" are noted as a distinctive contribution to world architecture. They developed great skill in weaving, created complex systems of irrigation, and domesticated turkeys. They fabricated tools, and their jewelry featured fine silverwork with turquoise. Their golden age appears to have been about 950-1200 A.D.
- The great expedition of Francisco Vásquez de Coronado crossed what is now New Mexico in 1540.
- On July 11, 1598, wealthy Don Juan de Onate established San Juan, the first European settlement in New Mexico (the second in the United States), at the Tewa pueblo of Yugeuingge. In 1605, Onate journeyed to the Gulf of California, and he carved his signature on famed Inscription Rock.
- Don Pedro de Peralta founded Santa Fe in the winter of 1609-10.
- By 1626 the Franciscan Fathers had established 43 missions, with 34,000 Indian converts.
- Because the Spaniards treated them so harshly, the Indians revolted under Pope, a Tewa medicine man, in 1680 and captured Santa Fe.
- The Indians ruled Santa Fe until 1692, when Governor Don Diego de Vagas recaptured it.
- Albuquerque was founded in 1706.
- On his expedition of 1806-07, Zebulon Pike was captured and taken to Santa Fe.
- During the Mexican War of 1846, U.S. military forces brought New Mexico under U.S. control.
- During the Civil War, Confederate forces captured Santa Fe on March 10, 1862, but General Henry H. Sibley recaptured the capital on April 8.
- The Plains Indians carried on warfare with the settlers for nearly 50 years, until Indian leader Geronimo surrendered in 1886.

So They Say

"Everything is quiet in Cimarron. Nobody has been killed for three days."

Las Vegas Gazette, on the lawlessness of the frontier

- In 1901 cowboy Jim White discovered a "hole in the ground." This proved to be a vast underground wonderland, and it became known as Carlsbad Caverns.
- On January 6, 1912, New Mexico became the 47th state.

• The atomic age was born at Alamogordo on July 16, 1945, with the test explosion of the first atomic bomb.

• In 1985 a major rating of American cities placed Albuquerque among the best places to live in the nation.

THAT'S INTERESTING

• Christopher Carson, known to everyone as Kit, began to trap in New Mexico as early as 1826. He gained much of his fame in other parts of the country. However, he kept his home in Taos, and he was buried in the Kit Carson Cemetery there.

• In the Four Corners region, where four states touch (New Mexico, Arizona, Utah, and Colorado), visitors often sprawl out so they can say they have slept in all four at once.

• Pueblo Bonito housed as many as 1,500 people in its 800 rooms, becoming perhaps the first "condominium."

• One of the principal attractions of Carlsbad Caverns is the evening flight of millions of bats. Winging their way out of the cavern entrance, the swarm of bats look like a column of smoke.

NEW MEXICO NOTABLES

William Henry (Billy the Kid) Bonney (New York, NY, 1859-1881), outlaw. **Christopher (Kit) Carson** (Madison City, KY, 1809-1868), trapper/Indian agent/soldier. **John Simpson Chisum** (Hardeman County, TN, 1824-1868), cattleman. **Emerson Hough** (Newton, IA, 1857-1923), author. **Jean Baptiste Lamy** (France, 1814-1888), religious leader. **David Herbert (D. H.) Lawrence** (England, 1885-1930), author. **Mangas Coloradas** (in southwest New Mexico, 1770?-1863), Indian leader. **William Henry (Bill) Mauldin** (Mountain Park, 1921-), cartoonist. **Georgia O'Keeffe** (Sun Prairie, WI, 1887-1986), artist. **Albert Pike** (Boston, MA, 1809-1891), lawyer/ soldier. **Eugene Manlove Rhodes** (Tecumseh, NE, 1869-1934), cowboy/author. **Ernest Thompson Seton** (England, 1860-1946), author/naturalist. **Frank Springer** (Wapella, IA, 1848-1927), lawyer/paleontologist.

GENERAL

Admitted to statehood: January 6, 1912
Origin of name: Spaniards in Mexico applied term to land north and west of Rio Grande in the 16th century

Capital: Santa Fe
Nickname: Land of Enchantment
Motto: *Crescit Eundo*—It grows as it goes
Animal: Black bear
Bird: Roadrunner
Fish: Cutthroat trout
Flower: Yucca
Gem: Turquoise
Song: "Asi Es Nuevo Mejico" and "O, Fair New Mexico"
Tree: Piñon

THE LAND

Area: 121,598 sq. mi., 5th
  Land: 121,364 sq. mi., 5th
  Water: 234 sq. mi., 47th
    Inland water: 234 sq. mi., 44th
Topography: Eastern third, Great Plains; central third, Rocky Mountains (85% of the state is over 4,000 ft. elevation); western third, high plateau
Number of counties: 33
Geographic center: Torrance, 12 mi. SSW of Willard
Length: 370 mi.; width: 343 mi.
Highest point: 13,161 ft. (Wheeler Peak), 8th
Lowest point: 2,842 ft. (Red Bluff Reservoir), 49th
Mean elevation: 5,700 ft., 4th

CLIMATE AND ENVIRONMENT

Temp., highest: 122 deg. on June 27, 1994, at Waste Isolat. Pilot Plt.; lowest: –50 deg. on Feb. 1, 1951, at Gavilan
Monthly average: highest: 92.8 deg., 10th; lowest: 22.3 deg., 30th; spread (high to low): 70.5 deg., 22nd
Hazardous waste sites (1997): 9, 39th
Endangered species: Animals: 16—Lesser bat, Mexican long-nosed bat, Whooping crane, American peregrine falcon, Southwestern willow flycatcher, Pecos gambusia, Socorro isopod, Jaguar, Rio Grande silvery minnow, Alamosa springsnail, Socorro springsnail, Razorback sucker, Least tern, Gila topminnow, Gila trout, Woundfin. Plants: 8

MAJOR CITIES
POPULATION, 1996
PERCENTAGE INCREASE, 1990-96

Albuquerque, 419,681; 9.0%
Las Cruces, 74,779; 19.9%

Santa Fe, 66,522; 17.7%
Roswell, 47,559; 7.5%
Rio Rancho, 46,565; 43.2%

THE PEOPLE

Population (1997): 1,729,751, 36th
  Percent change (1990-97): 14.17%, 9th
  Percent of total U.S. pop.: 0.65%, 36th
  Per sq. mi: 14.23, 46th
Population (2000 proj.): 1,859,000, 36th
  Percent change (1995-2000): 10.33%, 6th
Percent in metro. area (1996): 56.68%, 36th
Foreign born: 81,000, 28th
  Percent: 5.3%, 16th
Top three ancestries reported:
  German, 15.45%
  Mexican, 14.26%
  Spanish, 12.61%
White (1992): 1,384,000, 87.48%, 29th
Black (1992): 36,000, 2.28%, 40th
Native American (1992): 144,000, 9.10%, 2nd
Asian, Pacific Isle (1992): 18,000, 1.14%, 29th
Hispanic origin (1992): 614,000, 38.81%, 1st
Percent over 5 yrs. speaking language other than English at home: 35.5%, 1st
Percent males (1996): 49.35%, 15th; percent females: 50.65%, 37th
Percent never married: 25.8%, 24th
Marriages per 1,000 (1996): 9.35, 15th
Divorces per 1,000 (1996): 6.39, 4th
Median age (1996): 33.3
Under 5 years (1996): 8.04%, 6th
18 years and under (1996): 32.35%, 4th
65 years and over (1996): 11.04%, 45th
Percent increase among the elderly (1995-96): 1.90%, 6th

OF VITAL IMPORTANCE

Live births per 1,000 pop. (1996): 15.9, 8th
Infant mortality rate per 1,000 live births (1995): 6.2, 42nd
  Rate for whites: 6.1, 32nd
  Rate for blacks: NA
Births to unmarried women, % of total (1996): 42.1%, 5th
Births to teenage mothers, % of total (1996): 17.9%, 5th
Abortions (1992): 6,410, 38th
  Rate per 1,000 women 14-44 years old: 17.7, 29th
  Percent change (1988-92): –7%, 23rd
Average lifetime (1989-91): 75.74, 25th

Total death rate per 100,000 pop. (1995): 744.3, 44th
  Accidents and adverse effects: 54.6, 3rd
  Alzheimer's disease: 6.5, 42nd
  Cancer: 159.5, 47th
  Cerebrovascular diseases: 42.7, 49th
  Chronic liver disease and cirrhosis: 15.4, 2nd
  Chronic obstructive pulmonary diseases and allied conditions: 41.5, 22nd
  Diabetes mellitus: 26.1, 11th
  Diseases of heart: 196.1, 47th
  HIV infection: 9.1, 28th
  Homicide: 10.1, 14th
  Injury by firearms: 17.7, 11th
  Motor vehicle accidents: 26.7, 4th
  Pneumonia and influenza: 23.9, 47th
  Suicide: 17.6, 4th

KEEPING WELL

Active nonfederal physicians per 100,000 pop. (1995): 199, 29th
Dentists per 100,000 (1991): 41, 49th
Nurses per 100,000 (1995): 683, 45th
Hospitals per 100,000 (1995): 2.14, 28th
  Admissions per 1,000 (1995): 92.58, 44th
  Hospital beds per 1,000 (1995): 2.20, 48th
  Occupancy rate per 100 beds (1995): 56.76, 40th
  Average cost per patient per day (1995) $1,073, 11th
  Average cost per stay (1995): $5,358, 38th
AIDS cases (new, 1996): 205; per 100,000 12.0, 29th
Persons living with HIV infection (1996): NA
Other notifiable diseases, per 100,000 pop.:
  Gonorrhea (1995): 62.5, 32nd
  Syphilis (1995): 8.2, 31st
  Tuberculosis (1996): 5.2, 25th
Pop. without health insur. (1996): 22.3%, 3rd

HOUSEHOLDS BY TYPE

Total households (1996): 619,000, 37th
  Percent change (1990-96): 14.1%, 8th
  Per 1,000 pop. (1996) 361.35, 44th
  Percent of householders 65 yrs. and over (1996): 19.71%, 39th
  Persons per household (1996): 2.64, 17th
Family households: 391,487
  Percent of total: 72.14%, 14th
Nonfamily households: 151,222
  Percent of total: 27.86%, 38th
Pop. living in group quarters: 28,807
  Percent of pop.: 1.90%, 50th

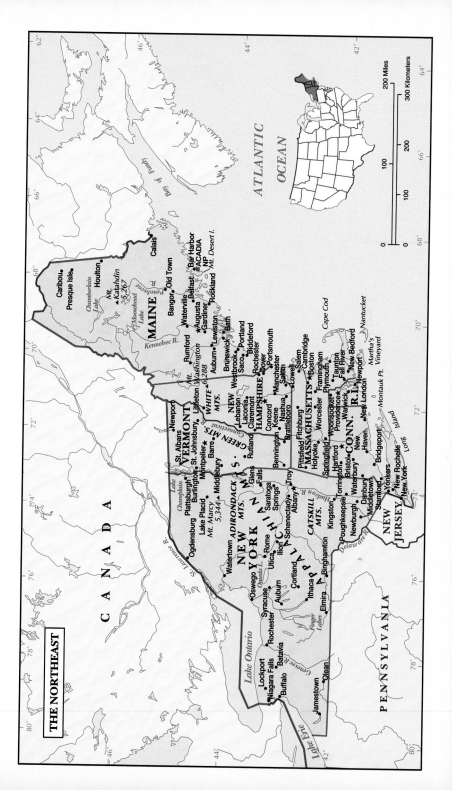

THE NORTHEAST

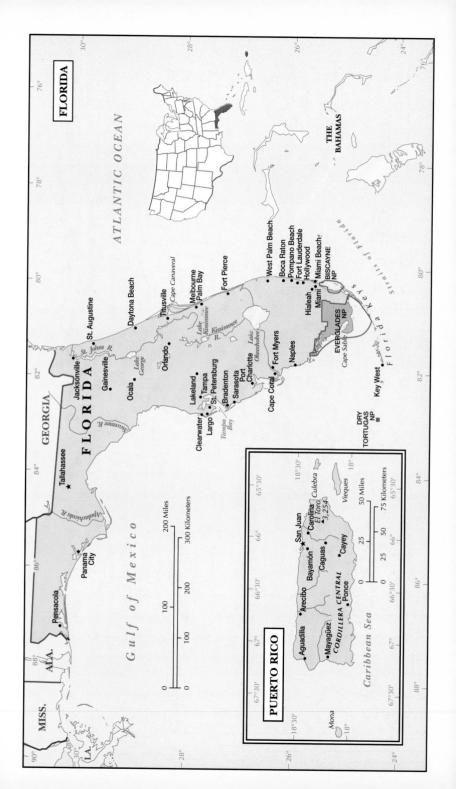

FLORIDA

ATLANTIC OCEAN

THE BAHAMAS

MISS. ALA. LA.

GEORGIA

F L O R I D A

Tallahassee

Panama City

Pensacola

Apalachicola R.

Gulf of Mexico

Jacksonville
St. Augustine
St. Johns R.
Gainesville
Suwannee R.
Ocala
Lake George
Orlando
Lakeland
Tampa
Clearwater
Largo
St. Petersburg
Tampa Bay
Bradenton
Sarasota
Port Charlotte
Cape Coral
Fort Myers
Naples
Lake Kissimmee
Kissimmee R.
Lake Okeechobee
Daytona Beach
Titusville
Cape Canaveral
Melbourne
Palm Bay
Fort Pierce
West Palm Beach
Boca Raton
Pompano Beach
Fort Lauderdale
Hollywood
Miami Beach
Miami
Hialeah
EVERGLADES NP
BISCAYNE NP
Cape Sable
Key West
F l o r i d a   Keys
Straits of Florida

DRY TORTUGAS NP

0   100   200 Miles
0   100   200   300 Kilometers

PUERTO RICO

San Juan
Carolina
El Toro 3,254
Bayamón
Caguas
Cayey
Arecibo
Aguadilla
Mayagüez
CORDILLERA CENTRAL
Ponce
Culebra
Vieques
Mona
Caribbean Sea

0   25   50 Miles
0   25   50   75 Kilometers

18°30'   18°   65°30'   66°   66°30'   67°   67°30'

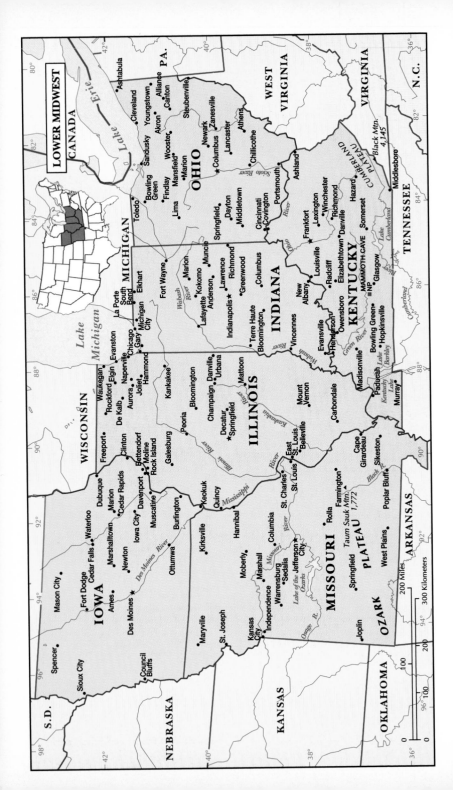

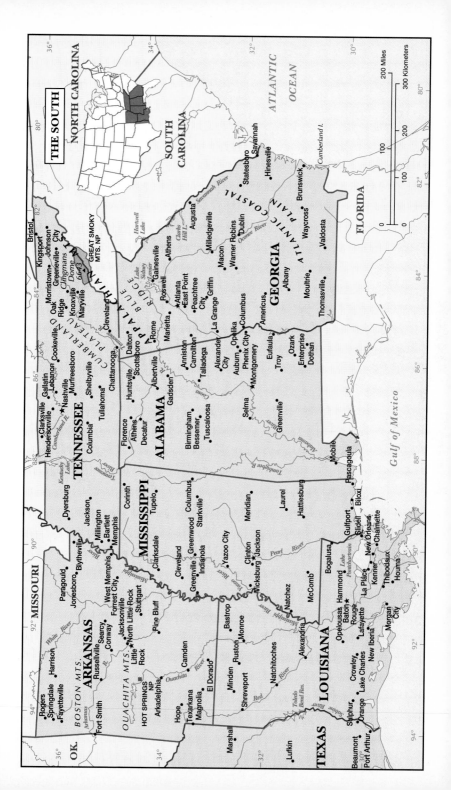

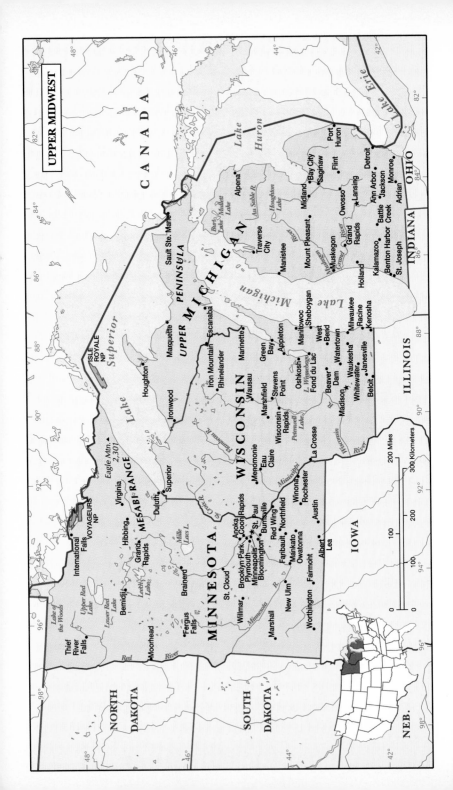

UPPER MIDWEST

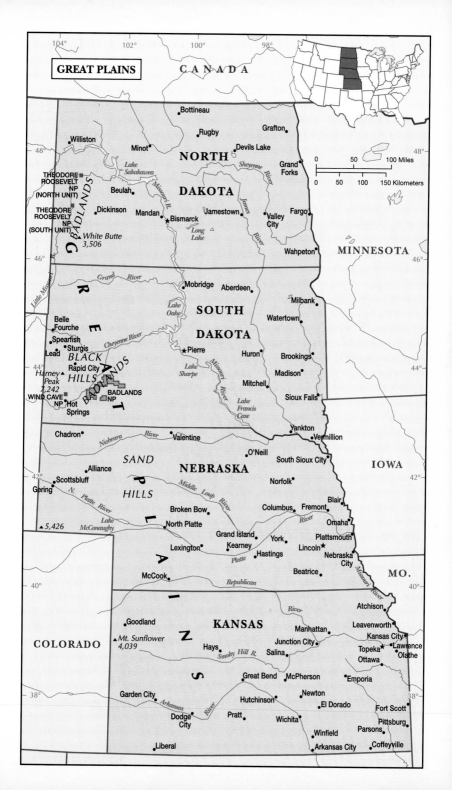

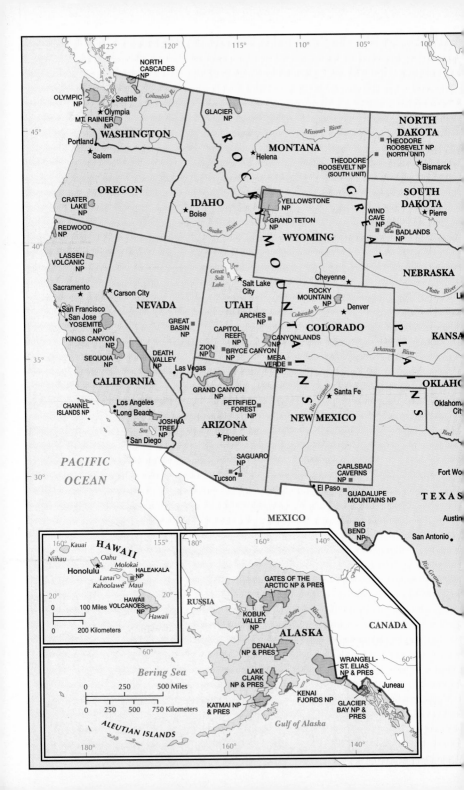

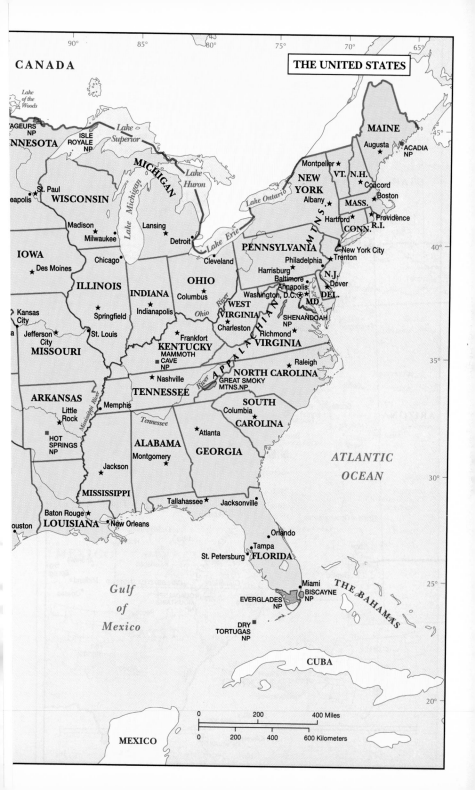

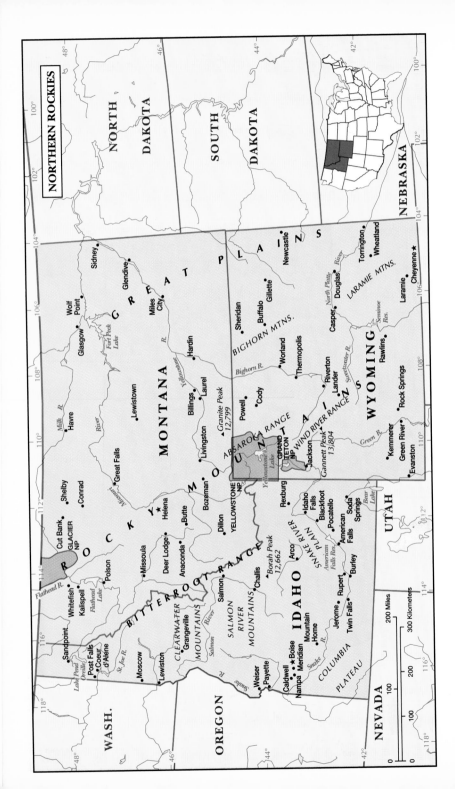

NORTHERN ROCKIES

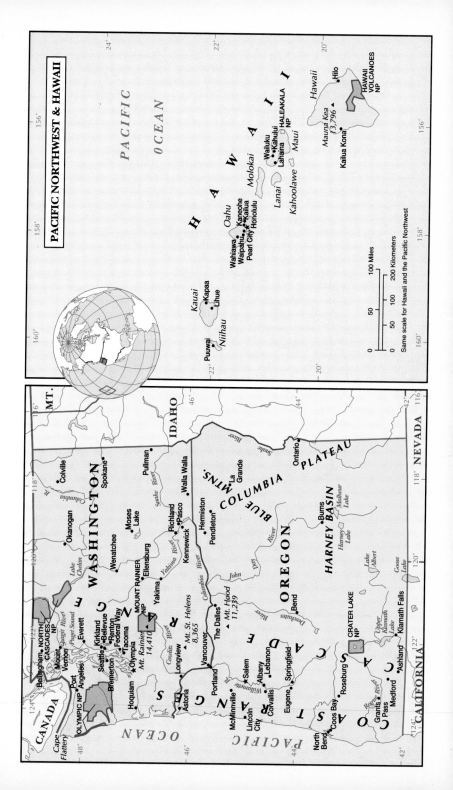

PACIFIC NORTHWEST & HAWAII

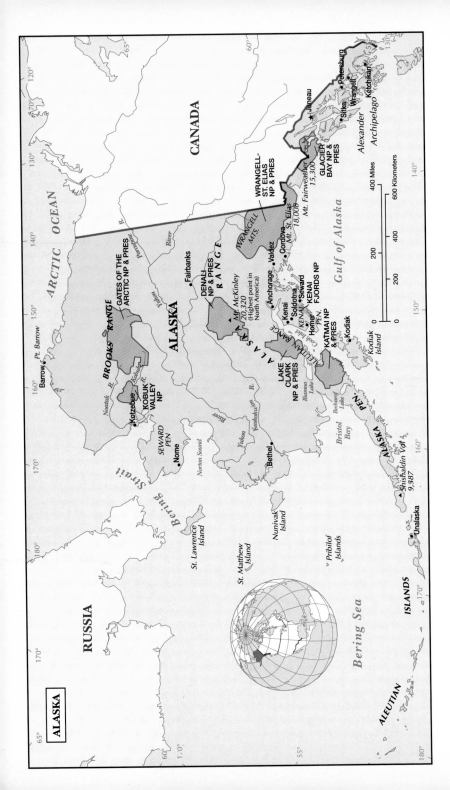

LIVING QUARTERS

Total housing units: 632,058
  Persons per unit: 2.40, 26th
Occupied housing units: 542,709
  Percent of total units: 85.86%, 40th
  Persons per unit: 2.69, 8th
  Percent of units with over 1 person per room: 7.89%, 6th
Owner-occupied units: 365,965
  Percent of total units: 57.90%, 31st
  Percent of occupied units: 67.43%, 25th
  Persons per unit: 2.85, 6th
  Median value: $70,100, 24th
Renter-occupied units: 176,744
  Percent of total units: 27.96%, 30th
  Percent of occupied units: 32.57%, 27th
  Persons per unit: 2.52, 8th
  Median contract rent: $312, 29th
  Rental vacancy rate: 11.4%, 10th
Mobile home, trailer & other as a percent of occupied housing units: 20.71%, 2nd
Persons in emergency shelters for homeless persons: 667, 0.044%, 29th
Persons visible in street locations: 164, 0.0108%, 18th
Nursing home population: 6,276, 0.41%, 46th

CRIME INDEX PER 100,000 (1996)

Total reported: 6,602.3, 5th
  Percent increase: 2.7%, 4th
  Violent: 840.6, 8th
    Percent increase: 2.6%, 3rd
    Murder & nonnegligent manslaughter: 11.5, 5th
    Forcible rape: 63.5, 2nd
    Aggravated assault: 603.2, 4th
    Robbery: 162.4, 23rd
  Property: 5,761.7, 6th
    Percent increase: 2.7%, 5th
    Burglary: 1,376.9, 3rd
    Larceny-theft: 3,802.6, 10th
    Motor vehicle theft: 582.2, 12th

TEACHING AND LEARNING

Pop. 3 and over enrolled in school (1996): 432,927, 35th
Percent of pop.: 25.27%, 6th
Public elementary & secondary schools (1996-97): 721, 40th
  Total enrollment (1996): 330,522, 35th
    Percent of school age pop.: 90.55%, 32nd
    Percent of total pop.: 19.29%, 7th

Teachers (1996): 19,608, 37th
  Percent of pop.: 1.14%, 14th
Pupil/teacher ratio (1995): 17.0, 19th
Teachers' avg. salary (1996-97): $29,715, 46th
Expenditure per capita (1992-93): $1,420.30, 18th
  Education as % of state govt. expenditures: 35.1%, 27th
Expenditure per pupil (1994-95): $4,586, 45th
  Percent increase (1993-94 & 1994-95): 7.63%, 4th
Percent at or above grade level, NAEP tests:
  Reading, grade 4 (1994): 2%1, 34th
  Math, grade 4 (1996): 51%, 38th
  Math, grade 8 (1996): 51%, 33rd
Percent of graduates taking SAT (1995): 11%, 34th
  Mean SAT verbal scores: 485, 16th
  Mean SAT mathematical scores: 530, 18th
Percent of graduates taking ACT (1997): 59%, 23rd
  Mean ACT scores: 20.3, 39th
Percent of pop. over 25 completing:
  Less than 9th grade: 11.4%, 15th
  High school: 75.1%, 33rd
  College degree(s): 20.4%, 22nd
Higher education, institutions (1996): 35, 34th
  Enrollment (1995-96): 102,405, 35th
    Percent increase in enroll. (1990-95): 19.8%, 3rd
    White non-Hispanic (1995): 57,229, 39th
      Percent of enroll.: 55.88%, 48th
    Total minority enroll. (1995): 43,383, 19th
      Percent of enroll.: 42.36%, 3rd
    Black non-Hispanic (1995): 2,593, 40th
      Percent of enroll.: 2.53%, 40th
    Hispanic (1995): 32,067, 7th
      Percent of enroll.: 31.31%, 1st
    Asian/Pacific Islander (1995): 1,694, 38th
      Percent of enroll.: 1.65%, 37th
    American Indian/AK native (1995): 7,029, 4th
      Percent of enroll.: 6.86%, 4th
    Nonresident alien (1995): 1,793, 40th
      Percent of enroll.: 1.75%, 45th
    Female (1995): 59,199, 35th
      Percent of enroll.: 57.81%, 6th
  Pub. institutions (1995-96): 24, 27th
    Enrollment: 97,220, 34th
      Percent increase in enrollment (1990-95): 16.6%, 5th
      Percent of enroll.: 94.94%, 4th

Private institutions (1995-96): 11, 41st
Enrollment: 5,185, 47th
Percent increase in enrollment (1990-95): 147.3%, 1st
Percent of enroll.: 5.06%, 48th
Tuition (in state), public 4-year institution (1996-97): $2,016, 43rd
Tuition (in state), public 2-year institution (1996-97): $689, 48th
Tuition, private 4-year institution (1996-97): $10,356, 30th
Public library systems (1994): 73, 36th
Books & serial vol. per capita: 3.3, 20th
Library visits per capita: NA
Circulation per capita: 6.5, 27th

LAW ENFORCEMENT AND CORRECTIONS

Police protection and corrections expenditures (1996): $231,227,000
Per capita: $134.99, 17th
Police per 10,000 pop. (1996): 23.03, 21st
Prisoners (1 year or more) per 100,000 pop. (1996): 261, 36th
Percent change (1995-96): 14.8%, 5th
Percent of inmates that are female: 8.0%, 3rd
Percent change: 36.0%, 3rd
Death penalty: yes, by lethal injection
Under sentence (Jan. 1998): 4, 33rd
Executed, 1976-97: 0

RELIGION, NUMBER AND PERCENT OF POPULATION

Agnostic: 10,683—1.00%, 10th
Buddhist: 1,068—0.10%, 17th
Christian: 910,216—85.20%, 32nd
Hindu: NA
Jewish: 7,478—0.70%, 21st
Muslim: NA
Unitarian: 3,205—0.30%, 15th
Other: 11,752—1.10%, 32nd
None: 106,833—10.00%, 11th
Refused to answer: 17,093—1.60%, 39th

MAKING A LIVING

Personal income per capita (1996): $18,770, 49th
Percent increase (1995-96): 2.8%, 29th
Disposable personal income per capita (1996): $16,674, 47th
Median income of households (average, 1995-96): $25,922, 50th
Percent of pop. below poverty level (1995-96): 25.4%, 1st

ECONOMY

In civilian labor force (1996): 800,000
Percent of total pop.: 63.0%, 45th
Percent of total pop. 65 years and over: 12.5%, 21st
Percent of total female pop.: 55.2%, 46th
Major employer industries (total nonagricultural, 1996):
Construction: 42,700—6.2%, 5th
Finance, insurance, & real estate: 31,500—4.5%, 39th
Government: 171,100—24.7%, 4th
Manufacturing: 45,900—6.6%, 45th
Service: 192,100—27.7%, 21st
Trade: 164,100—23.6%, 26th
Transportation, communications, public utilities: 31,200—4.5%, 41st
Unemployment rate (1996): 8.1%, 2nd
Male: 8.4%, 3rd
Female: 7.6%, 3rd
Total businesses (1995): 40,631, 36th
New business incorps. (1995): 3,584
Percent of total businesses: 8.82%, 25th
Business failures (1995): 405
Failures per 10,000 businesses: 99.7, 17th
Agriculture farm income:
Marketing (1996): $1,709,056,000, 34th
Average per farm: $126,597, 14th
Leading products (1997): Cattle, dairy products, hay, greenhouse, pecans, onions, chiles, corn, cotton
Average value land & build. per acre (1997): $280, 47th
Percent increase (1996-97): 9%, 5th
Govt. payments (1996): $59,000,000, 29th
Average per farm: $4,370, 13th
Construction, value of all (1996): $2,228,989,000, 36th
Per capita: $1,301, 22nd
Manufactures (1995):
Value added: $8,358,100,000
Per capita: $4,959, 37th
Leading products (1997): Foods, machinery, apparel, lumber, printing, transportation equipment, electronics, semiconductors
Value of nonfuel mineral production (1996): $963,000,000, 12th
Leading mineral products (1996): Natural gas, petroleum, coal, copper, potash, sand/gravel, cement, stone
Energy consumption per person (1994): 356.9 mil. Btu, 23rd

Retail sales (1995): $14,634,000,000
  Per household: $24,022, 34th
  Sales increase (1994-95): 3.8%, 30th
Tourism revenues (1994): $2.75 bil.
Foreign exports, in total value (1996): $931,000,000, 44th
  Per capita: $543, 49th
Gross state product per person (1994): $22,880, 38th
Public aid recipients (percent of resident pop. 1994): 8.7%, 10th
Medicaid recipients (percent of pop., 1995): 17.0%, 6th
Medicare enrollment per 1,000 pop. (1996): 127, 39th

TRAVEL AND TRANSPORTATION

Motor vehicle registrations (1996): 1,544,633, 34th
  Per 1,000 pop.: 902.63, 9th
Motorcycle registrations (1996): 31,578, 34th
  Per 1,000 pop.: 20.44, 24th
Licensed drivers (1996): 1,173,442, 36th
  Per 1,000 pop.: 694.41, 23rd
Public roads & streets (1996)
  Total mileage: 59,455, 34th
    Per 1,000 pop.: 134.70, 9th
    Rural mileage: 53,322, 32nd
    Per 1,000 pop.: 31.12, 9th
    Urban mileage: 6,133, 35th
    Per 1,000 pop.: 3.58, 10th
    Interstate mileage: 1,000, 17th
    Per 1,000 pop.: 0.58, 6th
Speed limit (max. interstate, autos, mi. per hr., 1997): 75
Annual vehicle-mi. of travel per driver (1996): 18,240, 2nd
Mean travel time for workers age 16+ who work away from home: 19.1 min., 36th

GOVERNMENT

Percent of voting age pop. registered (1996): 69.57%, 40th
  Percent of voting age pop. voting for president: (1996): 46.0%, 40th
  Percent of voting age pop. voting for U.S. representatives (1996): 45.3%, 35th
State legislators, total (1997): 112, 38th
  Women members (1997): 30
    Percent of legislature: 27%, 13th
U.S. Congress, House members (1998): 3
  Change (1988-98): 0
Revenues (1996):
  State govt.: $8,129,383,000
    Per capita: $4,745.70, 8th
    Parimutuel & amusement taxes & lotteries, revenue per capita (1995): $1.19, 44th
Expenditures (1996):
  State govt.: $6,740,498,000
    Per capita: $3,934.91, 10th
Debt outstanding (1996): $2,146,696,000
  Per capita: $1,253.18, 29th

LAWS AND REGULATIONS

Legal driving age: 16, 15 if completed driver education course
Marriage age without parental consent: 18
Divorce residence requirement: 6 mo.

ATTRACTIONS (1997)

Major opera companies: 2
Major symphony orchestras: 1
Major dance companies: 1
Per capita spending by the NEA (1997): $0.49, 17th
State Fair in mid-September at Albuquerque

SPORTS AND COMPETITION

NCAA (Division I) football and basketball teams: New Mexico State Univ. Aggies, Univ. of New Mexico Lobos

WEBSITES CONTAINING FURTHER INFORMATION

New Mexico Dept. of Tourism	http://www.nets.com/newmextourism
State of New Mexico Government Information Web	http://www.state.nm.us

NEW YORK

"We found a pleasant place between steep little hills...and from those hills a mighty, deep mouthed river ran into the sea."

Giovanni de Verrazano, explorer

Stretching from Niagara Falls in the west and the rugged Adirondacks in the northeast to the culturally rich and ethnically diverse "Big Apple"—Manhattan—in the southeast, New York is a state of dramatic contrasts. Although it no longer ranks first among the states in either population or manufacturing, New York State must still rank as the "Empire State" in its combination of rich historical tradition, cultural institutions, notable natives, commerce, industry, finance, and international influence, among other factors.

So They Say

"The roar of these waters [Niagara Falls] is like the roar when the mighty wave of democracy breaks on shores where kings lie couched in ease."

Writer Oscar Wilde (1882)

SUPERLATIVES

- World's most extensive deep water port.
- World's longest suspension bridge—the Verrazano-Narrows.
- World center of finance.
- First in publishing, the garment industry, and furs.
- First in the photographic industry.
- Historical center of Indian power.
- First capital of the United States—New York City.
- World center of tourism.
- Claims world's oldest chartered city—Albany.

MOMENTS IN HISTORY

- In 1524, the explorer Giovanni de Verrazano, in the employ of the French, probably was the first European to set foot on New York soil, and in that same year black Portuguese explorer Esteban Gómez may also have done so.
- In 1609 explorer Henry Hudson entered the Hudson River, sailing up as far as present-day Albany, and Samuel de Champlain found Lake Champlain.

So They Say

"...large lake filled with beautiful islands and with a fine country around it."

Samuel de Champlain,
on Lake Champlain

- Hudson's discoveries supported Dutch claims. In 1614 the Dutch built Fort Nassau, near present-day Albany, and settlers arrived at what is now New York City in 1624.
- In 1664 the Duke of York sent a large fleet to take over the area for England, and the Dutch surrendered.
- The acquittal of publisher John Peter Zenger in 1735 on libel charges was vital to the preservation of freedom of the press.

So They Say

"This city [New York] is situated upon the point of a small island, lying open to the bay on one side, and on the others included between the North and East rivers....It contains between two and three thousand houses, and 16 or 17,000 inhabitants, is tolerably well built, and has several good houses. The streets are paved and very clean, but in general narrow. There are two or three, indeed, which are spacious and airy, particularly the Broadway."

Sailing Captain Andrew Burnaby (1759)

- A century of warfare between the French and British for control of the area finally ended in 1761, with the British taking full control.
- In 1775, more than a year before national independence was agreed upon, 225 residents of Coxsackie signed a declaration of independence.
- New York became one of the main Revolutionary battlegrounds, suffering 92 engagements—almost a third of the total.
- New York City fell in the battles of Long Island and Fort Washington, in August and October 1776.
- The Battle of Saratoga is ranked as one of the most important in world history. The

British General John Burgoyne surrendered there on October 17, 1777.

- Indian power in western New York was broken in 1779.
- On July 26, 1788, New York became the 11th state.
- New York City was the capital of the new nation when George Washington took the presidential oath on the balcony of Federal Hall on April 30, 1789.
- The steamboat era began when Robert Fulton's *Clermont* chugged up the Hudson in 1807.
- During the War of 1812, much land fighting took place along the Canadian border, and the British fleet was destroyed on Lake Champlain in 1814.
- The Erie Canal opened on October 26, 1825, bringing New York City commerce to and from the far reaches of the Great Lakes.
- In 1883, New York became the first state with a civil service system for state employees.
- The Statue of Liberty was dedicated in 1886.
- President William McKinley received a fatal gunshot wound at the Pan-American Exposition at Buffalo in 1901.
- Lake Placid hosted the Winter Olympic Games in 1932 (and again in 1980).
- In 1953 the United Nations moved to New York City.
- New York transportation advances continued with the opening of the New York State Thruway in 1954 and the St. Lawrence Seaway in 1959.
- In 1993 the World Trade Center was devastated by a terrorist bomb that killed six people. A year later four terrorists tried for the crime were found guilty and received stiff prison sentences.

THAT'S INTERESTING

- A giant "prehistoric" man uncovered in 1896 at the town of Cardiff drew worldwide attention, until the "Cardiff Giant" was found to be a hoax, one of the most notable of all time.
- Like a giant three-dimensional jigsaw puzzle, the Statue of Liberty was assembled from parts shipped to New York in 214 packing crates.
- To delay British General John Burgoyne on his march through New York, General

Philip Schuyler's wife herself burned the wheat fields, slowing the enemy advance.

- Samuel Wilson, a Troy meat packer, was known as Uncle Sam as he furnished meat to the Army in the War of 1812. His reputation increased until the "real" Uncle Sam became the U.S. symbol.

NOTABLE NATIVES

Humphrey Bogart (New York City, 1899-1957), actor. **James Cagney** (New York City, 1899-1986), actor/dancer. **William George Fargo** (Pompey, 1818-1881), businessman. **Millard Fillmore** (Summerhill, 1800-1874), U.S. president. **Henry Louis (Lou) Gehrig** (New York City, 1903-1941), baseball player. **George Gershwin** (Brooklyn, 1898-1837), composer. **Jackie Gleason** (Brooklyn, 1916-1987), actor/comedian. **Edward Henry Harriman** (Hempstead, 1848-1909), financier. **Julia Ward Howe** (New York City, 1819-1910), author/social reformer. **Charles Evans Hughes** (Glens Falls, 1862-1948), chief justice of the United States. **George Inness** (Newburgh, 1825-1894), artist. **Washington Irving** (New York City, 1783-1859), author. **Henry James** (New York City, 1843-1916), author. **William James** (New York City, 1842-1910), psychologist/philosopher. **Michael Jeffrey Jordan** (Brooklyn, 1963-), basketball player. **Alfred A. Knopf** (New York City, 1892-1984), publisher. **Herman Melville** (New York City, 1819-1891), author. **John Wesley Powell** (Mt. Morris, now part of New York City, 1834-1902), geologist/ethnologist. **George Mortimer Pullman** (Brocton, 1831-1897), inventor/industrialist. **Frederic Remington** (Canton, 1861-1909), artist. **John Davison Rockefeller** (Richford, 1839-1937), industrialist/philanthropist. **Anna Eleanor Roosevelt** (New York City, 1884-1962), author/diplomat/humanitarian/U.S. first lady. **Franklin Delano Roosevelt** (Hyde Park, 1882-1945), U.S. president. **Theodore Roosevelt** (New York City, 1858-1919), U.S. president. **Jonas Edward Salk** (New York City, 1914-1995), physician/scientist. **William Henry Seward** (Florida, 1801-1872), public official. **Shenandoah** (near Oneida Castle, 1706?-1816), Indian leader. **Alfred Emanuel Smith** (New York City, 1873-1944), political leader. **Elizabeth Cady Stanton** (Johnstown, 1815-1902), social reformer. **Barbra Streisand** (New York City, 1942-), actress/singer. **Kateri Tekakwitha** (what is now Auriesville, 1656-1680), religious figure. **Louis Comfort Tiffany** (New York City, 1848-1933), painter/craftsman/ decorator. **Samuel Jones Tilden** (Lebanon, 1814-1886), public official. **Martin Van Buren** (Kinderhook, 1782-1862), U.S. president. **Edith Newbold Wharton** (New York City, 1862-1937), author. **Walt Whitman** (West Hills, 1819-1892) poet/philosopher. **Frank Winfield Woolworth** (Rodman, 1852-1919), merchant. **Linus Yale** (Salisbury, 1821-1868), inventor.

GENERAL

Admitted to statehood: July 26, 1788
Origin of name: For Duke of York and Albany, who received patent to New Netherland from his brother Charles II and sent an expedition to capture the territory in 1664
Capital: Albany
Nickname: Empire State
Motto: *Excelsior*—Ever upward
Animal: Beaver
Bird: Bluebird
Fish: Brook trout (brookies or speckles)
Flower: Rose
Gem: Garnet
Song: "I Love New York"
Tree: Sugar maple

THE LAND

Area: 53,989 sq. mi., 27th
  Land: 47,224 sq. mi., 30th
  Water: 6,765 sq. mi., 5th
    Inland water: 1,888 sq. mi., 10th
    Coastal water: 976 sq. mi., 8th
    Great Lakes: 3,901 sq. mi., 3rd
Topography: Highest and most rugged mountains in the NE Adirondack upland; St. Lawrence-Champlain lowlands extend from Lake Ontario NE along the Canadian border; Hudson-Mohawk lowland follows the flows of the rivers N and W, 10-30 mi. wide; Atlantic coastal plain in the SE; Appalachian Highlands, covering half the state westward from the Hudson Valley, include the Catskill Mountains Finger Lakes; plateau of Erie-Ontario lowlands
Number of counties: 62
Geographic center: Madison, 12 mi. S of Oneida and 26 mi. SW of Utica
Length: 330 mi.; width: 283 mi.
Highest point: 5,344 ft. (Mount Marcy), 21st
Lowest point: sea level (Atlantic Ocean), 3rd

Mean elevation: 1,000 ft., 26th
Coastline: 127 mi., 14th
Shoreline: 1,850 mi., 13th

CLIMATE AND ENVIRONMENT

Temp., highest: 108 deg. on July 22, 1926, at Troy; lowest: −52 deg. on Feb. 18, 1979, at Old Forge
Monthly average: highest: 85.3 deg., 38th; lowest: 11.9 deg., 12th; spread (high to low): 73.4 deg., 18th
Hazardous waste sites (1997): 77, 4th
Endangered species: Animals: 6—Indiana bat, Karner blue butterfly, American peregrine falcon, Dwarf wedge mussel, Roseate tern, Piping plover. Plants: 1

MAJOR CITIES
POPULATION, 1996
PERCENTAGE INCREASE, 1990-96

New York, 7,380,906; 0.8%
Buffalo, 310,548; −5.4%
Rochester, 221,594; −3.8%
Yonkers, 190,316; 1.2%
Syracuse, 155,865; −4.9%

THE PEOPLE

Population (1997): 18,137,226, 3rd
  Percent change (1990-97): 0.81%, 47th
  Percent of total U.S. pop.: 6.78%, 3rd
  Per sq. mi: 332.95, 7th
Population (2000 proj.): 18,160,000, 3rd
  Percent change (1995-2000): 0.13%, 50th
Percent in metro. area (1996): 91.79%, 7th
Foreign born: 2,852,000, 2nd
  Percent: 15.9%, 2nd
Top three ancestries reported:
  German, 16.11%
  Italian, 15.77%
  Irish, 15.56%
White (1992): 14,134,000, 78.05%, 40th
Black (1992): 3,118,000, 17.22%, 11th
Native American (1992): 68,000, 0.38%, 30th
Asian, Pacific Isle (1992): 790,000, 4.36%, 4th
Hispanic origin (1992): 2,362,000, 13.04%, 6th
Percent over 5 yrs. speaking language other than English at home: 23.3%, 5th
Percent males (1996): 48.18%, 46th; percent females: 51.82%, 6th
Percent never married: 32.1%, 3rd
Marriages per 1,000 (1996): 8.37, 24th

Divorces per 1,000 (1996): 3.34, 37th
Median age (1996): 35.3
Under 5 years (1996): 7.27%, 14th
18 years and under (1996): 27.54%, 40h
65 years and over (1996): 13.39%, 20th
Percent increase among the elderly (1995-96): 0.39%, 37th

OF VITAL IMPORTANCE

Live births per 1,000 pop. (1996): 14.9, 16th
Infant mortality rate per 1,000 live births (1995): 7.7, 21st
  Rate for whites: 6.2, 26th
  Rate for blacks: 13.9, 26th
Births to unmarried women, % of total (1996): 38.8%, 7th
Births to teenage mothers, % of total (1996): 9.2%, 45th
Abortions (1992): 195,390, 2nd
  Rate per 1,000 women 14-44 years old: 46.2, 2nd
  Percent change (1988-92): 7%, 7th
Average lifetime (1989-91): 74.68, 39th
Total death rate per 100,000 pop. (1995): 928.4, 21st
  Accidents and adverse effects: 27.5, 48th
  Alzheimer's disease: 3.6, 50th
  Cancer: 213.3, 24th
  Cerebrovascular diseases: 44.8, 47th
  Chronic liver disease and cirrhosis: 9.9, 17th
  Chronic obstructive pulmonary diseases and allied conditions: 33.8, 44th
  Diabetes mellitus: 19.4, 38th
  Diseases of heart: 350.2, 5th
  HIV infection: 44.1, 2nd
  Homicide: 8.7, 22nd
  Injury by firearms: 9.0, 41st
  Motor vehicle accidents: 9.9, 49th
  Pneumonia and influenza: 36.1, 11th
  Suicide: 7.6, 49th

KEEPING WELL

Active nonfederal physicians per 100,000 pop. (1995): 361, 3rd
Dentists per 100,000 (1991): 79, 3rd
Nurses per 100,000 (1995): 915, 17th
Hospitals per 100,000 (1995): 1.27, 46th
  Admissions per 1,000 (1995): 132.22, 13th
  Hospital beds per 1,000 (1995): 4.07, 14th
  Occupancy rate per 100 beds (1995): 79.97, 2nd

Average cost per patient per day (1995): $909, 29th
Average cost per stay (1995): $8,077, 4th
AIDS cases (new, 1996): 12,379; per 100,000: 68.1, 2nd
Persons living with HIV infection (1996): NA
Other notifiable diseases, per 100,000 pop.:
  Gonorrhea (1995): 143.3, 20th
  Syphilis (1995): 48.5, 6th
  Tuberculosis (1996): 14.2, 4th
Pop. without health insur. (1996): 17.0%, 11th

HOUSEHOLDS BY TYPE

Total households (1996): 6,737,000, 3rd
  Percent change (1990-96): 1.5%, 48th
  Per 1,000 pop. (1996) 370.47, 38th
  Percent of householders 65 yrs. and over (1996): 22.62%, 17th
  Persons per household (1996): 2.65, 13th
Family households: 4,489,312
  Percent of total: 67.62%, 46th
Nonfamily households: 2,150,010
  Percent of total: 32.38%, 6th
Pop. living in group quarters: 545,265
  Percent of pop.: 3.03%, 15th

LIVING QUARTERS

Total housing units: 7,226,891
  Persons per unit: 2.49, 8th
Occupied housing units: 6,639,322
  Percent of total units: 91.87%, 10th
  Persons per unit: 2.62, 12th
  Percent of units with over 1 person per room: 6.50%, 8th
Owner-occupied units: 3,464,436
  Percent of total units: 47.94%, 49th
  Percent of occupied units: 52.18%, 50th
  Persons per unit: 2.86, 5th
  Median value: $131,600, 7th
Renter-occupied units: 3,174,886
  Percent of total units: 43.93%, 2nd
  Percent of occupied units: 47.82%, 2nd
  Persons per unit: 2.38, 22nd
  Median contract rent: $428, 11th
  Rental vacancy rate: 4.9%, 50th
Mobile home, trailer & other as a percent of occupied housing units: 4.56%, 43rd
Persons in emergency shelters for homeless persons: 32,472, 0.180%, 2nd
Persons visible in street locations: 10,732, 0.0597%, 3rd
Nursing home population: 126,175, 0.70%, 27th

CRIME INDEX PER 100,000 (1996)

Total reported: 4,132.3, 37th
  Percent increase: –9.4%, 46th
  Violent: 727.0, 12th
    Percent increase: –13.6%, 47th
    Murder & nonnegligent manslaughter: 7.4, 21st
    Forcible rape: 23.0, 47th
    Aggravated assault: 356.7, 23rd
    Robbery: 340.0, 3rd
  Property: 3,405.3, 41st
    Percent increase: –8.4%, 45th
    Burglary: 713.9, 36th
    Larceny-theft: 2,197.0, 43rd
    Motor vehicle theft: 494.4, 18th

TEACHING AND LEARNING

Pop. 3 and over enrolled in school (1996): 3,866,566, 3rd
  Percent of pop.: 21.26%, 46th
Public elementary & secondary schools (1996-97): 4,149, 3rd
  Total enrollment (1996): 2,825,000, 3rd
    Percent of school age pop.: 87.73%, 45th
    Percent of total pop.: 15.53%, 45th
  Teachers (1996): 185,063, 3rd
    Percent of pop.: 1.02%, 29th
  Pupil/teacher ratio (1995): 15.5, 36th
  Teachers' avg. salary (1996-97): $49,560, 3rd
  Expenditure per capita (1992-93): $1,665.12, 3rd
    Education as % of state govt. expenditures: 28.2%, 47th
  Expenditure per pupil (1994-95): $9,623, 2nd
    Percent increase (1993-94 & 1994-95): 4.88%, 18th
Percent at or above grade level, NAEP tests:
  Reading, grade 4 (1994): 27%, 20th
  Math, grade 4 (1996): 64%, 22nd
  Math, grade 8 (1996): 61%, 20th
Percent of graduates taking SAT (1995): 74%, 3rd
  Mean SAT verbal scores: 419, 42nd
  Mean SAT mathematical scores: 473, 39th
Percent of graduates taking ACT (1997): 16%, 33rd
  Mean ACT scores: 21.9, 7th
Percent of pop. over 25 completing:
  Less than 9th grade: 10.2%, 20th
  High school: 74.8%, 34th
  College degree(s): 23.1%, 11th

Higher education, institutions (1996): 310, 2nd
  Enrollment (1995-96): 1,041,566, 2nd
    Percent increase in enroll. (1990-95): –0.6%, 40th
  White non-Hispanic (1995): 690,917, 2nd
    Percent of enroll.: 66.33%, 45th
  Total minority enroll. (1995): 306,102, 3rd
    Percent of enroll.: 29.39%, 10th
  Black non-Hispanic (1995): 135,813, 2nd
    Percent of enroll.: 13.04%, 14th
  Hispanic (1995): 99,972, 3rd
    Percent of enroll.: 9.60%, 6th
  Asian/Pacific Islander (1995): 66,543, 2nd
    Percent of enroll.: 6.39%, 4th
  American Indian/AK native (1995): 3,774, 9th
    Percent of enroll.: 0.36%, 41st
  Nonresident alien (1995): 44,547, 2nd
    Percent of enroll.: 4.28%, 6th
  Female (1995): 597,428, 2nd
    Percent of enroll.: 57.36%, 12th
  Pub. institutions (1995-96): 89, 3rd
    Enrollment: 588,491, 3rd
      Percent increase in enrollment (1990-95): –4.6%, 44th
    Percent of enroll.: 56.50%, 46th
  Private institutions (1995-96): 221, 1st
    Enrollment: 453,075, 1st
      Percent increase in enrollment (1990-95): 5%, 25th
    Percent of enroll.: 43.50%, 6th
  Tuition (in state), public 4-year institution (1996-97): $3,797, 13th
  Tuition (in state), public 2-year institution (1996-97): $2,519, 4th
  Tuition, private 4-year institution (1996-97): $14,559, 12th
Public library systems (1994): 741, 1st
  Books & serial vol. per capita: 4.2, 8th
  Library visits per capita: 4.9, 10th
  Circulation per capita: 7.1, 21st

LAW ENFORCEMENT AND CORRECTIONS

Police protection and corrections expenditures (1996): $2,730,599,000
  Per capita: $150.16, 9th
Police per 10,000 pop. (1996): 37.15, 2nd
Prisoners (1 year or more) per 100,000 pop. (1996): 383, 19th
  Percent change (1995-96): 1.8%, 42nd
  Percent of inmates that are female: 5.3%, 38th
    Percent change: 3.1%, 40th

Death penalty: yes, by lethal injection
  Under sentence (Jan. 1998): 0
  Executed, 1976-97: 0

RELIGION, NUMBER AND PERCENT OF POPULATION

Agnostic: 82,385—0.60%, 19th
Buddhist: 27,462—0.20%, 11th
Christian: 10,957,263—79.80%, 44th
Hindu: 82,385—0.60%, 1st
Jewish: 947,433—6.90%, 1st
Muslim: 109,847—0.80%, 1st
Unitarian: 41,193—0.30%, 15th
Other: 205,964—1.50%, 18th
None: 878,778—6.40%, 28th
Refused to answer: 398,196—2.90%, 9th

MAKING A LIVING

Personal income per capita (1996): $28,782, 5th
  Percent increase (1995-96): 2.1%, 41st
Disposable personal income per capita (1996): $24,380, 5th
Median income of households (average, 1995-96): $34,707, 27th
Percent of pop. below poverty level (1995-96): 16.6%, 11th

ECONOMY

In civilian labor force (1996): 8,639,000
  Percent of total pop.: 61.6, 50th
  Percent of total pop. 65 years and over: 11.1%, 32nd
  Percent of total female pop.: 53.9%, 50th
Major employer industries (total nonagricultural, 1996):
  Construction: 254,100—3.2%, 47th
  Finance, insurance, & real estate: 721,000—9.1%, 2nd
  Government: 1,382,300—17.5%, 22nd
  Manufacturing: 921,800—11.6%, 38th
  Service: 2,610,400—33.0%, 6th
  Trade: 1,620,600—20.5%, 49th
  Transportation, communications, public utilities: 402,200—5.1%, 22nd
Unemployment rate (1996): 6.2%, 9th
  Male: 6.5%, 7th
  Female: 5.9%, 13th
Total businesses (1995): 467,262, 2nd
New business incorps. (1995): 72,433
  Percent of total businesses: 15.50%, 5th
Business failures (1995): 5,060
  Failures per 10,000 businesses: 108.2, 15th
Agriculture farm income:
  Marketing (1996): $3,043,034,000, 27th
    Average per farm: $84,529, 29th

Leading products (1997): Dairy products, cattle, apples, grapes, strawberries, cherries, pears, onions, potatoes, cabbage, corn, green beans, cauliflower, corn, hay, wheat, oats, dry beans
Average value land & build. per acre (1997): $1,390, 24th
  Percent increase (1996-97): 4%, 35th
Govt. payments (1996): $43,289,000, 31st
  Average per farm: $1,202, 35th
Construction, value of all (1996): $13,893,300,000, 5th
  Per capita: $764, 49th
Manufactures (1995):
  Value added: $89,923,800,000
    Per capita: $4,958, 38th
  Leading products (1997): Books and periodicals, apparel, pharmaceuticals, machinery, instruments, toys and sporting goods, electronic equipment, automotive and aircraft components
Value of nonfuel mineral production (1996): $891,000,000, 15th
Leading mineral products (1996): Stone, cement, salt, sand/gravel, zinc
Energy consumption per person (1994): 213.1 mil. Btu, 51st
Retail sales (1995): $137,771,000,000
  Per household: $95,429, 1st
  Sales increase (1994-95): 2.5%, 41st
Tourism revenues (1995): $24.3 bil.
Foreign exports, in total value (1996): $34,230,000,000, 3rd
  Per capita: $1,882, 16th
Gross state product per person (1994): $31,427, 7th
Public aid recipients (percent of resident pop. 1994): 10.0%, 4th
Medicaid recipients (percent of pop., 1995): 16.7%, 8th
Medicare enrollment per 1,000 pop. (1996): 146, 24th

TRAVEL AND TRANSPORTATION

Motor vehicle registrations (1996): 10,635,602, 4th
  Per 1,000 pop.: 586.49, 50th
Motorcycle registrations (1996): 136,246, 9th
  Per 1,000 pop.: 12.81, 39th
Licensed drivers (1996): 10,473,731, 4th
  Per 1,000 pop.: 575.78, 51st
Public roads & streets (1996)
  Total mileage: 112,347, 13th
    Per 1,000 pop.: 16.18, 44th

Rural mileage: 71,701, 21st
  Per 1,000 pop.: 3.94, 43rd
Urban mileage: 40,646, 4th
  Per 1,000 pop.: 2.24, 48th
Interstate mileage: 1,499, 6th
  Per 1,000 pop.: 0.08, 45th
Speed limit (max. interstate, autos, mi. per hr., 1997): 65
Annual vehicle-mi. of travel per driver (1996): 11,317, 47th
Mean travel time for workers age 16+ who work away from home: 28.6 min., 1st

GOVERNMENT

Percent of voting age pop. registered (1996): 74.92%, 30th
  Percent of voting age pop. voting for president: (1996): 46.5%, 39th
  Percent of voting age pop. voting for U.S. representatives (1996): 40.9%, 42nd
State legislators, total (1997): 211, 4th
  Women members (1997): 39
    Percent of legislature: 18%, 32nd
U.S. Congress, House members (1998): 31
  Change (1988-98): −3
Revenues (1996):
  State govt.: $94,277,491,000
    Per capita: $5,184.35, 3rd
  Parimutuel & amusement taxes & lotteries, revenue per capita (1995): $156.07, 11th
Expenditures (1996):
  State govt.: $82,420,166,000
    Per capita: $4,532.32, 3rd
Debt outstanding (1996): $73,121,852,000
  Per capita: $4,021.00, 7th

LAWS AND REGULATIONS

Legal driving age: 18, 17 if completed driver education course
Marriage age without parental consent: 18
Divorce residence requirement: 1 yr., for qualifications check local statutes

ATTRACTIONS (1997)

Major opera companies: 15
Major symphony orchestras: 11
Major dance companies: 35
Major professional theater companies (nonprofit): 5
Per capita spending by the NEA (1997): $0.95, 6th
State Fair in late August–early September at Syracuse

SPORTS AND COMPETITION

NCAA (Division I) football and basketball teams: Canisius College Golden Griffins, Colgate Univ. Red Raiders, Columbia Univ.-Barnard College Lions, Cornell Univ. Big Red, Fordham Univ. Rams, Hofstra Univ. Flying Dutchmen, Iona College Gaels, Long Island Univ.-Brooklyn Blackbirds (basketball only), Manhattan College Jaspers (basketball only), Marist College Red Foxes, Niagara Univ. Purple Eagles (basketball only), Siena College Saints, St. Bonaventure Univ. Bonnies (basketball only), St. Francis College Terriers (basketball only), St. John's Univ. Red Storm, State Univ. of New York-Buffalo Bulls, Syracuse Univ. Orangemen, U.S. Military Academy Cadets/Black Knights, Wagner College Seahawks
Major league baseball teams: New York Mets (NL East), Shea Stadium; New York Yankees (AL East), Yankee Stadium
Major league soccer teams: NY/NJ Metro-Stars, Giants Stadium (NJ)
NBA basketball teams: New York Knicks, Madison Square Garden
WNBA basketball teams: New York Liberty, Madison Square Garden
NFL football teams: Buffalo Bills (AFC), Rich Stadium; New York Jets (AFC), Giants Stadium (NJ); New York Giants (NFC), Giants Stadium (NJ)
NHL hockey teams: New York Rangers, Madison Square Garden; Buffalo Sabres, Marine Midland Arena; New York Islanders, Nassau Veterans' Memorial Coliseum

WEBSITES CONTAINING FURTHER INFORMATION

Empire State Development Page	http://empire.state.ny.us
I Love NY— New York State Travel and Tourism	http://www.iloveny.state.ny.us
Welcome to New York	http://www.state.ny.us

NORTH CAROLINA

"In my honest and unbiased judgment, the Good Lord will place the Garden of Eden in North Carolina when He restores it to the earth. He will do this because He will have so few changes to make in order to achieve perfection."
Sam Irvin, Jr., local writer

North Carolina was the site of "mankind's single most significant event," as the Wright Brothers' first flight has been called. It also was the site of one of history's great mysteries—the disappearance of the Roanoke Island settlement. North Carolina is the "longest" state in the East, and Grandfather Mountain is said to be the world's oldest. The state's seacoast is unique in the country. Waves and winds continue to build up and change the shape and area of the coast, and the sea level still rises slowly. On land, near Nags Head, winds have built up the largest sand dunes on the Atlantic Coast. Windstorms also sometimes cut new channels or inlets clear through the sandy islands. By contrast, the Appalachian Mountains reach their highest levels in the state. Between the mountains and the sea lies a productive land.

SUPERLATIVES

- World's first heavier-than-air flight.
- First radio SOS, sent off shores of Cape Hatteras.
- First U.S. school of forestry.
- Leader in fine furniture production.
- First in the nation in tobacco cultivation and cigarette production.

MOMENTS IN HISTORY

- During his expedition of 1540, Hernando de Soto and his large party reached the western mountains, found no riches, and departed.
- After receiving rights to the North Carolina area, Sir Walter Raleigh sent Captains M. Philip Amadas and M. Arthur Barlowe to scout the area in 1584.

So They Say

"We found such plenty that I think in all the world the like abundance is not to be found." **Captain M. Arthur Barlowe**

- Raleigh responded by sending seven ships that landed on Roanoke Island in 1585, but the settlement failed.

- Under Governor John White, in 1587 another group restored the Roanoke settlement and added to it. There, Virginia Dare became the first child of English parents to be born in America. White returned to England to bring help to the colony.
- Coming back to America in August 1590, White found one of the great mysteries of the continent. The colony had been abandoned without a trace except for two cryptic carvings. Nothing further was ever learned about the fate of the settlers.

So They Say

"As we entered up the sandy bank, upon a tree...were curiously carved... Roman letters C R O....We passed toward the place where they were left in sundry houses, but we found the houses taken down...one of the chief trees...had the bark taken off, and five foot from the ground in fair capital letters, was graven CROATOAN, without any cross or sign of distress."

John White, on the abandonment of Roanoke

- In 1663, Charles II granted the Carolinas to eight "Lords Proprietors." A year later, Albemarle County was founded.
- Dissatisfied with their lot, in 1677 a group of Albemarle settlers led by John Culpeper took part in the short-lived "Culpeper's Rebellion," the first ever attempted by American colonists.
- The coasts were alive with pirates, and in 1718 the notorious pirate Blackbeard (real name, Edward Teach) was killed in a notable struggle.
- The king bought out the Lords Proprietors in 1729.
- The Regulators, a group protesting the injustice of British rule, were defeated in the Battle of Alamance. Although the movement collapsed in 1771, it has been called by some "the first battle of the Revolution."
- British Lord Cornwallis marched south and occupied Charlotte in 1780. In the Battle

of Kings Mountain, SC in that year, the North Carolina mountain men won a great victory.

• In 1781, Cornwallis returned, and the two forces met again in the terrible Battle of Guilford Court House. Cornwallis claimed victory, but he lost so many men that one of his staff said, "Another such victory would destroy the British army."

So They Say

"I never saw such fighting since God made me. The Americans fought like demons."   **Lord Cornwallis**

• North Carolina became the 12th state on November 21, 1789.

• The state legislature met at the new capital city of Raleigh for the first time in 1794.

• In 1838 the government began to remove the Cherokee to the West, from their ancestral lands. On the "Trail of Tears," 4,000 died, but a few managed to escape into the mountains. Cherokee leader Tsali and all but one of his family were murdered, but finally those who remained bought a reservation, where their descendants continue to live today.

• The August 1861 capture of forts Clark and Hatteras was the first substantial Union victory in the Civil War.

• On May 6, 1865, the last Confederate army in the state laid down its arms. North Carolina troops suffered the greatest losses of all the states.

• After the tragedy of Reconstruction, the economy began to revive.

• The state took the lead in cigarette production in 1884.

• Cotton mills multiplied, and by 1900 the state had achieved leadership in the production of fine furniture.

• The Wright Brothers' plane lifted off the sands of Kitty Hawk on December 17, 1903.

• When Hurricane Hazel struck in 1954, it was one of the most disastrous of such storms to hit the state.

• The year 1995 brought another tropical storm, this time carrying devastating floods.

THAT'S INTERESTING

• The rare shortia plant grows only in the North Carolina mountains and Japan.

• Trader John Lawson revealed that traders looked for the Indians with the smallest mouths. The Indians filled their mouths with as much rum as they could and spit it into a container before giving up a pelt.

• Colonel Benjamin Cleveland was noted not only for his courage in the Battle of Kings Mountain but also for his weight of 450 pounds.

• The women of Edenton opposed the British tax on tea by deciding not to drink it. A teapot-shaped monument pays tribute to this decision.

• Blowing Rock is a unique natural formation. When handkerchiefs are tossed over the ridge, the currents of air waft them back.

• Because of its location and variations in altitude, the state claims that "you can choose whatever climate you want and find it in North Carolina." The warm Gulf Stream almost reaches to the shore, keeping the weather mild year-round. The spicy air of the mountains has many admirers in winter and in summer. And between the two regions there are many variations.

• Indians of the region were fond of sports, and they invented a number of complicated, rough ball games.

• Thousands of schoolchildren contributed their pennies to a campaign to help bring the historic battleship *North Carolina* back to its home state, safely at last to anchor at Wilmington.

NOTABLE NATIVES

Thomas Hart Benton (Hillsboro, 1782-1858), public official. **Braxton Bragg** (Warrenton, 1817-1876), soldier. **Thomas Lanier Clingman** (Huntersville, 1812-1897), soldier/public official. **James Buchanan Duke** (Durham, 1856-1925), industrialist. **William Franklin (Billy) Graham** (Charlotte, 1918-), evangelist. **Jesse Louis Jackson** (Greenville, 1941-) civil rights leader. **Andrew Johnson** (Raleigh, 1808-1875), U.S. president. **Dolley Payne Madison** (Guilford City, 1768-1849), U.S. first lady. **Edward Roscoe Murrow** (Greensboro, 1908-1965), journalist/broadcaster. **James Knox Polk** (Mecklenburg County, 1795-1849), U.S. president. **William Sydney Porter (O. Henry)** (Greensboro, 1862-1910), author. **Matt Whittaker Ransom** (Warren County, 1826-1904), soldier/lawyer/legislator. **Zebulon Baird Vance** (Buncombe

County, 1830-1894), lawyer/public official.
Thomas Clayton Wolfe (Asheville, 1900-1938), author.

GENERAL

Admitted to statehood: November 21, 1789
Origin of name: Charles I gave a large patent to Sir Robert Heath, 1619, to be called Province of Carolana, from *Carolus*, Latin name for Charles. A new patent was granted by Charles II to Earl of Clarendon and others. Divided into North and South Carolina, 1710
Capital: Raleigh
Nickname: Tar Heel State, Old North State
Motto: *Esse Quam Videri*—To be, rather than to seem
Bird: Cardinal
Insect: Honeybee
Fish: Channel bass
Flower: Dogwood
Gem: Emerald
Song: "The Old North State"
Tree: Pine

THE LAND

Area: 52,672 sq. mi., 29th
  Land: 48,718 sq. mi., 29th
  Water: 3,954 sq. mi., 10th
    Inland water: 3,954 sq. mi., 6th
Topography: Coastal plain and tidewater, two-fifths of state, extending to the fall line of the rivers; piedmont plateau, another two-fifths, 200 mi. wide, of gentle to rugged hills; southern Appalachian Mountains contain Blue Ridge and Great Smoky Mountains
Number of counties: 100
Geographic center: Chatham, 10 mi. NW of Sanford
Length: 500 mi.; width: 150 mi.
Highest point: 6,684 ft. (Mount Mitchell), 16th
Lowest point: sea level (Atlantic Ocean), 3rd
Mean elevation: 700 ft., 35th
Coastline: 301 mi., 7th
Shoreline: 3,375 mi., 6th

CLIMATE AND ENVIRONMENT

Temp., highest: 110 deg. on Aug. 21, 1983, at Fayetteville; lowest: –34 deg. on Jan. 21, 1985, at Mount Mitchell
Monthly average: highest: 88.3 deg., 23rd; lowest: 27.3 deg., 39th; spread (high to low): 61.0 deg., 42nd

Hazardous waste sites (1997): 23, 17th
Endangered species: Animals: 15—Indiana bat, Virginia big-eared bat, Saint Francis' satyr butterfly, Appalachian elktoe, American peregrine falcon, Carolina heelsplitter, West Indian manatee, Dwarf wedge mussel, Little-wing pearlymussel, Cape Fear shiner, Spruce-fir moss spider, Tar River spinymussel, Carolina northern flying squirrel, Red wolf, Red-cockaded woodpecker. Plants: 17

MAJOR CITIES
POPULATION, 1996
PERCENTAGE INCREASE, 1990-96

Charlotte, 441,297; 5.2%
Raleigh, 243,835; 15.0%
Greensboro, 195,426; 6.3%
Winston-Salem, 153,541; 1.7%
Durham, 149,799; 7.9%

THE PEOPLE

Population (1997): 7,425,183, 11th
  Percent change (1990-97): 11.95%, 12th
  Percent of total U.S. pop.: 2.77%, 11th
  Per sq. mi: 137.96, 16th
Population (2000 proj.): 7,783,000, 11th
  Percent change (1995-2000): 8.17%, 10th
Percent in metro. area (1996): 66.82%, 33rd
Foreign born: 115,000, 21st
  Percent: 1.7%, 37th
Top three ancestries reported:
  African, 18.52%
  German, 16.75%
  English, 14.88%
White (1992): 5,178,000, 75.75%, 43rd
Black (1992): 1,514,000, 22.15%, 8th
Native American (1992): 84,000, 1.23%, 14th
Asian, Pacific Isle (1992): 61,000, 0.89%, 37th
Hispanic origin (1992): 84,000, 1.23%, 39th
Percent over 5 yrs. speaking language other than English at home: 3.9%, 42nd
Percent males (1996): 48.59%, 34th; percent females: 51.41%, 18th
Percent never married: 25.1%, 30th
Marriages per 1,000 (1996): 8.45, 22nd
Divorces per 1,000 (1996): 4.90, 13th
Median age (1996): 34.7
Under 5 years (1996): 7.12%, 18th
18 years and under (1996): 27.75%, 37th

65 years and over (1996): 12.52%, 31st

Percent increase among the elderly (1995-96): 1.56%, 12th

OF VITAL IMPORTANCE

Live births per 1,000 pop. (1996): 14.4, 20th

Infant mortality rate per 1,000 live births (1995): 9.2, 10th

Rate for whites: 6.7, 18th

Rate for blacks: 15.9, 15th

Births to unmarried women, % of total (1996): 32.0%, 23rd

Births to teenage mothers, % of total (1996): 15.0%, 14th

Abortions (1992): 36,180, 12th

Rate per 1,000 women 14-44 years old: 22.4, 22nd

Percent change (1988-92): −12%, 32nd

Average lifetime (1989-91): 74.48, 40th

Total death rate per 100,000 pop. (1995): 902.2, 27th

Accidents and adverse effects: 41.0, 20th

Alzheimer's disease: 9.2, 19th

Cancer: 206.8, 27th

Cerebrovascular diseases: 72.3, 10th

Chronic liver disease and cirrhosis: 9.4, 21st

Chronic obstructive pulmonary diseases and allied conditions: 39.7, 26th

Diabetes mellitus: 24.3, 19th

Diseases of heart: 269.5, 32nd

HIV infection: 14.1, 14th

Homicide: 9.6, 16th

Injury by firearms: 16.2, 14th

Motor vehicle accidents: 20.7, 17th

Pneumonia and influenza: 33.9, 16th

Suicide: 12.6, 22nd

KEEPING WELL

Active nonfederal physicians per 100,000 pop. (1995): 214, 23rd

Dentists per 100,000 (1991): 42, 46th

Nurses per 100,000 (1995): 820, 25th

Hospitals per 100,000 (1995): 1.65, 37th

Admissions per 1,000 (1995): 115.77, 24th

Hospital beds per 1,000 (1995): 3.15, 29th

Occupancy rate per 100 beds (1995): 68.28, 11th

Average cost per patient per day (1995): $832, 35th

Average cost per stay (1995): $5,631, 30th

AIDS cases (new, 1996): 895; per 100,000: 12.2, 28th

Persons living with HIV infection, not yet AIDS (1996): 6,502

Other notifiable diseases, per 100,000 pop.:

Gonorrhea (1995): 333.0, 3rd

Syphilis (1995): 42.5, 8th

Tuberculosis (1996): 7.6, 18th

Pop. without health insur. (1996): 16.0%, 16th

HOUSEHOLDS BY TYPE

Total households (1996): 2,796,000, 10th

Percent change (1990-96): 11.1%, 14th

Per 1,000 pop. (1996) 381.81, 19th

Percent of householders 65 yrs. and over (1996): 21.07%, 32nd

Persons per household (1996): 2.53, 37th

Family households: 1,812,053

Percent of total: 71.99%, 15th

Nonfamily households: 704,973

Percent of total: 28.01%, 37th

Pop. living in group quarters: 224,470

Percent of pop.: 3.39%, 10th

LIVING QUARTERS

Total housing units: 2,818,193

Persons per unit: 2.35, 35th

Occupied housing units: 2,517,026

Percent of total units: 89.31%, 26th

Persons per unit: 2.51, 30th

Percent of units with over 1 person per room: 2.89%, 28th

Owner-occupied units: 1,711,817

Percent of total units: 60.74%, 20th

Percent of occupied units: 68.01%, 21st

Persons per unit: 2.62, 46th

Median value: $65,800, 28th

Renter-occupied units: 805,209

Percent of total units: 28.57%, 29th

Percent of occupied units: 31.99%, 31st

Persons per unit: 2.39, 18th

Median contract rent: $284, 34th

Rental vacancy rate: 9.2%, 20th

Mobile home, trailer & other as a percent of occupied housing units: 18.04%, 7th

Persons in emergency shelters for homeless persons: 2,637, 0.040%, 36th

Persons visible in street locations: 259, 0.0039%, 34th

Nursing home population: 47,014, 0.71%, 26th

CRIME INDEX PER 100,000 (1996)

Total reported: 5,526.2, 16th

Percent increase: −2.0%, 23rd

Violent: 588.1, 21st
  Percent increase: −9.0%, 34th
  Murder & nonnegligent manslaughter:
    8.5, 14th
  Forcible rape: 31.3, 31st
  Aggravated assault: 384.5, 19th
  Robbery: 163.9, 22nd
Property: 4,938.1, 16th
  Percent increase: −1.1%, 23rd
  Burglary: 1,345.6, 4th
  Larceny-theft: 3,257.0, 19th
  Motor vehicle theft: 335.5, 37th

TEACHING AND LEARNING

Pop. 3 and over enrolled in school (1996):
  1,571,992, 10th
Percent of pop.: 21.47%, 40th
Public elementary & secondary schools (1996-
  97): 1,985, 14th
  Total enrollment (1996): 1,199,962, 11th
    Percent of school age pop.: 90.84%, 30th
    Percent of total pop.: 16.39%, 40th
  Teachers (1996): 73,839, 12th
    Percent of pop.: 1.01%, 31st
  Pupil/teacher ratio (1995): 16.2, 29th
  Teachers' avg. salary (1996-97): $31,225, 43rd
  Expenditure per capita (1992-93):
    $1,235.90, 34th
    Education as % of state govt. expendi-
      tures: 37.1%, 16th
  Expenditure per pupil (1994-95): $5,077,
    37th
    Percent increase (1993-94 & 1994-95):
      3.74%, 27th
Percent at or above grade level, NAEP tests:
  Reading, grade 4 (1994): 30%, 16th
  Math, grade 4 (1996): 64%, 22nd
  Math, grade 8 (1996): 56%, 27th
Percent of graduates taking SAT (1995): 60%,
  14th
  Mean SAT verbal scores: 411, 48th
  Mean SAT mathematical scores: 454, 48th
Percent of graduates taking ACT (1997):
  11%, 38th
  Mean ACT scores: 19.3, 48th
Percent of pop. over 25 completing:
  Less than 9th grade: 12.7%, 12th
  High school: 70.0%, 43rd
  College degree(s): 17.4%, 38th
Higher education, institutions (1996): 121,
  7th
  Enrollment (1995-96): 372,030, 10th
    Percent increase in enroll. (1990-95):
      5.6%, 21st

White non-Hispanic (1995): 277,844,
  10th
  Percent of enroll.: 74.68%, 34th
Total minority enroll. (1995): 88,486, 9th
  Percent of enroll.: 23.78%, 17th
Black non-Hispanic (1995): 73,185, 7th
  Percent of enroll.: 19.67%, 8th
Hispanic (1995): 4,438, 26th
  Percent of enroll.: 1.19%, 40th
Asian/Pacific Islander (1995): 7,074, 20th
  Percent of enroll.: 1.90%, 35th
American Indian/AK native (1995): 3,789,
  8th
  Percent of enroll.: 1.02%, 19th
Nonresident alien (1995): 5,700, 27th
  Percent of enroll.: 1.53%, 49th
Female (1995): 212,026, 10th
  Percent of enroll.: 56.99%, 15th
Pub. institutions (1995-96): 74, 4th
  Enrollment: 303,099, 9th
    Percent increase in enrollment (1990-
      95): 6.2%, 18th
    Percent of enroll.: 81.47%, 30th
Private institutions (1995-96): 47, 14th
  Enrollment: 68,931, 11th
    Percent increase in enrollment (1990-
      95): 3.3%, 30th
    Percent of enroll.: 18.53%, 22nd
Tuition (in state), public 4-year institution
  (1996-97): $1,841, 48th
Tuition (in state), public 2-year institution
  (1996-97): $581, 49th
Tuition, private 4-year institution (1996-
  97): $11,682, 24th
Public library systems (1994): 74, 35th
  Books & serial vol. per capita: 2.0, 39th
  Library visits per capita: 3.3, 29th
  Circulation per capita: 5.9, 32nd

LAW ENFORCEMENT AND
CORRECTIONS

Police protection and corrections expenditures
  (1996): $1,068,159,000
Per capita: $145.87, 11th
Police per 10,000 pop. (1996): 23.30, 20th
Prisoners (1 year or more) per 100,000 pop.
  (1996): 379, 20th
  Percent change (1995-96): 0.1%, 45th
  Percent of inmates that are female: 6.1%,
    27th
    Percent change: 6.7%, 31st
Death penalty: yes, by lethal gas, lethal injec-
  tion
  Under sentence (Jan. 1998): 197, 5th

Executed, 1976-97: 8, 13th
Executed in 1997: 0

RELIGION, NUMBER AND PERCENT OF POPULATION

Agnostic: 15,068—0.30%, 37th
Buddhist: 5,023—0.10%, 17th
Christian: 4,550,374—90.60%, 8th
Hindu: NA
Jewish: 25,112—0.50%, 27th
Muslim: 10,045—0.20%, 13th
Unitarian: 5,023—0.10%, 31st
Other: 85,382—1.70%, 14th
None: 241,079—4.80%, 42nd
Refused to answer: 85,382—1.70%, 35th

MAKING A LIVING

Personal income per capita (1996): $22,010, 33rd
Percent increase (1995-96): 3.9%, 17th
Disposable personal income per capita (1996): $19,110, 35th
Median income of households (average, 1995-96): $34,262, 28th
Percent of pop. below poverty level (1995-96): 12.4%, 21st

ECONOMY

In civilian labor force (1996): 3,796,000
Percent of total pop.: 68.5%, 23rd
Percent of total pop. 65 years and over: 13.6%, 15th
Percent of total female pop.: 61.5%, 23rd
Major employer industries (total nonagricultural, 1996):
Construction: 188,500—5.3%, 13th
Finance, insurance, & real estate: 153,500—4.3%, 45th
Government: 561,400—15.8%, 34th
Manufacturing: 846,800—23.9%, 2nd
Service: 817,000—23.0%, 46th
Trade: 811,000—22.8%, 40th
Transportation, communications, public utilities: 167,900—4.7%, 35th
Unemployment rate (1996): 4.3%, 39th
Male: 4.3%, 39th
Female: 4.5%, 38th
Total businesses (1995): 181,972, 10th
New business incorps. (1995): 16,021
Percent of total businesses: 8.80%, 27th
Business failures (1995): 962
Failures per 10,000 businesses: 52.9, 45th
Agriculture farm income:
Marketing (1996): $7,831,309,000, 8th
Average per farm: $135,023, 10th

Leading products (1997): Tobacco, broilers, hogs, turkeys, cotton, soybeans, corn, grains, wheat, peanuts, sweet potatoes
Average value land & build. per acre (1997): $2,050, 13th
Percent increase (1996-97): 4%, 35th
Govt. payments (1996): $75,702,000, 25th
Average per farm: $1,305, 33rd
Construction, value of all (1996): $12,433,627,000, 7th
Per capita: $1,698, 6th
Manufactures (1995):
Value added: $73,919,400,000
Per capita: $10,274, 2nd
Leading products (1997): Textiles, industrial machinery and equipment, tobacco products, electric and electronic equipment, chemical, furniture, food products, apparel
Value of nonfuel mineral production (1996): $731,000,000, 18th
Leading mineral products (1996): Stone, phosphate rock, lithium minerals, sand/gravel
Energy consumption per person (1994): 313.3 mil. Btu, 35th
Retail sales (1995): $65,781,000,000
Per household: $23,698, 35th
Sales increase (1994-95): 9.3%, 5th
Tourism revenues (1994): $8 bil.
Foreign exports, in total value (1996): $15,734,000,000, 10th
Per capita: $2,149, 12th
Gross state product per person (1994): $25,675, 21st
Public aid recipients (percent of resident pop. 1994): 7.2%, 18th
Medicaid recipients (percent of pop., 1995): 15.1%, 12th
Medicare enrollment per 1,000 pop. (1996): 144, 25th

TRAVEL AND TRANSPORTATION

Motor vehicle registrations (1996): 5,759,234, 11th
Per 1,000 pop.: 787.96, 29th
Motorcycle registrations (1996): 67,855, 20th
Per 1,000 pop.: 11.78, 42nd
Licensed drivers (1996): 5,028,421, 10th
Per 1,000 pop.: 698.17, 19th
Public roads & streets (1996)
Total mileage: 97,509, 16th
Per 1,000 pop.: 113.32, 33rd
Rural mileage: 75,077, 17th
Per 1,000 pop.: 10.25, 34th

Urban mileage: 22,432, 12th
    Per 1,000 pop.: 3.06, 27th
    Interstate mileage: 981, 18th
    Per 1,000 pop.: 0.13, 39th
Speed limit (max. interstate, autos, mi. per
    hr., 1997): 70
Annual vehicle-mi. of travel per driver (1996):
    15,217, 17th
Mean travel time for workers age 16+ who
    work away from home: 19.8 min.,
    31st

GOVERNMENT

Percent of voting age pop. registered (1996):
    78.24%, 23rd
    Percent of voting age pop. voting for presi-
        dent: (1996): 45.8%, 41st
    Percent of voting age pop. voting for U.S.
        representatives (1996): 45.7%, 32nd
State legislators, total (1997): 170, 15th
    Women members (1997): 29
    Percent of legislature: 17%, 36th
U.S. Congress, House members (1998): 12
    Change (1988-98): 1
Revenues (1996):
    State govt.: $23,387,492,000
    Per capita: $3,193.70, 34th
    Parimutuel & amusement taxes & lotter-
        ies, revenue per capita (1995): NA
Expenditures (1996):
    State govt.: $21,220,754,000
    Per capita: $2,897.82, 33rd
Debt outstanding (1996): $4,513,348,000
    Per capita: $616.33, 47th

LAWS AND REGULATIONS

Legal driving age: 18, 16 if completed driver
    education course

Marriage age without parental consent: 18
Divorce residence requirement: 6 mo.

ATTRACTIONS (1997)

Major opera companies: 1
Major symphony orchestras: 3
Major dance companies: 2
Per capita spending by the NEA (1997):
    $0.16, 43rd
State Fair in mid-October at Raleigh

SPORTS AND COMPETITION

NCAA (Division I) football and basketball
    teams: Appalachian State Univ. Moun-
    taineers, Campbell Univ. Fighting Camels
    (basketball only), Davidson College
    Wildcats, Duke Univ. Blue Devils, East
    Carolina Univ. Pirates, North Carolina
    A&T State Univ. Aggies, North Carolina
    State Univ. Wolfpack, Univ. of North
    Carolina-Asheville Bulldogs (basketball
    only), Univ. of North Carolina-Chapel
    Hill Tar Heels, Univ. of North Carolina-
    Charlotte 49ers (basketball only), Univ. of
    North Carolina-Greensboro Spartans
    (basketball only), Univ. of North Caro-
    lina-Wilmington Seahawks (basketball
    only), Wake Forest Univ. Demon Dea-
    cons, Western Carolina Univ. Cata-
    mounts
NBA basketball teams: Charlotte Hornets,
    Charlotte Coliseum
WNBA basketball teams: Charlotte Sting,
    Charlotte Coliseum
NFL football teams: Carolina Panthers (NFC),
    Ericsson Stadium
NHL hockey teams: Carolina Hurricanes,
    Greensboro Coliseum

WEBSITES CONTAINING FURTHER INFORMATION

State of North Carolina	http://www.state.nc.us
Welcome NCNetWorks	http://www.webpress.net/ncnetworks

NORTH DAKOTA

North Dakota is a land where the great plains have been transformed into lake country by enormous modern reservoirs. Ancient lakes figured in the state's present by depositing the rich soil that brings agricultural abundance. North Dakota is the state where Theodore Roosevelt developed his dynamic image, and the nation dedicated its only National Memorial Park on a portion of the land he once owned. The state is small in population but rich in natural resources (for example, it has the world's greatest reserves of lignite) and in its wealth of tradition.

SUPERLATIVES

- Novel skyscraper capitol.
- "Capital" of the lignite industry.
- First in spring wheat, rye, and flax.

MOMENTS IN HISTORY

- Pierre Gaultier de Varennes, Sieur de La Vérendrye, and his two sons arrived in what is now North Dakota in 1738 and reached the Mandan Indian village near present-day Menoken.
- Braving an unusually bitter winter, in 1797 the party of British scientist David Thompson visited the Mandan towns on the Missouri River.
- After the Louisiana Purchase, the first true picture of the region came with the detailed reports of the Lewis and Clark expedition. Meriwether Lewis and William Clark spent the winter of 1804 at what they called Fort Mandan, near the Mandan and Arikara villages of present Washburn. They lived in log cabins chinked with mud.
- As they left the winter camp on April 7, 1805, Lewis and Clark sent back to civilization a vast amount of information they had gathered to that point. This included numbers of new and unusual plants and animals and the most complete information on the Indian tribes yet noted.
- On their way back in 1806, Lewis and Clark stopped again to visit their Indian friends at Fort Mandan. The expedition was enormously important in keeping peace with the western Indians for many years.

So They Say

"I could but esteem this moment of my departure as among the most happy of my life. The party are in excellent health and spirits, zealously attached to the enterprise and anxious to proceed, not a whisper or murmur of discontent to be heard among them, but all act in unison, and with the most perfect harmony."
Meriwether Lewis

- Following the Lewis and Clark expedition, fur trading posts were opened, and in 1812, William Douglas established a Scottish settlement near present-day Pembina.
- Explorer David Thompson took part in the 1818 survey of the U.S.-Canadian border.
- In 1828 the American Fur Company began Fort Union on the North Dakota side of the Missouri River, and for about 40 years it remained the most important post in a vast region.
- Begun in 1857, Fort Abercrombie was the first federal stronghold located in what is now North Dakota.
- Dakota Territory was organized in 1861.
- Indian warfare went on over a long period, but by 1881 most of the Sioux people had turned to reservation life.
- Theodore Roosevelt arrived in North Dakota in 1883 and became a successful and popular rancher.
- One of the worst of many prairie fires swept the area on September 25, 1888.

So They Say

"...For at least 40 miles in width the fire burned off every vestige of grass unprotected by breaks. One could hardly recognize the charred land the next day. Thousands of bushels of grain were burned and many men lost all they had, grain, buildings and stock."
Newspaper account of the 1888 prairie fires

- Both Dakotas became states on November 2, 1889.
- After "Honest John" Burke was elected

governor in 1906, child labor laws and other modern laws were enacted.

- In 1919 the state began operating its own businesses, banks, and other formerly private enterprises—an action unique among the states.
- Discovery of oil in 1951 brought a new surge in the state's economy.
- Completion of vast artificial lakes and irrigation systems in the 1970s further enhanced the economy.
- By 1981, North Dakota had outstripped Kansas as the leading wheat state.
- In 1997 the Children's Rights Council chose North Dakota as the best place to raise a family.
- Severe flooding hit North Dakota in 1997. All 50,000 residents of Grand Forks were forced to evacuate.

THAT'S INTERESTING

- When he signed the statehood bills for the two Dakotas on the same day, President Benjamin Harrison would not reveal which one he signed first. Consequently, no one knows whether North Dakota is technically the 39th or the 40th state.
- Because it lies equally distant—about 1,500 miles from the Atlantic Ocean, the Pacific Ocean, the Arctic Ocean, and the Gulf of Mexico—geographers say that North Dakota is located in almost the exact center of the North American continent.
- North Dakota's lignite reserves are thought to be the largest single concentration of solid fuel in the world, enough to supply all of America's fuel needs for many generations to come.
- Inventor D. H. Houston named his new film Kodak, a variation of Dakota that became known around the world.
- A Portal golf course is probably the only place where a golfer might make a tee shot in the United States and end up in a hole in Canada.

NORTH DAKOTA NOTABLES

Maxwell Anderson (Atlantic, PA, 1888-1959), playwright. **George Catlin** (Wilkes-Barre, PA, 1796-1872), Indian expert/artist. **John Bernard Flannagan** (Fargo, 1895-1942), sculptor. **Roger Eugene Maris** (Hibbing, MN, 1934-1985), baseball player. **Lawrence Welk** (Strasburg, 1903-1992), entertainer.

GENERAL

Admitted to statehood: November 2, 1889
Origin of name: *Dakota* is Sioux for "friend" or "ally"
Capital: Bismarck
Nickname: Peach Garden State, Sioux State
Motto: Liberty and union, now and forever, one and inseparable
Bird: Western meadowlark
Fish: Northern pike
Flower: Wild prairie rose
Stone: Teredo petrified wood
Song: "North Dakota Hymn"
Tree: American elm

THE LAND

Area: 70,704 sq. mi., 18th
  Land: 68,994 sq. mi., 17th
  Water: 1,710 sq. mi., 18th
  Inland water: 1,710 sq. mi., 12th
Topography: Central lowland in the E comprises the flat Red River Valley and the rolling drift prairie; Missouri plateau of the Great Plains on the W
Number of counties: 53
Geographic center: Sheridan, 5 mi. SW of McClusky
Length: 340 mi.; width: 211 mi.
Highest point: 3,506 ft. (White Butte), 30th
Lowest point: 750 ft. (Red River), 45th
Mean elevation: 1,900 ft., 16th

CLIMATE AND ENVIRONMENT

Temp., highest: 121 deg. on July 6, 1936, at Steele; lowest: –60 deg. on Feb. 15, 1936, at Parshall
Monthly average: highest: 84.4 deg., 40th; lowest: –5.1 deg., 2nd; spread (high to low): 89.5 deg., 2nd
Hazardous waste sites (1997): 0, 50th
Endangered species: Animals: 7—Whooping crane, Eskimo curlew, American peregrine falcon, Black-footed ferret, Pallid sturgeon, Least tern, Gray wolf. Plants: 0

MAJOR CITIES
POPULATION, 1996
PERCENTAGE INCREASE, 1990-96

Fargo, 83,778; 13.1%
Bismarck, 53,514; 8.6%
Grand Forks, 50,675; 2.5%
Minot, 35,926; 4.0%
Dickinson, 16,094; 0.0%

THE PEOPLE

Population (1997): 640,883, 47th
  Percent change (1990-97): 0.33%, 48th
  Percent of total U.S. pop.: 0.24%, 47th
  Per sq. mi: 9.06, 48th
Population (2000 proj.): 643,000, 48th
  Percent change (1990-2000): 0.7%, 47th
Percent in metro. area (1996): 42.72%, 42nd
Foreign born: 9,000, 49th
  Percent: 1.5%, 43rd
Top three ancestries reported:
  German, 50.86%
  Norwegian, 29.58%
  Irish, 8.45%
White (1992): 599,000, 94.48%, 10th
Black (1992): 4,000, 0.63%, 45th
Native American (1992): 27,000, 4.26%, 7th
Asian, Pacific Isle (1992): 4,000, 0.63%, 44th
Hispanic origin (1992): 5,000, 0.79%, 44th
Percent over 5 yrs. speaking language other
    than English at home: 7.9%, 22nd
Percent males (1996): 49.94%, 7th; percent
    females: 50.06%, 45th
Percent never married: 25.9%, 23rd
Marriages per 1,000 (1996): 7.81, 34th
Divorces per 1,000 (1996): 3.48, 33rd
Median age (1996): 34.9
Under 5 years (1996): 6.46%, 42nd
18 years and under (1996): 29.38%, 17th
65 years and over (1996): 14.51%, 6th
Percent increase among the elderly (1995-96):
    0.08%, 49th

OF VITAL IMPORTANCE

Live births per 1,000 pop. (1996): 13.0, 42nd
Infant mortality rate per 1,000 live births
    (1995): 7.2, 31st
  Rate for whites: 6.7, 18th
  Rate for blacks: NA
Births to unmarried women, % of total
    (1996): 25.2%, 45th
Births to teenage mothers, % of total (1996):
    9.6%, 44th
Abortions (1992): 1,490, 49th
  Rate per 1,000 women 14-44 years old:
    10.7, 46th
  Percent change (1988-92): −28%, 50th
Average lifetime (1989-91): 77.62, 4th
Total death rate per 100,000 pop. (1995):
    931.6, 20th
  Accidents and adverse effects: 32.7, 40th
  Alzheimer's disease: 11.5, 7th
  Cancer: 214.4, 22nd
  Cerebrovascular diseases: 77.3, 5th

Chronic liver disease and cirrhosis: 6.4,
    45th
Chronic obstructive pulmonary diseases and
    allied conditions: 37.9, 33rd
Diabetes mellitus: 24.3, 19th
Diseases of heart: 304.3, 18th
HIV infection: NA
Homicide: NA
Injury by firearms: 10.8, 35th
Motor vehicle accidents: 13.1, 41st
Pneumonia and influenza: 32.1, 24th
Suicide: 14.7, 14th

KEEPING WELL

Active nonfederal physicians per 100,000 pop.
    (1995): 204, 28th
Dentists per 100,000 (1991): 47, 38th
Nurses per 100,000 (1995): 1,090, 5th
Hospitals per 100,000 (1995): 6.71, 2nd
  Admissions per 1,000 (1995): 138.85, 8th
  Hospital beds per 1,000 (1995): 6.55,
    2nd
  Occupancy rate per 100 beds (1995):
    64.29, 18th
  Average cost per patient per day (1995):
    $521, 49th
  Average cost per stay (1995): $5,589, 35th
AIDS cases (new, 1996): 12; per 100,000:
    1.9, 49th
Persons living with HIV infection, not yet
    AIDS (1996): 56
Other notifiable diseases, per 100,000 pop.:
  Gonorrhea (1995): 5.9, 50th
  Syphilis (1995): 0.0, 49th
  Tuberculosis (1996): 1.2, 50th
Pop. without health insur. (1996): 9.8%, 45th

HOUSEHOLDS BY TYPE

Total households (1996): 247,000, 47th
  Percent change (1990-96): 2.4%, 46th
  Per 1,000 pop. (1996) 383.54, 13th
  Percent of householders 65 yrs. and over
    (1996): 24.29%, 8th
  Persons per household (1996): 2.51, 41st
Family households: 166,270
  Percent of total: 69.03%, 37th
Nonfamily households: 74,608
  Percent of total: 30.97%, 15th
Pop. living in group quarters: 24,234
  Percent of pop.: 3.79%, 4th

LIVING QUARTERS

Total housing units: 276,340
  Persons per unit: 2.31, 39th

Occupied housing units: 240,878
  Percent of total units: 87.17%, 37th
  Persons per unit: 2.46, 43rd
  Percent of units with over 1 person per room: 1.98%, 43rd
Owner-occupied units: 157,950
  Percent of total units: 57.16%, 34th
  Percent of occupied units: 65.57%, 35th
  Persons per unit: 2.74, 22nd
  Median value: $50,800, 43rd
Renter-occupied units: 82,928
  Percent of total units: 30.01%, 22nd
  Percent of occupied units: 34.43%, 18th
  Persons per unit: 2.18, 49th
  Median contract rent: $266, 40th
  Rental vacancy rate: 9.0%, 22nd
Mobile home, trailer & other as a percent of occupied housing units: 12.30%, 23rd
Persons in emergency shelters for homeless persons: 279, 0.044%, 29th
Persons visible in street locations: 30, 0.0047%, 30th
Nursing home population: 8,159, 1.28%, 3rd

CRIME INDEX PER 100,000 (1996)

Total reported: 2,669.1, 50th
  Percent increase: −6.9%, 40th
  Violent: 84.0, 51st
    Percent increase: −3.1%, 18th
    Murder & nonnegligent manslaughter: 2.2, 46th
    Forcible rape: 24.1, 45th
    Aggravated assault: 46.7, 51st
    Robbery: 11.0, 51st
  Property: 2,585.1, 50th
    Percent increase: −7.0%, 40th
    Burglary: 309.2, 51st
    Larceny-theft: 2,085.9, 46th
    Motor vehicle theft: 190.1, 44th

TEACHING AND LEARNING

Pop. 3 and over enrolled in school (1996): 158,826, 46th
Percent of pop.: 24.66%, 10th
Public elementary & secondary schools (1996-97): 613, 42nd
  Total enrollment (1996): 118,427, 47th
    Percent of school age pop.: 93.25%, 20th
    Percent of total pop.: 18.39%, 11th
  Teachers (1996): 7,706, 47th
    Percent of pop.: 1.20%, 8th
  Pupil/teacher ratio (1995): 15.9, 31st
  Teachers' avg. salary (1996-97): $27,711, 50th

Expenditure per capita (1992-93): $1,516.13, 11th
  Education as % of state govt. expenditures: 37.7%, 13th
Expenditure per pupil (1994-95): $4,775, 42nd
  Percent increase (1993-94 & 1994-95): 2.16%, 41st
Percent at or above grade level, NAEP tests:
  Reading, grade 4 (1994): 38%, 2nd
  Math, grade 4 (1996): 75%, 2nd
  Math, grade 8 (1996): 77%, 2nd
Percent of graduates taking SAT (1995): 5%, 47th
  Mean SAT verbal scores: 515, 2nd
  Mean SAT mathematical scores: 592, 1st
Percent of graduates taking ACT (1997): 78%, 4th
  Mean ACT scores: 21.4, 19th
Percent of pop. over 25 completing:
  Less than 9th grade: 15.0%, 6th
  High school: 76.7%, 27th
  College degree(s): 18.1%, 31st
Higher education, institutions (1996): 21, 41st
  Enrollment (1995-96): 40,399, 47th
    Percent increase in enroll. (1990-95): 6.7%, 19th
  White non-Hispanic (1995): 35,871, 45th
    Percent of enroll.: 88.79%, 12th
  Total minority enroll. (1995): 2,968, 48th
    Percent of enroll.: 7.35%, 43rd
  Black non-Hispanic (1995): 343, 48th
    Percent of enroll.: 0.85%, 46th
  Hispanic (1995): 247, 50th
    Percent of enroll.: 0.61%, 48th
  Asian/Pacific Islander (1995): 302, 49th
    Percent of enroll.: 0.75%, 50th
  American Indian/AK native (1995): 2,076, 20th
    Percent of enroll.: 5.14%, 6th
  Nonresident alien (1995): 1,560, 42nd
    Percent of enroll.: 3.86%, 8th
  Female (1995): 20,457, 48th
    Percent of enroll.: 50.64%, 50th
  Pub. institutions (1995-96): 15, 38th
    Enrollment: 36,810, 44th
      Percent increase in enrollment (1990-95): 6.1%, 19th
    Percent of enroll.: 91.12%, 6th
  Private institutions (1995-96): 6, 46th
    Enrollment: 3,589, 48th
      Percent increase in enrollment (1990-95): 12.6%, 15th
    Percent of enroll.: 8.88%, 46th

Tuition (in state), public 4-year institution (1996-97): $2,381, 30th

Tuition (in state), public 2-year institution (1996-97): $1,783, 16th

Tuition, private 4-year institution (1996-97): $7,419, 46th

Public library systems (1994): 78, 34th

Books & serial vol. per capita: 3.5, 17th

Library visits per capita: 5.4, 3rd

Circulation per capita: 7.3, 20th

LAW ENFORCEMENT AND CORRECTIONS

Police protection and corrections expenditures (1996): $23,440,000

Per capita: $36.40, 50th

Police per 10,000 pop. (1996): 16.16, 50th

Prisoners (1 year or more) per 100,000 pop. (1996): 101, 51st

Percent change (1995-96): 19.5%, 1st

Percent of inmates that are female: 6.2%, 25th

Percent change: 55.2%, 1st

Death penalty: no

RELIGION, NUMBER AND PERCENT OF POPULATION

Agnostic: 1,854—0.40%, 34th

Buddhist: NA

Christian: 437,927—94.50%, 2nd

Hindu: NA

Jewish: 1,854—0.40%, 31st

Muslim: NA

Unitarian: NA

Other: 2,781—0.60%, 46th

None: 7,415—1.60%, 49th

Refused to answer: 11,585—2.50%, 18th

MAKING A LIVING

Personal income per capita (1996): $20,710, 39th

Percent increase (1995-96): 9.0%, 1st

Disposable personal income per capita (1996): $18,351, 37th

Median income of households (average, 1995-96): $30,709, 40th

Percent of pop. below poverty level (1995-96): 11.5%, 28th

ECONOMY

In civilian labor force (1996): 343,000

Percent of total pop.: 72.0%, 8th

Percent of total pop. 65 years and over: 14.5%, 9th

Percent of total female pop.: 66.4%, 8th

Major employer industries (total nonagricultural, 1996):

Construction: 15,000—4.9%, 19th

Finance, insurance, & real estate: 14,400—4.7%, 34th

Government: 70,700—22.9%, 5th

Manufacturing: 21,600—7.0%, 44th

Service: 84,600—27.4%, 24th

Trade: 80,200—26.0%, 2nd

Transportation, communications, public utilities: 18,400—6.0%, 8th

Unemployment rate (1996): 3.1%, 50th

Male: 3.1%, 50th

Female: 3.0%, 51st

Total businesses (1995): 20,269, 48th

New business incorps. (1995): 1,021

Percent of total businesses: 5.04%, 51st

Business failures (1995): 98

Failures per 10,000 businesses: 48.3, 47th

Agriculture farm income:

Marketing (1996): $3,532,393,000, 23rd

Average per farm: $113,948, 19th

Leading products (1997): Wheat, cattle, barley, sugar beets, flaxseed, oats, potatoes, beans, honey, soybeans, sunflowers, hay

Average value land & build. per acre (1997): $410, 43rd

Percent increase (1996-97): 7%, 14th

Govt. payments (1996): $351,520,000, 7th

Average per farm: $11,339, 1st

Construction, value of all (1996): $656,169,000, 49th

Per capita: $1,020, 41st

Manufactures (1995):

Value added: $1,559,300,000

Per capita: $2,431, 46th

Leading products (1997): Farm equipment, processed foods, fabricated metals, electronics

Value of nonfuel mineral production (1996): $30,300,000, 49th

Leading mineral products (1996): Petroleum, coal, natural gas, sand/gravel, lime, clays, gemstones

Energy consumption per person (1994): 538.9 mil. Btu, 5th

Retail sales (1995): $6,381,000,000

Per household: $25,897, 10th

Sales increase (1994-95): 3.2%, 34th

Tourism revenues (1992): $826 mil.

Foreign exports, in total value (1996): $707,000,000, 46th
  Per capita: $1,099, 38th
Gross state product per person (1994): $21,151, 44th
Public aid recipients (percent of resident pop. 1994): 3.9%, 47th
Medicaid recipients (percent of pop., 1995): 9.6%, 43rd
Medicare enrollment per 1,000 pop. (1996): 160, 10th

TRAVEL AND TRANSPORTATION

Motor vehicle registrations (1996): 679,047, 46th
  Per 1,000 pop.: 1,056.66, 3rd
Motorcycle registrations (1996): 16,394, 46th
  Per 1,000 pop.: 24.14, 14th
Licensed drivers (1996): 448,781, 48th
  Per 1,000 pop.: 699.57, 18th
Public roads & streets (1996)
  Total mileage: 86,808, 20th
      Per 1,000 pop.: 1134.89, 1st
    Rural mileage: 84,985, 14th
      Per 1,000 pop.: 132.06, 1st
    Urban mileage: 1,823, 48th
      Per 1,000 pop.: 2.83, 36th
    Interstate mileage: 571, 36th
      Per 1,000 pop.: 0.89, 5th
Speed limit (max. interstate, autos, mi. per hr., 1997): 70
Annual vehicle-mi. of travel per driver (1996): 15,006, 20th
Mean travel time for workers age 16+ who work away from home: 13.0 min., 51st

GOVERNMENT

Percent of voting age pop. registered (1996): NA
  Percent of voting age pop. voting for president: (1996): 56.3%, 16th
  Percent of voting age pop. voting for U.S. representatives (1996): 55.6%, 12th
State legislators, total (1997): 147, 25th
  Women members (1997): 25
    Percent of legislature: 17%, 37th
U.S. Congress, House members (1998): 1
  Change (1988-98): 0
Revenues (1996):
  State govt.: $2,568,635,000
    Per capita: $3,988.56, 15th
    Parimutuel & amusement taxes & lotteries, revenue per capita (1995): $17.15, 39th
Expenditures (1996):
  State govt.: $2,063,612,000
    Per capita: $3,204.37, 24th
Debt outstanding (1996): $819,003,000
  Per capita: $1,271.74, 28th

LAWS AND REGULATIONS

Legal driving age: 16
Marriage age without parental consent: 18
Divorce residence requirement: 6 mo.

ATTRACTIONS (1997)

Per capita spending by the NEA (1997): $0.78, 8th
State Fair in third week in July at Minot

SPORTS AND COMPETITION

NCAA (Division II) football and basketball teams: North Dakota State Univ. Bison, Univ. of North Dakota (Fighting) Sioux

WEBSITES CONTAINING FURTHER INFORMATION

State of North Dakota	http://www.state.nd.us
North Dakota Tourism	http://www.ndtourism.com

OHIO

"Ohio is the farthest west of the East and the farthest north of the South." *Attributed to author Louis Bromfield*

Without a historic agreement, Cleveland would have been in Connecticut. In another twist of history, Ohio did not enter the Union officially until 1953. Professional baseball got its start in Ohio. The hot dog was invented in the state, as well as floating soap (Ivory). On a more serious note, Ohio has long been one of the leaders in industry and cultural activities and was the birthplace of seven U.S. presidents, along with a near record number of other figures of world acclaim. Ohio has more than 50 accredited colleges and universities; Oberlin College, established in 1833, was the first institution of higher education in the United States to enroll both men and women. In 1995, Cleveland celebrated the opening of the Rock and Roll Hall of Fame.

SUPERLATIVES

- First professional baseball team—the Cincinnati Red Stockings.
- First in clay products manufacture.
- Pioneer leader in rubber products.
- World leader in machine tools.

MOMENTS IN HISTORY

- The first known European explorer in the Ohio region was the French emissary Robert Cavalier, Sieur de La Salle, in 1669-70. He claimed the entire vast region west of the Alleghenies for France.
- In 1749, to demonstrate his "discovery," the Sieur de Bienville planted a series of six lead plates along the banks of the Ohio River.
- On October 31, 1750, Ohio Company representative George Gist and his dog spent Christmas at the trading post of George Croghan. Gist and his faithful dog explored much of present-day Ohio, winning the Indians to the British cause.
- In 1754, George Washington was sent by the British to defend the Ohio country. He started to build a defense called Fort Necessity before the French attacked in the French and Indian War. The French attack came before the roof had been finished, and Washington was forced to give up—perhaps the only time this great patriot ever surrendered.

- In 1763 the French gave up all claims, and British claims were confirmed.
- Indian uprisings under chiefs including Pontiac and Cornstalk occupied British attention during most of the period before the Revolution.
- The Revolution brought no great battles to Ohio country. Most of the British cause was carried on by Indian raids. At war's end the new nation formally claimed the western lands after the Treaty of Paris in 1783.
- The claims to Ohio by Connecticut and Virginia were settled by agreements for Ohio to include the Western Reserve and the Virginia Military Survey.
- The Northwest Ordinance of 1787 established government in that whole region.
- In 1788 the first of many thousands of settlers floated down the Ohio River and founded Marietta.

- In 12 months in 1788-89, 10,000 settlers reached Ohio, most of them floating down the Ohio on flatboats, sometimes attacked by Indians or pirates.
- Indian troubles increased until, with the Treaty of Greenville in 1795, the Indians gave up much of their Ohio lands.
- In 1803, Ohio became the first state west of the Alleghenies.

• Many critical battles with British and Indian forces occurred in the state during the War of 1812.

• An American fleet led by Oliver Hazard Perry won a major victory over the British fleet at the Battle of Put-in-Bay off Ohio shores in September 1813.

So They Say

"We have met the enemy, and they are ours."

Oliver Hazard Perry's minimal report to his commander after his victory at Put-in-Bay

---

• The "border war" with Michigan in 1835 was settled, giving Ohio the area around Toledo.

• In the years before 1860, perhaps more slaves were spirited through Ohio on the Underground Railroad than through any other state.

• Several attacks by Confederate raiders plagued Ohio during the Civil War, which called 345,000 Ohioans into service.

• After the war, John D. Rockefeller founded the Standard Oil Company at Cleveland in 1870. National Cash Register was founded at Dayton in 1879, and, with many other industries, Ohio became one of the great industrial states.

• In 1937 the Ohio River region suffered the worst floods in the history of the Ohio-Mississippi watershed.

• The Ohio Turnpike opened in 1955.

• Famed Ohio astronaut John Glenn was elected to the U.S. Senate in 1974.

• Cincinnati's Contemporary Arts Center in 1990 was acquitted in a widely publicized obscenity trial, reaffirming freedom of speech and expression.

THAT'S INTERESTING

• One of the nation's important archaeological features is the great Serpent Mound, "gliding" across a field in seven sinuous curves, a reminder of the Hopewell peoples.

• The city of Cincinnati can claim a unique distinction. Needing a railroad into the South, the city undertook to do what no city had ever tried before—to build and operate a whole railroad. In 1880, Cincinnati finished the Southern Railroad, and goods began to flow southward.

• Technically, Ohio did not legally become a state until 1953 because the U.S. Congress had up to then neglected to give its formal approval to statehood.

• Harry M. Stevens of Niles saw a cartoon of a dachshund dog as a wiener. He called his sandwich invention a "hot dog."

• The first cash register was named a "mechanical money drawer" by its inventor, James Ritty.

NOTABLE NATIVES

Sherwood Anderson (Camden, 1876-1941), author. Neil Alden Armstrong (Wapakoneta, 1930-), astronaut. Erma Bombeck (Dayton, 1927-1996), humorist. Arthur Holly Compton (Wooster, 1892-1962), physicist. Cornstalk (Ohio-West Virginia frontier, 1720?-1777), Indian leader. George Armstrong Custer (New Rumley, 1839-1876), soldier. Clarence Seward Darrow (near Kinsman, 1857-1938), lawyer. Paul Laurence Dunbar (Dayton, 1872-1906), poet. Thomas Alva Edison (Milan, 1847-1931), inventor. Daniel Decatur Emmett (Mount Vernon, 1815-1904), entertainer/composer. Frederick Funston (New Carlisle, 1865-1917), soldier. Clark Gable (Cadiz, 1901-1960), actor. James Abram Garfield (Orange, 1831-1881), U.S. president. John Herschel Glenn (Cambridge, 1921-), astronaut/public official. Ulysses Simpson Grant (Point Pleasant, 1822-1885), U.S. president/soldier. Zane Grey (Zanesville, 1875-1939), author. Warren Gamaliel Harding (Blooming Grove, 1865-1923), U.S. president. Benjamin Harrison (North Bend, 1833-1901), U.S. president. Rutherford Birchard Hayes (Delaware, 1822-1893), U.S. president. Dean Martin (Steubenville, 1917-1995), singer/actor. William McKinley (Niles, 1843-1901), U.S. president. Paul Newman (Cleveland, 1925-), actor. Jack William Nicklaus (Columbus, 1940-), golfer. Pontiac (in northern Ohio, 1720?-1769), Indian leader. Edward Vernon Rickenbacker (Columbus, 1890-1973), aviator/businessman. Philip Henry Sheridan (Somerset?, 1831-1888), soldier. William Tecumseh Sherman (Lancaster, 1820-1891), soldier. Steven Spielberg (Cincinnati, 1947-), director. Robert Alphonso Taft (Cincinnati, 1889-1953), public official. William Howard Taft (Cincinnati, 1857-1930), U.S. president. James Grover Thurber (Columbus, 1894-

1961), humorist/cartoonist. **Orville Wright** (Dayton, 1811-1948), inventor/pioneer aviator.

GENERAL

Admitted to statehood: March 1, 1803
Origin of name: Iroquois word for "fine or good river"
Capital: Columbus
Nickname: Buckeye State
Motto: With God, all things are possible
Bird: Cardinal
Insect: Ladybug
Flower: Scarlet carnation
Stone: Ohio flint
Song: "Beautiful Ohio"
Tree: Buckeye

THE LAND

Area: 44,828 sq. mi., 34th
    Land: 40,953 sq. mi., 35th
    Water: 3,875 sq. mi., 11th
        Inland water: 376 sq. mi., 37th
        Great Lakes: 3,499 sq. mi., 4th
Topography: Generally rolling plain; Allegheny plateau located in the E; Lake Erie plains extend southward; central plains in the W
Number of counties: 88
Geographic center: Delaware, 25 mi. NNE of Columbus
Length: 220 mi.; width: 220 mi.
Highest point: 1,549 ft. (Campbell Hill), 43rd
Lowest point: 455 ft. (Ohio River), 36th
Mean elevation: 850 ft., 31st

CLIMATE AND ENVIRONMENT

Temp., highest: 113 deg. on July 21, 1934, near Gallipolis; lowest: −39 deg. on Feb. 10, 1899, at Milligan
Monthly average: highest: 85.8 deg., 34th; lowest: 15.5 deg., 18th; spread (high to low): 70.3 deg., 23rd
Hazardous waste sites (1997): 33, 10th
Endangered species: Animals: 14—Indiana bat, American burying beetle, Karner blue butterfly, Mitchell's satyr butterfly, Clubshell, Hine's emerald dragonfly, American peregrine falcon, Fanshell, Scioto madtom, Pink mucket pearlymussel, Purple cat's paw pearlymussel, White cat's paw pearlymussel, Piping plover, Northern riffleshell. Plants: 1

MAJOR CITIES POPULATION, 1996 PERCENTAGE INCREASE, 1990-96

Columbus, 657,053; 3.8%
Cleveland, 498,246; −1.5%
Cincinnati, 345,818; −5.0%
Toledo, 317,606; −4.6%
Akron, 216,882; −2.8%

THE PEOPLE

Population (1997): 11,186,331, 7th
    Percent change (1990-97): 3.13%, 40th
    Percent of total U.S. pop.: 4.18%, 7th
    Per sq. mi: 249.54, 10th
Population (2000 proj.): 11,335,500, 7th
    Percent change (1995-2000): 1.65%, 43rd
Percent in metro. area (1996): 81.05%, 19th
Foreign born: 260,000, 15th
    Percent: 2.4%, 33rd
Top three ancestries reported:
    German, 37.50%
    Irish, 17.48%
    English, 13.36%
White (1992): 9,692,000, 87.94%, 26th
Black (1992): 1,206,000, 10.94%, 19th
Native American (1992): 21,000, 0.19%, 46th
Asian, Pacific Isle (1992): 102,000, 0.93%, 34th
Hispanic origin (1992): 149,000, 1.35%, 36th
Percent over 5 yrs. speaking language other than English at home: 5.4%, 36th
Percent males (1996): 48.41%, 39th; percent females: 51.59%, 13th
Percent never married: 25.5%, 26th
Marriages per 1,000 (1996): 7.41, 38th
Divorces per 1,000 (1996): 4.00, 30th
Median age (1996): 35.3
Under 5 years (1996): 6.82%, 34th
18 years and under (1996): 28.29%, 30th
65 years and over (1996): 13.40%, 19th
Percent increase among the elderly (1995-96): 0.54%, 32nd

OF VITAL IMPORTANCE

Live births per 1,000 pop. (1996): 13.7, 32nd
Infant mortality rate per 1,000 live births (1995): 8.7, 13th
    Rate for whites: 7.3, 6th
    Rate for blacks: 17.5, 9th
Births to unmarried women, % of total (1996): 32.9%, 19th

Births to teenage mothers, % of total (1996): 13.3%, 22nd
Abortions (1992): 49,520, 9th
  Rate per 1,000 women 14-44 years old: 19.5, 25th
  Percent change (1988-92): –7%, 23rd
Average lifetime (1989-91): 75.32, 29th
Total death rate per 100,000 pop. (1995): 950.1, 14th
  Accidents and adverse effects: 29.1, 44th
  Alzheimer's disease: 9.0, 21st
  Cancer: 226.1, 13th
  Cerebrovascular diseases: 60.0, 28th
  Chronic liver disease and cirrhosis: 8.5, 32nd
  Chronic obstructive pulmonary diseases and allied conditions: 44.2, 17th
  Diabetes mellitus: 30.0, 5th
  Diseases of heart: 317.4, 11th
  HIV infection: 7.9, 31st
  Homicide: 4.8, 35th
  Injury by firearms: 9.5, 40th
  Motor vehicle accidents: 12.4, 43rd
  Pneumonia and influenza: 30.7, 29th
  Suicide: 9.7, 45th

KEEPING WELL

Active nonfederal physicians per 100,000 pop. (1995): 219, 20th
Dentists per 100,000 (1991): 54, 24th
Nurses per 100,000 (1995): 896, 18th
Hospitals per 100,000 (1995): 1.61, 39th
  Admissions per 1,000 (1995): 123.31, 18th
  Hospital beds per 1,000 (1995): 3.39, 25th
  Occupancy rate per 100 beds (1995): 58.73, 35th
  Average cost per patient per day (1995): $1,061, 16th
  Average cost per stay (1995): $6,141, 19th
AIDS cases (new, 1996): 1,161; per 100,000: 10.4, 31st
Persons living with HIV infection, not yet AIDS (1996): 3,195
Other notifiable diseases, per 100,000 pop.:
  Gonorrhea (1995): 207.8, 12th
  Syphilis (1995): 17.4, 20th
  Tuberculosis (1996): 2.7, 39th
Pop. without health insur. (1996): 11.5%, 35th

HOUSEHOLDS BY TYPE

Total households (1996): 4,260,000, 7th
  Percent change (1990-96): 4.2%, 38th
  Per 1,000 pop. (1996) 381.28, 21st

Percent of householders 65 yrs. and over (1996): 22.44%, 20th
Persons per household (1996): 2.54, 33rd
Family households: 2,895,223
  Percent of total: 70.83%, 25th
Nonfamily households: 1,192,323
  Percent of total: 29.17%, 27th
Pop. living in group quarters: 261,451
  Percent of pop.: 2.41%, 36th

LIVING QUARTERS

Total housing units: 4,371,945
  Persons per unit: 2.48, 10th
Occupied housing units: 4,087,546
  Percent of total units: 93.49%, 1st
  Persons per unit: 2.51, 30th
  Percent of units with over 1 person per room: 1.76%, 46th
Owner-occupied units: 2,758,149
  Percent of total units: 63.09%, 9th
  Percent of occupied units: 67.48%, 24th
  Persons per unit: 2.74, 22nd
  Median value: $63,500, 29th
Renter-occupied units: 1,329,397
  Percent of total units: 30.41%, 20th
  Percent of occupied units: 32.52%, 28th
  Persons per unit: 2.27, 36th
  Median contract rent: $296, 31st
  Rental vacancy rate: 7.5%, 35th
Mobile home, trailer & other as a percent of occupied housing units: 6.03%, 42nd
Persons in emergency shelters for homeless persons: 4,277, 0.039%, 38th
Persons visible in street locations: 188, 0.0017%, 47th
Nursing home population: 93,769, 0.86%, 18th

CRIME INDEX PER 100,000 (1996)

Total reported: 4,455.7, 32nd
  Percent increase: 1.1%, 8th
  Violent: 428.7, 31st
    Percent increase: –11.2%, 42nd
    Murder & nonnegligent manslaughter: 4.8, 28th
    Forcible rape: 41.3, 19th
    Aggravated assault: 218.4, 33rd
    Robbery: 164.1, 21st
  Property: 4,027.0, 31st
    Percent increase: 2.7%, 7th
    Burglary: 835.4, 29th
    Larceny-theft: 2,784.1, 32nd
    Motor vehicle theft: 407.5, 30th

TEACHING AND LEARNING

Pop. 3 and over enrolled in school (1996): 2,381,370, 7th
Percent of pop.: 21.31%, 45th
Public elementary & secondary schools (1996-97): 3,865, 5th
Total enrollment (1996): 1,841,095, 6th
Percent of school age pop.: 88.13%, 41st
Percent of total pop.: 16.48%, 37th
Teachers (1996): 104,583, 7th
Percent of pop.: 0.94%, 39th
Pupil/teacher ratio (1995): 17.1, 16th
Teachers' avg. salary (1996-97): $38,831, 16th
Expenditure per capita (1992-93): $1,253.43, 31st
Education as % of state govt. expenditures: 35.2%, 26th
Expenditure per pupil (1994-95): $6,162, 16th
Percent increase (1993-94 & 1994-95): 3.20%, 33rd
Percent at or above grade level, NAEP tests:
Reading, grade 4 (1994): NA
Math, grade 4 (1996): NA
Math, grade 8 (1996): NA
Percent of graduates taking SAT (1995): 23%, 28th
Mean SAT verbal scores: 460, 24th
Mean SAT mathematical scores: 515, 23rd
Percent of graduates taking ACT (1997): 60%, 21st
Mean ACT scores: 21.3, 23rd
Percent of pop. over 25 completing:
Less than 9th grade: 7.9%, 38th
High school: 75.7%, 30th
College degree(s): 17.0%, 40th
Higher education, institutions (1996): 156, 6th
Enrollment (1995-96): 540,275, 8th
Percent increase in enroll. (1990-95): –3.1%, 46th
White non-Hispanic (1995): 452,802, 6th
Percent of enroll.: 83.81%, 20th
Total minority enroll. (1995): 71,511, 13th
Percent of enroll.: 13.24%, 31st
Black non-Hispanic (1995): 50,853, 14th
Percent of enroll.: 9.41%, 19th
Hispanic (1995): 7,831, 15th
Percent of enroll.: 1.45%, 37th
Asian/Pacific Islander (1995): 10,782, 14th
Percent of enroll.: 2.00%, 32nd
American Indian/AK native (1995): 2,045, 21st
Percent of enroll.: 0.38%, 36th

Nonresident alien (1995): 15,962, 9th
Percent of enroll.: 2.95%, 19th
Female (1995): 298,235, 8th
Percent of enroll.: 55.20%, 36th
Pub. institutions (1995-96): 61, 8th
Enrollment: 409,818, 7th
Percent increase in enrollment (1990-95): -4.2%, 43rd
Percent of enroll.: 75.85%, 38th
Private institutions (1995-96): 95, 5th
Enrollment: 130,457, 6th
Percent increase in enrollment (1990-95): 0.3%, 37th
Percent of enroll.: 24.15%, 14th
Tuition (in state), public 4-year institution (1996-97): $3,834, 12th
Tuition (in state), public 2-year institution (1996-97): $2,323, 8th
Tuition, private 4-year institution (1996-97): $12,989, 18th
Public library systems (1994): 250, 12th
Books & serial vol. per capita: 3.6, 15th
Library visits per capita: 5.0, 9th
Circulation per capita: 11.8, 1st

LAW ENFORCEMENT AND CORRECTIONS

Police protection and corrections expenditures (1996): $1,335,785,000
Per capita: $119.56, 24th
Police per 10,000 pop. (1996): 19.28, 36th
Prisoners (1 year or more) per 100,000 pop. (1996): 413, 15th
Percent change (1995-96): 3.4%, 36th
Percent of inmates that are female: 6.1% 27th
Percent change: 0.4%, 43rd
Death penalty: yes, by electrocution, lethal injection
Under sentence (Jan. 1998): 179, 6th
Executed, 1976-97: 0

RELIGION, NUMBER AND PERCENT OF POPULATION

Agnostic: 40,237—0.50%, 27th
Buddhist: 8,047—0.10%, 17th
Christian: 6,928,786—86.10%, 26th
Hindu: 8,047—0.10%, 10th
Jewish: 56,332—0.70%, 23rd
Muslim: 32,190—0.40%, 5th
Unitarian: 8,047—0.10%, 31st
Other: 193,137—2.40%, 5th
None: 595,506—7.40%, 17th
Refused to answer: 177,042—2.20%, 23rd

MAKING A LIVING

Personal income per capita (1996): $23,537, 22nd

Percent increase (1995-96): 2.6%, 34th

Disposable personal income per capita (1996): $20,340, 22nd

Median income of households (average, 1995-96): $35,022, 23rd

Percent of pop. below poverty level (1995-96): 12.1%, 24th

ECONOMY

In civilian labor force (1996): 5,643,000

Percent of total pop.: 66.3%, 35th

Percent of total pop. 65 years and over: 11.6%, 26th

Percent of total female pop.: 58.6%, 36th

Major employer industries (total nonagricultural, 1996):

Construction: 212,700—4.0%, 36th

Finance, insurance, & real estate: 277,000—5.2%, 24th

Government: 751,700—14.2%, 43rd

Manufacturing: 1,093,900—20.7%, 9th

Service: 1,415,100—26.7%, 33rd

Trade: 1,300,100—24.5%, 15th

Transportation, communications, public utilities: 231,700—4.4%, 42nd

Unemployment rate (1996): 4.9%, 31st

Male: 5.0%, 27th

Female: 4.8%, 30th

Total businesses (1995): 263,739, 7th

New business incorps. (1995): 20,859

Percent of total businesses: 7.91%, 37th

Business failures (1995): 2,141

Failures per 10,000 businesses: 81.2, 24th

Agriculture farm income:

Marketing (1996): $5,121,783,000, 15th

Average per farm: $71,136, 37th

Leading products (1997): Soybeans, corn, dairy products, hay, wheat, oats

Average value land & build. per acre (1997): $2,110, 12th

Percent increase (1996-97): 6%, 20th

Govt. payments (1996): $163,120,000, 18th

Average per farm: $2,266, 25th

Construction, value of all (1996): $13,994,419,000, 4th

Per capita: $1,253, 25th

Manufactures (1995):

Value added: $103,713,100,000

Per capita: $9,301, 4th

Leading products (1997): Transportation equipment, machinery, primary and fabricated metal products

Value of nonfuel mineral production (1996): $934,000,000, 13th

Leading mineral products (1996): Coal, natural gas, petroleum, stone, salt, sand/gravel, lime, cement

Energy consumption per person (1994): 357.4 mil. Btu, 22nd

Retail sales (1995): $104,900,000,000

Per household: $24,837, 21st

Sales increase (1994-95): 6.7%, 16th

Tourism revenues (1992): $8 bil.

Foreign exports, in total value (1996): $22,677,000,000, 7th

Per capita: $2,030, 14th

Gross state product per person (1994): $24,756, 24th

Public aid recipients (percent of resident pop. 1994): 8.1%, 14th

Medicaid recipients (percent of pop., 1995): 13.8%, 15th

Medicare enrollment per 1,000 pop. (1996): 150, 17th

TRAVEL AND TRANSPORTATION

Motor vehicle registrations (1996): 9,770,484, 5th

Per 1,000 pop.: 875.27, 16th

Motorcycle registrations (1996): 219,719, 2nd

Per 1,000 pop.: 22.49, 18th

Licensed drivers (1996): 7,772,757, 6th

Per 1,000 pop.: 698.11, 21st

Public roads & streets (1996)

Total mileage: 114,642, 9th

Per 1,000 pop.: 110.26, 39th

Rural mileage: 81,451, 15th

Per 1,000 pop.: 7.29, 39th

Urban mileage: 33,191, 7th

Per 1,000 pop.: 2.97, 31st

Interstate mileage: 1,573, 5th

Per 1,000 pop.: 0.14, 36th

Speed limit (max. interstate, autos, mi. per hr., 1997): 65

Annual vehicle-mi. of travel per driver (1996): 13,128, 35th

Mean travel time for workers age 16+ who work away from home: 20.7 min., 24th

GOVERNMENT

Percent of voting age pop. registered (1996): 82.42%, 13th

Percent of voting age pop. voting for president: (1996): 54.3%, 21st

Percent of voting age pop. voting for U.S. representatives (1996): 52.5%, 18th

State legislators, total (1997): 132, 33rd

Women members (1997): 29

Percent of legislature: 22%, 27th

U.S. Congress, House members (1998): 19

Change (1988-98): –2

Revenues (1996):

State govt.: $43,823,449,000

Per capita: $3,922.26, 18th

Parimutuel & amusement taxes & lotteries, revenue per capita (1995): $185.31, 8th

Expenditures (1996):

State govt.: $35,517,336,000

Per capita: $3,178.85, 25th

Debt outstanding (1996): $12,627,741,000

Per capita: $1,130.20, 34th

LAWS AND REGULATIONS

Legal driving age: 18, 16 if completed driver education course

Marriage age without parental consent: 18

Divorce residence requirement: 6 mo.

ATTRACTIONS (1997)

Major opera companies: 6

Major symphony orchestras: 6

Major dance companies: 7

Major professional theater companies (non-profit): 3

Per capita spending by the NEA (1997): $0.14, 45th

State Fair in mid-August at Columbus

SPORTS AND COMPETITION

NCAA (Division I) football and basketball teams: Bowling Green State Univ. Falcons, Cleveland State Univ. Vikings (basketball only), Kent State Univ. Golden Flashes, Miami Univ. RedHawks, Ohio State Univ. Buckeyes, Ohio Univ. Bobcats, Univ. of Akron Zips, Univ. of Cincinnati Bearcats, Univ. of Dayton Flyers, Univ. of Toledo Rockets, Wright State Univ. Raiders (basketball only), Xavier Univ. Musketeers (basketball only), Youngstown State Univ. Penguins

Major league baseball teams: Cincinnati Reds (NL Central), Cinergy Field; Cleveland Indians (AL Central), Jacobs Field

Major league soccer teams: Columbus Crew, Ohio Stadium

NBA basketball teams: Cleveland Cavaliers, Gund Arena

ABL basketball teams: Columbus Quest, Battelle Hall, Columbus Convention Center

WNBA basketball teams: Cleveland Rockers, Gund Arena

NFL football teams: Cincinnati Bengals (AFC), Cinergy Field

WEBSITES CONTAINING FURTHER INFORMATION

State of Ohio Government Front Page   http://www.state.oh.us

OKLAHOMA

> "The state Oklahoma most resembles is of course Texas, if only because it too does everything with color and originality, but tell an Oklahoman that his state is a dependency of Texas and he will bite your eyes out."
>
> John Gunther, writer

Thousands of oil and natural gas wells dot the Oklahoma landscape, and there are millions of beef cattle on its ranches. Oklahoma is the home of about a third of the nation's Indian people, who speak more than 50 languages. Oklahomans have demonstrated their genius in government and diplomacy and celebrate such world-famous natives as humorist Will Rogers and athlete Jim Thorpe. It is the state of the "Sooners" and the "Boomers." When the Oklahoma territory was opened up for settlement in 1889, those who entered the territory to stake their homestead claims before the official time were called "Sooners." Those who entered legally at the appointed time were called "Boomers." Oklahoma is also a center of cowboy culture and preserves notable collections of Western art and customs.

SUPERLATIVES

• Has the only county touching four states—Cimarron County.
• The former home of five separate Indian nations.
• "Oil capital of the world"—Tulsa.
• Finest collection of Western and cowboy art—Woolaroc Museum, in Bartlesville.

MOMENTS IN HISTORY

• Claimed variously by Spain and France, the territory that is now Oklahoma was the starting point of a trail to Spanish Santa Fe blazed by French traders in 1750.
• Control of the region came to the United States in 1803 with the Louisiana Purchase.
• In 1817, Pierre Chouteau of the famed Chouteau family founded Grand Saline (Salina), first permanent European settlement in what is now Oklahoma.
• One of the most shameful episodes in U.S. history began in 1817 with the first removal of scattered groups of Indians from their native lands to Indian Territory. Formal establishment of the lands known as Indian Territory was decided in 1834.
• The resettlement process intensified with the brutal removal of the groups known as the

Five Civilized Tribes. When Congress in 1830 ordered the resettlement of the Creeks from their ancestral lands in parts of Georgia, Alabama, and Mississippi and areas of the Appalachians, they fought back fiercely, and they executed Chief William McIntosh for having ceded the tribal land. But their resistance was beaten down, and they started their tragic march to Oklahoma.
• In the early 1830s, the Chickasaw people were moved to Oklahoma over the infamous route that became known as the "Trail of Tears."
• Forced by the federal government in 1831-33, the Choctaw Indians also trudged over the "Trail of Tears." Before their removal there were about 20,000 Choctaws. By 1843 they numbered only about 12,000.
• Almost at once, however, the Choctaw began to prosper in their new homes. In 1834 the Choctaw nation adopted a new constitution, some of whose provisions are still a part of the Oklahoma constitution. The other Indian nations prospered in much the same way as the Choctaw.
• By 1838, U.S. armed forces had begun the evacuation of the Cherokee people. About 15,000 were marched over the "Trail of Tears" to Indian Territory under conditions of extreme hardship, and nearly 4,000 perished on the way.
• The Seminole wars in Florida ended in 1842 without a surrender or peace treaty. After the war some of the few remaining Seminole agreed to move to Oklahoma, forming the fifth of the Civilized Tribes.
• In 1844 the Cherokee nation published the *Cherokee Advocate*, the first newspaper in what is now Oklahoma, printed partly in English and partly in the new Cherokee alphabet.
• The five tribes gathered in 1859 for an intertribal council, resulting in a progressive code of laws.
• When the Civil War came, the Five Nations embraced the Confederate cause.
• The first Civil War struggle in what is now Oklahoma was the Battle of Round

Mountain near Keystone, on November 19, 1861.

• With the collapse of the Confederacy, the Five Nations faced ruin and the forfeiture of their lands and rights. However, the skill of the Indian negotiators in the late 1860s reduced the tribal losses to some of the western Oklahoma lands.

• Beginning in the 1870s, more than 25 other tribes were forced to move to Oklahoma on land bought or leased by the federal government.

• The displaced Indians caused much unrest, but in 1875, George Armstrong Custer defeated Indian forces in the Battle of the Washita, and most of the Indian conflict ended.

• The Five Nations made remarkable progress in education, government, and commerce. Oklahoma's first telephone line was built by the Cherokee in 1885.

• One of the most remarkable events in U.S. history occurred when the government opened "unassigned lands" to settlement. At high noon on April 22, 1889, thousands rushed across the border, and by nightfall the formerly empty site of what is now Oklahoma City had become a tent community of 10,000 people. Other towns were also founded that day.

So They Say

"I saw excited men jump from the windows of crowded coaches even before the train came to a stop...and rush off to stake out claims in a field that by noon next day was a busy tent city of 10,000 people....Rivals shot it out over claim disputes."

Anonymous eyewitness, on settlers arriving in Oklahoma

• In all, ten land openings brought settlers to Oklahoma during the period from 1889 to 1906.

• In May 1890, Oklahoma Territory was created, coexisting with Indian Territory.

• Oklahoma became a state on November 6, 1907, with a population of 1,414,177, including residents in Indian Territory.

• In 1908, 92 leading Oklahoma women gathered at Guthrie to take state jobs as seamstresses—jobs lasting only two days, without pay. While there, the women created the first

flag to carry the 46 stars, the last symbolizing their own state.

• In the drought of the 1930s, terrible dust storms swept the plowed lands and blanketed the skies. Thousands of "Okies" fled their devastated farms.

So They Say

"You could see it a-comin'...just a whole boil, roll and boil. The cloud crashed over Kenton, over Felt....[In Cimarron County] the day became darker than night. Car ignitions shorted out, windmills brushed by wind and dust became charged with electricity. People were lost a few hundred feet from home....The worst day [April 14, 1935]...known as Black Sunday...had given the name Dust Bowl."

Oklahoma resident Michael Parfit

• During World War II, 13 Oklahomans won the Medal of Honor.

• In the 1970s, the McClellan-Kerr Arkansas River Navigation System opened. Tulsa and Muskogee became inland "seaports."

• On April 19, 1995, a federal office building in Oklahoma City was bombed in the nation's worst terrorist attack; 168 people lost their lives.

THAT'S INTERESTING

• With a mountain being defined as any elevation over 2,000 feet, Oklahoma claims that the 1,999-foot rise known as Cavanal is the world's highest hill.

• In an attempt to scalp an enemy, Chief Pawhuska once pulled at a man's white hair. The man's wig came off in his hand. The chief kept this powerful "magic" the rest of his life and took the name meaning "white hair."

• More languages are spoken in Oklahoma than in Europe. Each of the state's 55 Indian tribes has a separate language or its own distinctive dialect.

• The Cherokee Indian generally known as Sequoyah—who moved to Oklahoma in 1828—has a unique distinction worldwide, as the only person to have created a written language and a system of mathematics. He later became a diplomatic representative of his people in Washington—all of this accomplished by someone who was an illiterate in any known language. This unique savant is one of the two representatives of Oklahoma to be honored in Statuary Hall in Washington, DC.

NOTABLE NATIVES

Acee Blue Eagle (near Anadarka, 1910-1959), artist. **Woodrow Wilson (Woody) Guthrie** (Okemah, 1912-1967), folk singer/composer. **Patrick Jay Hurley** (Indian Territory, 1883-1963), diplomat. **Karl Guthe Jansky** (Norman, 1905-1950), engineer. **Robert Samuel Kerr** (Ada, 1896-1963), political figure. **Mickey Charles Mantle** (Spavinaw, 1931-1995), baseball player. **Oral Roberts** (Ada, 1918-), evangelist. **William Penn Adair (Will) Rogers** (near Oologa, 1879-1935), humorist/actor. **Maria Tallchief** (Fairfax, 1925-), dancer. **James Francis (Jim) Thorpe** (Prague, 1888-1953), athlete.

GENERAL

Admitted to statehood: November 16, 1907
Origin of name: Choctaw word meaning "red man," proposed by Rev. Allen Wright, Choctaw-speaking Indian
Capital: Oklahoma City
Nickname: Sooner State
Motto: *Labor Omnia Vincit*—Labor conquers all things
Animal: Bison
Bird: Scissor-tailed flycatcher
Insect: Honeybee
Flower: Mistletoe
Stone: Rose rock (barite rose)
Song: "Oklahoma"
Tree: Redbud

THE LAND

Area: 69,903 sq. mi., 20th
  Land: 68,679 sq. mi., 19th
  Water: 1,224 sq. mi., 25th
    Inland water: 1,224 sq. mi., 17th
Topography: High plains predominate in the W, hills and small mountains in the E; the E central region is dominated by the Arkansas River Basin, and the Red River Plains are in the S
Number of counties: 77
Geographic center: 8 mi. N of Oklahoma City
Length: 400 mi.; width: 220 mi.
Highest point: 4,973 ft. (Black Mesa), 23rd
Lowest point: 289 ft. (Little River), 34th
Mean elevation: 1,300 ft., 20th

CLIMATE AND ENVIRONMENT

Temp., highest: 120 deg. on July 26, 1934, at Tishmoningo and on June 27, 1994, at Tipton; lowest: –27 deg. on Jan. 18, 1930, at Watts
Monthly average: highest: 93.9 deg., 5th; lowest: 24.8 deg., 36th; spread (high to low): 69.1 deg., 24th
Hazardous waste sites (1997): 10, 34th
Endangered species: Animals: 11—Gray bat, Indiana bat, American burying beetle, Whooping crane, Eskimo curlew, American peregrine falcon, Least tern, Black-capped vireo, Red-cockaded woodpecker, Ozark big-eared bat, Ouachita rock-pocketbook. Plants: 0

MAJOR CITIES
POPULATION, 1996
PERCENTAGE INCREASE, 1990-96

Oklahoma City, 469,852; 5.7%
Tulsa, 378,491; 3.0%
Norman, 90,228; 12.7%
Lawton, 82,582; .5%
Broken Arrow, 69,175; 19.2%

THE PEOPLE

Population (1997): 3,317,091, 27th
  Percent change (1990-97): 5.45%, 33rd
  Percent of total U.S. pop.: 1.24%, 27th
  Per sq. mi: 47.45, 35th
Population (2000 proj.): 3,371,500, 28th
  Percent change (1995-2000): 2.85%, 37th
Percent in metro. area (1996): 60.23%, 35th
Foreign born: 65,000, 29th
  Percent: 2.1%, 34th
Top three ancestries reported:
  German, 22.70%
  Irish, 20.41%
  American Indian, 14.91%
White (1992): 2,660,000, 83.00%, 33rd
Black (1992): 246,000, 7.68%, 25th
Native American (1992): 261,000, 8.14%, 3rd
Asian, Pacific Isle (1992): 39,000, 1.22%, 28th
Hispanic origin (1992): 94,000, 2.93%, 23rd
Percent over 5 yrs. speaking language other than English at home: 5.0%, 37th
Percent males (1996): 48.93%, 24th; percent females: 51.07%, 28th
Percent never married: 20.9%, 50th
Marriages per 1,000 (1996): 8.08, 29th

Divorces per 1,000 (1996): 5.84, 8th
Median age (1996): 34.9
Under 5 years (1996): 6.95%, 26th
18 years and under (1996): 29.67%, 13th
65 years and over (1996): 13.49%, 17th
Percent increase among the elderly (1995-96): 0.55%, 31st

OF VITAL IMPORTANCE

Live births per 1,000 pop. (1996): 14.0, 28th
Infant mortality rate per 1,000 live births (1995): 8.3, 15th
　Rate for whites: 8.0, 1st
　Rate for blacks: 15.1, 20th
Births to unmarried women, % of total (1996): 30.9%, 28th
Births to teenage mothers, % of total (1996): 17.2%, 6th
Abortions (1992): 8,940, 33rd
　Rate per 1,000 women 14-44 years old: 12.5, 40th
　Percent change (1988-92): –23%, 48th
Average lifetime (1989-91): 75.10, 33rd
Total death rate per 100,000 pop. (1995): 1,002.3, 7th
　Accidents and adverse effects: 44.9, 10th
　Alzheimer's disease: 6.3, 43rd
　Cancer: 217.9, 17th
　Cerebrovascular diseases: 72.5, 9th
　Chronic liver disease and cirrhosis: 9.7, 19th
　Chronic obstructive pulmonary diseases and allied conditions: 48.1, 9th
　Diabetes mellitus: 19.5, 36th
　Diseases of heart: 340.4, 7th
　HIV infection: 7.1, 32nd
　Homicide: 13.5, 4th
　Injury by firearms: 16.1, 15th
　Motor vehicle accidents: 22.1, 11th
　Pneumonia and influenza: 41.6, 5th
　Suicide: 15.3, 10th

KEEPING WELL

Active nonfederal physicians per 100,000 pop. (1995): 160, 45th
Dentists per 100,000 (1991): 48, 35th
Nurses per 100,000 (1995): 591, 50th
Hospitals per 100,000 (1995): 3.36, 11th
　Admissions per 1,000 (1995): 112.26, 29th
　Hospital beds per 1,000 (1995): 3.51, 23rd
　Occupancy rate per 100 beds (1995): 53.04, 48th
　Average cost per patient per day (1995): $861, 33rd
　Average cost per stay (1995): $5,188, 42nd

AIDS cases (new, 1996): 272; per 100,000: 8.2, 37th
Persons living with HIV infection, not yet AIDS (1996): 1,686
Other notifiable diseases, per 100,000 pop.:
　Gonorrhea (1995): 154.9, 17th
　Syphilis (1995): 17.8, 19th
　Tuberculosis (1996): 6.1, 22nd
Pop. without health insur. (1996): 17.0%, 11th

HOUSEHOLDS BY TYPE

Total households (1996): 1,265,000, 27th
　Percent change (1990-96): 4.9%, 33rd
　Per 1,000 pop. (1996) 383.22, 14th
　Percent of householders 65 yrs. and over (1996): 23.00%, 14th
　Persons per household (1996): 2.50, 46th
Family households: 855,321
　Percent of total: 70.91%, 24th
Nonfamily households: 350,814
　Percent of total: 29.09%, 28th
Pop. living in group quarters: 93,677
　Percent of pop.: 2.98%, 19th

LIVING QUARTERS

Total housing units: 1,406,499
　Persons per unit: 2.24, 42nd
Occupied housing units: 1,206,135
　Percent of total units: 85.75%, 41st
　Persons per unit: 2.50, 34th
　Percent of units with over 1 person per room: 3.31%, 23rd
Owner-occupied units: 821,188
　Percent of total units: 58.39%, 28th
　Percent of occupied units: 68.08%, 19th
　Persons per unit: 2.59, 49th
　Median value: $48,100, 46th
Renter-occupied units: 384,947
　Percent of total units: 27.37%, 36th
　Percent of occupied units: 31.92%, 33rd
　Persons per unit: 2.41, 16th
　Median contract rent: $259, 43rd
　Rental vacancy rate: 14.7%, 2nd
Mobile home, trailer & other as a percent of occupied housing units: 11.91%, 24th
Persons in emergency shelters for homeless persons: 2,222, 0.071%, 14th
Persons visible in street locations: 340, 0.0108%, 18th
Nursing home population: 29,666, 0.94%, 12th

CRIME INDEX PER 100,000 (1996)

Total reported: 5,652.9, 15th
  Percent increase: 1.0%, 9th
  Violent: 597.1, 19th
    Percent increase: –10.1%, 35th
    Murder & nonnegligent manslaughter: 6.8, 24th
    Forcible rape: 46.8, 11th
    Aggravated assault: 436.9, 12th
    Robbery: 106.6, 34th
  Property: 5,055.8, 15th
    Percent increase: 2.5%, 8th
    Burglary: 1,255.6, 8th
    Larceny-theft: 3,317.4, 17th
    Motor vehicle theft: 482.9, 22nd

TEACHING AND LEARNING

Pop. 3 and over enrolled in school (1996): 801,055, 27th
  Percent of pop.: 24.27%, 12th
Public elementary & secondary schools (1996-97): 1,830, 18th
  Total enrollment (1996): 620,379, 27th
    Percent of school age pop.: 95.00%, 11th
    Percent of total pop.: 18.79%, 9th
  Teachers (1996): 39,350, 24th
    Percent of pop.: 1.19%, 10th
  Pupil/teacher ratio (1995): 15.7, 33rd
  Teachers' avg. salary (1996-97): $29,270, 47th
  Expenditure per capita (1992-93): $1,224.08, 37th
    Education as % of state govt. expenditures: 38.5%, 8th
  Expenditure per pupil (1994-95): $4,845, 39th
    Percent increase (1993-94 & 1994-95): 2.34%, 39th
Percent at or above grade level, NAEP tests:
  Reading, grade 4 (1994): NA
  Math, grade 4 (1996): NA
  Math, grade 8 (1996): NA
Percent of graduates taking SAT (1995): 9%, 38th
  Mean SAT verbal scores: 491, 12th
  Mean SAT mathematical scores: 536, 15th
Percent of graduates taking ACT (1997): 66%, 12th
  Mean ACT scores: 20.6, 38th
Percent of pop. over 25 completing:
  Less than 9th grade: 9.8%, 22nd
  High school: 74.6%, 36th
  College degree(s): 17.8%, 33rd

Higher education, institutions (1996): 45, 28th
  Enrollment (1995-96): 180,676, 25th
    Percent increase in enroll. (1990-95): 4.3%, 23rd
    White non-Hispanic (1995): 137,276, 28th
      Percent of enroll.: 75.98%, 33rd
    Total minority enroll. (1995): 35,256, 26th
      Percent of enroll.: 19.51%, 20th
    Black non-Hispanic (1995): 13,147, 24th
      Percent of enroll.: 7.28%, 24th
    Hispanic (1995): 4,180, 27th
      Percent of enroll.: 2.31%, 23rd
    Asian/Pacific Islander (1995): 4,092, 27th
      Percent of enroll.: 2.26%, 27th
    American Indian/AK native (1995): 13,837, 2nd
      Percent of enroll.: 7.66%, 3rd
    Nonresident alien (1995): 8,144, 14th
      Percent of enroll.: 4.51%, 4th
    Female (1995): 98,406, 28th
      Percent of enroll.: 54.47%, 44th
  Pub. institutions (1995-96): 29, 24th
    Enrollment: 158,026, 26th
      Percent increase in enrollment (1990-95): 4.6%, 22nd
    Percent of enroll.: 87.46%, 13th
  Private institutions (1995-96): 16, 34th
    Enrollment: 22,650, 32nd
      Percent increase in enrollment (1990-95): 2.3%, 33rd
    Percent of enroll.: 12.54%, 39th
  Tuition (in state), public 4-year institution (1996-97): $1,936, 47th
  Tuition (in state), public 2-year institution (1996-97): $1,262, 31st
  Tuition, private 4-year institution (1996-97): $7,579, 45th
Public library systems (1994): 112, 27th
  Books & serial vol. per capita: 2.2, 35th
  Library visits per capita: 3.9, 22nd
  Circulation per capita: 6.4, 28th

LAW ENFORCEMENT AND CORRECTIONS

Police protection and corrections expenditures (1996): $347,319,000
  Per capita: $105.21, 30th
Police per 10,000 pop. (1996): 19.94, 33rd
Prisoners (1 year or more) per 100,000 pop. (1996): 591, 4th
  Percent change (1995-96): 7.9%, 17th
  Percent of inmates that are female: 9.9%, 1st
    Percent change: 6.9%, 30th

Death penalty: yes, by electrocution, firing squad, lethal injection
Under sentence (Jan. 1998): 118, 10th
Executed, 1976-97: 9, 11th
Executed in 1997: 1, 9th

RELIGION, NUMBER AND PERCENT OF POPULATION

Agnostic: 9,234—0.40%, 34th
Buddhist: 4,617—0.20%, 11th
Christian: 1,989,994—86.20%, 25th
Hindu: 2,309—0.10%, 10th
Jewish: 4,617—0.20%, 40th
Muslim: NA
Unitarian: 2,309—0.10%, 31st
Other: 48,480—2.10%, 9th
None: 150,058—6.50%, 25th
Refused to answer: 96,960—4.20%, 2nd

MAKING A LIVING

Personal income per capita (1996): $19,350, 45th
Percent increase (1995-96): 2.8%, 29th
Disposable personal income per capita (1996): $16,980, 44th
Median income of households (average, 1995-96): $27,263, 47th
Percent of pop. below poverty level (1995-96): 16.9%, 9th

ECONOMY

In civilian labor force (1996): 1,577,000
Percent of total pop.: 63.9%, 41st
Percent of total pop. 65 years and over: 11.7%, 25th
Percent of total female pop.: 55.8%, 44th
Major employer industries (total nonagricultural, 1996):
Construction: 50,300—3.7%, 42nd
Finance, insurance, & real estate: 67,300—5.0%, 29th
Government: 271,500—20.0%, 9th
Manufacturing: 173,600—12.8%, 34th
Service: 364,300—26.9%, 27th
Trade: 318,500—23.5%, 28th
Transportation, communications, public utilities: 77,200—5.7%, 15th
Unemployment rate (1996): 4.1%, 43rd
Male: 3.6%, 46th
Female: 4.6%, 32nd
Total businesses (1995): 81,395, 29th
New business incorps. (1995): 7,796
Percent of total businesses: 9.58%, 22nd
Business failures (1995): 1,311
Failures per 10,000 businesses: 161.1, 2nd

Agriculture farm income:
Marketing (1996): $3,565,551,000, 21st
Average per farm: $49,522, 46th
Leading products (1997): Cattle, wheat, cotton, hay, peanuts, grain sorghum, soybeans, corn, pecans, broilers
Average value land & build. per acre (1997): $570, 41st
Percent increase (1996-97): 4%, 35th
Govt. payments (1996): $236,707,000, 12th
Average per farm: $3,288, 20th
Construction, value of all (1996): $3,182,716,000, 33rd
Per capita: $964, 45th
Manufactures (1995):
Value added: $14,622,300,000
Per capita: $4,461, 42nd
Leading products (1997): Nonelectrical machinery, transportation equipment, food products, fabricated metal products
Value of nonfuel mineral production (1996): $372,000,000, 34th
Leading mineral products (1996): Natural gas, petroleum, coal, stone, cement, sand/gravel, gypsum
Energy consumption per person (1994): 424.2 mil. Btu, 12th
Retail sales (1995): $25,998,000,000
Per household: $20,727, 47th
Sales increase (1994-95): 1.5%, 45th
Tourism revenues (1995): $3 bil.
Foreign exports, in total value (1996): $2,365,000,000, 35th
Per capita: $716, 46th
Gross state product per person (1994): $20,315, 48th
Public aid recipients (percent of resident pop. 1994): 6.2%, 32nd
Medicaid recipients (percent of pop., 1995): 12.0%, 25th
Medicare enrollment per 1,000 pop. (1996): 140, 31st

TRAVEL AND TRANSPORTATION

Motor vehicle registrations (1996): 3,081,723, 24th
Per 1,000 pop.: 935.18, 7th
Motorcycle registrations (1996): 59,210, 22nd
Per 1,000 pop.: 19.21, 27th
Licensed drivers (1996): 2,155,558, 29th
Per 1,000 pop.: 658.21, 38th
Public roads & streets (1996)
Total mileage: 112,664, 12th
Per 1,000 pop.: 134.13, 10th

Rural mileage: 99,630, 7th
  Per 1,000 pop.: 30.18, 10th
Urban mileage: 13,034, 25th
  Per 1,000 pop.: 3.95, 5th
Interstate mileage: 930, 21st
  Per 1,000 pop.: 0.28, 15th
Speed limit (max. interstate, autos, mi. per hr., 1997): 75
Annual vehicle-mi. of travel per driver (1996): 16,457, 8th
Mean travel time for workers age 16+ who work away from home: 19.3 min., 34th

GOVERNMENT

Percent of voting age pop. registered (1996): 81.58%, 18th
  Percent of voting age pop. voting for president: (1996): 49.9%, 27th
  Percent of voting age pop. voting for U.S. representatives (1996): 48.8%, 24th
State legislators, total (1997): 149, 23rd
  Women members (1997): 15
  Percent of legislature: 10%, 49th
U.S. Congress, House members (1998): 6
  Change (1988-98): 0
Revenues (1996):
  State govt.: $10,609,104,000
  Per capita: $3,213.91, 33rd

Parimutuel & amusement taxes & lotteries, revenue per capita (1995): $4.89, 41st
Expenditures (1996):
  State govt.: $9,265,486,000
  Per capita: $2,806.87, 38th
Debt outstanding (1996): $3,889,324,000
  Per capita: $1,178.23, 33rd

LAWS AND REGULATIONS

Legal driving age: 16
Marriage age without parental consent: 18
Divorce residence requirement: 6 mo.

ATTRACTIONS (1997)

Major opera companies: 1
Major symphony orchestras: 2
Major dance companies: 1
Per capita spending by the NEA (1997): $0.16, 44th
State Fair in late August–early September at Oklahoma City

SPORTS AND COMPETITION

NCAA (Division I) football and basketball teams: Oklahoma State Univ. Cowboys, Oral Roberts Univ. Golden Eagles (basketball only), Univ. of Oklahoma Sooners, Univ. of Tulsa Golden Hurricane

WEBSITES CONTAINING FURTHER INFORMATION

Oklahoma Home Page   http://www.oklaosf.state.ok.us

OREGON

"The cabins rise, the fields are sown, and Oregon is theirs! They will take, they will hold; by the spade in the mold; by the seed in the soil, by the sweat and the toil; by the plow in the loam; by the school and the home!"
Arthur Guiterman, poet

Oregon stretches from one of the most spectacular coastlines on the west, to Hells Canyon, the nation's deepest gorge, on the east. Crater Lake is the deepest in the United States and one of the loveliest. The state boasts the greatest extent of standing timber in the nation, the biggest sand dunes, and the largest geyser. Oregon was the goal of the many thousands of pioneers who traveled overland on the Oregon Trail. Harvesting of lumber, and the manufacturing industries based upon it, help keep Oregon vital today. The state has also long been a leader in sound ecological legislation and forward-looking public servants.

SUPERLATIVES

- Largest reserves of standing timber.
- Leading U.S. timber producer.
- Produces most U.S. plywood.
- Leads in nickel production.
- Greatest profusion of agates.
- First pheasants in United States, in Linn County.

MOMENTS IN HISTORY

- In 1543 the Spanish expedition of Bartolome Ferrello passed the present-day coast of Oregon, but it is not known how far he went to the north.
- Britain's Sir Francis Drake may have reached as far north as the southern Oregon coast in 1579.
- The prominent promontory called Cape Blanco by Martin d'Augilar in 1603 was the first Oregon feature to be given a name by Europeans.
- Early explorers found the Chinook Indians living in luxury on the wonderful salmon that now bear their name. Many tribes gathered for an annual ceremony of the salmon to pray for the fish's favor.
- On August 17, 1775, the Spanish navigator Bruno Heceta discovered the mouth of the Columbia River.
- Famed English explorer Captain James Cook saw the Oregon coast and named Cape Foulweather in 1778.

- American Captain Robert Gray became the first white person known to have landed in Oregon, when he reached present-day Tillamook County in 1788. His men engaged in the first skirmish of white men with the Indians in Oregon. One sailor was killed.
- On May 11, 1792, Captain Gray became the first person to make the perilous entry into the Columbia River. He and his men sailed upstream about 15 miles and traded with the Indians, buying two salmon for one nail and a prime beaver skin for two spikes. He also bought 150 rare sea otters, worth $100 each in China. Gray named the river for his ship, the *Columbia*.
- As early as 1800, American ships controlled most of the fur trade of the northwest coast, but that trade diminished as they went into whaling.

So They Say

"...stately clippers of the China trade would leave New England ports, sail around Cape Horn and up to the Oregon coast. There they would trade their beads, trinkets, blankets, and a few tools or other items with the Indians for the precious sea otter, beaver and other furs. After taking on water and supplies, they would sail for China, usually stopping at the Hawaiian islands for more supplies. In China teas, spices, silks, and other goods of the Orient were acquired in exchange for furs. Sometimes as much as $250,000 was made in one voyage." **Anonymous**

- The great expedition of Lewis and Clark reached its coveted goal of the Pacific and built Fort Clatsop on Young's Bay, spending the winter of 1805-06 there.
- Lewis and Clark returned east in 1806, leaving behind certificates with Indian leaders that testified to their fair and hospitable treatment.
- John Jacob Astor's Pacific Fur Company set up headquarters in 1811 and established Fort Astoria, the first permanent white settlement in Oregon.

- During the War of 1812, the British seized Astoria, but the Americans retook it in 1817.
- In 1824 the great Hudson's Bay Company took over Astoria, under the remarkable leadership of John McLoughlin.
- In 1834 the Reverend Jason Lee established a mission station and school near present-day Salem.

- In May 1843, the settlers at Champoeg voted in favor of government by the United States and set up a provisional government of their own.
- By 1846, thousands of settlers were coming over the Oregon Trail in numbers that increased until the railroad began to take over in the 1870s.
- In 1856 a strange and troubling event took place when the Indians' burial canoes were removed from their resting place on land and sent off to sea to make room for a military blockhouse, while the Indians stood silently by.
- On February 14, 1859, Oregon gained statehood.

- During the Civil War, Indian troubles plagued the new state.
- In 1877, Chief Joseph of the Nez Percé and his people were forced out of their homeland in Oregon, Washington, and parts of Idaho.
- The transcontinental railroad reached Portland in 1883.
- Oregon pioneered U.S. primary elections and initiated a presidential preference primary in 1911.
- The Third Oregon Infantry was the first of the country's national guards to be mobilized and ready for World War I.
- The great Bonneville Dam began to transmit power in 1938.
- In one of the few Japanese attacks on the mainland during World War II, a Japanese sub shelled Fort Stevens on June 21, 1942.
- Oregon attracted so many new residents that beginning in the 1970s the state discouraged newcomers.
- The much publicized effort of cult leader Bhagwan Shree Rajneesh to establish a stronghold in Oregon failed, and he left the state in 1985.
- In 1990, ten new active volcanoes were discovered on the seabed off the Oregon coast.
- In 1995, Senator Robert Packwood resigned after a Senate committee found he had engaged in sexual misconduct.

THAT'S INTERESTING

- The Indians thought the squeaks of the wheels of the settlers' wagons sounded like their words "chik-chik-chaile-kikash," and that became their name for wagon.
- At 1,932 feet, Oregon's Crater Lake is the nation's deepest lake—and one of the most beautiful. It has neither inlet nor outlet, yet it remains at about the same level year in and year out.
- The world's highest sand dunes are found south of the Umpqua River. In the Coos Bay area, the jumbled rocks of the shore show what happened centuries ago when ancient earthquakes twisted the rocks into an untidy clutter. These include such landmarks as Tillamook Head and Otter Crescent. Another landmark, Haystack Rock on Cannon Beach, is the third largest rock monolith in the world. Smaller rock formations rise along most of the coast like a natural skyline.

• One of earth's deepest clefts is Hells Canyon. For 40 miles this jagged gash drops to an average of 6,000 feet below the rim on either side.

• Oregon's madrona tree sheds its bark as well as its leaves.

• The giant insect-eating cobra lily is another unusual form of plant life.

• Oregon students earn money for school by picking up the innumerable pinecones for seed.

• More than two centuries ago, the ship *Manzanita* foundered on the coast; beachcombers are still picking up lumps of beeswax from its cargo.

NOTABLE NATIVES

Homer Davenport (Silverton, 1867-1912), cartoonist. **Chief Joseph** (Wallowa Valley, near the Oregon/Idaho/Washington border, 1840?-1904), Indian leader. **Edwin Markham** (Oregon City, 1852-1940), poet. **Linus Carl Pauling** (Portland, 1901-1994), chemist. **John Reed** (Portland, 1887-1920), journalist/political radical.

GENERAL

Admitted to statehood: February 14, 1859
Origin of name: Origin unknown. One theory holds that the name may have come from the French word *ouragon*, meaning "hurricane"
Capital: Salem
Nickname: Beaver State
Motto: She flies with her own wings
Animal: Beaver
Bird: Western meadowlark
Fish: Chinook salmon
Flower: Oregon grape
Stone: Thunderegg
Song: "Oregon, My Oregon"
Tree: Douglas fir

THE LAND

Area: 97,131 sq. mi., 10th
  Land: 96,002 sq. mi., 10th
  Water: 1,129 sq. mi., 26th
    Inland water: 1,129 sq. mi., 19th
    Coastal water: 80 sq. mi., 19th
Topography: Rugged coast range; fertile Willamette River Valley to E and S; Cascade Mountain range of volcanic peaks E of the valley; plateau E of Cascades, remaining two-thirds of state

Number of counties: 36
Geographic center: Crook, 25 mi. SSE of Prineville
Length: 360 mi.; width: 261 mi.
Highest point: 11,239 ft. (Mount Hood), 13th
Lowest point: sea level (Pacific Ocean), 3rd
Mean elevation: 3,300 ft., 9th
Coastline: 296 mi., 8th
Shoreline: 1,410 mi., 16th

CLIMATE AND ENVIRONMENT

Temp., highest: 119 deg. on Aug. 10, 1898, at Pendleton; lowest: –54 deg. on Feb. 10, 1933, at Seneca
Monthly average: highest: 82.6 deg., 45th; lowest: 32.8 deg., 45th; spread (high to low): 49.8 deg., 50th
Hazardous waste sites (1997): 10, 34th
Endangered species: Animals: 7—Borax Lake chub, Oregon chub, Columbian white-tailed deer, American peregrine falcon, Brown pelican, Lost River sucker, Shortnose sucker. Plants: 5

MAJOR CITIES
POPULATION, 1996
PERCENTAGE INCREASE, 1990-96

Portland, 480,824; 3.7%
Eugene, 123,718; 9.7%
Salem, 122,566; 13.7%
Gresham, 81,583; 19.5%
Beaverton, 63,224; 18.6%

THE PEOPLE

Population (1997): 3,243,487, 29th
  Percent change (1990-97): 14.11%, 10th
  Percent of total U.S. pop.: 1.21%, 29th
  Per sq. mi: 32.97, 40th
Population (2000 proj.): 3,397,000, 27th
  Percent change (1995-2000): 8.15%, 11th
Percent in metro. area (1996): 70.19%, 25th
Foreign born: 139,000, 19th
  Percent: 4.9%, 18th
Top three ancestries reported:
  German, 30.93%
  English, 20.23%
  Irish, 16.43%
White (1992): 2,797,000, 94.11%, 12th
Black (1992): 51,000, 1.72%, 42nd
Native American (1992): 42,000, 1.41%, 12th
Asian, Pacific Isle (1992): 81,000, 2.73%, 12th

Hispanic origin (1992): 127,000, 4.27%, 20th
Percent over 5 yrs. speaking language other than English at home: 7.3%, 24th
Percent males (1996): 49.43%, 13th; percent females: 50.57%, 39th
Percent never married: 23.1%, 42nd
Marriages per 1,000 (1996): 7.98, 31st
Divorces per 1,000 (1996): 4.69, 18th
Median age (1996): 36.3
Under 5 years (1996): 6.72%, 37th
18 years and under (1996): 28.02%, 33rd
65 years and over (1996): 13.41%, 18th
Percent increase among the elderly (1995-96): 0.88%, 24th

OF VITAL IMPORTANCE

Live births per 1,000 pop. (1996): 13.6, 36th
Infant mortality rate per 1,000 live births (1995): 6.1, 43rd
  Rate for whites: 5.9, 39th
  Rate for blacks: NA
Births to unmarried women, % of total (1996): 29.7%, 32nd
Births to teenage mothers, % of total (1996): 13.2%, 24th
Abortions (1992): 16,060, 23rd
  Rate per 1,000 women 14-44 years old: 23.9, 18th
  Percent change (1988-92): 00%, 13th
Average lifetime (1989-91): 76.44, 18th
Total death rate per 100,000 pop. (1995): 898.4, 29th
  Accidents and adverse effects: 43.5, 15th
  Alzheimer's disease: 12.5, 3rd
  Cancer: 214.7, 20th
  Cerebrovascular diseases: 77.7, 3rd
  Chronic liver disease and cirrhosis: 9.2, 26th
  Chronic obstructive pulmonary diseases and allied conditions: 45.4, 12th
  Diabetes mellitus: 21.7, 33rd
  Diseases of heart: 240.1, 38th
  HIV infection: 9.2, 26th
  Homicide: 4.7, 36th
  Injury by firearms: 13.8, 27th
  Motor vehicle accidents: 18.9, 22nd
  Pneumonia and influenza: 28.8, 32nd
  Suicide: 15.8, 9th

KEEPING WELL

Active nonfederal physicians per 100,000 pop. (1995): 212, 26th
Dentists per 100,000 (1991): 69, 9th

Nurses per 100,000 (1995): 806, 30th
Hospitals per 100,000 (1995): 2.04, 29th
  Admissions per 1,000 (1995): 94.24, 42nd
  Hospital beds per 1,000 (1995): 2.29, 46th
  Occupancy rate per 100 beds (1995): 52.78, 49th
  Average cost per patient per day (1995): $1,141, 9th
  Average cost per stay (1995): $5,325, 40th
AIDS cases (new, 1996): 463; per 100,000: 14.5, 23rd
Persons living with HIV infection (1996): NA
Other notifiable diseases, per 100,000 pop.:
  Gonorrhea (1995): 27.2, 42nd
  Syphilis (1995): 2.1, 41st
  Tuberculosis (1996): 5.9, 23rd
Pop. without health insur. (1996): 15.3%, 19th

HOUSEHOLDS BY TYPE

Total households (1996): 1,249,000, 28th
  Percent change (1990-96): 13.2%, 11th
  Per 1,000 pop. (1996) 389.83, 5th
  Percent of householders 65 yrs. and over (1996): 21.86%, 24th
  Persons per household (1996): 2.51, 41st
Family households: 750,844
  Percent of total: 68.05%, 45th
Nonfamily households: 352,469
  Percent of total: 31.95%, 7th
Pop. living in group quarters: 66,205
  Percent of pop.: 2.33%, 40th

LIVING QUARTERS

Total housing units: 1,193,567
  Persons per unit: 2.38, 29th
Occupied housing units: 1,103,313
  Percent of total units: 92.44%, 7th
  Persons per unit: 2.48, 38th
  Percent of units with over 1 person per room: 3.64%, 21st
Owner-occupied units: 695,957
  Percent of total units: 58.31%, 29th
  Percent of occupied units: 63.08%, 41st
  Persons per unit: 2.62, 46th
  Median value: $67,100, 27th
Renter-occupied units: 407,356
  Percent of total units: 34.13%, 11th
  Percent of occupied units: 36.92%, 13th
  Persons per unit: 2.33, 28th
  Median contract rent: $344, 23rd
  Rental vacancy rate: 5.3%, 49th

Mobile home, trailer & other as a percent of occupied housing units: 13.16%, 21st

Persons in emergency shelters for homeless persons: 3,254, 0.114%, 4th

Persons visible in street locations: 564, 0.0198%, 9th

Nursing home population: 18,200, 0.64%, 31st

CRIME INDEX PER 100,000 (1996)

Total reported: 5,996.6, 10th
  Percent increase: −8.6%, 43rd
  Violent: 463.1, 27th
    Percent increase: −11.4%, 43rd
    Murder & nonnegligent manslaughter: 4.0, 34th
    Forcible rape: 39.7, 21st
    Aggravated assault: 297.2, 27th
    Robbery: 122.2, 29th
  Property: 5,533.6, 9th
    Percent increase: −8.4%, 44th
    Burglary: 988.3, 18th
    Larceny-theft: 4,014.3, 6th
    Motor vehicle theft: 531.0, 15th

TEACHING AND LEARNING

Pop. 3 and over enrolled in school (1996): 704,928, 28th
  Percent of pop.: 22.00%, 34th
Public elementary & secondary schools (1996-97): 1,216, 29th
  Total enrollment (1996): 537,783, 28th
    Percent of school age pop.: 90.08%, 35th
    Percent of total pop.: 16.78%, 32nd
  Teachers (1996): 26,757, 33rd
    Percent of pop.: 0.84%, 49th
  Pupil/teacher ratio (1995): 19.8, 4th
  Teachers' avg. salary (1996-97): $40,900, 14th
  Expenditure per capita (1992-93): $1,478.85, 12th
    Education as % of state govt. expenditures: 36.1%, 22nd
  Expenditure per pupil (1994-95): $6,436, 14th
    Percent increase (1993-94 & 1994-95): 2.76%, 36th
Percent at or above grade level, NAEP tests:
  Reading, grade 4 (1994): NA
  Math, grade 4 (1996): 65%, 20th
  Math, grade 8 (1996): 67%, 15th

Percent of graduates taking SAT (1995): 51%, 19th
  Mean SAT verbal scores: 448, 25th
  Mean SAT mathematical scores: 499, 25th
Percent of graduates taking ACT (1997): 12%, 37th
  Mean ACT scores: 22.3, 2nd
Percent of pop. over 25 completing:
  Less than 9th grade: 6.2%, 45th
  High school: 81.5%, 9th
  College degree(s): 20.6%, 21st
Higher education, institutions (1996): 45, 28th
  Enrollment (1995-96): 167,145, 30th
    Percent increase in enroll. (1990-95): 0.8%, 33rd
  White non-Hispanic (1995): 139,202, 27th
    Percent of enroll.: 83.28%, 22nd
  Total minority enroll. (1995): 21,555, 33rd
    Percent of enroll.: 12.90%, 33rd
  Black non-Hispanic (1995): 2,980, 39th
    Percent of enroll.: 1.78%, 42nd
  Hispanic (1995): 6,306, 17th
    Percent of enroll.: 3.77%, 15th
  Asian/Pacific Islander (1995): 9,683, 15th
    Percent of enroll.: 5.79%, 8th
  American Indian/AK native (1995): 2,586, 16th
    Percent of enroll.: 1.55%, 10th
  Nonresident alien (1995): 6,388, 22nd
    Percent of enroll.: 3.82%, 9th
  Female (1995): 90,139, 30th
    Percent of enroll.: 53.93%, 48th
  Pub. institutions (1995-96): 22, 30th
    Enrollment: 143,617, 29th
      Percent increase in enrollment (1990-95): −0.6%, 36th
    Percent of enroll.: 85.92%, 18th
  Private institutions (1995-96): 23, 26th
    Enrollment: 23,528, 31st
      Percent increase in enrollment (1990-95): 10.4%, 17th
    Percent of enroll.: 14.08%, 34th
  Tuition (in state), public 4-year institution (1996-97): $3,407, 17th
  Tuition (in state), public 2-year institution (1996-97): $1,524, 21st
  Tuition, private 4-year institution (1996-97): $14,766, 10th
Public library systems (1994): 124, 23rd
  Books & serial vol. per capita: 2.4, 33rd
  Library visits per capita: NA
  Circulation per capita: 9.6, 3rd

LAW ENFORCEMENT AND CORRECTIONS

Police protection and corrections expenditures (1996): $411,554,000
  Per capita: $128.45, 21st
Police per 10,000 pop. (1996): 16.44, 46th
Prisoners (1 year or more) per 100,000 pop. (1996): 226, 40th
  Percent change (1995-96): 12.3%, 10th
  Percent of inmates that are female: 6.6%, 20th
    Percent change: 22.8%, 10th
Death penalty: yes, by lethal injection
  Under sentence (Jan. 1998): 23, 22nd
  Executed, 1976-97: 2, 21st
  Executed in 1997: 1, 9th

RELIGION, NUMBER AND PERCENT OF POPULATION

Agnostic: 25,418—1.20%, 2nd
Buddhist: 10,591—0.50%, 2nd
Christian: 1,611,943—76.10%, 49th
Hindu: NA
Jewish: 8,473—0.40%, 31st
Muslim: 2,118—0.10%, 22nd
Unitarian: 8,473—0.40%, 8th
Other: 36,009—1.70%, 14th
None: 364,329—17.20%, 1st
Refused to answer: 50,837—2.40%, 20th

MAKING A LIVING

Personal income per capita (1996): $22,668, 28th
  Percent increase (1995-96): 4.8%, 9th
Disposable personal income per capita (1996): $19,189, 34th
Median income of households (average, 1995-96): $36,470, 20th
Percent of pop. below poverty level (1995-96): 11.5%, 28th

ECONOMY

In civilian labor force (1996): 1,721,000
  Percent of total pop.: 69.3%, 17th
  Percent of total pop. 65 years and over: 10.3%, 36th
  Percent of total female pop.: 62.2%, 19th
Major employer industries (total nonagricultural, 1996):
  Construction: 78,300—5.3%, 13th
  Finance, insurance, & real estate: 90,600—6.1%, 11th
  Government: 246,100—16.7%, 28th
  Manufacturing: 235,300—16.0%, 23rd
  Service: 384,700—26.1%, 35th
  Trade: 365,000—24.8%, 11th
  Transportation, communications, public utilities: 72,800—4.9%, 29th
Unemployment rate (1996): 5.9%, 13th
  Male: 6.0%, 8th
  Female: 5.8%, 15th
Total businesses (1995): 93,468, 25th
New business incorps. (1995): 9,730
  Percent of total businesses: 10.41%, 19th
Business failures (1995): 795
  Failures per 10,000 businesses: 85.1, 22nd
Agriculture farm income:
  Marketing (1996): $2,976,542,000, 28th
    Average per farm: $77,313, 33rd
  Leading products (1997): Cattle, greenhouse, dairy products, wheat, hay, grass seed, potatoes, onions, Christmas trees, pears, mint
  Average value land & build. per acre (1997): $1,000, 32nd
    Percent increase (1996-97): 8%, 10th
  Govt. payments (1996): $74,262,000, 28th
    Average per farm: $1,929, 30th
Construction, value of all (1996): $5,378,328,000, 25th
  Per capita: $1,679, 7th
Manufactures (1995):
  Value added: $19,677,300,000
    Per capita: $6,265, 25th
  Leading products (1997): Lumber and wood products, computer equipment, foods, machinery, primary and fabricated metals, paper
Value of nonfuel mineral production (1996): $251,000,000, 37th
Leading mineral products (1996): Stone, sand/gravel, cement, lime, diatomite
Energy consumption per person (1994): 336.3 mil. Btu, 29th
Retail sales (1995): $31,193,000,000
  Per household: $25,416, 16th
  Sales increase (1994-95): 17.2%, 1st
Tourism revenues (1995): $4.1 bil.
Foreign exports, in total value (1996): $8,948,000,000, 20th
  Per capita: $2,793, 8th
Gross state product per person (1994): $24,096, 31st
Public aid recipients (percent of resident pop. 1994): 5.1%, 40th

Medicaid recipients (percent of pop., 1995): 14.4%, 13th
Medicare enrollment per 1,000 pop. (1996): 232, 2nd

TRAVEL AND TRANSPORTATION

Motor vehicle registrations (1996): 2,851,048, 27th
Per 1,000 pop.: 891.98, 14th
Motorcycle registrations (1996): 60,841, 21st
Per 1,000 pop.: 21.34, 20th
Licensed drivers (1996): 2,541,873, 26th
Per 1,000 pop.: 807.24, 2nd
Public roads & streets (1996)
Total mileage: 83,190, 24th
Per 1,000 pop.: 125.97, 15th
Rural mileage: 73,039, 20th
Per 1,000 pop.: 22.80, 15th
Urban mileage: 10,151, 29th
Per 1,000 pop.: 3.17, 22nd
Interstate mileage: 728, 32nd
Per 1,000 pop.: 0.23, 20th
Speed limit (max. interstate, autos, mi. per hr., 1997): 65
Annual vehicle-mi. of travel per driver (1996): 11,605, 43rd
Mean travel time for workers age 16+ who work away from home: 19.6 min., 33rd

GOVERNMENT

Percent of voting age pop. registered (1996): 81.38%, 19th
Percent of voting age pop. voting for president: (1996): 57.5%, 10th
Percent of voting age pop. voting for U.S. representatives (1996): 55.7%, 11th
State legislators, total (1997): 90, 44th
Women members (1997): 23
Percent of legislature: 26%, 16th

U.S. Congress, House members (1998): 5
Change (1988-98): 0
Revenues (1996):
State govt.: $15,431,878,000
Per capita: $4,816.44, 7th
Parimutuel & amusement taxes & lotteries, revenue per capita (1995): $282.53, 4th
Expenditures (1996):
State govt.: $11,857,897,000
Per capita: $3,700.97, 14th
Debt outstanding (1996): $6,086,273,000
Per capita: $1,899.59, 15th

LAWS AND REGULATIONS

Legal driving age: 16
Marriage age without parental consent: 18
Divorce residence requirement: 6 mo., for qualifications check local statutes

ATTRACTIONS (1997)

Major opera companies: 1
Major symphony orchestras: 1
Major dance companies: 2
Major professional theater companies (non-profit): 1
Per capita spending by the NEA (1997): $0.26, 26th
State Fair in late August–early September at Salem

SPORTS AND COMPETITION

NCAA (Division I) football and basketball teams: Oregon State Univ. Beavers, Univ. of Oregon Ducks, Univ. of Portland Pilots (basketball only)
NBA basketball teams: Portland Trail Blazers, Rose Garden
ABL basketball teams: Portland Power, Memorial Coliseum

WEBSITES CONTAINING FURTHER INFORMATION

Welcome to Oregon On-Line!   http://www.state.or.us

PENNSYLVANIA

"Nowhere in this country, from sea to sea, does nature comfort us with such assurance of plenty, such rich and tranquil beauty as in those unsung unpainted hills of Pennsylvania."

Richard Harding Davis, journalist and author

To many, Pennsylvania is the most historic state—the birthplace of independence and of the Constitution, with a claim to more historic events and historic firsts than perhaps any other state. It often is called the "Birthstate of the Nation." All of the hard coal in the country is mined in Pennsylvania, and Pittsburgh is famous for the production of pig iron and steel. Originally a refuge for persecuted Quakers, Pennsylvania is also home to the Amish and the Mennonites, religious groups characterized by their distinctive dress and simple lifestyle. Many still speak a variation of German called Pennsylvania Dutch.

SUPERLATIVES

- Nation's first museum of art—the Philadelphia Academy of Arts.
- First natural history museum.
- First hospital—the Pennsylvania Hospital.
- First scientific society—the Franklin Institute, endowed by Benjamin Franklin.
- First circulating library.
- First medical college, founded in 1765 by John Morgan.
- First chamber of commerce.
- Greatest anthracite reserves.
- First in magnetite ore.
- First regular steamboat run.
- First steam locomotive on rails.
- First computer, at the University of Pennsylvania in the 1940s.

MOMENTS IN HISTORY

- The first known visit to the area was by Captain John Smith of Virginia in 1608.
- Henry Hudson's voyage in 1609 gave the Dutch claim to the region.
- Johan Printz established the first permanent European settlement (Swedish), on Tinicum Island in 1643.
- The Dutch seized the Swedish settlements in 1655, and the British took over in turn in 1664.
- William Penn arrived in Pennsylvania in October 1682, aboard the *Welcome,* to take over his enormous grant that later became Pennsylvania and Delaware.

> ### So They Say
> *"The air is sweet and clear, the Heavens serene...The country itself...is not to be despised...in some places a vast fat earth, like our best vales, in England."*
> **William Penn**

- In 1682, Penn's "Great Law" became one of the first documents safeguarding life, liberty, and property through jury trial.
- The 1701 Charter of Privileges contained most of the principles of present constitutions.
- George Washington won the first skirmish of the French and Indian War, the Battle of Laurel Mountain, May 28, 1754, in present-day Fayette County.
- In 1755, British General Edward Braddock's major defeat left much of Pennsylvania in French hands.
- Beginning in 1756, Fort Augusta was built, the first of a chain of British outposts in the wilderness.
- After widespread losses, the French relinquished their claims in 1763.
- As Revolutionary tensions grew, James Smith in 1769 captured Fort Bedford, first stronghold to fall to American rebels.
- The first Continental Congress, meeting at Philadelphia in 1774, marked that city as a national capital.
- With the signing of the Declaration of Independence in Philadelphia on July 4, 1776, the process of Revolution formally began. Philadelphia fell to Lord William Howe on September 26, 1777.
- By the spring of 1778, the hardships of Valley Forge were left behind.
- The first wagon trip westward in 1783 pioneered the way for the vast movement of settlers to western Pennsylvania.
- After the Articles of Confederation failed, delegates labored at Philadelphia from May to September 1787, to write a new Constitution. Held together, in part, by the will and skill of Benjamin Franklin, they brought forth a new nation.

- On December 12, 1787, Pennsylvania became the second state.
- In 1790, when Benjamin Franklin died, the world mourned the first citizen of Philadelphia and one of the most extraordinary figures America ever has produced. Some 20,000 people—the largest crowd in the history of Philadelphia to that time—turned out for his funeral.
- During the War of 1812, Oliver Hazard Perry's eventually triumphant fleet was built in the wilds near present-day Erie.

So They Say

"I never walked through the streets of any city with so much satisfaction as those of Philadelphia. The neatness and cleanliness of all animate and inanimate things, houses, pavements, and citizens, is not to be surpassed...the appearance of a finished and long-established metropolis."

British traveler Frances Wright (1819)

- In the 1830s, 1840s, and 1850s, Pennsylvania led the nation in science and culture.
- Pennsylvania played a key role in the Underground Railroad and gave Abraham Lincoln its vote in the 1860 election.
- Pennsylvania was the only Northern state in which a critical battle of the Civil War was fought. During the three days beginning on July 1, 1863, the Union successes in the Battle of Gettysburg marked a turning point of the war.

So They Say

"Troops under my command have repulsed the enemy's assault and we have gained a great victory. The enemy is now flying in all directions in my front."

Union General George Meade, at Gettysburg

- In 1876 the Centennial Exposition at Philadelphia celebrated the 100th birthday of the Declaration of Independence.
- The May 1889 flood at Johnstown was one of the nation's worst disasters, with 2,200 lives lost.
- In 1972, Hurricane Agnes brought Pennsylvania the worst-yet hurricane/flood damage in the history of the state.

- In 1991, Harris Wofford became the first Democrat elected to the U.S. Senate from Pennsylvania since 1962.

THAT'S INTERESTING

- William Penn received the greatest land grant ever given an English subject, for which he was required to pay only two beaver skins per year to the king.
- The carp in Lake Pymatuning sometimes crowd so closely together that ducks walk across the backs of the fish.
- When the Ringing Rocks near Upper Black Eddy are struck, the pitch depends on the size of the rock.

NOTABLE NATIVES

Louisa May Alcott (Germantown, 1832-1888), author. **Richard Allen** (Philadelphia, 1760-1831), religious leader. **Marian Anderson** (Philadelphia, 1902-1993), opera singer. **Maxwell Anderson** (Atlantic, 1888-1959), playwright. **Samuel Barber** (West Chester, 1910-1981), composer. **James Buchanan** (Mercersburg, 1791-1868), U.S. president. **Charles Wakefield Cadman** (Johnstown, 1881-1946), composer. **Simon Cameron** (Maytown, 1799-1889), public official/political leader. **Mary Cassatt** (Allegheny, now Pittsburgh, 1845-1926), artist. **W. C. Fields** (Philadelphia, 1880-1946), entertainer. **Stephen Collins Foster** (Lawrenceville, 1826-1864), composer. **Henry Clay Frick** (West Overton, 1849-1919), industrialist/philanthropist. **Henry John Heinz** (Pittsburgh, 1845-1919), industrialist. **Milton Snavely Hershey** (Dauphin County, 1857-1945), industrialist/philanthropist. **Lido Anthony (Lee) Iacocca** (Allentown, 1924-), business leader. **Harold LeClair Ickes** (Blair County, 1874-1952), public official. **Gene Kelly** (Pittsburgh, 1912-1996), actor/dancer. **Grace Kelly** (Philadelphia, 1929-1982), actress/princess of Monaco. **Walter Crawford Kelly** (Philadelphia, 1913-1973), cartoonist/illustrator. **George Catlett Marshall** (Uniontown, 1880-1959), soldier/public official. **George Brinton McClellan** (Philadelphia, 1826-1885), soldier. **William Holmes McGuffey** (near Claysville, 1800-1873), educator. **Andrew William Mellon** (Pittsburgh, 1855-1937), financier/art collector. **Ethelbert Woodbridge Nevin** (Edgeworth, 1862-1901), composer. **Maxfield Frederick Parrish** (Philadelphia, 1870-1966), artist. **Robert Edwin Peary** (Cresson, 1856-1920), explorer. **Mary Roberts Rinehart** (Pittsburgh, 1876-1958), author. **Washington Augustus Roebling** (Saxonburg, 1837-1926), engineer. **Charles Michael Schwab** (Williamsburg, 1862-1939), industrialist. **James Stewart** (Indiana, 1908-1997), actor. **William Tatem (Big Bill) Tilden, Jr.** (Germantown, 1893-1953), tennis player. **John Wanamaker** (Philadelphia, 1838-1922), merchant. **Anthony Wayne** (Wayneboro, 1745-1796), soldier. **Benjamin West** (Springfield, 1738-1820), artist.

GENERAL

Admitted to statehood: December 12, 1787

Origin of name: William Penn, the Quaker who was made full proprietor by King Charles II in 1681, suggested "Sylvania," or "woodland," as the name for his tract. Charles II added "Penn" to "Sylvania," contrary to the desires of the modest proprietor, in honor of Penn's father

Capital: Harrisburg

Nickname: Keystone State

Motto: Virtue, liberty, and independence

Animal: Whitetail deer

Bird: Ruffed grouse

Insect: Firefly

Fish: Brook trout

Flower: Mountain laurel

Song: "Pennsylvania"

Tree: Eastern hemlock

THE LAND

Area: 46,059 sq. mi., 33rd
  Land: 44,820 sq. mi., 32nd
  Water: 1,239 sq. mi., 23rd
    Inland water: 490 sq. mi., 45th
  Great Lakes: 749 sq. mi., 7th

Topography: Allegheny Mountains run SW to NE, with piedmont and coastal plain in the SE triangle; Allegheny Front a diagonal spine across the state's center; NW rugged plateau falls to Lake Erie lowland.

Number of counties: 67

Geographic center: Centre, 2.5 mi. SW of Bellefonte

Length: 283 mi.; width: 160 mi.

Highest point: 3,213 ft. (Mount Davis), 33rd

Lowest point: sea level (Delaware River), 3rd

Mean elevation: 1,100 ft., 23rd

Coastline: 0 mi.

Shoreline: 89 mi., 24th

CLIMATE AND ENVIRONMENT

Temp., highest: 111 deg. on July 10, 1936, at Phoenixville; lowest: –42 deg. on Jan. 5, 1904, at Smethport

Monthly average: highest: 86.2 deg., 32nd; lowest: 18.0 deg., 23rd; spread (high to low): 68.2 deg., 26th

Hazardous waste sites (1997): 97, 2nd

Endangered species: Animals: 11—Indiana bat, Clubshell, American peregrine falcon, Dwarf wedge mussel, Ring pink mussel, Cracking pearlymussel, Orangefoot pimple back pearlymussel, Pink mucket pearlymussel, Rough pigtoe, Northern rifleshell, Piping plover. Plants: 1

MAJOR CITIES
POPULATION, 1996
PERCENTAGE INCREASE, 1990-96

Philadelphia, 1,478,002; –6.8%

Pittsburgh, 350,363; –5.3%

Erie, 105,270; –3.2%

Allentown, 102,211; –2.9%

Scranton, 77,189; –5.6%

THE PEOPLE

Population (1997): 12,019,661, 5th
  Percent change (1990-97): 1.15%, 45th
  Percent of total U.S. pop.: 4.49%, 5th
  Per sq. mi: 260.97, 9th

Population (2000 proj.): 12,211,000, 5th
  Percent change (1995-2000): 1.15%, 45th

Percent in metro. area (1996): 84.55%, 12th

Foreign born: 369,000, 8th
  Percent: 3.1%, 25th

Top three ancestries reported:
  German, 36.31%
  Irish, 18.99%
  Italian, 11.55%

White (1992): 10,687,000, 89.10%, 25th

Black (1992): 1,134,000, 9.45%, 21st

Native American (1992): 16,000, 0.13%, 50th

Asian, Pacific Isle (1992): 159,000, 1.33%, 25th

Hispanic origin (1992): 254,000, 2.12%, 30th

Percent over 5 yrs. speaking language other than English at home: 7.3%, 24th

Percent males (1996): 48.15%, 47th; percent females: 51.85%, 5th
Percent never married: 27.3%, 16th
Marriages per 1,000 (1996): 5.82, 50th
Divorces per 1,000 (1996): 3.18, 42nd
Median age (1996): 36.9
Under 5 years (1996): 6.31%, 47th
Under 18 years (1996): 26.57%, 46th
65 years & older (1995): 15.86%, 2nd
Percent increase among the elderly (1995-96): 0.20%, 41st

OF VITAL IMPORTANCE

Live births per 1,000 pop. (1996): 12.4, 47th
Infant mortality rate per 1,000 live births (1995): 7.8, 19th
  Rate for whites: 6.2, 26th
  Rate for blacks: 17.6, 6th
Births to unmarried women, % of total (1996): 32.3%, 22nd
Births to teenage mothers, % of total (1996): 10.6%, 36th
Abortions (1992): 49,740, 8th
  Rate per 1,000 women 14-44 years old: 18.6, 26th
  Percent change (1988-92): –2%, 16th
Average lifetime (1989-91): 75.38, 28th
Total death rate per 100,000 pop. (1995): 1,059.2, 5th
  Accidents and adverse effects: 35.3, 30th
  Alzheimer's disease: 7.5, 33rd
  Cancer: 250.7, 4th
  Cerebrovascular diseases: 68.6, 17th
  Chronic liver disease and cirrhosis: 9.4, 21st
  Chronic obstructive pulmonary diseases and allied conditions: 43.9, 18th
  Diabetes mellitus: 28.2, 6th
  Diseases of heart: 359.7, 2nd
  HIV infection: 11.5, 18th
  Homicide: 6.5, 25th
  Injury by firearms: 11.6, 33rd
  Motor vehicle accidents: 13.1, 41st
  Pneumonia and influenza: 35.5, 13th
  Suicide: 12.1, 26th

KEEPING WELL

Active nonfederal physicians per 100,000 pop. (1995): 273, 8th
Dentists per 100,000 (1991): 66, 11th
Nurses per 100,000 (1995): 1,018, 10th
Hospitals per 100,000 (1995): 1.86, 31st
  Admissions per 1,000 (1995): 149.93, 3rd
  Hospital beds per 1,000 (1995): 4.02, 16th
  Occupancy rate per 100 beds (1995): 69.69, 9th

Average cost per patient per day (1995): $963, 22nd
Average cost per stay (1995): $6,482, 11th
AIDS cases (new, 1996): 2,348; per 100,000: 19.5, 15th
Persons living with HIV infection (1996): NA
Other notifiable diseases, per 100,000 pop.:
  Gonorrhea (1995): 108.0, 25th
  Syphilis (1995): 16.2, 21st
  Tuberculosis (1996): 4.8, 28th
Pop. without health insur. (1996): 9.5%, 46th

HOUSEHOLDS BY TYPE

Total households (1996): 4,594,000, 5th
  Percent change (1990-96): 2.2%, 47th
  Per 1,000 pop. (1996) 381.09, 23rd
  Percent of householders 65 yrs. and over (1996): 26.36%, 2nd
  Persons per household (1996): 2.58, 24th
Family households: 3,155,989
  Percent of total: 70.20%, 29th
Nonfamily households: 1,339,977
  Percent of total: 29.80%, 23rd
Pop. living in group quarters: 348,424
  Percent of pop.: 2.93%, 21st

LIVING QUARTERS

Total housing units: 4,938,140
  Persons per unit: 2.41, 25th
Occupied housing units: 4,495,966
  Percent of total units: 91.05%, 16th
  Persons per unit: 2.46, 44th
  Percent of units with over 1 person per room: 1.84%, 45th
Owner-occupied units: 3,176,121
  Percent of total units: 64.32%, 5th
  Percent of occupied units: 70.64%, 5th
  Persons per unit: 2.72, 28th
  Median value: $69,700, 25th
Renter-occupied units: 1,319,845
  Percent of total units: 26.73%, 39th
  Percent of occupied units: 29.36%, 47th
  Persons per unit: 2.19, 48th
  Median contract rent: $322, 28th
  Rental vacancy rate: 7.2%, 40th
Mobile home, trailer & other as a percent of occupied housing units: 7.12%, 35th
Persons in emergency shelters for homeless persons: 8,237, 0.069%, 15th
Persons visible in street locations: 1,312, 0.0110%, 16th
Nursing home population: 106,454, 0.90%, 17th

CRIME INDEX PER 100,000 (1996)

Total reported: 3,392.5, 45th
  Percent increase: 0.8%, 11th
  Violent: 432.5, 29th
    Percent increase: 1.2%, 8th
    Murder & nonnegligent manslaughter: 5.7, 27th
    Forcible rape: 25.3, 43rd
    Aggravated assault: 200.4, 38th
    Robbery: 201.1, 12th
  Property: 2,960.1, 45th
    Percent increase: 0.8%, 15th
    Burglary: 551.4, 48th
    Larceny-theft: 1,996.5, 48th
    Motor vehicle theft: 412.2, 29th

TEACHING AND LEARNING

Pop. 3 and over enrolled in school (1996): 2,425,009, 6th
  Percent of pop.: 20.11%, 49th
Public elementary & secondary schools (1996-97): 3,182, 7th
  Total enrollment (1996): 1,807,250, 7th
    Percent of school age pop.: 84.73%, 51st
    Percent of total pop.: 14.99%, 50th
  Teachers (1996): 106,400, 6th
    Percent of pop.: 0.88%, 46th
  Pupil/teacher ratio (1995): 17.0, 19th
  Teachers' avg. salary (1996-97): $47,429, 5th
  Expenditure per capita (1992-93): $1,402.93, 19th
    Education as % of state govt. expenditures: 36.8%, 19th
  Expenditure per pupil (1994-95): $7,109, 9th
    Percent increase (1993-94 & 1994-95): 1.80%, 45th
Percent at or above grade level, NAEP tests:
  Reading, grade 4 (1994): 30%, 16th
  Math, grade 4 (1996): 68%, 13th
  Math, grade 8 (1996): NA
Percent of graduates taking SAT (1995): 70%, 4th
  Mean SAT verbal scores: 419, 42nd
  Mean SAT mathematical scores: 461, 47th
Percent of graduates taking ACT (1997): 8%, 41st
  Mean ACT scores: 21.0, 30th
Percent of pop. over 25 completing:
  Less than 9th grade: 9.4%, 26th
  High school: 74.7%, 35th
  College degree(s): 17.9%, 32nd

Higher education, institutions (1996): 217, 3rd
  Enrollment (1995-96): 617,759, 6th
    Percent increase in enroll. (1990-95): 2.3%, 29th
    White non-Hispanic (1995): 516,552, 4th
      Percent of enroll.: 83.62%, 21st
    Total minority enroll. (1995): 84,254, 10th
      Percent of enroll.: 13.64%, 30th
    Black non-Hispanic (1995): 51,269, 13th
      Percent of enroll.: 8.30%, 21st
    Hispanic (1995): 11,171, 12th
      Percent of enroll.: 1.81%, 31st
    Asian/Pacific Islander (1995): 20,463, 9th
      Percent of enroll.: 3.31%, 18th
    American Indian/AK native (1995): 1,351, 26th
      Percent of enroll.: 0.22%, 51st
    Nonresident alien (1995): 16,953, 8th
      Percent of enroll.: 2.74%, 24th
    Female (1995): 339,831, 6th
      Percent of enroll.: 55.01%, 41st
  Pub. institutions (1995-96): 65, 6th
    Enrollment: 339,928, 8th
      Percent increase in enrollment (1990-95): -1.0%, 37th
    Percent of enroll.: 55.03%, 48th
  Private institutions (1995-96): 152, 3rd
    Enrollment: 277,831, 2nd
      Percent increase in enrollment (1990-95): 6.6%, 22nd
    Percent of enroll.: 44.97%, 4th
  Tuition (in state), public 4-year institution (1996-97): $4,994, 2nd
  Tuition (in state), public 2-year institution (1996-97): $2,012, 11th
  Tuition, private 4-year institution (1996-97): $14,908, 9th
Public library systems (1994): 445, 5th
  Books & serial vol. per capita: 2.1, 37th
  Library visits per capita: 3.0, 33rd
  Circulation per capita: 4.7, 39th

LAW ENFORCEMENT AND CORRECTIONS

Police protection and corrections expenditures (1996): $1,701,728,000
  Per capita: $141.15, 14th
Police per 10,000 pop. (1996): 26.39, 11th
Prisoners (1 year or more) per 100,000 pop. (1996): 286, 34th
  Percent change (1995-96): 6.5%, 22nd
  Percent of inmates that are female: 4.3%, 49th
    Percent change: −1.7%, 46th

Death penalty: yes, by lethal injection
Under sentence (Jan. 1998): 213, 4th
Executed, 1976-97: 2, 21st
Executed in 1997: 0

RELIGION, NUMBER AND PERCENT OF POPULATION

Agnostic: 63,608—0.70%, 17th
Buddhist: 9,087—0.10%, 17th
Christian: 7,987,326—87.90%, 19th
Hindu: 9,087—0.10%, 10th
Jewish: 154,476—1.70%, 10th
Muslim: 27,261—0.30%, 9th
Unitarian: 9,087—0.10%, 31st
Other: 208,997—2.30%, 6th
None: 445,255—4.90%, 40th
Refused to answer: 172,650—1.90%, 31st

MAKING A LIVING

Personal income per capita (1996): $24,668, 19th
Percent increase (1995-96): 2.4%, 38th
Disposable personal income per capita (1996): $21,410, 17th
Median income of households (average, 1995-96): $35,221, 21st
Percent of pop. below poverty level (1995-96): 11.9%, 26th

ECONOMY

In civilian labor force (1996): 5,903,000
Percent of total pop.: 63.6%, 42nd
Percent of total pop. 65 years and over: 10.8%, 34th
Percent of total female pop.: 55.6%, 45th
Major employer industries (total nonagricultural, 1996):
Construction: 201,700—3.8%, 41st
Finance, insurance, & real estate: 308,700—5.8%, 14th
Government: 720,900—13.6%, 49th
Manufacturing: 929,100—17.5%, 16th
Service: 1,651,200—31.1%, 9th
Trade: 1,205,300—22.7%, 43rd
Transportation, communications, public utilities: 271,900—5.1%, 22nd
Unemployment rate (1996): 5.3%, 20th
Male: 5.9%, 10th
Female: 4.6%, 32nd
Total businesses (1995): 283,998, 6th
New business incorps. (1995): 18,575
Percent of total businesses: 6.54%, 44th
Business failures (1995): 2,756
Failures per 10,000 businesses: 97.0, 18th

Agriculture farm income:
Marketing (1996): $4,142,509,000, 18th
Average per farm: $82,850, 30th
Leading products (1997): Dairy products, cattle, corn, hay, apples, potatoes, winter wheat, oats, vegetables, tobacco, grapes, mushrooms
Average value land & build. per acre (1997): $2,630, 7th
Percent increase (1996-97): 5%, 26th
Govt. payments (1996): $37,111,000, 33rd
Average per farm: $742, 39th
Construction, value of all (1996): $9,409,322,000, 11th
Per capita: $780, 48th
Manufactures (1995):
Value added: $84,581,800,000
Per capita: $7,007, 17th
Leading products (1997): Primary metals, foods, fabricated metal products, nonelectrical machinery, electrical machinery, printing and publishing, stone, clay, glass products
Value of nonfuel mineral production (1996): $1,040,000,000, 11th
Leading mineral products (1996): Coal, natural gas, stone, cement, lime, sand/gravel
Energy consumption per person (1994): 317.7 mil. Btu, 33rd
Retail sales (1995): $104,471,000,000
Per household: $22,749, 43rd
Sales increase (1994-95): 3.3%, 31st
Tourism revenues (1996): $14.2 bil.
Foreign exports, in total value (1996): $14,364,000,000, 12th
Per capita: $1,191, 34th
Gross state product per person (1994): $24,429, 27th
Public aid recipients (percent of resident pop. 1994): 7.2%, 18th
Medicaid recipients (percent of pop., 1995): 10.2%, 38th
Medicare enrollment per 1,000 pop. (1996): 172, 5th

TRAVEL AND TRANSPORTATION

Motor vehicle registrations (1996): 8,640,238, 7th
Per 1,000 pop.: 717.62, 41st
Motorcycle registrations (1996): 178,527, 4th
Per 1,000 pop.: 20.66, 22nd
Licensed drivers (1996): 8,154,055, 5th
Per 1,000 pop.: 676.11, 31st

Public roads & streets (1996)
  Total mileage: 118,952, 7th
    Per 1,000 pop.: 19.87, 40th
    Rural mileage: 85,750, 12th
    Per 1,000 pop.: 7.11, 40th
    Urban mileage: 33,202, 6th
    Per 1,000 pop.: 2.75, 38th
    Interstate mileage: 1,750, 4th
    Per 1,000 pop.: 0.15, 35th
Speed limit (max. interstate, autos, mi. per
  hr., 1997): 65
Annual vehicle-mi. of travel per driver (1996):
  11,756, 42nd
Mean travel time for workers age 16+ who
  work away from home: 21.6 min., 16th

GOVERNMENT

Percent of voting age pop. registered (1996):
  74.00%, 33rd
  Percent of voting age pop. voting for presi-
    dent: (1996): 49.0%, 30th
  Percent of voting age pop. voting for U.S.
    representatives (1996): 46.9%, 29th
State legislators, total (1997): 253, 2nd
  Women members (1997): 31
    Percent of legislature: 12%, 46th
U.S. Congress, House members (1998): 21
  Change (1988-98): –2
Revenues (1996):
  State govt.: $42,796,060,000
    Per capita: $3,549.77, 25th
    Parimutuel & amusement taxes & lotter-
      ies, revenue per capita (1995): $125.19,
      19th
Expenditures (1996):
  State govt.: $38,698,546,000
    Per capita: $3,209.90, 23rd
Debt outstanding (1996): $15,045,892,000
    Per capita: $1,248.00, 30th

LAWS AND REGULATIONS

Legal driving age: 18, 17 if completed driver
  education course

Marriage age without parental consent: 18
Divorce residence requirement: 6 mo.

ATTRACTIONS (1997)

Major opera companies: 5
Major symphony orchestras: 5
Major dance companies: 4
Major professional theater companies (non-
  profit): 2
Per capita spending by the NEA (1997):
  $0.26, 27th
State Fair during second week in January at
  Harrisburg

SPORTS AND COMPETITION

NCAA (Division I) football and basketball
  teams: Bucknell Univ. Bison, Drexel
  Univ. Dragons (basketball only), Du-
  quesne Univ. Dukes, Lafayette College
  Leopards, La Salle Univ. Explorers
  (basketball only), Lehigh Univ. Moun-
  tain Hawks (basketball only), Pennsyl-
  vania State Univ. Nittany Lions, Robert
  Morris College Colonials, St. Francis
  College Red Flash, St. Joseph's Univ.
  Hawks, Temple Univ. Owls, Univ. of
  Pennsylvania Red & Blue/Quakers,
  Univ. of Pittsburgh Panthers, Villanova
  Univ. Wildcats
Major league baseball teams: Pittsburgh Pi-
  rates (NL Central), Three Rivers Sta-
  dium; Philadelphia Phillies (NL East),
  Veterans Stadium
NBA basketball teams: Philadelphia 76ers,
  CoreStates Center
ABL basketball teams: Philadelphia Rage, The
  Palestra, The Apollo
NFL football teams: Pittsburgh Steelers (AFC),
  Three Rivers Stadium; Philadelphia Ea-
  gles (NFC), Veterans Stadium
NHL hockey teams: Philadelphia Flyers,
  CoreStates Center; Pittsburgh Pen-
  guins, Allegheny Energy Dome

WEBSITES CONTAINING FURTHER INFORMATION

Commonwealth of Pennsylvania Home Page   http://www.state.pa.us

RHODE ISLAND

"One views it as placed there by some refinement in the scheme of nature, just a touchstone of taste—with a beautiful little sense to be read with it by a few persons and nothing at all to be made of it, as to its essence, by most others."
                                                                    Henry James, novelist

The smallest state in area, Rhode Island could be fitted into enormous Alaska 425 times. However, despite its size, it has the longest official name. And it is an important industrial state, especially in textile and jewelry production. It lies on the beautiful Narragansett Bay—an arm of the Atlantic Ocean—and is a popular vacation area, to which boaters, fishermen, and other water-sports fans flock during the summer months. The big and the little have combined to weave the fascinating story of Rhode Island.

SUPERLATIVES

- Said to be the birthplace of the U.S. industrial revolution.
- Most heavily industrialized state in proportion to size.
- World's costume jewelry center.
- Birthplace of the poultry industry.
- Oldest synagogue in America—the Touro Synagogue in Newport.
- Largest unsupported dome in America, on the capitol.
- Nation's oldest indoor shopping center, at Providence.

MOMENTS IN HISTORY

- Giovanni de Verrazano made the first recorded European contact with what is now Rhode Island in 1524, at Narragansett Bay.
- In 1635, William Blackstone settled in Valley Falls, becoming the first European settler known in the Rhode Island area.
- Providence was founded by Roger Williams in 1636 on a grant of land ceded to him by the Narragansett Indians.
- In 1644, Williams obtained a charter for the colony; after the restoration of the English monarchy, a second, liberal charter for the colony was granted by King Charles II in 1663.

So They Say

"Having a sense of God's merciful providence unto me called this place Providence, desired it might be for a shelter for persons distressed for conscience."
                                                     Roger Williams

- The first law against slavery in North America was enacted by Rhode Island on May 18, 1652.
- King Philip, chief of the Wampanoag Indians, led his people in King Philip's War (1675-76); he was captured and executed on August 12, 1676, crippling Indian power in the region.
- Rhode Islanders were quick to protest the British tax laws. On June 9, 1772, the British sloop of war *Gaspee* was captured and burned in Narragansett Bay.
- Providence celebrated its own "tea party" on March 2, 1775, by burning a huge mound of captured tea.
- During the Revolutionary War many Rhode Island communities were captured. Heaviest fighting in the state was in the Battle of Rhode Island, August 28-29, 1778.
- Opposed to the new U.S. Constitution and its government, Rhode Island held out until May 29, 1790, when it became the last of the 13 original colonies to join.
- In 1793 the firm of Almy, Brown, and Slater built a new mill. Founder Samuel Slater is generally considered to have introduced modern manufacturing to the New World. The Slater Mill Historic Site is revered as the birthplace of the American textile industry.
- In 1824 women weavers of Pawtucket went on strike, in what was thought to be the first strike in the United States by women.
- In 1876, President Rutherford B. Hayes made a historic conversation over the newly invented telephone, from Rocky Point to Providence, a distance of 8 miles.
- In 1895 the Cornelius Vanderbilt mansion, the Breakers, became perhaps the nation's most elegant private home, expanding Newport's high social position.
- The America's Cup yacht race came to Newport in 1930. In 1983, Americans lost the race for the first time, to Australia.
- During World War II, working at Quonset Point near Davisville, the Navy Seabees designed a structure that became world renowned, known as the Quonset hut.
- In 1953, Newport was the scene of the

marriage of John F. Kennedy and Jacqueline Bouvier. When Kennedy was president of the United States, the first family was a frequent guest of the Bouviers at their summer home located at Newport.

- Newport held the first of its celebrated jazz festivals in 1954.

THAT'S INTERESTING

- The smallest state has the longest official name, the "State of Rhode Island and Providence Plantations."
- Many protests against the British tax on tea were made in Rhode Island. One man dashed around Providence crossing out the word "tea" on every sign he found.
- A lover of good jokes, Mrs. William Astor once invited Newport society to meet the Prince del Drago, who turned out to be a tiny monkey resplendent in a full dress suit.
- The Rhode Island red chicken is the only state bird to have been "developed" in a state.

NOTABLE NATIVES

Nelson Wilmarth Aldrich (Foster, 1841-1915), public official. **Zachariah Allen** (Providence, 1795-1882), inventor. **Nicholas Brown** (Providence, 1729-1791), manufacturer. **William Ellery Channing** (Newport, 1780-1842), religious leader. **George Michael Cohan** (Providence, 1878-1942), composer/actor. **George William Curtis** (Providence, 1824-1892), author/lecturer. **Thomas Wilson Dorr** (Providence, 1805-1854), political reformer. **Robert Gray** (Tiverton, 1755-1806), explorer. **Nathanael Greene** (Warwick, 1742-1786), Revolutionary soldier. **Stephen Hopkins** (Providence, 1707-1785), colonial adminstrator. **Napoleon (Larry) Lajoie** (Woonsocket, 1874-1959), baseball player. **Matthew Calbraith Perry** (Newport, 1794-1858), naval officer. **Oliver Hazard Perry** (South Kingston, 1785-1819), naval officer. **Gilbert Charles Stuart** (North Kingstown, 1755-1828), artist.

GENERAL

Admitted to statehood: May 29, 1790
Origin of name: Exact origin unknown. One theory notes that Giovanni de Verrazano recorded an island about the size of Rhodes in the Mediterranean in 1524, but others believe the state was named Roode Eylandt by Dutch explorer Adriaen Block because of its red clay

Capital: Providence
Nickname: Little Rhody, Ocean State
Motto: Hope
Bird: Rhode Island red
Flower: Violet
Stone: Cumberlandite
Song: "Rhode Island"
Tree: Red maple

THE LAND

Area: 1,231 sq. mi., 50th
   Land: 1,045 sq. mi., 50th
   Water: 186 sq. mi., 48th
      Inland water: 168 sq. mi., 46th
      Coastal water: 18 sq. mi., 20th
Topography: Eastern lowlands of Narragansett Basin; western uplands of flat and rolling hills
Number of counties: 5
Geographic center: Kent, 1 mile SSW of Crompton
Length: 40 mi.; width: 30 mi.
Highest point: 812 ft. (Jerimoth Hill), 46th
Lowest point: sea level (Atlantic Ocean), 3rd
Mean elevation: 200 ft., 47th
Coastline: 40 mi., 19th
Shoreline: 384 mi., 20th

CLIMATE AND ENVIRONMENT

Temp., highest: 104 deg. on Aug. 2, 1975, at Providence; lowest: -25 deg. on Feb. 5, 1996, at Greene
Monthly average: highest: 81.7 deg., 48th; lowest: 20.0 deg., 27th; spread (high to low): 61.7 deg., 39th
Hazardous waste sites (1997): 12, 29th
Endangered species: Animals: 3—American burying beetle, American peregrine falcon, Roseate tern. Plants: 1

MAJOR CITIES
POPULATION, 1996
PERCENTAGE INCREASE, 1990-96

Providence, 152,558; –5.1%
Warwick, 84,514; –1.1%
Cranston, 74,324; –2.3%
Pawtucket, 69,068; –4.9%
East Providence, 48,389; –4.0%

THE PEOPLE

Population (1997): 987,429, 43rd
   Percent change (1990-97): -1.60%, 50th
   Percent of total U.S. pop.: 0.37%, 43rd
   Per sq. mi: 639.11, 3rd

Population (2000 proj.): 993,500, 43rd
  Percent change (1995-2000): 0.35%, 48th
Percent in metro. area (1996): 91.64%, 8th
Foreign born: 95,000, 24th
  Percent: 9.5%, 7th
Top three ancestries reported:
  Irish, 21.34%
  Italian, 19.84%
  English, 16.05%
White (1992): 932,000, 93.11%, 14th
Black (1992): 45,000, 4.50%, 31st
Native American (1992): 4,000, 0.40%, 27th
Asian, Pacific Isle (1992): 20,000, 2.00%, 18th
Hispanic origin (1992): 51,000, 5.09%, 18th
Percent over 5 yrs. speaking language other than English at home: 17.0%, 9th
Percent males (1996): 48.12%, 48th; percent females: 51.88%, 4th
Percent never married: 29.6%, 6th
Marriages per 1,000 (1996): 7.91, 32nd
Divorces per 1,000 (1996): 3.26, 39th
Median age (1996): 35.8
Under 5 years (1996): 6.37%, 46th
18 years and under (1996): 26.20%, 48th
65 years and over (1996): 15.77%, 3rd
Percent increase among the elderly (1995-96): 0.16%, 44th

OF VITAL IMPORTANCE

Live births per 1,000 pop. (1996): 12.6, 45th
Infant mortality rate per 1,000 live births (1995): 7.2, 31st
  Rate for whites: 7.0, 13th
  Rate for blacks: NA
Births to unmarried women, % of total (1996): 32.9%, 19th
Births to teenage mothers, % of total (1996): 10.3%, 40th
Abortions (1992): 6,990, 36th
  Rate per 1,000 women 14-44 years old: 30.0, 8th
  Percent change (1988-92): –2%, 16th
Average lifetime (1989-91): 76.54, 16th
Total death rate per 100,000 pop. (1995): 975.7, 12th
  Accidents and adverse effects: 21.9, 50th
  Alzheimer's disease: 12.2, 4th
  Cancer: 250.4, 5th
  Cerebrovascular diseases: 64.8, 23rd
  Chronic liver disease and cirrhosis: 11.9, 7th
  Chronic obstructive pulmonary diseases and allied conditions: 42.0, 20th

Diabetes mellitus: 24.7, 16th
Diseases of heart: 334.1, 9th
HIV infection: 10.0, 23rd
Homicide: 3.5, 44th
Injury by firearms: 6.3, 48th
Motor vehicle accidents: 8.1, 50th
Pneumonia and influenza: 31.1, 28th
Suicide: 9.0, 47th

KEEPING WELL

Active nonfederal physicians per 100,000 pop. (1995): 298, 6th
Dentists per 100,000 (1991): 56, 20th
Nurses per 100,000 (1995): 1,136, 4th
Hospitals per 100,000 (1995): 1.11, 49th
  Admissions per 1,000 (1995): 120.20, 21st
  Hospital beds per 1,000 (1995): 2.73, 38th
  Occupancy rate per 100 beds (1995): 66.67, 12th
  Average cost per patient per day (1995): $1,092, 10th
  Average cost per stay (1995): $6,202, 16th
AIDS cases (new, 1996): 178; per 100,000: 18.0, 17th
Persons living with HIV infection (1996): NA
Other notifiable diseases, per 100,000 pop.:
  Gonorrhea (1995): 55.1, 36th
  Syphilis (1995): 9.1, 28th
  Tuberculosis (1996): 3.5, 33rd
Pop. without health insur. (1996): 9.9%, 44th

HOUSEHOLDS BY TYPE

Total households (1996): 378,000, 43rd
  Percent change (1990-96): –0.1%, 50th
  Per 1,000 pop. (1996) 381.82, 18th
  Percent of householders 65 yrs. and over (1996): 25.40%, 4th
  Persons per household (1996): 2.56, 28th
Family households: 258,886
  Percent of total: 68.49%, 43rd
Nonfamily households: 119,091
  Percent of total: 31.51%, 9th
Pop. living in group quarters: 38,595
  Percent of pop.: 3.85%, 3rd

LIVING QUARTERS

Total housing units: 414,572
  Persons per unit: 2.42, 21st
Occupied housing units: 337,977
  Percent of total units: 81.52%, 48th
  Persons per unit: 2.51, 30th
  Percent of units with over 1 person per room: 2.57%, 34th

Owner-occupied units: 224,792
  Percent of total units: 54.22%, 40th
  Percent of occupied units: 66.51%, 29th
  Persons per unit: 2.78, 17th
  Median value: $133,500, 6th
Renter-occupied units: 153,185
  Percent of total units: 36.95%, 7th
  Percent of occupied units: 45.32%, 4th
  Persons per unit: 2.23, 45th
  Median contract rent: $416, 13th
  Rental vacancy rate: 7.9%, 30th
Mobile home, trailer & other as a percent of occupied housing units: 2.62%, 47th
Persons in emergency shelters for homeless persons: 469, 0.047%, 25th
Persons visible in street locations: 44, 0.0044%, 31st
Nursing home population: 10,156, 1.01%, 10th

CRIME INDEX PER 100,000 (1996)

Total reported: 3,993.5, 39th
  Percent increase: −5.9%, 37th
  Violent: 347.2, 35th
    Percent increase: −5.7%, 26th
    Murder & nonnegligent manslaughter: 2.5, 45th
    Forcible rape: 29.0, 35th
    Aggravated assault: 232.4, 32nd
    Robbery: 83.2, 39th
  Property: 3,646.4, 38th
    Percent increase: −5.9%, 37th
    Burglary: 821.7, 30th
    Larceny-theft: 2,360.3, 42nd
    Motor vehicle theft: 464.3, 23rd

TEACHING AND LEARNING

Pop. 3 and over enrolled in school (1996): 225,281, 43rd
  Percent of pop.: 22.76%, 23rd
Public elementary & secondary schools (1996-97): 310, 48th
  Total enrollment (1996): 151,181, 44th
    Percent of school age pop.: 87.90%, 43rd
    Percent of total pop.: 15.27%, 48th
  Teachers (1996): 10,586, 43rd
    Percent of pop.: 1.07%, 26th
  Pupil/teacher ratio (1995): 14.3, 48th
  Teachers' avg. salary (1996-97): $43,019, 10th
  Expenditure per capita (1992-93): $1,337.95, 23rd
    Education as % of state govt. expenditures: 29.8%, 43rd

Expenditure per pupil (1994-95): $7,469, 6th
  Percent increase (1993-94 & 1994-95): 1.85%, 44th
Percent at or above grade level, NAEP tests:
  Reading, grade 4 (1994): 32%, 13th
  Math, grade 4 (1996): 61%, 27th
  Math, grade 8 (1996): 60%, 21st
Percent of graduates taking SAT (1995): 70%, 4th
  Mean SAT verbal scores: 425, 39th
  Mean SAT mathematical scores: 463, 46th
Percent of graduates taking ACT (1997): 2%, 50th
  Mean ACT scores: 21.4, 19th
Percent of pop. over 25 completing:
  Less than 9th grade: 11.1%, 18th
  High school: 72.0%, 41st
  College degree(s): 21.3%, 18th
Higher education, institutions (1996): 12, 46th
  Enrollment (1995-96): 74,100, 39th
    Percent increase in enroll. (1990-95): −5.3%, 50th
  White non-Hispanic (1995): 62,824, 37th
    Percent of enroll.: 84.78%, 17th
  Total minority enroll. (1995): 8,773, 40th
    Percent of enroll.: 11.84%, 35th
  Black non-Hispanic (1995): 3,200, 38th
    Percent of enroll.: 4.32%, 30th
  Hispanic (1995): 2,709, 32nd
    Percent of enroll.: 3.66%, 16th
  Asian/Pacific Islander (1995): 2,593, 33rd
    Percent of enroll.: 3.50%, 15th
  American Indian/AK native (1995): 271, 46th
    Percent of enroll.: 0.37%, 39th
  Nonresident alien (1995): 2,503, 36th
    Percent of enroll.: 3.38%, 14th
  Female (1995): 40,936, 39th
    Percent of enroll.: 55.24%, 35th
  Pub. institutions (1995-96): 3, 50th
    Enrollment: 38,653, 41st
      Percent increase in enrollment (1990-95): −8.7%, 50th
    Percent of enroll.: 52.16%, 49th
  Private institutions (1995-96): 9, 42nd
    Enrollment: 35,447, 25th
      Percent increase in enrollment (1990-95): −1.3%, 42nd
    Percent of enroll.: 47.84%, 3rd
  Tuition (in state), public 4-year institution (1996-97): $3,907, 10th

Tuition (in state), public 2-year institution (1996-97): $1,736, 17th

Tuition, private 4-year institution (1996-97): $15,644, 6th

Public library systems (1994): 51, 41st

　Books & serial vol. per capita: 4.1, 9th

　Library visits per capita: 5.4, 3rd

　Circulation per capita: 6.2, 30th

LAW ENFORCEMENT AND CORRECTIONS

Police protection and corrections expenditures (1996): $145,948,000

　Per capita: $147.42, 10th

Police per 10,000 pop. (1996): 23.95, 16th

Prisoners (1 year or more) per 100,000 pop. (1996): 205, 43rd

　Percent change (1995-96): 10.7%, 13th

　Percent of inmates that are female: 7.0%, 13th

　　Percent change: 45.9%, 2nd

Death penalty: no

RELIGION, NUMBER AND PERCENT OF POPULATION

Agnostic: 3,889—0.50%, 27th

Buddhist: NA

Christian: 680,552—87.50%, 21st

Hindu: NA

Jewish: 12,444—1.60%, 11th

Muslim: 3,111—0.40%, 5th

Unitarian: 3,111—0.40%, 8th

Other: 5,444—0.70%, 43rd

None: 46,666—6.00%, 32nd

Refused to answer: 22,555—2.90%, 9th

MAKING A LIVING

Personal income per capita (1996): $24,765, 18th

　Percent increase (1995-96): 1.8%, 45th

Disposable personal income per capita (1996): $21,659, 14th

Median income of households (average, 1995-96): $36,695, 18th

Percent of pop. below poverty level (1995-96): 10.8%, 36th

ECONOMY

In civilian labor force (1996): 496,000

　Percent of total pop.: 65.6%, 37th

　Percent of total pop. 65 years and over: 11.5%, 27th

　Percent of total female pop.: 58.9%, 35th

Major employer industries (total nonagricultural, 1996):

　Construction: 13,600—3.1%, 48th

　Finance, insurance, & real estate: 25,200—5.7%, 17th

　Government: 61,300—13.9%, 48th

　Manufacturing: 82,400—18.7%, 11th

　Service: 146,100—33.1%, 5th

　Trade: 98,200—22.2%, 45th

　Transportation, communications, public utilities: 14,900—3.4%, 50th

Unemployment rate (1996): 5.1%, 26th

　Male: 4.9%, 28th

　Female: 5.4%, 19th

Total businesses (1995): 27,766, 44th

New business incorps. (1995): 2,743

　Percent of total businesses: 9.88%, 20th

Business failures (1995): 129

　Failures per 10,000 businesses: 46.5, 49th

Agriculture farm income:

　Marketing (1996): $82,867,000, 49th

　　Average per farm: $118,381, 17th

　Leading products (1997): Greenhouse products, eggs, dairy products, potatoes, turf

　Average value land & build. per acre (1997): $7,900, 2nd

　　Percent increase (1996-97): 10%, 2nd

　Govt. payments (1996): $156,000, 50th

　　Average per farm: $223, 49th

Construction, value of all (1996): $657,522,000, 48th

　Per capita: $664, 51st

Manufactures (1995):

　Value added: $5,426,100,000

　　Per capita: $5,482, 33rd

　Leading products (1997): Costume jewelry, machinery, textiles, electronics

Value of nonfuel mineral production (1996): $31,900,000, 48th

Leading mineral products (1996): Sand/gravel, stone, gemstones

Energy consumption per person (1994): 249.5 mil. Btu, 45th

Retail sales (1995): $7,359,000,000

　Per household: $19,766, 48th

　Sales increase (1994-95): −2.4%, 51st

Tourism revenues (1995): $1.6 bil.

Foreign exports, in total value (1996): $919,000,000, 45th

　Per capita: $928, 43rd

Gross state product per person (1994): $23,945, 33rd

Public aid recipients (percent of resident pop. 1994): 8.6%, 11th

Medicaid recipients (percent of pop., 1995): 13.6%, 16th
Medicare enrollment per 1,000 pop. (1996): 171, 6th

TRAVEL AND TRANSPORTATION

Motor vehicle registrations (1996): 695,928, 45th
Per 1,000 pop.: 704.18, 44th
Motorcycle registrations (1996): 17,048, 44th
Per 1,000 pop.: 24.50, 13th
Licensed drivers (1996): 670,360, 43rd
Per 1,000 pop.: 675.97, 32nd
Public roads & streets (1996)
Total mileage: 6,001, 48th
Per 1,000 pop.: 16.06, 45th
Rural mileage: 1,360, 50th
Per 1,000 pop.: 1.37, 50th
Urban mileage: 4,641, 38th
Per 1,000 pop.: 4.69, 3rd
Interstate mileage: 69, 48th
Per 1,000 pop.: 0.07, 47th
Speed limit (max. interstate, autos, mi. per hr., 1997): 65
Annual vehicle-mi. of travel per driver (1996): 10,644, 49th
Mean travel time for workers age 16+ who work away from home: 19.2 min., 35th

GOVERNMENT

Percent of voting age pop. registered (1996): 80.25%, 20th
Percent of voting age pop. voting for president: (1996): 52.0%, 24th
Percent of voting age pop. voting for U.S. representatives (1996): 48.0%, 25th

State legislators, total (1997): 150, 22nd
Women members (1997): 39
Percent of legislature: 26%, 17th
U.S. Congress, House members (1998): 2
Change (1988-98): 0
Revenues (1996):
State govt.: $4,270,615,000
Per capita: $4,313.75, 13th
Parimutuel & amusement taxes & lotteries, revenue per capita (1995): $297.01, 2nd
Expenditures (1996):
State govt.: $4,061,406,000
Per capita: $4,102.43, 7th
Debt outstanding (1996): $5,505,683,000
Per capita: $5,561.30, 2nd

LAWS AND REGULATIONS

Legal driving age: 18, 16 if completed driver education course
Marriage age without parental consent: 18
Divorce residence requirement: 1 yr.

ATTRACTIONS (1997)

Major symphony orchestras: 1
Major professional theater companies (non-profit): 1
Per capita spending by the NEA (1997): $0.65, 11th
State Fair in mid-August at Richmond

SPORTS AND COMPETITION

NCAA (Division I) football and basketball teams: Brown Univ. Bears, Providence College Friars (basketball only), Univ. of Rhode Island Rams

WEBSITES CONTAINING FURTHER INFORMATION

Rhode Island Government Information Service	http://www.info.state.ri.us
RI Secretary of State's Public Information Kiosk	http://www.state.ri.us

SOUTH CAROLINA

"South Carolina in many ways epitomizes the American South. Historically, it was central in the events that preceded the Civil War....Since the Civil War, South Carolina has endured some of the worst effects of the reconstruction era and subsequently negotiated the economic shift from agriculture to industry that has been crucial to the development of other states in the deep South."
Robert O'Brien, historian

Two of the most important battles in the history of the United States were fought in South Carolina. The British were defeated in 1780 in the Battle of Kings Mountain, which was the turning point of the Revolutionary War in the South. And in 1861, Confederate batteries bombed Fort Sumter in Charleston Harbor, beginning the Civil War. The Palmetto State is the smallest in the Deep South and ranges from a lowland in the east, through sand hills, to the mountains in the west. The Indians called South Carolina's mountains "Sahkanga," which means "the great blue hills of God." Today they are known by the slightly less poetic name of the Blue Ridge Mountains. Charleston, the first capital—much older than the nation—boasts a restored residential section which, with its historic homes, ironwork, courtyards, piazza, and gardens, is one of the country's most delightful.

SUPERLATIVES

- First European settlement on the North American coast, 1526.
- First American Protestant settlement, 1652.
- Site of the most Revolutionary battles of any state.
- First state to secede from the Union.
- First shots of the Civil War.
- Leader in vermiculite.
- First U.S. railroad designed for steam.
- Nation's first cotton mill.
- Leader in glass fiber production.
- Nation's oldest theater building—the Street Theater on Charleston's Old Dock.

MOMENTS IN HISTORY

- The short-lived settlement San Miguel de Guadalupe was founded at present-day Winyah Bay by Spanish Captain Lucas Vasquez de Ayllon in 1526. It is said to have been the first European settlement on the coast of North America.
- Near modern Silver Bluff, the destructive 1540-41 expedition of Hernando de Soto

entered present-day western South Carolina, leaving a trail of disease and misery upon its departure.
- The Parris Island settlement by Huguenots in 1652, under the leadership of Jean Ribaut, was the first Protestant settlement in America.
- Charles II granted the Carolina region to loyal friends, the Lords Proprietors, and Charles Towne was founded in 1670. The settlement was moved to its present location ten years later, and it eventually was named Charleston.
- Plantations flourished after the first importation of slaves in 1670.
- Alarmed by seizure of their lands, in 1715 the Indians attacked and massacred widely in a struggle known as the Yamassee War.
- In 1718 the ravages of piracy were diminished when Blackbeard, scourge of the coast, was killed after a stupendous fight. Other pirates were captured, tried, and hanged.
- In 1749 a cruel plague known as the "Great Mortality" took hundreds of lives as a result of a disease now thought to have been influenza.
- Urged on by the French, the Cherokee began attacks on western settlements but were forced to surrender in 1761.
- Although prosperous, South Carolina resisted the despised British taxes and sent delegates to the Continental Congresses of 1774 and 1775.
- South Carolina experienced some of the fiercest fighting and suffering of the Revolutionary War, with 137 battles fought there.
- Francis Marion organized a guerrilla group in 1780. He became known as the "Swamp Fox" for his brilliant raids and disappearance into the swamps.
- A quickly assembled frontier force defeated the British at the Battle of Kings Mountain on October 7, 1780—in a major turning point of the Revolution because it upset the British timetable.

• Another important American victory occurred on January 17, 1781, at the Battle of Cowpens.

• In December 1782, British forces withdrew from Charleston.

• On May 23, 1788, South Carolina became the eighth state.

• By 1827 state leaders were threatening to nullify U.S. laws, and it appeared that South Carolina might secede from the Union in opposition to high tariffs, but the tariff rates were lowered.

So They Say

"...they can talk and write resolutions and print threats to their heart's content. But if one drop of blood is shed there in defiance of the laws of the United States, I will hang the first man of them I can get my hands on, to the first tree I can find."

Andrew Jackson, on nullification

• The country's divisions over slavery deepened, and on December 20, 1860, South Carolina became the first state to secede from the Union.

• On April 12, 1861, Fort Sumter in Charleston harbor was attacked. With that attack on the Union stronghold and the surrender of the fort, the Civil War had begun.

• The state suffered greatly during the war, and further suffering continued during Reconstruction until about 1876.

So They Say

"Thus began the darkest period in the State's history...from 1868 to 1874...the 'Rule of the Robbers.'...Votes in the legislature were bought. Furniture, jewelry, clothing, and groceries were purchased with public funds, while patients in the state hospital actually suffered for food, and threats were made to turn convicts out of the penitentiary because they could not be fed."

South Carolina: A Guide
to the Palmetto State

• The state constitution of 1895 deprived most of the state's blacks of the right to vote.

• During the period 1940 to 1960, the port of Charleston jumped from 57th place to 14th among the nation's ports.

• In 1975, Dr. James B. Edwards became the first Republican governor since Reconstruction days.

• The first female student was admitted to The Citadel military college in 1995, but she resigned after a short time.

THAT'S INTERESTING

• When the chief of an early Indian group died, his horse was buried alive with him. The sorrowing Indians would bind their leader's body to his faithful beast and bury horse and master as in life. There were so many such burials that Indian Hill is known as a mountain.

• On the way to a Lancaster cemetery, the body of Andrew Jackson's father was taken from bar to bar on a sled, until some mourner found it had disappeared. The body turned up in a snowbank and finally reached the intended burial place.

• Theodosia Burr Alston, Aaron Burr's daughter, was the wife of South Carolina Governor Joseph Alston. In 1812 she sailed from Charleston to New York and was never heard from again. Later, a pirate confessed that she had been made to walk the plank, but his story was never verified.

• Francis Marion was a hero to the people of South Carolina, but his fame was little noted elsewhere until parson Mason Locke Weems published his biography, with many tales. One of these told of the visit of a British general to the swamp camp under a flag of truce. The general was so impressed by the Swamp Fox that he returned to England and resigned his commission.

So They Say

Our band is few, but true and tried,
Our leader frank and bold:
The British soldier trembles
When Marion's name is told.

William Cullen Bryant,
on Francis Marion

NOTABLE NATIVES

Mary McLeod Bethune (Maysville, 1875-1955), educator. **James Francis Byrnes** (Charleston, 1879-1972), Supreme Court justice. **John Caldwell Calhoun** (Abbeville County, 1782-1850), public official/political leader. **Andrew Jackson** (Waxhaw's district, 1767-1845), U.S. president. **Henry Laurens** (Charleston, 1724-1792), political leader. **Francis (Swamp Fox) Marion** (Berkeley County, 1732?-1795), Revolutionary soldier. **Joel Roberts Poinsett** (Charleston, 1779-1851), diplomat.

GENERAL

Admitted to statehood: May 23, 1788
Origin of name: Charles I gave a large patent to Sir Robert Heath, 1619, to be called Province of Carolana, from *Carolus*, Latin name for Charles. A new patent was granted by Charles II to Earl of Clarendon and others. Divided into North and South Carolina, 1710
Capital: Columbia
Nickname: Palmetto State
Motto: *Animis Opibusque Parati*—Prepared in mind and resources; *Dum Spiro Spero*—While I breathe, I hope
Animal: White-tail deer
Bird: Carolina wren
Fish: Striped bass
Flower: Carolina (yellow) jessamine
Gem: Amethyst
Stone: Blue granite
Song: "Carolina" and "South Carolina on My Mind"
Tree: Palmetto

THE LAND

Area: 31,189 sq. mi., 40th
  Land: 30,111 sq. mi., 40th
  Water: 1,078 sq. mi., 28th
    Inland water: 1,006 sq. mi., 21st
    Coastal water: 72 sq. mi., 17th
Topography: Blue Ridge province in NW has highest peaks; piedmont lies between the mountains and the fall line; coastal plain covers two-thirds of the state.
Number of counties: 46
Geographic center: Richland, 13 mi. SE of Columbia
Length: 260 mi.; width: 200 mi.
Highest point: 3,560 ft. (Sassafras Mountain), 29th
Lowest point: sea level (Atlantic Ocean), 3rd
Mean elevation: 350 ft., 44th
Coastline: 187 mi.,1th
Shoreline: 2,876 mi., 11th

CLIMATE AND ENVIRONMENT

Temp., highest: 111 deg. on June 28, 1954, at Camden; lowest: −19 deg. on Jan. 21, 1985, at Caesars Head
Monthly average: highest: 91.9 deg., 14th; lowest: 31.2 deg., 43rd; spread (high to low): 60.7 deg., 43rd
Hazardous waste sites (1997): 26, 14th
Endangered species: Animals: 6—Indiana bat, American peregrine falcon, Carolina heelsplitter, West Indian manatee, Wood stork, Red-cockaded woodpecker. Plants: 13

MAJOR CITIES
POPULATION, 1996
PERCENTAGE INCREASE, 1990-96

Columbia, 112,773; 1.8%
Charleston, 71,052; −11.1%
North Charleston, 59,923; −14.8%
Greenville, 57,064; −2.0%
Rock Hill, 44,061; 5.9%

THE PEOPLE

Population (1997): 3,760,181, 26th
  Percent change (1990-97): 7.86%, 19th
  Percent of total U.S. pop.: 1.40%, 26th
  Per sq. mi: 117.48, 20th
Population (2000 proj.): 3,855,000, 26th
  Percent change (1995-2000): 4.96%, 23rd
Percent in metro. area (1996): 69.59%, 27th
Foreign born: 50,000, 34th
  Percent: 1.4%, 44th
Top three ancestries reported:
  African, 24.96%
  German, 14.34%
  Irish, 13.94%
White (1992): 2,489,000, 69.08%, 47th
Black (1992): 1,080,000, 29.98%, 4th
Native American (1992): 8,000, 0.22%, 39th
Asian, Pacific Isle (1992): 25,000, 0.69%, 41st
Hispanic origin (1992): 35,000, 0.97%, 41st
Percent over 5 yrs. speaking language other than English at home: 3.5%, 45th
Percent males (1996): 48.31%, 42nd; percent females: 51.69%, 10th
Percent never married: 26.4%, 21st
Marriages per 1,000 (1996): 11.66, 6th
Divorces per 1,000 (1996): 4.12, 27th
Median age (1996): 34.4
Under 5 years (1996): 6.92%, 29th
18 years and under (1996): 28.32%, 29th

65 years and over (1996): 12.08%, 36th
Percent increase among the elderly (1995-96): 1.47%, 15th

OF VITAL IMPORTANCE

Live births per 1,000 pop. (1996): 13.7, 32nd
Infant mortality rate per 1,000 live births (1995): 9.6, 5th
  Rate for whites: 6.7, 18th
  Rate for blacks: 14.6, 23rd
Births to unmarried women, % of total (1996): 37.2%, 8th
Births to teenage mothers, % of total (1996): 16.8%, 8th
Abortions (1992): 12,190, 30th
  Rate per 1,000 women 14-44 years old: 14.2, 36th
  Percent change (1988-92): –15%, 38th
Average lifetime (1989-91): 73.51, 46th
Total death rate per 100,000 pop. (1995): 912.7, 26th
  Accidents and adverse effects: 44.5, 11th
  Alzheimer's disease: 7.6, 32nd
  Cancer: 201.9, 34th
  Cerebrovascular diseases: 75.2, 6th
  Chronic liver disease and cirrhosis: 10.2, 13th
  Chronic obstructive pulmonary diseases and allied conditions: 38.4, 30th
  Diabetes mellitus: 27.4, 7th
  Diseases of heart: 277.6, 29th
  HIV infection: 15.2, 12th
  Homicide: 8.9, 18th
  Injury by firearms: 14.4, 24th
  Motor vehicle accidents: 23.1, 8th
  Pneumonia and influenza: 27.1, 41st
  Suicide: 11.9, 30th

KEEPING WELL

Active nonfederal physicians per 100,000 pop. (1995): 190, 37th
Dentists per 100,000 (1991): 42, 46th
Nurses per 100,000 (1995): 707, 43rd
Hospitals per 100,000 (1995): 1.80, 33rd
  Admissions per 1,000 (1995): 111.63, 31st
  Hospital beds per 1,000 (1995): 3.08, 32nd
  Occupancy rate per 100 beds (1995): 64.60, 17th
  Average cost per patient per day (1995): $923, 26th
  Average cost per stay (1995): $5,935, 23rd
AIDS cases (new, 1996): 869; per 100,000: 23.5, 13th
Persons living with HIV infection, not yet AIDS (1996): 5,670

Other notifiable diseases, per 100,000 pop.:
  Gonorrhea (1995): 329.9, 4th
  Syphilis (1995): 45.6, 7th
  Tuberculosis (1996): 9.4, 13th
Pop. without health insur. (1996): 17.1%, 10th

HOUSEHOLDS BY TYPE

Total households (1996): 1,376,000, 26th
  Percent change (1990-96): 9.4%, 18th
  Per 1,000 pop. (1996) 371.99, 37th
  Percent of householders 65 yrs. and over (1996): 21.00%, 34th
  Persons per household (1996): 2.64, 17th
Family households: 928,206
  Percent of total: 73.78%, 4th
Nonfamily households: 329,838
  Percent of total: 26.22%, 48th
Pop. living in group quarters: 116,543
  Percent of pop.: 3.34%, 12th

LIVING QUARTERS

Total housing units: 1,424,155
  Persons per unit: 2.45, 15th
Occupied housing units: 1,258,044
  Percent of total units: 88.34%, 33rd
  Persons per unit: 2.50, 34th
  Percent of units with over 1 person per room: 4.06%, 15th
Owner-occupied units: 878,704
  Percent of total units: 61.70%, 13th
  Percent of occupied units: 69.85%, 12th
  Persons per unit: 2.75, 21st
  Median value: $61,1000, 31st
Renter-occupied units: 379,340
  Percent of total units: 26.64%, 41st
  Percent of occupied units: 30.15%, 40th
  Persons per unit: 2.25, 39th
  Median contract rent: $276, 37th
  Rental vacancy rate: 11.5%, 9th
Mobile home, trailer & other as a percent of occupied housing units: 20.14%, 3rd
Persons in emergency shelters for homeless persons: 973, 0.028%, 48th
Persons visible in street locations: 102, 0.0029%, 38th
Nursing home population: 18,228, 0.52%, 44th

CRIME INDEX PER 100,000 (1996)

Total reported: 6,214.1, 8th
  Percent increase: 2.5%, 5th

Violent: 996.9, 3rd
  Percent increase: 1.5%, 6th
  Murder & nonnegligent manslaughter:
    9.0, 11th
  Forcible rape: 49.2, 9th
  Aggravated assault: 766.7, 2nd
  Robbery: 172.0, 15th
Property: 5,217.2, 11th
  Percent increase: 2.7%, 6th
  Burglary: 1,283.8, 6th
  Larceny-theft: 3,505.0, 12th
  Motor vehicle theft: 428.5, 27th

TEACHING AND LEARNING

Pop. 3 and over enrolled in school (1996):
    823,105, 26th
  Percent of pop.: 22.25%, 29th
Public elementary & secondary schools (1996-
    97): 1,095, 32nd
  Total enrollment (1996): 648,980, 26th
    Percent of school age pop.: 94.88%, 12th
    Percent of total pop.: 17.54%, 24th
  Teachers (1996): 40,640, 23rd
    Percent of pop.: 1.10%, 21st
  Pupil/teacher ratio (1995): 16.2, 29th
  Teachers' avg. salary (1996-97): $32,659,
    36th
  Expenditure   per   capita   (1992-93):
    $1,192.27, 39th
    Education as % of state govt. expendi-
      tures: 34.8%, 29th
  Expenditure per pupil (1994-95): $4,797,
    40th
    Percent increase (1993-94 & 1994-95):
      0.76%, 50th
Percent at or above grade level, NAEP tests:
  Reading, grade 4 (1994): 20%, 35th
  Math, grade 4 (1996): 48%, 39th
  Math, grade 8 (1996): 48%, 37th
Percent of graduates taking SAT (1995): 58%,
    15th
  Mean SAT verbal scores: 401, 51st
  Mean SAT mathematical scores: 443, 51st
Percent of graduates taking ACT (1997):
    13%, 36th
  Mean ACT scores: 18.9, 49th
Percent of pop. over 25 completing:
  Less than 9th grade: 13.6%, 9th
  High school: 68.3%, 45th
  College degree(s): 16.6%, 42nd
Higher education, institutions (1996): 59,
    22nd
  Enrollment (1995-96): 174,125, 28th
    Percent increase in enroll. (1990-95):
      9.3%, 9th

White non-Hispanic (1995): 127,856, 31st
  Percent of enroll.: 73.43%, 36th
Total minority enroll. (1995): 43,352, 20th
  Percent of enroll.: 24.90%, 15th
Black non-Hispanic (1995): 39,088, 16th
  Percent of enroll.: 22.45%, 6th
Hispanic (1995): 1,550, 37th
  Percent of enroll.: 0.89%, 43rd
Asian/Pacific Islander (1995): 2,232, 35th
  Percent of enroll.: 1.28%, 42nd
American Indian/AK native (1995): 482, 42nd
  Percent of enroll.: 0.28%, 46th
Nonresident alien (1995): 2,917, 34th
  Percent of enroll.: 1.68%, 47th
Female (1995): 101,479, 26th
  Percent of enroll.: 58.28%, 4th
Pub. institutions (1995-96): 33, 15th
  Enrollment: 148,706, 28th
    Percent increase in enrollment (1990-
      95): 13.4%, 6th
  Percent of enroll.: 85.40%, 20th
Private institutions (1995-96): 26, 24th
  Enrollment: 25,419, 30th
    Percent increase in enrollment (1990-
      95): −9.8%, 49th
  Percent of enroll.: 14.60%, 32nd
Tuition (in state), public 4-year institution
    (1996-97): $3,206, 19th
Tuition (in state), public 2-year institution
    (1996-97): $1,114, 36th
Tuition, private 4-year institution (1996-
    97): $10,253, 31st
Public library systems (1994): 40, 43rd
  Books & serial vol. per capita: 1.7, 49th
  Library visits per capita: 2.9, 35th
  Circulation per capita: 4.3, 44th

LAW ENFORCEMENT AND CORRECTIONS

Police protection and corrections expenditures
    (1996): $531,566,000
  Per capita: $143.70, 12th
Police per 10,000 pop. (1996): 22.13, 24th
Prisoners (1 year or more) per 100,000 pop.
    (1996): 532, 5th
  Percent change (1995-96): 3.9%, 33rd
  Percent of inmates that are female: 5.9%
    31st
    Percent change: 15.0%, 15th
Death penalty: yes, by electrocution, lethal
    injection
  Under sentence (Jan. 1998): 70, 16th
  Executed, 1976-97: 13, 9th
  Executed in 1997: 2, 6th

RELIGION, NUMBER AND PERCENT OF POPULATION

Agnostic: 5,133—0.20%, 42nd
Buddhist: 2,567—0.10%, 17th
Christian: 2,386,841—93.00%, 6th
Hindu: NA
Jewish: 7,700—0.30%, 35th
Muslim: 5,133—0.20%, 13th
Unitarian: NA
Other: 30,798—1.20%, 29th
None: 82,128—3.20%, 45th
Refused to answer: 46,197—1.80%, 34th

MAKING A LIVING

Personal income per capita (1996): $19,755, 42nd
Percent increase (1995-96): 2.5%, 35th
Disposable personal income per capita (1996): $17,467, 42nd
Median income of households (average, 1995-96): $32,297, 34th
Percent of pop. below poverty level (1995-96): 16.5%, 12th

ECONOMY

In civilian labor force (1996): 1,848,000
Percent of total pop.: 65.4%, 39th
Percent of total pop. 65 years and over: 9.1%, 41st
Percent of total female pop.: 58.2%, 39th
Major employer industries (total nonagricultural, 1996):
Construction: 93,500—5.6%, 10th
Finance, insurance, & real estate: 72,300—4.3%, 45th
Government: 298,900—17.8%, 20th
Manufacturing: 365,200—21.8%, 7th
Service: 373,400—22.3%, 49th
Trade: 397,600—23.7%, 25th
Transportation, communications, public utilities: 73,400—4.4%, 42nd
Unemployment rate (1996): 6.0%, 12th
Male: 5.8%, 13th
Female: 6.2%, 10th
Total businesses (1995): 87,990, 27th
New business incorps. (1995): 7,601
Percent of total businesses: 8.64%, 30th
Business failures (1995): 490
Failures per 10,000 businesses: 55.7, 43rd
Agriculture farm income:
Marketing (1996): $1,602,056,000, 35th
Average per farm: $74,514, 35th
Leading products (1997): Tobacco, broilers, cattle, soybeans, corn, cotton, peaches, hay

Average value land & build. per acre (1997): $1,400, 23rd
Percent increase (1996-97): 3%, 42nd
Govt. payments (1996): $42,868,000, 32nd
Average per farm: $1,994, 27th
Construction, value of all (1996): $5,438,753,000, 23rd
Per capita: $1,470, 16th
Manufactures (1995):
Value added: $31,467,400,000
Per capita: $8,567, 8th
Leading products (1997): Textiles, chemicals & chemical products, machinery & fabricated metal products, apparel & related products
Value of nonfuel mineral production (1996): $495,000,000, 27th
Leading mineral products (1996): Cement, stone, gold, sand/gravel
Energy consumption per person (1994): 373.2 mil. Btu, 20th
Retail sales (1995): $31,320,000,000
Per household: $23,205, 40th
Sales increase (1994-95): 5.3%, 24th
Tourism revenues (1996): $13.1 bil.
Foreign exports, in total value (1996): $6,698,000,000, 22nd
Per capita: $1,811, 21st
Gross state product per person (1994): $21,814, 42nd
Public aid recipients (percent of resident pop. 1994): 6.7%, 26th
Medicaid recipients (percent of pop., 1995): 13.5%, 18th
Medicare enrollment per 1,000 pop. (1996): 142, 28th

TRAVEL AND TRANSPORTATION

Motor vehicle registrations (1996): 2,790,575, 28th
Per 1,000 pop.: 750.83, 37th
Motorcycle registrations (1996): 39,219, 28th
Per 1,000 pop.: 14.05, 36th
Licensed drivers (1996): 2,542,139, 25th
Per 1,000 pop.: 693.25, 25th
Public roads & streets (1996)
Total mileage: 64,359, 31st
Per 1,000 pop.: 117.40, 26th
Rural mileage: 53,785, 31st
Per 1,000 pop.: 14.54, 26th
Urban mileage: 10,574, 27th
Per 1,000 pop.: 2.86, 35th
Interstate mileage: 829, 27th
Per 1,000 pop.: 0.22, 21st

Speed limit (max. interstate, autos, mi. per hr., 1997): 65

Annual vehicle-mi. of travel per driver (1996): 15,442, 15th

Mean travel time for workers age 16+ who work away from home: 20.5 min., 28th

GOVERNMENT

Percent of voting age pop. registered (1996): 65.49%, 45th

Percent of voting age pop. voting for president: (1996): 41.5%, 48th

Percent of voting age pop. voting for U.S. representatives (1996): 38.1%, 46th

State legislators, total (1997): 170, 16th

Women members (1997): 23

Percent of legislature: 14%, 43rd

U.S. Congress, House members (1998): 6

Change (1988-98): 0

Revenues (1996):

State govt.: $12,601,859,000

Per capita: $3,406.83, 28th

Parimutuel & amusement taxes & lotteries, revenue per capita (1995): $7.33, 40th

Expenditures (1996):

State govt.: $12,399,928,000

Per capita: $3,352.24, 20th

Debt outstanding (1996): $5,324,200,000

Per capita: $1,439.36, 22nd

LAWS AND REGULATIONS

Legal driving age: 16

Marriage age without parental consent: 18

Divorce residence requirement: 1 yr., for qualifications check local statutes

ATTRACTIONS (1997)

Major opera companies: 1

Major symphony orchestras: 1

Per capita spending by the NEA (1997): $0.18, 40th

State Fair in mid-October at Columbia

SPORTS AND COMPETITION

NCAA (Division I) football and basketball teams: Charleston Southern Univ. Buccaneers, The Citadel Bulldogs, Clemson Univ. Tigers, College of Charleston Cougars (basketball only), Coastal Carolina Univ. Chanticleers (basketball only), Furman Univ. Paladins, South Carolina State Univ. Bulldogs, Univ. of South Carolina Fighting Gamecocks, Winthrop Univ. Eagles (basketball only), Wofford College Terriers

WEBSITES CONTAINING FURTHER INFORMATION

South Carolina Home Page   http://www.state.sc.us

SOUTH DAKOTA

"Hard work is a legacy of the generations who settled the prairie, broke the soil, built the sod houses, fought the draughts and grasshoppers and penny-a-pound price for their products. It is a legacy that even those of us who leave carry with us. All of this work has produced what may be the largest collection of powerful hands in the world."
Tom Brokaw, newscaster

"When the prairie schooners of the pioneer rolled out of the woods upon the vast reaches of land of this region, it was like a gateway opening on a new world."
South Dakota Industrial Development & Expansion Agency

Visitors flock to South Dakota to see the world-famed "rock stars,"—that is, the four presidential faces of the Mount Rushmore Memorial. South Dakota is a land where "the great lakes" were created on barren prairie and where the Homestake Mine has produced more gold than any other gold mine worldwide. The history of South Dakota reads like an exciting adventure story, filled with daring fur trappers, battles between settlers and Indians, and such colorful characters as Calamity Jane, General George A. Custer, Sitting Bull, and Wild Bill Hickock. Today, the state continues to gain as a center of financial and other service industries.

SUPERLATIVES

- Highest point east of the Rockies—Harney Peak.
- Longest nonnavigable river—James River.
- World record total production of a single gold mine—Homestake Mine.
- Leader in bentonite production.
- World's largest portrait busts—those on Mount Rushmore.

So They Say

"This memorial will crown the height of land between the Rocky Mountains and the Atlantic seaboard, where coming generations may view it for all time ....On this towering wall...is to be inscribed a memorial which will represent some of the outstanding events of American history..."

President Calvin Coolidge, dedicating the Mount Rushmore Memorial (1929)

MOMENTS IN HISTORY

- On their expedition of 1743, brothers François and Louis-Joseph La Vérendrye are thought to have visited what is now South Dakota. On a hill overlooking the Missouri River, they buried a lead plate claiming the region for France.
- In 1794, Jean Baptiste Trudeau established a trading company in present-day Charles Mix County.
- On August 22, 1804, the great Meriwether Lewis and William Clark expedition camped at present-day Elk Point. The election they held for sergeant was the first in the entire Northwest.

So They Say

"This scenery already rich, pleasing and beautiful was still farther heightened by immense herds of buffalo, deer, elk and antelopes...I do not think I exaggerate when I estimate the number of buffalo, which could be comprehended at one view to amount to 3,000. This plain is entirely occupied by the burrows of the barking squirrel...in infinite numbers.... The shortness and verdure of grass gave the plain the appearance throughout its whole extent of beautiful bowling green...." **Meriwether Lewis**

- Fort Pierre Chouteau (Pierre), founded in 1831, was the oldest permanently occupied European settlement in the state.
- The first "Puffing Canoe" (steamboat), the *Yellowstone*, reached Fort Pierre in 1831.
- When Father Pierre Jean de Smet visited the Black Hills in 1848, an Indian chief of-

fered him a bag of glittering powder, which he recognized as gold but did not disclose to anyone, fearing for Indian rights.

• Dakota Territory was created on March 2, 1861.

• January 1, 1863, was one of the most significant dates in the history of South Dakota—when the Homestead Act took effect. Under this act, homesteaders could claim 160 acres of land by meeting certain conditions, principally that they live on their property for a specified time.

• During the Civil War the Santee Sioux began an uprising called the War of the Outbreak, settled in 1865 at a great council with the Indians near present-day Pierre.

• Fort Sisseton was established in 1864 at the unheard of cost of $2 million.

• The great military expedition of George Armstrong Custer entered the Black Hills in 1874, and gold was discovered by the party. A Chicago newspaper carried the news, and the rush for gold was on. One authority has claimed that the discovery was the most important single event in South Dakota history.

• By midsummer 1876, Dead Tree Gulch (later Deadwood) harbored 25,000 gold seekers, squatters on Indian lands. Deadwood became a rip-roaring prospecting town.

• On August 2, 1876, Wild Bill Hickock was killed at Deadwood.

• The winter of 1880-81 was the worst in history, followed by great floods, sweeping away villages.

• On the same day, November 2, 1889, South Dakota became a state along with North Dakota. President Benjamin Harrison never revealed which state he named first.

• Famed Chief Sitting Bull was killed by police action in 1890 at what is now Little Eagle.

• On December 28, 1890, the infamous "battle" at Wounded Knee resulted in the deaths of more than 200 Sioux men, women, and children, slain by government forces after an Indian shot an officer. This proved to be the country's last large-scale action between troops and Indians.

• After a contest between Mitchell and Pierre, the latter was chosen state capital by a vote in 1904.

• The year was 1913. "Look what I found!" exclaimed Hattie Foster. In a moment she and other children pulled a dirty piece of metal covered with obscure engravings from the ground. It turned out to be one of the historic objects of the continent. It had been buried overlooking the Missouri River in 1743 and it proclaimed that this exploring expedition of the French La Vérendrye brothers gave the ownership of the whole great region to Louis XV of France.

• The visit of President Calvin Coolidge to the Black Hills captured world attention. On August 10, 1927, President Coolidge dedicated the unfinished Mount Rushmore Memorial. His speech there was said by some to have been the finest of a career not noted for public eloquence.

• The Great Depression was made worse by a terrible drought from 1933 through 1936. The Sioux planned to revive their rain dance, but no one remembered it.

• With the increase in gold prices in 1933, gold mining returned to the Black Hills.

• In 1948, South Dakota became the nation's leading gold producer.

• The disastrous flood of 1972 at Rapid City killed nearly 250 persons.

• In 1973, Indians occupied Wounded Knee in protest against the massacre of unarmed Sioux in that 1890 battle.

• A 1980 Supreme Court ruling ordered the United States to pay the Sioux Indians of South Dakota more than $100 million in compensation for the seizure of their lands in the 19th century.

• In the early 1980s, Citicorp moved its credit card operation to Sioux Falls, and other business followed, bringing many new jobs to the state.

• In 1992 federal agents seized a priceless tyrannosaurus rex skeleton from fossil collectors, claiming it had been illegally removed from U.S. land.

THAT'S INTERESTING

• The Dacotah Indians felt that the dead should be buried high above the ground, and many early settlers told of seeing bodies placed in the lofty branches of such trees as the Three Sisters cottonwoods at Pierre.

• Chief Red Cloud of the Oglala Sioux was outraged at the destruction of the buffalo hunting grounds by settlers. He went to war, winning a series of brilliant victories over the Army. This is said to be the only time in history when the Army was defeated by an equal force of Indians.

• Explorer Meriwether Lewis took an Indian baby in his arms and predicted that some day he would be a great leader. Struck-by-the-Ree grew up to confirm the prophecy and, as a friend of the government, he saved the community of Yankton from Indian attack.

• On his visit to the Black Hills, President Calvin Coolidge gained a reputation as a golfer. He did not know that the greens had been altered for his benefit, so as to slope toward the holes.

So They Say

"As we rode [in the Badlands], or seemed to be floating upon a splendid winding road...we rose and fell between its delicate parallels of rose and cream and sublime shapes, chalk white, fretted against a blue sky, with high floating clouds."   Architect Frank Lloyd Wright

---

• When South Dakotans exclaim, "That damned Missouri," they mean a compliment. The three great dams on the Missouri River have transformed central South Dakota geography into a region sometimes called the Great Lakes of South Dakota.

• The Nystrom Bank at Wall did not close during Franklin D. Roosevelt's 1933 bank holiday—the only one in the country not to. No one had thought to notify the owner.

NOTABLE NATIVES

Crazy Horse (Oglala Sioux tribal site, 1849?-1877), Indian leader. **Hubert Horatio Humphrey** (Wallace, 1911-1978), U.S. senator/vice president. **Ernest Orlando Lawrence** (Canton, 1901-1958), physicist. **George Stanley McGovern** (Avon, 1922-), public official. **Sitting Bull** (Hunkpapa Sioux tribal site on Grand River, 1831?-1890), Indian leader.

GENERAL

Admitted to statehood: November 2, 1889
Origin of name: From the Sioux for "friend or ally"
Capital: Pierre
Nickname: Coyote State, Mount Rushmore State
Motto: Under God, the people rule
Animal: Coyote

Bird: Chinese ring-necked pheasant
Insect: Honeybee
Fish: Walleye
Flower: Pasqueflower
Gem: Fairburn agate
Mineral: Rose quartz
Stone: Black Hills gold
Song: "Hail, South Dakota"
Tree: Black Hills spruce

THE LAND

Area: 77,121 sq. mi., 17th
  Land: 75,896 sq. mi., 16th
  Water: 1,225 sq. mi., 24th
    Inland water: 1,225 sq. mi., 16th
Topography: Prairie plains in the E; rolling hills of the Great Plains in the W; the Black Hills, rising 3,500 ft. in the SW corner
Number of counties: 66
Geographic center: Hughes, 8 mi. NE of Pierre
Length: 380 mi.; width: 210 mi.
Highest point: 7,242 ft. (Harney Peak), 15th
Lowest point: 966 ft. (Big Stone Lake), 46th
Mean elevation: 2,200 ft., 13th

CLIMATE AND ENVIRONMENT

Temp., highest: 120 deg. on July 5, 1936, at Gannvalley; lowest: –58 deg. on Feb. 17, 1936, at McIntosh
Monthly average: highest: 86.5 deg., 31st; lowest: 1.9 deg., 4th; spread (high to low): 84.6 deg., 5th
Hazardous waste sites (1997): 2, 47th
Endangered species: Animals: 8—American burying beetle, Whooping crane, Eskimo curlew, American peregrine falcon, Black-footed ferret, Pallid sturgeon, Least tern, Gray wolf. Plants: 0

MAJOR CITIES
POPULATION, 1996
PERCENTAGE INCREASE, 1990-96

Sioux Falls, 113,223; 12.3%
Rapid City, 57,642; 5.7%
Aberdeen, 25,088; 0.4%
Watertown, 19,619; 11.3%
Brookings, 17,413; 7.0%

THE PEOPLE

Population (1997): 737,973, 45th
  Percent change (1990-97): 6.03%, 25th
  Percent of total U.S. pop.: 0.28%, 45th
  Per sq. mi: 9.57, 47th

Population (2000 proj.): 773,500, 45th
  Percent change (1995-2000): 6.10%, 19th
Percent in metro. area (1996): 33.28%, 46th
Foreign born: 8,000, 50th
  Percent: 1.1%, 46th
Top three ancestries reported:
  German, 51.01%
  Norwegian, 15.23%
  Irish, 12.64%
White (1992): 648,000, 91.53%, 19th
Black (1992): 4,000, 0.56%, 47th
Native American (1992): 53,000, 7.49%, 4th
Asian, Pacific Isle (1992): 4,000, 0.56%, 48th
Hispanic origin (1992): 6,000, 0.85%, 43rd
Percent over 5 yrs. speaking language other
    than English at home: 6.5%, 29th
Percent males (1996): 49.30%, 17th; percent
    females: 50.70%, 35th
Percent never married: 24.4%, 33rd
Marriages per 1,000 (1996): 9.19, 16th
Divorces per 1,000 (1996): 3.73, 31st
Median age (1996): 34.5
Under 5 years (1996): 7.03%, 24th
18 years and under (1996): 31.10%, 9th
65 years and over (1996): 14.40%, 8th
Percent increase among the elderly (1995-96):
    0.11%, 47th

OF VITAL IMPORTANCE

Live births per 1,000 pop. (1996): 14.3, 22nd
Infant mortality rate per 1,000 live births
    (1995): 9.5, 6th
  Rate for whites: 7.9, 2nd
  Rate for blacks: NA
Births to unmarried women, % of total
    (1996): 29.5%, 33rd
Births to teenage mothers, % of total (1996):
    11.5%, 31st
Abortions (1992): 1,040, 50th
  Rate per 1,000 women 14-44 years old: 6.8,
    50th
  Percent change (1988-92): 19%, 2nd
Average lifetime (1989-91): 76.91, 8th
Total death rate per 100,000 pop. (1995):
    948.5, 15th
  Accidents and adverse effects: 44.4, 12th
  Alzheimer's disease: 9.9, 14th
  Cancer: 214.5, 21st
  Cerebrovascular diseases: 73.2, 7th
  Chronic liver disease and cirrhosis: 10.4,
    11th
  Chronic obstructive pulmonary diseases and
    allied conditions: 44.4, 16th
  Diabetes mellitus: 23.0, 25th

Diseases of heart: 312.3, 14th
HIV infection: 2.9, 48th
Homicide: NA
Injury by firearms: 9.7, 39th
Motor vehicle accidents: 22.1, 11th
Pneumonia and influenza: 42.0, 3rd
Suicide: 11.8, 33rd

KEEPING WELL

Active nonfederal physicians per 100,000 pop.
    (1995): 166, 43rd
Dentists per 100,000 (1991): 45, 42nd
Nurses per 100,000 (1995): 1,077, 6th
Hospitals per 100,000 (1995): 6.86, 1st
  Admissions per 1,000 (1995): 128.94, 14th
  Hospital beds per 1,000 (1995): 6.31, 3rd
  Occupancy rate per 100 beds (1995):
    65.22, 13th
  Average cost per patient per day (1995):
    $476, 51st
  Average cost per stay (1995): $5,494, 36th
AIDS cases (new, 1996): 14; per 100,000:
    1.9, 50th
Persons living with HIV infection, not yet
    AIDS (1996): 153
Other notifiable diseases, per 100,000 pop.:
  Gonorrhea (1995): 32.5, 41st
  Syphilis (1995): 1.0, 45th
  Tuberculosis (1996): 2.6, 41st
Pop. without health insur. (1996): 9.5%,
    46th

HOUSEHOLDS BY TYPE

Total households (1996): 273,000, 46th
  Percent change (1990-96): 5.4%, 32nd
  Per 1,000 pop. (1996) 372.95, 35th
  Percent of householders 65 yrs. and over
    (1996): 24.91%, 6th
  Persons per household (1996): 2.56, 28th
Family households: 180,306
  Percent of total: 69.61%, 33rd
Nonfamily households: 78,728
  Percent of total: 30.39%, 19th
Pop. living in group quarters: 25,841
  Percent of pop.: 3.71%, 6th

LIVING QUARTERS

Total housing units: 292,436
  Persons per unit: 2.38, 30th
Occupied housing units: 259,034
  Percent of total units: 88.58%, 32nd
  Persons per unit: 2.53, 24th
  Percent of units with over 1 person per
    room: 2.96%, 26th

Owner-occupied units: 171,161
  Percent of total units: 58.53%, 27th
  Percent of occupied units: 66.08%, 32nd
  Persons per unit: 2.71, 29th
  Median value: $45,200, 50th
Renter-occupied units: 87,873
  Percent of total units: 30.05%, 21st
  Percent of occupied units: 33.92%, 21st
  Persons per unit: 2.34, 27th
  Median contract rent: $242, 46th
  Rental vacancy rate: 7.3%, 38th
Mobile home, trailer & other as a percent of occupied housing units: 13.21%, 20th
Persons in emergency shelters for homeless persons: 396, 0.057%, 18th
Persons visible in street locations: 71, 0.0102%, 20th
Nursing home population: 9,356, 1.34%, 1st

CRIME INDEX PER 100,000 (1996)

Total reported: 2,969.9, 48th
  Percent increase: –3.0%, 29th
  Violent: 177.2, 46th
    Percent increase: –14.6%, 49th
    Murder & nonnegligent manslaughter: 1.2, 51st
    Forcible rape: 41.0, 20th
    Aggravated assault: 116.1, 45th
    Robbery: 18.9, 49th
  Property: 2,792.8, 48th
    Percent increase: –2.1%, 26th
    Burglary: 557.0, 47th
    Larceny-theft: 2,121.9, 44th
    Motor vehicle theft: 113.9, 51st

TEACHING AND LEARNING

Pop. 3 and over enrolled in school (1996): 179,605, 45th
  Percent of pop.: 24.54%, 11th
Public elementary & secondary schools (1996-97): 824, 37th
  Total enrollment (1996): 142,910, 45th
    Percent of school age pop.: 93.41%, 17th
    Percent of total pop.: 19.52%, 6th
  Teachers (1996): 9,474, 45th
    Percent of pop.: 1.29%, 3rd
  Pupil/teacher ratio (1995): 15.0, 40th
  Teachers' avg. salary (1996-97): $26,764, 51st
  Expenditure per capita (1992-93): $1,214.45, 38th
    Education as % of state govt. expenditures: 35.7%, 25th

Expenditure per pupil (1994-95): $4,775, 42nd
  Percent increase (1993-94 & 1994-95): 4.12%, 25th
Percent at or above grade level, NAEP tests:
  Reading, grade 4 (1994): NA
  Math, grade 4 (1996): NA
  Math, grade 8 (1996): NA
Percent of graduates taking SAT (1995): 5%, 47th
  Mean SAT verbal scores: 505, 5th
  Mean SAT mathematical scores: 563, 5th
Percent of graduates taking ACT (1997): 68%, 10th
  Mean ACT scores: 21.3, 23rd
Percent of pop. over 25 completing:
  Less than 9th grade: 13.4%, 11th
  High school: 77.1%, 24th
  College degree(s): 17.2%, 39th
Higher education, institutions (1996): 21, 41st
  Enrollment (1995-96): 36,695, 48th
    Percent increase in enroll. (1990-95): 7.3%, 17th
  White non-Hispanic (1995): 32,509, 47th
    Percent of enroll.: 88.59%, 13th
  Total minority enroll. (1995): 3,189, 47th
    Percent of enroll.: 8.69%, 40th
  Black non-Hispanic (1995): 293, 49th
    Percent of enroll.: 0.80%, 48th
  Hispanic (1995): 178, 51st
    Percent of enroll.: 0.49%, 51st
  Asian/Pacific Islander (1995): 264, 50th
    Percent of enroll.: 0.72%, 51st
  American Indian/AK native (1995): 2,454, 18th
    Percent of enroll.: 6.69%, 5th
  Nonresident alien (1995): 997, 46th
    Percent of enroll.: 2.72%, 25th
  Female (1995): 20,499, 47th
    Percent of enroll.: 55.86%, 27th
  Pub. institutions (1995-96): 9, 43rd
    Enrollment: 29,693, 47th
      Percent increase in enrollment (1990-95): 11.6%, 8th
    Percent of enroll.: 80.92%, 32nd
  Private institutions (1995-96): 12, 38th
    Enrollment: 7,002, 45th
      Percent increase in enrollment (1990-95): –8.0%, 48th
    Percent of enroll.: 19.08%, 20th
  Tuition (in state), public 4-year institution (1996-97): $2,727, 24th
  Tuition (in state), public 2-year institution (1996-97): $3,430, 1st

Tuition, private 4-year institution (1996-97): $9,624, 35th
Public library systems (1994): 113, 26th
  Books & serial vol. per capita: 3.4, 18th
  Library visits per capita: 3.7, 25th
  Circulation per capita: 7.0, 23rd

LAW ENFORCEMENT AND CORRECTIONS

Police protection and corrections expenditures (1996): $63,870,000
  Per capita: $87.26, 41st
Police per 10,000 pop. (1996): 15.29, 51st
Prisoners (1 year or more) per 100,000 pop. (1996): 281, 35th
  Percent change (1995-96): 12.1%, 11th
  Percent of inmates that are female: 6.9%, 15th
    Percent change: 7.6%, 29th
Death penalty: yes, by lethal injection
  Under sentence (Jan. 1998): 2, 34th
  Executed, 1976-97: 0

RELIGION, NUMBER AND PERCENT OF POPULATION

Agnostic: 4,975—1.00%, 10th
Buddhist: NA
Christian: 467,690—94.00%, 4th
Hindu: NA
Jewish: 995—0.20%, 40th
Muslim: 1,491—0.30%, 9th
Unitarian: 1,493—0.30%, 15th
Other: 3,483—0.70%, 43rd
None: 12,439—2.50%, 48th
Refused to answer: 4,975—1.00%, 47th

MAKING A LIVING

Personal income per capita (1996): $21,516, 35th
  Percent increase (1995-96): 7.5%, 2nd
Disposable personal income per capita (1996): $19,381, 32nd
Median income of households (average, 1995-96): $29,989, 43rd
Percent of pop. below poverty level (1995-96): 13.2%, 19th

ECONOMY

In civilian labor force (1996): 390,000
  Percent of total pop.: 72.3%, 7th
  Percent of total pop. 65 years and over: 18.3%, 2nd
  Percent of total female pop.: 66.7%, 7th
Major employer industries (total nonagricultural, 1996):

Construction: 14,700—4.2%, 34th
Finance, insurance, & real estate: 19,800—5.7%, 17th
Government: 70,400—20.2%, 8th
Manufacturing: 47,800—13.7%, 30th
Service: 90,100—25.8%, 38th
Trade: 87,600—25.1%, 9th
Transportation, communications, public utilities: 16,400—4.7%, 35th
Unemployment rate (1996): 3.2%, 49th
  Male: 3.2%, 49th
  Female: 3.2%, 47th
Total businesses (1995): 22,708, 45th
New business incorps. (1995): 1,401
  Percent of total businesses: 6.17%, 47th
Business failures (1995): 182
  Failures per 10,000 businesses: 80.1, 25th
Agriculture farm income:
  Marketing (1996): $3,683,512,000, 19th
    Average per farm: $113,339, 20th
  Leading products (1997): Cattle, wheat, hogs, corn, oats, sunflowers, soybeans, sorghum
  Average value land & build. per acre (1997): $325, 45th
    Percent increase (1996-97): 5%, 26th
  Govt. payments (1996): $229,605,000, 13th
    Average per farm: $7,065, 7th
Construction, value of all (1996): $813,905,000, 46th
  Per capita: $1,111, 35th
Manufactures (1995):
  Value added: $3,927,300,000
    Per capita: $5,387, 34th
  Leading products (1997): Food and food products, machinery, electric and electronic equipment
Value of nonfuel mineral production (1996): $353,000,000, 35th
Leading mineral products (1996): Gold, cement, petroleum, sand/gravel, stone
Energy consumption per person (1994): 321.5 mil. Btu, 32nd
Retail sales (1995): $7,244,000,000
  Per household: $26,603, 8th
  Sales increase (1994-95): 5.7%, 21st
Tourism revenues (1995): $1.25 bil.
Foreign exports, in total value (1996): $443,000,000, 48th
  Per capita: $605, 47th
Gross state product per person (1994): $23,920, 34th

Public aid recipients (percent of resident pop. 1994): 4.4%, 45th

Medicaid recipients (percent of pop., 1995): 10.2%, 38th

Medicare enrollment per 1,000 pop. (1996): 161, 9th

TRAVEL AND TRANSPORTATION

Motor vehicle registrations (1996): 751,071, 44th
  Per 1,000 pop.: 1,018.32, 4th
Motorcycle registrations (1996): 24,734, 38th
  Per 1,000 pop.: 32.93, 5th
Licensed drivers (1996): 515,869, 46th
  Per 1,000 pop.: 707.15, 14th
Public roads & streets (1996)
  Total mileage: 83,375, 23rd
      Per 1,000 pop.: 1113.84, 2nd
  Rural mileage: 81,435, 16th
      Per 1,000 pop.: 111.19, 2nd
  Urban mileage: 1,940, 46th
      Per 1,000 pop.: 2.65, 42nd
  Interstate mileage: 678, 34th
      Per 1,000 pop.: 0.93, 4th
Speed limit (max. interstate, autos, mi. per hr., 1997): 75
Annual vehicle-mi. of travel per driver (1996): 15,074, 19th
Mean travel time for workers age 16+ who work away from home: 13.8 min., 50th

GOVERNMENT

Percent of voting age pop. registered (1996): 85.98%, 8th
  Percent of voting age pop. voting for president: (1996): 61.1%, 4th

Percent of voting age pop. voting for U.S. representatives (1996): 60.9%, 4th
State legislators, total (1997): 105, 40th
  Women members (1997): 19
    Percent of legislature: 18%, 33rd
U.S. Congress, House members (1998): 1
  Change (1988-98): 0
Revenues (1996):
  State govt.: $2,283,576,000
    Per capita: $3,119.64, 38th
    Parimutuel & amusement taxes & lotteries, revenue per capita (1995): $114.30, 22nd
Expenditures (1996):
  State govt.: $1,974,632,000
    Per capita: $2,697.58, 42nd
Debt outstanding (1996): $1,704,133,000
  Per capita: $2,328.05, 12th

LAWS AND REGULATIONS

Legal driving age: 16
Marriage age without parental consent: 18
Divorce residence requirement: For qualifications check local statutes

ATTRACTIONS (1997)

Per capita spending by the NEA (1997): $0.81, 7th
State Fair in late August–September at Huron

SPORTS AND COMPETITION

NCAA (Division II) football and basketball teams: Augustana College Vikings, Northern State Univ. Wolves, South Dakota State Univ. Jackrabbits, Univ. of South Dakota Coyotes

WEBSITES CONTAINING FURTHER INFORMATION

State of South Dakota	http://www.state.sd.us

TENNESSEE

"With his good tempered easiness of manners, the Tennessean has democratic feeling of equality....Whether of farm, mountain or city, he is like the Tennessee farmer, who, after hearing Martin Van Buren speak, stepped up, took the President's hand and invited him 'to come out and r'ar around with the boys.' "

Federal Writers' Project, Tennessee

Tennessee's borders touch eight other states, a record that is tied only by Missouri. Renowned for its scenery and natural wonders, Tennessee also has many other distinctions. In music it is known as the "Birthplace of the Blues" and home of Elvis Presley. Nashville, with its Grand Ole Opry and its many recording studios, is the nation's country music capital. The land in Tennessee slopes from its impressive mountains in the east to its lowlands along the Mississippi River in the west. The state has a long military tradition, and its famous military figures include John Sevier in the Revolutionary War, Andrew Jackson in the War of 1812, and Alvin C. York in World War I. More Civil War battles were fought in Tennessee than in any other state except for Virginia.

SUPERLATIVES

• Claims the greatest variety of birds in the United States.
• First in U.S. aluminum production.
• Leader in diverse hardwood products.
• The nation's largest and oldest national military park—Chickamauga-Chattanooga.
• Called "Birthplace of the Blues"—Memphis.
• Country music capital—Nashville.

MOMENTS IN HISTORY

• In April 1541, the great party of Spanish explorer Hernando de Soto reached the area of present-day Memphis and perhaps other Tennessee points.
• In 1673, Father Jacques Marquette and Louis Jolliet were greeted by Indians of the Memphis area, and in the same year, James Needham and Gabriel Arthur explored East Tennessee.
• Robert Cavelier, Sieur de La Salle, built primitive Fort Prudhomme in 1682.
• Spain, England, and France all claimed the region, but British interests seemed to prevail. In 1757, Fort Loudoun, near present-day Knoxville, was completed.

• In 1763 the French gave up all claims to the region.
• Defying a British ban on settlement, settlers arrived. Washington County was proclaimed, and Jonesboro was laid out in 1779 as its county seat, the oldest permanent European settlement in what is now Tennessee.
• During the Revolution, mountain men from the eastern section took an important part in the 1780 Battle of Kings Mountain, fought in northwestern South Carolina.
• In 1780, Fort Nashborough (Nashville) was founded.
• Ignored by the central government, settlers in 1784 in Jonesboro established what they called the (never-recognized) State of Franklin.

So They Say

Neglected by the central government, settlers met at Jonesboro in 1784, and three counties in present Tennessee attempted to form a new state, called the State of Franklin. They adopted a constitution, elected a governor, and continued for four years until the action was repealed.

The Enchantment of Tennessee

• In 1790, North Carolina gave up its claim to the region, and the federal government established a territory including present-day Tennessee.
• Major Indian troubles began in 1792.

So They Say

"News from this place is desperate. The Indians have killed whole families. ...You may hear the cries of some persons for their friends daily....Nothing but screams and the roaring of guns, and no man to assist me for some time."

Valentine Sevier, brother of Revolutionary leader John Sevier (November 11, 1794)

• Indian troubles diminished, population increased, and Tennessee became a state on June 1, 1796.

• In 1809, in one of the mysteries of American history, western explorer Meriwether Lewis met his death at an inn known as Grinder's Stand. He had been traveling along the old Natchez Trace road toward Washington. The death is officially called suicide, but many authorities feel that Lewis was murdered. A number of important papers that he had with him have never been found.

• The earthquake of 1811, said to be the most destructive in U.S. history, created Reelfoot Lake.

• Against their will, beginning in 1838, the Cherokee were driven from their ancestral lands in the mountain areas of Tennessee and other southern states and suffered the terrible hardships of the "Trail of Tears" on the journey west.

• Nashville was captured by Union forces on February 23, 1862.

• By 1864 most of Tennessee was in Union hands, but there were destructive Confederate raids.

• On February 25, 1865, Tennessee adopted a state constitutional amendment freeing the slaves, the only state to do this by popular vote.

So They Say

"The progress of seventy-five years has been wiped out by four years of war."

Anonymous, on the
Civil War in Tennessee

• Among the state's 91,180 serving in World War I, Sergeant Alvin C. York became one of the best known enlisted men, cited for outstanding bravery in that war.

• In 1925 world attention turned to Tennessee during the notorious "Monkey Trial" of Tennessee teacher John T. Scopes, who was convicted of teaching evolution.

• Begun in 1933, Norris Dam, near Andersonville, was the first of the great projects of the Tennessee Valley Authority.

• During World War II, Tennessee was the center of what has been called the best-kept secret in history. The government selected Oak Ridge for its atomic energy plant, and the end product resulted in the destruction of two Japanese cities and the end of the war in the Pacific.

• The progress in civil rights was shadowed by the murder of esteemed civil rights leader Dr. Martin Luther King, Jr., at Memphis on April 4, 1968.

• In 1977, Memphis mourned the death of a favorite son, Elvis Presley.

• The 1982 World's Fair at Knoxville attracted 11 million visitors.

THAT'S INTERESTING

• The 22 major lakes of Tennessee are known as the Great Lakes of the South. Most are manmade, and their waters lap at 10,000 miles of shoreline.

• The only known defeat of a naval force by cavalry was carried out in a Civil War raid by Confederate General Nathan Bedford Forrest. On November 4, 1864, Forrest's cavalry attacked the federal supply base at Johnsonville on the Tennessee River. The base, with its fleet of 30 gunboats, transports, and barges, was virtually destroyed.

• When Tennessean Andrew Jackson won the Battle of New Orleans during the War of 1812, his fans in Tennessee spread the word that Jackson had left immediately to conquer England.

• Confederate heroine Antoinette Polk was so close to capture by Union forces that they managed to pluck a feather from her hat, but she escaped to warn Confederate troops of Union plans.

• Near Nashville is a prehistoric village where fine pottery and other items were found just as their owners had left them. No one knows what circumstances caused the village to be evacuated suddenly. A shining black finish still covered the hard clay floors.

NOTABLE NATIVES

John Bell (Nashville, 1796-1869), public official. **Julian Bond** (Nashville, 1940-), social reformer/public official. **George Deforest Brush** (Shelbyville, 1855-1941), artist. **David (Davy) Crockett** (Greeneville, 1786-1836), frontiersman/public official. **David Glasgow Farragut** (near Knoxville, 1801-1870), naval officer. **Nathan Bedford Forrest** (Chapel Hill, 1821-1877), soldier. **Richard Halliburton** (Brownsville, 1900-1939), explorer/author. **Cordell Hull** (Overton County, 1871-1955), public official. **Opie Percival Read** (Nashville, 1842-1939), author. **Alvin Cullum York** (Pall Mall, 1887-1964), soldier.

GENERAL

Admitted to statehood: June 1, 1796

Origin of name: *Tanasi* was the name of Cherokee villages on the Little Tennessee River. From 1784 to 1788 this was the State of Franklin, or Frankland

Capital: Nashville

Nickname: Volunteer State

Motto: Agriculture and commerce

Slogan: Tennessee—America at its best

Animal: Raccoon

Bird: Mockingbird

Insect: Firefly and ladybug

Flower: Iris

Gem: Tennessee River pearl

Rock: Limestone

Stone: Agate

Song: "When It's Iris Time in Tennessee," "Tennessee Waltz," "My Homeland Tennessee," "My Tennessee," and "Rocky Top"

Tree: Tulip poplar

THE LAND

Area: 42,145 sq. mi., 36th
    Land: 41,219 sq. mi., 34th
    Water: 926 sq. mi., 30th
       Inland water: 926 sq. mi., 24th

Topography: Rugged country in the E; Great Smoky Mountains of the Unakas; low ridges of the Appalachian Valley; the flat Cumberland Plateau; slightly rolling terrain and knobs of the interior low plateau, the largest region; Eastern Gulf coastal plain to the W, laced with meandering streams; Mississippi alluvial plain, a narrow strip of swamp and flood plain in the extreme W

Number of counties: 95

Geographic center: Rutherford, 5 mi. NE of Murfreesboro

Length: 440 mi.; width: 120 mi.

Highest point: 6,643 ft. (Clingmans Dome), 17th

Lowest point: 178 ft. (Mississippi River), 29th

Mean elevation: 900 ft., 30th

CLIMATE AND ENVIRONMENT

Temp., highest: 113 deg. on Aug. 9, 1930, at Perryville; lowest: –32 deg. on Dec. 30, 1917, at Mountain City

Monthly average: highest: 91.5 deg., 16th; lowest: 27.8 deg., 41st; spread (high to low): 63.7 deg., 34th

Hazardous waste sites (1997): 14, 26th

Endangered species: Animals: 57—Southern acornshell, Gray bat, Indiana bat, Ovate clubshell, Southern clubshell, Cumberlandian combshell, Upland combshell, Nashville crayfish, Amber darter, Bluemask darter, Boulder darter, Duskytail darter, Appalachian elktoe, Cumberland elktoe, American peregrine falcon, Fanshell, Triangular kidneyshell, Alabama lampmussel, Conasauga logperch, Pygmy madtom, Smoky madtom, Marstonia, Coosa moccasinshell, Oyster mussel, Ring pink mussel, Winged mapleleaf mussel, Appalachian monkeyface pearlymussel, Birdwing pearlymussel, Cracking pearlymussel, Cumberland bean pearlymussel, Cumberland monkeyface pearlymussel, Dromedary pearlymussel, Green-blossom pearlymussel, Little-wing pearlymussel, Orange-foot pimple back pearlymussel, Pale lilliput pearlymussel, Pink mucket pearlymussel, Purple bean (mussel), Purple cat's paw pearlymussel, Tubercled-blossom pearlymussel, Turgid-blossom pearlymussel, White wartyback pearlymussel, Yellow-blossom pearlymussel, Cumberland pigtoe, Fine-rayed pigtoe, Rough pigtoe, Shiny pigtoe, Southern pigtoe, Rough rabbitsfoot, Tan riffleshell, Anthony's riversnail, Spruce-fir moss spider, Carolina northern flying squirrel, Pallid sturgeon, Least tern, Red wolf, Red-cockaded woodpecker. Plants: 13

MAJOR CITIES
POPULATION, 1996
PERCENTAGE INCREASE, 1990-96

Memphis, 596,725; –3.5%
Nashville-Davidson, 511,263; 4.7%
Knoxville, 167,535; –1.3%
Chattanooga, 150,425; –1.3%
Clarksville, 94,879; 25.6%

THE PEOPLE

Population (1997): 5,368,198, 17th
    Percent change (1990-97): 10.07%, 14th
    Percent of total U.S. pop.: 2.01%, 17th
    Per sq. mi: 127.37, 17th
Population (2000 proj.): 5,662,500, 16th
    Percent change (1995-2000): 7.73%, 12th

Percent in metro. area (1996): 67.73%, 31st
Foreign born: 59,000, 31st
   Percent: 1.2%, 45th
Top three ancestries reported:
   Irish, 17.94%
   German, 14.85%
   English, 14.19%
White (1992): 4,170,000, 82.99%, 34th
Black (1992): 808,000, 16.08%, 12th
Native American (1992): 11,000, 0.22%, 39th
Asian, Pacific Isle (1992): 36,000, 0.72%, 39th
Hispanic origin (1992): 38,000, 0.76%, 45th
Percent over 5 yrs. speaking language other than English at home: 2.9%, 46th
Percent males (1996): 48.36%, 41st; percent females: 51.64%, 11th
Percent never married: 23.2%, 41st
Marriages per 1,000 (1996): 15.43, 3rd
Divorces per 1,000 (1996): 6.47, 3rd
Median age (1996): 35.3
Under 5 years (1996): 6.94%, 27th
18 years and under (1996): 27.66%, 38th
65 years and over (1996): 12.55%, 29th
Percent increase among the elderly (1995-96): 1.01%, 22nd

OF VITAL IMPORTANCE

Live births per 1,000 pop. (1996): 13.9, 29th
Infant mortality rate per 1,000 live births (1995): 9.3, 9th
   Rate for whites: 6.8, 16th
   Rate for blacks: 17.9, 5th
Births to unmarried women, % of total (1996): 33.4%, 16th
Births to teenage mothers, % of total (1996): 16.8%, 8th
Abortions (1992): 19,060, 20th
   Rate per 1,000 women 14-44 years old: 16.2, 31st
   Percent change (1988-92): −14%, 36th
Average lifetime (1989-91): 74.32, 43rd
Total death rate per 100,000 pop. (1995): 976.1, 11th
   Accidents and adverse effects: 47.3, 7th
   Alzheimer's disease: 8.8, 23rd
   Cancer: 220.9, 15th
   Cerebrovascular diseases: 79.8, 2nd
   Chronic liver disease and cirrhosis: 9.3, 25th
   Chronic obstructive pulmonary diseases and allied conditions: 41.9, 21st
   Diabetes mellitus: 23.4, 22nd

Diseases of heart: 308.2, 16th
HIV infection: 9.7, 24th
Homicide: 11.1, 11th
Injury by firearms: 18.6, 9th
Motor vehicle accidents: 24.5, 6th
Pneumonia and influenza: 36.0, 12th
Suicide: 13.0, 19th

KEEPING WELL

Active nonfederal physicians per 100,000 pop. (1995): 226, 16th
Dentists per 100,000 (1991): 53, 29th
Nurses per 100,000 (1995): 869, 20th
Hospitals per 100,000 (1995): 2.40, 21st
   Admissions per 1,000 (1995): 140.79, 7th
   Hospital beds per 1,000 (1995): 3.98, 17th
   Occupancy rate per 100 beds (1995): 59.81, 29th
   Average cost per patient per day (1995): $871, 32nd
   Average cost per stay (1995): $5,355, 39th
AIDS cases (new, 1996): 826; per 100,000: 15.5, 22nd
Persons living with HIV infection, not yet AIDS (1996): 3,852
Other notifiable diseases, per 100,000 pop.:
   Gonorrhea (1995): 264.3, 7th
   Syphilis (1995): 49.6, 5th
   Tuberculosis (1996): 9.5, 12th
Pop. without health insur. (1996): 15.2%, 20th

HOUSEHOLDS BY TYPE

Total households (1996): 2,041,000, 17th
   Percent change (1990-96): 10.1%, 15th
   Per 1,000 pop. (1996) 383.65, 12th
   Percent of householders 65 yrs. and over (1996): 21.12%, 31st
   Persons per household (1996): 2.52, 40th
Family households: 1,348,019
   Percent of total: 72.72%, 9th
Nonfamily households: 505,706
   Percent of total: 27.28%, 43rd
Pop. living in group quarters: 129,129
   Percent of pop.: 2.65%, 31st

LIVING QUARTERS

Total housing units: 2,026,067
   Persons per unit: 2.41, 24th
Occupied housing units: 1,853,725
   Percent of total units: 91.49%, 13th
   Persons per unit: 2.51, 30th
   Percent of units with over 1 person per room: 2.74%, 31st

Owner-occupied units: 1,261,118
  Percent of total units: 62.24%, 11th
  Percent of occupied units: 68.03%, 20th
  Persons per unit: 2.66, 40th
  Median value: $58,400, 37th
Renter-occupied units: 592,607
  Percent of total units: 29.25%, 26th
  Percent of occupied units: 31.97%, 32nd
  Persons per unit: 2.35, 25th
  Median contract rent: $273, 38th
  Rental vacancy rate: 9.6%, 16th
Mobile home, trailer & other as a percent of occupied housing units: 11.19%, 25th
Persons in emergency shelters for homeless persons: 1,864, 0.038%, 39th
Persons visible in street locations: 357, 0.0073%, 23rd
Nursing home population: 35,192, 0.72%, 25th

CRIME INDEX PER 100,000 (1996)

Total reported: 5,449.3, 18th
  Percent increase: 1.6%, 7th
  Violent: 774.0, 10th
    Percent increase: 0.3%, 10th
    Murder & nonnegligent manslaughter: 9.5, 9th
    Forcible rape: 46.5, 12th
    Aggravated assault: 494.3, 9th
    Robbery: 223.7, 10th
  Property: 4,675.4, 19th
    Percent increase: 1.8%, 9th
    Burglary: 1,163.5, 10th
    Larceny-theft: 2,864.8, 30th
    Motor vehicle theft: 647.1, 8th

TEACHING AND LEARNING

Pop. 3 and over enrolled in school (1996): 1,137,063, 18th
  Percent of pop.: 21.37%, 42nd
Public elementary & secondary schools (1996-97): 1,563, 20th
  Total enrollment (1996): 891,101, 16th
    Percent of school age pop.: 93.02%, 22nd
    Percent of total pop.: 16.75%, 34th
  Teachers (1996): 51,369, 17th
    Percent of pop.: 0.97%, 37th
  Pupil/teacher ratio (1995): 16.7, 25th
  Teachers' avg. salary (1996-97): $33,789, 32nd
  Expenditure per capita (1992-93): $955.86, 51st
    Education as % of state govt. expenditures: 31.1%, 40th

Expenditure per pupil (1994-95): $4,388, 48th
  Percent increase (1993-94 & 1994-95): 5.76%, 11th
Percent at or above grade level, NAEP tests:
  Reading, grade 4 (1994): 27%, 20th
  Math, grade 4 (1996): 58%, 30th
  Math, grade 8 (1996): 53%, 31st
Percent of graduates taking SAT (1995): 12%, 33rd
  Mean SAT verbal scores: 497, 8th
  Mean SAT mathematical scores: 543, 12th
Percent of graduates taking ACT (1997): 83%, 1st
  Mean ACT scores: 19.7, 46th
Percent of pop. over 25 completing:
  Less than 9th grade: 16.0%, 3rd
  High school: 67.1%, 46th
  College degree(s): 16.0%, 44th
Higher education, institutions (1996): 76, 17th
  Enrollment (1995-96): 245,962, 21st
    Percent increase in enroll. (1990-95): 8.7%, 11th
    White non-Hispanic (1995): 198,271, 20th
      Percent of enroll.: 80.61%, 23rd
    Total minority enroll. (1995): 42,824, 21st
      Percent of enroll.: 17.41%, 24th
    Black non-Hispanic (1995): 36,165, 17th
      Percent of enroll.: 14.70%, 11th
    Hispanic (1995): 2,346, 33rd
      Percent of enroll.: 0.95%, 42nd
    Asian/Pacific Islander (1995): 3,563, 31st
      Percent of enroll.: 1.45%, 41st
    American Indian/AK native (1995): 750, 38th
      Percent of enroll.: 0.30%, 45th
    Nonresident alien (1995): 4,867, 31st
      Percent of enroll.: 1.98%, 43rd
    Female (1995): 137,634, 21st
      Percent of enroll.: 55.96%, 24th
  Pub. institutions (1995-96): 24, 27th
    Enrollment: 193,136, 21st
      Percent increase in enrollment (1990-95): 10.3%, 11th
      Percent of enroll.: 78.52%, 35th
  Private institutions (1995-96): 52, 11th
    Enrollment: 52,826, 20th
      Percent increase in enrollment (1990-95): 3.2%, 32nd
      Percent of enroll.: 21.48%, 17th
  Tuition (in state), public 4-year institution (1996-97): $2,051, 41st

Tuition (in state), public 2-year institution (1996-97): $1,046, 39th

Tuition, private 4-year institution (1996-97): $10,387, 29th

Public library systems (1994): 140, 21st
Books & serial vol. per capita: 1.7, 49th
Library visits per capita: 2.5, 39th
Circulation per capita: 3.9, 48th

LAW ENFORCEMENT AND CORRECTIONS

Police protection and corrections expenditures (1996): $531,860,000
Per capita: $99.98, 33rd
Police per 10,000 pop. (1996): 21.80, 29th
Prisoners (1 year or more) per 100,000 pop. (1996): 292, 32nd
Percent change (1995-96): 2.8%, 39th
Percent of inmates that are female: 4.4%, 48th
Percent change: 5.2%, 35th
Death penalty: yes, by electrocution
Under sentence (Jan. 1998): 110, 12th
Executed, 1976-97: 0

RELIGION, NUMBER AND PERCENT OF POPULATION

Agnostic: 7,321—0.20%, 42nd
Buddhist: 3,661—0.10%, 17th
Christian: 3,316,487—90.60%, 9th
Hindu: NA
Jewish: 10,982—0.30%, 35th
Muslim: 3,661—0.10%, 22nd
Unitarian: 3,661—0.10%, 31st
Other: 36,606—1.00%, 34th
None: 219,635—6.00%, 32nd
Refused to answer: 58,570—1.60%, 39th

MAKING A LIVING

Personal income per capita (1996): $21,764, 34th
Percent increase (1995-96): 2.5%, 35th
Disposable personal income per capita (1996): $19,441, 30th
Median income of households (average, 1995-96): $30,331, 42nd
Percent of pop. below poverty level (1995-96): 15.7%, 16th

ECONOMY

In civilian labor force (1996): 2,751,000
Percent of total pop.: 67.0%, 32nd
Percent of total pop. 65 years and over: 16.3%, 5th
Percent of total female pop.: 60.8%, 26th

Major employer industries (total nonagricultural, 1996):
Construction: 112,700—4.4%, 30th
Finance, insurance, & real estate: 117,200—4.6%, 35th
Government: 383,100—15.1%, 38th
Manufacturing: 522,200—20.6%, 10th
Service: 655,500—25.9%, 37th
Trade: 596,300—23.5%, 28th
Transportation, communications, public utilities: 142,800—5.6%, 18th
Unemployment rate (1996): 5.2%, 23rd
Male: 4.9%, 28th
Female: 5.4%, 19th
Total businesses (1995): 124,814, 19th
New business incorps. (1995): 8,194
Percent of total businesses: 6.56%, 43rd
Business failures (1995): 991
Failures per 10,000 businesses: 79.4, 27th
Agriculture farm income:
Marketing (1996): $2,371,873,000, 30th
Average per farm: $29,648, 49th
Leading products (1997): Cattle, dairy products, tobacco, soybeans, cotton, lint, grain, corn
Average value land & build. per acre (1997): $1,650, 16th
Percent increase (1996-97): 8%, 10th
Govt. payments (1996): $79,917,000, 24th
Average per farm: $999, 37th
Construction, value of all (1996): $8,285,391,000, 15th
Per capita: $1,558, 11th
Manufactures (1995):
Value added: $43,125,600,000
Per capita: $8,205, 9th
Leading products (1997): Chemicals, food, industrial machinery & equipment, fabricated metal products, transportation equipment, rubber & plastic products, paper & allied products, printing & publishing
Value of nonfuel mineral production (1996): $651,000,000, 19th
Leading mineral products (1996): Coal, stone, zinc, cement, sand/gravel, clays
Energy consumption per person (1994): 377.8 mil. Btu, 18th
Retail sales (1995): $49,132,000,000
Per household: $24,299, 30th
Sales increase (1994-95): 7.0%, 13th
Tourism revenues (1995): $7.7 bil.

Foreign exports, in total value (1996): $8,094,000,000, 21st
Per capita: $1,522, 26th
Gross state product per person (1994): $24,451, 26th
Public aid recipients (percent of resident pop. 1994): 9.0%, 9th
Medicaid recipients (percent of pop., 1995): 27.9%, 1st
Medicare enrollment per 1,000 pop. (1996): 148, 22nd

TRAVEL AND TRANSPORTATION

Motor vehicle registrations (1996): 4,830,482, 14th
Per 1,000 pop.: 910.14, 8th
Motorcycle registrations (1996): 78,869, 17th
Per 1,000 pop.: 16.33, 33rd
Licensed drivers (1996): 3,739,043, 15th
Per 1,000 pop.: 712.64, 12th
Public roads & streets (1996)
Total mileage: 85,795, 21st
Per 1,000 pop.: 116.13, 27th
Rural mileage: 68,518, 24th
Per 1,000 pop.: 12.88, 27th
Urban mileage: 17,277, 17th
Per 1,000 pop.: 3.25, 18th
Interstate mileage: 1,062, 16th
Per 1,000 pop.: 0.20, 26th
Speed limit (max. interstate, autos, mi. per hr., 1997): 65
Annual vehicle-mi. of travel per driver (1996): 15,355, 16th
Mean travel time for workers age 16+ who work away from home: 21.5 min., 19th

GOVERNMENT

Percent of voting age pop. registered (1996): 70.63%, 38th
Percent of voting age pop. voting for president: (1996): 47.1%, 37th
Percent of voting age pop. voting for U.S. representatives (1996): 44.3%, 36th
State legislators, total (1997): 132, 33rd

Women members (1997): 18
Percent of legislature: 14%, 44th
U.S. Congress, House members (1998): 9
Change (1988-98): 0
Revenues (1996):
State govt.: $14,749,141,000
Per capita: $2,772.39, 49th
Parimutuel & amusement taxes & lotteries, revenue per capita (1995): NA
Expenditures (1996):
State govt.: $13,829,307,000
Per capita: $2,599.49, 47th
Debt outstanding (1996): $3,069,027,000
Per capita: $576.88, 48th

LAWS AND REGULATIONS

Legal driving age: 16
Marriage age without parental consent: 18
Divorce residence requirement: 6 mo., for qualifications check local statutes

ATTRACTIONS (1997)

Major opera companies: 3
Major symphony orchestras: 4
Major dance companies: 1
Per capita spending by the NEA (1997): $0.13, 48th
State Fair in late September at Nashville

SPORTS AND COMPETITION

NCAA (Division I) football and basketball teams: Austin Peay State Univ. Governors, Belmont Univ. Bruins (basketball only), East Tennessee State Univ. Buccaneers, Middle Tennessee State Univ. Blue Raiders, Tennessee State Univ. Tigers, Tennessee Tech Univ. Golden Eagles, Univ. of Memphis Tigers, Univ. of Tennessee-Chattanooga Moccasins, Univ. of Tennessee-Knoxville Volunteers, Univ. of Tennessee-Martin Skyhawks, Vanderbilt Univ. Commodores
NFL football teams: Tennessee Oilers (AFC), Liberty Bowl Memorial Stadium

WEBSITES CONTAINING FURTHER INFORMATION

Tenn.net	http://www.tenn.net
Tennessee's WWW Site	http://www.state.tn.us

T E X A S

"The province of Techas will be the richest state of our union, without any exception."   President Thomas Jefferson

Novelist Edna Ferber labeled Texas as a giant, and she was right. The total wealth of its natural resources surpasses that of all the other states. As a separate country it would rank 11th in wealth among the nations. Texas leads the nation in total productivity, and its history retells one of the nation's most heroic events, the defense of the Alamo. Texans are friendly—indeed, "Friendship" is their state motto. Once the typical Texan was a frontier cowboy with a ten-gallon hat, but today the state's symbol might more appropriately be an oil field worker or a laboratory scientist. Texas is still a frontier state, but nowadays the frontier is the space program. Perhaps it is typical and appropriate that this giant state has constructed the largest of all the state capitols as a symbol of its strength.

SUPERLATIVES

- Greatest variety of flowers.
- Greatest variety of reptiles.
- Leader in helium production.
- First in petroleum refining.
- First in asphalt production.
- First in cotton production.
- Produces the greatest quantity of chemicals from seawater.
- Only state with five major ports.

MOMENTS IN HISTORY

- The shipwrecked party of Alvar Nuñez Cabéza de Vaca escaped from Indian captivity on an island off the Texas coast in 1535 and made an incredible journey across country back to Mexico.
- The renowned expedition of Francisco Vásquez de Coronado crossed the Rio Grande in 1541.
- In 1598 dashing Don Juan de Onate crossed the Rio Grande into Texas and claimed the land for Spain.
- The first permanent European settlement in what is now Texas was Ysleta, founded in 1682.
- In the first half of the 1700s, about a dozen missions became outposts of civilization in Texas.
- The Sabine and Red rivers were established as northern and eastern boundaries in 1819.

- Moses and Stephen Austin established an American foothold in Texas before Moses died in the 1820s, and the American presence grew in the early 1830s.
- By 1835 the Americans in Texas realized that they must seek independence from Mexico, and they laid siege to San Antonio, which fell in December.
- In February 1836, Mexican leader Antonio Lopez de Santa Anna arrived to recapture San Antonio, finding the defenders at an old mission called the Alamo. He faced the heroic stand of a handful of men under the brave leadership of Commander William Barret Travis. After a long siege, Santa Anna's forces overwhelmed and slaughtered them on March 6. Santa Anna then captured and murdered 330 Texans at Goliad.

So They Say

"The enemy has demanded a surrender at discretion, or otherwise, the garrison are to be put to the sword. . .I shall never surrender or retreat—victory or death."

Alamo Commander William Barret Travis

- Texan dynamo Sam Houston led his forces eastward and lured Santa Anna into a difficult position. Santa Anna was defeated and captured at the decisive Battle of San Jacinto, on April 21, 1836.

So They Say

"This morning we are in preparation to meet Santa Anna. It is the only chance of saving Texas. Texas could have started 4,000 men. We will only have about seven hundred. We go to conquer."

Later—"Victory is certain. Trust in God and fear not. And remember the Alamo!"   **Sam Houston**

- Later that year, the people held an election and chose Sam Houston as the first president of the independent Republic of Texas.
- After ten years of independence, on December 29, 1845, Texas became the 28th state.

• As the divisions over slavery increased, Sam Houston became governor in 1859.

• Despite Houston's objection, the state voted to secede and join the Confederacy on January 28, 1861, and Houston resigned as governor.

• During the Civil War, Texas furnished enormous quantities of essential materials and food.

• Texas was readmitted to the Union on March 30, 1870, and a new constitution became law on February 15, 1876.

• Between the years 1870 and 1890, 10 million cattle were shipped from Texas to the nation's markets.

So They Say

"With an area of more than a quarter of a million square miles, with an unlimited variety of soil, climate and productions, with a capacity for growth and prosperity beyond calculation, with a steady stream of immigration converging from all parts of the world, with her vast prairies, her rivers, her streams, her enterprise, her history, her sacred memories and her teeming future, Texas is indeed the Coming Empire."

Writer Oscar Wilde (1882)

• The terrible hurricane at Galveston on September 8, 1900, killed at least 6,000 and left 8,000 homeless.

• An explosion at a New London school in 1937 brought death to more than 300 pupils and teachers.

• Texan Lyndon Baines Johnson succeeded to the presidency following the assassination of John F. Kennedy at Dallas on November 22, 1963.

So They Say

"All I have I would have given gladly not to be standing here today."

Lyndon Johnson, assuming the presidency after the Kennedy assassination

---

• A highly controversial federal raid on the Branch Davidian compound at Waco ended in a tragic fire on April 19, 1993; more than 70 cult members were killed.

• In 1997, San Antonio experienced almost unprecedented floods.

THAT'S INTERESTING

• Only in Texas do all of the four major divisions of the North American continent come together.

• Many people think of Texas as flat and arid, but it has extremely varied terrain including mountains. Although dry in parts, Texas has many miles of inland water.

• Near Odessa a 10-acre crater marks the spot where a meteor of nickel and iron, weighing an estimated 625 tons, crashed far into the earth in a cloud of smoke and shower of sparks.

• Rockwall is a strange formation of rock in the county of the same name—as thin and vertical as a wall.

• The Karnakawa Indians had a strange habit of spending most of the daytime hours in the leafy treetops, coming down to the ground for night raids on terrified neighbors.

• Someone has said that the Rio Grande is a mile wide and a foot deep—too thin to plow and too thick to drink. It is among the longest on the continent.

• At statehood, Texas retained the right to divide itself into five new states. This could still be done if the people wished.

• Fifteen thousand carloads of Texas pink granite were required to build the Texas capitol, the largest outside Washington, DC. This material was donated by the owners of Granite Mountain, near Marble Falls.

NOTABLE NATIVES

Joan Crawford (San Antonio, 1908-1977), actress. **James Frank Dobie** (Live Oak County, 1888-1964), folklorist/educator. **Dwight David Eisenhower** (Denison, 1890-1969), U.S. president/soldier. **James Edward Ferguson** (Temple, 1871-1944), public official. **Miriam A. (Ma) Ferguson** (Bell County, 1875-1961), public official. **John Nance Garner** (Red River County, 1868-1967), U.S. vice president. **Howard Robard Hughes** (Houston, 1905-1976), industrialist/aviator/producer. **Lyndon Baines Johnson** (near Stonewall, 1908-1973), U.S. president. **Barbara Jordan** (Houston, 1936-1996), public official. **Audie Murphy** (Kingston, 1924-1971), soldier/actor. **Chester William Nimitz** (Fredericksburg, 1885-1966), naval officer. **Sandra Day O'Connor** (El Paso, 1930-), Supreme Court justice. **Katherine Anne Porter** (Indian Creek, 1890-1980), author. **Wiley Post** (near Grand Saline, 1899-1925), aviator. **Mildred Ella**

Didrikson (Babe) Zaharias (Port Arthur, 1914-1956), athlete.

GENERAL

Admitted to statehood: December 29, 1845
Origin of name: Variant of word used by Caddo and other Indians meaning "friends" or "allies" and applied to them by the Spanish in eastern Texas. Also written *texias, tejas, teysas*
Capital: Austin
Nickname: Lone Star State
Motto: Friendship
Bird: Mockingbird
Flower: Bluebonnet
Gem: Topaz
Stone: Petrified palmwood
Song: "Texas, Our Texas"
Tree: Pecan

THE LAND

Area: 267,277 sq. mi., 2nd
  Land: 261,914 sq. mi., 2nd
  Water: 5,363 sq. mi., 8th
    Inland water: 4,959 sq. mi., 2nd
    Coastal water: 404 sq. mi., 14th
Topography: Gulf Coast Plain in the S and SE; North Central Plains slope upward with some hills; Great Plains extend over the Panhandle, are broken by low mountains; Trans-Pecos are southern extension of the Rockies.
Number of counties: 254
Geographic center: McCulloch, 15 mi. NE of Brady
Length: 790 mi.; width: 660 mi.
Highest point: 8,749 ft. (Guadalupe Peak), 14th
Lowest point: sea level (Gulf of Mexico), 3rd
Mean elevation: 1,700 ft., 17th
Coastline: 367 mi., 6th
Shoreline: 3,359 mi., 7th

CLIMATE AND ENVIRONMENT

Temp., highest: 120 deg. on Aug. 12, 1936, at Seymour; lowest: −23 deg. on Feb. 8, 1933, at Seminole
Monthly average: highest: 98.5 deg., 4th; lowest: 21.7 deg., 29th; spread (high to low): 76.8 deg., 13th
Hazardous waste sites (1997): 26, 14th
Endangered species: Animals: 35—Mexican long-nosed bat, Coffin Cave mold beetle, Kretschmarr Cave mold beetle, Tooth Cave ground beetle, Whooping crane, Eskimo curlew, Fountain darter, American peregrine falcon, Northern aplomado falcon, Southwestern willow flycatcher, Big Bend gambusia, Clear Creek gambusia, Pecos gambusia, San Marcos gambusia, Bee Creek Cave harvestman, Bone Cave harvestman, Jaguar, Jaguarundi, West Indian manatee, Rio Grande silvery minnow, Ocelot, Brown pelican, Attwater's greater prairie-chicken, Tooth Cave pseudoscorpion, Comanche Springs pupfish, Leon Springs pupfish, Barton Springs salamander, Texas blind salamander, Tooth Cave spider, Least tern, Houston toad, Kemp's turtle, Black-capped vireo, Golden-cheeked warbler, Red-cockaded woodpecker. Plants: 23

MAJOR CITIES
POPULATION, 1996
PERCENTAGE INCREASE, 1990-96

Houston, 1,744,058; 6.5%
San Antonio, 1,067,816; 11.3%
Dallas, 1,053,292; 4.5%
El Paso, 599,865; 16.4%
Austin, 541,278; 14.7%

THE PEOPLE

Population (1997): 19,439,337, 2nd
  Percent change (1990-97): 14.44%, 8th
  Percent of total U.S. pop.: 7.26%, 2nd
  Per sq. mi: 72.37, 30th
Population (2000 proj.): 20,148,500, 2nd
  Percent change (1995-2000): 7.61%, 13th
Percent in metro. area (1996): 84.16%, 13th
Foreign born: 1,524,000, 4th
  Percent: 9.0%, 9th
Top three ancestries reported:
  Mexican, 20.03%
  German, 17.37%
  Irish, 13.95%
White (1992): 15,083,000, 85.30%, 30th
Black (1992): 2,139,000, 12.10%, 18th
Native American (1992): 77,000, 0.44%, 25th
Asian, Pacific Isle (1992): 385,000, 2.18%, 14th
Hispanic origin (1992): 4,689,000, 26.52%, 3rd
Percent over 5 yrs. speaking language other than English at home: 25.4%, 3rd

Percent males (1996): 49.41%, 14th; percent females: 50.59%, 38th
Percent never married: 25.1%, 30th
Marriages per 1,000 (1996): 9.39, 14th
Divorces per 1,000 (1996): NA
Median age (1996): 32.6
Under 5 years (1996): 8.42%, 3rd
18 years and under (1996): 31.53%, 6th
65 years and over (1996): 10.20%, 47th
Percent increase among the elderly (1995-96): 1.73%, 10th

OF VITAL IMPORTANCE

Live births per 1,000 pop. (1996): 17.1, 3rd
Infant mortality rate per 1,000 live births (1995): 6.5, 38th
  Rate for whites: 5.9, 39th
  Rate for blacks: 11.7, 32nd
Births to unmarried women, % of total (1996): 30.5%, 29th
Births to teenage mothers, % of total (1996): 16.2%, 12th
Abortions (1992): 97,400, 3rd
  Rate per 1,000 women 14-44 years old: 23.1, 20th
  Percent change (1988-92): –7%, 23rd
Average lifetime (1989-91): 75.14, 32nd
Total death rate per 100,000 pop. (1995): 736.1, 45th
  Accidents and adverse effects: 34.3, 34th
  Alzheimer's disease: 7.9, 29th
  Cancer: 168.9, 45th
  Cerebrovascular diseases: 52.3, 41st
  Chronic liver disease and cirrhosis: 10.0, 16th
  Chronic obstructive pulmonary diseases and allied conditions: 33.3, 45th
  Diabetes mellitus: 24.4, 18th
  Diseases of heart: 222.9, 42nd
  HIV infection: 14.8, 13th
  Homicide: 9.6, 16th
  Injury by firearms: 15.2, 17th
  Motor vehicle accidents: 17.8, 24th
  Pneumonia and influenza: 20.5, 49th
  Suicide: 11.9, 30th

KEEPING WELL

Active nonfederal physicians per 100,000 pop. (1995): 189, 38th
Dentists per 100,000 (1991): 48, 35th
Nurses per 100,000 (1995): 647, 46th
Hospitals per 100,000 (1995): 2.22, 24th
  Admissions per 1,000 (1995): 108.36, 33rd
  Hospital beds per 1,000 (1995): 3.05, 34th
  Occupancy rate per 100 beds (1995): 54.55, 46th
  Average cost per patient per day (1995): $1,063, 15th
  Average cost per stay (1995): $5,879, 27th
AIDS cases (new, 1996): 4,830; per 100,000: 25.3, 12th
Persons living with HIV infection (1996): NA
Other notifiable diseases, per 100,000 pop.:
  Gonorrhea (1995): 164.5, 15th
  Syphilis (1995): 42.3, 9th
  Tuberculosis (1996): 11.0, 6th
Pop. without health insur. (1996): 24.3%, 1st

HOUSEHOLDS BY TYPE

Total households (1996): 6,894,000, 2nd
  Percent change (1990-96): 13.6%, 9th
  Per 1,000 pop. (1996) 360.41, 47th
  Percent of householders 65 yrs. and over (1996): 17.99%, 47th
  Persons per household (1996): 2.69, 8th
Family households: 4,343,878
  Percent of total: 71.55%, 17th
Nonfamily households: 1,727,059
  Percent of total: 28.45%, 35th
Pop. living in group quarters: 393,447
  Percent of pop.: 2.32%, 41st

LIVING QUARTERS

Total housing units: 7,008,999
  Persons per unit: 2.42, 20th
Occupied housing units: 6,070,937
  Percent of total units: 86.62%, 39th
  Persons per unit: 2.70, 6th
  Percent of units with over 1 person per room: 8.15%, 5th
Owner-occupied units: 3,695,115
  Percent of total units: 52.72%, 45th
  Percent of occupied units: 60.87%, 44th
  Persons per unit: 2.85, 6th
  Median value: $59,600, 35th
Renter-occupied units: 2,375,822
  Percent of total units: 33.90%, 12th
  Percent of occupied units: 39.13%, 9th
  Persons per unit: 2.55, 7th
  Median contract rent: $328, 27th
  Rental vacancy rate: 13.0%, 4th
Mobile home, trailer & other as a percent of occupied housing units: 10.39%, 27th
Persons in emergency shelters for homeless persons: 7,816, 0.046%, 27th
Persons visible in street locations: 1,442, 0.0085%, 22nd
Nursing home population: 101,005, 0.59%, 38th

CRIME INDEX PER 100,000 (1996)

Total reported: 5,708.9, 14th
  Percent increase: 0.4%, 12th
  Violent: 644.4, 14th
    Percent increase: –2.9%, 16th
    Murder & nonnegligent manslaughter: 7.7, 17th
    Forcible rape: 43.8, 14th
    Aggravated assault: 421.4, 16th
    Robbery: 171.5, 16th
  Property: 5,064.5, 14th
    Percent increase: 0.9%, 11th
    Burglary: 1,068.5, 14th
    Larceny-theft: 3,447.4, 13th
    Motor vehicle theft: 548.6, 14th

TEACHING AND LEARNING

Pop. 3 and over enrolled in school (1996): 4,761,711, 2nd
  Percent of pop.: 24.89%, 8th
Public elementary & secondary schools (1996-97): 6,638, 2nd
  Total enrollment (1996): 3,809,186, 2nd
    Percent of school age pop.: 98.43%, 2nd
    Percent of total pop.: 19.91%, 5th
  Teachers (1996): 247,526, 1st
    Percent of pop.: 1.29%, 3rd
  Pupil/teacher ratio (1995): 15.6, 35th
  Teachers' avg. salary (1996-97): $32,644, 37th
  Expenditure per capita (1992-93): $1,338.71, 22nd
    Education as % of state govt. expenditures: 39.1%, 6th
  Expenditure per pupil (1994-95): $5,222, 33rd
    Percent increase (1993-94 & 1994-95): 6.61%, 7th
Percent at or above grade level, NAEP tests:
  Reading, grade 4 (1994): 26%, 23rd
  Math, grade 4 (1996): 69%, 11th
  Math, grade 8 (1996): 59%, 22nd
Percent of graduates taking SAT (1995): 47%, 22nd
  Mean SAT verbal scores: 419, 42nd
  Mean SAT mathematical scores: 474, 38th
Percent of graduates taking ACT (1997): 30%, 29th
  Mean ACT scores: 20.2, 41st
Percent of pop. over 25 completing:
  Less than 9th grade: 13.5%, 10th
  High school: 72.1%, 40th
  College degree(s): 20.3%, 24th

Higher education, institutions (1996): 179, 4th
  Enrollment (1995-96): 952,525, 3rd
    Percent increase in enroll. (1990-95): 5.7%, 20th
    White non-Hispanic (1995): 590,137, 3rd
      Percent of enroll.: 61.96%, 47th
    Total minority enroll. (1995): 336,140, 2nd
      Percent of enroll.: 35.29%, 5th
    Black non-Hispanic (1995): 93,660, 3rd
      Percent of enroll.: 9.83%, 18th
    Hispanic (1995): 195,377, 2nd
      Percent of enroll.: 20.51%, 2nd
    Asian/Pacific Islander (1995): 42,311, 3rd
      Percent of enroll.: 4.44%, 13th
    American Indian/AK native (1995): 4,792, 6th
      Percent of enroll.: 0.50%, 28th
    Nonresident alien (1995): 26,248, 3rd
      Percent of enroll.: 2.76%, 23rd
    Female (1995): 514,350, 3rd
      Percent of enroll.: 54.00%, 47th
  Pub. institutions (1995-96): 107, 2nd
    Enrollment: 836,851, 2nd
      Percent increase in enrollment (1990-95): 4.3%, 23rd
    Percent of enroll.: 87.86%, 11th
  Private institutions (1995-96): 72, 8th
    Enrollment: 115,674, 7th
      Percent increase in enrollment (1990-95): 16.7%, 12th
    Percent of enroll.: 12.14%, 41st
  Tuition (in state), public 4-year institution (1996-97): $2,022, 42nd
  Tuition (in state), public 2-year institution (1996-97): $788, 46th
  Tuition, private 4-year institution (1996-97): $9,385, 36th
Public library systems (1994): 496, 4th
  Books & serial vol. per capita: 2.0, 39th
  Library visits per capita: 3.0, 33rd
  Circulation per capita: 4.3, 44th

LAW ENFORCEMENT AND CORRECTIONS

Police protection and corrections expenditures (1996): $2,642,953,000
  Per capita: $138.17, 16th
Police per 10,000 pop. (1996): 22.60, 22nd
Prisoners (1 year or more) per 100,000 pop. (1996): 686, 2nd
  Percent change (1995-96): 3.6%, 35th
  Percent of inmates that are female: 7.5%, 4th
    Percent change: 25.2%, 7th

Death penalty: yes, by lethal injection
  Under sentence (Jan. 1998): 428, 2nd
  Executed, 1976-97: 144, 1st
  Executed in 1997: 37, 1st

RELIGION, NUMBER AND PERCENT OF POPULATION

Agnostic: 72,904—0.60%, 19th
Buddhist: 24,301—0.20%, 11th
Christian: 10,935,604—90.00%, 11th
Hindu: NA
Jewish: 85,055—0.70%, 23rd
Muslim: 24,301—0.20%, 13th
Unitarian: 24,301—0.20%, 23rd
Other: 194,411—1.60%, 17th
None: 595,383—4.90%, 40th
Refused to answer: 194,411—1.60%, 39th

MAKING A LIVING

Personal income per capita (1996): $22,045, 32nd
  Percent increase (1995-96): 4.0%, 15th
Disposable personal income per capita (1996): $19,621, 29th
Median income of households (average, 1995-96): $33,029, 33rd
Percent of pop. below poverty level (1995-96): 17.0%, 8th

ECONOMY

In civilian labor force (1996): 9,748,000
  Percent of total pop.: 69.0%, 20th
  Percent of total pop. 65 years and over: 15.2%, 7th
  Percent of total female pop.: 59.7%, 33rd
Major employer industries (total nonagricultural, 1996):
  Construction: 435,900—5.3%, 13th
  Finance, insurance, & real estate: 444,000—5.4%, 21st
  Government: 1,454,400—17.6%, 21st
  Manufacturing: 1,054,300—12.8%, 34th
  Service: 2,220,700—26.9%, 27th
  Trade: 1,988,300—24.1%, 20th
  Transportation, communications, public utilities: 488,200—5.9%, 12th
Unemployment rate (1996): 5.6%, 15th
  Male: 5.3%, 20th
  Female: 6.1%, 12th
Total businesses (1995): 438,262, 3rd
New business incorps. (1995): 38,122
  Percent of total businesses: 8.70%, 29th
Business failures (1995): 6,152
  Failures per 10,000 businesses: 140.4, 6th

Agriculture farm income:
  Marketing (1996): $13,053,234,000, 2nd
    Average per farm: $63,674, 43rd
  Leading products (1997): Cattle, cotton, grain sorghum, grains, vegetables, citrus & other fruits, pecans, peanuts
  Average value land & build. per acre (1997): $600, 38th
    Percent increase (1996-97): 5%, 26th
  Govt. payments (1996): $764,778,000, 1st
    Average per farm: $3,731, 17th
Construction, value of all (1996): $24,969,136,000, 2nd
  Per capita: $1,305, 21st
Manufactures (1995):
  Value added: $112,425,100,000
    Per capita: $6,004, 28th
  Leading products (1997): Industrial machinery & equipment, foods, electric and electronic equipment, chemicals and chemical products, apparel
Value of nonfuel mineral production (1996): $1,780,000,000, 5th
Leading mineral products (1996): Petroleum, natural gas, cement, sand/gravel, stone, magnesium, lime
Energy consumption per person (1994): 564.2 mil. Btu, 4th
Retail sales (1995): $165,526,000,000
  Per household: $24,665, 24th
  Sales increase (1994-95): 8.0%, 7th
Tourism revenues (1994): $24.6 bil.
Foreign exports, in total value (1996): $66,862,000,000, 2nd
  Per capita: $3,495, 5th
Gross state product per person (1994): $26,106, 18th
Public aid recipients (percent of resident pop. 1994): 6.3%, 31st
Medicaid recipients (percent of pop., 1995): 13.6%, 16th
Medicare enrollment per 1,000 pop. (1996): 111, 46th

TRAVEL AND TRANSPORTATION

Motor vehicle registrations (1996): 13,486,868, 2nd
  Per 1,000 pop.: 706.44, 43rd
Motorcycle registrations (1996): 148,815, 8th
  Per 1,000 pop.: 11.03, 47th
Licensed drivers (1996): 12,369,243, 2nd
  Per 1,000 pop.: 657.89, 39th
Public roads & streets (1996)

Total mileage: 296,259, 1st
  Per 1,000 pop.: 115.49, 29th
  Rural mileage: 214,062, 1st
  Per 1,000 pop.: 11.19, 30th
  Urban mileage: 82,197, 2nd
  Per 1,000 pop.: 4.30, 4th
  Interstate mileage: 3,234, 1st
  Per 1,000 pop.: 0.17, 32nd
Speed limit (max. interstate, autos, mi. per hr., 1997): 70
Annual vehicle-mi. of travel per driver (1996): 14,750, 22nd
Mean travel time for workers age 16+ who work away from home: 22.2 min., 12th

GOVERNMENT

Percent of voting age pop. registered (1996): 77.52%, 24th
  Percent of voting age pop. voting for president: (1996): 41.2%, 49th
  Percent of voting age pop. voting for U.S. representatives (1996): 38.3%, 45th
State legislators, total (1997): 181, 11th
  Women members (1997): 34
  Percent of legislature: 19%, 30
U.S. Congress, House members (1998): 30
  Change (1988-98): 3
Revenues (1996):
  State govt.: $51,118,112,000
  Per capita: $2,672.42, 50th
  Parimutuel & amusement taxes & lotteries, revenue per capita (1995): $148.26, 14th
Expenditures (1996):
  State govt.: $46,081,839,000
  Per capita: $2,409.13, 49th
Debt outstanding (1996): $14,575,675,000
  Per capita: $762.01, 44th

LAWS AND REGULATIONS

Legal driving age: 18, 16 if completed driver education course
Marriage age without parental consent: 18
Divorce residence requirement: 6 mo., for qualifications check local statutes

ATTRACTIONS (1997)

Major opera companies: 4
Major symphony orchestras: 6
Major dance companies: 5
Major professional theater companies (nonprofit): 2
Per capita spending by the NEA (1997): $0.14, 46th
State Fair in mid-October at Dallas

SPORTS AND COMPETITION

NCAA (Division I) football and basketball teams: Baylor Univ. Bears, Lamar Univ. Cardinals (basketball only), Prairie View A&M Univ. Panthers, Rice Univ. Owls, Sam Houston State Univ. Bearkats, Southern Methodist Univ. Mustangs, Southwest Texas State Univ. Bobcats, Stephen F. Austin State Univ. Lumberjacks, Texas A&M Univ. Aggies, Texas Christian Univ. Horned Frogs, Texas Southern Univ. Tigers, Texas Tech Univ. Red Raiders, Univ. of Houston Cougars, Univ. of North Texas Mean Green Eagles/Eagles, Univ. of Texas-Arlington Mavericks (basketball only), Univ. of Texas-Austin Longhorns, Univ. of Texas-El Paso Miners, Univ. of Texas-Pan American Broncs (basketball only), Univ. of Texas-San Antonio Roadrunners (basketball only)
Major league baseball teams: Houston Astros (NL Central), The Astrodome; Texas Rangers (AL West), The Ballpark in Arlington
Major league soccer teams: Dallas Burn, Cotton Bowl
NBA basketball teams: San Antonio Spurs, Alamodome; Dallas Mavericks, Reunion Arena; Houston Rockets, The Compaq Center
WNBA basketball teams: Houston Comets, The Compaq Center
NFL football teams: Dallas Cowboys (NFC), Texas Stadium
NHL hockey teams: Dallas Stars, Reunion Arena

WEBSITES CONTAINING FURTHER INFORMATION

State of Texas Government
Information   http://www.state.tx.us

UTAH

"...that the physical obstacles to the occupation of a region so unpromising were sufficient to discourage the most sanguine imagination and to appall the stoutest heart, the mind is filled with wonder at witnessing the immense results which have been accomplished in so short a time, and from a beginning apparently so insignificant."   Howard Stansbury, explorer and civil engineer

Utah is a land that was settled because no one else wanted it, and it soon blossomed under the dedication of an unusual people, the Mormons. It is a "desert" land swarming with seagulls and pelicans, where the faithful erected a monument to a bird. Its broad expanses possess some of the nation's most spectacular natural formations, many found nowhere else, such as Rainbow Bridge. Today the capital, Salt Lake City, is the smallest city in the country to boast a top-ranked symphony, dance company, and opera company. Utah is a fascinating land described as "wonderful, outrageous, mysterious, and strange."

So They Say

"....A state as different from the rest of the Union in faith, manners, and customs as it is widely separated by the vast plains and inhospitable deserts that surround it...[given] the indomitable energy the unity and concentration of actions...which seems to possess the entire Mormon community."

John James Abert, traveler on the Mormon Trail (1852)

SUPERLATIVES

- Bear River, the continent's longest river not reaching the sea.
- Largest salt lake in North America—Great Salt Lake.
- Nation's only major east-west range—the Uintas.
- Highest and largest natural arch—Rainbow Bridge.
- World center of genealogical research.

MOMENTS IN HISTORY

- Little was known of the region until Catholic priests Silvestre Velez de Escalante and Francisco Atanasio Dominguez passed through the area in 1776, looking for a route to California. They left present-day Utah at Padre Creek. Many Spanish expeditions followed the padres' route to California.
- The winter of 1824-25 brought Jim Bridger, the first European explorer known to have arrived at the shores of Great Salt Lake. Bridger told of a terrible winter which "froze" all the buffalo there.
- In 1826 the fur business of Jackson and Sublette was organized in the region, and the great frontiersman Jedediah Strong Smith made a thorough exploration of the area.
- A "rendezvous" of fur traders and trappers was held in 1826 at present-day Ogden. These gatherings in the wilderness, which became annual events, took on a carnival atmosphere, with games, races, singing, and storytelling, brightened by the colorful Indian costumes or frontier garb of all the participants.
- The explorations of John C. Frémont in 1843, 1844, 1845, and 1854 did much to make the region known.
- In 1845, guided by Kit Carson, Frémont crossed the central Salt Desert.
- The first permanent European-style settlement in Utah was Fort Buenaventura (later Ogden), built in 1844-45 by Miles Goodyear.
- Driven from their three prosperous settlements in the East, the first of vast numbers of members of the Church of Jesus Christ of the Latter-Day Saints (Mormons) reached their "Promised Land" on July 24, 1847. Their leader, Brigham Young, looked out from a hill over the site of present-day Salt Lake City and said, "This is the place"—a region so remote and forlorn he expected never again to be driven out.

So They Say

"When my husband said 'This is the place,' I cried, for it seemed to me the most desolate in all the world."

Clara Decker Young, wife of Brigham Young

- The fall of 1847 found the Mormons ready to reap substantial crops, until a swarm of crickets threatened all. The crops were saved by the arrival of flights of seagulls, who ate the crickets and gave the Mormons their "symbol of deliverance."

• By 1849 the broad streets of Salt Lake City had been laid out; there were gristmills and sawmills run by waterpower, carding machines, and other advances. That year, the thousands of 49ers began to pass by on their way to the California gold fields, and the Mormons prospered by supplying their desperate needs.

So They Say

"At our feet...lay the waters of the Great Salt Lake...They were clear and calm and stretched far to the south and west....The stillness of the grave seemed to pervade...and, excepting here and there a solitary wild duck...not a living thing was to be seen....The bleak and naked shores...presented a scene so different from what I had pictured...of the beauties of this far-famed spot, that my disappointment was extreme."

Explorer/engineer Howard Stansbury (1852)

• With incredible Mormon energy, by 1855, Ogden, Provo, Utah Valley, Manti, Sanpete Valley, Tooele, Nephi, Fillmore, Brigham City, Cedar City, and Santa Clara had been established in Utah, along with Las Vegas in Nevada, and Morgan, Moab, and Fort Lemhi in Idaho—all by the Mormons.

• From 1855 to 1860, more than 4,000 Mormon converts from Europe crossed the plains to Utah, pulling and pushing their handcarts from the eastern railheads, the only "transportation" the leaders at Salt Lake City could provide for them.

So They Say

"They are expected to walk and draw their carts across the plains. Sufficient teams will be furnished to haul the aged, infirm and those unable to walk. A few good cows will be sent along to furnish milk and some beef cattle."

Brigham Young

• In 1861 the overland telegraph was completed to Utah. At last the isolated region could communicate with the rest of the country at the speed of electricity.

• Indian warfare plagued the settlers until about 1868.

• In 1869 the first transcontinental railroad was completed with the pounding of the golden spike at Promontory Point.

• On January 4, 1896, Utah became the 45th state.

• The magnificent Rainbow Bridge was discovered in 1909. In 1910, President Taft proclaimed it a national monument.

• World War I called 21,000 Utahans to service, and the Mormon Relief Societies made substantial contributions to the starving of Europe.

• During World War II, 70,000 Utah men and women saw service.

• In 1983 the heaviest rains and snowfalls of record brought the most widespread flooding ever experienced there. Great Salt Lake rose 10 feet in two years.

• A presidential executive order created Utah's Grand Staircase-Escalante National Monument in 1996.

THAT'S INTERESTING

• Authorities believe that prehistoric peoples lit their sacred fires at the base of Rainbow Bridge and paid awed tribute to their gods.

• Early travelers brought back such terrifying descriptions of the awesome character and uselessness of the land that the Spanish to the south left it alone for over 200 years.

• The beautiful Seagull monument at Salt Lake City pays tribute to the bird that saved the first Mormon crops.

• Celebrating the completion of the first transcontinental railroad, Governor Leland Stanford of California swung his sledgehammer at the gold spike—and missed.

• Zion Narrows canyon is so narrow and deep that even in bright daylight stars are visible from the canyon bottom.

NOTABLE NATIVES

Maude Adams (Salt Lake City, 1872-1953), actress. **John Moses Browning** (Ogden, 1855-1926), inventor. **Bernard Augustine De Voto** (Ogden, 1897-1955), author. **Marriner Stoddard Eccles** (Logan, 1890-1977), banker. **Philo Taylor Farnsworth** (Beaver, 1906-1971), engineer/inventor. **Harvey Fletcher** (Provo, 1884-

1981), physicist. **John Held, Jr.** (Salt Lake City, 1889-1958), illustrator/author. **Mahonri Mackintosh Young** (Salt Lake City, 1877-1957), sculptor/painter/etcher.

GENERAL

Admitted to statehood: January 4, 1896

Origin of name: From Navajo word meaning "upper," or "higher up," as applied to a Shoshone tribe called Ute. Spanish form is *Yutta*, English *Uta* or *Utah*. Proposed name *Deseret*, "land of honeybees," from Book of Mormon, was rejected by Congress

Capital: Salt Lake City

Nickname: Beehive State

Motto: Industry

Bird: Seagull

Flower: Sego lily

Gem: Topaz

Song: "Utah, We Love Thee"

Tree: Blue spruce

THE LAND

Area: 84,904 sq. mi., 13th
  Land: 82,168 sq. mi., 12th
  Water: 2,736 sq. mi., 14th
    Inland water: 2,736 sq. mi., 7th
Topography: High Colorado plateau cut by brilliantly colored canyons of the SE; broad, flat, desert-like Great Basin of the W; the Great Salt Lake and Bonneville Salt Flats to the NW; Middle Rockies in the NE running E-W; valleys and plateaus of the Wasatch Front
Number of counties: 29
Geographic center: Sanpete, 3 mi. N of Manti
Length: 350 mi.; width: 270 mi.
Highest point: 13,528 ft. (Kings Peak), 7th
Lowest point: 2,000 ft. (Beaverdam Wash), 48th
Mean elevation: 6,100 ft., 3rd

CLIMATE AND ENVIRONMENT

Temp., highest: 117 deg. on July 5, 1985, at Saint George; lowest: –69 deg. on Feb. 1, 1985, at Peter's Sink
Monthly average: highest: 93.2 deg., 8th; lowest: 19.7 deg., 26th; spread (high to low): 73.5 deg., 17th
Hazardous waste sites (1997): 12, 29th
Endangered species: Animals: 13—Kanab ambersnail, Bonytail chub, Humpback chub, Virgin River chub, Whooping crane, American peregrine falcon, Black-footed ferret, Southwestern willow flycatcher, Utah valvata snail, Colorado squawfish, June sucker, Razorback sucker, Woundfin. Plants: 9

MAJOR CITIES
POPULATION, 1996
PERCENTAGE INCREASE, 1990-96

Salt Lake City, 172,575; 7.9%
Provo, 99,606; 14.7%
West Valley City, 99,136; 14.0%
Sandy, 94,593; 25.7%
Orem, 79,736; 18.0%

THE PEOPLE

Population (1997): 2,059,148, 34th
  Percent change (1990-97): 19.52%, 4th
  Percent of total U.S. pop.: 0.77%, 34th
  Per sq. mi: 24.25, 42nd
Population (2000 proj.): 2,211,500, 34th
  Percent change (1995-2000): 13.35%, 4th
Percent in metro. area (1996): 76.86%, 21st
Foreign born: 59,000, 31st
  Percent: 3.4%, 23rd
Top three ancestries reported:
  English, 43.53%
  German, 17.35%
  Danish, 9.46%
White (1992): 1,731,000, 95.58%, 8th
Black (1992): 13,000, 0.72%, 44th
Native American (1992): 27,000, 1.49%, 11th
Asian, Pacific Isle (1992): 39,000, 2.15%, 15th
Hispanic origin (1992): 94,000, 5.19%, 17th
Percent over 5 yrs. speaking language other than English at home: 7.8%, 23rd
Percent males (1996): 49.82%, 8th; percent females: 50.18%, 43rd
Percent never married: 25.5%, 26th
Marriages per 1,000 (1996): 11.02, 9th
Divorces per 1,000 (1996): 4.64, 20th
Median age (1996): 26.8
Under 5 years (1996): 9.62%, 1st
18 years and under (1996): 38.15%, 1st
65 years and over (1996): 8.76%, 50th
Percent increase among the elderly (1995-96): 1.86%, 7th

OF VITAL IMPORTANCE

Live births per 1,000 pop. (1996): 20.7, 1st
Infant mortality rate per 1,000 live births (1995): 5.4, 50th

Rate for whites: 5.3, 47th
Rate for blacks: NA
Births to unmarried women, % of total (1996): 16.0%, 51st
Births to teenage mothers, % of total (1996): 10.6%, 36th
Abortions (1992): 3,940, 42nd
Rate per 1,000 women 14-44 years old: 9.3, 47th
Percent change (1988-92): −27%, 49th
Average lifetime (1989-91): 77.70, 3rd
Total death rate per 100,000 pop. (1995): 560.6, 50th
Accidents and adverse effects: 32.4, 41st
Alzheimer's disease: 6.9, 39th
Cancer: 108.6, 50th
Cerebrovascular diseases: 39.9, 50th
Chronic liver disease and cirrhosis: 5.3, 51st
Chronic obstructive pulmonary diseases and allied conditions: 24.1, 49th
Diabetes mellitus: 21.3, 35th
Diseases of heart: 148.1, 50th
HIV infection: 4.8, 40th
Homicide: 3.9, 41st
Injury by firearms: 11.5, 34th
Motor vehicle accidents: 17.2, 27th
Pneumonia and influenza: 24.5, 45th
Suicide: 14.8, 13th

KEEPING WELL

Active nonfederal physicians per 100,000 pop. (1995): 134, 51st
Dentists per 100,000 (1991): 65, 13th
Nurses per 100,000 (1995): 647, 46th
Hospitals per 100,000 (1995): 2.15, 27th
Admissions per 1,000 (1995): 87.65, 48th
Hospital beds per 1,000 (1995): 2.15, 49th
Occupancy rate per 100 beds (1995): 52.38, 51st
Average cost per patient per day (1995): $1,213, 6th
Average cost per stay (1995): $5,676, 29th
AIDS cases (new, 1996): 196; per 100,000: 9.8, 35th
Persons living with HIV infection, not yet AIDS (1996): 765
Other notifiable diseases, per 100,000 pop.:
Gonorrhea (1995): 15.7, 43rd
Syphilis (1995): 2.6, 40th
Tuberculosis (1996): 2.9, 36th
Pop. without health insur. (1996): 12.0%, 33rd

HOUSEHOLDS BY TYPE

Total households (1996): 639,000, 35th
Percent change (1990-96): 19.0%, 4th
Per 1,000 pop. (1996) 319.50, 51st
Percent of householders 65 yrs. and over (1996): 17.53%, 48th
Persons per household (1996): 3.06, 1st
Family households: 410,862
Percent of total: 76.47%, 1st
Nonfamily households: 126,411
Percent of total: 23.53%, 51st
Pop. living in group quarters: 29,048
Percent of pop.: 1.69%, 51st

LIVING QUARTERS

Total housing units: 598,388
Persons per unit: 2.88, 1st
Occupied housing units: 537,273
Percent of total units: 89.79%, 23rd
Persons per unit: 3.03, 1st
Percent of units with over 1 person per room: 5.51%, 13th
Owner-occupied units: 365,979
Percent of total units: 61.16%, 16th
Percent of occupied units: 68.12%, 18th
Persons per unit: 3.38, 1st
Median value: $68,900, 26th
Renter-occupied units: 171,294
Percent of total units: 28.63%, 28th
Percent of occupied units: 31.88%, 34th
Persons per unit: 2.67, 3rd
Median contract rent: $300, 30th
Rental vacancy rate: 8.6%, 23rd
Mobile home, trailer & other as a percent of occupied housing units: 7.64%, 34th
Persons in emergency shelters for homeless persons: 925, 0.054%, 21st
Persons visible in street locations: 276, 0.0160%, 10th
Nursing home population: 6,222, 0.36%, 48th

CRIME INDEX PER 100,000 (1996)

Total reported: 5,985.9, 12th
Percent increase: −1.7%, 21st
Violent: 331.9, 38th
Percent increase: 0.9%, 9th
Murder & nonnegligent manslaughter: 3.2, 42nd
Forcible rape: 41.8, 16th
Aggravated assault: 218.1, 34th
Robbery: 68.9, 40th
Property: 5,654.0, 8th
Percent increase: −1.9%, 25th

Burglary: 848.3, 26th
Larceny-theft: 4,377.1, 3rd
Motor vehicle theft: 428.6, 26th

TEACHING AND LEARNING

Pop. 3 and over enrolled in school (1996): 625,409, 33rd
Percent of pop.: 31.27%, 1st
Public elementary & secondary schools (1996-97): 735, 38th
Total enrollment (1996): 478,085, 32nd
Percent of school age pop.: 97.57%, 3rd
Percent of total pop.: 23.90%, 1st
Teachers (1996): 20,224, 35th
Percent of pop.: 1.01%, 31st
Pupil/teacher ratio (1995): 23.8, 2nd
Teachers' avg. salary (1996-97): $31,750, 41st
Expenditure per capita (1992-93): $1,429.69, 16th
Education as % of state govt. expenditures: 42.1%, 1st
Expenditure per pupil (1994-95): $3,656, 51st
Percent increase (1993-94 & 1994-95): 6.31%, 8th
Percent at or above grade level, NAEP tests:
Reading, grade 4 (1994): 30%, 16th
Math, grade 4 (1996): 69%, 11th
Math, grade 8 (1996): 70%, 9th
Percent of graduates taking SAT (1995): 4%, 50th
Mean SAT verbal scores: 513, 3rd
Mean SAT mathematical scores: 563, 5th
Percent of graduates taking ACT (1997): 69%, 8th
Mean ACT scores: 21.5, 16th
Percent of pop. over 25 completing:
Less than 9th grade: 3.4%, 51st
High school: 85.1%, 2nd
College degree(s): 22.3%, 15th
Higher education, institutions (1996): 17, 44th
Enrollment (1995-96): 147,324, 32nd
Percent increase in enroll. (1990-95): 21.5%, 2nd
White non-Hispanic (1995): 132,566, 30th
Percent of enroll.: 89.98%, 8th
Total minority enroll. (1995): 9,416, 38th
Percent of enroll.: 6.39%, 46th
Black non-Hispanic (1995): 904, 44th
Percent of enroll.: 0.61%, 50th
Hispanic (1995): 3,821, 29th
Percent of enroll.: 2.59%, 21st

Asian/Pacific Islander (1995): 3,088, 32nd
Percent of enroll.: 2.10%, 30th
American Indian/AK native (1995): 1,603, 23rd
Percent of enroll.: 1.09%, 18th
Nonresident alien (1995): 5,342, 30th
Percent of enroll.: 3.63%, 10th
Female (1995): 73,452, 32nd
Percent of enroll.: 49.86%, 51st
Pub. institutions (1995-96): 10, 41st
Enrollment: 110,560, 32nd
Percent increase in enrollment (1990-95): 28.4%, 1st
Percent of enroll.: 75.05%, 39th
Private institutions (1995-96): 7, 44th
Enrollment: 36,764, 24th
Percent increase in enrollment (1990-95): 4.5%, 27th
Percent of enroll.: 24.95%, 13th
Tuition (in state), public 4-year institution (1996-97): $2,010, 44th
Tuition (in state), public 2-year institution (1996-97): $1,392, 25th
Tuition, private 4-year institution (1996-97): $3,073, 50th
Public library systems (1994): 69, 37th
Books & serial vol. per capita: 2.7, 28th
Library visits per capita: NA
Circulation per capita: 8.9, 8th

LAW ENFORCEMENT AND CORRECTIONS

Police protection and corrections expenditures (1996): $201,181,000
Per capita: $100.59, 32nd
Police per 10,000 pop. (1996): 17.80, 42nd
Prisoners (1 year or more) per 100,000 pop. (1996): 194, 44th
Percent change (1995-96): 14.1%, 6th
Percent of inmates that are female: 5.3%, 38th
Percent change: 30.4%, 5th
Death penalty: yes, by firing squad, lethal injection
Under sentence (Jan. 1998): 11, 28th
Executed, 1976-97: 5, 16th
Executed in 1997: 0

RELIGION, NUMBER AND PERCENT OF POPULATION

Agnostic: 9,859—0.90%, 14th
Buddhist: 1,095—0.10%, 17th
Christian: 959,576—87.60%, 20th
Hindu: NA

Jewish: 7,668—0.70%, 23rd
Muslim: NA
Unitarian: 1,095—0.10%, 31st
Other: NA
None: 85,442—7.80%, 16th
Refused to answer: 31,767—2.90%, 9th

MAKING A LIVING

Personal income per capita (1996): $19,156, 46th
  Percent increase (1995-96): 5.4%, 7th
Disposable personal income per capita (1996): $16,436, 50th
Median income of households (average, 1995-96): $37,298, 17th
Percent of pop. below poverty level (1995-96): 8.1%, 49th

ECONOMY

In civilian labor force (1996): 998,000
  Percent of total pop.: 71.3%, 12th
  Percent of total pop. 65 years and over: NA
  Percent of total female pop.: 61.6%, 22nd
Major employer industries (total nonagricultural, 1996):
  Construction: 60,200—6.3%, 4th
  Finance, insurance, & real estate: 50,400—5.3%, 22nd
  Government: 166,600—17.5%, 22nd
  Manufacturing: 129,400—13.6%, 31st
  Service: 255,500—26.8%, 30th
  Trade: 230,500—24.1%, 20th
  Transportation, communications, public utilities: 54,000—5.7%, 15th
Unemployment rate (1996): 3.5%, 47th
  Male: 3.3%, 48th
  Female: 3.7%, 45th
Total businesses (1995): 45,882, 35th
New business incorps. (1995): 5,917
  Percent of total businesses: 12.90%, 10th
Business failures (1995): 344
  Failures per 10,000 businesses: 75.0, 30th
Agriculture farm income:
  Marketing (1996): $873,143,000, 37th
    Average per farm: $65,160, 42nd
  Leading products (1997): Cattle, hay, turkeys, corn, wheat, barley, apples, potatoes, cherries, onions, peaches, pears
  Average value land & build. per acre (1997): $750, 36th
    Percent increase (1996-97): 8%, 10th
  Govt. payments (1996): $21,006,000, 37th
    Average per farm: $1,568, 32nd

Construction, value of all (1996): $3,737,673,000, 30th
  Per capita: $1,868, 5th
Manufactures (1995):
  Value added: $9,497,500,000
    Per capita: $4,867, 41st
  Leading products (1997): Medical instruments, electronic components, food products, fabricated metals, transportation equipment, steel, copper
Value of nonfuel mineral production (1996): $1,560,000,000, 7th
  Leading mineral products (1996): Petroleum, coal, copper
Energy consumption per person (1994): 311.6 mil. Btu, 36th
Retail sales (1995): $15,331,000,000
  Per household: $24,920, 20th
  Sales increase (1994-95): 7.5%, 10th
Tourism revenues (1995): $3.6 bil.
Foreign exports, in total value (1996): $3,296,000,000, 32nd
  Per capita: $1,648, 22nd
Gross state product per person (1994): $21,834, 41st
Public aid recipients (percent of resident pop. 1994): 3.6%, 49th
Medicaid recipients (percent of pop., 1995): 8.2%, 47th
Medicare enrollment per 1,000 pop. (1996): 96, 47th

TRAVEL AND TRANSPORTATION

Motor vehicle registrations (1996): 1,445,088, 36th
  Per 1,000 pop.: 716.25, 42nd
Motorcycle registrations (1996): 23,171, 39th
  Per 1,000 pop.: 16.03, 34th
Licensed drivers (1996): 1,255,460, 35th
  Per 1,000 pop.: 641.09, 41st
Public roads & streets (1996)
  Total mileage: 41,718, 37th
    Per 1,000 pop.: 120.85, 22nd
  Rural mileage: 35,306, 37th
    Per 1,000 pop.: 17.65, 21st
  Urban mileage: 6,412, 34th
    Per 1,000 pop.: 3.21, 19th
  Interstate mileage: 940, 20th
    Per 1,000 pop.: 0.47, 9th
Speed limit (max. interstate, autos, mi. per hr., 1997): 75
Annual vehicle-mi. of travel per driver (1996): 14,811, 21st
Mean travel time for workers age 16+ who work away from home: 18.9 min., 40th

GOVERNMENT

Percent of voting age pop. registered (1996): 78.80%, 22nd

Percent of voting age pop. voting for president: (1996): 50.3%, 26th

Percent of voting age pop. voting for U.S. representatives (1996): 50.2%, 23rd

State legislators, total (1997): 104, 41st
Women members (1997): 16
Percent of legislature: 15%, 41st

U.S. Congress, House members (1998): 3
Change (1988-98): 0

Revenues (1996):
State govt.: $6,773,191,000
Per capita: $3,386.60, 29th
Parimutuel & amusement taxes & lotteries, revenue per capita (1995): NA

Expenditures (1996):
State govt.: $6,171,775,000
Per capita: $3,085.89, 27th

Debt outstanding (1996): $2,464,177,000
Per capita: $1,232.09, 31st

LAWS AND REGULATIONS

Legal driving age: 16

Marriage age without parental consent: 18, county to provide premarital counseling if under 19 or divorced

Divorce residence requirement: 3 mo., for qualifications check local statutes

ATTRACTIONS (1997)

Major opera companies: 2
Major symphony orchestras: 1
Major dance companies: 2
Per capita spending by the NEA (1997): $0.37, 20th
State Fair in early September at Salt Lake City

SPORTS AND COMPETITION

NCAA (Division I) football and basketball teams: Brigham Young Univ. Cougars, Southern Utah Univ. Thunderbirds, Univ. of Utah Utes, Utah State Univ. Aggies, Weber State Univ. Wildcats

NBA basketball teams: Utah Jazz, Delta Center

WNBA basketball teams: Utah Starzz, Delta Center

WEBSITES CONTAINING FURTHER INFORMATION

| State of Utah WWW Homepage | http://www.state.ut.us |

VERMONT

Up where the north wind blows just a little keener,
Up where the grasses grow just a little greener,
Up where the mountain peaks rise a little higher
Up where the human kind draws just a little nigher,
That's where Vermont comes in.
                                     Charles Hial Darling, poet

Vermont is known for the independent nature of its people. They were so opposed to slavery that the Georgia legislature once voted humorously that "...the whole state should be made into an island and towed out to sea." Vermonters are so "politically correct" that their legislature declared war on Germany before the United States did. Every year, the spectacular Green Mountains attract thousands of skiers and other tourists. Farming is more important in Vermont than in the other New England states. Three-fifths of the state is covered by forests, and lumbering and wood processing are major industries, as is the quarrying of granite, marble, and slate. Only about a third of the people reside in cities and towns.

SUPERLATIVES

- Claims only breed of horse produced in the United States.
- Leader in marble production.
- World granite center.
- First in maple syrup production.
- First U.S. patent issued.

MOMENTS IN HISTORY

- On July 4, 1609, during the first known European visit to present-day Vermont, French explorer Samuel de Champlain discovered a lake he named Champlain.
- In 1666, French Captain de La Motte built a fortress on present-day La Motte Island in Lake Champlain.
- In 1690 the English built a fort at Chimney Point.
- The outpost of Fort Dummer, begun in 1724, was the first permanent settlement in present-day Vermont.
- The 1741 proclamation of King George II of England appeared to include present-day Vermont in New Hampshire, but the boundaries were long disputed.
- In 1764, King George III set the boundary at the Connecticut River, leaving present-day Vermont in New York territory.
- The owners of New Hampshire grants contested the New York claims and were supported by Ethan Allen and his Green Mountain Boys. They withstood a New York attack in 1771.
- On May 10, 1775, Allen and Colonel Benedict Arnold captured Fort Ticonderoga in one of the early actions of the Revolution.
- After British General John Burgoyne recaptured Fort Ticonderoga on July 6, 1777, he pursued American General Arthur St. Clair. The next day the Americans defeated Burgoyne in the Battle of Hubbardton, the only battle of the Revolution fought on Vermont soil.
- The Battle of Bennington, in August 1777, was fought just across the New York border but was led by General John Stark and Seth Warner of Vermont. Vermont men played the key role in this struggle.

> ## So They Say
> *"There are the Red Coats and they are ours, or this night Molly Stark sleeps a widow!"*
> **General John Stark**

- Indian attacks terrorized the countryside during the Revolution; the worst saw plundering, burning, and taking of prisoners from Tunbridge to Royalton during October 1780.
- Vermont operated as an independent republic from 1777 to 1791, but this was not recognized by the Continental Congress or New York State.
- On March 4, 1791, Vermont became the first state added to the Union following the original 13 colonies.
- During the War of 1812, the Battle of Plattsburgh in September 1814 brought U.S. control to Lake Champlain and thwarted the British invasion of Vermont.
- Vermont's Chester A. Arthur became president of the United States in 1881.
- Montpelier native Admiral George Dewey emerged the hero of the Spanish-American War of 1898.
- Admiral Henry T. Mayo of Burlington was the principal commander of the U.S. Atlantic fleet during World War I.

• On the death of President Warren G. Harding, in the flicker of kerosene lamps at Plymouth, Calvin Coolidge on August 3, 1923, took the oath of office as U.S. president—administered by his justice-of-the-peace father.

> ### So They Say
>
> "Never before or since has a president taken the oath of office from his own father, in his own home, and under such unique surroundings."
>
> **Vermont Board of Historic Sites, on Coolidge's taking the oath of office**

• In 1941 the good people of Vermont got so enraged at the Nazis that they declared war on Germany two months before the United States did.

• In 1985, Democrat Madeleine M. Kunin became the first woman governor of Vermont.

THAT'S INTERESTING

• In the late 1700s, schoolteacher Justin Morgan developed the Morgan horse, the only breed originating in the United States.

• The Indians were so devoted to the chapel they had built at Swanton that when the French were driven out, the faithful Indians went with them and took the chapel apart, rebuilding it stone by stone at their new home in Canada.

• James Johns of Huntington printed by hand every copy of every issue of the newspaper he published for 40 years.

NOTABLE NATIVES

Chester Alan Arthur (Fairfield, 1829-1886), U.S. president. **Calvin Coolidge** (Plymouth, 1872-1933), U.S. president. **John Deere** (Rutland, 1804-1886), inventor/industrialist. **George Dewey** (Montpelier, 1837-1917), naval officer. **John Dewey** (Burlington, 1859-1952), philosopher/psychologist/educator. **Stephen Arnold Douglas** (Brandon, 1813-1861), public official/political leader. **James Fisk** (Bennington, 1834-1872), financier. **Joseph Smith** (Sharon, 1805-1844), religious leader. **Brigham Young** (Whitingham, 1801-1877), religious leader.

GENERAL

Admitted to statehood: March 4, 1791
Origin of name: From French words *vert* (green) and *mont* (mountain). The Green Mountains were said to have been named by Samuel de Champlain. When the state was formed, 1777, Dr. Thomas Young suggested combining *vert* and *mont* into Vermont

Capital: Montpelier
Nickname: Green Mountain State
Motto: Freedom and unity
Animal: Morgan horse
Bird: Hermit thrush
Insect: Honeybee
Fish: Brook trout, walleye pike
Flower: Red clover
Song: "Hail, Vermont"
Tree: Sugar maple

THE LAND

Area: 9,615 sq. mi., 43rd
  Land: 9,249 sq. mi., 43rd
  Water: 366 sq. mi., 44th
    Inland water: 366 sq. mi., 40th
Topography: Green Mountains create N-S backbone 20-36 mi. wide; average altitude, 1,000 ft.
Number of counties: 14
Geographic center: Washington, 3 mi. E of Roxbury
Length: 160 mi.; width: 80 mi.
Highest point: 4,393 ft. (Mount Mansfield), 26th
Lowest point: 95 ft. (Lake Champlain), 28th
Mean elevation: 1,000 ft., 27th

CLIMATE AND ENVIRONMENT

Temp., highest: 105 deg. on July 4, 1911, at Vernon; lowest: –50 deg. on Dec. 30, 1933, at Bloomfield
Monthly average: highest: 80.5 deg., 49th; lowest: 7.7 deg., 7th; spread (high to low): 72.8 deg., 20th
Hazardous waste sites (1997): 8, 40th
Endangered species: Animals: 3—Indiana bat, American peregrine falcon, Dwarf wedge mussel. Plants: 2

MAJOR CITIES
POPULATION, 1996
PERCENTAGE INCREASE, 1990-96

Burlington, 39,004; –0.3%
Rutland, 17,605; –3.4%
South Burlington, 13,860; 8.2%
Essex Junction, 8,546; 1.79%
Barre, 9,206; –2.91%

THE PEOPLE

Population (1997): 588,978, 49th
  Percent change (1990-97): 4.66%, 37th
  Percent of total U.S. pop.: 0.22%, 49th
  Per sq. mi: 61.26, 31st
Population (2000 proj.): 612,000, 49th
  Percent change (1995-2000): 4.62%, 25th
Percent in metro. area (1996): 32.37%, 47th
Foreign born: 18,000, 46th
  Percent: 3.1%, 25th
Top three ancestries reported:
  English, 26.11%
  French, 23.62%
  Irish, 17.94%
White (1992): 564,000, 98.77%, 1st
Black (1992): 2,000, 0.35%, 51st
Native American (1992): 2,000, 0.35%, 31st
Asian, Pacific Isle (1992): 4,000, 0.70%, 40th
Hispanic origin (1992): 4,000, 0.70%, 46th
Percent over 5 yrs. speaking language other
    than English at home: 5.8%, 31st
Percent males (1996): 49.27%, 18th; percent
    females: 50.73%, 34th
Percent never married: 27.6%, 12th
Marriages per 1,000 (1996): 10.06, 12th
Divorces per 1,000 (1996): 4.23, 26th
Median age (1996): 35.7
Under 5 years (1996): 6.06%, 49th
18 years and under (1996): 27.57%, 39th
65 years and over (1996): 12.11%, 35th
Percent increase among the elderly (1995-96):
    0.89%, 23rd

OF VITAL IMPORTANCE

Live births per 1,000 pop. (1996): 11.5, 49th
Infant mortality rate per 1,000 live births
    (1995): 6.0, 45th
  Rate for whites: 6.2, 26th
  Rate for blacks: NA
Births to unmarried women, % of total
    (1996): 26.4%, 42nd
Births to teenage mothers, % of total (1996):
    8.9%, 46th
Abortions (1992): 2,900, 46th
  Rate per 1,000 women 14-44 years old:
    21.2, 24th
  Percent change (1988-92): −18%, 45th
Average lifetime (1989-91): 76.54, 16th
Total death rate per 100,000 pop. (1995):
    846.7, 34th
  Accidents and adverse effects: 32.8, 39th
  Alzheimer's disease: 7.4, 36th
  Cancer: 198.9, 36th
  Cerebrovascular diseases: 57.1, 33rd

Chronic liver disease and cirrhosis: 6.0,
    48th
Chronic obstructive pulmonary diseases and
    allied conditions: 41.2, 25th
Diabetes mellitus: 24.5, 17th
Diseases of heart: 278.2, 28th
HIV infection: 4.6, 41st
Homicide: NA
Injury by firearms: 10.6, 36th
Motor vehicle accidents: 16.1, 30th
Pneumonia and influenza: 29.0, 31st
Suicide: 13.0, 19th

KEEPING WELL

Active nonfederal physicians per 100,000 pop.
    (1995): 270, 9th
Dentists per 100,000 (1991): 56, 20th
Nurses per 100,000 (1995): 924, 16th
Hospitals per 100,000 (1995): 2.39, 22nd
  Admissions per 1,000 (1995): 94.02, 43rd
  Hospital beds per 1,000 (1995): 3.08,
    32nd
  Occupancy rate per 100 beds (1995):
    72.22, 5th
  Average cost per patient per day (1995):
    $714, 43rd
  Average cost per stay (1995): $5,883, 25th
AIDS cases (new, 1996): 25; per 100,000:
    4.2, 44th
Persons living with HIV infection (1996): NA
Other notifiable diseases, per 100,000 pop.:
  Gonorrhea (1995): 11.8, 45th
  Syphilis (1995): 0.0, 49th
  Tuberculosis (1996): 0.7, 51st
Pop. without health insur. (1996): 11.1%,
    40th

HOUSEHOLDS BY TYPE

Total households (1996): 227,000, 49th
  Percent change (1990-96): 7.5%, 22nd
  Per 1,000 pop. (1996) 385.40, 11th
  Percent of householders 65 yrs. and over
    (1996): 19.82%, 38th
  Persons per household (1996): 2.57, 26th
Family households: 144,895
  Percent of total: 68.78%, 39th
Nonfamily households: 65,755
  Percent of total: 31.22%, 13th
Pop. living in group quarters: 21,642
  Percent of pop.: 3.85%, 2nd

LIVING QUARTERS

Total housing units: 271,241
  Persons per unit: 2.07, 51st

Occupied housing units: 210,650
  Percent of total units: 77.66%, 51st
  Persons per unit: 2.48, 38th
  Percent of units with over 1 person per room: 1.71%, 49th
Owner-occupied units: 145,368
  Percent of total units: 53.59%, 43rd
  Percent of occupied units: 69.01%, 15th
  Persons per unit: 2.73, 26th
  Median value: $95,500, 13th
Renter-occupied units: 65,282
  Percent of total units: 24.07%, 49th
  Percent of occupied units: 30.99%, 37th
  Persons per unit: 2.22, 46th
  Median contract rent: $374, 17th
  Rental vacancy rate: 7.5%, 35th
Mobile home, trailer & other as a percent of occupied housing units: 13.57%, 19th
Persons in emergency shelters for homeless persons: 232, 0.041%, 33rd
Persons visible in street locations: 16, 0.0028%, 41st
Nursing home population: 4,809, 0.85%, 19th

CRIME INDEX PER 100,000 (1996)

Total reported: 3,002.9, 47th
  Percent increase: −12.5%, 50th
  Violent: 121.2, 49th
    Percent increase: 2.5%, 4th
    Murder & nonnegligent manslaughter: 1.9, 48th
    Forcible rape: 27.0, 40th
    Aggravated assault: 76.9, 49th
    Robbery: 15.4, 50th
  Property: 2,881.7, 46th
    Percent increase: −13.1%, 50th
    Burglary: 673.0, 40th
    Larceny-theft: 2,058.4, 47th
    Motor vehicle theft: 150.3, 48th

TEACHING AND LEARNING

Pop. 3 and over enrolled in school (1996): 141,672, 50th
  Percent of pop.: 24.05%, 13th
Public elementary & secondary schools (1996-97): 384, 47th
  Total enrollment (1996): 106,607, 49th
    Percent of school age pop.: 96.04%, 7th
    Percent of total pop.: 18.10%, 13th
  Teachers (1996): 7,952, 46th
    Percent of pop.: 1.35%, 2nd
  Pupil/teacher ratio (1995): 13.8, 50th
  Teachers' avg. salary (1996-97): $37,200, 21st

Expenditure per capita (1992-93): $1,540.41, 10th
  Education as % of state govt. expenditures: 39.3%, 5th
Expenditure per pupil (1994-95): $6,750, 13th
  Percent increase (1993-94 & 1994-95): 2.27%, 40th
Percent at or above grade level, NAEP tests:
  Reading, grade 4 (1994): NA
  Math, grade 4 (1996): 67%, 16th
  Math, grade 8 (1996): 72%, 8th
Percent of graduates taking SAT (1995): 68%, 8th
  Mean SAT verbal scores: 429, 35th
  Mean SAT mathematical scores: 472, 40th
Percent of graduates taking ACT (1997): 7%, 42nd
  Mean ACT scores: 21.9, 7th
Percent of pop. over 25 completing:
  Less than 9th grade: 8.7%, 31st
  High school: 80.8%, 12th
  College degree(s): 24.3%, 9th
Higher education, institutions (1996): 22, 40th
  Enrollment (1995-96): 35,065, 49th
    Percent increase in enroll. (1990-95): −3.7%, 47th
    White non-Hispanic (1995): 32,242, 48th
      Percent of enroll.: 91.95%, 4th
    Total minority enroll. (1995): 2,033, 51st
      Percent of enroll.: 5.80%, 48th
    Black non-Hispanic (1995): 477, 46th
      Percent of enroll.: 1.36%, 44th
    Hispanic (1995): 481, 47th
      Percent of enroll.: 1.37%, 39th
    Asian/Pacific Islander (1995): 676, 47th
      Percent of enroll.: 1.93%, 33rd
    American Indian/AK native (1995): 399, 45th
      Percent of enroll.: 1.14%, 17th
    Nonresident alien (1995): 790, 48th
      Percent of enroll.: 2.25%, 35th
    Female (1995): 20,228, 49th
      Percent of enroll.: 57.69%, 8th
  Pub. institutions (1995-96): 6, 45th
    Enrollment: 20,470, 50th
      Percent increase in enrollment (1990-95): −2.1%, 39th
      Percent of enroll.: 58.38%, 45th
  Private institutions (1995-96): 16, 34th
    Enrollment: 14,595, 38th
      Percent increase in enrollment (1990-95): −5.8%, 47th
      Percent of enroll.: 41.62%, 7th

Tuition (in state), public 4-year institution (1996-97): $6,538, 1st

Tuition (in state), public 2-year institution (1996-97): $2,516, 5th

Tuition, private 4-year institution (1996-97): $16,378, 4th

Public library systems (1994): 200, 17th

Books & serial vol. per capita: 4.8, 2nd

Library visits per capita: NA

Circulation per capita: 7.1, 21st

LAW ENFORCEMENT AND CORRECTIONS

Police protection and corrections expenditures (1996): $77,149,000

Per capita: $130.98, 20th

Police per 10,000 pop. (1996): 23.91, 17th

Prisoners (1 year or more) per 100,000 pop. (1996): 137, 48th

Percent change (1995-96): –23.0%, 51st

Percent of inmates that are female: 2.8%, 50th

Percent change: –27.3%, 51st

Death penalty: no

RELIGION, NUMBER AND PERCENT OF POPULATION

Agnostic: 5,036—1.20%, 2nd

Buddhist: NA

Christian: 350,848—83.60%, 39th

Hindu: NA

Jewish: 4,616—1.10%, 15th

Muslim: NA

Unitarian: 4,616—1.10%, 1st

Other: 3,777—0.90%, 35th

None: 47,843—11.40%, 8th

Refused to answer: 2,938—0.70%, 48th

MAKING A LIVING

Personal income per capita (1996): $22,124, 31st

Percent increase (1995-96): 3.5%, 20th

Disposable personal income per capita (1996): $19,381, 32nd

Median income of households (average, 1995-96): $33,591, 32nd

Percent of pop. below poverty level (1995-96): 11.5%, 28th

ECONOMY

In civilian labor force (1996): 324,000

Percent of total pop.: 71.6%, 11th

Percent of total pop. 65 years and over: NA

Percent of total female pop.: 66.3%, 9th

Major employer industries (total nonagricultural, 1996):

Construction: 12,600—4.6%, 25th

Finance, insurance, & real estate: 12,200—4.4%, 43rd

Government: 45,300—16.5%, 30th

Manufacturing: 45,900—16.7%, 19th

Service: 81,500—29.7%, 14th

Trade: 64,600—23.5%, 28th

Transportation, communications, public utilities: 12,200—4.4%, 42nd

Unemployment rate (1996): 4.6%, 34th

Male: 4.5%, 37th

Female: 4.6%, 32nd

Total businesses (1995): 20,542, 47th

New business incorps. (1995): 1,630

Percent of total businesses: 7.93%, 36th

Business failures (1995): 148

Failures per 10,000 businesses: 72.0, 34th

Agriculture farm income:

Marketing (1996): $534,666,000, 41st

Average per farm: $89,111, 26th

Leading products (1997): Dairy products, cattle, greenhouse, apples, maple syrup, vegetables, small fruits

Average value land & build. per acre (1997): $1,550, 19th

Percent increase (1996-97): 1%, 44th

Govt. payments (1996): $4,035,000, 42nd

Average per farm: $673, 40th

Construction, value of all (1996): $591,775,000, 51st

Per capita: $1,005, 42nd

Manufactures (1995):

Value added: $3,444,900,000

Per capita: $5,891, 29th

Leading products (1997): Machine tools, furniture, scales, books, computer components, specialty foods

Value of nonfuel mineral production (1996): $66,800,000, 46th

Leading mineral products (1996): Sand/gravel, stone, talc and pyrophyllite, gemstones

Energy consumption per person (1994): 263.0 mil. Btu, 41st

Retail sales (1995): $5,144,000,000

Per household: $23,129, 42nd

Sales increase (1994-95): 0.4%, 47th

Tourism revenues (1995): $2.2 bil.

Foreign exports, in total value (1996): $3,302,000,000, 31st

Per capita: $5,609, 1st

Gross state product per person (1994): $22,892, 37th

Public aid recipients (percent of resident pop. 1994): 7.0%, 22nd
Medicaid recipients (percent of pop., 1995): 17.0%, 6th
Medicare enrollment per 1,000 pop. (1996): 144, 25th

TRAVEL AND TRANSPORTATION

Motor vehicle registrations (1996): 503,139, 50th
Per 1,000 pop.: 857.92, 17th
Motorcycle registrations (1996): 18,256, 43rd
Per 1,000 pop.: 36.28, 4th
Licensed drivers (1996): 455,606, 47th
Per 1,000 pop.: 779.11, 4th
Public roads & streets (1996)
Total mileage: 14,192, 46th
Per 1,000 pop.: 124.11, 16th
Rural mileage: 12,858, 42nd
Per 1,000 pop.: 21.84, 16th
Urban mileage: 1,334, 51st
Per 1,000 pop.: 2.27, 47th
Interstate mileage: 320, 46th
Per 1,000 pop.: 0.54, 7th
Speed limit (max. interstate, autos, mi. per hr., 1997): 65
Annual vehicle-mi. of travel per driver (1996): 13,601, 33rd
Mean travel time for workers age 16+ who work away from home: 18.0 min., 42nd

GOVERNMENT

Percent of voting age pop. registered (1996): 86.59%, 7th
Percent of voting age pop. voting for president: (1996): 58.6%, 6th
Percent of voting age pop. voting for U.S. representatives (1996): 57.8%, 7th
State legislators, total (1997): 180, 12th
Women members (1997): 58
Percent of legislature: 32%, 6th
U.S. Congress, House members (1998): 1
Change (1988-98): 0
Revenues (1996):
State govt.: $2,146,205,000
Per capita: $ 3,643.81, 23rd
Parimutuel & amusement taxes & lotteries, revenue per capita (1995): $123.53, 20th
Expenditures (1996):
State govt.: $2,061,059,000
Per capita: $3,499.25, 18th
Debt outstanding (1996): $1,717,898,000
Per capita: $2,916.63, 9th

LAWS AND REGULATIONS

Legal driving age: 18
Marriage age without parental consent: 18
Divorce residence requirement: 6 mo., for qualifications check local statutes

ATTRACTIONS (1997)

Per capita spending by the NEA (1997): $0.96, 5th
State Fair in early September at Rutland

SPORTS AND COMPETITION

NCAA (Division I) football and basketball teams: Univ. of Vermont Catamounts (basketball only)

WEBSITES CONTAINING FURTHER INFORMATION

State of Vermont Home Page	http://www.state.vt.us
Vermont/New Hampshire Map of WWW Resources	http://www.destek.net/Maps/VT-NH.html
Vermont: The Green Mountain State	http://mole.uvm.edu/Vermont

VIRGINIA

Of all the states, but three will live in story,
Old Massachusetts with her Plymouth Rock,
And old Virginia with her noble stock,
And sunny Kansas with her woes and glory.   Eugene Fitch Ware, poet

Before the Europeans arrived, Virginia was the realm of a great Indian emperor, Powhatan. During its epic years, Virginia became both the "Mother of Presidents" (eight) and the "Mother of the Frontier." Having given up claims to Illinois, Indiana, Ohio, Michigan, Wisconsin, and parts of Minnesota, it also is known as "Mother of the States." Virginia was in the forefront of the Revolutionary War, which ended when Lord Cornwallis surrendered to Washington in Yorktown. In the Civil War, more battles were fought on Virginia soil than in any other state. Virginia is a land of stately mansions, battlefields, old churches, and colonial homes. In 1989 the state was the first since Reconstruction to elect an African-American governor, L. Douglas Wilder.

SUPERLATIVES

- Most native presidents—eight.
- First manufacturing in the United States—in a glass factory, 1608.
- First iron furnace, 1619.
- Leads in synthetic fiber production.
- Pioneer in tobacco farming.
- Country's first canal—in 1790, running the 7 miles between Richmond and Westham.

MOMENTS IN HISTORY

- Early explorers must have passed the shores of Virginia. By the 1580s, the Spanish Jesuit missionaries had a mission on Aquia Creek in the Potomac region, but they were massacred by the Indians.
- On May 14, 1607, three English ships anchored in the James River and next day James Town (Jamestown) was begun, the first permanent English American settlement.
- Captain John Smith, leader of the settlement, made peace with powerful Chief Powhatan, probably with the somewhat legendary help of the chief's daughter, Pocahontas. Smith returned to England in October 1609, to care for an injury.
- The 65 survivors of the "starving time" of 1609-1610 were rescued by Lord De la Warr, who brought supplies and new settlers.

> ### So They Say
>
> The ships "...moored to the trees in 6 fathoms of water...." The Indians came "...creeping upon all foures from the Hills, like Beares with their Bowes in their mouthes." Next morning, May 15, 1607, the pioneers "...set to work about the fortifications."
>
> **Captain John Smith, on landing and settling in Virginia**

- In 1619 the colonists organized a House of Burgesses, claimed as the first democratically elected legislative body in the New World.
- After the death of Powhatan in 1618, Indian troubles began and continued until 1646, when King Opechancanough was shot.
- Nathaniel Bacon rallied the people against the government of Sir William Berkeley in 1676 with "America's first declaration of independence," but he died soon after, and Berkeley hanged some 20 of his followers.
- The frontiers pushed westward, and Augusta County was organized in 1738, claiming lands to the Mississippi.
- As discontent over taxes and other acts of the government grew, Patrick Henry entered the House of Burgesses in 1765 and became a leader in opposing the government.

> ### So They Say
>
> "Gentlemen may cry, peace, peace— but there is no peace. The war is actually begun!...Is life so dear, or peace so sweet, as to be purchased at the price of chains and slavery? Forbid it, Almighty God! I know not what course others may take; but as for me, give me liberty, or give me death!"
>
> **Patrick Henry (1775)**

- On May 6, 1776, the fifth Virginia Convention declared that the colony was free and independent.
- Sponsored by Virginia, the work of General George Rogers Clark during the

American Revolution kept the western area in the hands of the colonies.

• American armies laid siege to Yorktown, and General Lord Cornwallis surrendered in October 1781.

• After the failure of the Articles of Confederation, Virginian George Washington presided at the convention that finally created a new government, and Virginia became the tenth state on June 25, 1788.

• On April 30, 1789, Washington became the first of the long succession of Virginians who were to hold the office of president.

So They Say

"Here was buried Thomas Jefferson, author of the Declaration of American Independence, of the Statute of Virginia for religious freedom, and father of the University of Virginia."

Thomas Jefferson,
author of his own epitaph

• As early as 1778, Virginia had made the slave trade a criminal offense, but most Virginians supported slavery, and Richmond became the capital of the Confederacy on May 29, 1861.

• Many important battles of the Civil War were fought in Virginia until, on April 9, 1865, General Robert E. Lee surrendered his exhausted forces at Virginia's Appomattox Court House.

• On January 26, 1870, Virginia once more became a sovereign state.

• The great financial and human losses of the Civil War caused many hardships, but by the 1890s, prosperity was returning.

• In 1924, Virginia native Woodrow Wilson died, broken in health after suffering a stroke in 1919. During the late years of his second administration, his second wife, Edith Bolling Galt, was believed to have carried on many of the functions of the presidency.

• During the administration of Governor Harry Flood Byrd, in 1927 the government was simplified and improved, but segregation became law.

• Virginia's third constitution was approved in 1970, and the state elected its first Republican governor since 1886.

• In 1989, L. Douglas Wilder was elected as the first African-American governor since Reconstruction.

THAT'S INTERESTING

• When John Rolfe married the Indian princess Pocahontas, the king of England was distressed that her planter husband, a commoner, had married a royal person without the crown's permission.

• The old apothecary shop in Alexandria, where Martha Washington bought castor oil in quarts, remained as a landmark. One jokester said she probably used it to make her candy.

• The annual jousting tournament near Staunton is said to be the nation's oldest continuously operating sporting event.

• In the Civil War battle at Marye's Heights, Union General Ambrose Burnside sent wave after wave of his infantry to the slaughter. Darkness finally brought an end to the butchery, but not before seven Union divisions had dashed themselves against a stone wall. The Confederate defenders lost only 1,200 men.

• When stationed at Fredericksburg in the winter of 1862, Union and Confederate pickets across the Rappahannock River from each other made little sailboats that they floated back and forth with items to trade.

NOTABLE NATIVES

Stephen Fuller Austin (Austinville, 1793-1836), colonizer/political leader. **Richard Evelyn Byrd** (Winchester, 1888-1957), naval officer/explorer. **Willa Sibert Cather** (Winchester, 1873-1947), author. **George Rogers Clark** (Charlottesville, 1752-1818), frontier leader/soldier. **William Clark** (Caroline County, 1770-1838), soldier/explorer. **Henry Clay** (Hanover County, 1777-1852), political leader. **William Henry Harrison** (Berkeley, 1773-1841), U.S. president. **Thomas Jefferson** (Goochland, now Albemarle County, 1743-1826), U.S. president. **Joseph Eggleston Johnston** (Farmville, 1807-1891), soldier. **Henry (Light-Horse Harry) Lee** (Prince William County, 1756-1818) soldier/public official. **Robert Edward Lee** (Westmoreland County, 1807-1870), soldier. **Meriwether Lewis** (Albemarle County, 1774-1809), soldier/explorer/public official. **Charles Lynch** (Lynchburg, 1736-1779), planter/patriot. **James Madison** (Port Conway, 1751-1836), U.S. president. **John Marshall** (Fauquier County, 1755-1835), chief justice of the U.S.

Cyrus Hall McCormick (Rockbridge County, 1809-1884), inventor/industrialist. James Monroe (Westmoreland County, 1758-1831), U.S. president. Pocahontas (probably near Jamestown, 1595?-1617), Indian figure. Powhatan (in Virginia, 1550?-1618), Indian leader. Peyton Randolph (Williamsburg?, 1721?-1775), politician. Walter Reed (Gloucester County, 1851-1902), physician. George Campbell Scott (Wise, 1927-), actor. William Clark Styron, Jr. (Newport News, 1925-), author. Zachary Taylor (Orange County, 1784-1850), U.S. president/soldier. John Tyler (Greenway, 1790-1862), U.S. president. Booker Taliaferro Washington (Franklin County, 1856-1915), educator. George Washington (Westmoreland County, 1732-1799), U.S. president/soldier. Thomas Woodrow Wilson (Staunton, 1856-1924), U.S. president/educator.

GENERAL

Admitted to statehood: June 25, 1788
Origin of name: Named by Sir Walter Raleigh, who fitted out the expedition of 1584 to the New World in honor of Queen Elizabeth, the Virgin Queen of England
Capital: Richmond
Nickname: Old Dominion, Mother of Presidents
Motto: *Sic Semper Tyrannis*—Thus always to tyrants
Animal: Fox hound
Bird: Cardinal
Flower: Dogwood
Tree: Dogwood

THE LAND

Area: 42,326 sq. mi., 35th
  Land: 39,598 sq. mi., 37th
  Water: 2,728 sq. mi., 15th
    Inland water: 1,000 sq. mi., 22nd
    Coastal water: 1,728 sq. mi., 5th
Topography: Mountain and valley region in the W, including the Blue Ridge Mountains; rolling piedmont plateau; tidewater, or coastal plain, including the E shore
Number of counties: 95
Geographic center: 5 mi. SW of Buckingham
Length: 430 mi.; width: 200 mi.
Highest point: 5,729 ft. (Mount Rogers), 19th
Lowest point: sea level (Atlantic Ocean), 3rd

Mean elevation: 950 ft., 28th
Coastline: 112 mi., 15th
Shoreline: 3,315 mi., 8th

CLIMATE AND ENVIRONMENT

Temp., highest: 110 deg. on July 15, 1954, at Balcony Falls; lowest: –30 deg. on Jan. 22, 1985, at Mountain Lake Biological Station
Monthly average: highest: 88.4 deg., 22nd; lowest: 26.2 deg., 37th; spread (high to low): 62.2 deg., 37th
Hazardous waste sites (1997): 25, 16th
Endangered species: Animals: 31—Gray bat, Indiana bat, Virginia big-eared bat, Purple bean mussel, Cumberlandian combshell, Duskytail darter, American peregrine falcon, Fanshell, Lee County cave isopod, Roanoke logperch, Dwarf wedge mussel, Oyster mussel, Appalachian monkeyface pearlymussel, Birdwing pearlymussel, Cracking pearlymussel, Cumberland monkeyface pearlymussel, Dromedary pearlymussel, Green-blossom pearlymussel, Littlewing pearlymussel, Pink mucket pearlymussel, Fine-rayed pigtoe, Rough pigtoe, Shiny pigtoe, Rough rabbitsfoot, Tan riffleshell, Shenandoah salamander, Virginia fringed mountain snail, James River spinymussel, Delmarva Peninsula fox squirrel, Virginia northern flying squirrel, Red-cockaded woodpecker. Plants: 4

MAJOR CITIES
POPULATION, 1996
PERCENTAGE INCREASE, 1990-96

Virginia Beach, 430,385; 9.5%
Norfolk, 233,430; –10.6%
Richmond, 198,267; –2.2%
Chesapeake, 192,342; 26.6%
Newport News, 176,122; 2.7%

THE PEOPLE

Population (1997): 6,733,996, 12th
  Percent change (1990-97): 8.80%, 17th
  Percent of total U.S. pop.: 2.52%, 12th
  Per sq. mi: 157.45, 15th
Population (2000 proj.): 6,981,000, 12th
  Percent change (1995-2000): 5.49%, 21st
Percent in metro. area (1996): 77.87%, 20th
Foreign born: 312,000, 12th
  Percent: 5.0%, 17th

Top three ancestries reported:
German, 19.16%
English, 16.98%
African, 15.67%
White (1992): 4,964,000, 77.64%, 41st
Black (1992): 1,228,000, 19.21%, 9th
Native American (1992): 17,000, 0.27%, 37th
Asian, Pacific Isle (1992): 186,000, 2.91%, 9th
Hispanic origin (1992): 178,000, 2.78%, 25th
Percent over 5 yrs. speaking language other than English at home: 7.3%, 24th
Percent males (1996): 49.01%, 22nd; percent females: 50.99%, 30th
Percent never married: 27.1%, 18th
Marriages per 1,000 (1996): 9.80, 13th
Divorces per 1,000 (1996): 4.29, 25th
Median age (1996): 34.5
Under 5 years (1996): 6.87%, 32nd
18 years and under (1996): 27.17%, 42nd
65 years and over (1996): 11.19%, 44th
Percent increase among the elderly (1995-96): 1.48%, 14th

OF VITAL IMPORTANCE

Live births per 1,000 pop. (1996): 13.8, 30th
Infant mortality rate per 1,000 live births (1995): 7.8, 19th
Rate for whites: 5.7, 43rd
Rate for blacks: 15.3, 16th
Births to unmarried women, % of total (1996): 28.8%, 34th
Births to teenage mothers, % of total (1996): 11.0%, 34th
Abortions (1992): 35,020, 13th
Rate per 1,000 women 14-44 years old: 22.7, 21st
Percent change (1988-92): −5%, 20th
Average lifetime (1989-91): 75.22, 31st
Total death rate per 100,000 pop. (1995): 799.9, 41st
Accidents and adverse effects: 33.4, 36th
Alzheimer's disease: 7.9, 29th
Cancer: 190.4, 38th
Cerebrovascular diseases: 57.5, 31st
Chronic liver disease and cirrhosis: 7.2, 41st
Chronic obstructive pulmonary diseases and allied conditions: 34.1, 43rd
Diabetes mellitus: 17.6, 44th
Diseases of heart: 240.2, 37th
HIV infection: 12.6, 16th
Homicide: 7.8, 23rd

Injury by firearms: 14.4, 24th
Motor vehicle accidents: 13.9, 38th
Pneumonia and influenza: 28.5, 33rd
Suicide: 12.5, 23rd

KEEPING WELL

Active nonfederal physicians per 100,000 pop. (1995): 227, 14th
Dentists per 100,000 (1991): 54, 24th
Nurses per 100,000 (1995): 816, 28th
Hospitals per 100,000 (1995): 1.45, 42nd
Admissions per 1,000 (1995): 104.11, 36th
Hospital beds per 1,000 (1995): 2.81, 37th
Occupancy rate per 100 beds (1995): 61.83, 20th
Average cost per patient per day (1995): $901, 31st
Average cost per stay (1995): $5,423, 37th
AIDS cases (new, 1996): 1,195; per 100,000: 17.9, 18th
Persons living with HIV infection, not yet AIDS (1996): 6,079
Other notifiable diseases, per 100,000 pop.:
Gonorrhea (1995): 156.2, 16th
Syphilis (1995): 24.0, 14th
Tuberculosis (1996): 5.2, 25th
Pop. without health insur. (1996): 12.5%, 30th

HOUSEHOLDS BY TYPE

Total households (1996): 2,511,000, 12th
Percent change (1990-96): 9.6%, 17th
Per 1,000 pop. (1996) 376.18, 33rd
Percent of householders 65 yrs. and over (1996): 18.68%, 45th
Persons per household (1996): 2.61, 20th
Family households: 1,629,490
Percent of total: 71.10%, 21st
Nonfamily households: 662,340
Percent of total: 28.90%, 31st
Pop. living in group quarters: 209,300
Percent of pop.: 3.38%, 11th

LIVING QUARTERS

Total housing units: 2,496,334
Persons per unit: 2.48, 11th
Occupied housing units: 2,291,830
Percent of total units: 91.81%, 11th
Persons per unit: 2.57, 17th
Percent of units with over 1 person per room: 2.84%, 29th
Owner-occupied units: 1,519,521
Percent of total units: 60.87%, 19th
Percent of occupied units: 66.30%, 31st

Persons per unit: 2.70, 33rd
Median value: $91,000, 16th
Renter-occupied units: 772,309
Percent of total units: 30.94%, 18th
Percent of occupied units: 33.70%, 22nd
Persons per unit: 2.43, 15th
Median contract rent: $411, 14th
Rental vacancy rate: 8.1%, 28th
Mobile home, trailer & other as a percent of occupied housing units: 7.95%, 33rd
Persons in emergency shelters for homeless persons: 2,657, 0.043%, 32nd
Persons visible in street locations: 319, 0.0052%, 28th
Nursing home population: 37,762, 0.61%, 35th

CRIME INDEX PER 100,000 (1996)

Total reported: 3,968.3, 40th
Percent increase: −0.5%, 15th
Violent: 341.3, 36th
Percent increase: −5.6%, 23rd
Murder & nonnegligent manslaughter: 7.5, 18th
Forcible rape: 26.7, 41st
Aggravated assault: 184.5, 41st
Robbery: 122.6, 28th
Property: 3,627.0, 39th
Percent increase: 0.0%, 17th
Burglary: 588.1, 45th
Larceny-theft: 2,760.1, 33rd
Motor vehicle theft: 278.8, 39th

TEACHING AND LEARNING

Pop. 3 and over enrolled in school (1996): 1,452,012, 12th
Percent of pop.: 21.75%, 38th
Public elementary & secondary schools (1996-97): 1,889, 16th
Total enrollment (1996): 1,096,093, 12th
Percent of school age pop.: 93.13%, 21st
Percent of total pop.: 16.42%, 39th
Teachers (1996): 80,896, 11th
Percent of pop.: 1.21%, 7th
Pupil/teacher ratio (1995): 14.4, 46th
Teachers' avg. salary (1996-97): $35,837, 26th
Expenditure per capita (1992-93): $1,280.34, 29th
Education as % of state govt. expenditures: 37.8%, 11th
Expenditure per pupil (1994-95): $5,327, 32nd
Percent increase (1993-94 & 1994-95): 4.27%, 21st

Percent at or above grade level, NAEP tests:
Reading, grade 4 (1994): 26%, 23rd
Math, grade 4 (1996): 62%, 26th
Math, grade 8 (1996): 58%, 23rd
Percent of graduates taking SAT (1995): 65%, 11th
Mean SAT verbal scores: 428, 37th
Mean SAT mathematical scores: 468, 43rd
Percent of graduates taking ACT (1997): 6%, 43rd
Mean ACT scores: 20.7, 35th
Percent of pop. over 25 completing:
Less than 9th grade: 11.2%, 16th
High school: 75.2%, 32nd
College degree(s): 24.5%, 7th
Higher education, institutions (1996): 89, 14th
Enrollment (1995-96): 355,919, 11th
Percent increase in enroll. (1990-95): 0.7%, 34th
White non-Hispanic (1995): 264,430, 12th
Percent of enroll.: 74.29%, 35th
Total minority enroll. (1995): 83,662, 11th
Percent of enroll.: 23.51%, 18th
Black non-Hispanic (1995): 56,981, 10th
Percent of enroll.: 16.01%, 9th
Hispanic (1995): 8,080, 14th
Percent of enroll.: 2.27%, 24th
Asian/Pacific Islander (1995): 17,231, 11th
Percent of enroll.: 4.84%, 12th
American Indian/AK native (1995): 1,370, 25th
Percent of enroll.: 0.38%, 36th
Nonresident alien (1995): 7,827, 17th
Percent of enroll.: 2.20%, 37th
Female (1995): 200,955, 11th
Percent of enroll.: 56.46%, 18th
Pub. institutions (1995-96): 39, 12th
Enrollment: 293,127, 10th
Percent increase in enrollment (1990-95): 0.6%, 34th
Percent of enroll.: 82.36%, 26th
Private institutions (1995-96): 50, 12th
Enrollment: 62,792, 16th
Percent increase in enrollment (1990-95): 1%, 36th
Percent of enroll.: 17.64%, 26th
Tuition (in state), public 4-year institution (1996-97): $3,962, 9th
Tuition (in state), public 2-year institution (1996-97): $1,465, 22nd
Tuition, private 4-year institution (1996-97): $11,149, 25th

Public library systems (1994): 90, 31st
  Books & serial vol. per capita: 2.5, 31st
  Library visits per capita: 4.4, 18th
  Circulation per capita: 7.0, 23rd

LAW ENFORCEMENT AND CORRECTIONS

Police protection and corrections expenditures (1996): $1,121,832,000
  Per capita: $168.07, 5th
Police per 10,000 pop. (1996): 21.86, 28th
Prisoners (1 year or more) per 100,000 pop. (1996): 404, 18th
  Percent change (1995-96): –7.0%, 50th
  Percent of inmates that are female: 6.1%, 27th
    Percent change: 1.7%, 42nd
Death penalty: yes, by electrocution, lethal injection
  Under sentence (Jan. 1998): 41, 19th
  Executed, 1976-97: 46, 2nd
  Executed in 1997: 9, 2nd

RELIGION, NUMBER AND PERCENT OF POPULATION

Agnostic: 28,096—0.60%, 19th
Buddhist: 18,731—0.40%, 5th
Christian: 4,092,610—87.40%, 23rd
Hindu: 4,683—0.10%, 10th
Jewish: 51,509—1.10%, 15th
Muslim: 9,365—0.20%, 13th
Unitarian: 9,365—0.20%, 23rd
Other: 79,605—1.70%, 14th
None: 299,688—6.40%, 28th
Refused to answer: 88,970—1.90%, 31st

MAKING A LIVING

Personal income per capita (1996): $24,925, 15th
  Percent increase (1995-96): 2.7%, 33rd
Disposable personal income per capita (1996): $21,434, 16th
Median income of households (average, 1995-96): $38,252, 14th
Percent of pop. below poverty level (1995-96): 11.3%, 31st

ECONOMY

In civilian labor force (1996): 3,389,000
  Percent of total pop.: 67.3%, 30th
  Percent of total pop. 65 years and over: 12.5%, 21st
  Percent of total female pop.: 60.8%, 26th

Major employer industries (total nonagricultural, 1996):
  Construction: 174,800—5.6%, 10th
  Finance, insurance, & real estate: 162,200—5.2%, 24th
  Government: 597,100—19.1%, 14th
  Manufacturing: 398,500—12.7%, 36th
  Service: 911,400—29.1%, 16th
  Trade: 713,700—22.8%, 40th
  Transportation, communications, public utilities: 161,800—5.2%, 21st
Unemployment rate (1996): 4.4%, 38th
  Male: 4.2%, 40th
  Female: 4.6%, 32nd
Total businesses (1995): 162,378, 12th
New business incorps. (1995): 19,172
  Percent of total businesses: 11.81%, 13th
Business failures (1995): 1,713
  Failures per 10,000 businesses: 105.5, 16th
Agriculture farm income:
  Marketing (1996): $2,378,146,000, 29th
    Average per farm: $49,545, 45th
  Leading products (1997): Broilers, cattle, dairy products, tobacco, soybeans, corn, peanuts, grains
  Average value land & build. per acre (1997): $2,030, 14th
    Percent increase (1996-97): 6%, 20th
  Govt. payments (1996): $30,423,000, 34th
    Average per farm: $634, 41st
Construction, value of all (1996): $9,213,203,000, 12th
  Per capita: $1,380, 18th
Manufactures (1995):
  Value added: $40,133,700,000
    Per capita: $6,064, 27th
  Leading products (1997): Textiles, transportation equipment, electric & electronic equipment, food processing, chemicals, printing, lumber & wood products, apparel
Value of nonfuel mineral production (1996): $529,000,000, 22nd
Leading mineral products (1996): Coal, stone, cement, sand/gravel, lime, kyanite
Energy consumption per person (1994): 304.8 mil. Btu, 39th
Retail sales (1995): $66,648,000,000
  Per household: $26,932, 6th
  Sales increase (1994-95): 7.0%, 13th
Tourism revenues (1994): $9.4 bil.
Foreign exports, in total value (1996): $12,215,000,000, 14th
  Per capita: $1,830, 20th

Gross state product per person (1994): $27,125, 15th

Public aid recipients (percent of resident pop. 1994): 4.8%, 41st

Medicaid recipients (percent of pop., 1995): 10.3%, 35th

Medicare enrollment per 1,000 pop. (1996): 125, 41st

TRAVEL AND TRANSPORTATION

Motor vehicle registrations (1996): 5,576,132, 12th
  Per 1,000 pop.: 836.48, 19th
Motorcycle registrations (1996): 57,561, 23rd
  Per 1,000 pop.: 10.32, 49th
Licensed drivers (1996): 4,628,886, 12th
  Per 1,000 pop.: 699.73, 17th
Public roads & streets (1996)
  Total mileage: 69,384, 30th
    Per 1,000 pop.: 110.39, 38th
  Rural mileage: 50,854, 33rd
    Per 1,000 pop.: 7.62, 38th
  Urban mileage: 18,530, 15th
    Per 1,000 pop.: 2.78, 37th
  Interstate mileage: 1,107, 14th
    Per 1,000 pop.: 0.17, 32nd
Speed limit (max. interstate, autos, mi. per hr., 1997): 65
Annual vehicle-mi. of travel per driver (1996): 15,196, 18th
Mean travel time for workers age 16+ who work away from home: 24.0 min., 7th

GOVERNMENT

Percent of voting age pop. registered (1996): 65.36%, 46th
Percent of voting age pop. voting for president: (1996): 47.5%, 34th
Percent of voting age pop. voting for U.S. representatives (1996): 43.2%, 37th
State legislators, total (1997): 140, 28th
  Women members (1997): 21
    Percent of legislature: 15%, 42nd
U.S. Congress, House members (1998): 11
  Change (1988-98): 1

Revenues (1996):
  State govt.: $20,072,003,000
    Per capita: $3,007.04, 44th
    Parimutuel & amusement taxes & lotteries, revenue per capita (1995): $133.31, 15th
Expenditures (1996):
  State govt.: $17,717,140,000
    Per capita: $2,654.25, 45th
Debt outstanding (1996): $8,792,968,000
    Per capita: $1,317.30, 27th

LAWS AND REGULATIONS

Legal driving age: 19, 16 if completed driver education course
Marriage age without parental consent: 18
Divorce residence requirement: 6 mo., for qualifications check local statutes

ATTRACTIONS (1997)

Major opera companies: 2
Major symphony orchestras: 2
Major dance companies: 1
Per capita spending by the NEA (1997): $0.18, 41st
State Fair in late September–early October at Richmond

SPORTS AND COMPETITION

NCAA (Division I) football and basketball teams: College of William & Mary Tribe, George Mason Univ. Patriots (basketball only), Hampton Univ. Pirates, James Madison Univ. Dukes, Liberty Univ. Flames, Norfolk State Univ. Spartans (basketball only), Old Dominion Univ. Monarchs (basketball only), Radford Univ. Highlanders, Univ. of Richmond Spiders, Univ. of Virginia Cavaliers, Virginia Commonwealth Univ. Rams (basketball only), Virginia Military Institute Keydets, Virginia Polytechnic Institute & State Univ. Gobblers/ Hokies

WEBSITES CONTAINING FURTHER INFORMATION

Welcome to Virginia   http://www.state.va.us

WASHINGTON

> "But, however inviting may be the soil, the remote distance and savage aspect of the boundless wilderness along the Pacific seem to defer the colonization of such a region to a period far beyond the present generation [early 1800s] and yet, if we consider the rapid progress of civilization in other new and equally remote countries, we might still indulge the hope of seeing this, at no distant time, one of the most flourishing countries on the globe."
>
> Alexander Ross, fur trader and chronicler

Smallest in area of the conterminous states west of Iowa, Washington is a state with a split personality—the rainy lands to the west and the desert land east of the Cascade Mountains, which stretch for miles without a single tree. Both sides are known for their production of major crops. Ships from all parts of the world dock in the ports of Washington, and fishing fleets catch salmon, halibut, and other fish in the Pacific Ocean. Washington is a lumbering state as well as a leader in dairy farming and flower-bulb production, cattle raising, and wheat, fruit, and vegetable crops. Grand Coulee Dam, on the Columbia River, is the mightiest piece of masonry in the world. Seattle has often been ranked as the "most livable" U.S. city.

So They Say

"...an incomparable harbor, vast tracts of timber, salmon-filled waters, good farmland, benign climate. There seemed to be everything needed for a good life in Puget Sound."

Anonymous 19th-century observer

SUPERLATIVES

- Provides 10% of all U.S. annual timber growth.
- Produces 30% of the nation's hydroelectric power.
- World leader in apple production.
- World's largest farm reclamation project.
- Leader in vegetable seed production.
- Unique temperate rain forest—Olympic Peninsula.

MOMENTS IN HISTORY

- Juan de Fuca may have sailed the Washington shores in 1592, but the first recorded visit was made by Juan Perez in 1774.
- Bruno Heceta and Juan de Bodega y Quadra in 1775 were the first Europeans known to have touched present-day Washington, and they claimed the land for the King of Spain.
- Captain George Vancouver discovered Puget Sound in 1792.
- In 1792, Captain Robert Gray reached the Columbia River, sailed into its treacherous mouth, and landed his ship the *Columbia* at present-day Fort Columbia.
- The great expedition of Meriwether Lewis and William Clark made the dangerous passage down the Snake and Columbia rivers and arrived at the coast in November 1805.

So They Say

"Great joy in camp, we are in view of the Ocean, this great Pacific Ocean which we been so long anxious to see, and the roreing or noise made by the waves...may be heard distinctly."

Meriwether Lewis

- Lewis and Clark began their return journey on March 23, 1806, trading with the Indians they encountered and considerably treating their ailments.
- David Thompson established the trading post of Spokane House in 1810.
- Several mergers extended the Hudson's Bay Company interests in the area, and they established Fort Vancouver in 1824. It became the first permanent European settlement in present-day Washington.
- By 1828, Fort Vancouver had become a civilization in the wilderness, under the direction of a British fur trader named Dr. John McLoughlin, who was known throughout the West for his hospitality and kindness to those in difficulty. McLoughlin's actions got him in trouble with both American and British authorities, and he ended up as a "man without a country."

So They Say

"The fort dining hall was a noble apartment capable of seating 500 guests. A huge map of the Indian country covered the wall...the long tables began to fill. With a wave of the hand the stately governor [McLoughlin] seated his guests according to rank. Before them cut-glass and silver, with the McLoughlin coat of arms, shone side by side with modern queen's ware and rare old china...the branching candelabra sent out an odor of perfumed wax."

Writer Eva Dye, on Dr. John McLoughlin's hospitality

• In 1836, Dr. Marcus Whitman established a mission called Waiilatpu, near present-day Walla Walla.

• In 1843 the first large group of settlers came overland from the United States by covered wagon, establishing the famous Oregon Trail.

• The rival claims of Britain and the United States appeared to be leading to war, but in 1846 the present boundaries of Washington were settled.

• In 1847 the Cayuse Indians attacked the Waiilatpu mission and killed Dr. and Mrs. Whitman.

• Oregon Territory—Washington, Oregon, and parts of Idaho—was established in 1848, and development came rapidly.

• The Indian wars came to a virtual halt in 1858.

• The cities of Vancouver, Ellensburg, Spokane, and Seattle were all swept by fire in 1889.

• On November 11, 1889, Washington became a state.

• Seattle hosted the Alaska-Yukon-Pacific Exposition in 1909.

• During World War II the super-secret installations at Richland turned out nuclear materials, and the state's production of airplanes and ships made a vital contribution to the war effort.

• Seattle (1962) and Spokane (1974) held world's fairs.

• The explosion of Mount St. Helens volcano, on May 18, 1980, was one of the worst disasters of an era.

• In 1988 state apple growers lost more than $145 million in wake of reports that alar, a growth-inducing chemical sprayed on apples, causes cancer.

• The 1991 collision of a Japanese fishing vessel and a Chinese freighter covered the beaches in Olympic National Park with oil from the resulting spill.

• In 1992 experts claimed the world's largest living organism, a 1,500-acre fungus, was growing south of Mount Adams.

THAT'S INTERESTING

• The drowned valley of Puget Sound is dotted with the tops of hills, plateaus, and mountains that were too high to be covered with water. These became the 300 islands of the sound. Whidbey Island is the largest, and the San Juan group forms a cluster of 150 islands.

• Beacon Rock near Skamania is the second largest single rock (monolith) in the world. It rises steeply for 900 feet from the edge of the Columbia River. Only Gibraltar is higher.

• A weather novelty, especially unusual in dry areas, is the will-o'-the-wisps. These are dim, flickering lights often seen darting over the Horse Heaven Hills. Residents of the area claim to have seen "balls of fire" dashing over the surface.

• Point Roberts on the mainland is American territory but juts out from Canada and cannot be reached by land from the rest of the United States.

• Some of the coastal Indian lodges were enormous, and many related families lived in them. The Old-Man-House of the Suquamish Indians may have covered more than an acre. Inside there were 40 apartments divided by split logs.

• The Nez Percé were noted for developing and riding their beautiful spotted Appaloosa ponies, one of the truly distinct and remarkable breeds.

• Early Seattle had a shortage of females. Asa Mercer went east and persuaded 11 girls of good families to return to meet the many eligible bachelors. Several prominent families trace their roots back to the Mercer girls.

NOTABLE NATIVES

Harry Lillis (Bing) Crosby (Tacoma, 1904-1977), singer/actor. **William Henry (Bill) Gates** (Seattle, 1955-), businessman/software pioneer. **Chief Joseph** (Wallowa Valley, near the Washington/Idaho/Oregon border,

1840?-1904), Indian leader. **Mary Therese McCarthy** (Seattle, 1912-1989), author. **Seattle** or **Sealth** (near Seattle, 1786?-1866), Indian leader. **Minoru Yamasaki** (Seattle, 1912-1986), architect.

GENERAL

Admitted to statehood: November 11, 1889
Origin of name: Named after George Washington. When the bill creating the territory of Columbia was introduced in the 32nd Congress, the name was changed to Washington
Capital: Olympia
Nickname: Evergreen State
Motto: *Al-ki*—By and by
Bird: Willow goldfinch
Fish: Steelhead trout
Flower: Western rhododendron
Song: "Washington, My Home"
Tree: Western hemlock

THE LAND

Area: 70,637 sq. mi., 19th
  Land: 66,581 sq. mi., 20th
  Water: 4,056 sq. mi., 9th
    Inland water: 1,545 sq. mi., 14th
    Coastal water: 2,511 sq. mi., 2nd
Topography: Olympic Mountains on NW peninsula; open land along coast to Columbia River; flat terrain of Puget Sound lowland; Cascade Mountains' high peaks to the E of lowland; Columbia Basin in central portion; highlands to the NE; mountains to the SE
Number of counties: 39
Geographic center: Chelan, 10 mi. WSW of Wenatchee
Length: 360 mi.; width: 240 mi.
Highest point: 14,410 ft. (Mount Rainier), 4th
Lowest point: sea level (Pacific Ocean), 3rd
Mean elevation: 1,700 ft., 18th
Coastline: 157 mi., 12th
Shoreline: 3,026 mi., 10th

CLIMATE AND ENVIRONMENT

Temp., highest: 118 deg. on Aug. 5, 1961, at Ice Harbor Dam; lowest: –48 deg. on Dec. 30, 1968, at Mazama and Winthrop
Monthly average: highest: 84.0 deg., 41st; lowest: 20.0 deg., 27th; spread (high to low): 64.0 deg., 33rd

Hazardous waste sites (1997): 48, 7th
Endangered species: Animals: 5—Woodland caribou, Columbian white-tailed deer, American peregrine falcon, Brown pelican, Gray wolf. Plants: 2

MAJOR CITIES
POPULATION, 1996
PERCENTAGE INCREASE, 1990-96

Seattle, 524,704; 1.6%
Spokane, 186,562; 5.3%
Tacoma, 179,114; 1.4%
Bellevue, 92,267; 6.2%
Everett, 81,028; 14.2%

THE PEOPLE

Population (1997): 5,610,362, 15th
  Percent change (1990-97): 15.28%, 7th
  Percent of total U.S. pop.: 2.10%, 15th
  Per sq. mi: 78.68, 27th
Population (2000 proj.): 5,843,500, 15th
  Percent change (1995-2000): 7.60%, 14th
Percent in metro. area (1996): 82.77%, 15th
Foreign born: 322,000, 10th
  Percent: 6.6%, 14th
Top three ancestries reported:
  German, 28.56%
  English, 18.43%
  Irish, 15.78%
White (1992): 4,636,000, 90.14%, 22nd
Black (1992): 165,000, 3.21%, 36th
Native American (1992): 93,000, 1.81%, 9th
Asian, Pacific Isle (1992): 249,000, 4.84%, 3rd
Hispanic origin (1992): 242,000, 4.71%, 19th
Percent over 5 yrs. speaking language other than English at home: 9.0%, 19th
Percent males (1996): 49.81%, 10th; percent females: 50.19%, 42nd
Percent never married: 24.8%, 32nd
Marriages per 1,000 (1996): 7.08, 42nd
Divorces per 1,000 (1996): 4.79, 17th
Median age (1996): 34.9
Under 5 years (1996): 7.08%, 19th
18 years and under (1996): 28.74%, 25th
65 years and over (1996): 11.59%, 38th
Percent increase among the elderly (1995-96): 1.49%, 13th

OF VITAL IMPORTANCE

Live births per 1,000 pop. (1996): 14.5, 18th
Infant mortality rate per 1,000 live births (1995): 5.9, 46th

Rate for whites: 5.6, 44th
Rate for blacks: 16.2, 14th
Births to unmarried women, % of total (1996): 27.3%, 39th
Births to teenage mothers, % of total (1996): 11.3%, 32nd
Abortions (1992): 33,190, 14th
Rate per 1,000 women 14-44 years old: 27.7, 11th
Percent change (1988-92): 0%, 13th
Average lifetime (1989-91): 76.82, 12th
Total death rate per 100,000 pop. (1995): 751.0, 43rd
Accidents and adverse effects: 34.9, 32nd
Alzheimer's disease: 9.0, 21st
Cancer: 183.0, 42nd
Cerebrovascular diseases: 60.7, 27th
Chronic liver disease and cirrhosis: 8.2, 36th
Chronic obstructive pulmonary diseases and allied conditions: 39.7, 26th
Diabetes mellitus: 19.4, 38th
Diseases of heart: 208.6, 45th
HIV infection: 10.9, 20th
Homicide: 5.5, 30th
Injury by firearms: 12.2, 32nd
Motor vehicle accidents: 13.7, 39th
Pneumonia and influenza: 28.1, 35th
Suicide: 14.4, 16th

KEEPING WELL

Active nonfederal physicians per 100,000 pop. (1995): 224, 17th
Dentists per 100,000 (1991): 62, 16th
Nurses per 100,000 (1995): 798, 31st
Hospitals per 100,000 (1995): 1.62, 38th
Admissions per 1,000 (1995): 85.99, 49th
Hospital beds per 1,000 (1995): 1.99, 51st
Occupancy rate per 100 beds (1995): 56.48, 42nd
Average cost per patient per day (1995): $1,318, 3rd
Average cost per stay (1995): $6,180, 18th
AIDS cases (new, 1996): 804; per 100,000: 14.5, 24th
Persons living with HIV infection (1996): NA
Other notifiable diseases, per 100,000 pop.:
Gonorrhea (1995): 50.9, 37th
Syphilis (1995): 3.9, 36th
Tuberculosis (1996): 5.2, 25th
Pop. without health insur. (1996): 13.5%, 24th

HOUSEHOLDS BY TYPE

Total households (1996): 2,139,000, 15th
Percent change (1990-96): 14.2%, 7th
Per 1,000 pop. (1996) 386.59, 9th
Percent of householders 65 yrs. and over (1996): 18.98%, 44th
Persons per household (1996): 2.53, 37th
Family households: 1,264,934
Percent of total: 67.56%, 47th
Nonfamily households: 607,497
Percent of total: 32.44%, 5th
Pop. living in group quarters: 120,531
Percent of pop.: 2.48%, 35th

LIVING QUARTERS

Total housing units: 2,032,378
Persons per unit: 2.39, 27th
Occupied housing units: 1,872,431
Percent of total units: 92.13%, 8th
Persons per unit: 2.49, 36th
Percent of units with over 1 person per room: 3.89%, 19th
Owner-occupied units: 1,171,580
Percent of total units: 57.65%, 32nd
Percent of occupied units: 62.57%, 42nd
Persons per unit: 2.68, 36th
Median value: $93,400, 15th
Renter-occupied units: 700,851
Percent of total units: 34.48%, 10th
Percent of occupied units: 37.43%, 12th
Persons per unit: 2.30, 32nd
Median contract rent: $383, 16th
Rental vacancy rate: 5.8%, 47th
Mobile home, trailer & other as a percent of occupied housing units: 11.07%, 26th
Persons in emergency shelters for homeless persons: 4,565, 0.094%, 8th
Persons visible in street locations: 772, 0.0159%, 11th
Nursing home population: 32,840, 0.67%, 30th

CRIME INDEX PER 100,000 (1996)

Total reported: 5,909.4, 13th
Percent increase: −5.7%, 36th
Violent: 431.2, 30th
Percent increase: −11.0%, 39th
Murder & nonnegligent manslaughter: 4.6, 31st
Forcible rape: 51.1, 7th
Aggravated assault: 256.4, 30th
Robbery: 119.0, 30th

Property: 5,478.2, 10th
  Percent increase: −5.3%, 36th
  Burglary: 1,057.5, 15th
  Larceny-theft: 3,898.5, 9th
  Motor vehicle theft: 522.2, 17th

TEACHING AND LEARNING

Pop. 3 and over enrolled in school (1996): 1,257,722, 15th
  Percent of pop.: 22.73%, 24th
Public elementary & secondary schools (1996-97): 2,124, 12th
  Total enrollment (1996): 971,903, 14th
    Percent of school age pop.: 92.47%, 25th
    Percent of total pop.: 17.57%, 23rd
  Teachers (1996): 47,479, 20th
    Percent of pop.: 0.86%, 48th
  Pupil/teacher ratio (1995): 20.4, 3rd
  Teachers' avg. salary (1996-97): $37,860, 19th
  Expenditure per capita (1992-93): $1,630.78, 5th
    Education as % of state govt. expenditures: 34.3%, 31st
  Expenditure per pupil (1994-95): $5,906, 23rd
    Percent increase (1993-94 & 1994-95): 2.70%, 37th
Percent at or above grade level, NAEP tests:
  Reading, grade 4 (1994): 27%, 20th
  Math, grade 4 (1996): 67%, 16th
  Math, grade 8 (1996): 67%, 15th
Percent of graduates taking SAT (1995): 48%, 20th
  Mean SAT verbal scores: 443, 30th
  Mean SAT mathematical scores: 494, 27th
Percent of graduates taking ACT (1997): 16%, 33rd
  Mean ACT scores: 22.4, 1st
Percent of pop. over 25 completing:
  Less than 9th grade: 5.5%, 49th
  High school: 83.8%, 4th
  College degree(s): 22.9%, 13th
Higher education, institutions (1996): 64, 19th
  Enrollment (1995-96): 285,819, 17th
    Percent increase in enroll. (1990-95): 8.5%, 13th
  White non-Hispanic (1995): 228,386, 17th
    Percent of enroll.: 79.91%, 28th
  Total minority enroll. (1995): 48,472, 18th
    Percent of enroll.: 16.96%, 26th
  Black non-Hispanic (1995): 10,599, 28th
    Percent of enroll.: 3.71%, 33rd

Hispanic (1995): 10,197, 13th
  Percent of enroll.: 3.57%, 17th
Asian/Pacific Islander (1995): 22,451, 7th
  Percent of enroll.: 7.85%, 3rd
American Indian/AK native (1995): 5,225, 5th
  Percent of enroll.: 1.83%, 8th
Nonresident alien (1995): 8,961, 12th
  Percent of enroll.: 3.14%, 16th
Female (1995): 159,320, 16th
  Percent of enroll.: 55.74%, 31st
Pub. institutions (1995-96): 37, 14th
  Enrollment: 246,635, 14th
    Percent increase in enrollment (1990-95): 8.3%, 16th
    Percent of enroll.: 86.29%, 16th
Private institutions (1995-96): 27, 23rd
  Enrollment: 39,184, 23rd
    Percent increase in enrollment (1990-95): 9.6%, 19th
    Percent of enroll.: 13.71%, 36th
Tuition (in state), public 4-year institution (1996-97): $2,928, 21st
Tuition (in state), public 2-year institution (1996-97): $1,445, 23rd
Tuition, private 4-year institution (1996-97): $13,794, 14th
Public library systems (1994): 69, 37th
  Books & serial vol. per capita: 2.8, 26th
  Library visits per capita: NA
  Circulation per capita: 10.1, 2nd

LAW ENFORCEMENT AND CORRECTIONS

Police protection and corrections expenditures (1996): $668,970,000
  Per capita: $120.91, 23rd
Police per 10,000 pop. (1996): 16.39, 47th
Prisoners (1 year or more) per 100,000 pop. (1996): 224, 41st
  Percent change (1995-96): 7.8%, 18th
  Percent of inmates that are female: 7.3%, 10th
    Percent change: 16.0%, 14th
Death penalty: yes, by Hanging, lethal injection
  Under sentence (Jan. 1998): 11, 27th
  Executed, 1976-97: 2, 21st
  Executed in 1997: 0

RELIGION, NUMBER AND PERCENT OF POPULATION

Agnostic: 50,474—1.40%, 1st
Buddhist: 18,027—0.50%, 2nd

Christian: 2,779,690—77.10%, 47th
Hindu: 3,605—0.10%, 10th
Jewish: 14,421—0.40%, 31st
Muslim: NA
Unitarian: 18,027—0.50%, 6th
Other: 97,343—2.70%, 2nd
None: 504,743—14.00%, 2nd
Refused to answer: 118,975—3.30%, 4th

MAKING A LIVING

Personal income per capita (1996): $24,838, 16th
  Percent increase (1995-96): 4.2%, 13th
Disposable personal income per capita (1996): $21,740, 13th
Median income of households (average, 1995-96): $36,647, 19th
Percent of pop. below poverty level (1995-96): 12.2%, 23rd

ECONOMY

In civilian labor force (1996): 2,887,000
  Percent of total pop.: 68.9%, 22nd
  Percent of total pop. 65 years and over: NA
  Percent of total female pop.: 61.1%, 25th
Major employer industries (total nonagricultural, 1996):
  Construction: 127,200—5.3%, 13th
  Finance, insurance, & real estate: 123,800—5.1%, 26th
  Government: 450,400—18.7%, 17th
  Manufacturing: 344,100—14.3%, 29th
  Service: 649,200—26.9%, 27th
  Trade: 590,900—24.5%, 15th
  Transportation, communications, public utilities: 122,900—5.1%, 22nd
Unemployment rate (1996): 6.5%, 7th
  Male: 5.9%, 10th
  Female: 7.2%, 4th
Total businesses (1995): 151,925, 14th
New business incorps. (1995): 13,340
  Percent of total businesses: 8.78%, 28th
Business failures (1995): 2,384
  Failures per 10,000 businesses: 156.9, 3rd
Agriculture farm income:
  Marketing (1996): $5,680,980,000, 13th
    Average per farm: $157,805, 6th
  Leading products (1997): Cattle, apples, dairy products, potatoes, hay, farm forest products
  Average value land & build. per acre (1997): $1,230, 27th
    Percent increase (1996-97): 10%, 2nd

Govt. payments (1996): $156,039,000, 20th
    Average per farm: $4,334, 14th
Construction, value of all (1996): $8,403,400,000, 14th
  Per capita: $1,519, 15th
Manufactures (1995):
  Value added: $28,150,400,000
    Per capita: $5,183, 35th
  Leading products (1997): Aircraft, pulp & paper, lumber & plywood, aluminum, processed fruits & vegetables, machinery, electronics, computer software
Value of nonfuel mineral production (1996): $626,000,000, 20th
Leading mineral products (1996): Sand/gravel, magnesium, cement, stone, gold
Energy consumption per person (1994): 391.2 mil. Btu, 15th
Retail sales (1995): $49,551,000,000
  Per household: $23,562, 37th
  Sales increase (1994-95): 2.2%, 42nd
Tourism revenues (1994): $7.5 bil.
Foreign exports, in total value (1996): $26,482,000,000, 5th
  Per capita: $4,786, 3rd
Gross state product per person (1994): $26,926, 16th
Public aid recipients (percent of resident pop. 1994): 7.1%, 20th
Medicaid recipients (percent of pop., 1995): 11.7%, 27th
Medicare enrollment per 1,000 pop. (1996): 127, 39th

TRAVEL AND TRANSPORTATION

Motor vehicle registrations (1996): 4,602,920, 16th
  Per 1,000 pop.: 833.93, 20th
Motorcycle registrations (1996): 104,450, 12th
  Per 1,000 pop.: 22.69, 17th
Licensed drivers (1996): 3,765,376, 14th
  Per 1,000 pop.: 691.18, 26th
Public roads & streets (1996)
  Total mileage: 79,555, 25th
    Per 1,000 pop.: 114.38, 31st
  Rural mileage: 61,908, 29th
    Per 1,000 pop.: 11.19, 31st
  Urban mileage: 17,647, 16th
    Per 1,000 pop.: 3.19, 21st
  Interstate mileage: 763, 29th
    Per 1,000 pop.: 0.14, 36th
Speed limit (max. interstate, autos, mi. per hr., 1997): 70
Annual vehicle-mi. of travel per driver (1996): 12,641, 39th

Mean travel time for workers age 16+ who work away from home: 22.0 min., 13th

GOVERNMENT

Percent of voting age pop. registered (1996): 74.80%, 31st
  Percent of voting age pop. voting for president: (1996): 54.7%, 19th
  Percent of voting age pop. voting for U.S. representatives (1996): 52.7%, 17th
State legislators, total (1997): 147, 25th
  Women members (1997): 57
  Percent of legislature: 39%, 2nd
U.S. Congress, House members (1998): 9
  Change (1988-98): 1
Revenues (1996):
  State govt.: $24,790,010,000
  Per capita: $4,480.39, 10th
    Parimutuel & amusement taxes & lotteries, revenue per capita (1995): $74.32, 31st
Expenditures (1996):
  State govt.: $21,085,737,000
  Per capita: $3,810.90, 12th
Debt outstanding (1996): $8,991,106,000
  Per capita: $1,625.00, 20th

LAWS AND REGULATIONS

Legal driving age: 18, 16 if completed driver education course

Marriage age without parental consent: 18
Divorce residence requirement: Bona fide resident

ATTRACTIONS (1997)

Major opera companies: 1
Major symphony orchestras: 2
Major dance companies: 1
Major professional theater companies (non-profit): 3
Per capita spending by the NEA (1997): $0.31, 23rd
State fair: Western Washington, mid-August at Puyallup; Eastern Washington, late September at Ellensburg

SPORTS AND COMPETITION

NCAA (Division I) football and basketball teams: Eastern Washington Univ. Eagles, Gonzaga Univ. Bulldogs/Zags (basketball only), Univ. of Washington Huskies, Washington State Univ. Cougars
Major league baseball teams: Seattle Mariners (AL West), The Kingdome
NBA basketball teams: Seattle SuperSonics, Key Arena
ABL basketball teams: Seattle Reign, Mercer Arena, Seattle Center
NFL football teams: Seattle Seahawks (AFC), The Kingdome

WEBSITES CONTAINING FURTHER INFORMATION

| Home Page Washington—Home | http://www.wa.gov/home.htm |

WEST VIRGINIA

"We West Virginians are very tired of being considered inhabitants of just a dominion of Old Dominion....Some inhabitants take a very strong line about this and always refer to it in conversation as 'West—By God—Virginia!'"
John Knowles, novelist

"The world's most beautiful place!"
Pearl Buck, novelist

West Virginia's "birth" during the Civil War, when the region refused to secede from the Union, made it unique among the states. Its mountains have given it the loftiest average height east of the Rockies. The state contains some of the most rugged land in the country: There are no large areas of level ground, except along major rivers. Its beautiful mountain scenery and mineral springs attract many tourists. Its surface shelters an unusual variety of plants, ranging from Arctic types to those of the semitropics. Beneath the surface lie minerals, including coal, in which the state has long been a leader. This war-born state suffered terribly during the Civil War. One city changed hands an incredible 56 times. But West Virginia is a state that always seems able to bounce back from disaster.

SUPERLATIVES

- "Highest state" east of the Mississippi.
- Only state carved from another without its permission.
- Pioneer in natural gas production and leads the eastern states.
- Noted for record sizes of individual trees.

MOMENTS IN HISTORY

- The earliest known Europeans in what is now West Virginia came with the party of Walter Austin in 1641.
- Noted for its heavy drinking, the party of Governor Alexander Spotswood of Virginia may have staggered as far as present-day Pendleton County in 1716.
- Laid out in 1732, Shepherdstown became the oldest permanent settlement in West Virginia.
- In 1749 famed explorer Pierre Joseph, Celeron de Bienville, undertook his renowned trip down the Ohio River, a journey designed to reinforce the claims of France to all the lands west of the Allegheny Mountains.
- By 1753 settlers were arriving in substantial numbers.

- The French and Indian War caused great hardship, diminishing when the French lost the continent in 1763.

> ### So They Say
> "I am too little acquainted, Sir, with pathetic language to attempt a description of the people's distresses—I see inevitable destruction in so clear a light, that, unless vigorous measures are taken by the Assembly and speedy assistance sent...the poor inhabitants that are now in the Fort [Edwards] must unavoidably fall...."
>
> **George Washington,**
> **on French and Indian War attacks**

- In 1774 the entire family of Mingo Indian leader James Logan was murdered in his absence.

> ### So They Say
> "...in cold blood and unprovoked, [white men] cut off all the relatives of Logan, not sparing even my women and chilldren. There runs not a drop of my blood in the veins of any creature. This called on me for revenge. I have fully glutted my vengeance...."
>
> **Indian leader James Logan,**
> **who reputedly took**
> **some 30 white scalps in revenge**

- A battle with the Indians at Point Pleasant in 1774 has been labeled "the first battle of the Revolution."
- During the Revolution, Indian wars again erupted in 1777. A principal cause was the cold-blooded murder of Chief Cornstalk, who was on a peaceful mission.
- The Battle of Fort Henry (Wheeling), called the "Last Battle of the Revolution," was fought in September 1782, long after war had ceased in the East.
- In 1784, George Washington issued a certificate of confidence to West Virginia inventor James Rumsey—the first official indi-

cation that Rumsey was the inventor of the steamboat, preceding both John Fitch and Robert Fulton. Fulton was said to have spied on Rumsey to study his work.

> ## So They Say
>
> "We got on board the steamboat which was to convey us to Wheeling....She was a noble boat, by far the finest we had seen....In front of the ladies' cabin was an ample balcony, sheltered by an awning...chairs and sofas were placed there, and even at that early season, nearly all the female passengers passed the whole day there."
>
> **British travel writer Frances Trollope (1832)**

• The most notorious episode of the growing hostility over slavery took place in 1859 when "Isaac Smith" led his followers across the Potomac and captured the federal arsenal at Harpers Ferry. Of course, he was really the abolitionist John Brown, who was quickly tried and executed.

> ## So They Say
>
> "Let no man pray that Brown be spared. Let Virginia make him a martyr. Now he has only blundered. His cause was noble, his work miserable. But a cord and a gibbet would redeem all that, and round up Brown's failure with a heroic success."
>
> **Clergyman Henry Ward Beecher, on John Brown**

• When Virginia seceded in 1861, the West Virginia legislators voted against it but were overruled.

• The skirmish at Philippi on June 3, 1861, is considered to have been the first land battle of the Civil War. It was important because it shut off the Confederates from the coal fields of the region.

• On two different occasions, the people of West Virginia voted to separate from Virginia. On June 20, 1863, the wartime state of West Virginia was born by acceptance of the federal government.

• Civil War battles brought much destruction, especially to industry. The state's last major encounter of the war was the Battle of Droop Mountain, on November 6, 1863,

but Confederate raids continued. Romney changed hands 56 times between Union and Confederate troops.

• After much controversy, the capital was moved permanently to Charleston in 1885.

• A mine explosion in 1907 at Monongah was one of the worst in the state's history, causing 361 deaths.

• The state capitol burned on January 3, 1921, and that same year a miners' disagreement came to be known as the Battle of Blair Mountain.

• The 1937 Ohio River floods were the worst yet recorded, with some cities overwhelmed by water more than 20 feet above flood stage.

• During World War II the famed Greenbrier Hotel became an internment center for enemy diplomats, then a government hospital, serving more than 20,000 patients.

• The state's coal production reached its all-time high in 1947, declined, then was reborn in the mid-1970s.

• By 1997 there was concern over the coal mining practice of "shearing the mountaintops" and its effect on the environment and public health.

THAT'S INTERESTING

• West Virginia has an unusual geographical outline. As a result, Chester is farther north than Pittsburgh, PA, making West Virginia a northern state; Bluefield is farther south than Richmond, VA, making it a southern state; Kenova is farther west than Port Huron, MI, making it a midwestern state; and Harpers Ferry is farther east than Rochester, NY, making it an eastern state.

• In 1896, four Rural Free Delivery mail routes were set up as a trial of that new postal system. A West Virginia mail carrier began delivering before the official date, giving the state its unofficial early lead in such service.

• When the Tug Fork was chosen as the boundary river by mistake, West Virginia lost 1,000 square miles of territory that might have been hers.

• The West Virginia "panhandle" is so narrow that the city of Weirton stretches from border to border. The only U.S. city that extends from one state border to another, it is wedged in between Ohio and Pennsylvania.

• A touring circus is said to have decided the choice of Charleston as state capital. Its supporters lured voters statewide with a flamboyant circus and won handily.

• Ann Royall became the first woman journalist to interview a president. While John Quincy Adams was swimming, she stole his clothes and would not return them until he gave her a hearing.

• The community of Shepherdstown in West Virginia was on George Washington's list for choice of a national capital, but it lost out in the final selection.

NOTABLE NATIVES

Newton Diehl Baker (Martinsburg, 1871-1937), public official. **Pearl Sydenstricker Buck** (Hillsboro, 1892-1973), author. **Cornstalk** (Ohio-West Virginia frontier, 1720?-1777), Indian leader. **John William Davis** (Clarksburg, 1873-1955), politician. **Thomas Jonathan (Stonewall) Jackson** (Clarksburg, 1824-1863), soldier. **Dwight Whitney Morrow** (Huntington, 1873-1931), banker/diplomat. **Walter Philip Reuther** (Wheeling, 1907-1970), labor leader. **Charles Elwood (Chuck) Yeager** (Myra, 1923-), aviator.

GENERAL

Admitted to statehood: June 20, 1863
Origin of name: Virginia was named by Sir Walter Raleigh, who fitted out the expedition of 1584, in honor of Queen Elizabeth, the Virgin Queen of England. It became West Virginia when western counties of Virginia refused to secede from the United States in 1863
Capital: Charleston
Nickname: Mountain State
Motto: *Montani Semper Liberi*—Mountaineers are always free
Animal: Black bear
Bird: Cardinal
Fish: Brook trout
Flower: Big rhododendron
Song: "West Virginia, My Home Sweet Home," "The West Virginia Hills," and "This Is My West Virginia"
Tree: Sugar maple

THE LAND

Area: 24,232 sq. mi., 41st
  Land: 24,087 sq. mi., 41st
  Water: 145 sq. mi., 49th
    Inland water: 145 sq. mi., 48th
Topography: Ranging from hilly to mountainous; Allegheny plateau, in the W, covers two-thirds of the state; mountains here are the highest in the state, over 4,000 ft.
Number of counties: 55
Geographic center: Braxton, 4 mi. E of Sutton
Length: 240 mi.; width: 130 mi.
Highest point: 4,861 ft. (Spruce Knob), 24th
Lowest point: 240 ft. (Potomac River), 31st
Mean elevation: 1,500 ft., 19th

CLIMATE AND ENVIRONMENT

Temp., highest: 112 deg. on July 10, 1936, at Martinsburg; lowest: –37 deg. on Dec. 30, 1917, at Lewisburg
Monthly average: highest: 85.6 deg., 35th; lowest: 23.9 deg., 33rd; spread (high to low): 61.7 deg., 39th
Hazardous waste sites (1997): 6, 44th
Endangered species: Animals: 11—Indiana bat, Virginia big-eared bat, Clubshell, American peregrine falcon, Fanshell, Ring pink mussel, Pink mucket pearlymussel, Tubercled-blossom pearlymussel, Northern riffleshell, James River spinymussel, Virginia northern flying squirrel. Plants: 4

MAJOR CITIES POPULATION, 1996 PERCENTAGE INCREASE, 1990-96

Charleston, 56,098; –2.1%
Huntington, 53,941; –1.6%
Wheeling, 33,311; –4.5%
Parkersburg, 32,766; –3.2%
Morgantown, 26,919; 4.0%

THE PEOPLE

Population (1997): 1,815,787, 35th
  Percent change (1990-97): 1.24%, 44th
  Percent of total U.S. pop.: 0.68%, 35th
  Per sq. mi: 74.94, 29th
Population (2000 proj.): 1,837,000, 37th
  Percent change (1995-2000): 0.49%, 47th
Percent in metro. area (1996): 41.83%, 43rd
Foreign born: 16,000, 47th
  Percent: 0.9%, 49th
Top three ancestries reported:
  German, 26.16%
  Irish, 19.41%
  English, 15.06%
White (1992): 1,741,000, 96.24%, 7th
Black (1992): 57,000, 3.15%, 37th
Native American (1992): 2,000, 0.11%, 51st
Asian, Pacific Isle (1992): 8,000, 0.44%, 51st
Hispanic origin (1992): 9,000, 0.50%, 51st

Percent over 5 yrs. speaking language other than English at home: 2.6%, 50th

Percent males (1996): 48.27%, 43rd; percent females: 51.73%, 8th

Percent never married: 22.2%, 47th

Marriages per 1,000 (1996): 6.06, 49th

Divorces per 1,000 (1996): 4.39, 23rd

Median age (1996): 37.7

Under 5 years (1996): 5.85%, 50th

18 years and under (1996): 26.22%, 47th

65 years and over (1996): 15.21%, 4th

Percent increase among the elderly (1995-96): 0.19%, 42nd

OF VITAL IMPORTANCE

Live births per 1,000 pop. (1996): 11.3, 50th

Infant mortality rate per 1,000 live births (1995): 7.9, 18th

Rate for whites: 7.6, 4th

Rate for blacks: NA

Births to unmarried women, % of total (1996): 31.4%, 25th

Births to teenage mothers, % of total (1996): 16.8%, 8th

Abortions (1992): 3,140, 45th

Rate per 1,000 women 14-44 years old: 7.7, 48th

Percent change (1988-92): 2%, 10th

Average lifetime (1989-91): 74.26, 44th

Total death rate per 100,000 pop. (1995): 1,107.0, 2nd

Accidents and adverse effects: 40.4, 21st

Alzheimer's disease: 8.6, 26th

Cancer: 259.4, 3rd

Cerebrovascular diseases: 67.9, 19th

Chronic liver disease and cirrhosis: 11.0, 9th

Chronic obstructive pulmonary diseases and allied conditions: 60.0, 1st

Diabetes mellitus: 32.8, 3rd

Diseases of heart: 378.9, 1st

HIV infection: 4.3, 42nd

Homicide: 5.5, 30th

Injury by firearms: 16.6, 12th

Motor vehicle accidents: 21.2, 15th

Pneumonia and influenza: 33.9, 16th

Suicide: 15.1, 12th

KEEPING WELL

Active nonfederal physicians per 100,000 pop. (1995): 196, 33rd

Dentists per 100,000 (1991): 45, 42nd

Nurses per 100,000 (1995): 793, 33rd

Hospitals per 100,000 (1995): 3.23, 12th

Admissions per 1,000 (1995): 148.25, 4th

Hospital beds per 1,000 (1995): 4.43, 7th

Occupancy rate per 100 beds (1995): 60.49, 27th

Average cost per patient per day (1995): $763, 39th

Average cost per stay (1995): $4,974, 46th

AIDS cases (new, 1996): 121; per 100,000: 6.6, 39th

Persons living with HIV infection, not yet AIDS (1996): 388

Other notifiable diseases, per 100,000 pop.:

Gonorrhea (1995): 47.0, 39th

Syphilis (1995): 3.6, 37th

Tuberculosis (1996): 3.1, 35th

Pop. without health insur. (1996): 14.9%, 21st

HOUSEHOLDS BY TYPE

Total households (1996): 714,000, 34th

Percent change (1990-96): 3.7%, 41st

Per 1,000 pop. (1996) 391.02, 4th

Percent of householders 65 yrs. and over (1996): 26.19%, 3rd

Persons per household (1996): 2.50, 46th

Family households: 500,259

Percent of total: 72.65%, 11th

Nonfamily households: 188,298

Percent of total: 27.35%, 41st

Pop. living in group quarters: 36,911

Percent of pop.: 2.06%, 48th

LIVING QUARTERS

Total housing units: 781,295

Persons per unit: 2.30, 41st

Occupied housing units: 688,557

Percent of total units: 88.13%, 34th

Persons per unit: 2.48, 37th

Percent of units with over 1 person per room: 1.91%, 44th

Owner-occupied units: 510,058

Percent of total units: 65.28%, 1st

Percent of occupied units: 74.08%, 1st

Persons per unit: 2.63, 44th

Median value: $47,900, 47th

Renter-occupied units: 178,499

Percent of total units: 22.85%, 51st

Percent of occupied units: 25.92%, 51st

Persons per unit: 2.33, 28th

Median contract rent: $221, 49th

Rental vacancy rate: 10.1%, 15th

Mobile home, trailer & other as a percent of occupied housing units: 18.61%, 6th

Persons in emergency shelters for homeless persons: 451, 0.025%, 49th

Persons visible in street locations: 33, 0.0018%, 46th

Nursing home population: 12,591, 0.70%, 27th

CRIME INDEX PER 100,000 (1996)

Total reported: 2,483.4, 51st
  Percent increase: 1.0%, 9th
  Violent: 210.1, 45th
    Percent increase: 0.0%, 11th
    Murder & nonnegligent manslaughter: 3.8, 37th
    Forcible rape: 19.6, 51st
    Aggravated assault: 146.3, 43rd
    Robbery: 40.4, 43rd
  Property: 2,273.3, 51st
    Percent increase: 1.1%, 10th
    Burglary: 546.5, 49th
    Larceny-theft: 1,549.8, 51st
    Motor vehicle theft: 176.9, 46th

TEACHING AND LEARNING

Pop. 3 and over enrolled in school (1996): 389,475, 37th
  Percent of pop.: 21.33%, 44th
Public elementary & secondary schools (1996-97): 877, 36th
  Total enrollment (1996): 303,441, 36th
    Percent of school age pop.: 96.33%, 5th
    Percent of total pop.: 16.62%, 35th
  Teachers (1996): 20,642, 34th
    Percent of pop.: 1.13%, 17th
  Pupil/teacher ratio (1995): 14.6, 43rd
  Teachers' avg. salary (1996-97): $33,159, 35th
  Expenditure per capita (1992-93): $1,323.61, 25th
    Education as % of state govt. expenditures: 37.9%, 10th
  Expenditure per pupil (1994-95): $6,107, 19th
    Percent increase (1993-94 & 1994-95): 6.90%, 5th
Percent at or above grade level, NAEP tests:
  Reading, grade 4 (1994): 26%, 23rd
  Math, grade 4 (1996): 63%, 25th
  Math, grade 8 (1996): 54%, 29th
Percent of graduates taking SAT (1995): 17%, 30th
  Mean SAT verbal scores: 448, 25th
  Mean SAT mathematical scores: 484, 31st
Percent of graduates taking ACT (1997): 57%, 24th
  Mean ACT scores: 20.0, 45th

Percent of pop. over 25 completing:
  Less than 9th grade: 16.8%, 2nd
  High school: 66.0%, 49th
  College degree(s): 12.3%, 51st
Higher education, institutions (1996): 28, 38th
  Enrollment (1995-96): 86,034, 37th
    Percent increase in enroll. (1990-95): 1.5%, 32nd
  White non-Hispanic (1995): 79,347, 35th
    Percent of enroll.: 92.23%, 3rd
  Total minority enroll. (1995): 4,961, 43rd
    Percent of enroll.: 5.77%, 49th
  Black non-Hispanic (1995): 3,395, 37th
    Percent of enroll.: 3.95%, 32nd
  Hispanic (1995): 469, 48th
    Percent of enroll.: 0.55%, 49th
  Asian/Pacific Islander (1995): 900, 43rd
    Percent of enroll.: 1.05%, 45th
  American Indian/AK native (1995): 197, 50th
    Percent of enroll.: 0.23%, 50th
  Nonresident alien (1995): 1,726, 41st
    Percent of enroll.: 2.01%, 42nd
  Female (1995): 47,995, 37th
    Percent of enroll.: 55.79%, 28th
  Pub. institutions (1995-96): 16, 37th
    Enrollment: 74,857, 37th
      Percent increase in enrollment (1990-95): 1%, 31st
    Percent of enroll.: 87.01%, 14th
  Private institutions (1995-96): 12, 38th
    Enrollment: 11,177, 41st
      Percent increase in enrollment (1990-95): 4.6%, 26th
    Percent of enroll.: 12.99%, 38th
  Tuition (in state), public 4-year institution (1996-97): $2,088, 40th
  Tuition (in state), public 2-year institution (1996-97): $1,376, 26th
  Tuition, private 4-year institution (1996-97): $10,805, 28th
Public library systems (1994): 97, 29th
  Books & serial vol. per capita: 2.5, 31st
  Library visits per capita: 3.4, 28th
  Circulation per capita: 4.6, 40th

LAW ENFORCEMENT AND CORRECTIONS

Police protection and corrections expenditures (1996): $121,314,000
  Per capita: $66.40, 49th
Police per 10,000 pop. (1996): 19.35, 35th

Prisoners (1 year or more) per 100,000 pop. (1996): 150, 47th
  Percent change (1995-96): 9.9%, 15th
  Percent of inmates that are female: 5.4%, 37th
    Percent change: 14.7%, 16th
Death penalty: no

RELIGION, NUMBER AND PERCENT OF POPULATION

Agnostic: 2,700—0.20%, 42nd
Buddhist: 1,350—0.10%, 17th
Christian: 1,167,664—86.50%, 24th
Hindu: 1,350—0.10%, 10th
Jewish: 1,350—0.10%, 43rd
Muslim: 1,350—0.10%, 22nd
Unitarian: 1,350—0.10%, 31st
Other: 39,147—2.90%, 1st
None: 107,992—8.00%, 15th
Refused to answer: 25,648—1.90%, 31st

MAKING A LIVING

Personal income per capita (1996): $18,444, 50th
  Percent increase (1995-96): 2.0%, 43rd
Disposable personal income per capita (1996): $16,494, 49th
Median income of households (average, 1995-96): $25,431, 51st
Percent of pop. below poverty level (1995-96): 17.6%, 6th

ECONOMY

In civilian labor force (1996): 808,000
  Percent of total pop.: 55.6%, 51st
  Percent of total pop. 65 years and over: 7.8%, 42nd
  Percent of total female pop.: 47.7%, 51st
Major employer industries (total nonagricultural, 1996):
  Construction: 34,300—4.9%, 19th
  Finance, insurance, & real estate: 27,100—3.9%, 49th
  Government: 138,800—19.9%, 12th
  Manufacturing: 81,900—11.7%, 36th
  Service: 191,300—27.4%, 24th
  Trade: 160,100—22.9%, 37th
  Transportation, communications, public utilities: 39,200—5.6%, 18th
Unemployment rate (1996): 7.5%, 4th
  Male: 8.3%, 4th
  Female: 6.6%, 7th
Total businesses (1995): 40,599, 37th
New business incorps. (1995): 2,535
  Percent of total businesses: 6.24%, 46th
Business failures (1995): 287
  Failures per 10,000 businesses: 70.7, 37th

Agriculture farm income:
  Marketing (1996): $388,170,000, 46th
    Average per farm: $19,409, 50th
  Leading products (1997): Cattle, broilers, dairy products, turkeys, apples, peaches, hay, tobacco, corn, wheat, oats
  Average value land & build. per acre (1997): $1,000, 32nd
    Percent increase (1996-97): 4%, 35th
  Govt. payments (1996): $4,538,000, 41st
    Average per farm: $227, 48th
Construction, value of all (1996): $1,232,476,000, 40th
  Per capita: $675, 50th
Manufactures (1995):
  Value added: $8,947,700,000
    Per capita: $4,894, 40th
  Leading products (1997): Machinery, plastic & hardwood products, fabricated metals, chemicals, aluminum, steel, automotive parts
Value of nonfuel mineral production (1996): $191,000,000, 39th
Leading mineral products (1996): Coal, natural gas, petroleum, stone, cement, sand/gravel, lime, salt
Energy consumption per person (1994): 448.1 mil. Btu, 6th
Retail sales (1995): $13,616,000,000
  Per household: $19,197, 50th
  Sales increase (1994-95): 4.3%, 27th
Tourism revenues (1992): $2.6 bil.
Foreign exports, in total value (1996): $2,169,000,000, 36th
  Per capita: $1,188, 35th
Gross state product per person (1994): $19,020, 50th
Public aid recipients (percent of resident pop. 1994): 9.6%, 6th
Medicaid recipients (percent of pop., 1995): 21.3%, 3rd
Medicare enrollment per 1,000 pop. (1996): 182, 4th

TRAVEL AND TRANSPORTATION

Motor vehicle registrations (1996): 1,406,285, 37th
  Per 1,000 pop.: 772.51, 33rd
Motorcycle registrations (1996): 16,075, 47th
  Per 1,000 pop.: 11.43, 44th
Licensed drivers (1996): 1,304,539, 34th
  Per 1,000 pop.: 714.72, 11th
Public roads & streets (1996)
  Total mileage: 35,130, 39th
    Per 1,000 pop.: 119.24, 23rd

Rural mileage: 31,953, 38th
  Per 1,000 pop.: 17.50, 22nd
Urban mileage: 3,177, 40th
  Per 1,000 pop.: 1.74, 50th
Interstate mileage: 550, 39th
  Per 1,000 pop.: 0.30, 12th
Speed limit (max. interstate, autos, mi. per hr., 1997): 70
Annual vehicle-mi. of travel per driver (1996): 13,883, 29th
Mean travel time for workers age 16+ who work away from home: 21.0 min., 23rd

GOVERNMENT

Percent of voting age pop. registered (1996): 68.51%, 42nd
  Percent of voting age pop. voting for president: (1996): 45.0%, 44th
  Percent of voting age pop. voting for U.S. representatives (1996): 36.9%, 47th
State legislators, total (1997): 134, 32nd
  Women members (1997): 21
    Percent of legislature: 16%, 39th
U.S. Congress, House members (1998): 3
  Change (1988-98): –1
Revenues (1996):
  State govt.: $6,866,159,000

Per capita: $3,760.22, 20th
  Parimutuel & amusement taxes & lotteries, revenue per capita (1995): $88.92, 26th
Expenditures (1996):
  State govt.: $6,969,795,000
    Per capita: $3,816.97, 11th
Debt outstanding (1996): $2,830,217,000
  Per capita: $1,549.95, 21st

LAWS AND REGULATIONS

Legal driving age: 18, 16 if completed driver education course
Marriage age without parental consent: 18
Divorce residence requirement: 1 yr., for qualifications check local statutes

ATTRACTIONS (1997)

Major symphony orchestras: 1
Per capita spending by the NEA (1997): $0.26, 28th
State Fair during late August at Lewisburg (Fairlea)

SPORTS AND COMPETITION

NCAA (Division I) football and basketball teams: Marshall Univ. Thundering Herd, West Virginia Univ. Mountaineers

WEBSITES CONTAINING FURTHER INFORMATION

West Virginia K-12 Home Page   http://access.K12.wv.us

WISCONSIN

"Wisconsin is the soul of a great people. She manifests the spirit of the conqueror, whose strength has subdued the forest, quickened the soil, harnessed the forces of Nature and multiplied production. From her abundance she served food to the world."

Fred L. Holmes, author

Wisconsin is a state of progress and leadership in many areas. Spurred by Robert La Follette, the state pioneered in progressive social legislation. It leads the nation in number of milk cows, in production of milk, and in value of milk products. It also produces 40% of the nation's cheese and 20% of its butter. But manufacturing is Wisconsin's chief industry. It is a leader in the manufacturing of machinery and produces more paper than any other state. The state's nickname (the Badger State) began with a group of burrowing miners—all adding to the state's many contrasts.

SUPERLATIVES

- First U.S. kindergarten—opened by Mrs. Carl Schurz in Watertown, 1865.
- Pioneer in social legislation.
- Leads nation in dairy and paper products.
- Smallest city with a major pro football team—the Green Bay Packers.
- World's oldest continuously operating radio station—WHA, in Madison.

MOMENTS IN HISTORY

- In 1634, French explorer Jean Nicolet became the first European in the area.
- Pierre Esprit Radisson and Medart Chouart, Sieur de Groseillier, explored in 1654-56, opening the area to fur trade.

So They Say

"I liked noe country as I have that wherein we wintered Washington Island, Wisconsin; for whatever a man could desire was to be had in great plenty; viz. staggs, fishes in abundance, and all sort of meat, corne enough."

Explorer Pierre Esprit Radisson, in later memoirs

- After crossing the state and pioneering a route from the east, on June 17, 1673, the explorers Father Jacques Marquette and Louis Jolliet discovered the long-sought upper reaches of the Mississippi River at the mouth of the Wisconsin River.

So They Say

As he marveled at the Mississippi's great flow, Father Marquette felt "...a joy that I cannot express."

- Daniel Greysolon, Sieur de Lhut, in 1678 explored the western end of Lake Superior and claimed the land in the name of France.
- With the 1763 Treaty of Paris, the British gained control.
- Augustin Monet de Langlade founded Green Bay in 1764, a thriving fur trading post and the first permanent European settlement.
- Prairie du Chien was founded in 1781 on the site of a large Indian village.
- The 1783 Treaty of Paris gave the area to the United States, but the British continued to claim the region until after the War of 1812.
- By 1822 lead mining was in full swing in southwest Wisconsin. Many miners burrowed into the hillside like badgers, giving the "Badger State" its nickname.
- During the Black Hawk War, Chief Black Hawk fled into Wisconsin. On August 2, 1832, the Battle of Bad Axe ended the war. Trying to escape across the Mississippi River, many of the men, women, and children were massacred.

So They Say

"Bad, and cruel, as our people were treated by the whites, not one of them was hurt or molested by any of my band...This is a lesson worthy for the white man to learn...." **Chief Black Hawk**

- In 1835 the first steamboat arrived at the trading port that became Milwaukee.
- Madison was selected as the territorial capital in 1836, although still wilderness.
- After it became the 30th state on May 29, 1848, Wisconsin attracted waves of Scandinavian, German, and other immigrants.

- In 1851 the first train chugged over new tracks from Milwaukee to Waukesha.
- In 1856 at Watertown, Mrs. Carl Schurz opened the first kindergarten to be operated in America, basing the effort on her experience in German kindergartens.
- The October 8, 1871, forest fire devastated the lumber town of Peshtigo, killing nearly 1,200.
- In 1890, Stephen M. Babcock developed a machine and method of testing the amount of butterfat in milk, giving a new boost to the "Dairy State."
- Robert M. La Follette became the first native-born governor of Wisconsin in 1901, bringing many widely copied reforms.
- In 1904 fire partially destroyed the statehouse. The third capitol in Madison, the present one, was built between 1906 and 1917, as the state mobilized for World War I.
- In 1919, as a result of careful and scientific development, Wisconsin took the lead in milk and milk products and has been among the top-ranking dairy states ever since.
- During the Great Depression of the 1930s, Wisconsin passed the first unemployment compensation legislation.
- The Depression squeeze on dairy workers sparked the state's milk strikes of 1934, and thousands of gallons of milk were dumped in protest of conditions.
- The baseball Braves came to Milwaukee in 1953 and won the World Series in 1957. (They moved on to Atlanta in 1966.)
- The opening of the St. Lawrence Seaway in 1959 brought many benefits to Wisconsin's ports.
- The 1992 Wautoma tornado cut through the city, causing two deaths and heavy property damage.

THAT'S INTERESTING

- Believing that he had reached China and the Far East, Jean Nicolet stepped ashore near the Winnebago village of Red Bank, shooting pistols and wearing embroidered Chinese silk robes, to the astonishment of the Indians.
- Prairie du Chien (Prairie of the Dog) was named for Chief Alim, a prominent Indian whose native name means Dog.
- During the early 1800s, Wisconsin was a frontier. There were gunfights and gang brawls, and a social evening usually consisted of relaxing in the "lighthouses"—as the saloons were

called—drinking "fusel oil" or "forty-rod," playing poker for a month's wages, or watching a horse race or a wolf fight.

- German settlers came to Milwaukee and eastern Wisconsin in large numbers. They brought with them many of their customs, including the Christmas tree and other holiday traditions that have spread over the rest of the country.
- Christopher Latham Sholes developed one of the world's most important inventions. After making 25 different models and spending six years perfecting his idea, he introduced the first practical commercial typewriter.
- Green Bay is the oldest permanent European settlement in the state. It is also the smallest city in the nation to boast its own major league football team—the Green Bay Packers.
- A group called the Phalanx was organized near Ripon as a community, with all property held in the name of the group. Members lived in one long house and ate at one long table. The venture was notable for its financial success. Before many years, it had grown so rich that its members decided to disband and divide the profits.

So They Say

"So she's young and poor, is she. Well that's nothing agin' her....You may tell her she can come."

Abraham Lincoln, on agreeing to sit for his sculpture by Vinnie Ream Hoxie, Madison native and first woman sculptor commissioned by Congress

---

NOTABLE NATIVES

Carrie Chapman Catt (Ripon, 1859-1947), social reformer. **Zona Gale** (Portage, 1874-1938), author. **Hamlin Garland** (West Salem, 1860-1940), author. **King Camp Gillette** (Fond du Lac, 1855-1932), industrialist. **Vinnie Ream Hoxie** (Madison, 1847-1914), sculptor. **Robert Marion La Follette** (Primrose, 1855-1925), political leader. **William Hubbs Rehnquist** (Milwaukee, 1924-), chief justice of the United States. **Spencer Tracy** (Milwaukee, 1900-1967), actor. **George Orson Welles** (Kenosha, 1915-1985), director/actor. **James Walsh** (Two Rivers, 1859-1933), public official. **Thornton Niven Wilder** (Madison, 1897-1975), author/playwright. **Thomas Frank Lloyd Wright** (Richland Center, 1867-1959), architect.

GENERAL

Admitted to statehood: May 29, 1848

Origin of name: An Indian name, spelled *Ouisconsin* and *Mesconsing* by the early chroniclers. Believed to mean "grassy place" in Chippewa. Congress made it *Wisconsin*

Capital: Madison

Nickname: Badger State

Motto: Forward

Animal: Badger

Bird: Robin

Insect: Honeybee

Fish: Muskellunge

Flower: Wood violet

Mineral: Galena

Stone: Red granite

Song: "On, Wisconsin!"

Tree: Sugar maple

THE LAND

Area: 65,500 sq. mi., 22nd
    Land: 54,314 sq. mi., 25th
    Water: 11,186 sq. mi., 3rd
        Inland water: 1,831 sq. mi., 11th
        Great Lakes: 9,355 sq. mi., 2nd

Topography: Narrow Lake Superior lowland plain met by Northern highland, which slopes gently to the sandy crescent central plain; Western upland in the SW; three broad parallel limestone ridges running N-S are separated by wide and shallow lowland in the SE

Number of counties: 72

Geographic center: Wood, 9 mi. SE of Marshfield

Length: 310 mi.; width: 260 mi.

Highest point: 1,951 ft. (Timms Hill), 39th

Lowest point: 581 ft. (Lake Michigan), 41st

Mean elevation: 1,050 ft., 24th

CLIMATE AND ENVIRONMENT

Temp., highest: 114 deg. on July 13, 1936, at Wisconsin Dells; lowest: –54 deg. on Jan. 24, 1922, at Danbury

Monthly average: highest: 82.8 deg., 44th; lowest: 5.4 deg., 5th; spread (high to low): 77.4 deg., 10th

Hazardous waste sites (1997): 39, 8th

Endangered species: Animals: 8—Karner blue butterfly, Hine's emerald dragonfly, American peregrine falcon, Winged mapleleaf mussel, Higgins' eye pearlymussel, Piping plover, Kirtland's warbler, Gray wolf. Plants: 0

MAJOR CITIES POPULATION, 1996 PERCENTAGE INCREASE, 1990-96

Milwaukee, 590,503; –6.0%

Madison, 197,630; 3.6%

Green Bay, 102,076; 5.8%

Kenosha, 86,888; 8.0%

Racine, 82,572; –2.0%

THE PEOPLE

Population (1997): 5,169,677, 18th
    Percent change (1990-97): 5.68%, 31st
    Percent of total U.S. pop.: 1.93%, 18th
    Per sq. mi: 78.92, 26th

Population (2000 proj.): 5,325,000, 18th
    Percent change (1995-2000): 3.94%, 33rd

Percent in metro. area (1996): 67.74%, 30th

Foreign born: 122,000, 20th
    Percent: 2.5%, 31st

Top three ancestries reported:
    German, 53.78%
    Irish, 12.51%
    Polish, 10.34%

White (1992): 4,625,000, 92.63%, 16th

Black (1992): 263,000, 5.27%, 30th

Native American (1992): 42,000, 0.84%, 19th

Asian, Pacific Isle (1992): 62,000, 1.24%, 27th

Hispanic origin (1992): 102,000, 2.04%, 31st

Percent over 5 yrs. speaking language other than English at home: 5.8%, 31st

Percent males (1996): 49.20%, 21st; percent females: 50.80%, 31st

Percent never married: 27.1%, 18th

Marriages per 1,000 (1996): 7.02, 43rd

Divorces per 1,000 (1996): 3.36, 36th

Median age (1996): 35.1

Under 5 years (1996): 6.58%, 39th

18 years and under (1996): 28.92%, 21st

65 years and over (1996): 13.29%, 21st

Percent increase among the elderly (1995-96): 0.62%, 29th

OF VITAL IMPORTANCE

Live births per 1,000 pop. (1996): 13.0, 42nd

Infant mortality rate per 1,000 live births (1995): 7.3, 30th
    Rate for whites: 6.3, 24th
    Rate for blacks: 18.6, 4th

Births to unmarried women, % of total (1996): 27.4%, 38th

Births to teenage mothers, % of total (1996): 10.6%, 36th

Abortions (1992): 15,450, 25th
  Rate per 1,000 women 14-44 years old: 13.6, 37th
  Percent change (1988-92): −15%, 38th
Average lifetime (1989-91): 76.87, 11th
Total death rate per 100,000 pop. (1995): 880.1, 30th
  Accidents and adverse effects: 35.6, 29th
  Alzheimer's disease: 10.2, 10th
  Cancer: 206.3, 28th
  Cerebrovascular diseases: 69.8, 14th
  Chronic liver disease and cirrhosis: 6.9, 42nd
  Chronic obstructive pulmonary diseases and allied conditions: 36.7, 36th
  Diabetes mellitus: 21.6, 34th
  Diseases of heart: 281.4, 26th
  HIV infection: 4.3, 42nd
  Homicide: 4.7, 36th
  Injury by firearms: 10.1, 38th
  Motor vehicle accidents: 15.1, 33rd
  Pneumonia and influenza: 33.1, 20th
  Suicide: 12.1, 26th

KEEPING WELL

Active nonfederal physicians per 100,000 pop. (1995): 213, 25th
Dentists per 100,000 (1991): 62, 16th
Nurses per 100,000 (1995): 882, 19th
Hospitals per 100,000 (1995): 2.48, 20th
  Admissions per 1,000 (1995): 107.36, 35th
  Hospital beds per 1,000 (1995): 3.32, 27th
  Occupancy rate per 100 beds (1995): 60.59, 25th
  Average cost per patient per day (1995): $794, 38th
  Average cost per stay (1995): $5,679, 28th
AIDS cases (new, 1996): 270; per 100,000: 5.2, 43rd
Persons living with HIV infection, not yet AIDS (1996): 1,908
Other notifiable diseases, per 100,000 pop.:
  Gonorrhea (1995): 107.8, 26th
  Syphilis (1995): 11.3, 26th
  Tuberculosis (1996): 2.2, 43rd
Pop. without health insur. (1996): 8.4%, 51st

HOUSEHOLDS BY TYPE

Total households (1996): 1,943,000, 18th
  Percent change (1990-96): 6.6%, 31st
  Per 1,000 pop. (1996) 376.55, 32nd
  Percent of householders 65 yrs. and over (1996): 22.23%, 22nd
  Persons per household (1996): 2.61, 20th

Family households: 1,275,172
  Percent of total: 69.98%, 30th
Nonfamily households: 546,946
  Percent of total: 30.02%, 22nd
Pop. living in group quarters: 133,598
  Percent of pop.: 2.73%, 26th

LIVING QUARTERS

Total housing units: 2,055,774
  Persons per unit: 2.38, 31st
Occupied housing units: 1,822,118
  Percent of total units: 88.63%, 31st
  Persons per unit: 2.53, 24th
  Percent of units with over 1 person per room: 2.10%, 41st
Owner-occupied units: 1,215,350
  Percent of total units: 59.12%, 25th
  Percent of occupied units: 66.70%, 28th
  Persons per unit: 2.79, 15th
  Median value: $62,500, 30th
Renter-occupied units: 606,768
  Percent of total units: 29.52%, 25th
  Percent of occupied units: 33.30%, 24th
  Persons per unit: 2.26, 38th
  Median contract rent: $331, 26th
  Rental vacancy rate: 4.7%, 51st
Mobile home, trailer & other as a percent of occupied housing units: 7.10%, 36th
Persons in emergency shelters for homeless persons: 1,555, 0.032%, 47th
Persons visible in street locations: 71, 0.0015%, 48th
Nursing home population: 50,345, 1.03%, 8th

CRIME INDEX PER 100,000 (1996)

Total reported: 3,821.4, 42nd
  Percent increase: −1.7%, 21st
  Violent: 252.7, 43rd
    Percent increase: −10.1%, 35th
    Murder & nonnegligent manslaughter: 4.0, 34th
    Forcible rape: 21.0, 48th
    Aggravated assault: 131.1, 44th
    Robbery: 96.6, 36th
  Property: 3,568.7, 40th
    Percent increase: −1.0%, 22nd
    Burglary: 588.3, 44th
    Larceny-theft: 2,634.5, 35th
    Motor vehicle theft: 345.9, 35th

TEACHING AND LEARNING

Pop. 3 and over enrolled in school (1996): 1,184,961, 16th
  Percent of pop.: 22.96%, 22nd

Public elementary & secondary schools (1996-97): 2,037, 13th
  Total enrollment (1996): 884,738, 17th
    Percent of school age pop.: 87.95%, 42nd
    Percent of total pop.: 17.15%, 28th
  Teachers (1996): 55,296, 16th
    Percent of pop.: 1.07%, 26th
  Pupil/teacher ratio (1995): 15.8, 32nd
  Teachers' avg. salary (1996-97): $38,950, 15th
  Expenditure per capita (1992-93): $1,590.24, 8th
    Education as % of state govt. expenditures: 37.5%, 14th
  Expenditure per pupil (1994-95): $6,930, 12th
    Percent increase (1993-94 & 1994-95): 3.17%, 34th
Percent at or above grade level, NAEP tests:
  Reading, grade 4 (1994): 35%, 6th
  Math, grade 4 (1996): 74%, 5th
  Math, grade 8 (1996): 75%, 5th
Percent of graduates taking SAT (1995): 9%, 38th
  Mean SAT verbal scores: 501, 7th
  Mean SAT mathematical scores: 572, 4th
Percent of graduates taking ACT (1997): 64%, 17th
  Mean ACT scores: 22.3, 2nd
Percent of pop. over 25 completing:
  Less than 9th grade: 9.5%, 24th
  High school: 78.6%, 21st
  College degree(s): 17.7%, 36th
Higher education, institutions (1996): 66, 18th
  Enrollment (1995-96): 300,223, 14th
    Percent increase in enroll. (1990-95): 0.1%, 38th
    White non-Hispanic (1995): 265,457, 11th
      Percent of enroll.: 88.42%, 14th
    Total minority enroll. (1995): 27,864, 29th
      Percent of enroll.: 9.28%, 38th
    Black non-Hispanic (1995): 12,670, 25th
      Percent of enroll.: 4.22%, 31st
    Hispanic (1995): 6,283, 18th
      Percent of enroll.: 2.09%, 29th
    Asian/Pacific Islander (1995): 6,452, 21st
      Percent of enroll.: 2.15%, 29th
    American Indian/AK native (1995): 2,459, 17th
      Percent of enroll.: 0.82%, 23rd
    Nonresident alien (1995): 6,902, 21st
      Percent of enroll.: 2.30%, 33rd
    Female (1995): 167,856, 14th
      Percent of enroll.: 55.91%, 26th
  Pub. institutions (1995-96): 30, 21st
    Enrollment: 245,770, 15th
      Percent increase in enrollment (1990-95): –3.1%, 40th
      Percent of enroll.: 81.86%, 28th
  Private institutions (1995-96): 36, 19th
    Enrollment: 54,453, 19th
      Percent increase in enrollment (1990-95): 17.7%, 9th
      Percent of enroll.: 18.14%, 24th
  Tuition (in state), public 4-year institution (1996-97): $2,747, 22nd
  Tuition (in state), public 2-year institution (1996-97): $1,942, 13th
  Tuition, private 4-year institution (1996-97): $12,492, 19th
Public library systems (1994): 381, 6th
  Books & serial vol. per capita: 3.2, 22nd
  Library visits per capita: 5.2, 6th
  Circulation per capita: 8.7, 10th

LAW ENFORCEMENT AND CORRECTIONS

Police protection and corrections expenditures (1996): $574,295,000
  Per capita: $111.30, 26th
Police per 10,000 pop. (1996): 23.31, 19th
Prisoners (1 year or more) per 100,000 pop. (1996): 230, 39th
  Percent change (1995-96): 15.4%, 2nd
  Percent of inmates that are female: 5.2%, 40th
    Percent change: 32.1%, 4th
Death penalty: no

RELIGION, NUMBER AND PERCENT OF POPULATION

Agnostic: 10,808—0.30%, 37th
Buddhist: 10,808—0.30%, 8th
Christian: 3,249,714—90.20%, 10th
Hindu: NA
Jewish: 14,411—0.40%, 31st
Muslim: 7,206—0.20%, 13th
Unitarian: 7,206—0.20%, 23rd
Other: 28,822—0.80%, 37th
None: 219,770—6.10%, 31st
Refused to answer: 54,042—1.50%, 42nd

MAKING A LIVING

Personal income per capita (1996): $23,269, 24th
  Percent increase (1995-96): 3.1%, 26th

Disposable personal income per capita (1996): $19,858, 26th

Median income of households (average, 1995-96): $41,082, 7th

Percent of pop. below poverty level (1995-96): 8.7%, 46th

ECONOMY

In civilian labor force (1996): 2,918,000
Percent of total pop.: 74.7%, 1st
Percent of total pop. 65 years and over: 14.9%, 8th
Percent of total female pop.: 69.6%, 1st
Major employer industries (total nonagricultural, 1996):
Construction: 105,300—4.0%, 36th
Finance, insurance, & real estate: 138,300—5.3%, 22nd
Government: 383,200—14.7%, 41st
Manufacturing: 601,200—23.1%, 4th
Service: 655,400—25.2%, 40th
Trade: 595,200—22.9%, 37th
Transportation, communications, public utilities: 120,700—4.6%, 38th
Unemployment rate (1996): 3.5%, 47th
Male: 3.8%, 45th
Female: 3.2%, 47th
Total businesses (1995): 133,238, 17th
New business incorps. (1995): 8,818
Percent of total businesses: 6.62%, 42nd
Business failures (1995): 1,140
Failures per 10,000 businesses: 85.6, 21st
Agriculture farm income:
Marketing (1996): $6,061,542,000, 10th
Average per farm: $76,728, 34th
Leading products (1997): Dairy products, cattle, corn, hogs, canned & frozen vegetables
Average value land & build. per acre (1997): $1,250, 26th
Percent increase (1996-97): 6%, 20th
Govt. payments (1996): $156,849,000, 19th
Average per farm: $1,985, 28th
Construction, value of all (1996): $5,993,948,000, 22nd
Per capita: $1,162, 28th
Manufactures (1995):
Value added: $50,988,900,000
Per capita: $9,953, 3rd
Leading products (1997): Food products, motor vehicles & equipment, paper products, medical instruments & supplies, printing, plastics
Value of nonfuel mineral production (1996): $399,000,000, 33rd

Leading mineral products (1996): Stone, sand/gravel, copper, lime

Energy consumption per person (1994): 337.3 mil. Btu, 27th

Retail sales (1995): $41,473,000,000
Per household: $25,738, 13th
Sales increase (1994-95): 6.7%, 16th
Tourism revenues (1995): $6.1 bil.
Foreign exports, in total value (1996): $9,504,000,000, 18th
Per capita: $1,842, 19th
Gross state product per person (1994): $24,661, 25th
Public aid recipients (percent of resident pop. 1994): 6.5%, 28th
Medicaid recipients (percent of pop., 1995): 9.0%, 45th
Medicare enrollment per 1,000 pop. (1996): 149, 20th

TRAVEL AND TRANSPORTATION

Motor vehicle registrations (1996): 3,971,550, 18th
Per 1,000 pop.: 771.74, 34th
Motorcycle registrations (1996): 169,594, 6th
Per 1,000 pop.: 42.70, 3rd
Licensed drivers (1996): 3,601,619, 17th
Per 1,000 pop.: 703.15, 15th
Public roads & streets (1996)
Total mileage: 111,435, 15th
Per 1,000 pop.: 121.60, 21st
Rural mileage: 95,453, 8th
Per 1,000 pop.: 18.50, 20th
Urban mileage: 15,982, 20th
Per 1,000 pop.: 3.10, 24th
Interstate mileage: 745, 31st
Per 1,000 pop.: 0.14, 36th
Speed limit (max. interstate, autos, mi. per hr., 1997): 65
Annual vehicle-mi. of travel per driver (1996): 14,175, 27th
Mean travel time for workers age 16+ who work away from home: 18.3 min., 41st

GOVERNMENT

Percent of voting age pop. registered (1996): NA
Percent of voting age pop. voting for president: (1996): 57.4%, 11th
Percent of voting age pop. voting for U.S. representatives (1996): 56.2%, 9th
State legislators, total (1997): 132, 33rd
Women members (1997): 31
Percent of legislature: 23%, 24th

U.S. Congress, House members (1998): 9
  Change (1988-98): 0
Revenues (1996):
  State govt.: $25,072,066,000
    Per capita: $ 4,858.93, 6th
    Parimutuel & amusement taxes & lotteries,
      revenue per capita (1995): $97.59, 24th
Expenditures (1996):
  State govt.: $16,989,913,000
    Per capita: $3,292.62, 21st
Debt outstanding (1996): $9,126,746,000
  Per capita: $1,768.75, 17th

LAWS AND REGULATIONS

Legal driving age: 18, 16 if completed driver
  education course
Marriage age without parental consent: 18
Divorce residence requirement: 6 mo.

ATTRACTIONS (1997)

Major opera companies: 2
Major symphony orchestras: 1
Major dance companies: 1
Major professional theater companies (non-
  profit): 1
Per capita spending by the NEA (1997):
  $0.22, 34th
State Fair in early August at West Allis

SPORTS AND COMPETITION

NCAA (Division I) football and basketball
  teams: Marquette Univ. Golden Eagles
  (basketball only), Univ. of Wisconsin-
  Green Bay Phoenix (basketball only),
  Univ. of Wisconsin-Madison Badgers,
  Univ. of Wisconsin-Milwaukee Pan-
  thers (bastketball only)
Major league baseball teams: Milwaukee
  Brewers (NL Central), County Sta-
  dium
NBA basketball teams: Milwaukee Bucks,
  Bradley Center
NFL football teams: Green Bay Packers
  (NFC), Lambeau Field

WEBSITES CONTAINING FURTHER INFORMATION

State of Wisconsin Web Page	http://www.state.wi.us
Wisconsin Information and Web Sites	http://infomad.com/wisconsin
Wisconsin On-Line	http://www.wistravel.com

WYOMING

"The scenery from the 'divide' was in beautiful contrast with that of the country left behind us. Broad and grassy valleys were spread out before us, bounded by low rounded hills covered with verdure, over which ranged bands of buffalo, while little flocks of antelope bounded gracefully around us. The low bottom of the Medicine-bow, upon which we are encamped, is thickly covered with excellent grass, and the stream has an extensive fringe of willows and rose-bushes, with occasional groves of cottonwood and aspens."
Howard Stansbury, Wyoming pioneer (1852)

Small in population, rich in history, Wyoming lives up to its nickname of "the Equality State." It boasts the nation's first elected woman official, as well as the first woman governor and the greatest plainswoman of the West. It relishes such mysteries as the prehistoric Medicine Wheel. Among its notable scenic attractions, Wyoming claims the first national park (Yellowstone), the first national monument (Devils Tower), and the first national forest (Shoshone). More than 80% of its land is used for cattle grazing, and thousands of oil wells dot the prairies. To emphasize its Western past, Wyoming celebrates with one of the nation's most notable annual festivals, Frontier Days at Cheyenne.

SUPERLATIVES

- World's largest elk (wapiti) herd—Jackson Elk Refuge.
- Largest U.S. coal reserves.
- First "dude ranch"—Eaton Brothers, near Dayton.

MOMENTS IN HISTORY

- In 1743, brothers François and Louis-Joseph La Vérendrye entered the area of present-day Wyoming.
- In 1807, John Colter, the first native of the United States known to enter present-day Wyoming, discovered Yellowstone and the Tetons.
- In 1811, Wilson Price Hunt's party crossed much of the present state.
- In 1812, Robert Stuart and a group of fur traders called the Astorians returned from a trip to the Pacific Coast and crossed the Continental Divide in the vicinity of South Pass. They built the first known cabin in Wyoming.
- Wyoming's first substantial trading post was set up by Antonio Mateo in 1828, near the Powder River forks.

- In 1832 the expedition of Captain B. L. E. de Bonneville pioneered parts of the Oregon Trail and built Fort Bonneville near present-day Daniel.
- Fort Laramie, the first permanent trading post in Wyoming, was established by William Sublette and Robert Campbell in 1834. It became the first European-style community in the state.
- Sponsored by General William H. Ashley, a series of meetings known as rendezvous gathered annually in various locations from 1834 through the 1840s. These attracted a picturesque group of trappers, traders, and Indians, who traded and brawled uproariously.
- In 1843, Fort Bridger, the second permanent settlement, was established by Jim Bridger and Louis Vasquez. It served as a military post from 1858 to 1890.
- During the California gold rush, in 1850 alone, more than 60,000 people and 90,000 domestic animals crossed the state.
- A period of Indian troubles extended from about 1862 to 1868, with 1865 known as "the bloody year on the plains."

So They Say

"...All were killed. Within a small space most were found, horribly mutilated. I loaded the wagons with as many of the bodies as they could contain...the soldiers being so overcome with horror as almost unable to obey orders..."

Captain Tenadore Ten Eyck, on a bloody massacre of the 1860s

- The transcontinental railroad arrived at Cheyenne in 1867 and was completed to California two years later. Cities sprang up almost overnight.
- In 1869 the Wyoming Territory was organized. John A. Campbell, the first territorial

governor, on December 10 signed a bill giving Wyoming women the right to vote.

• In the early 1870s the first scientific party reached Yellowstone and reported on its many natural wonders.

• On March 1, 1872, Yellowstone became the first national park.

• In 1886 the University of Wyoming opened.

• Although the Wyoming population of 62,500 was not enough to qualify for statehood, on July 10, 1890, Wyoming nevertheless became a state.

• Devils Tower became the nation's first national monument in 1906.

• In 1978 the largest radio telescope in the world was built, to be operated by the University of Wyoming.

• The forest fires of 1988 swept through much of the timberland of Yellowstone National Park.

THAT'S INTERESTING

• When the Indians saw the first two white women in Wyoming, they were astonished that such pale creatures could survive the trip, and they killed the fattest dogs to prepare a feast for their guests.

• The Indian name for Bull Lake was "the lake that roars." The strange sound comes from the action of the wind on the ice.

• The prehistoric Medicine Wheel is similar to Stonehenge in England and one in the Gobi Desert. It remains a mystery to scholars.

WYOMING NOTABLES

James Bridger (Richmond, VA, 1804-1881), frontiersman/trader/scout. Martha Jane (Calamity Jane) Cannary Burk (Princeton, MO, 1852?-1903), frontierswoman. William Frederick (Buffalo Bill) Cody (Scott County, IA, 1846-1917), frontiersman/entertainer. Crazy Horse (Oglala Sioux tribe site, 1849?-1877), Indian leader. Emerson Hough (Newton, IA, 1857-1923), author. Thomas Moran (England, 1837-1926), artist. Edgar Wilson (Bill) Nye (Shirley, ME, 1850-1896), humorist. Paul Jackson Pollock (Cody, 1912-1956), artist. Red Cloud (north-central Nebraska, 1822-1909), Indian leader. Nellie Tayloe Ross (St. Joseph, MO, 1880?-1977), public official. Washakie (in Montana, 1804-1900), Indian leader. Owen Wister (Philadelphia, PA, 1860-1938), author.

GENERAL

Admitted to statehood: July 10, 1890

Origin of name: Taken from Wyoming Valley, Pennsylvania, which was the site of an Indian massacre in 1778 and became widely known from Thomas Campbell's account in the poem "Gertrude of Wyoming." The Algonquin word means "large prairie place," and the Delaware Indian word means "mountains and valleys alternating"

Capital: Cheyenne

Nickname: Equality State

Motto: Equal rights

Bird: Meadowlark

Flower: Indian paintbrush

Stone: Jade

Song: "Wyoming"

Tree: Cottonwood

THE LAND

Area: 97,819 sq. mi., 9th
   Land: 97,105 sq. mi., 9th
   Water: 714 sq. mi., 35th
      Inland water: 714 sq. mi., 30th

Topography: Eastern Great Plains rise to the foothills of the Rocky Mountains; Continental Divide crosses the state from the NW to the SE.

Number of counties: 23

Geographic center: Fremont, 58 mi. ENE of Lander

Length: 360 mi.; width: 280 mi.

Highest point: 13,804 ft. (Gannett Peak), 5th

Lowest point: 3,099 ft. (Belle Fourche River), 50th

Mean elevation: 6,700 ft., 2nd

CLIMATE AND ENVIRONMENT

Temp., highest: 114 deg. on July 12, 1900, at Basin; lowest: –66 deg. on Feb. 9, 1933, at Riverside R.S.

Monthly average: highest: 87.1 deg., 26th, lowest: 11.9 deg., 12th; spread (high to low): 75.2 deg., 15th

Hazardous waste sites (1997): 3, 46th

Endangered species: Animals: 8—Whooping crane, Kendall Warm Springs dace, American peregrine falcon, Black footed ferret, Colorado squawfish, Razorback sucker, Wyoming toad, Gray wolf. Plants: 0

MAJOR CITIES
POPULATION, 1996
PERCENTAGE INCREASE, 1990-96

Cheyenne, 53,729; 7.4%
Casper, 48,800; 4.4%
Laramie, 26,583; –0.4%
Rock Springs, 19,742; 3.6%
Gillette, 19,202; 9.4%

THE PEOPLE

Population (1997): 479,743, 51st
  Percent change (1990-97): 5.77%, 28th
  Percent of total U.S. pop.: 0.18%, 51st
  Per sq. mi: 4.90, 50th
Population (2000 proj.): 522,000, 51st
Foreign born: 8,000, 50th
  Percent change (1995-2000): 8.75%, 8th
Percent in metro. area (1996): 29.72%, 50th
  Percent: 1.7%, 37th
Foreign born: 8,000, 50th
  Percent: 0.9%, 49th
Top three ancestries reported:
  German, 34.80%
  English, 22.25%
  Irish, 16.08%
White (1992): 448,000, 96.34%, 6th
Black (1992): 4,000, 0.86%, 43rd
Native American (1992): 10,000, 2.15%, 8th
Asian, Pacific Isle (1992): 3,000, 0.65%, 42nd
Hispanic origin (1992): 27,000, 5.81%, 14th
Percent over 5 yrs. speaking language other
    than English at home: 5.7%, 33rd
Percent males (1996): 50.35%, 4th; percent
    females: 49.65%, 48th
Percent never married: 21.7%, 48th
Marriages per 1,000 (1996): 10.17, 11th
Divorces per 1,000 (1996): 6.49, 2nd
Median age (1996): 34.9
Under 5 years (1996): 6.53%, 41st
18 years and under (1996): 31.12%, 8th
65 years and over (1996): 11.22%, 43rd
Percent increase among the elderly (1995-96):
    1.77%, 9th

OF VITAL IMPORTANCE

Live births per 1,000 pop. (1996): 13.1, 41st
Infant mortality rate per 1,000 live births
    (1995): 7.7, 21st
  Rate for whites: 6.8, 16th
  Rate for blacks: NA
Births to unmarried women, % of total
    (1996): 27.0%, 40th
Births to teenage mothers, % of total (1996):
    14.4%, 17th

Abortions (1992): 460, 51st
  Per 1,000 women 14-44 years old: 4.3, 51st
  Percent change (1988-92): –16%, 41st
Average lifetime (1989-91): 76.21, 21st
Total death rate per 100,000 pop. (1995):
    774.7, 42nd
  Accidents and adverse effects: 50.0, 5th
  Alzheimer's disease: 9.4, 16th
  Cancer: 186.6, 41st
  Cerebrovascular diseases: 55.8, 36th
  Chronic liver disease and cirrhosis: 12.5,
    6th
  Chronic obstructive pulmonary diseases and
    allied conditions: 55.4, 2nd
  Diabetes mellitus: 22.1, 31st
  Diseases of heart: 203.3, 46th
  HIV infection: NA
  Homicide: NA
  Injury by firearms: 15.0, 21st
  Motor vehicle accidents: 27.1, 2nd
  Pneumonia and influenza: 28.5, 33rd
  Suicide: 17.1, 6th

KEEPING WELL

Active nonfederal physicians per 100,000 pop.
    (1995): 150, 48th
Dentists per 100,000 (1991): 50, 33rd
Nurses per 100,000 (1995): 798, 31st
Hospitals per 100,000 (1995): 5.21, 5th
  Admissions per 1,000 (1995): 89.58, 46th
  Hospital beds per 1,000 (1995): 4.17, 12th
  Occupancy rate per 100 beds (1995):
    55.00, 45th
  Average cost per patient per day (1995):
    $545, 48th
  Average cost per stay (1995): $4,817, 48th
AIDS cases (new, 1996): 7; per 100,000: 1.5,
    51st
Persons living with HIV infection, not yet
    AIDS (1996): 59
Other notifiable diseases, per 100,000 pop.:
  Gonorrhea (1995): 10.6, 46th
  Syphilis (1995): 0.4, 47th
  Tuberculosis (1996): 1.5, 47th
Pop. without health insur. (1996): 13.5%,
    24th

HOUSEHOLDS BY TYPE

Total households (1996): 184,000, 51st
  Percent change (1990-96): 8.8%, 20th
  Per 1,000 pop. (1996) 382.54, 16th
  Percent of householders 65 yrs. and over
    (1996): 19.02%, 43rd
  Persons per household (1996): 2.55, 31st

Family households: 119,825
  Percent of total: 70.97%, 23rd
Nonfamily households: 49,014
  Percent of total: 29.03%, 29th
Pop. living in group quarters: 10,240
  Percent of pop.: 2.26%, 44th

LIVING QUARTERS

Total housing units: 203,411
  Persons per unit: 2.23, 44th
Occupied housing units: 168,839
  Percent of total units: 83.00%, 45th
  Persons per unit: 2.57, 17th
  Percent of units with over 1 person per room: 2.78%, 30th
Owner-occupied units: 114,544
  Percent of total units: 56.31%, 37th
  Percent of occupied units: 67.84%, 23rd
  Persons per unit: 2.74, 22nd
  Median value: $61,600, 32nd
Renter-occupied units: 54,295
  Percent of total units: 26.69%, 40th
  Percent of occupied units: 32.16%, 29th
  Persons per unit: 2.39, 18th
  Median contract rent: $270, 39th
  Rental vacancy rate: 14.4%, 3rd
Mobile home, trailer & other as a percent of occupied housing units: 21.24%, 1st
Persons in emergency shelters for homeless persons: 183, 0.040%, 36th
Persons visible in street locations: 13, 0.0029%, 38th
Nursing home population: 2,679, 0.59%, 38th

CRIME INDEX PER 100,000 (1996)

Total reported: 4,254.1, 35th
  Percent increase: −1.5%, 20th
  Violent: 249.7, 44th
    Percent increase: −1.8%, 13th
    Murder & nonnegligent manslaughter: 3.3, 41st
    Forcible rape: 29.1, 34th
    Aggravated assault: 196.9, 39th
    Robbery: 20.4, 47th
  Property: 4,004.4, 32nd
    Percent increase: −1.5%, 24th
    Burglary: 662.0, 42nd
    Larceny-theft: 3,203.3, 20th
    Motor vehicle theft: 139.1, 50th

TEACHING AND LEARNING

Pop. 3 and over enrolled in school (1996): 128,953, 51st
  Percent of pop.: 26.81%, 3rd

Public elementary & secondary schools (1996-97): 410, 46th
  Total enrollment (1996): 98,777, 50th
    Percent of school age pop.: 96.84%, 4th
    Percent of total pop.: 20.54%, 4th
  Teachers (1996): 6,700, 49th
    Percent of pop.: 1.39%, 1st
  Pupil/teacher ratio (1995): 14.8, 42nd
  Teachers' avg. salary (1996-97): $31,721, 42nd
  Expenditure per capita (1992-93): $1,873.80, 2nd
    Education as % of state govt. expenditures: 36.7%, 20th
  Expenditure per pupil (1994-95): $6,160, 17th
    Percent increase (1993-94 & 1994-95): 4.42%, 20th
Percent at or above grade level, NAEP tests:
  Reading, grade 4 (1994): 32%, 13th
  Math, grade 4 (1996): 64%, 22nd
  Math, grade 8 (1996): 68%, 11th
Percent of graduates taking SAT (1995): 10%, 37th
  Mean SAT verbal scores: 476, 20th
  Mean SAT mathematical scores: 525, 19th
Percent of graduates taking ACT (1997): 70%, 7th
  Mean ACT scores: 21.4, 19th
Percent of pop. over 25 completing:
  Less than 9th grade: 5.7%, 47th
  High school: 83.0%, 5th
  College degree(s): 18.8%, 28th
Higher education, institutions (1996): 9, 49th
  Enrollment (1995-96): 30,176, 50th
    Percent increase in enroll. (1990-95): −3.7%, 47th
    White non-Hispanic (1995): 27,517, 49th
      Percent of enroll.: 91.19%, 6th
    Total minority enroll. (1995): 2,212, 50th
      Percent of enroll.: 7.33%, 44th
    Black non-Hispanic (1995): 254, 50th
      Percent of enroll.: 0.84%, 47th
    Hispanic (1995): 1,269, 39th
      Percent of enroll.: 4.21%, 13th
    Asian/Pacific Islander (1995): 236, 51st
      Percent of enroll.: 0.78%, 49th
    American Indian/AK native (1995): 453, 43rd
      Percent of enroll.: 1.50%, 12th
    Nonresident alien (1995): 447, 51st
      Percent of enroll.: 1.48%, 50th
    Female (1995): 17,101, 51st
      Percent of enroll.: 56.67%, 16th

Pub. institutions (1995-96): 8, 44th
Enrollment: 29,420, 48th
Percent increase in enrollment (1990-95): –3.9%, 42nd
Percent of enroll.: 97.49%, 2nd
Private institutions (1995-96): 1, 51st
Enrollment: 756, 51st
Percent increase in enrollment (1990-95): 7.5%, 21st
Percent of enroll.: 2.51%, 50th
Tuition (in state), public 4-year institution (1996-97): $2,144, 39th
Tuition (in state), public 2-year institution (1996-97): $1,046, 40th
Tuition, private 4-year institution (1996-97): $—, 51st
Public library systems (1994): 23, 48th
Books & serial vol. per capita: 4.7, 3rd
Library visits per capita: 4.7, 13th
Circulation per capita: 8.1, 11th

LAW ENFORCEMENT AND CORRECTIONS

Police protection and corrections expenditures (1996): $43,832,000
Per capita: $91.12, 37th
Police per 10,000 pop. (1996): 25.89, 12th
Prisoners (1 year or more) per 100,000 pop. (1996): 307, 29th
Percent change (1995-96): 6.3%, 26th
Percent of inmates that are female: 7.4%, 6th
Percent change: 3.8%, 39th
Death penalty: yes, by lethal injection, lethal gas
Under sentence (Jan. 1998): 0
Executed, 1976-97: 1, 25th
Executed in 1997: 0

RELIGION, NUMBER AND PERCENT OF POPULATION

Agnostic: 1,590—0.50%, 27th
Buddhist: NA
Christian: 260,494—81.90%, 41st
Hindu: 636—0.20%, 3rd
Jewish: NA
Muslim: NA
Unitarian: NA
Other: 1,908—0.60%, 46th
None: 42,939—13.50%, 3rd
Refused to answer: 10,496—3.30%, 4th

MAKING A LIVING

Personal income per capita (1996): $21,245, 36th

Percent increase (1995-96): 1.1%, 48th
Disposable personal income per capita (1996): $18,614, 36th
Median income of households (average, 1995-96): $31,707, 37th
Percent of pop. below poverty level (1995-96): 12.1%, 24th

ECONOMY

In civilian labor force (1996): 258,000
Percent of total pop.: 71.0%, 13th
Percent of total pop. 65 years and over: NA
Percent of total female pop.: 63.5%, 13th
Major employer industries (total nonagricultural, 1996):
Construction: 14,200—6.4%, 3rd
Finance, insurance, & real estate: 7,900—3.6%, 51st
Government: 58,700—26.5%, 3rd
Manufacturing: 10,800—4.9%, 48th
Service: 48,100—21.7%, 51st
Trade: 52,100—23.5%, 28th
Transportation, communications, public utilities: 13,800—6.2%, 6th
Unemployment rate (1996): 5.0%, 30th
Male: 5.1%, 24th
Female: 5.0%, 27th
Total businesses (1995): 17,133, 51st
New business incorps. (1995): 2,159
Percent of total businesses: 12.60%, 12th
Business failures (1995): 108
Failures per 10,000 businesses: 63.0, 39th
Agriculture farm income:
Marketing (1996): $661,979,000, 40th
Average per farm: $72,745, 36th
Leading products (1997): Cattle, sugar beets, hay, sheep, wheat, beans, barley, oats
Average value land & build. per acre (1997): $220, 48th
Percent increase (1996-97): 7%, 14th
Govt. payments (1996): $24,381,000, 35th
Average per farm: $2,679, 22nd
Construction, value of all (1996): $641,873,000, 50th
Per capita: $1,333, 19th
Manufactures (1995):
Value added: $1,029,800,000
Per capita: $2,145, 48th
Leading products (1997): Refined petroleum, foods, wood products, stone & clay products, electronic devices, sporting apparel, aircraft

Value of nonfuel mineral production (1996): $918,000,000, 14th

Leading mineral products (1996): Petroleum, coal, natural gas, soda ash, clays, helium, cement, stone

Energy consumption per person (1994): 862.8 mil. Btu, 3rd

Retail sales (1995): $4,501,000,000
Per household: $24,785, 23rd
Sales increase (1994-95): 2.6%, 39th

Tourism revenues (1992): $1.5 bil.

Foreign exports, in total value (1996): $481,000,000, 47th
Per capita: $999, 40th

Gross state product per person (1994): $32,900, 5th

Public aid recipients (percent of resident pop. 1994): 4.5%, 44th

Medicaid recipients (percent of pop., 1995): 10.7%, 33rd

Medicare enrollment per 1,000 pop. (1996): 128, 37th

TRAVEL AND TRANSPORTATION

Motor vehicle registrations (1996): 562,048, 48th
Per 1,000 pop.: 1,170.91, 1st

Motorcycle registrations (1996): 14,954, 48th
Per 1,000 pop.: 26.61, 11th

Licensed drivers (1996): 346,299, 50th
Per 1,000 pop.: 722.67, 8th

Public roads & streets (1996)
Total mileage: 34,115, 41st
Per 1,000 pop.: 170.87, 4th
Rural mileage: 31,794, 39th
Per 1,000 pop.: 66.04, 4th
Urban mileage: 2,321, 44th
Per 1,000 pop.: 4.82, 1st
Interstate mileage: 913, 22nd
Per 1,000 pop.: 1.90, 1st

Speed limit (max. interstate, autos, mi. per hr., 1997): 75

Annual vehicle-mi. of travel per driver (1996): 21,452, 1st

Mean travel time for workers age 16+ who work away from home: 15.4 min., 48th

GOVERNMENT

Percent of voting age pop. registered (1996): 67.62%, 44th
Percent of voting age pop. voting for president: (1996): 60.1%, 5th
Percent of voting age pop. voting for U.S. representatives (1996): 59.7%, 5th

State legislators, total (1997): 90, 45th
Women members (1997): 17
Percent of legislature: 19%, 31st

U.S. Congress, House members (1998): 1
Change (1988-98): 0

Revenues (1996)
State govt.: $2,347,858,000
Per capita: $4,881.20, 5th
Parimutuel & amusement taxes & lotteries, revenue per capita (1995): NA

Expenditures (1996):
State govt.: $2,062,116,000
Per capita: $4,287.14, 5th

Debt outstanding (1996): $799,017,000
Per capita: $1,661.16, 19th

LAWS AND REGULATIONS

Legal driving age: 16

Marriage age without parental consent: 18

Divorce residence requirement: 2 mo., for qualifications check local statutes

ATTRACTIONS (1997)

Per capita spending by the NEA (1997): $1.10, 3rd

State Fair in late August at Douglas

SPORTS AND COMPETITION

NCAA (Division I) football and basketball teams: Univ. of Wyoming Cowboys

WEBSITES CONTAINING FURTHER INFORMATION

Welcome to the State of Wyoming   http://www.state.wy.us

OUTLYING AREAS

CARIBBEAN ISLANDS

Commonwealth of Puerto Rico

It is spring all year in Puerto Rico, a land that someone has said is "more than half Spanish and more than half American." Puerto Rico is the smallest of the islands known as the Greater Antilles. The Atlantic Ocean lies to the north and the Caribbean to the south. The Dominican Republic is the neighbor to the west; the American Virgin Islands lie to the east. Vieques is the largest of the outlying islands. The main island is mountainous, rising to massive El Yunque near the east coast. Puerto Rico's climate is ideal, with little variation year-round, making it a mecca for tourists. There are beautiful beaches, high mountains, unique animal life, one of the world's largest caverns, ancient cities, and modern attractions. However, Puerto Rico is also subject to destructive hurricanes.

Christopher Columbus reached the island in 1493, and by early 1511, the island became the first Spanish colony in the New World. It suffered many attacks by the English. After almost 400 years of Spanish rule, Spain ceded Puerto Rico to the United States after the Spanish-American War of 1898.

Puerto Ricans received U.S. citizenship in 1917, and the island became an internally self-governing commonwealth in 1952. Its relationship to the United States is a matter of continuing concern, with many Puerto Ricans preferring the present system, others desiring statehood, and others advocating independence. The people do not vote in national elections, except for primaries. Puerto Rico is represented in the U.S. House of Representatives by a nonvoting delegate.

General

Name: Commonwealth of Puerto Rico (Estado Libre Asociado de Puerto Rico)
Capital: San Juan
Motto: *Joannes Est Norman Eius* (John is his name)
Bird: Reinita
Flower: Maga
Song: "La Borinqueña"
Tree: Ceiba

The Land and Climate

Area: 3,508 sq. mi.
    Land: 3,427 sq. mi.

Topography: Mountainous area covering three-fourths of the rectangular island, surrounded by a broken coastal plain
Highest point: 4,389 ft. (Cerro de Punta)
Lowest point: Sea level (Atlantic Ocean)
Climate: Mildly tropical, with a mean temperature of 77 deg; rainfall is plentiful, except in some arid regions in the south

The People

Population (1996 est.): 3,782,862
Per sq. mi.: 1,103.8
Percent urban (1990): 66.8%

Principal Cities

Bayamón, Caguas, Carolina, Ponce, San Juan

Government

Chief of state: President of the United States
Head of government: Governor of Puerto Rico
Legislature: Bicameral legislature (Senate and House of Representatives)

Economy

Principal industries: Manufacturing
Manufactured goods: Pharmaceuticals, chemicals, machinery and metals, electric machinery and equipment, petroleum refining, food products, apparel
Agricultural products: Sugarcane, coffee, pineapples, plantains, bananas, yams, pigeon peas, peppers, pumpkins, coriander, lettuce, tobacco
Minerals: Cement, crushed stone
GDP (1995): $28.4 bil.
Per capita income (1996): $7,882
Unemployment rate (1996): 13.4%

Virgin Islands

In 1493, Columbus became the first European to reach the Virgin Islands, which he named in honor of the Virgins of St. Ursula. Before Columbus, the islands had been inhabited by the Siboney Indians, by the Arawak from South America, and by the fierce Caribes (whose name was given to the Caribbean).

Pirates swarmed over the islands, which have been claimed by Holland, Spain, France, England, and Denmark. In 1917 the United States bought its present portion of the Virgins from Denmark, to keep them from falling into German hands during World War I.

In 1927 the people became American nationals; they achieved limited self-government in 1936, and their rights were expanded in 1954. Today the Virgin Islands has a republican form of government, with an elected governor and lieutenant governor; the people elect a nonvoting member to the U.S. House of Representatives.

General

Name: Virgin Islands of the United States
Capital: Charlotte Amalie, St. Thomas
Bird: Yellow breast
Flower: Yellow elder or yellow trumpet
Song: "Virgin Islands March"

The Land and Climate

Area: 171 sq. mi. (land)
Land: 134 sq. mi.
Topography: Mostly hilly to rugged and mountainous with little level land
Highest point: 1,556 ft. (Crown Mountain, St. Thomas)
Lowest point: Sea level (Atlantic Ocean)
Climate: Subtropical, tempered by easterly trade winds; relatively low humidity; little seasonal temperature variation; rainy season from May to November

The People

Population (1996 est.): 97,120
Per sq. mi: 724.7

Principal Cities

Charlotte Amalie, Saint Croix, Saint Thomas

Government

Chief of state: President of the United States
Head of government: Governor of the Virgin Islands
Legislature: Unicameral

Economy

Principal industries: Tourism, rum, alumina production, petroleum refining, watch assembly, textiles, electronics
Manufactured goods: Rum, textiles, pharmaceuticals, perfume
Agricultural products: Truck garden produce, food crops (small scale), fruit, sorghum, cattle
Minerals: Sand, gravel
Per capita income (1989): $11,052
Unemployment rate (1992): 2.8%

Other Caribbean Islands

Navassa, which is uninhabited, lies between Jamaica and Haiti and has an area of about 3 square miles. It is administered by the U.S. Coast Guard, which operates an automatic lighthouse.

The United States laid claim to the uninhabited islands of **Quita Sueno Bank, Roncador**, and **Serrana** until 1981, when the claim of Colombia to the islands was recognized.

PACIFIC ISLANDS

American Samoa

This unincorporated territory of seven small islands of the Samoan group is the most southerly region under U.S. jurisdiction. The islands lie 2,300 miles southwest of Honolulu, Hawaii. The main islands are mountainous and volcanic, surrounded by coral reefs. Swains Island came under U.S. control in 1925 and is organized as a part of the Samoan group.

Native Polynesians probably reached the islands about 1000 B.C. The Dutch explorer Jacob Roggeveen visited the islands in 1722. The United States, Britain, and France claimed trade and other privileges in the islands, and the United States established a naval station at Pago Pago in 1878. An agreement of 1899 recognized the U.S. right to govern present American Samoa. In 1978 a governor was popularly elected for the first time.

The islands retain much of their original Polynesian culture, clinging to traditional dress. Siva, the traditional dance, is popular with both locals and the increasing number of tourists.

Principal exports are fish products, mostly tuna, packed by leading producers. The cocoa of the island is ranked among the world's best. The Samoan people are known for their fine craft work, particularly tapa cloth, pounded from the bark of the paper mulberry trees. Baskets and laufala floor mats are woven from palm leaves.

General

Name: Territory of American Samoa
Capital: Pago Pago, Island of Tutuila
Motto: *Samoa Muamua le Atua* (In Samoa, God is first)
Flower: Paogo (Ula-fala)
Song: "Amerika Samoa"

The Land and Climate

Area: 90 sq. mi.
  Land: 77 sq. mi.
Topography: Five volcanic islands with rugged peaks and limited coastal plains; two coral atolls
Highest point: 3,160 ft. (Lata Mountain, Tau Island)
Lowest point: Sea level (Pacific Ocean)
Climate: Tropical marine, moderated by southeast tradewinds; little seasonal temperature variation; rainy season from November to April, dry season from May to October

The People

Population (1996 est.:): 59,566
Per sq. mi.: 773.6
Largest city: Pago Pago

Government

Chief of state: President of the United States
Head of government: Governor of American Samoa
Legislature: Bicameral legislative assembly (Fono)

Economy

Principal industries: Tuna fishing and processing, meat canning, handicrafts
Agricultural products: Bananas, coconuts, vegetables, taro, breadfruit, yams, copra, pineapples, papayas, dairy products
GDP (1991): $128 million
Unemployment rate (1991): 12%

Guam

The explorer Ferdinand Magellan reached Guam in the Marianas chain in 1521. Spanish missionaries began colonization in 1668.

After the Spanish-American War of 1898, Spain ceded the island to the United States. Its residents are U.S. citizens but do not vote for president. Guam is represented in the U.S. House of Representatives by a nonvoting delegate.

Guam is the largest and most southerly of the Marianas, with a tropical climate. The government is the principal employer, and tourism is important.

General

Name: Territory of Guam
Capital: Agana
Nickname: Where America's Day Begins
Bird: Toto (fruit dove)
Flower: Puti Tai Nobio (bougainvillea)
Song: "Stand Ye Guamanians"
Tree: Ifit (intsiabijuga)

The Land and Climate

Area: 217 sq. mi.
  Land: 210 sq. mi.
Topography: Coralline limestone plateaus in the north, southern chain of low volcanic mountains sloping gently to the west, more steeply to coastal cliffs on the east
Highest point: 1,332 ft. (Mount Lamlam, Agat District)
Lowest point: Sea level (Pacific Ocean)
Climate: Tropical, with temperatures from 70 deg. to 90 deg.

The People

Population (1996 est.): 156,974
Per sq. mi.: 747.5

Principal Cities

Dededo, Mangilao, Santa Rita, Tamuning, Yigo

Government

Chief of state: President of the United States
Head of Government: Governor of Guam
Legislature: Unicameral

Economy

Principal industries: Tourism, U.S. military construction, transshipment services, concrete products, printing and publishing, food processing, textiles
Manufactured goods: Textiles, foods
Agricultural products: Fruits, vegetables, eggs, pork, poultry, beef, copra
GDP (1993): $2.917 bil.
Per capita income (1992): $10,834
Unemployment rate (1996): 6.7%

Small Pacific Islands

With its sister islands, Wilkes and Peale, **Wake Island** is an important outpost on the route from Hawaii to Hong Kong. These islands formally became a U.S. possession in 1899. Administered by the U.S. Air Force, they have a population mainly associated with the Air Force.

With Sand and Eastern Island in the North Pacific, 1,150 miles northwest of Hawaii, **Midway** came under U.S. control in

1867. The Midway Islands are administered by the U.S. Navy and occupied only by military personnel.

South of Hawaii, **Johnston Atoll** occupies only about 1 square mile and is under the U.S. Defense Nuclear Agency, Fish and Wildlife Service, and Department of the Interior. **Kingman Reef** was discovered in 1874 by American explorers. Less than half a mile square, it is under U.S. Navy control.

Howland, Jarvis, and **Baker Islands,** lying some 1,500 miles southwest of Hawaii, are uninhabited islets under control of the U.S. Interior Department.

Palmyra is a 2-square-mile island privately owned and administered by the U.S. Interior Department.

Micronesia

Several Pacific Island groups, collectively known as Micronesia, were placed under U.S. trusteeship after World War II. The trusteeship has since been dissolved. The Northern Mariana Islands is a U.S. commonwealth; the other island groups are now independent states, with close ties to the United States.

Commonwealth of the Northern Mariana Islands is an archipelago of 14 islands stretching for 300 miles, with a total land area of 179 square miles. The population, of Chamorro descent, is 52,284, concentrated on three main islands: Saipan, Rota, and Tinian. The group has been self-governing since 1978, under a constitution adopted by the people in free association with the United States. There is a governor and a bicameral legislature. Tourism is increasing and is the principal industry on these islands.

Stretching for 1,800 miles along the archipelago of the Caroline Islands are the four **Federated States of Micronesia.** The states are

Pohnpei (population 52,000), with the capital city of Palikir; **Kosrae** (16,500); **Truk** (31,000); and **Yap** (12,000)—each made up of several small islands. The island federation lies southwest of Honolulu and southeast of Guam. The population is diverse, with several languages. The Federated States of Micronesia is now a sovereign self-governing state, with guarantees of U.S. defense and aid. Major economic activities are subsistence farming and fishing. Geographical isolation and a poor infrastructure impede long-term growth.

Republic of the Marshall Islands is a sovereign, self-governing state consisting of two clusters of atolls. Each atoll is a cluster of a number of small islands surrounding a lagoon. The total land area is 70 square miles. The total population is 60,652, with 20,000 in the capital, Majuro. The main economic activities are agriculture (producing coconuts, tomatoes, melons, and breadfruit) and tourism. The United States remains responsible for defense and retains certain other responsibilities.

The 200 islands of the Caroline Island chain form the **Republic of Palau.** Eight are permanently inhabited, with a total population of 17,240, with more than 10,000 of these on the island of Koror. The economy consists of subsistence agriculture and farming, plus some tourism. The United States recognized the constitution of Palau, which became effective in 1980. There is a bicameral legislature and an elected president and vice president, advised by a council of chiefs.

Palau was the last remaining entity of the U.S. Trust Territory of the Pacific Islands, established in 1947. The government of Palau and the United States signed a compact of free association, which was eventually approved—by a plebiscite of Palau voters in 1993. Palau became independent in 1994.

PART III:
THE STATES
COMPARED

NOTE TO THE READER

The data in the following tables are listed state by state in "Descending Numerical Order" ("Desc. Num. Order"), except where otherwise noted. Where two or more listings are equal in rank, ranks are assigned here in alphabetical order by state; in Part II: Portrait of the States, however, equal rankings are assigned the same number.

Some percents may not add to 100% because of rounding. Where no year is given for statistics they are as of 1990.

States are referred to by their postal abbreviations:

AL	Alabama	KY	Kentucky	ND	North Dakota
AK	Alaska	LA	Louisiana	OH	Ohio
AZ	Arizona	ME	Maine	OK	Oklahoma
AR	Arkansas	MD	Maryland	OR	Oregon
CA	California	MA	Massachusetts	PA	Pennsylvania
CO	Colorado	MI	Michigan	RI	Rhode Island
CT	Connecticut	MN	Minnesota	SC	South Carolina
DE	Delaware	MS	Mississippi	SD	South Dakota
DC	District of Columbia	MO	Missouri	TN	Tennessee
FL	Florida	MT	Montana	TX	Texas
GA	Georgia	NE	Nebraska	UT	Utah
HI	Hawaii	NV	Nevada	VT	Vermont
ID	Idaho	NH	New Hampshire	VA	Virginia
IL	Illinois	NJ	New Jersey	WA	Washington
IN	Indiana	NM	New Mexico	WV	West Virginia
IA	Iowa	NY	New York	WI	Wisconsin
KS	Kansas	NC	North Carolina	WY	Wyoming

GENERAL

HISTORICAL HIGHLIGHTS

1st Permanent European Settlement		Date Entered Union		Chron. Order
FL	1565	DE	Dec. 7, 1787	1
NM	1598	PA	Dec. 12, 1787	2
VA	1607	NJ	Dec. 18, 1787	3
NY	1614	GA	Jan. 2, 1788	4
NJ	1618	CT	Jan. 9, 1788	5
MA	1620	MA	Feb. 6, 1788	6
ME	1622	MD	April 28, 1788	7
NH	1623	SC	May 23, 1788	8
MD	1631	NH	June 21, 1788	9
CT	1634	VA	June 25, 1788	10
RI	1635	NY	July 26, 1788	11
DE	1638	NC	Nov. 21, 1789	12
PA	1643	RI	May 29, 1790	13
NC	1664	VT	March 4, 1791	14
MI	1668	KY	June 1, 1792	15
SC	1670	TN	June 1, 1796	16
TX	1682	OH	March 1, 1803	17
AR	1686	LA	April 30, 1812	18
IL	1699	IN	Dec. 11, 1816	19
MS	1699	MS	Dec. 10, 1817	20
AL	1702	IL	Dec. 3, 1818	21
LA	1714	AL	Dec. 14, 1819	22
VT	1724	ME	March 15, 1820	23
IN	1727?	MO	Aug. 10, 1821	24
WV	1732	AR	June 15, 1836	25
GA	1733	MI	Jan. 26, 1837	26
MO	1735	FL	March 3, 1845	27
DC	1751	TX	Dec. 29, 1845	28
AZ	1752	IA	Dec. 28, 1846	29
WI	1764	WI	May 29, 1848	30
CA	1769	CA	Sept. 9, 1850	31
KY	1774	MN	May 11, 1858	32
TN	1779	OR	Feb. 14, 1859	33
AK	1784	KS	Jan. 29, 1861	34
IA	1788	WV	June 20, 1863	35
OH	1788	NV	Oct. 31, 1864	36
MT	1807	NE	March 1, 1867	37
WA	1810	CO	Aug. 1, 1876	38
OR	1811	ND	Nov. 2, 1889	39
ND	1812	SD	Nov. 2, 1889	40
OK	1817	MT	Nov. 8, 1889	41
HI	1820	WA	Nov. 11, 1889	42
MN	1820	ID	July 3, 1890	43
NE	1823	WY	July 10, 1890	44
KS	1827	UT	Jan. 4, 1896	45
SD	1831	OK	Nov. 16, 1907	46
CO	1832	NM	Jan. 6, 1912	47
WY	1834	AZ	Feb. 14, 1912	48
UT	1844	AK	Jan. 3, 1959	49
NV	1849	HI	Aug. 21, 1959	50
ID	1860	DC	NA	51

THE LAND

AREA

	Total Area, Sq. Miles		Land, Sq. Miles		Water, Sq. Miles	Desc. Num. Order
AK	615,230	AK	570,374	AK	44,856	1
TX	267,277	TX	261,914	MI	39,896	2
CA	158,869	CA	155,973	WI	11,186	3
MT	147,046	MT	145,556	MN	7,326	4
NM	121,598	NM	121,364	NY	6,765	5
AZ	114,006	AZ	113,642	LA	6,084	6
NV	110,567	NV	109,806	FL	5,991	7
CO	104,100	CO	103,729	TX	5,363	8
WY	97,819	WY	97,105	WA	4,056	9
OR	97,131	OR	96,002	NC	3,954	10
MI	96,705	ID	82,751	OH	3,875	11
MN	86,943	UT	82,168	CA	2,896	12
UT	84,904	KS	81,823	ME	2,876	13
ID	83,574	MN	79,617	UT	2,736	14
KS	82,282	NE	76,878	VA	2,728	15
NE	77,359	SD	75,896	MD	2,522	16
SD	77,121	ND	68,994	IL	2,325	17
ND	70,704	MO	68,896	ND	1,710	18
WA	70,637	OK	68,679	MT	1,490	19
OK	69,903	WA	66,581	AL	1,487	20
MO	69,709	GA	57,919	MA	1,403	21
WI	65,500	MI	56,809	MS	1,372	22
FL	59,928	IA	55,875	PA	1,239	23
GA	58,977	IL	55,593	SD	1,225	24
IL	57,918	WI	54,314	OK	1,224	25
IA	56,276	FL	53,937	OR	1,129	26
NY	53,989	AR	52,075	AR	1,107	27
AR	53,182	AL	50,750	SC	1,078	28
NC	52,672	NC	48,718	GA	1,058	29
AL	52,237	NY	47,224	TN	926	30
LA	49,650	MS	46,914	ID	823	31
MS	48,286	PA	44,820	MO	811	32
PA	46,059	LA	43,566	NJ	796	33
OH	44,828	TN	41,219	NV	761	34
VA	42,326	OH	40,953	WY	714	35
TN	42,145	KY	39,732	CT	699	36
KY	40,411	VA	39,598	KY	679	37
IN	36,420	IN	35,870	IN	550	38
ME	33,741	ME	30,865	NE	481	39
SC	31,189	SC	30,111	KS	459	40
WV	24,232	WV	24,087	DE	442	41
MD	12,297	MD	9,775	IA	401	42
VT	9,615	VT	9,249	CO	371	43
NH	9,283	NH	8,969	VT	366	44
MA	9,241	MA	7,838	AZ	364	45
NJ	8,215	NJ	7,419	NH	314	46
HI	6,459	HI	6,423	NM	234	47
CT	5,544	CT	4,845	RI	186	48
DE	2,397	DE	1,955	WV	145	49
RI	1,231	RI	1,045	HI	36	50
DC	68	DC	61	DC	7	51

Source: U.S. Bureau of the Census

CLIMATE AND ENVIRONMENT

MONTHLY AVERAGE TEMPERATURES, IN DEG. F

Highest		Lowest[1]		Spread (High to Low)			Difference	Desc. Num. Order
AZ	105.0	AK	−21.6	AK	(71.8	21.6)	93.4	1
NV	104.5	ND	−5.1	ND	(84.4	−5.1)	89.5	2
CA	98.8	MN	−2.9	MN	(83.4	−2.9)	86.3	3
TX	98.5	SD	1.9	NV	(104.5	19.5)	85.0	4
OK	93.9	WI	5.4	SD	(86.5	1.9)	84.6	5
AR	93.6	IA	6.3	NE	(89.5	8.9)	80.6	6
LA	93.3	VT	7.7	IA	(86.2	6.3)	79.9	7
UT	93.2	MT	8.1	MT	(86.6	8.1)	78.5	8
KS	92.9	NE	8.9	CO	(92.2	14.3)	77.9	9
NM	92.8	NH	9.0	WI	(82.8	5.4)	77.4	10
MS	92.5	IL	9.8	IL	(87.1	9.8)	77.3	11
CO	92.2	ME	11.9	KS	(92.9	15.7)	77.2	12
GA	92.2	NY	11.9	TX	(98.5	21.7)	76.8	13
SC	91.9	WY	11.9	ID	(90.6	15.1)	75.5	14
FL	91.7	MI	14.0	WY	(87.1	11.9)	75.2	15
AL	91.5	CO	14.3	NH	(82.6	9.0)	73.6	16
TN	91.5	ID	15.1	UT	(93.2	19.7)	73.5	17
ID	90.6	OH	15.5	NY	(85.3	11.9)	73.4	18
MO	90.5	MA	15.6	IN	(88.8	15.8)	73.0	19
NE	89.5	KS	15.7	VT	(80.5	7.7)	72.8	20
IN	88.8	IN	15.8	MO	(90.5	19.4)	71.1	21
VA	88.4	CT	16.7	NM	(92.8	22.3)	70.5	22
NC	88.3	PA	18.0	OH	(85.8	15.5)	70.3	23
DC	87.9	MO	19.4	MI	(83.1	14.0)	69.1	24
KY	87.6	NV	19.5	OK	(93.9	24.8)	69.1	25
HI	87.1	UT	19.7	PA	(86.2	18.0)	68.2	26
IL	87.1	RI	20.0	CT	(84.8	16.7)	68.1	27
MD	87.1	WA	20.0	AR	(93.6	26.6)	67.0	28
WY	87.1	TX	21.7	ME	(78.9	11.9)	67.0	29
MT	86.6	NM	22.3	AZ	(105.0	38.1)	66.9	30
SD	86.5	KY	23.1	MA	(81.8	15.6)	66.2	31
IA	86.2	DE	23.2	KY	(87.6	23.1)	64.5	32
PA	86.2	WV	23.9	WA	(84.0	20.0)	64.0	33
OH	85.8	NJ	24.2	TN	(91.5	27.8)	63.7	34
DE	85.6	MD	24.3	MD	(87.1	24.3)	62.8	35
NJ	85.6	OK	24.8	DE	(85.6	23.2)	62.4	36
WV	85.6	VA	26.2	VA	(88.4	26.2)	62.2	37
NY	85.3	AR	26.6	CA	(98.8	36.8)	62.0	38
CT	84.8	NC	27.3	RI	(81.7	20.0)	61.7	39
ND	84.4	DC	27.5	WV	(85.6	23.9)	61.7	40
WA	84.0	TN	27.8	NJ	(85.6	24.2)	61.4	41
MN	83.4	AL	31.0	NC	(88.3	27.3)	61.0	42
MI	83.1	SC	31.2	SC	(91.9	31.2)	60.7	43
WI	82.8	GA	32.6	AL	(91.5	31.0)	60.5	44
NH	82.6	OR	32.8	DC	(87.9	27.5)	60.4	45
OR	82.6	MS	34.9	GA	(92.2	32.6)	59.6	46
MA	81.8	LA	36.2	MS	(92.5	34.9)	57.6	47
RI	81.7	CA	36.8	LA	(93.3	36.2)	57.1	48
VT	80.5	AZ	38.1	FL	(91.7	39.9)	51.8	49
ME	78.9	FL	39.9	OR	(82.6	32.8)	49.8	50
AK	71.8	HI	65.3	HI	(87.1	65.3)	21.8	51

[1]Ranked lowest to highest.

Source: National Climatic Data Center, NOAA, U.S. Dept. of Commerce

MAJOR CITIES

MOST POPULOUS CITIES IN EACH STATE

	Pop., 1996		Pop., % Inc., 1990–96	Desc. Num. Order
New York City, NY	7,380,906	Las Vegas, NV	46.0%	1
Los Angeles, CA	3,553,638	Boise, ID	20.6%	2
Chicago, IL	2,721,547	Phoenix, AZ	17.7%	3
Houston, TX	1,744,058	Fargo, ND	13.1%	4
Philadelphia, PA	1,478,002	Billings, MT	12.4%	5
Phoenix, AZ	1,159,014	Honolulu, HI	12.3%	6
Detroit, MI	1,000,272	Sioux Falls, SD	12.3%	7
Indianapolis, IN	746,737	Anchorage, AK	10.7%	8
Jacksonville, FL	679,792	Virginia Beach, VA	9.5%	9
Baltimore, MD	675,401	Albuquerque, NM	9.0%	10
Columbus, OH	657,053	Salt Lake City, UT	7.9%	11
Memphis, TN	596,725	Cheyenne, WY	7.4%	12
Milwaukee, WI	590,503	Jacksonville, FL	7.0%	13
Boston, MA	558,394	Denver, CO	6.5%	14
Washington, DC	543,213	Houston, TX	6.5%	15
Seattle, WA	524,704	Omaha, NE	6.2%	16
Denver, CO	497,840	Oklahoma City, OK	5.7%	17
Portland, OR	480,824	Wichita, KS	5.4%	18
New Orleans, LA	476,625	Charlotte, NC	5.2%	19
Oklahoma City, OK	469,852	Columbus, OH	3.8%	20
Charlotte, NC	441,297	Portland, OR	3.7%	21
Kansas City, MO	441,259	Indianapolis, IN	2.1%	22
Virginia Beach, VA	430,385	Los Angeles, CA	2.0%	23
Honolulu, HI	423,475	Atlanta, GA	2.0%	24
Albuquerque, NM	419,681	Columbia, SC	1.8%	25
Atlanta, GA	401,907	Manchester, NH	1.6%	26
Las Vegas, NV	376,906	Seattle, WA	1.6%	27
Omaha, NE	364,253	Kansas City, MO	1.5%	28
Minneapolis, MN	358,785	New York City, NY	0.8%	29
Wichita, KS	320,395	Des Moines, IA	0.1%	30
Newark, NJ	268,510	Little Rock, AR	0.0%	31
Louisville, KY	260,689	Burlington, VT	−0.3%	32
Birmingham, AL	258,543	Portland, ME	−1.6%	33
Anchorage, AK	250,505	Charleston, WV	−2.1%	34
Des Moines, IA	193,422	Chicago, IL	−2.2%	35
Jackson, MS	192,923	Newark, NJ	−2.4%	36
Little Rock, AR	175,752	Birmingham, AL	−2.6%	37
Salt Lake City, UT	172,575	Bridgeport, CT	−2.6%	38
Boise, ID	152,737	Minneapolis, MN	−2.6%	39
Providence, RI	152,558	Detroit, MI	−2.7%	40
Bridgeport, CT	137,990	Boston, MA	−2.8%	41
Sioux Falls, SD	113,223	Wilmington, DE	−2.9%	42
Columbia, SC	112,773	Louisville, KY	−3.3%	43
Manchester, NH	100,967	Memphis, TN	−3.5%	44
Billings, MT	91,195	New Orleans, LA	−4.1%	45
Fargo, ND	83,778	Jackson, MS	−4.5%	46
Wilmington, DE	69,490	Providence, RI	−5.1%	47
Portland, ME	63,123	Milwaukee, WI	−6.0%	48
Charleston, WV	56,098	Philadelphia, PA	−6.8%	49
Cheyenne, WY	53,729	Baltimore, MD	−8.2%	50
Burlington, VT	39,004	Washington, DC	−10.5%	51

Source: Bureau of the Census, U.S. Dept. of Commerce

THE PEOPLE

POPULATION

	1997		% Increase, 1990-97		% of Tot. U.S. Pop., 1997	Desc. Num. Order
CA	32,268,301	NV	39.54%	CA	12.06%	1
TX	19,439,337	AZ	24.27%	TX	7.26%	2
NY	18,137,226	ID	20.21%	NY	6.78%	3
FL	14,653,945	UT	19.52%	FL	5.48%	4
PA	12,019,661	CO	18.16%	PA	4.49%	5
IL	11,895,849	GA	15.56%	IL	4.44%	6
OH	11,186,331	WA	15.28%	OH	4.18%	7
MI	9,773,892	TX	14.44%	MI	3.65%	8
NJ	8,052,849	NM	14.17%	NJ	3.01%	9
GA	7,486,242	OR	14.11%	GA	2.80%	10
NC	7,425,183	FL	13.26%	NC	2.77%	11
VA	6,733,996	NC	11.95%	VA	2.52%	12
MA	6,117,520	AK	10.78%	MA	2.29%	13
IN	5,864,108	TN	10.07%	IN	2.19%	14
WA	5,610,362	MT	9.98%	WA	2.10%	15
MO	5,402,058	DE	9.82%	MO	2.02%	16
TN	5,368,198	VA	8.80%	TN	2.01%	17
WI	5,169,677	CA	8.33%	WI	1.93%	18
MD	5,094,289	SC	7.86%	MD	1.90%	19
MN	4,685,549	AR	7.33%	MN	1.75%	20
AZ	4,554,966	MN	7.08%	AZ	1.70%	21
LA	4,351,769	HI	7.07%	LA	1.63%	22
AL	4,319,154	AL	6.90%	AL	1.61%	23
KY	3,908,124	MD	6.56%	KY	1.46%	24
CO	3,892,644	SD	6.03%	CO	1.45%	25
SC	3,760,181	MS	6.02%	SC	1.40%	26
OK	3,317,091	KY	6.00%	OK	1.24%	27
CT	3,269,858	IN	5.77%	CT	1.22%	28
OR	3,243,487	WY	5.77%	OR	1.21%	29
IA	2,852,423	NH	5.72%	IA	1.07%	30
MS	2,730,501	WI	5.68%	MS	1.02%	31
KS	2,594,840	MO	5.57%	KS	0.97%	32
AR	2,522,819	OK	5.45%	AR	0.94%	33
UT	2,059,148	MI	5.15%	UT	0.77%	34
WV	1,815,787	NE	4.97%	WV	0.68%	35
NM	1,729,751	KS	4.73%	NM	0.65%	36
NV	1,676,809	VT	4.66%	NV	0.63%	37
NE	1,656,870	IL	4.07%	NE	0.62%	38
ME	1,242,051	NJ	3.94%	ME	0.46%	39
ID	1,210,232	OH	3.13%	ID	0.45%	40
HI	1,186,602	LA	3.08%	HI	0.44%	41
NH	1,172,709	IA	2.72%	NH	0.44%	42
RI	987,429	MA	1.68%	RI	0.37%	43
MT	878,810	WV	1.24%	MT	0.33%	44
SD	737,973	ME	1.15%	SD	0.28%	45
DE	731,581	PA	1.15%	DE	0.27%	46
ND	640,883	NY	0.81%	ND	0.24%	47
AK	609,311	ND	0.33%	AK	0.23%	48
VT	588,978	CT	−0.53%	VT	0.22%	49
DC	528,964	RI	−1.60%	DC	0.20%	50
WY	479,743	DC	−12.84%	WY	0.18%	51

Source: Bureau of the Census, U.S. Dept. of Commerce

POPULATION CHARACTERISTICS

	Pop. per Sq. Mi., 1997		% of Pop. in Metro. Areas, 1996		Foreign-Born, 1990		% of Pop. Foreign-Born	Desc. Num. Order
DC	7,778.88	DC	100.00%	CA	6,459,000	CA	21.7%	1
NJ	923.28	NJ	100.00%	NY	2,852,000	NY	15.9%	2
RI	639.11	MA	98.49%	FL	1,663,000	HI	14.7%	3
CT	589.80	CA	96.65%	TX	1,524,000	FL	12.9%	4
MA	579.59	FL	92.92%	NJ	967,000	NJ	12.5%	5
MD	410.60	MD	92.76%	IL	952,000	DC	9.7%	6
NY	332.95	NY	91.79%	MA	574,000	MA	9.5%	7
DE	293.93	RI	91.64%	PA	369,000	RI	9.5%	8
PA	260.97	CT	91.30%	MI	355,000	TX	9.0%	9
OH	249.54	NV	85.68%	WA	322,000	NV	8.7%	10
FL	222.85	AZ	85.05%	MD	313,000	CT	8.5%	11
IL	205.39	PA	84.55%	VA	312,000	IL	8.3%	12
CA	197.11	TX	84.16%	CT	279,000	AZ	7.6%	13
IN	161.01	IL	84.11%	AZ	278,000	MD	6.6%	14
VA	157.45	WA	82.77%	OH	260,000	WA	6.6%	15
NC	137.96	MI	82.45%	GA	173,000	NM	5.3%	16
TN	127.37	DE	81.90%	HI	163,000	VA	5.0%	17
GA	125.94	CO	81.18%	CO	142,000	OR	4.9%	18
NH	125.41	OH	81.05%	OR	139,000	AK	4.5%	19
SC	117.48	VA	77.87%	WI	122,000	CO	4.3%	20
HI	108.54	UT	76.86%	NC	115,000	MI	3.8%	21
MI	100.96	LA	75.18%	MN	113,000	NH	3.7%	22
KY	96.71	HI	73.65%	NV	105,000	UT	3.4%	23
LA	83.94	IN	71.69%	RI	95,000	DE	3.3%	24
AL	82.39	OR	70.19%	IN	94,000	PA	3.1%	25
WI	78.92	MN	69.72%	LA	87,000	VT	3.1%	26
WA	78.68	SC	69.59%	MO	84,000	ME	3.0%	27
MO	77.49	GA	68.51%	NM	81,000	ID	2.9%	28
WV	74.94	MO	67.99%	OK	65,000	GA	2.7%	29
TX	72.37	WI	67.74%	KS	63,000	MN	2.6%	30
VT	61.26	TN	67.73%	DC	59,000	KS	2.5%	31
MS	56.38	AL	67.72%	TN	59,000	WI	2.5%	32
MN	53.89	NC	66.82%	UT	59,000	OH	2.4%	33
IA	50.69	NH	62.32%	SC	50,000	LA	2.1%	34
OK	47.45	OK	60.23%	AL	44,000	OK	2.1%	35
AR	47.44	NM	56.68%	IA	43,000	NE	1.8%	36
AZ	39.95	KS	55.42%	NH	41,000	IN	1.7%	37
CO	37.39	NE	51.27%	ME	36,000	MT	1.7%	38
ME	35.10	KY	48.23%	KY	34,000	NC	1.7%	39
OR	32.97	AR	45.25%	ID	29,000	WY	1.7%	40
KS	31.54	IA	44.33%	NE	28,000	IA	1.6%	41
UT	24.25	ND	42.72%	AK	25,000	MO	1.6%	42
NE	21.42	WV	41.83%	AR	25,000	ND	1.5%	43
NV	15.17	AK	41.27%	DE	22,000	SC	1.4%	44
ID	14.48	ME	40.04%	MS	20,000	TN	1.2%	45
NM	14.23	SD	33.28%	VT	18,000	AL	1.1%	46
SD	9.57	VT	32.37%	WV	16,000	AR	1.1%	47
ND	9.06	MS	31.37%	MT	14,000	SD	1.1%	48
MT	5.98	ID	31.33%	ND	9,000	KY	0.9%	49
WY	4.90	WY	29.72%	SD	8,000	WV	0.9%	50
AK	0.93	MT	23.55%	WY	8,000	MS	0.8%	51

Source: Bureau of the Census, U.S. Dept. of Commerce

RACIAL AND ETHNIC GROUPS, BY PERCENT OF POPULATION (1992)

	Whites		Blacks		Native Americans		Asian or Pacific Islanders		Those of Hispanic Origin[1]	Desc. Num. Order
VT	98.77%	DC	65.64%	AK	15.48%	HI	63.41%	NM	38.81%	1
ME	98.46%	MS	35.83%	NM	9.10%	CA	10.67%	CA	27.04%	2
NH	98.30%	LA	31.25%	OK	8.14%	WA	4.84%	TX	26.52%	3
ID	97.19%	SC	29.98%	SD	7.49%	NY	4.36%	AZ	19.60%	4
IA	96.82%	GA	27.40%	MT	5.96%	NJ	4.05%	CO	13.19%	5
WY	96.34%	MD	25.67%	AZ	5.90%	AK	3.91%	NY	13.04%	6
WV	96.24%	AL	25.45%	ND	4.26%	NV	3.59%	FL	12.85%	7
UT	95.58%	NC	22.15%	WY	2.15%	MD	3.25%	NV	11.15%	8
NE	94.50%	VA	19.21%	WA	1.81%	VA	2.91%	NJ	10.32%	9
ND	94.48%	DE	17.51%	NV	1.72%	IL	2.77%	IL	8.40%	10
MN	94.34%	NY	17.22%	UT	1.49%	DC	2.74%	HI	7.79%	11
OR	94.11%	TN	16.08%	ID	1.41%	OR	2.73%	CT	6.95%	12
MT	93.19%	AR	15.91%	OR	1.41%	MA	2.72%	DC	5.98%	13
RI	93.11%	IL	15.12%	NC	1.23%	TX	2.18%	WY	5.81%	14
CO	92.81%	MI	14.17%	MN	1.19%	UT	2.15%	ID	5.53%	15
WI	92.63%	FL	14.11%	CA	0.95%	MN	2.04%	MA	5.24%	16
KY	92.17%	NJ	14.08%	CO	0.95%	CO	2.02%	UT	5.19%	17
KS	91.69%	TX	12.10%	KS	0.91%	RI	2.00%	RI	5.09%	18
SD	91.53%	OH	10.94%	WI	0.84%	CT	1.77%	WA	4.71%	19
MA	91.26%	MO	10.88%	NE	0.81%	AZ	1.75%	OR	4.27%	20
IN	91.07%	PA	9.45%	MI	0.61%	DE	1.59%	KS	4.02%	21
WA	90.14%	CT	8.78%	AR	0.54%	KS	1.43%	AK	3.40%	22
CT	89.23%	IN	7.95%	HI	0.52%	FL	1.36%	OK	2.93%	23
AZ	89.12%	CA	7.71%	ME	0.49%	GA	1.36%	MD	2.91%	24
PA	89.10%	OK	7.68%	LA	0.44%	PA	1.33%	VA	2.78%	25
OH	87.94%	KY	7.17%	TX	0.44%	MI	1.26%	NE	2.62%	26
MO	87.81%	NV	6.89%	RI	0.40%	WI	1.24%	DE	2.60%	27
NV	87.80%	KS	5.96%	AL	0.39%	OK	1.22%	LA	2.29%	28
NM	87.48%	MA	5.79%	MO	0.39%	NM	1.14%	MI	2.28%	29
TX	85.30%	WI	5.27%	NY	0.38%	LA	1.10%	PA	2.12%	30
FL	84.21%	RI	4.50%	VT	0.35%	ID	1.03%	WI	2.04%	31
MI	83.95%	CO	4.24%	MS	0.34%	IA	1.03%	IN	1.87%	32
OK	83.00%	AK	4.08%	FL	0.30%	NE	0.94%	GA	1.83%	33
TN	82.99%	NE	3.75%	DE	0.29%	OH	0.93%	MT	1.58%	34
AR	82.96%	AZ	3.26%	IA	0.29%	MO	0.92%	MN	1.39%	35
IL	81.90%	WA	3.21%	MD	0.28%	NH	0.90%	OH	1.35%	36
NJ	81.65%	WV	3.15%	VA	0.27%	NC	0.89%	IA	1.32%	37
CA	80.67%	HI	2.51%	IN	0.23%	IN	0.74%	MO	1.27%	38
DE	80.61%	MN	2.44%	GA	0.22%	TN	0.72%	NC	1.23%	39
NY	78.05%	NM	2.28%	IL	0.22%	VT	0.70%	NH	1.08%	40
VA	77.64%	IA	1.86%	MA	0.22%	SC	0.69%	SC	0.97%	41
AK	76.53%	OR	1.72%	NJ	0.22%	ME	0.65%	AR	0.92%	42
NC	75.75%	WY	0.86%	SC	0.22%	WY	0.65%	SD	0.85%	43
AL	73.56%	UT	0.72%	TN	0.22%	ND	0.63%	ND	0.79%	44
GA	71.03%	NH	0.63%	CT	0.21%	MT	0.61%	TN	0.76%	45
MD	70.82%	ND	0.63%	OH	0.19%	AL	0.60%	VT	0.70%	46
SC	69.08%	SD	0.56%	NH	0.18%	AR	0.58%	AL	0.65%	47
LA	67.21%	ME	0.40%	DC	0.17%	SD	0.56%	MS	0.65%	48
MS	63.29%	ID	0.38%	KY	0.16%	MS	0.54%	KY	0.61%	49
HI	33.48%	MT	0.36%	PA	0.13%	KY	0.53%	ME	0.57%	50
DC	31.62%	VT	0.35%	WV	0.11%	WV	0.44%	WV	0.50%	51

[1] Persons of Hispanic origin may be of any race.

Source: Bureau of the Census, U.S. Dept. of Commerce

GENDER AND MARITAL STATUS (1996)

	% Male		% Female		Marriages per 1,000 Pop.		Divorces per 1,000 Pop.	Desc. Num. Order
AK	52.60%	DC	53.17%	NV	88.09	NV	9.94	1
NV	50.99%	MS	51.97%	HI	16.45	WY	6.49	2
HI	50.46%	AL	51.93%	TN	15.43	TN	6.47	3
WY	50.35%	RI	51.88%	AR	14.44	NM	6.39	4
CA	50.08%	PA	51.85%	ID	12.59	AR	6.07	5
ID	50.00%	NY	51.82%	SC	11.66	AL	6.03	6
ND	49.94%	LA	51.79%	KY	11.15	ID	5.90	7
MT	49.82%	MA	51.73%	AL	11.08	OK	5.84	8
UT	49.82%	WV	51.73%	UT	11.02	AZ	5.83	9
WA	49.81%	SC	51.69%	FL	10.41	MS	5.78	10
CO	49.61%	TN	51.64%	WY	10.17	FL	5.57	11
AZ	49.52%	AR	51.62%	VT	10.06	KY	5.46	12
OR	49.43%	OH	51.59%	VA	9.80	MO	4.90	13
TX	49.41%	MO	51.53%	TX	9.39	NC	4.90	14
NM	49.35%	NJ	51.48%	NM	9.35	GA	4.88	15
MN	49.34%	FL	51.43%	SD	9.19	MT	4.83	16
SD	49.30%	KY	51.42%	CO	9.01	WA	4.79	17
VT	49.27%	NC	51.41%	LA	8.95	OR	4.69	18
NH	49.24%	CT	51.39%	AK	8.94	AK	4.66	19
KS	49.23%	MD	51.31%	AZ	8.86	UT	4.64	20
WI	49.20%	GA	51.27%	MO	8.60	DE	4.62	21
VA	49.01%	IN	51.27%	NC	8.45	KS	4.54	22
NE	48.98%	IA	51.27%	IN	8.42	WV	4.39	23
OK	48.93%	DE	51.26%	NY	8.37	NH	4.30	24
ME	48.84%	MI	51.25%	IA	8.36	VA	4.29	25
IL	48.83%	IL	51.17%	NH	8.36	VT	4.23	26
MI	48.75%	ME	51.16%	MD	8.24	SC	4.12	27
DE	48.74%	OK	51.07%	GA	8.17	HI	4.06	28
GA	48.73%	NE	51.02%	OK	8.08	MI	4.03	29
IN	48.73%	VA	50.99%	KS	8.01	OH	4.00	30
IA	48.73%	WI	50.80%	OR	7.98	SD	3.73	31
MD	48.69%	KS	50.77%	RI	7.91	NE	3.69	32
CT	48.61%	NH	50.76%	MS	7.86	ND	3.48	33
NC	48.59%	VT	50.73%	ND	7.81	IA	3.47	34
KY	48.58%	SD	50.70%	NE	7.72	IL	3.41	35
FL	48.57%	MN	50.66%	IL	7.61	WI	3.36	36
NJ	48.52%	NM	50.65%	MT	7.53	NY	3.34	37
MO	48.47%	TX	50.59%	OH	7.41	MN	3.27	38
OH	48.41%	OR	50.57%	MI	7.20	RI	3.26	39
AR	48.38%	AZ	50.48%	DE	7.17	CT	3.22	40
TN	48.36%	CO	50.39%	MN	7.12	MD	3.22	41
SC	48.31%	WA	50.19%	WA	7.08	PA	3.18	42
MA	48.27%	MT	50.18%	WI	7.02	NJ	3.14	43
WV	48.27%	UT	50.18%	CA	6.87	MA	2.03	44
LA	48.21%	ND	50.06%	MA	6.66	CA	NA	45
NY	48.18%	ID	50.00%	CT	6.54	CO	NA	46
PA	48.15%	CA	49.92%	NJ	6.47	DC	NA	47
RI	48.12%	WY	49.65%	DC	6.19	IN	NA	48
AL	48.07%	HI	49.54%	WV	6.06	LA	NA	49
MS	48.03%	NV	49.01%	PA	5.82	ME	NA	50
DC	46.83%	AK	47.40%	ME	NA	TX	NA	51

Source: Bureau of the Census, U.S. Dept. of Commerce

AGE (1996)

	% of Pop. Under 5 Years		% of Pop. 18 & Under		% of Pop. 65 Years & Over		% Inc. in the Elderly, 1995-96	Desc. Num. Order
UT	9.62%	UT	38.15%	FL	18.45%	AK	4.62%	1
CA	8.67%	AK	33.72%	PA	15.86%	NV	4.49%	2
TX	8.42%	ID	32.87%	RI	15.77%	HI	2.49%	3
AK	8.24%	NM	32.35%	WV	15.21%	AZ	2.32%	4
NV	8.06%	LA	31.62%	IA	15.17%	CO	1.93%	5
NM	8.04%	TX	31.53%	ND	14.51%	NM	1.90%	6
AZ	7.97%	MS	31.17%	AR	14.44%	DE	1.86%	7
IL	7.76%	WY	31.12%	SD	14.40%	UT	1.86%	8
HI	7.74%	SD	31.10%	CT	14.35%	WY	1.77%	9
ID	7.74%	CA	30.48%	MA	14.10%	TX	1.73%	10
GA	7.66%	NE	29.79%	ME	13.95%	CA	1.65%	11
MS	7.57%	KS	29.68%	DC	13.89%	NC	1.56%	12
LA	7.56%	OK	29.67%	MO	13.85%	WA	1.49%	13
NY	7.27%	MT	29.63%	NE	13.84%	VA	1.48%	14
CO	7.21%	MN	29.57%	NJ	13.77%	SC	1.47%	15
NJ	7.20%	GA	29.42%	KS	13.68%	GA	1.40%	16
MD	7.14%	ND	29.38%	OK	13.49%	ID	1.38%	17
NC	7.12%	IL	29.37%	OR	13.41%	NH	1.34%	18
WA	7.08%	AR	29.26%	OH	13.40%	MD	1.27%	19
IN	7.07%	MI	29.25%	NY	13.39%	FL	1.20%	20
AR	7.04%	WI	28.92%	WI	13.29%	MT	1.19%	21
KS	7.04%	CO	28.91%	AZ	13.23%	TN	1.01%	22
MI	7.04%	AZ	28.82%	MT	13.19%	VT	0.89%	23
SD	7.03%	MO	28.82%	AL	13.04%	OR	0.88%	24
AL	6.98%	HI	28.74%	HI	12.89%	AL	0.76%	25
OK	6.95%	WA	28.74%	DE	12.76%	MI	0.76%	26
TN	6.94%	IN	28.59%	KY	12.60%	LA	0.67%	27
DE	6.93%	NV	28.40%	IN	12.58%	NJ	0.67%	28
NE	6.92%	SC	28.32%	TN	12.55%	WI	0.62%	29
SC	6.92%	OH	28.29%	IL	12.54%	KY	0.57%	30
MO	6.89%	IA	28.21%	NC	12.52%	OK	0.55%	31
VA	6.87%	AL	28.19%	MI	12.44%	IN	0.54%	32
MN	6.86%	OR	28.02%	MN	12.39%	OH	0.54%	33
CT	6.82%	KY	28.01%	MS	12.27%	ME	0.52%	34
OH	6.82%	NH	27.87%	VT	12.11%	CT	0.50%	35
FL	6.74%	MD	27.80%	SC	12.08%	MN	0.48%	36
OR	6.72%	NC	27.75%	NH	12.01%	NY	0.39%	37
KY	6.71%	TN	27.66%	WA	11.59%	MS	0.37%	38
NH	6.58%	VT	27.57%	NV	11.44%	AR	0.34%	39
WI	6.58%	NY	27.54%	LA	11.41%	MA	0.30%	40
WY	6.53%	NJ	27.32%	MD	11.39%	PA	0.20%	41
ND	6.46%	VA	27.17%	ID	11.35%	WV	0.19%	42
MA	6.44%	DE	26.87%	WY	11.22%	MO	0.18%	43
IA	6.40%	ME	26.79%	VA	11.19%	RI	0.16%	44
MT	6.40%	CT	26.68%	NM	11.04%	IL	0.15%	45
RI	6.37%	PA	26.57%	CA	11.03%	NE	0.14%	46
PA	6.31%	WV	26.22%	TX	10.20%	SD	0.11%	47
DC	6.17%	RI	26.20%	CO	10.06%	KS	0.09%	48
VT	6.06%	FL	26.09%	GA	9.92%	ND	0.08%	49
WV	5.85%	MA	25.68%	UT	8.76%	IA	−0.09%	50
ME	5.75%	DC	22.20%	AK	5.15%	DC	−0.98%	51

Source: Bureau of the Census, U.S. Dept. of Commerce

OF VITAL IMPORTANCE

BIRTH RATES; INFANT MORTALITY

Live Birth Rate per 1,000 Pop.[1]		Infant Mortality Rate[2]		Infant Mortality, Whites[3]		Infant Mortality, Blacks[3]		Births to Unmarried, % of Tot.[4]		Births to Teenagers, % of Tot.[4]		Desc. Num. Order
UT	20.7	DC	16.2	OK	8.0	IA	21.2	DC	66.0	MS	21.3	1
AZ	18.0	MS	10.5	SD	7.9	DC	19.6	MS	45.1	AR	19.8	2
TX	17.1	AL	9.8	IA	7.8	IL	18.7	LA	43.4	LA	18.9	3
CA	16.9	LA	9.8	WV	7.6	WI	18.6	NV	42.7	AL	18.3	4
AK	16.7	SC	9.6	KY	7.4	TN	17.9	NM	42.1	NM	17.9	5
NV	16.2	SD	9.5	IN	7.3	KS	17.6	AZ	39.0	OK	17.2	6
ID	16.0	GA	9.4	NE	7.3	MN	17.6	NY	38.8	KY	17.0	7
NM	15.9	IL	9.4	OH	7.3	PA	17.6	SC	37.2	DC	16.8	8
GA	15.6	TN	9.3	AZ	7.2	IN	17.5	FL	36.0	SC	16.8	9
IL	15.6	NC	9.2	AR	7.2	OH	17.5	DE	35.5	TN	16.8	10
HI	15.5	MD	8.9	IL	7.2	MI	17.3	GA	35.0	WV	16.8	11
KS	15.4	AR	8.8	AL	7.1	AZ	17.0	AR	33.9	TX	16.2	12
DC	15.3	OH	8.7	MS	7.0	CO	16.8	MI	33.8	GA	15.9	13
MS	15.3	IN	8.4	MT	7.0	WA	16.2	IL	33.7	AZ	15.0	14
LA	15.2	MI	8.3	RI	7.0	NC	15.9	AL	33.5	NC	15.0	15
NY	14.9	OK	8.3	TN	6.8	LA	15.3	MD	33.4	IN	14.5	16
CO	14.6	IA	8.2	WY	6.8	MD	15.3	TN	33.4	WY	14.4	17
AR	14.5	WV	7.9	NC	6.7	VA	15.3	MO	33.1	MO	14.1	18
WA	14.5	PA	7.8	ND	6.7	AL	15.2	OH	32.9	DE	13.7	19
AL	14.4	VA	7.8	SC	6.7	GA	15.1	RI	32.9	ID	13.5	20
NC	14.4	AK	7.7	CT	6.5	OK	15.1	IN	32.6	FL	13.4	21
IN	14.3	NY	7.7	GA	6.5	MS	14.7	PA	32.3	NV	13.3	22
MI	14.3	WY	7.7	MO	6.4	SC	14.6	NC	32.0	OH	13.3	23
NJ	14.3	KY	7.6	ME	6.3	CA	14.4	CA	31.6	OR	13.2	24
SD	14.3	AZ	7.5	WI	6.3	AR	14.3	WV	31.4	KS	13.1	25
DE	14.1	DE	7.5	KS	6.2	NY	13.9	AK	31.3	IL	12.7	26
NE	14.1	FL	7.5	LA	6.2	MO	13.8	CT	31.3	MT	12.5	27
OK	14.0	MO	7.4	MI	6.2	NJ	13.3	OK	30.9	MI	12.2	28
TN	13.9	NE	7.4	NY	6.2	DE	13.1	TX	30.5	CA	12.0	29
MO	13.8	WI	7.3	PA	6.2	FL	13.0	HI	30.2	CO	11.9	30
VA	13.8	CT	7.2	VT	6.2	CT	12.6	KY	29.8	SD	11.5	31
MD	13.7	ND	7.2	AK	6.1	TX	11.7	OR	29.7	WA	11.3	32
MN	13.7	RI	7.2	NM	6.1	KY	10.7	SD	29.5	AK	11.2	33
OH	13.7	KS	7.0	CO	6.0	MA	9.0	VA	28.8	IA	11.0	34
SC	13.7	MT	7.0	DE	6.0	AK	NA	ME	28.7	VA	11.0	35
KY	13.6	MN	6.7	FL	6.0	HI	NA	NJ	27.9	NE	10.6	36
OR	13.6	NJ	6.6	MD	6.0	ID	NA	MT	27.8	PA	10.6	37
CT	13.5	CO	6.5	MN	6.0	ME	NA	WI	27.4	UT	10.6	38
FL	13.2	ME	6.5	OR	5.9	MT	NA	WA	27.3	WI	10.6	39
MA	13.2	TX	6.5	TX	5.9	NE	NA	WY	27.0	HI	10.3	40
WY	13.1	CA	6.3	CA	5.8	NV	NA	KS	26.9	MD	10.3	41
IA	13.0	NM	6.2	ID	5.8	NH	NA	VT	26.4	RI	10.3	42
ND	13.0	ID	6.1	VA	5.7	NM	NA	IA	26.3	ME	9.7	43
WI	13.0	OR	6.1	WA	5.6	ND	NA	MA	25.6	ND	9.6	44
RI	12.6	VT	6.0	NV	5.5	OR	NA	ND	25.2	NY	9.2	45
NH	12.5	WA	5.9	NH	5.5	RI	NA	CO	24.8	VT	8.9	46
PA	12.4	HI	5.8	NJ	5.3	SD	NA	NE	24.7	MN	8.5	47
MT	12.2	NV	5.7	UT	5.3	UT	NA	MN	24.4	CT	8.2	48
VT	11.5	NH	5.5	MA	4.7	VT	NA	NH	23.4	NJ	7.7	49
WV	11.3	UT	5.4	DC	NA	WV	NA	ID	21.3	NH	7.4	50
ME	11.1	MA	5.2	HI	NA	WY	NA	UT	16.0	MA	7.3	51

[1] 1996 [2] Per 1,000 live births, 1995 [3] 1995 [4] 1996
Source: National Center for Health Statistics, U.S. Dept. of Health and Human Services

DEATH RATES, TOTAL AND FROM SELECTED CAUSES (1995)

Total Death Rate per 100,000 Pop.		Cancer, Rate per 100,000		Heart Disease, Rate per 100,000		Suicide, Rate per 100,000		HIV Infection, Rate per 100,000		Desc. Num. Order
DC	1,244.2	DC	267.2	WV	378.9	NV	25.8	DC	117.8	1
WV	1,107.0	FL	263.5	PA	359.7	MT	23.1	NY	44.1	2
FL	1,081.3	WV	259.4	MS	356.0	AZ	19.1	FL	30.8	3
AR	1,075.1	PA	250.7	FL	351.6	NM	17.6	NJ	30.7	4
PA	1,059.2	RI	250.4	NY	350.2	CO	17.5	MD	25.6	5
MO	1,021.9	AR	244.7	MO	345.3	AK	17.1	DE	22.7	6
OK	1,002.3	ME	242.9	OK	340.4	WY	17.1	GA	22.0	7
MS	1,002.0	MA	231.9	AR	339.8	ID	16.0	CA	20.4	8
AL	996.1	NJ	231.9	RI	334.1	OR	15.8	CT	18.4	9
IA	986.0	MO	230.7	IA	332.0	FL	15.3	LA	16.8	10
TN	976.1	KY	229.2	OH	317.4	OK	15.3	MA	15.5	11
RI	975.7	DE	227.3	KY	315.8	WV	15.1	SC	15.2	12
KY	963.7	OH	226.1	AL	314.2	UT	14.8	TX	14.8	13
OH	950.1	AL	221.4	SD	312.3	ND	14.7	NC	14.1	14
SD	948.5	TN	220.9	NE	312.0	AR	14.5	NV	13.2	15
ME	946.8	IA	219.1	TN	308.2	WA	14.4	VA	12.6	16
KS	933.0	OK	217.9	IL	304.4	MO	13.5	IL	12.1	17
NE	932.6	IN	216.3	ND	304.3	AL	13.2	AZ	11.5	18
NJ	932.5	CT	215.6	NJ	303.3	ME	13.0	PA	11.5	19
ND	931.6	OR	214.7	DC	302.4	TN	13.0	CO	10.9	20
NY	928.4	SD	214.5	CT	298.9	VT	13.0	WA	10.9	21
IN	918.2	ND	214.4	KS	297.7	NC	12.6	HI	10.4	22
IL	916.9	LA	214.3	MI	294.8	LA	12.5	RI	10.0	23
LA	914.4	NY	213.3	IN	294.3	VA	12.5	TN	9.7	24
MA	913.4	MS	213.1	ME	293.9	KY	12.4	MS	9.5	25
SC	912.7	IL	212.2	WI	281.4	PA	12.1	AL	9.2	26
NC	902.2	NC	206.8	LA	279.4	WI	12.1	OR	9.2	27
CT	899.5	WI	206.3	VT	278.2	HI	12.0	NM	9.1	28
OR	898.4	NE	206.2	SC	277.6	IN	12.0	MO	8.8	29
WI	880.1	KS	205.9	DE	276.1	NH	11.9	MI	8.4	30
MT	876.6	NH	205.2	MA	275.8	SC	11.9	OH	7.9	31
MI	876.1	MI	203.5	NC	269.5	TX	11.9	OK	7.1	32
DE	875.9	MT	203.4	NH	256.9	IA	11.8	AR	6.8	33
VT	846.7	MD	201.9	NV	246.9	MS	11.8	IN	6.7	34
AZ	837.9	SC	201.9	AZ	242.6	SD	11.8	ME	6.1	35
MD	829.8	VT	198.9	GA	242.4	CA	11.7	KS	5.6	36
NV	818.6	NV	194.5	VA	240.2	GA	11.5	KY	5.6	37
MN	813.7	VA	190.4	OR	240.1	NE	11.4	MN	5.6	38
GA	810.8	AZ	190.1	MD	236.4	KS	11.3	AK	5.0	39
NH	803.6	MN	188.6	MT	230.3	MN	11.3	UT	4.8	40
VA	799.9	WY	186.6	MN	225.2	DE	11.2	VT	4.6	41
WY	774.7	WA	183.0	TX	222.9	MI	10.3	WV	4.3	42
WA	751.0	GA	177.3	CA	216.3	MD	10.1	WI	4.3	43
NM	744.3	ID	172.4	ID	212.3	CT	9.9	NH	4.1	44
TX	736.1	TX	168.9	WA	208.6	OH	9.7	ID	3.7	45
ID	732.1	CA	162.8	WY	203.3	IL	9.5	NE	3.7	46
CA	709.8	NM	159.5	NM	196.1	RI	9.0	IA	3.1	47
CO	667.6	HI	156.4	HI	196.0	MA	8.1	SD	2.9	48
HI	643.1	CO	145.9	CO	172.1	NY	7.6	MT	2.6	49
UT	560.6	UT	108.6	UT	148.1	NJ	7.3	ND	NA	50
AK	423.0	AK	95.1	AK	90.6	DC	7.0	WY	NA	51

Source: National Center for Health Statistics and U.S. Centers for Disease Control and Prevention, Dept. of Health and Human Services

KEEPING WELL

PHYSICIANS, NURSES; INSURANCE

Physicians per 100,000 Pop., 1995		Nurses per 100,000 Pop., 1995		% of Pop. Without Health Insur., 1996		Desc. Num. Order
DC	662	DC	1,699	TX	24.3%	1
MA	387	FL	1,699	AZ	24.1%	2
NY	361	MA	1,195	NM	22.3%	3
MD	349	RI	1,136	AR	21.7%	4
CT	334	ND	1,090	LA	20.9%	5
RI	298	SD	1,077	CA	20.1%	6
NJ	276	DE	1,067	FL	18.9%	7
PA	273	ME	1,059	MS	18.5%	8
VT	270	CT	1,032	GA	17.8%	9
HI	248	PA	1,018	SC	17.1%	10
IL	244	AK	1,011	NY	17.0%	11
CA	241	NH	993	OK	17.0%	12
MN	239	MN	955	NJ	16.7%	13
CO	227	MO	940	CO	16.6%	14
VA	227	NE	940	ID	16.5%	15
TN	226	VT	924	NC	16.0%	16
WA	224	NY	915	NV	15.6%	17
LA	222	OH	896	KY	15.4%	18
FL	220	WI	882	OR	15.3%	19
OH	219	TN	869	TN	15.2%	20
MO	218	IN	866	WV	14.9%	21
DE	217	MD	854	DC	14.8%	22
NH	214	NJ	850	MT	13.6%	23
NC	214	CO	830	AK	13.5%	24
WI	213	MI	820	WA	13.5%	25
OR	212	NC	820	WY	13.5%	26
MI	210	GA	818	DE	13.4%	27
ND	204	VA	816	MO	13.2%	28
NE	199	KS	814	AL	12.9%	29
NM	199	OR	806	VA	12.5%	30
AZ	198	WA	798	MA	12.4%	31
ME	198	WY	798	ME	12.1%	32
GA	196	WV	793	UT	12.0%	33
WV	196	IA	784	IA	11.6%	34
KS	195	ID	766	OH	11.5%	35
KY	193	AL	763	KS	11.4%	36
SC	190	AZ	760	MD	11.4%	37
TX	189	KY	756	NE	11.4%	38
AL	184	MT	751	IL	11.3%	39
MT	181	HI	733	VT	11.1%	40
IN	180	LA	724	CT	11.0%	41
AR	171	MS	709	IN	10.6%	42
IA	166	SC	707	MN	10.2%	43
SD	166	AR	690	RI	9.9%	44
OK	160	NM	683	ND	9.8%	45
NV	157	TX	647	NH	9.5%	46
AK	153	UT	647	PA	9.5%	47
WY	150	NV	611	SD	9.5%	48
MS	138	IL	595	MI	8.9%	49
ID	137	OK	591	HI	8.6%	50
UT	134	CA	574	WI	8.4%	51

Source: American Medical Assoc. (copyright); Health Resources and Services Administration, U.S. Dept. of Health and Human Services; Bureau of the Census, U.S. Dept. of Commerce

HOSPITALS (1995)

Hosp. per 100,000 Pop.		Admissions per 1,000 Pop.		Hosp. Beds per 1,000 Pop.		Occupancy Rate per 100 Beds		Avg. Cost per Patient per Day		Avg. Cost Per Patient Per Stay		Desc. Num. Order
SD	6.86	DC	277.98	DC	6.86	HI	80.00	DC	$1,346	DC	$8,632	1
ND	6.71	AL	150.95	ND	6.55	NY	79.97	AK	$1,341	HI	$8,445	2
MT	6.32	PA	149.93	SD	6.31	DE	78.95	WA	$1,318	AK	$8,282	3
NE	5.56	WV	148.25	MT	4.83	CT	73.33	CA	$1,315	NY	$8,077	4
WY	5.21	MS	143.86	NE	4.83	VT	72.22	CT	$1,264	CT	$7,358	5
KS	5.15	LA	143.25	MS	4.67	NJ	71.57	UT	$1,213	DE	$7,298	6
IA	4.08	TN	140.79	IA	4.43	DC	71.05	AZ	$1,191	CA	$7,111	7
MS	3.60	ND	138.85	WV	4.43	MA	69.84	MA	$1,157	MA	$7,099	8
ID	3.53	KY	138.34	LA	4.40	PA	69.69	OR	$1,141	NJ	$7,007	9
AR	3.42	AR	137.68	AL	4.30	MD	68.78	RI	$1,092	IL	$6,584	10
OK	3.36	NJ	134.42	KS	4.21	NC	68.28	NM	$1,073	PA	$6,482	11
WV	3.23	MO	134.11	WY	4.17	RI	66.67	NV	$1,072	CO	$6,289	12
ME	3.14	NY	132.22	MO	4.11	SD	65.22	CO	$1,069	MN	$6,241	13
MN	3.08	SD	128.94	AR	4.07	MI	65.20	MD	$1,064	MO	$6,228	14
LA	2.99	IA	127.02	NY	4.07	ME	65.00	TX	$1,063	MI	$6,218	15
AK	2.81	FL	125.09	PA	4.02	MN	64.94	OH	$1,061	RI	$6,202	16
AL	2.70	MA	123.64	TN	3.98	SC	64.60	DE	$1,058	NH	$6,188	17
KY	2.69	OH	123.31	KY	3.91	MT	64.29	IL	$1,050	WA	$6,180	18
NH	2.53	IL	122.74	MN	3.77	ND	64.29	FL	$1,004	OH	$6,141	19
WI	2.48	IN	120.45	NJ	3.76	VA	61.83	MI	$994	ME	$6,083	20
TN	2.40	RI	120.20	GA	3.62	ID	61.76	MO	$967	FL	$6,040	21
VT	2.39	GA	119.29	IL	3.55	NH	61.76	IN	$963	NV	$6,014	22
MO	2.37	MI	117.29	FL	3.51	MS	61.11	PA	$963	SC	$5,935	23
GA	2.22	NC	115.77	OK	3.51	NV	61.11	NJ	$962	MD	$5,899	24
TX	2.22	ME	114.42	OH	3.39	WI	60.59	HI	$956	VT	$5,883	25
DC	2.17	MD	113.84	IN	3.34	GA	60.54	SC	$923	NE	$5,880	26
UT	2.15	KS	113.45	WI	3.32	WV	60.49	ME	$915	TX	$5,879	27
NM	2.14	DE	112.97	ME	3.22	CA	60.13	NH	$915	WI	$5,679	28
OR	2.04	OK	112.26	NC	3.15	TN	59.81	NY	$909	UT	$5,676	29
IN	1.98	NE	111.79	MA	3.11	IL	59.76	LA	$902	NC	$5,631	30
PA	1.86	SC	111.63	MI	3.10	KY	59.60	VA	$901	GA	$5,618	31
CO	1.84	MT	110.34	SC	3.08	AR	59.41	TN	$871	AZ	$5,613	32
SC	1.80	TX	108.36	VT	3.08	FL	59.15	OK	$861	LA	$5,612	33
HI	1.77	MN	107.59	TX	3.05	AL	59.02	GA	$836	IN	$5,610	34
IL	1.75	WI	107.36	NH	2.96	OH	58.73	NC	$832	ND	$5,589	35
MI	1.75	VA	104.11	ID	2.92	IN	58.25	AL	$819	SD	$5,494	36
NC	1.65	CT	103.21	VA	2.81	CO	58.06	KY	$795	VA	$5,423	37
WA	1.62	AZ	101.23	RI	2.73	MO	57.53	WI	$794	NM	$5,358	38
OH	1.61	NV	97.39	DE	2.65	NE	56.96	WV	$763	TN	$5,355	39
MA	1.58	CA	95.89	HI	2.53	NM	56.76	MN	$736	OR	$5,325	40
FL	1.50	NH	95.82	MD	2.50	AZ	56.57	KS	$732	KS	$5,308	41
AZ	1.45	OR	94.24	CO	2.48	WA	56.48	ID	$719	OK	$5,188	42
VA	1.45	VT	94.02	CA	2.37	IA	56.35	VT	$714	MT	$5,184	43
CA	1.34	NM	92.58	AZ	2.35	LA	56.02	AR	$704	IA	$5,049	44
NV	1.31	CO	90.74	NV	2.35	WY	55.00	IA	$702	AL	$5,028	45
NY	1.27	WY	89.58	CT	2.29	TX	54.55	NE	$661	WV	$4,974	46
NJ	1.16	ID	89.42	OR	2.29	AK	53.85	MS	$584	KY	$4,838	47
DE	1.12	UT	87.65	NM	2.20	OK	53.04	WY	$545	WY	$4,817	48
RI	1.11	WA	85.99	AK	2.15	KS	52.78	ND	$521	ID	$4,686	49
CT	1.04	HI	81.72	UT	2.15	OR	52.78	MT	$493	AR	$4,459	50
MD	0.99	AK	66.23	WA	1.99	UT	52.38	SD	$476	MS	$4,265	51

Source: American Hospital Assoc. (copyright)

HOUSEHOLDS

NUMBER, SIZE, THOSE WITH ELDERLY (1996)

	Total House-holds		% Inc. in Households, 1990-96		House-holds per 1,000 Pop.		% of House-holders 65 & Over		Persons per House-hold	Desc. Num. Order
CA	11,101,000	NV	32.8%	DC	425.41	FL	28.85%	UT	3.06	1
TX	6,894,000	AZ	23.3%	FL	394.72	PA	26.36%	HI	2.97	2
NY	6,737,000	ID	19.1%	CO	392.89	WV	26.19%	DE	2.82	3
FL	5,684,000	UT	19.0%	WV	391.02	RI	25.40%	CA	2.79	4
PA	4,594,000	CO	17.1%	OR	389.83	IA	24.93%	AK	2.76	5
IL	4,352,000	GA	15.1%	ME	388.58	SD	24.91%	NJ	2.75	6
OH	4,260,000	WA	14.2%	MT	387.94	AR	24.82%	MD	2.70	7
MI	3,576,000	NM	14.1%	IA	386.75	ND	24.29%	TX	2.69	8
NJ	2,889,000	TX	13.6%	WA	386.59	NJ	23.33%	ID	2.68	9
NC	2,796,000	AK	13.4%	NV	386.15	CT	23.31%	LA	2.67	10
GA	2,723,000	OR	13.2%	VT	385.40	NE	23.30%	MI	2.66	11
VA	2,511,000	DE	11.4%	TN	383.65	MO	23.29%	MS	2.66	12
MA	2,322,000	MT	11.3%	ND	383.54	MA	23.08%	CT	2.65	13
IN	2,209,000	NC	11.1%	OK	383.22	OK	23.00%	GA	2.65	14
WA	2,139,000	TN	10.1%	MO	382.91	KS	22.81%	IL	2.65	15
MO	2,052,000	FL	10.0%	WY	382.54	MS	22.68%	NY	2.65	16
TN	2,041,000	VA	9.6%	NE	381.96	NY	22.62%	NM	2.64	17
WI	1,943,000	SC	9.4%	RI	381.82	AL	22.60%	SC	2.64	18
MD	1,871,000	HI	9.0%	NC	381.81	ME	22.57%	NH	2.62	19
MN	1,763,000	WY	8.8%	KS	381.80	OH	22.44%	MA	2.61	20
AZ	1,687,000	AL	7.8%	OH	381.28	HI	22.37%	VA	2.61	21
AL	1,624,000	VT	7.5%	MA	381.16	WI	22.23%	WI	2.61	22
LA	1,572,000	MS	7.4%	PA	381.09	MT	21.99%	AZ	2.59	23
CO	1,502,000	KY	7.1%	AZ	380.98	OR	21.86%	MN	2.58	24
KY	1,478,000	MD	7.0%	DE	380.69	KY	21.79%	PA	2.58	25
SC	1,376,000	MN	7.0%	KY	380.54	AZ	21.70%	IN	2.57	26
OK	1,265,000	CA	6.9%	AL	380.06	DC	21.65%	VT	2.57	27
OR	1,249,000	IN	6.9%	AR	378.88	IL	21.65%	AL	2.56	28
CT	1,231,000	AR	6.7%	MN	378.49	MI	21.39%	RI	2.56	29
IA	1,103,000	NH	6.7%	IN	378.19	IN	21.37%	SD	2.56	30
KS	982,000	WI	6.6%	NH	377.80	TN	21.12%	KY	2.55	31
MS	979,000	SD	5.4%	WI	376.55	NC	21.07%	WY	2.55	32
AR	951,000	OK	4.9%	VA	376.18	DE	21.01%	KS	2.54	33
WV	714,000	LA	4.8%	CT	375.99	SC	21.00%	ME	2.54	34
UT	639,000	NE	4.8%	SD	372.95	MN	20.76%	NE	2.54	35
NE	631,000	MI	4.6%	MI	372.73	LA	20.61%	OH	2.54	36
NV	619,000	MO	4.6%	SC	371.99	ID	20.00%	NV	2.53	37
NM	619,000	OH	4.2%	NY	370.47	VT	19.82%	NC	2.53	38
ME	483,000	KS	3.9%	GA	370.33	NM	19.71%	WA	2.53	39
NH	439,000	ME	3.8%	MD	368.89	CA	19.39%	TN	2.52	40
ID	430,000	WV	3.7%	IL	367.35	NH	19.36%	AR	2.51	41
HI	389,000	IL	3.6%	NJ	361.67	MD	19.03%	IA	2.51	42
RI	378,000	IA	3.6%	ID	361.65	WY	19.02%	MO	2.51	43
MT	341,000	NJ	3.4%	NM	361.35	WA	18.98%	ND	2.51	44
DE	276,000	MA	3.3%	LA	361.30	VA	18.68%	OR	2.51	45
SD	273,000	ND	2.4%	MS	360.46	NV	18.58%	MT	2.50	46
ND	247,000	PA	2.2%	TX	360.41	TX	17.99%	OK	2.50	47
DC	231,000	NY	1.5%	AK	352.55	UT	17.53%	WV	2.50	48
VT	227,000	CT	0.0%	CA	348.23	GA	17.08%	CO	2.47	49
AK	214,000	RI	−0.1%	HI	328.55	CO	16.38%	FL	2.45	50
WY	184,000	DC	−7.3%	UT	319.50	AK	9.35%	DC	2.24	51

Source: Bureau of the Census, U.S. Dept. of Commerce

LIVING QUARTERS

RENTAL HOUSING UNITS

As % of Housing Units		As % of Occupied Units		Persons per Unit		Median Contract Rent		Vacancy Rate		Desc. Num. Order
DC	54.77%	DC	61.10%	HI	2.78	HI	$599	AZ	15.3%	1
NY	43.93%	NY	47.82%	CA	2.74	CA	$561	OK	14.7%	2
HI	42.16%	HI	46.13%	UT	2.67	NJ	$521	WY	14.4%	3
CA	41.20%	RI	45.32%	MS	2.65	CT	$510	TX	13.0%	4
NV	40.65%	NV	45.23%	AK	2.58	MA	$506	LA	12.5%	5
MA	37.03%	CA	44.38%	LA	2.57	AK	$503	FL	12.4%	6
RI	36.95%	AK	43.90%	TX	2.55	NH	$479	GA	12.2%	7
AK	35.65%	MA	40.75%	NM	2.52	MD	$473	NH	11.8%	8
MD	34.97%	TX	39.13%	ID	2.51	NV	$445	SC	11.5%	9
WA	34.48%	MD	37.83%	GA	2.49	DC	$441	CO	11.4%	10
OR	34.13%	CO	37.76%	AR	2.48	NY	$428	NM	11.4%	11
TX	33.90%	WA	37.43%	AZ	2.46	DE	$425	KS	11.1%	12
IL	33.35%	OR	36.92%	MD	2.45	RI	$416	MO	10.7%	13
CO	32.78%	AZ	35.82%	AL	2.44	VA	$411	AR	10.4%	14
CT	32.02%	IL	35.77%	VA	2.43	FL	$402	WV	10.1%	15
NJ	31.91%	NJ	35.11%	OK	2.41	WA	$383	MT	9.6%	16
GA	31.45%	GA	35.07%	NJ	2.40	VT	$374	TN	9.6%	17
VA	30.94%	ND	34.43%	FL	2.39	AZ	$370	MS	9.5%	18
NE	30.57%	CT	34.38%	KY	2.39	IL	$369	AL	9.3%	19
OH	30.41%	LA	34.10%	NC	2.39	CO	$362	NC	9.2%	20
SD	30.05%	SD	33.92%	WY	2.39	ME	$358	NV	9.1%	21
ND	30.01%	VA	33.70%	DE	2.38	MN	$348	ND	9.0%	22
LA	29.79%	NE	33.53%	NY	2.38	GA	$344	UT	8.6%	23
AZ	29.55%	WI	33.30%	IL	2.37	OR	$344	AK	8.5%	24
WI	29.52%	FL	32.77%	NV	2.35	MI	$343	ME	8.4%	25
TN	29.25%	MT	32.75%	TN	2.35	WI	$331	IN	8.3%	26
KS	29.02%	NM	32.57%	SD	2.34	TX	$328	KY	8.2%	27
UT	28.63%	OH	32.52%	OR	2.33	PA	$322	VA	8.1%	28
NC	28.57%	WY	32.16%	WV	2.33	NM	$312	IL	8.0%	29
NM	27.96%	KS	32.07%	KS	2.31	UT	$300	DC	7.9%	30
IA	27.89%	NC	31.99%	MI	2.31	OH	$296	MN	7.9%	31
MO	27.85%	TN	31.97%	CT	2.30	IN	$291	RI	7.9%	32
KY	27.83%	OK	31.92%	IN	2.30	KS	$285	DE	7.8%	33
MT	27.76%	UT	31.88%	WA	2.30	NC	$284	NE	7.7%	34
FL	27.58%	NH	31.81%	MT	2.28	MO	$282	OH	7.5%	35
OK	27.37%	MO	31.23%	NE	2.27	NE	$282	VT	7.5%	36
IN	27.36%	VT	30.99%	OH	2.27	SC	$276	NJ	7.4%	37
AR	27.11%	AR	30.44%	WI	2.26	TN	$273	ID	7.3%	38
PA	26.73%	KY	30.39%	CO	2.25	WY	$270	SD	7.3%	39
WY	26.69%	SC	30.15%	IA	2.25	ND	$266	MI	7.2%	40
SC	26.64%	IA	29.97%	SC	2.25	ID	$261	PA	7.2%	41
AL	26.63%	ID	29.94%	MA	2.24	LA	$260	CT	6.9%	42
ID	26.13%	DE	29.77%	MO	2.24	OK	$259	MA	6.9%	43
NH	25.96%	IN	29.75%	NH	2.24	MT	$251	MD	6.8%	44
MI	25.77%	AL	29.53%	RI	2.23	KY	$250	IA	6.4%	45
MS	25.71%	ME	29.53%	VT	2.22	SD	$242	CA	5.9%	46
DE	25.42%	PA	29.36%	ME	2.20	AR	$230	WA	5.8%	47
MN	25.11%	MI	29.00%	PA	2.19	AL	$229	HI	5.4%	48
VT	24.07%	MS	28.50%	ND	2.18	WV	$221	OR	5.3%	49
ME	23.41%	MN	28.17%	DC	2.12	IA	$216	NY	4.9%	50
WV	22.85%	WV	25.92%	MN	2.08	MS	$215	WI	4.7%	51

Source: Bureau of the Census, U.S. Dept. of Commerce

OWNER-OCCUPIED HOUSING UNITS

As % of Housing Units		As % of Occupied Units		Persons per Unit		Median Value		Desc. Num. Order
WV	65.28%	WV	74.08%	UT	3.38	HI	$245,300	1
IA	65.17%	MN	71.83%	HI	3.19	CA	$195,500	2
IN	64.60%	MS	71.50%	AK	2.97	CT	$177,800	3
MS	64.49%	MI	71.00%	NJ	2.87	MA	$162,800	4
PA	64.32%	PA	70.64%	NY	2.86	NJ	$162,300	5
MN	64.04%	AL	70.47%	NM	2.85	RI	$133,500	6
KY	63.74%	ME	70.47%	TX	2.85	NY	$131,600	7
AL	63.57%	IN	70.25%	CA	2.84	NH	$129,400	8
MI	63.09%	DE	70.23%	LA	2.83	DC	$123,900	9
OH	63.09%	ID	70.06%	ID	2.82	MD	$116,500	10
TN	62.24%	IA	70.03%	MA	2.82	DE	$100,100	11
AR	61.95%	SC	69.85%	IL	2.81	NV	$95,700	12
SC	61.70%	KY	69.61%	MI	2.80	VT	$95,500	13
KS	61.46%	AR	69.56%	NH	2.80	AK	$94,400	14
MO	61.33%	VT	69.01%	MD	2.79	WA	$93,400	15
UT	61.16%	MO	68.77%	WI	2.79	VA	$91,000	16
ID	61.15%	NH	68.19%	MN	2.78	ME	$87,400	17
CT	61.13%	UT	68.12%	MS	2.78	CO	$82,700	18
VA	60.87%	OK	68.08%	RI	2.78	IL	$80,900	19
NC	60.74%	TN	68.03%	GA	2.76	AZ	$80,100	20
NE	60.61%	NC	68.01%	SC	2.75	FL	$77,100	21
MD	60.11%	KS	67.93%	CT	2.74	MN	$74,000	22
DE	59.95%	WY	67.84%	ND	2.74	GA	$71,300	23
IL	59.90%	OH	67.48%	OH	2.74	NM	$70,100	24
WI	59.12%	NM	67.43%	WY	2.74	PA	$69,700	25
NJ	58.97%	MT	67.25%	IN	2.73	UT	$68,900	26
SD	58.53%	FL	67.23%	VT	2.73	OR	$67,100	27
OK	58.39%	WI	66.70%	PA	2.72	NC	$65,800	28
OR	58.31%	RI	66.51%	AZ	2.71	OH	$63,500	29
GA	58.25%	NE	66.47%	DE	2.71	WI	$62,500	30
NM	57.90%	VA	66.30%	ME	2.71	WY	$61,600	31
WA	57.65%	SD	66.08%	SD	2.71	SC	$61,100	32
LA	57.56%	LA	65.89%	AL	2.70	MI	$60,600	33
ND	57.16%	CT	65.62%	VA	2.70	MO	$59,800	34
MT	57.01%	ND	65.57%	KY	2.69	TX	$59,600	35
FL	56.59%	MD	65.03%	NE	2.68	LA	$58,500	36
WY	56.31%	GA	64.93%	WA	2.68	TN	$58,400	37
ME	55.85%	NJ	64.89%	MO	2.67	ID	$58,200	38
NH	55.64%	IL	64.23%	NV	2.67	MT	$56,600	39
RI	54.22%	AZ	64.18%	CO	2.66	IN	$53,900	40
CO	54.03%	OR	63.08%	TN	2.66	AL	$53,700	41
MA	53.85%	WA	62.57%	MT	2.65	KS	$52,200	42
VT	53.59%	CO	62.24%	KS	2.64	ND	$50,800	43
AZ	52.94%	TX	60.87%	IA	2.63	KY	$50,500	44
TX	52.72%	MA	59.25%	WV	2.63	NE	$50,400	45
CA	51.63%	AK	56.10%	NC	2.62	OK	$48,100	46
HI	49.23%	CA	55.62%	OR	2.62	WV	$47,900	47
NV	49.22%	NV	54.77%	AR	2.61	AR	$46,300	48
NY	47.94%	HI	53.87%	OK	2.59	MS	$45,600	49
AK	45.57%	NY	52.18%	DC	2.50	SD	$45,200	50
DC	34.87%	DC	38.90%	FL	2.49	IA	$15,900	51

Source: Bureau of the Census, U.S. Dept. of Commerce

CRIME

CRIME RATE PER 100,000 POPULATION (1996)

Total		Violent Crime[1]		Murder & Nonnegligent Manslaughter		Forcible Rape		Robbery		Aggrav. Assault	
DC	11,896.7	DC	2,469.8	DC	73.1	AK	65.6	DC	1,186.7	DC	1,162.1
FL	7,497.4	FL	1,051.0	LA	17.5	NM	63.5	MD	393.2	SC	766.7
AZ	7,067.0	SC	996.9	NV	13.7	DE	62.6	NY	340.0	FL	702.2
LA	6,838.8	MD	931.2	MD	11.6	MI	57.0	NV	307.6	NM	603.2
NM	6,602.3	LA	929.1	NM	11.5	NV	53.4	CA	295.6	LA	593.5
HI	6,584.5	IL	886.2	MS	11.1	FL	52.1	FL	289.2	IL	562.6
GA	6,309.7	CA	862.7	AL	10.4	WA	51.1	IL	279.4	AK	537.7
SC	6,214.1	NM	840.6	IL	10.0	MN	50.0	LA	276.6	CA	525.8
MD	6,061.9	NV	811.3	TN	9.5	SC	49.2	NJ	235.8	TN	494.3
OR	5,996.6	TN	774.0	CA	9.1	DC	47.9	TN	223.7	MD	488.8
NV	5,992.0	AK	727.7	SC	9.0	OK	46.8	GA	205.4	MA	482.9
UT	5,985.9	NY	727.0	AR	8.7	TN	46.5	PA	201.1	OK	436.9
WA	5,909.4	DE	668.3	GA	8.6	CO	46.2	DE	179.9	NV	436.6
TX	5,708.9	TX	644.4	AZ	8.5	TX	43.8	MI	176.2	AZ	424.0
OK	5,652.9	MA	642.2	NC	8.5	KS	42.6	SC	172.0	DE	421.5
NC	5,526.2	GA	638.7	MO	8.1	UT	41.8	TX	171.5	TX	421.4
AK	5,450.4	MI	635.3	TX	7.7	AR	41.7	MO	170.6	MI	394.6
TN	5,449.3	AZ	631.5	FL	7.5	LA	41.5	CT	169.6	GA	392.8
IL	5,315.8	OK	597.1	MI	7.5	OH	41.3	AZ	167.8	NC	384.5
CA	5,207.8	MO	590.9	VA	7.5	SD	41.0	AL	166.7	MO	383.1
CO	5,118.5	NC	588.1	AK	7.4	OR	39.7	OH	164.1	IN	371.6
MI	5,117.5	AL	565.4	NY	7.4	MD	37.6	NC	163.9	AR	359.8
MO	5,084.0	IN	537.0	IN	7.2	MS	36.1	NM	162.4	NY	356.7
DE	4,894.9	NJ	531.5	OK	6.8	NH	34.8	HI	135.6	AL	355.6
AL	4,820.1	AR	524.3	KS	6.6	IL	34.2	MS	134.2	NE	341.1
AR	4,699.2	MS	488.3	KY	5.9	IN	34.1	MA	127.7	MS	306.8
KS	4,681.7	OR	463.1	PA	5.7	AL	32.7	IN	124.1	OR	297.2
MS	4,522.9	NE	434.7	CT	4.8	CA	32.1	VA	122.6	KS	268.3
IN	4,498.2	PA	432.5	OH	4.8	GA	32.1	OR	122.2	NJ	266.7
MT	4,493.6	WA	431.2	CO	4.7	KY	31.7	WA	119.0	WA	256.4
MN	4,463.1	OH	428.7	WA	4.6	NC	31.3	AK	117.0	CO	255.4
OH	4,455.7	KS	413.8	DE	4.3	AZ	31.2	MN	115.6	RI	232.4
NE	4,436.6	CT	412.0	NJ	4.2	MO	29.2	AR	114.1	OH	218.4
NJ	4,332.9	CO	404.5	OR	4.0	WY	29.1	OK	106.6	UT	218.1
WY	4,254.1	RI	347.2	WI	4.0	MA	29.0	CO	98.2	ID	217.0
CT	4,227.7	VA	341.3	MT	3.9	RI	29.0	WI	96.6	CT	214.6
NY	4,132.3	MN	338.8	WV	3.8	HI	27.5	KS	96.3	IA	205.9
ID	4,012.5	UT	331.9	ID	3.6	MT	27.1	KY	93.8	PA	200.4
RI	3,993.5	KY	320.5	MN	3.6	NE	27.1	RI	83.2	WY	196.9
VA	3,968.3	HI	280.6	HI	3.4	VT	27.0	UT	68.9	KY	189.2
MA	3,837.1	IA	272.5	WY	3.3	VA	26.7	NE	63.7	VA	184.5
WI	3,821.4	ID	267.2	UT	3.2	ID	26.3	IA	45.1	MN	169.7
IA	3,648.9	WI	252.7	NE	2.9	PA	25.3	WV	40.4	WV	146.3
ME	3,394.1	WY	249.7	MA	2.6	NJ	24.7	MT	29.7	WI	131.1
PA	3,392.5	WV	210.1	RI	2.5	ND	24.1	NH	27.3	SD	116.1
KY	3,166.3	SD	177.2	ND	2.2	CT	23.1	ME	23.5	HI	114.0
VT	3,002.9	MT	161.0	ME	2.0	NY	23.0	WY	20.4	MT	100.3
SD	2,969.9	ME	124.9	IA	1.9	WI	21.0	ID	20.3	ME	78.5
NH	2,823.5	VT	121.2	VT	1.9	ME	20.9	SD	18.9	VT	76.9
ND	2,669.1	NH	118.2	NH	1.7	IA	19.7	VT	15.4	NH	54.4
WV	2,483.4	ND	84.0	SD	1.2	WV	19.6	ND	11.0	ND	46.7

[1] Violent crimes include murder, forcible rape, robbery, and aggravated assault.
Source: FBI, *Uniform Crime Reports*

CRIME RATE PER 100,000 POPULATION (1996) (CONTINUED)

Property Crime[2]		Burglary		Larceny-Theft		Motor Vehicle Theft		Desc. Num. Order
DC	9,426.9	DC	1,809.9	DC	5,779.9	DC	1,837.0	1
FL	6,446.3	FL	1,521.2	HI	4,620.0	AZ	926.7	2
AZ	6,435.5	NM	1,376.9	UT	4,377.1	CA	760.6	3
HI	6,304.0	NC	1,345.6	AZ	4,252.5	FL	720.6	4
LA	5,909.7	LA	1,295.8	FL	4,204.5	MD	711.4	5
NM	5,761.7	SC	1,283.8	OR	4,014.3	MI	700.5	6
GA	5,671.0	AZ	1,256.3	LA	3,982.3	NV	698.3	7
UT	5,654.0	OK	1,255.6	GA	3,927.7	TN	647.1	8
OR	5,533.6	NV	1,220.1	WA	3,898.5	LA	631.6	9
WA	5,478.2	TN	1,163.5	NM	3,802.6	GA	628.5	10
SC	5,217.2	MS	1,132.4	MT	3,518.5	HI	604.5	11
NV	5,180.7	GA	1,114.8	SC	3,505.0	NM	582.2	12
MD	5,130.7	HI	1,079.5	TX	3,447.4	NJ	581.3	13
TX	5,064.5	TX	1,068.5	MD	3,427.0	TX	548.6	14
OK	5,055.8	WA	1,057.5	CO	3,415.5	OR	531.0	15
NC	4,938.1	AL	1,002.1	AK	3,386.7	MA	528.2	16
AK	4,722.7	MD	992.3	OK	3,317.4	WA	522.2	17
CO	4,714.0	OR	988.3	NV	3,262.3	NY	494.4	18
TN	4,675.4	KS	981.3	NC	3,257.0	AK	492.9	19
MO	4,493.0	CA	979.4	WY	3,203.3	IL	490.2	20
MI	4,482.2	AR	953.2	MO	3,151.1	CT	489.4	21
IL	4,429.6	IL	913.2	NE	3,045.7	OK	482.9	22
CA	4,345.1	CO	900.8	KS	3,038.3	RI	464.3	23
MT	4,332.7	MI	895.4	IL	3,026.2	MO	447.7	24
KS	4,268.0	MO	894.2	DE	2,988.3	DE	434.2	25
AL	4,254.7	UT	848.3	MN	2,977.1	UT	428.6	26
DE	4,226.6	AK	843.3	AR	2,908.8	SC	428.5	27
AR	4,174.9	CT	842.2	AL	2,886.7	IN	424.9	28
MN	4,124.3	OH	835.4	MI	2,886.3	PA	412.2	29
MS	4,034.6	RI	821.7	TN	2,864.8	OH	407.5	30
OH	4,027.0	DE	804.1	ID	2,848.8	CO	397.8	31
WY	4,004.4	NJ	791.9	OH	2,784.1	MN	384.8	32
NE	4,001.8	IN	783.8	VA	2,760.1	AL	365.8	33
IN	3,961.2	MN	762.5	IN	2,752.6	MS	350.8	34
CT	3,815.6	ME	748.4	WI	2,634.5	WI	345.9	35
NJ	3,801.4	NY	713.9	CA	2,605.1	NE	341.6	36
ID	3,745.3	ID	709.1	MS	2,551.5	NC	335.5	37
RI	3,646.4	MA	704.1	IA	2,520.8	AR	312.9	38
VA	3,627.0	KY	688.4	CT	2,484.1	VA	278.8	39
WI	3,568.7	VT	673.0	NJ	2,428.2	KY	261.1	40
NY	3,405.3	IA	664.6	ME	2,377.9	MT	255.7	41
IA	3,376.4	WY	662.0	RI	2,360.3	KS	248.4	42
ME	3,269.2	NE	614.5	NY	2,197.0	IA	191.1	43
MA	3,194.9	WI	588.3	SD	2,121.9	ND	190.1	44
PA	2,960.1	VA	588.1	NH	2,118.0	ID	187.5	45
VT	2,881.7	MT	558.4	ND	2,085.9	WV	176.9	46
KY	2,845.8	SD	557.0	VT	2,058.4	NH	151.6	47
SD	2,792.8	PA	551.4	PA	1,996.5	VT	150.3	48
NH	2,705.3	WV	546.5	MA	1,962.6	ME	142.9	49
ND	2,585.1	NH	435.7	KY	1,896.3	WY	139.1	50
WV	2,273.3	ND	309.2	WV	1,549.8	SD	113.9	51

[2] Property crimes include burglary, larceny-theft, and motor vehicle theft and do not include arson.

TEACHING AND LEARNING

ENROLLMENTS, PUBLIC SCHOOLS, TEACHERS

Pop. 3 & Over in School, 1996		% of Pop. 3+ in School, 1996		Public Schools, 1996-97		Teachers, 1996		Pupil/ Teacher Ratio, 1995		Desc. Num. Order
CA	7,352,354	UT	31.27%	CA	7,876	TX	247,526	CA	24.0	1
TX	4,761,711	DC	28.81%	TX	6,638	CA	228,028	UT	23.8	2
NY	3,866,566	WY	26.81%	NY	4,149	NY	185,063	WA	20.4	3
FL	2,877,586	ID	25.64%	IL	4,142	FL	120,450	OR	19.8	4
IL	2,679,153	AK	25.60%	OH	3,865	IL	115,859	MI	19.7	5
PA	2,425,009	NM	25.27%	MI	3,748	PA	106,400	AZ	19.6	6
OH	2,381,370	KS	24.99%	PA	3,182	OH	104,583	NV	19.1	7
MI	2,210,439	TX	24.89%	FL	2,760	NJ	90,703	ID	19.0	8
GA	1,635,951	NE	24.69%	NJ	2,279	MI	84,200	FL	18.9	9
NC	1,571,992	ND	24.66%	MO	2,256	GA	81,683	CO	18.5	10
NJ	1,554,844	SD	24.54%	MN	2,157	VA	80,896	HI	17.8	11
VA	1,452,012	OK	24.27%	WA	2,124	NC	73,839	MN	17.8	12
MA	1,350,588	VT	24.05%	WI	2,037	MA	65,863	IN	17.5	13
IN	1,274,225	MN	23.99%	NC	1,985	MO	59,222	MS	17.5	14
WA	1,257,722	CO	23.96%	IN	1,924	IN	56,412	AK	17.3	15
WI	1,184,961	MT	23.84%	VA	1,889	WI	55,296	AR	17.1	16
MO	1,174,863	IA	23.78%	MA	1,850	TN	51,369	IL	17.1	17
TN	1,137,063	AZ	23.12%	OK	1,830	LA	48,047	OH	17.1	18
MN	1,117,516	MS	23.08%	GA	1,763	MN	47,600	NM	17.0	19
MD	1,085,257	CA	23.06%	TN	1,563	WA	47,479	PA	17.0	20
AZ	1,023,740	MI	23.04%	IA	1,556	MD	47,005	AL	16.9	21
LA	981,505	WI	22.96%	KS	1,487	AL	42,492	KY	16.9	22
AL	967,545	RI	22.76%	CO	1,486	SC	40,640	DE	16.8	23
CO	916,177	WA	22.73%	LA	1,470	OK	39,350	MD	16.8	24
KY	841,929	AL	22.64%	NE	1,411	AZ	39,315	TN	16.7	25
SC	823,105	IL	22.61%	KY	1,402	KY	39,235	LA	16.6	26
OK	801,055	LA	22.56%	AL	1,319	CT	36,800	GA	16.5	27
OR	704,928	NH	22.28%	MD	1,276	CO	35,900	MT	16.4	28
CT	680,749	GA	22.25%	OR	1,216	IA	32,549	NC	16.2	29
IA	678,346	SC	22.25%	AZ	1,133	KS	30,750	SC	16.2	30
KS	642,783	MA	22.17%	AR	1,098	MS	29,237	ND	15.9	31
MS	626,858	ME	22.13%	SC	1,095	AR	29,194	WI	15.8	32
UT	625,409	AR	22.12%	CT	1,045	OR	26,757	NH	15.7	33
AR	555,256	OR	22.00%	MS	1,011	WV	20,642	OK	15.7	34
NM	432,927	MO	21.92%	MT	894	UT	20,224	TX	15.6	35
NE	407,839	NV	21.83%	WV	877	NE	20,109	IA	15.5	36
WV	389,475	IN	21.82%	SD	824	NM	19,608	NY	15.5	37
NV	349,957	VA	21.75%	UT	735	NV	14,723	MO	15.4	38
ID	304,818	KY	21.68%	ME	726	ME	14,458	KS	15.1	39
ME	275,107	NC	21.47%	NM	721	ID	13,059	DC	15.0	40
NH	258,908	MD	21.40%	ID	618	NH	12,394	SD	15.0	41
HI	251,683	TN	21.37%	ND	613	HI	10,675	WY	14.8	42
RI	225,281	DE	21.36%	AK	495	RI	10,586	MA	14.6	43
MT	209,583	WV	21.33%	NH	460	MT	10,110	WV	14.6	44
SD	179,605	OH	21.31%	NV	423	SD	9,474	NE	14.5	45
ND	158,826	HI	21.26%	WY	410	VT	7,952	CT	14.4	46
DC	156,436	NY	21.26%	VT	384	ND	7,706	VA	14.4	47
AK	155,363	CT	20.79%	RI	310	AK	7,644	RI	14.3	48
DE	154,856	PA	20.11%	HI	246	WY	6,700	ME	13.9	49
VT	141,672	FL	19.98%	DC	186	DE	6,642	NJ	13.8	50
WY	128,953	NJ	19.46%	DE	181	DC	5,398	VT	13.8	51

Source: Bureau of the Census, U.S. Dept. of Commerce; National Center for Education Statistics, U.S. Dept. of Education

PUBLIC SCHOOLS: SALARIES AND EXPENDITURES

Teachers' Avg. Salary, 1996-97		Expend. per Capita, 1992-93		Expend. per Pupil, 1994-95		Desc. Num. Order
AK	$50,647	AK	$2,443.96	NJ	$9,774	1
CT	$50,426	WY	$1,873.80	NY	$9,623	2
NY	$49,560	NY	$1,665.12	DC	$9,335	3
NJ	$49,349	DE	$1,656.86	AK	$8,963	4
PA	$47,429	WA	$1,630.78	CT	$8,817	5
DC	$45,012	NJ	$1,607.71	RI	$7,469	6
MI	$44,251	MN	$1,592.45	MA	$7,287	7
MA	$43,806	WI	$1,590.24	MD	$7,245	8
CA	$43,474	MI	$1,562.94	PA	$7,109	9
RI	$43,019	VT	$1,540.41	DE	$7,030	10
IL	$42,679	ND	$1,516.13	MI	$6,994	11
DE	$41,436	OR	$1,478.85	WI	$6,930	12
MD	$41,148	NE	$1,473.44	VT	$6,750	13
OR	$40,900	IA	$1,448.41	OR	$6,436	14
WI	$38,950	CT	$1,448.21	ME	$6,428	15
OH	$38,831	UT	$1,429.69	OH	$6,162	16
IN	$38,575	KS	$1,428.26	WY	$6,160	17
MN	$37,975	NM	$1,420.30	IL	$6,136	18
WA	$37,860	PA	$1,402.93	WV	$6,107	19
NV	$37,340	CO	$1,383.94	HI	$6,078	20
VT	$37,200	MT	$1,366.02	MN	$6,000	21
NH	$36,867	TX	$1,338.71	NE	$5,935	22
CO	$36,175	RI	$1,337.95	WA	$5,906	23
GA	$36,042	MD	$1,335.17	NH	$5,859	24
HI	$35,842	WV	$1,323.61	IN	$5,826	25
KS	$35,837	IN	$1,308.98	KS	$5,817	26
VA	$35,837	ME	$1,303.65	FL	$5,718	27
MO	$34,342	AZ	$1,303.18	MT	$5,692	28
KY	$33,950	VA	$1,280.34	IA	$5,483	29
FL	$33,881	CA	$1,263.19	CO	$5,443	30
ME	$33,800	OH	$1,253.43	MO	$5,383	31
TN	$33,789	DC	$1,244.05	VA	$5,327	32
AZ	$33,350	IL	$1,241.48	TX	$5,222	33
IA	$33,275	NC	$1,235.90	KY	$5,217	34
WV	$33,159	HI	$1,234.67	GA	$5,193	35
SC	$32,659	NH	$1,227.49	NV	$5,160	36
TX	$32,644	OK	$1,224.08	NC	$5,077	37
AL	$32,549	SD	$1,214.45	CA	$4,992	38
ID	$31,818	SC	$1,192.27	OK	$4,845	39
NE	$31,768	NV	$1,170.67	SC	$4,797	40
UT	$31,750	ID	$1,165.61	AZ	$4,778	41
WY	$31,721	GA	$1,157.24	ND	$4,775	42
NC	$31,225	AR	$1,151.93	SD	$4,775	43
AR	$29,975	LA	$1,150.41	LA	$4,761	44
MT	$29,950	MA	$1,106.92	NM	$4,586	45
NM	$29,715	KY	$1,100.46	AR	$4,459	46
OK	$29,270	FL	$1,087.70	AL	$4,405	47
LA	$28,347	AL	$1,060.70	TN	$4,388	48
MS	$27,720	MS	$1,052.79	ID	$4,210	49
ND	$27,711	MO	$1,052.79	MS	$4,080	50
SD	$26,764	TN	$955.86	UT	$3,656	51

Source: Bureau of the Census, U.S. Dept. of Commerce; National Center for Education Statistics, U.S. Dept. of Education

SAT AND ACT TESTS

% of Grads. Taking SAT, 1995		Mean SAT Verbal Scores		Mean SAT Math Scores		% of Grads. Taking ACT, 1997		Mean ACT Scores		Desc. Num. Order
CT	81%	IA	516	ND	592	TN	83%	WA	22.4	1
MA	80%	ND	515	IA	583	LA	80%	NH	22.3	2
NY	74%	UT	513	MN	579	MS	79%	OR	22.3	3
NH	70%	MN	506	WI	572	ND	78%	WI	22.3	4
NJ	70%	SD	505	SD	563	KS	74%	IA	22.1	5
PA	70%	KS	503	UT	563	NE	73%	MN	22.1	6
RI	70%	WI	501	IL	560	WY	70%	MT	21.9	7
DE	68%	TN	497	KS	557	IL	69%	NY	21.9	8
ME	68%	MS	496	NE	556	UT	69%	VT	21.9	9
VT	68%	MO	495	MO	550	MI	68%	CT	21.7	10
GA	65%	NE	494	MI	549	SD	68%	KS	21.7	11
VA	65%	AL	491	TN	543	AR	66%	NE	21.7	12
MD	64%	OK	491	MS	540	OK	66%	HI	21.6	13
NC	60%	IL	488	AL	538	KY	65%	MA	21.6	14
IN	58%	LA	486	MT	536	IA	64%	CO	21.5	15
SC	58%	NM	485	OK	536	MO	64%	ME	21.5	16
HI	57%	MI	484	LA	535	WI	64%	MO	21.5	17
DC	53%	AR	482	NM	530	CO	62%	UT	21.5	18
OR	51%	KY	477	WY	525	ID	62%	ID	21.4	19
FL	48%	WY	476	AR	523	AL	61%	ND	21.4	20
WA	48%	MT	473	KY	522	MN	60%	RI	21.4	21
AK	47%	ID	468	CO	518	OH	60%	WY	21.4	22
TX	47%	CO	462	OH	515	NM	59%	MI	21.3	23
CA	45%	OH	460	ID	511	WV	57%	NV	21.3	24
NV	30%	AZ	448	OR	499	MT	55%	OH	21.3	25
CO	29%	OR	448	AZ	496	NV	39%	SD	21.3	26
AZ	27%	WV	448	WA	494	FL	36%	IL	21.2	27
OH	23%	AK	445	NH	491	AK	32%	IN	21.2	28
MT	21%	NH	444	AK	489	TX	30%	AZ	21.1	29
WV	17%	WA	443	CA	485	AZ	27%	AK	21.0	30
ID	15%	NV	434	WV	484	IN	19%	CA	21.0	31
IL	13%	CT	431	NV	483	HI	17%	DE	21.0	32
TN	12%	MD	430	HI	482	GA	16%	PA	21.0	33
KY	11%	MA	430	MD	479	NY	16%	NJ	20.8	34
MI	11%	DE	429	NJ	478	WA	16%	FL	20.7	35
NM	11%	VT	429	CT	477	SC	13%	MD	20.7	36
WY	10%	VA	428	MA	477	OR	12%	VA	20.7	37
KS	9%	ME	427	TX	474	CA	11%	OK	20.6	38
LA	9%	RI	425	NY	473	MD	11%	AR	20.3	39
MN	9%	FL	420	VT	472	NC	11%	NM	20.3	40
MO	9%	NJ	420	FL	469	PA	8%	AL	20.2	41
NE	9%	NY	419	ME	469	VT	7%	GA	20.2	42
OK	9%	PA	419	DE	468	MA	6%	TX	20.2	43
WI	9%	TX	419	VA	468	VA	6%	KY	20.1	44
AL	8%	CA	417	IN	467	DC	5%	WV	20.0	45
AR	6%	IN	415	RI	463	NH	4%	TN	19.7	46
IA	5%	DC	412	PA	461	CT	3%	LA	19.4	47
ND	5%	NC	411	NC	454	DE	3%	NC	19.3	48
SD	5%	HI	407	GA	448	NJ	3%	SC	18.9	49
MS	4%	GA	406	DC	445	ME	2%	MS	18.7	50
UT	4%	SC	401	SC	443	RI	2%	DC	17.2	51

Source: SAT: National Center for Education Statistics, U.S. Dept. of Education; ACT: American College Testing Program

HIGHER EDUCATION INSTITUTIONS

Higher Education Instits., 1996		Total Enrollment, 1995-96		% Inc. in Enrollment, 1990-95		Minority Enrollment, 1995		Minority % of Enrollment, 1995		Desc. Num. Order
CA	349	CA	1,817,042	GA	25.0%	CA	832,127	HI	64.31%	1
NY	310	NY	1,041,566	UT	21.5%	TX	336,140	CA	45.80%	2
PA	217	TX	952,525	NM	19.8%	NY	306,102	NM	42.36%	3
TX	179	IL	717,854	MT	18.9%	FL	191,314	DC	41.29%	4
IL	169	FL	637,303	ID	14.8%	IL	190,803	TX	35.29%	5
OH	156	PA	617,759	HI	12.0%	NJ	92,089	MS	30.99%	6
NC	121	MI	548,339	MN	10.6%	MI	91,310	LA	30.83%	7
GA	120	OH	540,275	NV	9.9%	GA	91,064	FL	30.02%	8
MA	116	MA	413,794	SC	9.3%	NC	88,486	MD	29.83%	9
FL	114	NC	372,030	LA	9.1%	PA	84,254	NY	29.39%	10
MI	109	VA	355,919	TN	8.7%	VA	83,662	GA	28.94%	11
MN	106	NJ	333,831	AR	8.6%	MD	79,438	NJ	27.59%	12
MO	101	GA	314,712	KS	8.5%	OH	71,511	AL	26.58%	13
VA	89	WI	300,223	WA	8.5%	MA	67,405	SC	25.56%	14
AL	82	MO	291,536	FL	8.4%	AZ	66,658	AZ	24.90%	15
IN	78	IN	289,615	NH	8.1%	LA	62,880	NC	24.33%	16
TN	76	WA	285,819	SD	7.3%	AL	57,663	VA	23.78%	17
WI	66	MN	280,816	CO	6.9%	WA	48,472	VA	23.51%	18
WA	64	AZ	273,981	ND	6.7%	NM	43,383	NV	20.54%	19
KY	61	MD	266,310	TX	5.7%	SC	43,352	OK	19.51%	20
NJ	61	TN	245,962	NC	5.6%	TN	42,824	AK	18.86%	21
CO	59	CO	242,739	DE	5.5%	CO	42,071	DE	18.22%	22
IA	59	AL	225,612	OK	4.3%	HI	40,643	AR	17.48%	23
SC	59	LA	203,935	AZ	3.7%	MO	38,051	TN	17.41%	24
MD	57	OK	180,676	AL	3.2%	MS	38,027	CO	17.33%	25
KS	54	KY	178,858	NJ	2.9%	OK	35,256	WA	16.96%	26
MS	46	KS	177,643	NE	2.6%	DC	31,906	MI	16.65%	27
AZ	45	SC	174,125	MD	2.5%	IN	30,578	CT	16.34%	28
OK	45	IA	173,835	PA	2.3%	WI	27,864	MA	16.29%	29
OR	45	OR	167,145	IA	1.9%	CT	25,763	PA	13.64%	30
CT	42	CT	157,695	IN	1.7%	MN	24,305	OH	13.24%	31
AR	38	UT	147,324	WV	1.5%	KS	21,926	MO	13.05%	32
LA	36	MS	122,690	OR	0.8%	OR	21,555	OR	12.90%	33
NE	35	NE	115,718	VA	0.7%	AR	17,163	KS	12.34%	34
NM	35	NM	102,405	KY	0.6%	KY	15,977	RI	11.84%	35
ME	33	AR	98,180	MO	0.6%	NV	13,929	MT	11.08%	36
NH	30	WV	86,034	CA	0.5%	IA	12,419	IN	10.56%	37
MT	28	DC	77,277	WI	0.1%	UT	9,416	WI	9.28%	38
WV	28	RI	74,100	MS	-0.2%	NE	8,784	KY	8.93%	39
VT	22	NV	67,826	NY	-0.6%	RI	8,773	SD	8.69%	40
ND	21	NH	64,327	MA	-1.0%	DE	8,071	MN	8.66%	41
SD	21	HI	63,198	ME	-1.1%	AK	5,534	NE	7.59%	42
DC	18	ID	59,566	AK	-1.6%	WV	4,961	ND	7.35%	43
HI	17	ME	56,547	IL	-1.6%	MT	4,729	WY	7.33%	44
UT	17	DE	44,307	DC	-2.9%	ID	3,740	IA	7.14%	45
ID	12	MT	42,674	OH	-3.1%	NH	3,280	UT	6.39%	46
RI	12	ND	40,399	VT	-3.7%	SD	3,189	ID	6.28%	47
NV	10	SD	36,695	WY	-3.7%	ND	2,968	VT	5.80%	48
AK	9	VT	35,065	MI	-3.8%	ME	2,712	WV	5.77%	49
DE	9	WY	30,176	RI	-5.3%	WY	2,212	NH	5.10%	50
WY	9	AK	29,348	CT	-6.5%	VT	2,033	ME	4.80%	51

Source: National Center for Education Statistics, U.S. Dept. of Education

PUBLIC LIBRARIES (1994)

Library Systems		Books & Serial Vols. per Capita		Library Visits per Capita		Circulation per Capita		Desc. Num. Order
NY	741	ME	4.9	CT	6.3	OH	11.8	1
IL	606	VT	4.8	IN	5.7	WA	10.1	2
IA	518	MA	4.7	ND	5.4	IN	9.6	3
TX	496	WY	4.7	RI	5.4	OR	9.6	4
PA	445	KS	4.4	IL	5.3	MN	9.4	5
WI	381	NH	4.4	IA	5.2	KS	9.2	6
MI	380	CT	4.3	WI	5.2	MD	9.1	7
MA	373	NY	4.2	KS	5.1	IA	8.9	8
KS	324	RI	4.1	OH	5.0	UT	8.9	9
NJ	309	MO	4.0	ID	4.9	WI	8.7	10
NE	269	IA	3.9	NY	4.9	CT	8.1	11
OH	250	NE	3.8	NH	4.8	WY	8.1	12
IN	238	NJ	3.8	AZ	4.7	ID	7.9	13
ME	232	IN	3.7	NJ	4.7	CO	7.8	14
NH	229	DC	3.6	WY	4.7	MO	7.8	15
AL	207	OH	3.6	MN	4.6	NE	7.8	16
VT	200	ND	3.5	MD	4.5	ME	7.6	17
CT	194	IL	3.4	VA	4.4	IL	7.5	18
CA	170	SD	3.4	CO	4.3	NH	7.5	19
MO	147	ID	3.3	MO	4.3	ND	7.3	20
TN	140	NM	3.3	CA	4.0	NY	7.1	21
MN	132	WI	3.2	OK	3.9	VT	7.1	22
OR	124	AK	3.1	AK	3.8	SD	7.0	23
CO	120	MT	3.1	MI	3.8	VA	7.0	24
KY	116	MI	2.9	SD	3.7	MA	6.9	25
SD	113	MN	2.8	DC	3.5	AZ	6.8	26
OK	112	WA	2.8	MT	3.5	NM	6.5	27
ID	107	MD	2.7	WV	3.4	OK	6.4	28
FL	97	UT	2.7	AL	3.3	AK	6.3	29
WV	97	CO	2.6	DE	3.3	RI	6.2	30
VA	90	VA	2.5	NC	3.3	MT	6.0	31
AK	87	WV	2.5	NV	3.1	NC	5.9	32
MT	82	OR	2.4	PA	3.0	NJ	5.8	33
ND	78	HI	2.3	TX	3.0	HI	5.7	34
NC	74	LA	2.2	HI	2.9	MI	5.4	35
NM	73	OK	2.2	SC	2.9	FL	5.1	36
UT	69	AR	2.1	GA	2.8	KY	5.1	37
WA	69	PA	2.1	KY	2.6	NV	4.8	38
LA	65	AL	2.0	MS	2.5	PA	4.7	39
GA	54	AZ	2.0	TN	2.5	CA	4.6	40
RI	51	KY	2.0	AR	2.3	WV	4.6	41
MS	47	MS	2.0	LA	2.3	GA	4.4	42
SC	40	NV	2.0	FL	NA	LA	4.4	43
AZ	39	NC	2.0	ME	NA	DE	4.3	44
AR	35	TX	2.0	MA	NA	SC	4.3	45
DE	29	CA	1.9	NE	NA	TX	4.3	46
MD	24	DE	1.9	NM	NA	AR	4.0	47
NV	23	GA	1.8	OR	NA	AL	3.9	48
WY	23	FL	1.7	UT	NA	TN	3.9	49
DC	1	SC	1.7	VT	NA	DC	3.1	50
HI	1	TN	1.7	WA	NA	MS	3.1	51

Source: U.S. Dept. of Education, National Center for Education Statistics, *Public Libraries of the U.S.-1994*

LAW ENFORCEMENT AND CORRECTIONS

EXPENDITURES, POLICE, PRISONERS (1996)

Expend., Police, & Corrections		Expend. per Capita		Police per 10,000 Pop.		Prisoners per 100,000 Pop.		Desc. Num. Order
CA	$4,855,524,000	AK	$334.74	DC	66.89	DC	1,609	1
NY	$2,730,599,000	DE	$222.06	NY	37.15	TX	686	2
TX	$2,642,953,000	MD	$200.63	NJ	36.67	LA	615	3
FL	$1,942,357,000	CT	$174.38	LA	32.71	OK	591	4
PA	$1,701,728,000	VA	$168.07	GA	29.97	SC	532	5
MI	$1,469,964,000	MA	$166.81	DE	28.82	NV	502	6
OH	$1,335,785,000	MI	$153.22	IL	27.45	MS	498	7
IL	$1,167,743,000	CA	$152.31	MD	27.05	AL	492	8
NJ	$1,133,265,000	NY	$150.16	CT	26.90	AZ	481	9
VA	$1,121,832,000	RI	$147.42	MA	26.41	GA	462	10
NC	$1,068,159,000	NC	$145.87	PA	26.39	CA	451	11
MD	$1,017,567,000	SC	$143.70	WY	25.89	MI	440	12
MA	$1,016,198,000	NJ	$141.87	KS	24.87	FL	439	13
GA	$966,600,000	PA	$141.15	NV	24.58	DE	428	14
WA	$668,970,000	AZ	$139.92	FL	24.15	OH	413	15
AZ	$619,555,000	TX	$138.17	RI	23.95	MD	412	16
WI	$574,295,000	NM	$134.99	VT	23.91	MO	409	17
CT	$570,894,000	FL	$134.89	CO	23.88	VA	404	18
LA	$550,563,000	GA	$131.46	WI	23.31	NY	383	19
TN	$531,860,000	VT	$130.98	NC	23.30	AK	379	20
SC	$531,566,000	OR	$128.45	NM	23.03	NC	379	21
IN	$523,285,000	LA	$126.54	TX	22.60	AR	357	22
MO	$442,133,000	WA	$120.91	CA	22.23	NJ	343	23
OR	$411,554,000	OH	$119.56	SC	22.13	KY	331	24
CO	$405,922,000	NV	$118.49	NH	21.92	IL	327	25
MN	$390,793,000	WI	$111.30	AL	21.90	CO	322	26
OK	$347,319,000	MT	$109.69	HI	21.88	ID	319	27
KY	$341,092,000	ID	$107.65	VA	21.86	CT	314	28
AL	$306,982,000	CO	$106.18	TN	21.80	WY	307	29
MS	$282,796,000	OK	$105.21	MO	21.16	MA	302	30
IA	$245,084,000	MS	$104.13	MI	20.87	KS	301	31
KS	$235,528,000	UT	$100.59	AZ	20.40	TN	292	32
NM	$231,227,000	TN	$99.98	OK	19.94	IN	287	33
AR	$223,063,000	IL	$98.57	AR	19.65	PA	286	34
AK	$203,187,000	HI	$96.80	WV	19.35	SD	281	35
UT	$201,181,000	KS	$91.58	OH	19.28	NM	261	36
NV	$189,936,000	WY	$91.12	NE	18.83	HI	249	37
DE	$160,996,000	IN	$89.59	MS	18.80	MT	235	38
RI	$145,948,000	AR	$88.87	AK	18.32	WI	230	39
NE	$136,396,000	KY	$87.82	KY	18.01	OR	226	40
ID	$127,995,000	SD	$87.26	ID	17.88	WA	224	41
WV	$121,314,000	IA	$85.94	UT	17.80	IA	222	42
HI	$114,615,000	MN	$83.90	IN	17.35	RI	205	43
ME	$98,060,000	NE	$82.56	MT	16.61	NE	194	44
MT	$96,413,000	MO	$82.51	IA	16.51	UT	194	45
NH	$88,467,000	ME	$78.89	OR	16.44	NH	177	46
VT	$77,149,000	NH	$76.13	WA	16.39	WV	150	47
SD	$63,870,000	AL	$71.85	MN	16.33	VT	137	48
WY	$43,832,000	WV	$66.40	ME	16.31	ME	112	49
ND	$23,440,000	ND	$36.40	ND	16.16	MN	110	50
DC	NA	DC	NA	SD	15.29	ND	101	51

Source: FBI, *Uniform Crime Reports*; Bureau of Justice Statistics, U.S. Dept. of Justice

RELIGION

POPULATION 18 AND OVER, BY RELIGIOUS PREFERENCES

Christian		Jewish		Muslim		Hindu		Buddhist	
LA	94.70%	NY	6.90%	NY	0.80%	NY	0.60%	CA	0.70%
ND	94.50%	NJ	4.30%	CA	0.60%	NJ	0.30%	NH	0.50%
MS	94.20%	FL	3.60%	DC	0.60%	CO	0.20%	OR	0.50%
SD	94.00%	MA	3.50%	NJ	0.60%	GA	0.20%	WA	0.50%
AL	93.30%	MD	2.80%	IL	0.40%	IL	0.20%	MA	0.40%
SC	93.00%	CT	2.40%	MA	0.40%	MD	0.20%	NV	0.40%
GA	91.10%	CA	2.30%	OH	0.40%	MI	0.20%	VA	0.40%
NC	90.60%	DC	2.30%	RI	0.40%	NE	0.20%	DC	0.30%
TN	90.60%	CO	1.80%	GA	0.30%	WY	0.20%	KS	0.30%
WI	90.20%	PA	1.70%	MI	0.30%	AL	0.10%	WI	0.30%
TX	90.00%	AZ	1.60%	PA	0.30%	CA	0.10%	AR	0.20%
KS	89.90%	RI	1.60%	SD	0.30%	CT	0.10%	CT	0.20%
KY	89.80%	IL	1.50%	AL	0.20%	FL	0.10%	ID	0.20%
AR	89.60%	DE	1.40%	AZ	0.20%	IA	0.10%	NY	0.20%
IA	89.30%	VT	1.10%	MD	0.20%	KS	0.10%	OK	0.20%
MN	89.30%	VA	1.10%	NH	0.20%	ME	0.10%	TX	0.20%
MO	88.70%	NH	1.00%	NC	0.20%	MA	0.10%	AZ	0.10%
NE	88.40%	NV	0.90%	SC	0.20%	MN	0.10%	CO	0.10%
PA	87.90%	MI	0.80%	TX	0.20%	OH	0.10%	FL	0.10%
UT	87.60%	MN	0.80%	VA	0.20%	OK	0.10%	GA	0.10%
IN	87.50%	NM	0.70%	WI	0.20%	PA	0.10%	IL	0.10%
RI	87.50%	OH	0.70%	CT	0.10%	VA	0.10%	IN	0.10%
VA	87.40%	TX	0.70%	FL	0.10%	WA	0.10%	KY	0.10%
WV	86.50%	UT	0.70%	IN	0.10%	WV	0.10%	LA	0.10%
OK	86.20%	MS	0.60%	KS	0.10%	AK	NA	ME	0.10%
OH	86.10%	MO	0.60%	LA	0.10%	AZ	NA	MD	0.10%
IL	85.60%	GA	0.50%	MN	0.10%	AR	NA	MI	0.10%
NV	85.50%	NE	0.50%	OR	0.10%	DE	NA	MN	0.10%
CT	85.40%	NC	0.50%	TN	0.10%	DC	NA	MO	0.10%
DE	85.40%	ME	0.40%	WV	0.10%	HI	NA	NE	0.10%
DC	85.30%	ND	0.40%	AK	NA	ID	NA	NJ	0.10%
NM	85.20%	OR	0.40%	AR	NA	IN	NA	NM	0.10%
MT	85.00%	WA	0.40%	CO	NA	KY	NA	NC	0.10%
NJ	85.00%	WI	0.40%	DE	NA	LA	NA	OH	0.10%
ME	84.90%	IN	0.30%	HI	NA	MS	NA	PA	0.10%
MD	84.80%	KS	0.30%	ID	NA	MO	NA	SC	0.10%
MI	84.70%	SC	0.30%	IA	NA	MT	NA	TN	0.10%
FL	84.20%	TN	0.30%	KY	NA	NV	NA	UT	0.10%
VT	83.60%	KY	0.20%	ME	NA	NH	NA	WV	0.10%
MA	82.30%	LA	0.20%	MS	NA	NM	NA	AL	NA
ID	81.90%	OK	0.20%	MO	NA	NC	NA	AK	NA
WY	81.90%	SD	0.20%	MT	NA	ND	NA	DE	NA
CO	79.90%	AL	0.10%	NE	NA	OR	NA	HI	NA
NY	79.80%	AR	0.10%	NV	NA	RI	NA	IA	NA
AZ	79.50%	WV	0.10%	NM	NA	SC	NA	MS	NA
NH	78.30%	AK	NA	ND	NA	SD	NA	MT	NA
WA	77.10%	HI	NA	OK	NA	TN	NA	ND	NA
CA	77.00%	ID	NA	UT	NA	TX	NA	RI	NA
OR	76.10%	IA	NA	VT	NA	UT	NA	SD	NA
AK	NA	MT	NA	WA	NA	VT	NA	VT	NA
HI	NA	WY	NA	WY	NA	WI	NA	WY	NA

Source: *Religious Composition of State Population, 1990*, a report by The National Survey of Religious Identification

POPULATION 18 AND OVER, BY RELIGIOUS PREFERENCES (CONTINUED)

	Unitarian		Agnostic		Other		None		Refused to Respond	Desc. Num. Order
VT	1.10%	WA	1.40%	WV	2.90%	OR	17.20%	DE	5.70%	1
NV	0.90%	CA	1.20%	NH	2.70%	WA	14.00%	OK	4.20%	2
MA	0.80%	NH	1.20%	WA	2.70%	WY	13.50%	CT	3.90%	3
CO	0.70%	OR	1.20%	DC	2.50%	NH	13.40%	WA	3.30%	4
ME	0.60%	VT	1.20%	OH	2.40%	CA	13.00%	WY	3.30%	5
NE	0.50%	AZ	1.10%	AZ	2.30%	AZ	12.20%	AR	3.20%	6
WA	0.50%	CO	1.10%	MI	2.30%	ID	11.90%	ID	3.10%	7
CA	0.40%	ID	1.10%	PA	2.30%	CO	11.40%	MA	3.10%	8
ID	0.40%	IA	1.10%	OK	2.10%	VT	11.40%	NY	2.90%	9
IL	0.40%	FL	1.00%	CO	2.00%	MT	10.20%	RI	2.90%	10
KS	0.40%	MA	1.00%	IA	2.00%	ME	10.00%	UT	2.90%	11
MN	0.40%	NM	1.00%	CA	1.90%	NM	10.00%	AZ	2.80%	12
OR	0.40%	SD	1.00%	IN	1.90%	MI	8.70%	CA	2.80%	13
RI	0.40%	ME	0.90%	NC	1.70%	NV	8.10%	CO	2.80%	14
CT	0.30%	NV	0.90%	OR	1.70%	WV	8.00%	IL	2.80%	15
FL	0.30%	UT	0.90%	VA	1.70%	UT	7.80%	MT	2.70%	16
MD	0.30%	MD	0.70%	TX	1.60%	IN	7.40%	NJ	2.70%	17
MI	0.30%	PA	0.70%	NE	1.50%	OH	7.40%	NH	2.50%	18
MT	0.30%	IL	0.60%	NY	1.50%	MA	7.30%	ND	2.50%	19
NM	0.30%	KS	0.60%	GA	1.40%	DE	7.20%	OR	2.40%	20
NY	0.30%	MN	0.60%	ID	1.40%	FL	7.20%	IN	2.30%	21
SD	0.30%	MT	0.60%	IL	1.40%	MD	7.20%	MD	2.30%	22
AZ	0.20%	NJ	0.60%	MD	1.40%	IL	7.00%	DC	2.20%	23
AR	0.20%	NY	0.60%	CT	1.30%	NE	7.00%	ME	2.20%	24
KY	0.20%	TX	0.60%	FL	1.30%	KY	6.50%	MN	2.20%	25
MO	0.20%	VA	0.60%	MS	1.30%	MO	6.50%	MO	2.20%	26
NH	0.20%	CT	0.50%	MO	1.30%	OK	6.50%	OH	2.20%	27
TX	0.20%	DC	0.50%	NV	1.30%	NY	6.40%	FL	2.10%	28
VA	0.20%	MI	0.50%	KY	1.20%	VA	6.40%	MI	2.10%	29
WI	0.20%	MS	0.50%	MT	1.20%	DC	6.30%	NV	2.00%	30
AL	0.10%	OH	0.50%	SC	1.20%	WI	6.10%	PA	1.90%	31
GA	0.10%	RI	0.50%	MA	1.10%	RI	6.00%	VA	1.90%	32
IN	0.10%	WY	0.50%	NM	1.10%	TN	6.00%	WV	1.90%	33
IA	0.10%	MO	0.40%	TN	1.00%	IA	5.90%	SC	1.80%	34
NJ	0.10%	ND	0.40%	KS	0.90%	AR	5.80%	KS	1.70%	35
NC	0.10%	OK	0.40%	VT	0.90%	CT	5.80%	KY	1.70%	36
OH	0.10%	GA	0.30%	AL	0.80%	KS	5.70%	NE	1.70%	37
OK	0.10%	IN	0.30%	LA	0.80%	MN	5.60%	NC	1.70%	38
PA	0.10%	KY	0.30%	ME	0.80%	NJ	5.50%	NM	1.60%	39
TN	0.10%	NC	0.30%	MN	0.80%	PA	4.90%	TN	1.60%	40
UT	0.10%	WI	0.30%	NJ	0.80%	TX	4.90%	TX	1.60%	41
WV	0.10%	AL	0.20%	WI	0.80%	NC	4.80%	IA	1.50%	42
AK	NA	AR	0.20%	AR	0.70%	GA	4.60%	WI	1.50%	43
DE	NA	SC	0.20%	RI	0.70%	AL	3.90%	GA	1.40%	44
DC	NA	TN	0.20%	SD	0.70%	SC	3.20%	AL	1.30%	45
HI	NA	WV	0.20%	ND	0.60%	LA	2.90%	LA	1.20%	46
LA	NA	NE	0.10%	WY	0.60%	MS	2.80%	SD	1.00%	47
MS	NA	AK	NA	DE	0.30%	SD	2.50%	VT	0.70%	48
ND	NA	DE	NA	AK	NA	ND	1.60%	MS	0.60%	49
SC	NA	HI	NA	HI	NA	AK	NA	AK	NA	50
WY	NA	LA	NA	UT	NA	HI	NA	HI	NA	51

MAKING A LIVING

INCOME, POVERTY STATUS

Personal Income per Capita, 1996		% Inc. in Personal Income per Capita, 1995-96		Disposable Income per Capita, 1996		% of Pop. Below Poverty Level, 1995-96		Desc. Num. Order
DC	$34,932	ND	9.0%	DC	$29,567	NM	25.4%	1
CT	$33,189	SD	7.5%	CT	$27,706	DC	23.2%	2
NJ	$31,053	NV	6.9%	NJ	$26,570	MS	22.1%	3
MA	$29,439	NE	6.1%	MA	$24,720	LA	20.1%	4
NY	$28,782	IA	6.0%	NY	$24,380	AZ	18.3%	5
DE	$27,622	MN	5.6%	DE	$23,654	WV	17.6%	6
MD	$27,221	UT	5.4%	NH	$23,329	AL	17.1%	7
IL	$26,598	AZ	5.2%	MD	$23,158	TX	17.0%	8
NH	$26,520	OR	4.8%	IL	$22,778	OK	16.9%	9
MN	$25,580	CO	4.6%	NV	$21,805	CA	16.8%	10
NV	$25,451	KS	4.6%	HI	$21,776	NY	16.6%	11
HI	$25,159	GA	4.4%	CA	$21,760	SC	16.5%	12
CA	$25,144	WA	4.2%	WA	$21,740	MT	16.2%	13
CO	$25,084	FL	4.1%	RI	$21,659	AR	16.1%	14
VA	$24,925	DE	4.0%	MN	$21,597	KY	15.9%	15
WA	$24,838	TX	4.0%	VA	$21,434	TN	15.7%	16
MI	$24,810	ID	3.9%	PA	$21,410	FL	15.2%	17
RI	$24,765	NC	3.9%	MI	$21,376	GA	13.5%	18
PA	$24,668	AR	3.6%	AK	$21,277	ID	13.2%	19
AK	$24,558	VT	3.5%	CO	$21,265	SD	13.2%	20
FL	$24,104	IL	3.4%	FL	$21,185	NC	12.4%	21
OH	$23,537	MS	3.3%	OH	$20,340	IL	12.3%	22
KS	$23,281	CA	3.2%	KS	$20,225	WA	12.2%	23
WI	$23,269	MA	3.2%	NE	$20,180	OH	12.1%	24
NE	$23,047	MO	3.2%	MO	$19,906	WY	12.1%	25
MO	$22,864	IN	3.1%	WI	$19,858	PA	11.9%	26
GA	$22,709	WI	3.1%	IA	$19,723	MI	11.7%	27
OR	$22,668	NH	2.9%	GA	$19,664	ND	11.5%	28
IA	$22,560	AL	2.8%	TX	$19,621	OR	11.5%	29
IN	$22,440	KY	2.8%	TN	$19,441	VT	11.5%	30
VT	$22,124	NM	2.8%	IN	$19,433	VA	11.3%	31
TX	$22,045	OK	2.8%	SD	$19,381	HI	11.2%	32
NC	$22,010	VA	2.7%	VT	$19,381	ME	11.2%	33
TN	$21,764	OH	2.6%	OR	$19,189	KS	11.0%	34
SD	$21,516	LA	2.5%	NC	$19,110	IA	10.9%	35
WY	$21,245	SC	2.5%	WY	$18,614	RI	10.8%	36
AZ	$20,989	TN	2.5%	ND	$18,351	CT	10.7%	37
ME	$20,826	NJ	2.4%	AZ	$18,308	MA	10.6%	38
ND	$20,710	PA	2.4%	ME	$18,219	MD	10.2%	39
AL	$20,055	CT	2.2%	LA	$17,786	NE	9.9%	40
LA	$19,824	MI	2.1%	AL	$17,785	CO	9.7%	41
SC	$19,755	NY	2.1%	SC	$17,467	NV	9.6%	42
KY	$19,687	MT	2.0%	KY	$17,192	DE	9.5%	43
ID	$19,539	WV	2.0%	OK	$16,980	MN	9.5%	44
OK	$19,350	MD	1.8%	AR	$16,783	MO	9.5%	45
UT	$19,156	RI	1.8%	ID	$16,722	WI	8.7%	46
MT	$19,047	ME	1.7%	NM	$16,674	IN	8.6%	47
AR	$18,928	WY	1.1%	MT	$16,656	NJ	8.5%	48
NM	$18,770	AK	0.7%	WV	$16,494	UT	8.1%	49
WV	$18,444	DC	0.6%	UT	$16,436	AK	7.7%	50
MS	$17,471	HI	0.0%	MS	$15,911	NH	5.9%	51

Source: Bureau of Economic Analysis, U.S. Dept. of Commerce

ECONOMY

CIVILIAN LABOR FORCE (1996)

	Civ. Labor Force		% of Pop. in Labor Force		% of Pop. 65+ in Labor Force		% of Females in Labor Force	Desc. Num. Order
CA	15,596,000	MN	74.7%	KS	18.8%	WI	69.6%	1
TX	9,748,000	WI	74.7%	SD	18.3%	MN	68.7%	2
NY	8,639,000	AK	74.2%	NE	17.8%	AK	68.2%	3
FL	6,938,000	NE	74.2%	IA	16.4%	IA	68.1%	4
IL	6,100,000	IA	73.6%	TN	16.3%	NE	67.7%	5
PA	5,903,000	CO	72.4%	MD	15.3%	MD	66.8%	6
OH	5,643,000	SD	72.3%	TX	15.2%	SD	66.7%	7
MI	4,807,000	MD	72.0%	WI	14.9%	ND	66.4%	8
NJ	4,124,000	ND	72.0%	ND	14.5%	MO	66.3%	9
NC	3,796,000	MO	71.8%	MT	14.4%	VT	66.3%	10
GA	3,753,000	VT	71.6%	IL	14.3%	CO	65.7%	11
VA	3,389,000	UT	71.3%	HI	14.2%	DE	63.7%	12
MA	3,189,000	WY	71.0%	MN	14.1%	ME	63.5%	13
IN	3,072,000	ID	70.4%	MO	13.7%	WY	63.5%	14
WI	2,918,000	NH	70.2%	NH	13.6%	KS	63.2%	15
MO	2,898,000	KS	70.1%	NC	13.6%	ID	62.9%	16
WA	2,887,000	OR	69.3%	NV	13.4%	NH	62.9%	17
MD	2,786,000	IN	69.2%	ID	13.3%	CT	62.5%	18
TN	2,751,000	NV	69.1%	NJ	12.8%	OR	62.2%	19
MN	2,609,000	ME	69.0%	AR	12.6%	HI	61.9%	20
AZ	2,249,000	TX	69.0%	NM	12.5%	IN	61.9%	21
CO	2,102,000	WA	68.9%	VA	12.5%	UT	61.6%	22
AL	2,088,000	DE	68.5%	DC	12.2%	MA	61.5%	23
LA	1,997,000	IL	68.5%	ME	12.0%	NC	61.5%	24
KY	1,867,000	NC	68.5%	OK	11.7%	WA	61.1%	25
SC	1,848,000	HI	68.3%	OH	11.6%	NV	60.8%	26
OR	1,721,000	CT	68.2%	GA	11.5%	TN	60.8%	27
CT	1,720,000	GA	67.8%	KY	11.5%	VA	60.8%	28
IA	1,599,000	MA	67.5%	RI	11.5%	IL	60.7%	29
OK	1,577,000	VA	67.3%	DE	11.4%	MT	60.6%	30
KS	1,340,000	NJ	67.2%	MA	11.2%	GA	60.2%	31
MS	1,262,000	TN	67.0%	NY	11.1%	DC	60.1%	32
AR	1,234,000	MT	66.6%	IN	11.0%	TX	59.7%	33
UT	998,000	AZ	66.4%	CA	10.8%	NJ	59.5%	34
NE	913,000	MI	66.3%	PA	10.8%	RI	58.9%	35
NV	844,000	OH	66.3%	OR	10.3%	MI	58.6%	36
WV	808,000	RI	65.6%	FL	10.1%	OH	58.6%	37
NM	800,000	CA	65.5%	AL	9.5%	AR	58.4%	38
ME	669,000	SC	65.4%	MI	9.5%	AZ	58.2%	39
NH	624,000	AR	64.7%	MS	9.4%	SC	58.2%	40
ID	619,000	OK	63.9%	SC	9.1%	CA	56.4%	41
HI	591,000	AL	63.6%	WV	7.8%	AL	56.3%	42
RI	496,000	DC	63.6%	AK	NA	KY	56.1%	43
MT	447,000	PA	63.6%	AZ	NA	OK	55.8%	44
SD	390,000	NM	63.0%	CO	NA	PA	55.6%	45
DE	382,000	KY	62.5%	CT	NA	LA	55.2%	46
ND	343,000	MS	62.3%	LA	NA	NM	55.2%	47
VT	324,000	LA	62.0%	UT	NA	FL	54.8%	48
AK	316,000	FL	62.0%	VT	NA	MS	54.7%	49
DC	272,000	NY	61.6%	WA	NA	NY	53.9%	50
WY	258,000	WV	55.6%	WY	NA	WV	47.7%	51

Sources: Bureau of Labor Statistics, U.S. Dept. of Labor

PERCENTAGE OF STATES' WORKERS IN SELECTED INDUSTRIES (1996)

Finance, Insur., Real Estate		Govt.		Manu-facturing		Service		Trade		Transport., Commun., Public Util.		Desc. Num. Order
DE	11.5%	DC	38.7%	IN	24.0%	NV	43.1%	MT	27.2%	AK	8.6%	1
NY	9.1%	AK	27.8%	NC	23.9%	DC	42.1%	FL	26.0%	HI	7.7%	2
CT	8.3%	WY	26.5%	AR	23.4%	MA	35.0%	ND	26.0%	NJ	7.0%	3
HI	7.0%	NM	24.7%	WI	23.1%	FL	34.3%	NH	25.9%	CO	6.3%	4
MA	6.9%	ND	22.9%	MS	22.5%	RI	33.1%	HI	25.6%	GA	6.3%	5
IL	6.8%	MT	21.3%	MI	22.3%	NY	33.0%	GA	25.4%	MO	6.2%	6
FL	6.4%	HI	20.8%	SC	21.8%	MD	32.4%	ID	25.4%	WY	6.2%	7
NE	6.4%	SD	20.2%	AL	21.0%	HI	31.4%	ME	25.2%	AR	6.0%	8
NJ	6.4%	LA	20.0%	OH	20.7%	PA	31.1%	SD	25.1%	LA	6.0%	9
CO	6.2%	MS	20.0%	TN	20.6%	NJ	30.8%	NE	24.9%	NE	6.0%	10
AZ	6.1%	OK	20.0%	NH	18.7%	CA	30.7%	OR	24.8%	ND	6.0%	11
OR	6.1%	WV	19.9%	RI	18.7%	CT	30.4%	IA	24.7%	TX	5.9%	12
MN	5.9%	ID	19.8%	KY	18.6%	CO	29.8%	KS	24.7%	IL	5.8%	13
MD	5.8%	KS	19.1%	IA	17.9%	VT	29.7%	AZ	24.6%	MT	5.8%	14
MO	5.8%	MD	19.1%	MN	17.6%	AZ	29.6%	CO	24.5%	KS	5.7%	15
PA	5.8%	VA	19.1%	PA	17.5%	VA	29.1%	OH	24.5%	OK	5.7%	16
CA	5.7%	AL	18.7%	CT	17.4%	NH	29.0%	WA	24.5%	UT	5.7%	17
RI	5.7%	WA	18.7%	IL	17.1%	IL	28.9%	MN	24.4%	KY	5.6%	18
SD	5.7%	NE	18.2%	VT	16.7%	MT	28.4%	IN	24.2%	TN	5.6%	19
IA	5.6%	SC	17.8%	GA	16.6%	ME	27.9%	TX	24.1%	WV	5.6%	20
TX	5.4%	TX	17.6%	ME	16.3%	NM	27.7%	UT	24.1%	VA	5.2%	21
UT	5.3%	NY	17.5%	MO	16.1%	MN	27.6%	KY	24.0%	FL	5.1%	22
WI	5.3%	UT	17.5%	KS	16.0%	MO	27.6%	MD	24.0%	NY	5.1%	23
OH	5.2%	KY	17.3%	OR	16.0%	ND	27.4%	MO	23.9%	PA	5.1%	24
VA	5.2%	ME	17.2%	DE	15.4%	WV	27.4%	SC	23.7%	WA	5.1%	25
GA	5.1%	AZ	16.9%	ID	14.7%	DE	27.1%	MI	23.6%	CA	5.0%	26
ID	5.1%	IA	16.8%	MA	14.6%	OK	26.9%	NM	23.6%	IN	5.0%	27
WA	5.1%	OR	16.7%	CA	14.5%	TX	26.9%	NJ	23.5%	NV	5.0%	28
NH	5.0%	CA	16.6%	WA	14.3%	WA	26.9%	OK	23.5%	AL	4.9%	29
OK	5.0%	AR	16.5%	SD	13.7%	LA	26.8%	TN	23.5%	AZ	4.9%	30
ME	4.9%	VT	16.5%	NE	13.6%	MI	26.8%	VT	23.5%	MN	4.9%	31
IN	4.8%	CO	16.3%	UT	13.6%	UT	26.8%	WY	23.5%	OR	4.9%	32
KS	4.8%	GA	16.1%	NJ	13.3%	OH	26.7%	CA	23.3%	MD	4.8%	33
ND	4.7%	NC	15.8%	OK	12.8%	NE	26.4%	LA	23.3%	MS	4.8%	34
DC	4.6%	MN	15.6%	TX	12.8%	OR	26.1%	AL	23.0%	ID	4.7%	35
LA	4.6%	MO	15.6%	VA	12.7%	IA	26.0%	IL	23.0%	NC	4.7%	36
MI	4.6%	NJ	15.6%	WV	11.7%	TN	25.9%	MA	22.9%	SD	4.7%	37
TN	4.6%	TN	15.1%	NY	11.6%	SD	25.8%	WV	22.9%	CT	4.6%	38
AL	4.5%	FL	15.0%	AZ	10.5%	GA	25.6%	WI	22.9%	IA	4.6%	39
MT	4.5%	MI	14.8%	LA	10.4%	WI	25.2%	AR	22.8%	WI	4.6%	40
NV	4.5%	WI	14.7%	CO	10.3%	KS	24.5%	NC	22.8%	NM	4.5%	41
NM	4.5%	IL	14.3%	FL	7.9%	KY	24.4%	VA	22.8%	OH	4.4%	42
AK	4.4%	OH	14.2%	MD	7.9%	AK	23.7%	PA	22.7%	SC	4.4%	43
VT	4.4%	CT	14.1%	ND	7.0%	ID	23.3%	DE	22.3%	VT	4.4%	44
NC	4.3%	NH	14.1%	MT	6.6%	IN	23.2%	RI	22.2%	MA	4.3%	45
SC	4.3%	DE	14.0%	NM	6.6%	NC	23.0%	CT	21.9%	DE	4.2%	46
AR	4.0%	IN	14.0%	AK	6.2%	AR	22.7%	MS	21.3%	ME	4.1%	47
KY	4.0%	RI	13.9%	WY	4.9%	MS	22.6%	AK	20.7%	MI	3.9%	48
WV	3.9%	PA	13.6%	NV	4.6%	SC	22.3%	NY	20.5%	NH	3.5%	49
MS	3.8%	MA	13.2%	HI	3.1%	AL	22.2%	NV	20.1%	RI	3.4%	50
WY	3.6%	NV	12.0%	DC	2.1%	WY	21.7%	DC	8.0%	DC	3.1%	51

Source: Bureau of Labor Statistics, U.S. Dept. of Labor

THE STATES COMPARED

UNEMPLOYMENT, PUBLIC AID, MEDICAID

Unemployment Rate, 1996		Male Unemployment, 1996		Female Unemployment, 1996		% of Pop. Receiving Pub. Aid, 1994		% of Pop. Receiving Medicaid, 1995		Desc. Num. Order
DC	8.5%	AK	9.1%	DC	8.4%	DC	16.6%	TN	27.9%	1
NM	8.1%	DC	8.7%	LA	8.0%	CA	11.7%	DC	25.0%	2
AK	7.8%	NM	8.4%	NM	7.6%	MS	10.9%	WV	21.3%	3
WV	7.5%	WV	8.3%	CA	7.2%	NY	10.0%	MS	19.3%	4
CA	7.2%	CA	7.2%	MS	7.2%	LA	9.7%	LA	18.1%	5
LA	6.7%	HI	6.9%	WA	7.2%	WV	9.6%	NM	17.0%	6
WA	6.5%	NY	6.5%	WV	6.6%	KY	9.3%	VT	17.0%	7
HI	6.4%	NJ	6.0%	NJ	6.4%	MI	9.1%	NY	16.7%	8
NJ	6.2%	OR	6.0%	AK	6.3%	TN	9.0%	KY	16.6%	9
NY	6.2%	MT	5.9%	NV	6.2%	NM	8.7%	CA	15.9%	10
MS	6.1%	PA	5.9%	SC	6.2%	RI	8.6%	GA	15.9%	11
SC	6.0%	WA	5.9%	TX	6.1%	IL	8.3%	NC	15.1%	12
OR	5.9%	DE	5.8%	KY	5.9%	GA	8.2%	OR	14.4%	13
CT	5.7%	SC	5.8%	NY	5.9%	OH	8.1%	AR	14.2%	14
KY	5.6%	CT	5.7%	AZ	5.8%	AK	7.5%	OH	13.8%	15
TX	5.6%	LA	5.6%	HI	5.8%	MA	7.5%	RI	13.6%	16
AZ	5.5%	AR	5.4%	OR	5.8%	ME	7.4%	TX	13.6%	17
AR	5.4%	KY	5.4%	CT	5.7%	NC	7.2%	SC	13.5%	18
NV	5.4%	ME	5.4%	AL	5.4%	PA	7.2%	IL	13.2%	19
IL	5.3%	AZ	5.3%	AR	5.4%	MO	7.1%	MO	13.1%	20
MT	5.3%	IL	5.3%	FL	5.4%	WA	7.1%	AL	12.7%	21
PA	5.3%	TX	5.3%	ID	5.4%	VT	7.0%	ME	12.4%	22
DE	5.2%	MS	5.2%	RI	5.4%	HI	6.9%	MI	12.3%	23
ID	5.2%	ID	5.1%	TN	5.4%	AL	6.8%	FL	12.2%	24
TN	5.2%	MI	5.1%	GA	5.3%	FL	6.8%	MA	12.0%	25
AL	5.1%	WY	5.1%	IL	5.2%	SC	6.7%	OK	12.0%	26
FL	5.1%	OH	5.0%	KS	5.0%	AR	6.6%	WA	11.7%	27
ME	5.1%	AL	4.9%	WY	5.0%	AZ	6.5%	CT	11.6%	28
RI	5.1%	MD	4.9%	MD	4.9%	WI	6.5%	AZ	11.5%	29
WY	5.0%	MA	4.9%	ME	4.8%	CT	6.4%	AK	11.3%	30
MD	4.9%	MO	4.9%	OH	4.8%	TX	6.3%	MT	11.3%	31
MI	4.9%	RI	4.9%	MI	4.6%	OK	6.2%	DE	11.0%	32
OH	4.9%	TN	4.9%	MT	4.6%	NJ	6.0%	IA	10.7%	33
GA	4.6%	FL	4.8%	OK	4.6%	MD	5.9%	WY	10.7%	34
MO	4.6%	MN	4.8%	PA	4.6%	MT	5.6%	MN	10.3%	35
VT	4.6%	NV	4.8%	VT	4.6%	IA	5.4%	NE	10.3%	36
KS	4.5%	VT	4.5%	VA	4.6%	MN	5.4%	VA	10.3%	37
VA	4.4%	CO	4.4%	DE	4.5%	DE	5.2%	PA	10.2%	38
MA	4.3%	NC	4.3%	NH	4.5%	IN	5.2%	SD	10.2%	39
NC	4.3%	VA	4.2%	NC	4.5%	OR	5.1%	KS	10.0%	40
CO	4.2%	KS	4.1%	IN	4.4%	VA	4.8%	ID	9.9%	41
NH	4.2%	GA	4.0%	MO	4.3%	CO	4.7%	NJ	9.9%	42
IN	4.1%	IN	3.9%	IA	4.1%	KS	4.7%	IN	9.6%	43
OK	4.1%	NH	3.9%	CO	4.0%	WY	4.5%	ND	9.6%	44
MN	4.0%	WI	3.8%	MA	3.7%	SD	4.4%	WI	9.0%	45
IA	3.8%	OK	3.6%	UT	3.7%	NE	4.0%	NH	8.4%	46
UT	3.5%	IA	3.5%	NE	3.2%	ND	3.9%	MD	8.2%	47
WI	3.5%	UT	3.3%	SD	3.2%	NV	3.8%	UT	8.2%	48
SD	3.2%	SD	3.2%	WI	3.2%	UT	3.6%	CO	7.8%	49
ND	3.1%	ND	3.1%	MN	3.1%	NH	3.5%	NV	6.9%	50
NE	2.9%	NE	2.7%	ND	3.0%	ID	3.4%	HI	4.4%	51

Source: Bureau of Labor Statistics, U.S. Dept. of Labor; U.S. Bureau of the Census, U.S. Dept. of Commerce; Health Care Financing Admin., U.S. Dept. of Health and Human Services

BUSINESSES (1995)

Total Bus.		New Bus. Incorps.		As % of Total Bus.		Bus. Failures		Failures per 10,000 Bus.		Desc. Num. Order
CA	740,583	FL	98,066	DE	238.65%	CA	16,307	CA	220.2	1
NY	467,262	NY	72,433	NV	50.85%	TX	6,152	OK	161.1	2
TX	438,262	DE	50,094	FL	24.63%	NY	5,060	WA	156.9	3
FL	398,232	CA	41,913	NJ	17.13%	FL	2,904	MD	147.4	4
IL	293,694	TX	38,122	NY	15.50%	NJ	2,779	AZ	141.6	5
PA	283,998	NJ	37,861	GA	15.08%	PA	2,756	TX	140.4	6
OH	263,739	IL	34,495	MD	14.72%	WA	2,384	KS	133.6	7
MI	226,973	MI	31,254	MI	13.77%	OH	2,141	NJ	125.8	8
NJ	220,991	GA	26,990	CO	12.95%	MA	1,927	CO	125.3	9
NC	181,972	OH	20,859	UT	12.90%	MD	1,804	AR	122.4	10
GA	179,006	VA	19,172	HI	12.66%	VA	1,713	NV	121.7	11
VA	162,378	NV	18,926	WY	12.60%	IL	1,696	MA	120.2	12
MA	160,350	PA	18,575	VA	11.81%	MI	1,681	ID	117.7	13
WA	151,925	MD	18,014	IL	11.75%	CO	1,481	NH	112.3	14
IN	141,253	NC	16,021	DC	11.60%	GA	1,481	NY	108.2	15
MO	139,980	CO	15,309	LA	11.30%	AZ	1,410	VA	105.5	16
WI	133,238	MA	13,479	AZ	10.91%	OK	1,311	NM	99.7	17
MN	125,927	WA	13,340	AR	10.46%	WI	1,140	PA	97.0	18
TN	124,814	IN	12,451	OR	10.41%	MO	1,109	HI	90.2	19
MD	122,350	MN	12,203	RI	9.88%	TN	991	ME	87.3	20
CO	118,192	LA	11,082	MN	9.69%	NC	962	WI	85.6	21
AZ	99,583	AZ	10,866	OK	9.58%	KS	947	OR	85.1	22
LA	98,063	MO	10,743	KY	9.12%	MN	903	GA	82.7	23
AL	96,053	OR	9,730	NH	8.93%	IN	798	OH	81.2	24
OR	93,468	WI	8,818	NM	8.82%	OR	795	SD	80.1	25
CT	91,189	TN	8,194	IN	8.81%	AR	737	DC	79.7	26
SC	87,990	OK	7,796	NC	8.80%	KY	659	TN	79.4	27
KY	85,123	KY	7,764	WA	8.78%	IA	573	MO	79.2	28
OK	81,395	AL	7,686	TX	8.70%	AL	547	KY	77.4	29
IA	78,464	SC	7,601	SC	8.64%	SC	490	UT	75.0	30
KS	70,894	AR	6,298	MA	8.41%	CT	485	MI	74.1	31
AR	60,231	IA	5,925	AK	8.27%	LA	456	IA	73.0	32
MS	57,095	UT	5,917	MS	8.20%	NV	453	FL	72.9	33
NE	47,128	CT	4,830	AL	8.00%	NM	405	VT	72.0	34
UT	45,882	MS	4,680	ID	7.95%	NH	389	AK	71.8	35
NM	40,631	KS	4,475	VT	7.93%	ID	388	MN	71.7	36
WV	40,599	HI	3,792	OH	7.91%	UT	344	WV	70.7	37
NV	37,219	NM	3,584	ME	7.73%	NE	323	NE	68.5	38
ME	36,298	NE	3,360	MO	7.67%	ME	317	WY	63.0	39
NH	34,647	NH	3,095	IA	7.55%	WV	287	IL	57.7	40
ID	32,972	ME	2,805	NE	7.13%	HI	270	AL	56.9	41
HI	29,942	RI	2,743	WI	6.62%	MS	232	IN	56.5	42
MT	29,109	ID	2,622	TN	6.56%	SD	182	SC	55.7	43
RI	27,766	WV	2,535	PA	6.54%	DC	155	CT	53.2	44
SD	22,708	DC	2,256	KS	6.31%	MT	152	NC	52.9	45
DE	20,991	WY	2,159	WV	6.24%	VT	148	MT	52.2	46
VT	20,542	MT	1,767	SD	6.17%	RI	129	ND	48.3	47
ND	20,269	VT	1,630	MT	6.07%	AK	124	LA	46.5	48
DC	19,451	AK	1,428	CA	5.66%	WY	108	RI	46.5	49
AK	17,264	SD	1,401	CT	5.30%	ND	98	MS	40.6	50
WY	17,133	ND	1,021	ND	5.04%	DE	45	DE	21.4	51

Source: Dun & Bradstreet; Bureau of Economic Analysis, U.S. Dept. of Commerce

AGRICULTURE

	Farm Income Mktg., 1996		Farm Income Avg. per Farm, 1996		Avg. Value of Prop. per Acre, 1997		Govt. Payments, 1996		Govt. Pay., Avg. per Farm, 1996	Desc. Num. Order
CA	$23,309,526,000	DE	$302,814	NJ	$8,290	TX	$764,778,000	ND	$11,339	1
TX	$13,053,234,000	AZ	$286,189	RI	$7,900	KS	$555,139,000	MT	$10,949	2
IA	$12,852,687,000	CA	$284,263	CT	$7,500	IA	$501,694,000	AR	$8,414	3
NE	$9,454,041,000	CO	$172,630	MA	$6,200	NE	$388,819,000	KS	$8,411	4
IL	$9,049,998,000	NE	$168,822	MD	$4,000	IL	$386,767,000	AZ	$7,732	5
MN	$8,808,931,000	WA	$157,805	DE	$3,170	AR	$361,818,000	CO	$7,188	6
KS	$7,869,209,000	ID	$154,998	PA	$2,630	ND	$351,520,000	SD	$7,065	7
NC	$7,831,309,000	FL	$153,266	NH	$2,600	MN	$348,804,000	NE	$6,943	8
FL	$6,130,658,000	AR	$136,902	CA	$2,510	CA	$295,460,000	LA	$6,536	9
WI	$6,061,542,000	NC	$135,023	FL	$2,300	MO	$289,279,000	ID	$5,273	10
AR	$5,886,786,000	GA	$132,257	IL	$2,210	MT	$240,874,000	IA	$5,119	11
GA	$5,687,046,000	IA	$131,150	OH	$2,110	OK	$236,707,000	IL	$5,089	12
WA	$5,680,980,000	CT	$128,714	NC	$2,050	SD	$229,605,000	NM	$4,370	13
IN	$5,558,099,000	NM	$126,597	VA	$2,030	IN	$213,703,000	WA	$4,334	14
OH	$5,121,783,000	KS	$119,230	IN	$1,970	MS	$184,925,000	MS	$4,203	15
MO	$4,950,421,000	IL	$119,079	TN	$1,650	LA	$176,471,000	MN	$4,009	16
CO	$4,229,447,000	RI	$118,381	MI	$1,600	CO	$176,101,000	TX	$3,731	17
PA	$4,142,509,000	NV	$114,401	IA	$1,570	OH	$163,120,000	CA	$3,603	18
SD	$3,683,512,000	ND	$113,948	VT	$1,550	WI	$156,849,000	IN	$3,503	19
MI	$3,642,927,000	SD	$113,339	AL	$1,480	WA	$156,039,000	OK	$3,288	20
OK	$3,565,551,000	MD	$111,954	KY	$1,450	ID	$116,009,000	MO	$2,782	21
KY	$3,550,232,000	HI	$104,911	GA	$1,430	GA	$114,524,000	WY	$2,679	22
ND	$3,532,393,000	MN	$101,252	SC	$1,400	MI	$109,585,000	GA	$2,663	23
MS	$3,462,784,000	MT	$92,147	NY	$1,390	TN	$79,917,000	AK	$2,516	24
ID	$3,409,945,000	IN	$91,116	ME	$1,300	NC	$75,702,000	OH	$2,266	25
AL	$3,173,595,000	VT	$89,111	WI	$1,250	AL	$75,550,000	MI	$2,068	26
NY	$3,043,034,000	NJ	$87,061	LA	$1,230	KY	$74,542,000	SC	$1,994	27
OR	$2,976,542,000	LA	$86,743	WA	$1,230	OR	$74,262,000	WI	$1,985	28
VA	$2,378,146,000	NY	$84,529	MN	$1,040	NM	$59,000,000	DE	$1,955	29
TN	$2,371,873,000	PA	$82,850	AR	$1,010	AZ	$57,993,000	OR	$1,929	30
LA	$2,342,068,000	MS	$78,700	MO	$1,010	NY	$43,289,000	AL	$1,679	31
AZ	$2,146,417,000	MA	$78,311	OR	$1,000	SC	$42,868,000	UT	$1,568	32
MT	$2,027,226,000	OR	$77,313	WV	$1,000	PA	$37,111,000	NC	$1,305	33
NM	$1,709,056,000	WI	$76,728	ID	$960	VA	$30,423,000	MD	$1,288	34
SC	$1,602,056,000	SC	$74,514	MS	$950	WY	$24,381,000	NY	$1,202	35
MD	$1,533,770,000	WY	$72,745	UT	$750	FL	$22,872,000	NV	$1,042	36
UT	$873,143,000	OH	$71,136	NE	$680	UT	$21,006,000	TN	$999	37
NJ	$800,958,000	AL	$70,524	TX	$600	MD	$17,647,000	KY	$847	38
DE	$757,036,000	MI	$68,734	CO	$590	DE	$4,888,000	PA	$742	39
WY	$661,979,000	NH	$67,045	KS	$575	ME	$4,638,000	VT	$673	40
VT	$534,666,000	ME	$65,556	OK	$570	WV	$4,538,000	VA	$634	41
CT	$489,113,000	UT	$65,160	AZ	$420	VT	$4,035,000	ME	$627	42
ME	$485,111,000	TX	$63,674	ND	$410	NJ	$3,258,000	FL	$572	43
HI	$482,589,000	AK	$58,836	NV	$350	NV	$2,605,000	CT	$471	44
MA	$477,698,000	VA	$49,545	SD	$325	CT	$1,791,000	NH	$455	45
WV	$388,170,000	OK	$49,522	MT	$305	MA	$1,548,000	NJ	$354	46
NV	$286,002,000	MO	$47,600	NM	$280	AK	$1,258,000	MA	$254	47
NH	$160,907,000	KY	$40,344	WY	$220	NH	$1,093,000	WV	$227	48
RI	$82,867,000	TN	$29,648	AK	NA	HI	$580,000	RI	$223	49
AK	$29,418,000	WV	$19,409	DC	NA	RI	$156,000	HI	$126	50
DC	NA	DC	NA	HI	NA	DC	NA	DC	NA	51

Source: Economic Research Service, U.S. Dept. of Agriculture

CONSTRUCTION, MANUFACTURES, NONFUEL MINERALS, RETAIL SALES

Construction Value, 1996	Manufactures, Value Added, 1995	Manufactures per Capita, 1995	Nonfuel Mineral Production Value, 1996	Retail Sales per Household, 1995
CA $31,734,190,000	CA $178,358,400,000	IN $10,510	AZ $3,530,000,000	NY $95,429
TX $24,969,136,000	TX $112,425,100,000	NC $10,274	NV $3,230,000,000	HI $32,912
FL $22,314,402,000	OH $103,713,100,000	WI $9,953	CA $2,840,000,000	NH $30,240
OH $13,994,419,000	IL $93,762,800,000	OH $9,301	MN $1,800,000,000	AK $30,198
NY $13,893,300,000	NY $89,923,800,000	IA $9,225	TX $1,780,000,000	DE $28,048
IL $12,567,052,000	MI $87,397,500,000	MI $9,152	GA $1,720,000,000	VA $26,932
NC $12,433,627,000	PA $84,581,800,000	KY $8,712	UT $1,560,000,000	NV $26,900
GA $12,302,301,000	NC $73,919,400,000	SC $8,567	FL $1,540,000,000	SD $26,603
MI $10,784,198,000	IN $60,991,800,000	TN $8,205	MI $1,510,000,000	NJ $25,979
AZ $9,790,758,000	WI $50,988,900,000	IL $7,926	MO $1,250,000,000	ND $25,897
PA $9,409,322,000	GA $50,219,600,000	DE $7,900	PA $1,040,000,000	MI $25,867
VA $9,213,203,000	NJ $48,260,400,000	CT $7,631	NM $963,000,000	CT $25,847
IN $8,931,472,000	TN $43,125,600,000	NH $7,541	OH $934,000,000	WI $25,738
WA $8,403,400,000	MA $41,900,700,000	AR $7,505	WY $918,000,000	FL $25,688
TN $8,285,391,000	VA $40,133,700,000	MO $7,464	NY $891,000,000	MO $25,589
CO $7,960,610,000	MO $39,736,700,000	MN $7,062	IL $817,000,000	OR $25,416
MA $7,674,078,000	FL $37,933,600,000	PA $7,007	AL $735,000,000	MN $25,371
NJ $7,123,588,000	KY $33,632,000,000	LA $7,002	NC $731,000,000	ID $25,308
NV $7,034,658,000	MN $32,553,400,000	GA $6,974	TN $651,000,000	NE $25,073
MD $6,470,321,000	SC $31,467,400,000	KS $6,916	WA $626,000,000	UT $24,920
MO $6,042,038,000	LA $30,404,600,000	MA $6,899	IN $617,000,000	OH $24,837
WI $5,993,948,000	AL $29,078,500,000	AL $6,837	VA $529,000,000	CO $24,823
SC $5,438,753,000	WA $28,150,400,000	ID $6,819	CO $528,000,000	WY $24,785
MN $5,420,761,000	IA $26,215,200,000	MS $6,467	KS $524,000,000	TX $24,665
OR $5,378,328,000	CT $24,988,200,000	OR $6,265	AK $523,000,000	GA $24,643
LA $4,874,998,000	AZ $20,911,600,000	NJ $6,074	MT $523,000,000	MD $24,552
AL $4,793,865,000	OR $19,677,300,000	VA $6,064	SC $495,000,000	AZ $24,544
KY $4,693,285,000	CO $18,943,000,000	TX $6,004	IA $486,000,000	IA $24,536
KS $3,772,052,000	AR $18,639,600,000	VT $5,891	AR $453,000,000	ME $24,349
UT $3,737,673,000	KS $17,742,600,000	NE $5,718	KY $453,000,000	TN $24,299
MS $3,562,977,000	MS $17,442,500,000	ME $5,663	LA $428,000,000	LA $24,271
CT $3,423,652,000	MD $17,147,800,000	CA $5,646	ID $411,000,000	IN $24,264
OK $3,182,716,000	OK $14,622,300,000	RI $5,482	WI $399,000,000	IL $24,093
AR $2,795,210,000	UT $9,497,500,000	SD $5,387	OK $372,000,000	NM $24,022
IA $2,795,137,000	NE $9,360,600,000	WA $5,183	SD $353,000,000	NC $23,698
NM $2,228,989,000	WV $8,947,700,000	CO $5,056	MD $324,000,000	MA $23,652
ID $1,877,973,000	NH $8,658,500,000	NM $4,959	OR $251,000,000	WA $23,562
NE $1,869,209,000	NM $8,358,100,000	AZ $4,958	NJ $222,000,000	CA $23,427
HI $1,805,439,000	ID $7,931,900,000	NY $4,958	MA $191,000,000	KS $23,371
WV $1,232,476,000	ME $7,030,300,000	WV $4,894	WV $191,000,000	SC $23,205
NH $1,211,543,000	DE $5,665,700,000	UT $4,867	NE $147,000,000	MT $23,182
DC $1,162,103,000	RI $5,426,100,000	OK $4,461	MS $140,000,000	VT $23,129
ME $983,416,000	SD $3,927,300,000	MD $3,401	HI $112,000,000	PA $22,749
AK $983,379,000	VT $3,444,900,000	DC $2,952	CT $103,000,000	KY $22,663
MT $916,046,000	NV $2,991,100,000	FL $2,678	ME $73,100,000	AL $22,430
SD $813,905,000	MT $1,779,000,000	ND $2,431	VT $66,800,000	AR $22,100
DE $799,621,000	DC $1,636,400,000	AK $2,416	NH $43,900,000	OK $20,727
RI $657,522,000	ND $1,559,300,000	WY $2,145	RI $31,900,000	RI $19,766
ND $656,169,000	HI $1,488,500,000	MT $2,044	ND $30,300,000	MS $19,763
WY $641,873,000	AK $1,458,600,000	NV $1,955	DE $10,700,000	WV $19,194
VT $591,775,000	WY $1,029,800,000	HI $1,254	DC NA	DC $16,405

Source: F.W. Dodge Market Analysis Group, Lexington, MA; U.S. Bureau of the Census, Manufact. & Constr. Div., U.S. Dept. of Commerce; U.S. Geological Survey, U.S. Dept. of Interior; National Retail Institute (copyright)

FOREIGN EXPORTS, GROSS STATE PRODUCT, ENERGY CONSUMPTION

	Exports Value, 1996		Exports per Capita, 1996		State Product per Person, 1994		Energy Consumption per Person, 1994[1]	Desc. Num. Order
CA	$93,418,000,000	VT	$5,609	DC	$84,234	AK	1,050.8	1
TX	$66,862,000,000	LA	$4,980	DE	$37,796	LA	884.5	2
NY	$34,230,000,000	WA	$4,786	AK	$37,475	WY	862.8	3
MI	$27,553,000,000	AK	$4,743	CT	$33,722	TX	564.2	4
WA	$26,482,000,000	TX	$3,495	WY	$32,900	ND	538.9	5
IL	$24,176,000,000	CA	$2,930	NJ	$32,255	WV	448.1	6
OH	$22,677,000,000	MI	$2,872	NY	$31,427	AL	446.3	7
LA	$21,667,000,000	OR	$2,793	HI	$31,155	KY	445.5	8
FL	$20,744,000,000	MA	$2,384	MA	$30,822	ME	441.3	9
NC	$15,734,000,000	AZ	$2,372	NV	$30,170	IN	439.3	10
MA	$14,524,000,000	DE	$2,199	IL	$28,324	MT	430.8	11
PA	$14,364,000,000	NC	$2,149	CA	$27,861	OK	424.2	12
NJ	$13,119,000,000	IL	$2,041	CO	$27,291	KS	420.2	13
VA	$12,215,000,000	OH	$2,030	MN	$27,290	MS	398.0	14
IN	$10,984,000,000	MN	$1,931	VA	$27,125	WA	391.2	15
GA	$10,982,000,000	NY	$1,882	WA	$26,926	AR	389.9	16
AZ	$10,503,000,000	IN	$1,881	MD	$26,507	ID	389.0	17
WI	$9,504,000,000	CT	$1,863	TX	$26,106	TN	377.8	18
MN	$8,992,000,000	WI	$1,842	GA	$25,944	DE	374.9	19
OR	$8,948,000,000	VA	$1,830	NH	$25,855	SC	373.2	20
TN	$8,094,000,000	SC	$1,811	NC	$25,675	IA	365.5	21
SC	$6,698,000,000	UT	$1,648	NE	$25,484	OH	357.4	22
KY	$6,385,000,000	KY	$1,644	MI	$25,314	NM	356.9	23
CT	$6,100,000,000	NJ	$1,642	OH	$24,756	NV	351.8	24
MO	$5,404,000,000	IA	$1,543	WI	$24,661	NE	344.8	25
AL	$5,170,000,000	TN	$1,522	TN	$24,451	MN	342.1	26
MD	$5,019,000,000	GA	$1,493	PA	$24,429	WI	337.3	27
CO	$4,883,000,000	KS	$1,471	MO	$24,294	GA	336.9	28
IA	$4,400,000,000	FL	$1,441	KS	$24,180	OR	336.3	29
KS	$3,784,000,000	ID	$1,321	IA	$24,140	MI	325.6	30
VT	$3,302,000,000	CO	$1,277	OR	$24,096	NJ	322.3	31
UT	$3,296,000,000	NH	$1,274	IN	$24,024	SD	321.5	32
AK	$2,879,000,000	AL	$1,210	RI	$23,945	PA	317.7	33
MS	$2,623,000,000	PA	$1,191	SD	$23,920	IL	315.3	34
OK	$2,365,000,000	WV	$1,188	LA	$23,430	NC	313.3	35
WV	$2,169,000,000	NE	$1,154	AZ	$23,090	UT	311.6	36
AR	$2,003,000,000	ME	$1,110	VT	$22,892	DC	310.3	37
NE	$1,907,000,000	ND	$1,099	NM	$22,880	MO	305.6	38
DE	$1,594,000,000	MO	$1,008	FL	$22,779	VA	304.8	39
ID	$1,571,000,000	WY	$999	KY	$22,600	CO	286.9	40
NH	$1,481,000,000	MD	$990	UT	$21,834	VT	263.0	41
ME	$1,380,000,000	MS	$966	SC	$21,814	MD	256.6	42
NV	$1,268,000,000	RI	$928	ID	$21,345	AZ	253.5	43
NM	$931,000,000	AR	$798	ND	$21,151	NH	251.8	44
RI	$919,000,000	NV	$791	ME	$21,020	RI	249.5	45
ND	$707,000,000	OK	$716	AL	$21,016	MA	246.2	46
WY	$481,000,000	SD	$605	AR	$20,620	CT	243.4	47
SD	$443,000,000	DC	$561	OK	$20,315	FL	242.3	48
MT	$440,000,000	NM	$543	MT	$19,698	CA	240.6	49
DC	$305,000,000	MT	$500	WV	$19,020	HI	220.3	50
HI	$284,000,000	HI	$240	MS	$18,953	NY	213.1	51

[1]In million Btu.

Source: U.S. Bureau of the Census, *U.S. Merchandise Trade*; U.S. Bureau of Economic Analysis, *Survey of Current Business*; Energy Information Admin.

TRAVEL AND TRANSPORTATION

VEHICLE REGISTRATIONS (1996)

	Motor Vehicle Reg.		Reg. per 1,000 Pop.		Motor-cycle Reg.		Reg. per 1,000 Pop.	Desc. Num. Order
CA	25,213,707	WY	1,170.91	CA	526,048	NH	46.66	1
TX	13,486,868	MT	1,109.95	OH	219,719	IA	45.95	2
FL	10,888,596	ND	1,056.66	FL	203,334	WI	42.70	3
NY	10,635,602	SD	1,018.32	PA	178,527	VT	36.28	4
OH	9,770,484	IA	1,007.52	IL	171,091	SD	32.93	5
IL	8,816,876	NH	958.54	WI	169,594	ID	32.07	6
PA	8,640,238	OK	935.18	MI	149,971	HI	31.96	7
MI	8,010,396	TN	910.14	TX	148,815	MN	30.09	8
GA	6,282,672	NM	902.63	NY	136,246	ME	27.92	9
NJ	5,821,536	CO	899.67	IA	131,851	CO	27.44	10
NC	5,759,234	NE	896.80	MN	116,189	WY	26.61	11
VA	5,576,132	IN	894.90	WA	104,450	AK	24.71	12
IN	5,215,572	ID	893.51	IN	96,518	RI	24.50	13
TN	4,830,482	OR	891.98	CO	94,217	ND	24.14	14
MA	4,702,389	AK	877.76	NJ	91,995	AZ	24.10	15
WA	4,602,920	OH	875.27	MA	90,844	KS	23.15	16
MO	4,350,440	VT	857.92	TN	78,869	WA	22.69	17
WI	3,971,550	GA	856.62	GA	73,492	OH	22.49	18
MN	3,860,894	VA	836.48	AZ	71,873	MT	21.45	19
MD	3,634,579	WA	833.93	NC	67,855	OR	21.34	20
CO	3,433,287	MN	830.55	OR	60,841	CA	20.86	21
AL	3,323,683	MI	823.19	OK	59,210	PA	20.66	22
LA	3,318,205	DE	819.66	VA	57,561	NV	20.51	23
OK	3,081,723	KS	818.03	MO	54,118	NM	20.44	24
AZ	2,982,523	MO	811.09	NH	51,890	IL	19.40	25
IA	2,869,445	MS	804.84	KS	48,835	MA	19.32	26
OR	2,851,048	CT	798.47	CT	48,328	OK	19.21	27
SC	2,790,575	CA	791.45	SC	39,219	MI	18.72	28
KY	2,695,985	NC	787.96	MD	37,936	FL	18.67	29
CT	2,608,831	AL	775.26	LA	37,072	CT	18.52	30
MS	2,181,727	ME	774.01	AL	36,706	IN	18.51	31
KS	2,109,814	MA	772.73	KY	36,603	DE	16.84	32
AR	1,633,343	WV	772.51	ID	34,034	TN	16.33	33
NM	1,544,633	WI	771.74	NM	31,578	UT	16.03	34
NE	1,478,558	LA	764.42	MS	30,162	NJ	15.80	35
UT	1,445,088	FL	755.16	ME	26,768	SC	14.05	36
WV	1,406,285	SC	750.83	HI	25,114	MS	13.82	37
NH	1,112,113	IL	744.33	SD	24,734	KY	13.58	38
NV	1,095,676	NJ	727.52	UT	23,171	NY	12.81	39
ID	1,061,125	MD	718.25	NV	22,471	NE	12.58	40
MT	973,074	PA	717.62	MT	20,868	MO	12.44	41
ME	958,659	UT	716.25	NE	18,596	NC	11.78	42
HI	785,917	TX	706.44	VT	18,256	GA	11.70	43
SD	751,071	RI	704.18	RI	17,048	WV	11.43	44
RI	695,928	KY	694.47	AR	16,490	LA	11.17	45
ND	679,047	NV	684.45	ND	16,394	AL	11.04	46
DE	593,007	AZ	672.60	WV	16,075	TX	11.03	47
WY	562,048	HI	664.37	WY	14,954	MD	10.44	48
AK	531,017	AR	651.70	AK	13,122	VA	10.32	49
VT	503,139	NY	586.49	DE	9,985	AR	10.10	50
DC	237,415	DC	440.25	DC	1,600	DC	6.74	51

Source: Federal Highway Administration, U.S. Dept. of Transportation

TRENDS AMONG DRIVERS

	Licensed Drivers, 1996		Licenses per 1,000 Pop., 1996		Avg. Trip for Workers, 1990	Desc. Num. Order
CA	20,139,586	AL	813.93	NY	28.6 min.	1
TX	12,369,243	OR	807.24	DC	27.1 min.	2
FL	11,024,064	NH	784.77	MD	27.0 min.	3
NY	10,473,731	VT	779.11	NJ	25.3 min.	4
PA	8,154,055	FL	777.21	IL	25.1 min.	5
OH	7,772,757	DE	732.16	CA	24.6 min.	6
IL	7,210,972	CO	727.83	VA	24.0 min.	7
MI	6,658,750	WY	722.67	HI	23.8 min.	8
NJ	5,403,671	AK	720.92	GA	22.7 min.	9
NC	5,028,421	CT	718.20	MA	22.7 min.	10
GA	4,840,495	WV	714.72	LA	22.3 min.	11
VA	4,628,886	TN	712.64	TX	22.2 min.	12
MA	4,211,029	AR	711.94	WA	22.0 min.	13
WA	3,765,376	SD	707.15	NH	21.9 min.	14
TN	3,739,043	WI	703.15	FL	21.8 min.	15
IN	3,706,182	NE	702.63	AZ	21.6 min.	16
WI	3,601,619	VA	699.73	MO	21.6 min.	17
MO	3,587,086	ND	699.57	PA	21.6 min.	18
AL	3,456,100	NC	698.17	TN	21.5 min.	19
MD	3,344,125	MI	698.13	AL	21.2 min.	20
MN	2,761,121	OH	698.11	MI	21.2 min.	21
CO	2,727,570	ME	697.94	CT	21.1 min.	22
AZ	2,626,222	NM	694.41	WV	21.0 min.	23
LA	2,593,509	MA	693.62	CO	20.7 min.	24
SC	2,542,139	SC	693.25	KY	20.7 min.	25
OR	2,541,873	WA	691.18	OH	20.7 min.	26
KY	2,535,463	ID	691.11	MS	20.6 min.	27
CT	2,349,051	KS	690.74	SC	20.5 min.	28
OK	2,155,558	NV	681.20	IN	20.4 min.	29
IA	1,905,450	NJ	679.75	DE	20.0 min.	30
KS	1,770,786	PA	676.11	NV	19.8 min.	31
AR	1,769,012	RI	675.97	NC	19.8 min.	32
MS	1,693,159	MO	674.35	OR	19.6 min.	33
WV	1,304,539	GA	671.48	OK	19.3 min.	34
UT	1,255,460	IA	670.21	RI	19.2 min.	35
NM	1,173,442	MD	663.66	MN	19.1 min.	36
NE	1,151,764	MT	659.22	NM	19.1 min.	37
NV	1,044,609	OK	658.21	AR	19.0 min.	38
NH	901,104	TX	657.89	ME	19.0 min.	39
ME	864,447	KY	657.39	UT	18.9 min.	40
ID	805,911	UT	641.09	WI	18.3 min.	41
HI	732,508	IN	639.33	VT	18.0 min.	42
RI	670,360	CA	638.03	ID	17.3 min.	43
MT	573,749	MS	627.98	KS	17.2 min.	44
DE	524,992	HI	621.19	AK	16.7 min.	45
SD	515,869	IL	611.60	IA	16.2 min.	46
VT	455,606	DC	610.52	NE	15.8 min.	47
ND	448,781	AZ	610.04	WY	15.4 min.	48
AK	434,389	MN	598.34	MT	14.8 min.	49
WY	346,299	LA	597.85	SD	13.8 min.	50
DC	338,549	NY	575.78	ND	13.0 min.	51

Source: Federal Highway Administration, U.S. Dept. of Transportation

ROADWAY MILEAGE (1996)

Public Roads & Streets, Total Mileage		Total Mileage per 1,000 Pop.		Rural Mileage		Rural Mileage per 1,000 Pop.		Desc. Num. Order
TX	296,259	ND	1,134.89	TX	214,062	ND	132.06	1
CA	170,506	SD	1,113.84	KS	123,629	SD	111.19	2
IL	137,577	MT	179.39	MN	115,232	MT	76.63	3
KS	133,386	WY	170.87	MO	106,333	WY	66.04	4
MN	130,613	NE	156.17	IA	103,359	NE	53.07	5
MO	122,748	KS	151.86	IL	101,888	KS	48.06	6
PA	118,952	ID	150.18	OK	99,630	ID	47.01	7
MI	117,620	IA	139.52	WI	95,453	IA	36.24	8
OH	114,642	NM	134.70	MI	89,478	NM	31.12	9
FL	114,422	OK	134.13	NE	87,684	OK	30.18	10
IA	112,708	AR	130.98	CA	87,397	AR	27.91	11
OK	112,664	NV	128.09	PA	85,750	NV	24.79	12
NY	112,347	MN	128.04	GA	85,091	MN	24.74	13
GA	111,746	MS	126.95	ND	84,985	MS	24.03	14
WI	111,435	OR	125.97	OH	81,451	OR	22.80	15
NC	97,509	VT	124.11	SD	81,435	VT	21.84	16
AL	93,340	MO	122.91	NC	75,077	MO	19.84	17
IN	92,970	CO	122.18	IN	73,326	AK	18.88	18
NE	92,805	AL	121.84	AL	73,224	CO	18.61	19
ND	86,808	AK	121.84	OR	73,039	WI	18.50	20
TN	85,795	WI	121.60	NY	71,701	UT	17.65	21
CO	84,797	UT	120.85	CO	71,139	WV	17.50	22
SD	83,375	WV	119.24	AR	70,048	AL	17.14	23
OR	83,190	KY	118.84	TN	68,518	KY	16.19	24
WA	79,555	ME	118.16	MT	67,389	ME	16.06	25
AR	77,746	SC	117.40	FL	66,083	SC	14.54	26
MS	73,202	TN	116.13	MS	65,281	TN	12.88	27
KY	73,158	IN	115.92	KY	62,875	IN	12.55	28
MT	69,809	TX	115.49	WA	61,908	GA	11.57	29
VA	69,384	GA	115.20	ID	55,901	TX	11.19	30
SC	64,359	WA	114.38	SC	53,785	WA	11.19	31
LA	60,667	LA	113.94	NM	53,322	LA	10.73	32
ID	59,674	NC	113.32	VA	50,854	NH	10.49	33
NM	59,455	NH	112.99	LA	46,702	NC	10.25	34
AZ	54,895	AZ	112.40	NV	39,741	MI	9.33	35
NV	45,039	MI	112.26	AZ	38,662	AZ	8.73	36
UT	41,718	IL	111.61	UT	35,306	IL	8.60	37
NJ	35,924	VA	110.39	WV	31,953	VA	7.62	38
WV	35,130	OH	110.26	WY	31,794	OH	7.29	39
MA	34,725	PA	19.87	ME	19,962	PA	7.11	40
WY	34,115	FL	17.95	MD	15,781	DE	5.15	41
MD	29,680	DE	17.88	VT	12,858	FL	4.59	42
ME	22,577	CT	16.29	NH	12,190	NY	3.94	43
CT	20,600	NY	16.18	MA	12,050	MD	3.11	44
NH	15,106	RI	16.06	NJ	11,683	CA	2.74	45
VT	14,192	MD	15.85	AK	11,460	CT	2.72	46
AK	13,255	MA	15.70	CT	8,920	MA	1.98	47
RI	6,001	CA	15.35	DE	3,733	HI	1.94	48
DE	5,715	NJ	14.50	HI	2,291	NJ	1.46	49
HI	4,142	HI	13.50	RI	1,360	RI	1.37	50
DC	1,413	DC	12.60	DC	0	DC	0.00	51

Source: Federal Highway Administration, U.S. Dept. of Transportation

ROADWAY MILEAGE (1996) (CONTINUED)

	Urban Mileage		Urban Mileage per 1,000 Pop.		Interstate Mileage		Interstate Mileage per 1,000 Pop.	Desc. Num. Order
CA	83,109	WY	4.82	TX	3,234	WY	1.90	1
TX	82,197	AL	4.71	CA	2,424	AK	1.79	2
FL	48,339	RI	4.69	IL	2,163	MT	1.35	3
NY	40,646	TX	4.30	PA	1,750	SD	0.93	4
IL	35,689	OK	3.95	OH	1,573	ND	0.89	5
PA	33,202	KS	3.79	NY	1,499	NM	0.58	6
OH	33,191	MA	3.72	FL	1,471	VT	0.54	7
MI	28,142	AZ	3.67	GA	1,241	ID	0.51	8
GA	26,655	GA	3.62	MI	1,239	UT	0.47	9
NJ	24,241	NM	3.58	MT	1,190	NV	0.35	10
MA	22,675	CO	3.57	MO	1,178	KS	0.34	11
NC	22,432	CT	3.57	IN	1,172	ME	0.30	12
AL	20,116	FL	3.36	AZ	1,169	WV	0.30	13
IN	19,644	IN	3.36	VA	1,107	NE	0.29	14
VA	18,530	MN	3.30	AK	1,086	OK	0.28	15
WA	17,647	NV	3.30	TN	1,062	IA	0.27	16
TN	17,277	IA	3.28	NM	1,000	AZ	0.26	17
MO	16,415	TN	3.25	NC	981	CO	0.25	18
AZ	16,233	LA	3.21	CO	954	MS	0.25	19
WI	15,982	UT	3.21	UT	940	OR	0.23	20
MN	15,381	WA	3.19	OK	930	AR	0.22	21
LA	13,965	ID	3.17	MN	913	MO	0.22	22
MD	13,899	OR	3.17	WY	913	SC	0.22	23
CO	13,658	NE	3.10	AL	904	AL	0.21	24
OK	13,034	WI	3.10	LA	893	LA	0.21	25
CT	11,680	AR	3.07	KS	872	IN	0.20	26
SC	10,574	MO	3.06	SC	829	KY	0.20	27
KY	10,283	NC	3.06	IA	781	MN	0.20	28
OR	10,151	NJ	3.03	WA	763	TN	0.20	29
KS	9,757	IL	3.01	KY	762	NH	0.19	30
IA	9,349	OH	2.97	WI	745	IL	0.18	31
MS	7,921	AK	2.96	OR	728	GA	0.17	32
AR	7,698	MI	2.93	MS	685	TX	0.17	33
UT	6,412	MS	2.92	SD	678	VA	0.17	34
NM	6,133	SC	2.86	ID	611	PA	0.15	35
NV	5,298	ND	2.83	ND	571	OH	0.14	36
NE	5,121	VA	2.78	MA	565	WA	0.14	37
RI	4,641	MT	2.75	NV	563	WI	0.14	38
ID	3,773	PA	2.75	WV	550	MI	0.13	39
WV	3,177	MD	2.74	AR	541	NC	0.13	40
NH	2,916	DE	2.73	MD	482	CT	0.11	41
ME	2,615	KY	2.65	NE	480	FL	0.10	42
MT	2,420	SD	2.65	NJ	422	MD	0.10	43
WY	2,321	CA	2.61	ME	368	MA	0.09	44
DE	1,982	DC	2.60	CT	344	CA	0.08	45
SD	1,940	NH	2.51	VT	320	NY	0.08	46
HI	1,851	VT	2.27	NH	224	RI	0.07	47
ND	1,823	NY	2.24	RI	69	DE	0.06	48
AK	1,795	ME	2.10	HI	43	NJ	0.05	49
DC	1,413	WV	1.74	DE	41	HI	0.04	50
VT	1,334	HI	1.56	DC	13	DC	0.02	51

GOVERNMENT

REVENUES

	Total Revenue, 1996		Total Revenue per Capita, 1996		Gaming Revenue per Capita, 1995[1]	Desc. Num. Order
CA	$123,342,274,000	AK	$13,597.28	MA	$437.09	1
NY	$94,277,491,000	HI	$5,391.34	RI	$297.01	2
TX	$51,118,112,000	NY	$5,184.35	NV	$293.55	3
OH	$43,823,449,000	DE	$4,991.31	OR	$282.53	4
PA	$42,796,060,000	WY	$4,881.20	CT	$244.28	5
FL	$41,679,890,000	WI	$4,858.93	NJ	$225.62	6
MI	$38,047,205,000	OR	$4,816.44	MD	$197.12	7
IL	$36,990,605,000	NM	$4,745.70	OH	$185.31	8
NJ	$35,857,209,000	NJ	$4,488.88	GA	$179.64	9
MA	$25,196,723,000	WA	$4,480.39	FL	$156.12	10
WI	$25,072,066,000	MN	$4,406.46	NY	$156.07	11
WA	$24,790,010,000	CT	$4,382.86	DE	$152.30	12
NC	$23,387,492,000	RI	$4,313.75	IL	$151.26	13
GA	$22,408,977,000	MA	$4,136.03	TX	$148.26	14
MN	$20,525,269,000	ND	$3,988.56	VA	$133.31	15
VA	$20,072,003,000	MI	$3,965.73	MI	$133.19	16
MO	$17,050,787,000	MT	$3,954.11	KY	$129.92	17
IN	$16,549,937,000	OH	$3,922.26	ME	$126.41	18
MD	$16,041,152,000	CA	$3,869.20	PA	$125.19	19
OR	$15,431,878,000	WV	$3,760.22	VT	$123.53	20
TN	$14,749,141,000	NV	$3,741.35	NH	$122.99	21
CT	$14,349,487,000	ID	$3,686.86	SD	$114.30	22
LA	$14,296,187,000	VT	$3,643.81	IN	$97.62	23
KY	$13,788,272,000	KY	$3,550.02	WI	$97.59	24
AL	$12,741,148,000	PA	$3,549.77	CO	$90.60	25
SC	$12,601,859,000	AR	$3,447.33	WV	$88.92	26
AZ	$12,594,269,000	ME	$3,432.73	MO	$84.32	27
CO	$11,865,786,000	SC	$3,406.83	MN	$83.14	28
OK	$10,609,104,000	UT	$3,386.60	ID	$77.26	29
IA	$9,244,859,000	LA	$3,285.72	IA	$75.69	30
MS	$8,864,863,000	MS	$3,263.94	WA	$74.32	31
AR	$8,652,790,000	IA	$3,241.54	MS	$70.99	32
AK	$8,253,549,000	OK	$3,213.91	CA	$67.62	33
NM	$8,129,383,000	NC	$3,193.70	KS	$66.16	34
KS	$7,864,247,000	MO	$3,181.71	LA	$66.07	35
WV	$6,866,159,000	MD	$3,162.69	AZ	$64.53	36
UT	$6,773,191,000	IL	$3,122.36	NE	$55.61	37
HI	$6,383,347,000	SD	$3,119.64	MT	$35.68	38
NV	$5,997,387,000	CO	$3,103.79	ND	$17.15	39
NE	$4,998,908,000	NH	$3,064.40	SC	$7.33	40
ID	$4,383,680,000	KS	$3,057.64	OK	$4.89	41
RI	$4,270,615,000	GA	$3,047.60	AR	$4.84	42
ME	$4,266,881,000	NE	$3,025.97	AK	$3.32	43
DE	$3,618,697,000	VA	$3,007.04	NM	$1.19	44
NH	$3,560,835,000	AL	$2,981.78	AL	$1.17	45
MT	$3,475,665,000	FL	$2,894.44	WY	NA	46
ND	$2,568,635,000	AZ	$2,844.23	HI	NA	47
WY	$2,347,858,000	IN	$2,833.41	NC	NA	48
SD	$2,283,576,000	TN	$2,772.39	TN	NA	49
VT	$2,146,205,000	TX	$2,672.42	UT	NA	50
DC	NA	DC	NA	DC	NA	51

[1]Revenues from parimutuel and amusement taxes and lotteries
Source: Bureau of the Census, U.S. Dept. of Commerce

EXPENDITURES AND DEBT (1996)

	Total Expend.		Expend. per Capita		Debt Outstanding		Debt Out- standing per Capita	Desc. Num. Order
CA	$113,361,355,000	AK	$9,274.30	NY	$73,121,852,000	DE	$5,901.43	1
NY	$82,420,166,000	HI	$5,022.53	CA	$45,859,003,000	RI	$5,561.30	2
TX	$46,081,839,000	NY	$4,532.32	MA	$29,294,682,000	AK	$5,233.28	3
PA	$38,698,546,000	DE	$4,480.24	NJ	$25,601,576,000	NH	$5,019.77	4
FL	$36,454,217,000	WY	$4,287.14	IL	$22,676,430,000	CT	$5,013.85	5
OH	$35,517,336,000	CT	$4,132.44	CT	$16,415,336,000	MA	$4,808.71	6
MI	$35,079,667,000	RI	$4,102.43	FL	$15,514,762,000	HI	$4,321.78	7
IL	$34,111,276,000	MA	$4,095.49	PA	$15,045,892,000	NY	$4,021.00	8
NJ	$32,314,887,000	NJ	$4,045.43	TX	$14,575,675,000	NJ	$3,205.00	9
MA	$24,949,729,000	NM	$3,934.91	MI	$13,667,509,000	VT	$2,916.63	10
NC	$21,220,754,000	WV	$3,816.97	OH	$12,627,741,000	MT	$2,553.13	11
WA	$21,085,737,000	WA	$3,810.90	MD	$9,690,915,000	ME	$2,541.99	12
GA	$20,013,038,000	MN	$3,719.47	WI	$9,126,746,000	SD	$2,328.05	13
VA	$17,717,140,000	OR	$3,700.97	WA	$8,991,106,000	IL	$1,914.11	14
MN	$17,325,287,000	MI	$3,656.42	VA	$8,792,968,000	MD	$1,910.67	15
WI	$16,989,913,000	MT	$3,567.92	LA	$7,452,387,000	OR	$1,899.59	16
MD	$15,554,009,000	CA	$3,556.10	MO	$7,128,377,000	KY	$1,810.11	17
IN	$15,367,687,000	VT	$3,499.25	KY	$7,030,482,000	WI	$1,768.75	18
LA	$14,029,815,000	ME	$3,410.97	GA	$6,199,913,000	LA	$1,712.80	19
TN	$13,829,307,000	SC	$3,352.24	IN	$6,116,873,000	WY	$1,661.16	20
CT	$13,529,622,000	WI	$3,292.62	OR	$6,086,273,000	WA	$1,625.00	21
MO	$12,841,102,000	LA	$3,224.50	NH	$5,832,969,000	WV	$1,549.95	22
SC	$12,399,928,000	PA	$3,209.90	RI	$5,505,683,000	SC	$1,439.36	23
AL	$12,126,587,000	ND	$3,204.37	SC	$5,324,200,000	CA	$1,438.58	24
AZ	$11,898,144,000	OH	$3,178.85	HI	$5,116,982,000	MI	$1,424.59	25
OR	$11,857,897,000	IA	$3,104.19	MN	$4,858,281,000	NV	$1,408.94	26
KY	$11,842,386,000	UT	$3,085.89	NC	$4,513,348,000	MO	$1,330.17	27
CO	$10,311,855,000	MD	$3,066.64	DE	$4,278,539,000	VA	$1,317.30	28
OK	$9,265,486,000	KY	$3,049.02	OK	$3,889,324,000	ND	$1,271.74	29
IA	$8,853,150,000	MS	$3,025.36	AL	$3,645,292,000	NM	$1,253.18	30
MS	$8,216,867,000	NV	$3,013.94	CO	$3,576,722,000	PA	$1,248.00	31
KS	$7,275,754,000	ID	$2,944.74	AK	$3,176,601,000	UT	$1,232.09	32
AR	$7,050,461,000	NC	$2,897.82	ME	$3,159,694,000	ID	$1,222.50	33
WV	$6,969,795,000	IL	$2,879.32	TN	$3,069,027,000	OK	$1,178.23	34
NM	$6,740,498,000	AL	$2,837.96	AZ	$2,936,004,000	OH	$1,130.20	35
UT	$6,171,775,000	KS	$2,828.83	WV	$2,830,217,000	FL	$1,077.41	36
HI	$5,946,676,000	AR	$2,808.95	UT	$2,464,177,000	IN	$1,047.23	37
AK	$5,629,502,000	OK	$2,806.87	NV	$2,258,523,000	MN	$1,043.00	38
NV	$4,831,342,000	NH	$2,788.33	MT	$2,244,202,000	CO	$935.58	39
NE	$4,489,725,000	GA	$2,721.75	MS	$2,232,015,000	AR	$853.49	40
ME	$4,239,839,000	NE	$2,717.75	NM	$2,146,696,000	AL	$853.10	41
RI	$4,061,406,000	SD	$2,697.58	AR	$2,142,271,000	NE	$848.53	42
ID	$3,501,298,000	CO	$2,697.32	IA	$2,064,507,000	GA	$843.18	43
DE	$3,248,174,000	AZ	$2,687.02	VT	$1,717,898,000	MS	$821.80	44
NH	$3,240,034,000	VA	$2,654.25	SD	$1,704,133,000	TX	$762.01	45
MT	$3,136,205,000	IN	$2,631.00	ID	$1,453,555,000	IA	$723.88	46
ND	$2,063,612,000	TN	$2,599.49	NE	$1,401,777,000	AZ	$663.05	47
WY	$2,062,116,000	FL	$2,531.54	KS	$1,161,470,000	NC	$616.33	48
VT	$2,061,059,000	TX	$2,409.13	ND	$819,003,000	TN	$576.88	49
SD	$1,974,632,000	MO	$2,396.18	WY	$799,017,000	KS	$451.58	50
DC	NA	DC	NA	DC	NA	DC	NA	51

Source: Bureau of the Census, U.S. Dept. of Commerce

INDEXES

Below you will find three separate indexes to *The World Almanac of the U.S.A.*

The INDEX TO PEOPLE lists not only individuals but also groups of people such as the Creek Indians or the Amish. The INDEX TO PLACES includes each of the fifty states, islands under U.S. jurisdiction, cities (followed by state abbreviation), and geographical features such as mountain ranges and lakes. Page ranges in **boldface** indicate the main article on each state in Part II: Portraits of the States. THE INDEX TO TOPICS covers Parts I and III of the text only. Information on most topics listed within that index can also be found in each state article in Part II.

INDEX TO PLACES

INDEX TO TOPICS

WIN A FREE HOMETOWN USA™ MULTIMEDIA CD-ROM

Enter *The World Almanac of the U.S.A.* "Gateway to the U.S.A." Contest and win a free copy of the *HomeTown USA* CD-ROM, produced by GeoSystems Global Corporation.

To enter, send a letter including your name, address, daytime phone number, and the name of the place you think is the most interesting place to visit in the U.S.A. Send your entry to:

> WORLD ALMANAC BOOKS
> U.S.A. Essay Contest
> 1 International Blvd.
> Suite #444
> Mahwah, NJ 07495

All entries must be received no later than February 28, 1999. At that time, 1,000 winning entries will be chosen in a random drawing and each winner will receive a copy of the *HomeTown USA* CD-ROM.

ABOUT THE HOMETOWN USA CD-ROM

Having *HomeTown USA* is like having road maps showing every street in the U.S.A., all on one handy CD-ROM. You can search for locations by city, state, zip, or street, pan in or out through 10 levels of map detail, and create personalized maps to any size and scale. In addition to virtually every street in the U.S.A., it also locates airports, historic sites, parks, recreation areas, schools, colleges and universities, places of worship, and much more.

The *HomeTown USA* CD-ROM is produced by GeoSystems Global Corporation, one of the world's leading cartographers. GeoSystems produces quality mapping products for such companies as National Geographic, Reader's Digest, the National Park Service, and the American Automobile Association, as well as the maps found in *The World Almanac, The World Almanac for Kids,* and *The World Almanac of the U.S.A.* GeoSystems is also the creator and publisher of MapQuest® (www.mapquest.com), the most popular and powerful interactive mapping service on the Internet.

The World Almanac of the U.S.A. "Gateway to the U.S.A." Contest Rules

1. No purchase necessary.
2. Sweepstakes will be open to all residents of the 50 United States and Washington, DC. Employees of World Almanac Books and PRIMEDIA Reference Inc. ("Sponsors"), their subsidiaries, affiliates, advertising and promotion agencies, and their family/household members are not eligible to enter.
3. Enter by sending your name, address, and daytime phone number to: World Almanac Books, U.S.A. Essay Contest, 1 International Blvd., Mahwah, NJ 07495. Entries must be received by February 28, 1999. Multiple entries are not permitted. Sponsors shall not be responsible for lost, late, mutilated, or misdirected mail. Entries that are printed by machine, mechanically reproduced, tampered with, illegible, or incomplete are not eligible.
4. The prize winners will be selected by random drawing from all entries on or about February 28, 1999. The drawing will take place under the supervision of the Sponsors. Participants agree to be bound by these rules and the decision of the judges, whose decisions are final. Odds of winning will be determined by the total number of entries received. The winners will be notified by March 31, 1999. To obtain a list of winners, send a self-addressed, stamped envelope after March 31, 1999, to World Almanac Books, U.S.A. Essay Contest, 1 International Blvd., Mahwah, NJ 07495.
5. Each winner will receive a copy of the *HomeTown USA* CD-ROM (approximate retail value: $29.95). Sponsors make no warranties with regard to the prizes. Prizes are not transferable. No substitutions of prize allowed by winner, but Sponsors reserve the right to substitute a prize of equal or greater value. Prizes are not redeemable by winner for cash value.
6. All entries become the property of the Sponsors and will not be acknowledged or returned.
7. All taxes on prizes are solely the responsibility of the winners.
8. All entrants release the Sponsors, their affiliates, subsidiaries, directors, officers, employees, and agents, and all others associated with the development and execution of this sweepstakes from any and all liability from injury, loss, or damage of any kind resulting from participation in this promotion or acceptance or use of any prize.
9. Prizes must be claimed by June 30, 1999. Failure to execute and return any requested document within 30 days of postmark, or return of notification or prize as undeliverable may result in forfeiture of prize. An alternate winner will be selected. All reasonable effort will be made to contact the winner.
10. Void where prohibited by law. All federal, state, and local laws and regulations apply.